D1521023

Inside the Firm

IZA Prize in Labor Economics Series

Since 2002, the Institute for the Study of Labor (IZA) has awarded the annual IZA Prize in Labor Economics for outstanding contributions to policy-relevant labor market research and methodological progress in this sub-discipline of economic science. The IZA Prize is the only international science prize awarded exclusively to labor economists. This special focus acknowledges the global significance of high-quality basic research in labor economics and sound policy advice based on these research findings. As issues of employment and unemployment are among the most urgent challenges of our time, labor economists have an important task and responsibility. The IZA Prize in Labor Economics is today considered one of the most prestigious international awards in the field. It aims to stimulate further research on topics that have enormous implications for our future. All prize-winners contribute a volume to the IZA Prize in Labor Economics Series published by Oxford University Press, which has been established to provide an overview of the laureates' most significant findings.

The IZA Prize in Labor Economics has become an integral part of the institute's manifold activities to promote progress in labor market research. Based on nominations submitted by the IZA Research Fellows, a high-ranking IZA Prize Committee selects the prize-winner. In conjunction with the Award Ceremony the IZA Prize Conference brings together a number of renowned experts to discuss topical labor market issues.

It is not by coincidence that the IZA Prize in Labor Economics Series is published by Oxford University Press. This well-reputed publishing house has shown a great interest in the project from the very beginning as this exclusive series perfectly complements their range of publications. We gratefully acknowledge their excellent cooperation.

1L. F. Jimmermann

Klaus F. Zimmermann, IZA Director

Winners of the IZA Prize in Labor Economics

2010	Francine D. Blau (Cornell University)
2009	Richard A. Easterlin (University of Southern California)
2008	Richard Layard (London School of Economics)
	Stephen J. Nickell (Nuffield College)
2007	Richard B. Freeman (Harvard University)
2006	David Card (University of California, Berkeley)
	Alan B. Krueger (Princeton University)
2005	Dale T. Mortensen (Northwestern University)
	Christopher A. Pissarides (London School of Economics)
2004	Edward P. Lazear (Stanford University)
2003	Orley C. Ashenfelter (Princeton University)
2002	Jacob Mincer (Columbia University)

Edward P. Lazear
2004 IZA Prize Laureate

Inside the Firm

Contributions to Personnel Economics

Edward P. Lazear

Edited by
Steffen Altmann
Klaus F. Zimmermann

OXFORD
UNIVERSITY PRESS

OXFORD
UNIVERSITY PRESS

Great Clarendon Street, Oxford ox2 6DP

Oxford University Press is a department of the University of Oxford.
It furthers the University's objective of excellence in research, scholarship,
and education by publishing worldwide in

Oxford New York

Auckland Cape Town Dar es Salaam Hong Kong Karachi
Kuala Lumpur Madrid Melbourne Mexico City Nairobi
New Delhi Shanghai Taipei Toronto

With offices in

Argentina Austria Brazil Chile Czech Republic France Greece
Guatemala Hungary Italy Japan Poland Portugal Singapore
South Korea Switzerland Thailand Turkey Ukraine Vietnam
Oxford is a registered trade mark of Oxford University Press
in the UK and in certain other countries

Published in the United States
by Oxford University Press Inc., New York

British Library Cataloguing in Publication Data

Data available

Library of Congress Cataloging in Publication Data

Data available

Typeset by the IZA
Printed in Great Britain
on acid-free paper by
MPG Books Group, Bodmin and King's Lynn

ISBN 978–0–19–969339–9

1 3 5 7 9 10 8 6 4 2

Award Statement
of the IZA Prize Committee

The IZA Prize in Labor Economics 2004 is awarded to Edward P. Lazear (Jack Steele Parker Professor of Human Resources Management and Economics at the Graduate School of Business and Morris A. Cox Senior Fellow at the Hoover Institution at Stanford University), for his fundamental contributions to the field.

Edward Lazear is an exceptional scholar, a path-breaking researcher and an eminent economist with a vision, who has shaped the research agenda in labor economics. His leadership and entrepreneurial spirit have boosted the recognition of the field. Lazear's research is both original and fundamental. He builds models that provide novel and often surprising insights. Combining such new and highly important theoretical insights with down-to-earth empirical work, his papers are exemplary in applied theory. Lazear has brought great rigor to the analysis of compensation schemes, incentives in labor relations, and to the study of other human resource practices. His pioneering work in personnel economics has a decisive influence on modern labor economics.

His article "Why Is There Mandatory Retirement?" (Journal of Political Economy, 1979) marks the start of a sequence of studies that investigate the effects of various compensation schemes on productivity. In this paper, he argues that firms pay workers less than their marginal product early during the employment relationship and compensate them by paying higher wages at longer tenure in order to induce workers to provide efficient levels of effort throughout the employment relationship. Such compensation schemes make work around retirement age appear to be too attractive from the worker's point of view. Since workers would therefore not retire at the time when they optimally should withdraw from the labor market, firms make retirement mandatory. Lazear explains in "Agency, Earnings

Profiles, Productivity, and Hours Restrictions" (American Economic Review, 1981) why efficient labor contracts with deferred compensation have hours requirements and restrictions. In "Incentives, Productivity, and Labor Contracts" (Quarterly Journal of Economics, 1984), a co-authored paper with Robert Moore, he argues that increasing age-earnings profiles largely result from contractual arrangements with back loaded wages that reflect the firms' desire to provide lifecycle incentives rather than human capital accumulation.

"Rank-Order Tournaments as Optimum Labor Contracts" (Journal of Political Economy, 1981), an article jointly written with Sherwin Rosen, shows under which conditions rank-order tournaments, in which workers striving for promotions to better paying jobs on higher levels exert optimal levels of effort, can be superior incentive mechanisms compared to piece-rate schemes. In "Salaries and Piece Rates" (Journal of Business, 1986) Lazear illuminates the question why some workers are paid piece rates based on output while others are paid salaries for their input. Lazear emphasizes that the choice between salaries and piece rates is affected by weighting quality and quantity of output, by sorting considerations, monitoring costs, and asymmetric information. Lazear's article "Performance Pay and Productivity" (American Economic Review, 2000) studies empirically the effect of the introduction of piece rates at a company that installs windshields and shows that productivity gains among workers on piece rates result as workers work harder and because more productive workers are attracted by the piece-rate scheme.

Lazear has also shed light on other practices in employment relationships. In "Pay Equality and Industrial Politics" (Journal of Political Economy, 1989), he explains that some level of wage compression is efficient as it reduces uncooperative behavior that is detrimental to the firm. "Peer Pressure and Partnerships" (Journal of Political Economy, 1992), an article with Eugene Kandel, studies whether profit-sharing fosters peer pressure and how factors such as norms, shame, guilt, and empathy interact to create incentives in firms. Lazear's article "Job Security Provisions and Employment" (Quarterly Journal of Economics, 1990) makes the important point that government mandated severance pay can be offset by an optimal contract in a competitive labor market when payments by the firm are received by the worker, but that payments to third-party intermediaries necessarily distort incentives. He then analyzes the employment effects when the conditions under which severance payments are neutral are not met. Influential is also the paper with Sherwin Rosen entitled "Male-Female Wage Differentials in Job Ladders" (Journal of Labor Economics, 1990) in which they argue that observed male-female wage differentials reflect lower promotion probabilities of women, for whom promotion standards are higher.

Lazear's leadership and research has been an important impetus to the creation of the economics of personnel as a separate research field in economics, which finds expression in the fact that a new JEL code (M5) has been created for the discipline "Personnel Economics". Starting with "The Job as a Concept", a contribution to the book Performance Measurement, Evaluation, and Incentives edited by William J. Bruns in 1992, and continuing with his Presidential Address to the Society of Labor Economists in 1998 entitled "Personnel Economics: Past Lessons and Future Directions" (Journal of Labor Economics, 1999), he has set the research agenda and inspired a large and growing literature. This field keeps attracting the interest of many scholars and researchers; and Lazear's intellectual influence on other scholars who will be producing in this area is just beginning. Lazear is more than a guiding force behind this literature. His work has shaped the way that modern labor economics studies actually work. Personnel economics has revolutionized the teaching of human resources in business schools worldwide, and is nowadays taught in many universities. Lazear is responsible for much of its success. His textbooks make relatively complicated models and ideas accessible to undergraduates, MBA students, and even the public.

Lazear has founded the Journal of Labor Economics, which today is probably the world's top journal in the labor field. Thanks to Edward Lazear's entrepreneurial spirit, a forum was thus created that has improved the exchange of ideas among labor economists, stimulated scientific debate among scholars everywhere, and enhanced the visibility and respect for the entire field.

The IZA Prize in Labor Economics 2004 honors the work of a brilliant scholar who has greatly shaped and advanced the empirical and theoretical research in a new field of labor economics.

George A. Akerlof	University of California, Berkeley, IZA
Gary S. Becker	University of Chicago
Armin Falk	IZA; University of Bonn
Richard Portes	Centre for Economic Policy Research (CEPR)
Klaus F. Zimmermann	IZA; University of Bonn

Acknowledgments

This book is a product of the 2004 IZA Prize in Labor Economics. In reading the notification that went along with the award statement, I concluded that the award was primarily for my work in personnel economics, although a number of other areas were mentioned as well. Personnel economics is primarily about personnel or human resources policy.

Let me begin by expressing my gratitude. I have many people to thank. First are the two Klauses. As the CEO of Deutsche Post, Klaus Zumwinkel had the vision to support an organization like IZA. He was able to see that the activities of IZA would have payoff both in the short and long run to academics, business people, and policy makers. Klaus F. Zimmermann, a significant scholar in his own right, is certainly one of the most important academic entrepreneurs in our field. Klaus has had a huge impact on economics in general, and on labor economics in particular, not only through his own work but by being able to motivate and organize the work of others.

I owe much to my two most important academic role models, Gary Becker and Sherwin Rosen. Becker is not just one of the finest economists in the history of this field but more broadly he is one of the greatest social scientists of the 20th century. Sherwin Rosen was my colleague and teacher for almost 30 years. A leading, if not the leading labor economist in the world, Sherwin surely would have preceded me in receiving the IZA Prize were he alive. Finally, there are many who have supported me professionally by making my work environment a positive one. I have many deans to thank, and maybe most specifically, John Raisian, Director of the Hoover Institution, and Michael Spence, former Dean of the Graduate School of Business at Stanford.

With respect to this book, I express my deepest gratitude to Steffen Altmann, and his assistants, Benedikt Kliche, Stephan Luck, Jan Müller, Michael Siekemeier, Franziska Tausch, and Thomas Wasilewski for their help in putting together much of the material for this book, especially the new references on which the introductory and concluding chapters are based.

How did I get into personnel economics? The answer is: by accident. Producing good research is, in large part, luck. I remember one day, over 30 years ago, I was tuned into a news discussion about mandatory retirement, which was soon to become illegal in the United States. I remember thinking that the abolition of mandatory retirement might have dramatic effects on the labor market, but then wondered why mandatory retirement existed in the first place. Most people simply took it for granted. But discontinuities such as those that require that a worker leaves on his 65th birthday are difficult for economists to explain. I considered all the traditional explanations for mandatory retirement and decided that each was logically flawed. As a young person I looked around and also noticed that many of my senior colleagues who had high earnings were not necessarily producing so much. Their most productive years had occurred when they were younger but the highest wages occurred when they were older. The provision of incentives was at the heart of the matter and high wages for senior workers create an incentive for all to work hard. But high senior worker pay discourages retirement. As a result mandatory retirement was a necessary byproduct of this type of incentives scheme. In 1979 my first paper in personnel economics, "Why is there mandatory retirement?" was published in the Journal of Political Economy.

About the same time, Sherwin Rosen and I had been working on the pay of politicians. Being a successful politician was like winning a contest, so I started thinking about the executive labor market as being like a tournament. We discovered that tournaments are an alternative to piece rates in motivating workers and wrote the draft of the tournament paper that eventually became the 1981 Journal of Political Economy article.

The other factor that pushed me into personnel economics was that I started teaching business students. Initially, I taught the traditional topics in labor economics including supply and demand for labor, unions, unemployment, and so forth. Much to my chagrin, the MBAs found the material neither interesting nor useful. Mandatory retirement and tournaments were on my mind at the time so I brought those subjects into the classroom and found that the students liked the topics. I realized that this was a field that not only had intellectual appeal but also might have business relevance. Throughout my career I have attempted to write papers that were not only academically serious, but also answered questions that people in the business community found interesting.

The academic production function involves luck but it also involves the inputs of others. I have already mentioned my two most important role models, Sherwin Rosen and Gary Becker. Sherwin taught me discipline and rigor. But more importantly, Sherwin thought deeply about subjects and revisited them often in his career. Among all the economists I have known, Sherwin is arguably the deepest. I have tried to follow his example, with only mixed success. But I have, on many occasions, written papers that followed on topics that I had first worked on many years before. I have found this to be a very effective strategy because scholars understand questions at a very different level after the questions have been floating around in their brains for five to ten years. Sherwin was a master at doing this and it is a model that is worth mimicking.

Gary Becker more than anyone else taught me to reach for the stars. It is impossible to know Gary or even to read his work without realizing that he is a man who has never been afraid to be creative. Gary has used his tools to consider questions far outside the realm of traditional economics. A few years back, I was asked to write a paper on the extension of economics to other areas for the Millennium Issue of the Quarterly Journal of Economics. I wrote a paper called "Economic Imperialism" which discusses how economics has been successful in moving into and informing other areas of social science and the law. Gary is featured prominently in that essay, and there are many others as well. Watching Gary work gave me the confidence to extend the tools that I used to other areas, some of which are also considered outside the realm of economics. In this vein, the areas of culture and education, examined in this book, reflect the extension of the methodology of personnel economics to other areas.

Like many who will read this book, I have tried to produce good research that advances our knowledge and is consistent with my students' interests. That is a worthy goal, and the many fine researchers who now work in the area of personnel economics have made great progress toward that end.

Edward P. Lazear

Contents

Contents

Contents

Contents

Contents

1 Edward P. Lazear: A Founding Father of Personnel Economics

Steffen Altmann and Klaus F. Zimmermann

The IZA Prize in Labor Economics was awarded to Edward Lazear on October 25, 2004, in Berlin, Germany. The IZA Prize is given annually for outstanding contributions to policy-relevant research and methodological progress in the field of labor economics. Based on nominations submitted by IZA Research Fellows, the Prize Committee including Nobel Laureates George A. Akerlof and Gary S. Becker, as well as Armin Falk, Richard Portes, and Klaus F. Zimmermann, selected Ed Lazear as the third IZA Prize Winner.

In her laudation during the Berlin Prize Ceremony, Uschi Backes-Gellner (University of Zurich) named Ed Lazear the "jack-of-all-trades" of labor economics, alluding to Lazear's theory that being equipped well with many different skills rather than being a specialist in one particular area constitutes a good entrepreneur (Lazear 2005, see Chapter 16). Indeed, Ed Lazear seems to have many entrepreneurial qualities.

As a founding editor, Lazear has played a major role in successfully establishing the Journal of Labor Economics. Only a few years after its foundation, the journal was widely regarded as the world's top field journal in labor economics. Since then, the journal—for which Lazear continued to serve as an editor until 2001—has consolidated this role. As a forum for scientific debate among labor economists, the journal has enhanced the visibility and respect for the entire field and thereby fuelled its growth.

1

Ed Lazear has also proven his talent as an advisor outside the world of academia. Most notably, he served as Chairman of the President's Council of Economic Advisers from 2006 until 2009. During his time as the chief economic advisor at the White House, he dealt with many important issues in economic policy, most importantly the breakout of the global financial crisis. Previous to his work for the US government, many other countries, such as Czechoslovakia, Georgia, Romania, Russia, and Ukraine, have sought Lazear's advice for economic policy.

Moreover, Ed Lazear is a role model of an academic who does not lose sight of his students' needs. According to Lazear, his initial motivation to do research in personnel economics was the fact that his students at the Chicago Graduate School of Business found the traditional topics in labor economics to be lacking in relevance for their future careers (see Part II of this book). He has written several textbooks, both for students and for personnel practitioners. His book on personnel economics (Lazear 1995) has been selected as "Outstanding Book" by MIT Press in 1996 and was named one of the ten most important books in labor economics in the same year. Acknowledging his accomplishments, Stanford University awarded him the "Distinguished Teaching Award" in 1994.

Finally, Ed Lazear is an exceptional scholar. Few other economists have shaped the research agenda in labor economics in a similar manner. It is this domain where the jack-of-all-trades analogy does not completely match Lazear's record. Rather, he seems to be an example of a rare species that has the skills for being a successful entrepreneur and at the same time has the talents to be an excellent specialist in a certain field. On the one hand, his scientific contributions underline his qualities as a "research entrepreneur": Lazear has worked on a very diverse set of topics, ranging from labor market institutions such as mandatory retirement or works councils (Chapter 1, Chapter 4), compensation structures and their effects on employee behavior (Chapters 6-9) to cultural assimilation (Chapter 12). However, Lazear also qualifies as a "research specialist": in all of the mentioned areas, he developed ideas that have profoundly shaped the research agenda for many subsequent researchers.

The IZA Prize 2004 was awarded primarily for Ed Lazear's contributions to the field of personnel economics. This subfield of labor economics opens the "black box" of the production process and analyzes what happens inside firms. Most importantly, personnel economics studies the institutions and incentives that shape interactions between employees and employers and those amongs employees. The questions addressed in personnel economics can be organized according to the different phases of an employment relationship: How should employers select their employees? How do performance incentives influence sorting of workers, i.e., which aspects of a compensation scheme attract a certain "type" of worker? What is it that defines a position or "job" in the first place? How should employers structure their compensation schemes such that employees are motivated to work hard? Why do we observe different compensation schemes in different occupations, and why do different compensation structures sometimes even coexist within the same occupation? How do labor market institutions such as wage bargaining mechanisms or works councils interact with workplace performance? How does the relationship between co-workers impact behavior? For instance, how do the performance and compensation of teammates influence a worker's motivation and productivity? Finally, how do institutions that govern the termination of an employment relationship, e.g., retirement regulation or employment protection legislation, affect the behavior of employers and employees during the period of employment?

In a relatively short time, personnel economics has become an integral part of research in labor economics. Pioneering articles by Ed Lazear and other early contributors have inspired many other scholars to take up an economic approach for studying human resource questions. Meanwhile, a JEL classification code has been created for the field, and numerous articles on personnel economics appear in high-ranking general interest and field journals. The success of personnel economics is also reflected in the curricula of universities and business schools throughout the world, where a large number of courses on human resource practices or personnel management are now taught by economists.

What explains the success of personnel economics? First, as outlined above, personnel economics studies a multitude of important questions that many practitioners are confronted with in their daily business. Importantly, it does so in the unifying framework of economic theory. In particular, personnel economists can rely on the methodology of non-cooperative game theory and contract theory: in rigorously analyzing the information structures, incentives, and institutions that shape interactions in the workplace, personnel economics has generated a stream of novel—and sometimes surprising—insights on the above questions.

A particularly important finding is that workers' wages do not necessarily have to coincide with their marginal productivities. As a result of moral hazard problems caused by informational asymmetries (which are the rule rather than the exception in most employment relationships), it can be optimal for firms to implement earnings profiles that do not equalize pay and productivity at every point in time. For instance, simple rank-order based compensation schemes can be equally effective as or sometimes even superior to more elaborate incentive mechanisms (see Chapter 6). In a similar vein, career-based incentives that offer an increasing earnings profile can help to mitigate moral hazard problems, since the prospect of earning future rents gives workers an incentive not to behave opportunistically (see Chapter 1). A further fundamental insight of research in personnel economics is that a firm's compensation policy and its hiring strategy cannot be regarded as separate systems. Rather, compensation policy affects both workers' performance incentives and the selection of workers (see Chapter 7 and Chapter 8). Research in personnel economics has also shed new light on the functioning of labor market institutions, showing that these institutions can have important effects on the provision of incentives and, thus, on workplace behavior in general (see Chapters 1-5).

A second reason for the success of personnel economics is that it lends itself to rigorous empirical testing. Though almost a tautology, it is this testing of theories and the identification of causal effects that scientific progress crucially relies on. Again, Ed Lazear has been on the forefront of this development. Not only has he developed some of the most relevant theories, but he has also set standards in the empirical literature on personnel economics. Many of the chapters in this volume start out from an empirical observation, develop a theoretical model to explain the stylized facts, and continue by empirically testing the theory's implications. Lazear's work on compensation based on labor input or production output stands exemplary for such fruitful combination of theoretical and empirical analysis. In "Salaries and Piece Rates" (Lazear 1986b, see Chapter 7), he developed the relevant theory, showing that the choice between the two compensation systems has implications for workers' performance, but also for the type of workers that are attracted by the firm (in terms of productivity or other personal characteristics). Subsequently, in "Performance Pay and Productivity" (Lazear 2000b, see Chapter 8), he tested the theory's implications using data from personnel records of a firm that switched from hourly wages to a piece rate incentive scheme.

The theoretical models developed in personnel economics guide empirical researchers to structure their research questions and to identify the key variables needed for testing the theories' empirical validity. Starting in the 1990s, recent years have shown a rapid increase of empirical research in personnel economics. This is mainly due to the fact that researchers succeeded in gaining access to high-quality micro-level data. Firm-based data sets as well as matched employer-employee data have increasingly become available. These data allow the researcher to observe relevant variables in great detail and therefore make it possible to test numerous theoretical implications, e.g., regarding promotion patterns of employees, compensation schemes in different occupations, turnover rates and composition of the workforce, etc. It can even be speculated that the increased willingness of firms to open their personnel records for researchers is itself the best signal that the research done in personnel economics is considered useful by practitioners.

A second, and complementary, set of empirical studies in personnel economics relies on economic experiments. Experiments are particularly useful to study questions in personnel economics because of two main reasons. First, they give the researcher much tighter control over variables that are crucial for direct tests of theoretical models, such as workers' effort cost functions, production technologies, or the information structures which employers and employees are assumed to face. In addition, experiments allow the researcher to implement true ceteris paribus variations, which is crucial when one is interested in causal identification, e.g., of the "pure" incentive effect of a change in the compensation system.

The empirical findings in personnel economics have been both reassuring and inspiring for the field. On the one hand, the theories' most important implications have been confirmed empirically. To say it in Ed Lazear's (1999) words, many empirical studies have shown that "personnel economics is real": for instance, workers react to performance incentives largely as predicted by theory (see Prendergast 1999 for an excellent review of early empirical results), compensation schemes have been shown to affect the composition of the workforce (see, e.g., Chapter 8 or Dohmen and Falk 2010), and many empirical regularities on real-world hierarchies are consistent with the predictions of promotion-based incentive schemes (e.g., Ehrenberg and Bognanno 1990, Eriksson 1999, Bognanno 2001).

On the other hand, empirical studies have also found some interesting departures from theoretical predictions. Probably the most important one is the finding that incentives generated through compensation structures can sometimes have unintended consequences due to employees' non-pecuniary motives. Examples of such motives that play a role for employee behavior include concerns for distributional fairness or equity (Adams 1963, Fehr and Falk 2002, Abeler et al. 2010), social ties and social comparison (Bandiera, Barankay and Rasul 2009, Fließbach et al. 2007), or the tendency to reciprocate perceived (un)kind treatment even if—from a purely pecuniary viewpoint—this is suboptimal (Fehr, Gächter and Kirchsteiger 1997, Fehr, Klein and Schmidt 2007).

It is important, however, to point out that these findings do not reject the personnel economics approach. Rather, they suggest that the objective function of agents might be more complex than traditionally assumed. This, in turn, has led to the development—and further testing—of new theories that account for these empirical regularities. For instance, models that incorporate employee envy (Grund and Sliwka 2005, Kräkel 2008) or a joy of winning (Parco, Rapoport and Amaldoss 2005, Amaldoss and Rapoport 2009) are consistent with the observation of "dropouts" or excess effort provision that have been documented in experimental studies on tournament incentives (Müller and Schotter 2010; Altmann, Falk and Wibral 2011).

It is nearly impossible to overstate Ed Lazear's contributions to personnel economics. As one of the founding fathers of personnel economics, his work has profoundly shaped the field. The impact of Ed Lazear on subsequent scholars who study human resources can easily be seen by the fact that the papers in this volume alone have been cited more than 2100 times according to the Social Science Citation Index (SSCI) and more than 8000 times according to Google Scholar. Without Lazear's impetus, the economics of personnel would probably not exist as a field or, at least, would not be one of the most vital and active fields of research within labor economics today.

IZA follows the tradition of Ed Lazear's pioneering work in its research program area "Behavioral and Personnel Economics". Initiated in 2003, the program area mirrors the comprehensiveness of the personnel economics approach: researchers and fellows come from a variety of different backgrounds such as micro theory, empirical labor economics, management and business economics, as well as behavioral and experimental economics. The conferences and workshops organized by IZA in the past years have witnessed a committed scientific community that discusses novel developments in theoretical and empirical research on human resources while keeping closely personnel practitioners and their questions. In his acceptance speech at the 2004 prize ceremony in Berlin, Ed Lazear expressed the belief "that this new research initiative promises to be one of IZA's most fertile areas for research." More than five years later this expectation is increasingly becoming reality, both at IZA and in the labor economics profession as a whole.

II What Is Personnel Economics?

About a half-century ago, business analysis and education was highly descriptive. It focused on institution detail, it lacked unifying themes, and generally ignored frameworks that used the scientific method, where refutable hypotheses are presented and tested. In subsequent decades, the business curriculum was transformed. It became much more rigorous, but for the most part still maintained its connection with the real world, where normative instruction is as important as positive description. Modern finance is perhaps the best example of a successful evolution of thought, but other fields, such as marketing using the tools of standard price theory, accounting with its use of information economics, and business strategy, which incorporated game theory and more traditional industrial organization, have also enjoyed significant advances over the past twenty to thirty years.

Personnel economics is among the fields that stands out as one that has changed the thinking in a primarily business-oriented topic, namely the management of people. Since the typical business spends between sixty and seventy percent of its resources on labor, understanding the human part of business is of paramount importance. But for the most part, business leaders paid lip service to the importance of human resources management but rarely treated the questions posed by the field and subsequent analyses with much respect. The growth of personnel economics has begun to change this picture. Personnel economics not only draws heavily on modern economics and statistical methods, it does so in a way that is useful in both describing behavior and providing a reliable set of prescriptions for businesses to follow.

My own involvement in personnel economics came when, in 1978, I moved from the Economics Department at the University of Chicago to that university's Graduate School of Business, and then later to Stanford's business school. My students, many of whom would later become important actors in business throughout the world, found the traditional labor economics topics that I was teaching to be lacking in relevance to their world. Issues involving labor supply and demand, public policy analysis, and even investment in education, unemployment, and other policy relevant aspects of labor studies, while intellectually interesting, were not particularly germane to their careers. They needed tools that would help guide them as they managed the people in their organizations. They also needed to understand methods that would allow them to do this in ways that made both firms and workers better off. Were they to ignore the latter, they would find themselves losing exactly the resources necessary to get the job done.

The confrontation with the reality that what I was teaching was not relevant to most of my students forced me to change the focus of my research. But I was unwilling to relinquish the discipline provided by economic theory and econometrics. Economics is powerful precisely because it concentrates on the important and strips away the extraneous. Its parsimonious structure, coupled with its formal approach, is a major guide to clarity of thought. I have never given up my attachment to economic theory, statistics, and their methodology. Instead, I have used them to answer questions that were, until that point, generally deemed to be outside the realm of economic analysis. But far from being non-economic, the issues that were the central focus of human resources could be informed by economics, and the approach, which was new to that set of issues, made rapid progress in changing the field.

So what is personnel economics?[1] Personnel economics is defined as the application of microeconomic principles to human resources issues that are of concern to most businesses. The field arose for three primary reasons. First, as already mentioned, those of us who were teaching standard labor economics to business students encountered an uninterested audience. Their boredom with what we had to sell signaled that a change in the product might be warranted. Second, the issues studied by human resources specialists were of interest to economists, but the approach taken by the non-economist was unsatisfying to those with formal training. The field of human resources management was too loose, unfocused, ad hoc, for our tastes. It lacked the general, rigorous framework to which economists have grown accustomed. Third, the technology of economics changed. As a result of some breakthroughs, particularly those dealing with agency and contract theory, economists were better equipped to tackle problems that had evaded them in the past.[2]

Personnel economics is an attempt to look inside the black box. It is an imperialistic attempt by economists to do what Alfred Marshall (1890) said that "economists do not do." Personnel economists are more willing to reject Marshall's famous statement that it is not the economist's business to tell the brewer how to brew beer. Although personnel economists may not be the best brewmeisters, they have made progress using the tools of economics to understand and sometimes even to guide practitioners and consultants in hiring, motivating, and managing labor. And personnel economics is real. Personnel economics is not an intellectual exercise. It is useful in helping us to understand actual behavior in the real world.

Personnel Economics or Personnel?

Like other subfields of economics, personnel economics differs from other social sciences in three ways. First, personnel economics assumes that the worker and the firm are rational maximizing agents. Constrained maximization is the basic building block of the theory that forms the foundation of personnel economics. Even when evidence suggests that the theories are wrong, the personnel economist does not drop the assumption of maximization. Instead, the approach is to think more carefully about the nature of the model set up, but not about the rationality of the individuals making the choices. Some may view this as an ostrich-like defect. I do not. When data refute a theory, it is necessary to rethink the theory, its specifications, its assumptions, what it includes and what it leaves out. It is not a call to reject the elegance and power of maximization. The economic approach allows for imperfect information, transaction costs, and other intervening variables which make things somewhat more complicated, but the essence of personnel economics is to assume that behavior is determined primarily by the interaction of the agents and not by forces beyond their control. The success of personnel economics is in large part a result of simply assuming maximization because doing so allows the analyst to express complicated concepts in relatively simple, albeit sometimes abstract, terms. The language of economics allows the personnel economist to remove complexity. Details may add to the richness of the description, but the details also prevent the researcher from seeing what is essential.

In many respects, this is personnel economics' main selling point. The typical human resources text is verbose and short on general principle. Indeed, many books eschew generalization, arguing that each situation is different. The economist's approach is the opposite. Rather than thinking of each human resources event as separate, the scientific method that economists use places a premium on finding the underlying general principle and on downplaying other factors.

The second feature that distinguishes personnel economics from other forms of human resource analysis is that personnel economists focus on equilibrium. Like the physical sciences, almost all theories in personnel economics are consistent with some notion of equilibrium. For example, workers in firms are assumed to react in a particular way where each side generally takes the actions of the others into account. When this is done, a particular equilibrium results which, again, assists in making very specific predictions about outcomes in the real world. As obvious as this may seem, the restrictions implied by requiring equilibrium are an important and unique feature of the economic approach not only to human resources, but to social science in general. Equilibrium is not central to psychology, because there the subject is the individual, and not how the behavior of many individuals combine to form a system. Sociology, which does study systems, tends to do so absent any formal notion of equilibrium. And certainly in human resources management, equilibrium is an unmentioned concept.

Third, efficiency is a central concept of personnel economics. Adam Smith's early notion of the invisible hand makes its way into personnel economics. Individuals who maximize their own utility and interact with firms that maximize profits generate behavior that usually makes both parties better off. When efficiency suffers, say, as a result of moral hazard problems that arise in the agency literature, the economist pushes the analysis to another level, asking what actions might firms and/or workers take to alleviate such inefficiency. Taking this further step assists in making better positive predictions and also normative prescriptions for the business student.

Much of personnel economics is quite consistent with traditional labor economics. Agency theory concentrates on inducing workers to put forth effort and bears a very close resemblance to the theory of labor supply. There are two differences. First, labor supply usually refers to hours of work or the proportion of the population that is in the labor force. In the case of personnel economics, much of the discussion is about effort. Hours worked is merely one metric of effort. Second, because effort is a central variable, the inability to observe effort is at the heart of much of the discussion. The tension between the interests of the workers and the firm, although present in the study of labor supply, is more problematic when effort is considered because firms cannot simply pay on the basis of observable input or output.

Personnel economics differs from other forms of human resource analysis in that, as in all branches of economics, there is no free lunch. Firms hire workers in a competitive labor market and cannot simply take advantage of them. Workers cannot be induced to do things that they do not want to do without appropriate compensation, either in the form of money or some other non-monetary reward. But, unlike other fields that analyze workers at the level of the firm, personnel economics is willing to express all compensation in terms of money, even if money is not the only or most important factor in compensation. Non-monetary factors can be expressed in terms of money simply by finding its monetary equivalent through a standard hedonic approach.[3]

In an analogous vein, personnel economists think in terms of substitution, where other human resources specialists do not. For example, most firms have a benefits department that is distinct from the compensation department. Compensation is defined specifically to include monetary remuneration only and to exclude benefits. There is no explicit recognition of trade-offs, and non-economists frequently think in terms of providing some market level of each job attribute rather than thinking in terms of a total package of utility.

Personnel Economics Is Useful

Personnel economics must be judged by its ability to be used. Use must be defined in two ways. First, the field should be an effective descriptive device. It should provide positive analyses that provide testable hypotheses that are both not obvious and explain the real world. Second, the field should be helpful in assisting managers to think through their human resources strategies, for hiring, motivating, and training an effective workforce. I will argue that personnel economics has succeeded on both counts and will do so by summarizing some of my own work in the area, which is the subject of this book.

The structure is to consider four distinct aspects of personnel economics. First, personnel economics attempted to explain the existence of institutions that appeared puzzling on first blush. The existence of mandatory retirement, the structure of pension payments, the use of worker-firm decision making, and some apparently bizarre promotion practices all fit into this section.

Second, much of personnel economics examines particular aspects of compensation. Workers are sometimes paid straight salaries, sometimes given bonuses, sometimes motivated through raises and promotion, and sometimes rewarded with non-monetary compensation in lieu of monetary payments. To what extent and when should these various methods be used?

Third, personnel economics does not ignore the interaction between workers. Peer effects and social interactions form an important part of the subject. To be sure, this is one of the newer and least documented aspects of the field, but a couple of examples of the framework and the use thereof are provided in this book.

Finally, skill formation is a major factor in the workplace, both before the worker joins the firm, through formal education, and after, through on-the-job training. Although this book is not about human capital per se, the acquisition of human capital, the choice of skills to acquire, and the interaction of those skills with occupation and industry structure are important parts of personnel economics.

The chapters that comprise each part of the book are what I believe to have been my most significant contributions to that particular area. The chapters are very close to the original papers to preserve the historical context. References are not updated to include more recent work that extends, derives from, or criticizes the original articles. Because a substantial body of literature has emerged in the field of personnel economics, I conclude the book by summarizing some of these more significant developments and recent work. I also discuss the impact that personnel economics has had on the study of business and especially the labor component of business operations.

III Explaining Labor Institutions in Business

Introduction

Among the earliest work in personnel economics was my paper, published in 1979, entitled "Why is there mandatory retirement?" (see Chapter 1). As discussed in the introduction, my encounters with business students made clear that my work had to address issues that were of interest to them. In light of recent and impending changes in discrimination law in the United States (the prior existence and soon complete elimination of the institution of mandatory retirement), the question of why the institution existed in the first place needed to be answered. It was impossible to anticipate the effects on business of a law that would make mandatory retirement illegal without knowing what mandatory retirement did in the first place.

There were a number of possible explanations of mandatory retirement. Most took as given that a worker's productivity declined after some age. Many believed that mandatory retirement was a way to deal with workers in a uniform fashion, forcing them all out so that the employer did not have to address the sometimes daunting task of differentiating among workers. Relatedly, other explanations suggested that mandatory retirement was a way to improve morale among workers, again because similar treatment would prevent some from feeling mistreated. A somewhat different argument was that mandatory retirement created room for young workers to move up in the firm. After examining the logic of these explanations, I found them all lacking. Either they were inconsistent with basic logic, or they were contradicted by other behavior in the labor market. For example, it is unsatisfactory to merely claim that firms want to treat older workers uniformly with respect to retirement when they treat them differently in so many other respects (wages, promotions, and even retirement—some are allowed to return as "consultants," others are not).

The explanation offered in this chapter is that mandatory retirement was a necessary byproduct of a desirable incentive structure. Young workers were underpaid and older workers were overpaid as part of an optimal lifetime motivation mechanism. But the motivation structure creates the wrong labor supply incentives. Because wages exceed productivity for older workers, they do not choose to retire when productivity falls below their alternative use of time. As such, mandatory retirement assists in making contracts efficient. Workers can receive higher lifetime wages because they are provided with this incentive mechanism. They agree to mandatory retirement because the age of mandatory retirement is efficient, which means that they could not be made better off by being allowed to work additional years. Doing so would result in additional compensation that falls short of the value of the foregone leisure.

The mandatory retirement work was as much about incentives in a life cycle context as it was about the existence of mandatory retirement. It led to other papers on incentives, but retirement and more generally, separation particularly of older workers, was an important part of the discussion. In "Pensions as Severance Pay" (see Chapter 2) the ideas are generalized. Once it is recognized that wages can deviate from spot productivity, then it becomes clear that not only is the retirement decision distorted, but so too is the decision to leave the firm at other ages. Using data from a large sample of U.S. pension plans, I find that defined benefit pension plans were structured in a way that allowed the interpretation that they served as an efficient severance pay structure. Specifically, suppose that a 55-year-old worker who is currently overpaid relative to his productivity, is worth more to an outside firm than he is to his current one. Efficiency considerations dictate that the worker should leave the firm. The problem is that since wage exceeds productivity, it is possible that the current wage exceeds the wage the alternative firm would offer because outside productivity, which is above inside productivity, still lies below the current wage. There is an arbitrage opportunity. The current firm can "buy out" the worker, offering him something less than what he is currently "owed" by the firm, but enough so that when combined with the wage offer at the outside firm, the worker will be better off accepting the buyout. Implicit in defined benefit pension formulas is exactly such a buyout. Once the worker reaches a certain age, staying additional years costs the worker in pension benefits. The annual flow of benefits rises with seniority but not by enough to compensate for the lost years of pension benefits. By examining the pension formula, it is possible to infer the implicit buyout offered for early retirement. Furthermore, this gives a fix on the difference between wages and productivity for senior workers. The numbers obtained from this study suggest that not only is the theory of mandatory retirement a logical possibility, but the magnitudes are consistent with common sense about how large the wage-productivity deviations are and how much is necessary to motivate workers.

Another line of work on labor institutions is in the area of employment protection. Like mandatory retirement, this is an important institution that requires understanding in order to know what the effects of instituting or eliminating employment protection might be. Many European countries have adopted employment protection legislation. In addition to the view that this would provide desired benefits to workers, it was also believed that the policies might be employment enhancing because the laws might spread the work around and would force employers to retain workers. Unfortunately, this is only one side of the story. As I show in "Job Security Provisions and Employment" (Chapter 3), theory tells us that employers may be able to offset these constraints. To the extent that complete offsets are not possible, one expects that hiring will be affected adversely by the existence of severance restrictions. Firms that know that they cannot fire workers will be reluctant to hire them in the first place. This is shown empirically in the chapter, using data from a number of countries over a significant period of time.

European labor markets differ from American ones in a variety of ways. One important difference is the use of worker/management co-determination to a much greater extent in Europe than in the United States. Once again, it is important to understand the reason for and effects of these institutions. In "An Economic Analysis of Works Councils" with Richard Freeman (Chapter 4), it is shown that worker empowerment (say through a works council) may enhance productivity, but at the same time it allows workers to extract a larger share of the rents. Consequently, firms will cede workers less than the socially optimal amount of power. Conversely, workers left to their own devices would choose more power than is socially optimal, because they are interested not in maximizing the overall size of the pie, but rather the size of the piece that they receive. This suggests a role for government in constraining firms and workers to choose the right amount of worker authority. But governments, too, are subject to manipulation. Allowing governments to mandate works councils as a solution to the problem replaces industrial politics with national politics. It is unclear whether the outcomes are better when determined centrally by a government body than they are when determined by the interaction of firm and worker groups in a bargaining context.

Finally, there are other institutions that have been discussed by organization behavior specialists for many years. One is the "Peter Principle," which says that people are promoted to their level of incompetence. Earlier explanations relied on politics, influence, favoritism, and other adverse forces that result in the wrong individual being promoted. In "The Peter Principle: A Theory of Decline" (Chapter 5), I reject such explanations in favor of a simpler one that is completely rational. The Peter Principle results from a statistical artifact. If individuals are promoted because their productivity exceeded some (actually any) cutoff level, then in subsequent periods, productivity will be expected to fall. This results from transitory components of productivity regressing toward their mean values. Not only does this explanation fit the observation for promotions and productivity, but it reconciles a large variety of seemingly unrelated phenomena, such as the "Sports Illustrated Curse," where athletes who appear on the cover do worse in subsequent months or years, and the fact that movie sequels perform worse than the originals on which they are based.

The essence of the following five chapters is that simple economics and statistics can be used to explain institutional puzzles in a fully rational way without resorting to ad hoc, ex post explanations.

1

Why Is There Mandatory Retirement?

Mandatory retirement has recently become an important issue. Congress has enacted legislation that extends coverage under the Age Discrimination in Employment Act to workers up to age 70 rather than to age 65 as it previously stood. This essentially outlaws the use of mandatory retirement at age 65, a common practice. Furthermore, Congress is considering the extension of the Age Discrimination Act such that exemption would be eliminated entirely. The current legislation already does this for federal workers. In order to understand whether or not legislation outlawing mandatory retirement would benefit society, it is first essential to ask why this institution exists. The primary task of this chapter is to offer an analysis of that institution, with testable implications, and then to discuss policy proposals that are consistent with and implied by this analysis. As an outgrowth, a theory of agency is presented which provides insight on how to compensate an agent in a manner that creates a harmony of interest between the principal and the agent.

There are many defenses and explanations of mandatory retirement. Most rely on the notion that a worker's productivity declines significantly after some age, say 65, and that mandatory retirement is the employer's way to deal with this reduced productivity. Yet, there is a significant diversity of talent in the labor force. No one claims that only the most talented individuals are the ones who can find

The original version of this chapter was published as: Lazear, E. P. (1979). Why is there Mandatory Retirement?, in: Journal of Political Economy, 87(6), 1261-1284. University of Chicago Press. © 1979 University of Chicago. The author wishes to thank Charles Brown, Dennis Carlton, Linda Edwards, Victor Fuchs, Nathaniel Gregory, Victoria Lazear, Jacob Mincer, Sam Peltzman, Melvin Reder, Sherwin Rosen, and Lester Telser for useful suggestions. Victoria Lazear provided substantial assistance in solving the problem discussed in Section 1.1 of the text.

jobs. Instead, economists believe that differences in wage rates reflect differences in productivity. The same is true of older workers. If older workers are less productive than younger workers, employers in a competitive labor market would be forced to pay older workers a lower wage rate than they pay younger workers. There is no necessity to lay off the older workers simply because their productivity is not as high as the younger workers'. In fact, very young workers earn less than middle-aged workers as a reflection of their lower productivity. Yet, we do not find researchers arguing that the minimum age for employment should be 45. The correct question then is, why does employment rather than wage adjust?

Some have argued that morale would be adversely affected by lowering the wages of older workers. But it is not obvious that terminating workers rather than lowering their wages will improve the morale of the remaining workforce. A 60-year-old worker who is faced with approaching termination is not necessarily going to have a better attitude than one who knows his wage rate will be lowered 5 years from now. Another view often expressed is that one cannot judge the decrease in productivity so that it would be impossible to adjust wages accordingly. But laying off a worker adjusts his wage rate to zero. This is a poorer approximation of his true productivity decline than any smooth wage adjustment. Furthermore, employers face the problem of gauging productivity for all workers. There is nothing unique about 65-year-olds in this regard. Thus, a productivity decline is not a sufficient explanation for the existence of mandatory retirement. One must ask why the productivity decline is dealt with by terminating the worker rather than by reducing his wages.[1]

Another "explanation" is that a uniform retirement policy avoids the disadvantage of discrimination between employees. Two questions arise. First, there is nothing that requires that a uniform retirement policy be one that has a provision for mandatory retirement. One could easily set up a flexible retirement scheme, where payment varies with length of service, that is invariant across individuals but does not require mandatory retirement at any given age. The second problem is that employers discriminate between employees at every level: some are promoted, others are terminated, others experience wage gains while others do not, and the existence of differences between workers is dealt with in many ways. Why should employers or employees favor a system that reduces the ability of the employer to compensate workers differentially?

Another "explanation" is that mandatory retirement creates promotion possibilities for younger workers. This explanation ignores at least two factors: First, young workers know that they will become old workers at some date in the future. They care about the present value of some lifetime wage path rather than the present value of any segment of it. Although they would prefer to be promoted when young, they also would, if their retirement is truly mandatory, prefer to continue working when old. Second, promotion may be interpreted as an increase in one's wage rate (and perhaps a change in the accompanying job title) that occurs as one's productivity rises over the life cycle. The firm will, in competition, pay the worker his marginal product, no matter how old he is. Thus, there would be no incentive for a firm to mandatorily retire a worker whose marginal product was equal to or greater than his wage rate to "promote" a younger worker.

Needless to say, none of the so-called explanations satisfactorily describes why it is optimal to terminate a worker at a certain age rather than reduce his wages accordingly and in a continuous fashion. In fact, explanations of mandatory retirement suffer from the same drawback as explanations of layoffs. Economists have been puzzled by layoffs as an alternative to spot VMP payments as well. I suggest that the two phenomena are linked.

The purpose of this chapter is to give a theoretical explanation for the existence of mandatory retirement that is consistent with economic theory and then to test this theory empirically. Before proceeding, it is important to make clear what is meant by "mandatory retirement." The phenomenon that we wish to explain has the following characteristics: First, there is a definite date when a contract (either explicit or implicit) ends. Second, at that date there will be some workers who will wish to remain with the firm at their previous wage rates, but whom the firm will not choose to employ at that wage.[2]

Thus, mandatory retirement has the characteristic that at some time T, the worker earned some wage $\overline{W}$. But at $T + \varepsilon$, the firm is no longer willing to employ the worker at wage $\overline{W}$, nor is the firm's wage-offer function continuous at that point (i.e., it takes a discrete jump downward for some workers). This story, by definition, implies that at T the firm is paying some workers more than the value of their marginal products. This is a necessary condition for the firm to desire to terminate the worker, and this is the bottom line to virtually all explanations of mandatory retirement. The argument here will be that, for reasons discussed below, it will be optimal for firms and workers to have a payment scheme such that the worker receives less than his marginal product when young and more than his marginal product when old. This implies that there be some date at which the firm is no longer willing to pay the worker his current wage. He is, therefore, mandatorily retired.

Feldstein (1976) has employed the notion that a worker's commitment to the firm tends to be permanent. He presents evidence which reveals that a large proportion of total job separations consist of layoffs, and, further, that layoffs are, in large part, temporary. That is, the worker is reemployed by the same firm which has laid him off in the first place. The lifetime commitment to the firm is the starting point from which we attempt to explain the existence of mandatory retirement. A sketch of that explanation follows.

Workers care about the present value of their wage stream over the lifetime (i.e., their wealth), whereas firms care about the present value of the worker's marginal product over his lifetime. Other things equal, a worker would be indifferent between a wage path which paid him a constant dollar amount over his lifetime and another one which had the same present value but paid him less when he was young and more when he was old. Other things equal, the firm would be indifferent between paying the two streams. But other things are not equal. It will be shown that a wage profile which pays workers less when they are young and more when they are old will allow the worker and firm to behave in such a way as to raise the present value of marginal product over the lifetime. For example, by deferring payment a firm may induce a worker to perform at a higher level of effort. Both firm and worker may prefer this high wage/high effort combination to a lower wage/lower effort path that results from a payment scheme that creates incentives to shirk. Thus, it may pay the firm and worker to set up a scheme such that the worker is paid less than his marginal product when he is young and more than his marginal product when he is old to compensate.

The efficiency condition for retirement is that the value of the worker's marginal product is just equal to his reservation wage. This will determine the optimal date of retirement. But if workers are paid less than their marginal products when they are young and more when old, their wage rate at T (the optimal retirement date) will exceed VMP and, therefore, the reservation wage. Although this is the efficient and equilibrium date of retirement (the date such that the present value of the lifetime marginal product equals the present value of the lifetime wage payment), the worker will not voluntarily retire at this date because wage exceeds reservation wage. Wage exceeds reservation wage at this point because that payment scheme produces a superior lifetime profile which workers prefer ex ante. Therefore, mandatory retirement is required to induce them to leave the firm at the optimal date. Thus, the existence of mandatory retirement is optimal from the worker's point of view. The worker is actually better off as the result of a contract which specifies a mandatory termination date. This allows the worker's present value of marginal product to be higher than it would be in the absence of such a contract, and these "rents" will spill over to the worker.

1.1. The Model

Consider an individual who has a value of marginal product over his lifetime, $V^*(t)$, and a wage rate $W^*(t)$ as illustrated in Figure 1.1. This worker is receiving an amount less than his VMP for $t < t^*$ and an amount greater than his marginal product for $t > t^*$. Let T be the point such that

$$(1) \qquad\qquad V^*(T) = \widetilde{W}(T),$$

where $\widetilde{W}(t)$ is the individual's reservation wage at t. Any $W^*(t)$ path that satisfies the condition that

$$(2) \qquad\qquad \int_0^T W^*(t)e^{-rt}dt = \int_0^T V^*(t)e^{-rt}dt$$

will be an equilibrium path.[3] That is, other things equal, a worker is indifferent between a path which pays him his spot VMP at each point in time and one which pays him a wage less than VMP initially and more than VMP later. As long as each path yields the same present value, workers have no preference. The argument in this chapter, however, is that other things are not equal. A path which pays less than VMP when young and more than VMP when old may yield the worker a higher lifetime wealth. The reason is that a steeper path reduces the worker's incentive to cheat, shirk, and engage in malfeasant behavior. That is, it affects the amount of output per hour worked by altering the worker's incentive structure. This generates a preference for a path that has a wage greater than VMP at the date when VMP equals the reservation wage. Since this is the point when retirement should occur, and since workers would not voluntarily leave at this point (since $W^*[T] > \widetilde{W}[T]$), "mandatory" retirement is a necessary consequence. But what is important here is that retirement is "mandatory" only in an ex post sense. It is negotiated in advance and is part of an optimal contractual arrangement which insures that firm-worker separation occurs at the appropriate time.[4]

Figure 1.1
$\widetilde{W}, W^*, V^*$

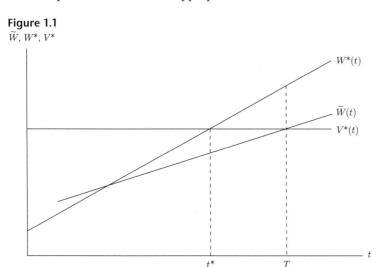

1.1.1.   Incentives-induced Mandatory Retirement

A steeper-than-VMP wage path is generated when we consider the notion of optimal effort, honesty, and malfeasance on the job.[5] These are treated symmetrically because performing at a level of effort lower than expected is merely a special type of worker "cheating."

Let a worker's marginal product at time t be given by $V^*(t)$; his reservation wage is $\widetilde{W}(t)$, and the optimal wage path is $W^*(t)$ (as defined above). Worker "cheating" is assumed to be detectable immediately and the worker is dismissed when he cheats.[6] A worker will cheat when the present value of cheating exceeds the cost of cheating.

The major cost of cheating is the loss of the current job which carries with it earnings greater than the individual's reservation wage. This immediately suggests that if wage paths are steeper than VMP paths (and reservation wage paths as the result), this will discourage cheating by workers since it raises the costs of termination. Stated otherwise, a firm which withholds payment until the end of an individual's work life is less likely to experience worker cheating than one that pays workers more at the beginning and less at the end of the worker's career. But if the former path discourages cheating, it results in a higher expected lifetime value of the marginal product. Thus, workers produce more and are paid more if their wage paths are steeper than VMP. But this implies that $W^*(T) > \widetilde{W}(T)$. Given that, the worker would not choose to retire at T. Since his VMP is equal to his reservation wage at T, however, it is optimal for him to leave the firm. Therefore, both worker and firm will, at $t = 0$, agree on a "mandatory" retirement date of T. I reiterate that it is only mandatory in the sense that, once at T, the worker would prefer to continue working at $W^*(T)$ if it were available. It is not available because his VMP is less than $W^*(T)$, his reservation wage equals his VMP at that point, and he has been paid exactly the full present value of his lifetime VMP at point T. Time T is the date of ex post mandatory, but ex ante voluntary, retirement.

In order to determine the exact shape of the $W^*(t)$ path, it is necessary to formalize the model: To make the model completely general, we start out with the possibility not only of worker cheating, but of firm cheating as well. Firm "cheating" takes the form of promising a worker a stream $W^*(t)$ from 0 to T, but dismissing the honest worker at some $t < T$ and depriving him of the promised wage stream. The firm's cheating may be intentional or may be "unintentional," if, for example, the firm goes bankrupt before T.[7] Initially, let us assume that firm cheating is unintentional or exogenous and that the distribution of dates t at which the firm "cheats" on the worker is known and given by $\tilde{g}(t)$. Exogeneity of $\tilde{g}(t)$ will be dropped below, but it is useful to adopt the assumption for comparison's sake.

Let the ith worker be assigned a $\theta_i \sim f(\theta_i)$, where θ is defined as the benefit that the worker derives from cheating. It may reflect the utility increase he derives when he works at a low effort level rather than the high effort level promised, or it may reflect something as tangible as revenue from the sale of stolen merchandise. For simplicity, assume that θ_i is constant over the worker's lifetime. If the worker "cheats", assume that he is caught with certainty and that as a result he is terminated. (The problem is complicated somewhat if there is a time lag for detection. As it turns out, that will necessitate pensions as part of the optimal wage path. For now this is ignored.)[8] The expected rent to a worker at time t is

(3) $R(t) = e^{rt} \int_t^T \left\{ W^*(\tau) - \widetilde{W}(\tau) - \tilde{g}(\tau) e^{r\tau} \int_\tau^T [W^*(\delta) - \widetilde{W}(\delta)] e^{-r\delta} d\delta \right\} e^{-r\tau} d\tau.$

This rather complicated expression is the value in period t dollars of nominal rents to the worker $[W^*(t) - \widetilde{W}(t)]$ minus the probability that the firm will cheat on the worker in the form of early termination $(\tilde{g}[\tau])$ times the cost to the worker of that cheating $(e^{r\tau} \int_\tau^T [W^*(\delta) - \widetilde{W}(\delta)] e^{-r\delta} d\delta)$. The worker cheats at time t if $\theta_i > R(t)$. From this, $\tilde{f}(t)$, the probability of worker cheating at time t, is derived:

(4) $\tilde{f}(t) = \begin{cases} F[R(0)] & \text{for} \quad t = 0, \\ f[R(t)][R'(t)] & \text{for} \quad R' < 0 \quad \text{and} \quad t > 0, \\ 0 & \text{for} \quad R' > 0 \quad \text{and} \quad t > 0, \end{cases}$

where $F \equiv 1 - \int_{-\infty}^R f(\theta) d\theta$. That is, at $t = 0$, some individuals, $F[R(0)]$, will have $\theta > R(0)$ and will choose to cheat. If $R'(t) > 0$, then those who did not cheat at $t = 0$ are even less likely to do so now or $\tilde{f}(t) = 0$. If $R'(t) < 0$, some individuals who did not cheat at zero, namely, $f[R(t)][R'(t)]$, will now find it profitable to cheat, so $\tilde{f}(t) = f[R(t)][R'(t)]$.

The problem then for the firm is to choose T and $W^*(t)$ so as to maximize the payment to the worker subject to the constraints that lifetime earnings equal lifetime expected VMP and that T is efficient. This can be written:

(5) $\max_{T, W^*(t)} \text{wealth} = \int_0^T \left\{ W^*(t) + \tilde{f}(t) \left[\theta - e^{rt} \int_t^T W^*(\tau) e^{-r\tau} d\tau \right] \right.$
$\left. - \tilde{g}(t) e^{rt} \int_t^T W^*(\tau) e^{-r\tau} d\tau \right\} e^{-rt} dt$

subject to

$$\text{wealth} = \text{expected VMP}$$

(6)
$$= \int_0^T \left[V^*(t) - \tilde{f}(t)e^{rt} \int_t^T V^*(\tau)e^{-r\tau}d\tau - \tilde{f}(t)c(t) \right. $$
$$\left. - \tilde{g}(t)e^{rt} \int_t^T V^*(\tau)e^{-r\tau}d\tau \right] e^{-rt}dt - \xi,$$

where ξ are hiring costs and the boundary condition is

(7)
$$V^*(T) - \tilde{f}(T)c(T) = \tilde{W}(T).$$

Equation (5) says wealth is equal to the wage rate ($W^*[t]$) plus the probability of worker cheating, $\tilde{f}(t)$, times the gain from worker cheating to the worker (θ) minus the cost to the worker ($e^{rt} \int_t^T W^*[\tau]e^{-r\tau}d\tau$), minus the probability of firm cheating, $[\tilde{g}(t)]$, times the cost to the worker ($e^{rt} \int_t^T W^*[\tau]e^{-r\tau}d\tau$). Expected VMP consists of nominal VMP, [$V^*(t)$], minus the costs imposed by worker cheating equal to the sum of the loss of his output between t and T ($e^{rt} \int_t^T V^*[\tau]e^{-r\tau}d\tau$), and exogenous costs imposed on the firm, $c(t)$,[9] times the probability that the worker cheats, [$\tilde{f}(t)$], minus the probability that the firm cheats, [$\tilde{g}(t)$], times the effect on marginal product ($e^{rt} \int_t^T V^*[\tau]e^{-r\tau}d\tau$), minus hiring costs, ξ. Equation (7) says that net VMP at T must equal the reservation wage $\tilde{W}(t)$ for efficiency. The complete solution to the problem is complicated and relegated to an appendix.[10] We merely sketch the solution here.

If $\tilde{g}(t)$ is exogenous, that is, the probability of the firm cheating on the worker is independent of $W^*(t)$, the solution boils down to choosing $W^*(t)$ so as to set $\tilde{f}(t) = 0$, that is, completely eliminating worker cheating. Payment should be weighted sufficiently toward the end of the career so that at every point t it does not pay for the worker to cheat. The exact form of the solution depends upon the distribution of θ_i. In the simplest case, where all workers have $\theta_i = \bar{\theta}$, the solution is indeterminate, but it has the characteristic that at $W^*(T)$, $W^*(T) - \tilde{W}(T) \geq \bar{\theta}$, and that $V^*(T) = \tilde{W}(T)$.[11] The intuition behind this solution is clear: If the worker cheats, he imposes cost $c(t)$ on the firm, but receives $\bar{\theta}$. Therefore, the cheating lifetime net VMP and wealth is

$$\int_0^T V^*(t)e^{-rt}dt + [\bar{\theta} - c(t^*)]e^{-rt^*}$$

if the worker cheats at t^*. If he never cheats, his lifetime VMP and wealth is simply $\int_0^T V^*(t)e^{-rt}dt$. As long as $c(t) > \bar{\theta}$, the cost imposed on the firm by worker cheating exceeds the value of cheating to the worker (stolen machines sell at a price less than the replacement cost to the firm) and the zero-cheating path will be preferred. The zero-cheating equilibrium is produced by paths having $R(t) > \theta$ for all t.

Figure 1.2 illustrates some possible $W^*(t)$ paths. One path is ABP. Here the worker receives a constant amount less than his VMP over his lifetime, but receives a large lump sum at T to set present values of payment and marginal products equal. There is no worker cheating because $R(t)$ is always greater than $\bar{\theta}$; it never pays to cheat. Another possibility is the more conventional LQ curve. Again, there is no worker cheating, and at T the worker receives more than his marginal product. Again, of course, present values of lifetime earnings and marginal products are equal. Another possibility is $LKHQ$. This is the Becker-Stigler (1974) solution where the worker posts a "bond" equal to LM, is paid interest on it (KM), and gets back the principal at T $(HQ = LM)$. A fourth possibility is $LHNX$. Here the worker is paid less than his VMP initially, more at T, and receives a pension equal to NX. As long as the present value of remaining rent exceeds $\bar{\theta}$ and the present value of earnings equals present value of payments, this will be an optimal path. This path is probably the most typical.

Figure 1.2

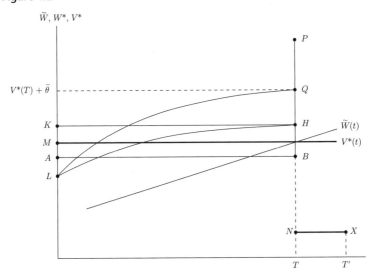

27

The important point that comes out of the above analysis is that in all these cases, $W^*(T) > \widetilde{W}(T)$. That is, if the worker could continue to earn $W^*(T)$, he would not choose to retire. If he were paid $V^*(T)$, on the other hand, he would choose to retire. Mandatory retirement is warranted because it is optimal for the worker to retire at T, but paying him a wage that would induce him to do so voluntarily would result in more than the optimal amount of cheating. Thus, a path that is optimal from a cheating point of view coupled with mandatory retirement is superior for both worker and firm.

Without going into the details of the analysis, suffice it to say that when $\widetilde{g}(t)$, the probability of firm cheating, is endogenous and influenced by the amount owed to the worker, the indeterminacy disappears (as it does for certain distributions of θ_i). The complete analysis is contained in an appendix.[12] The sense of the main result is this: As the amount owed to the worker above his marginal product increases, the gains to the firm from cheating on the worker increase. Therefore, minimizing the sum of cheating costs (which is essentially what (5) does) will trade off reduced worker cheating against increased firm cheating as $W^*(t)$ becomes more end weighted. This eliminates the indeterminacy and tends to reduce the end weighting of the payment stream. Mandatory retirement will still be required, however, since $W^*(T) > \widetilde{W}(T)$.

As an aside, it is interesting to ask whether or not $\widetilde{g}(t)$ is endogenous. That is, does the firm have a greater incentive to cheat when it owes the worker more? In a world of perfect (or unbiased)[13] information and infinitely lived firms, the answer appears to be "No." In that case, any cheating by the firm would affect the next generation of workers' assessments of $\widetilde{g}(t)$. This would raise the wage that the firm has to pay to attract workers, and this cost should just offset the benefit. However, if either of these assumptions is dropped, $\widetilde{g}(t)$ may well become endogenous.[14]

A second result is that as firm cheating becomes more profitable and $\widetilde{g}(t)$ increases, T declines. That is, mandatory retirement should occur at earlier ages in industries where the incentive for firms to cheat on their workers is higher. This is because the left-hand side of equation (7) is reduced as $\widetilde{f}(t)$ increases and less end weighting of the wage path produces a higher $\widetilde{f}(t)$.

One final and important implication results from the analysis: Other things constant (including education, ability, etc.), workers who have steeper profiles are more likely to have entered a long-term contract designed to prevent cheating. A necessary consequence of this contract is mandatory retirement. Therefore, individuals whose lifetime wage growth rate is higher than anticipated are more likely to have mandatory retirement. This somewhat counterintuitive implication that the high-performing, honest workers, with high wage growth rates, are more likely to have mandatory retirement is tested in the empirical section. The prediction is unequivocally supported by that evidence.

Note that pensions are a possibility, but not a necessity up to this point. Path $LHNX$ in Figure 1.2, for example, is one possible path. Two added considerations make pensions part of the optimal determinate wage path. The first, and most obvious, is a progressive income tax structure which makes a lump-sum payment at T less desirable than a smooth pension flow from T to T'. The second is relaxation of the assumption that cheating is observed immediately. If there were a lag time required for detection, then it would be optimal to withhold some payment until after T, or until the results were in, as it were. Pensions would act as such a holdback. This argument is somewhat less compelling than the first, however, because it requires that firms be allowed to terminate pension payments after they have already begun to make them. As an empirical phenomenon, the significance of midstream termination is doubtful.[15]

1.1.2.   Stochastic Variation

Another consideration is important. There is a potential inefficiency in this model which is tied to the question of early retirement. One observes that individuals sometimes leave the firm before T, the date of mandatory retirement. Does this suggest a mistake or inefficiency implicit in the lifetime contract? The answer is no. Consider Figure 1.3.

Suppose that we introduce a stochastic component to the analysis such that at time t^*, the worker receives an unexpected offer of $\widetilde{W}_{t^*}$ from another firm. Under these circumstances, the worker would not leave the original firm, because $W^*(t^*) > \widetilde{W}_{t^*}$. However, if $\widetilde{W}_{t^*}$ measures his VMP in the alternative firm, it is inefficient for him to remain with the original firm since $\widetilde{W}_{t^*} > V(t^*)$. That is, his social value is greater at the alternative firm, yet he remains with the original firm only because his wage rate is higher there. This is clearly inefficient, and it is unnecessary. An appropriate severance payment will eliminate the inefficiency which seems at first glance to be a necessary consequence of long-term contracts. At t^*, the original firm still "owes" the worker area $ABCD$ as payment (with interest) for service rendered between 0 and t_0.

Figure 1.3

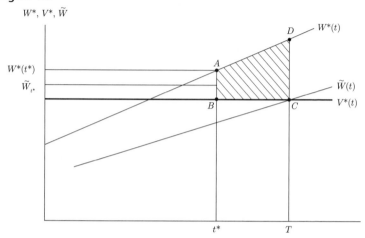

If the firm were to make a lump-sum payment to the worker at t^* equal to area $ABCD$ in t^* dollars, the firm would have paid out over the worker's lifetime an amount exactly equal to the present value of his marginal product. This is the equilibrium condition for the firm's payment through T, so the firm suffers no loss by allowing the worker to quit at t^* with severance pay. The worker, however, is better off. As the result of taking the job at the alternative firm and receiving severance pay, he will receive the present value of $W(t)$ from 0 to T plus the present value of the difference $\widetilde{W}(t^*) - V(t)$ from t^* to T. That is,

$$
\begin{aligned}
\text{the present value} \atop \text{of earnings} &= \int_0^{t^*} W^*(\tau)e^{-r\tau} + \int_{t^*}^T [W^*(\tau) - V^*(\tau)]e^{-r\tau} \\
&\quad + \int_{t^*}^T \widetilde{W}(t^*)e^{-r\tau}d\tau \\
&= \int_0^T W^*(\tau)e^{-r\tau}d\tau - \int_{t^*}^T V^*(\tau)e^{-r\tau}d\tau + \int_{t^*}^T \widetilde{W}(t^*)e^{-r\tau}d\tau \\
&= \int_0^T W^*(\tau)e^{-r\tau}d\tau + \int_{t^*}^T \left[\widetilde{W}(t^*) - V^*(\tau)\right]e^{-r\tau}d\tau,
\end{aligned}
$$

which exceeds his earnings at the original firm $[= \int_0^T W^*(\tau)e^{-r\tau}d\tau]$ by the difference between $\tilde{W}(t^*)$ and V^* for the appropriate period. Thus, the worker and firm behave efficiently as long as severance pay is permitted.

One form that the severance-pay arrangement may take is increased pension benefits. Thus, we expect that workers who retire early would receive a larger expected pension than those who work through T. This is a characteristic of many pension plans (as will be discussed below).

The qualification raised in the last few paragraphs is an important one because it reconciles the phenomenon of early retirement with the lifetime payment scheme suggested earlier. It is also important because it means that unexpected changes either in the alternative use of time (as another employment offer or a change in the value of leisure, say, due to poor health) or in the value of the marginal product at the original firm (say, due to business-cycle conditions) do not result in an inefficiency. This long-term contract carries no immobility costs as long as severance pay (or pension adjustment) is permitted.

1.1.3. The Choice of T

The past few pages have argued that mandatory retirement is the necessary consequence of an optimal wage scheme which makes both workers and firms better off. There, the existence of some T or date of mandatory retirement was determined optimal. But one important issue remains: The formal model presented in Section 1.1.1 yields a solution for T given the parameters. However, one observes that the actual distribution of T is not as smooth as one might expect from that model. That is, the reservation wage functions are likely to be smooth, and this would imply a smooth distribution of T. The real world seems to be characterized by a set of T's that take particular values. One source (Banker's Trust 1975), which sampled firms which employed a total of 8.4 million workers (about 10 percent of the civilian labor force) in 1970-75, reports that of firms which stated an age of mandatory retirement, over 87 percent had that age equal to 65. This suggests that there is some exogenous factor which pulls T to age 65. An obvious candidate for prime mover is the social security provision which becomes available at age 65. Consider the reservation wage function in Figures 1.1 and 1.2. If at 65 an individual becomes eligible for a social security subsidy to leisure, the reservation wage $\widetilde{W}(t)$ is likely to take a discrete jump upward at 65. This means that voluntary retirement takes a discrete jump at age 65 as well, which implies that the choice of T such that age equals 65 is most likely. An implication of this argument is that before social security, the distribution of mandatory-retirement ages among firms with mandatory retirement would have been more dispersed. Unfortunately, no data are available on this point.

Social security is one possible determinant of T. There may be others as well. Social security payments do not affect all individuals in the same way. High-wage workers, for example, may find the social security subsidy to leisure relatively less attractive than do low-wage workers. As a result, ages of mandatory retirement might vary by the characteristics of the workers. An obvious determinant of retirement date is education. If education increases the value of work by more than the value of leisure, one would expect more educated workers to retire later. This positive relationship is found by Bowen and Finegan (1969). If, as this chapter claims, mandatory retirement is the outgrowth of an optimal long-term contract, we might then expect that conditional upon having mandatory retirement, education and the age of mandatory retirement will be positively correlated. This is explored in the empirical analysis below. In addition, anything that affects $\tilde{f}(t)$ and $\tilde{g}(t)$ will affect the choice of T. If either probability of cheating is higher, T will be lower. Thus, the age of mandatory retirement will be negatively related to the probability of early termination.

1.2. Some Implications of the Model

In the previous section, a model was presented which has implications for the incidence of mandatory retirement by job and demographic characteristics. In this section I will explore these implications in greater detail and outline the empirical tests which will be discussed in the next section.

The first and most important implication of the model is that mandatory retirement is more likely to be found where job tenure is long. That is, we portray mandatory retirement as the consequence of an optimal long-term contract between a worker and firm. If contracts are short term, say week by week or even year by year, profiles where wages are below VMP early in life and above VMP late in life are unfeasible. Mandatory retirement is only useful in a long-term context.

Another implication, already discussed, is that unanticipated wage growth and the existence of mandatory retirement should be positively correlated. This, too, can be tested easily. By looking at an individual's work history and corresponding wage growth one can see how it relates to mandatory retirement. The argument on wage growth relates to the part that is unobservable at $t = 0$. Some differences are anticipated. We know, for example, from the outset that more educated workers learn more rapidly than the less educated. We therefore want to compare two individuals with the same observable characteristics.[16] The one with the most rapid wage growth, given these characteristics, is then the one with the higher probability of mandatory retirement under the incentives view. We therefore expect the probability of mandatory retirement to be positively related to the difference between actual wage growth and predicted (at time $t = 0$) wage growth.

Wage growth and job tenure are not exogenous variables. They are themselves the result of a choice process that is based on lifetime optimization. This suggests that mandatory retirement will be correlated with those variables that underlie wage growth and job tenure determination. That is, a reduced form, as well as structural approach, may prove interesting. For example, to the extent that whites have longer job tenure than nonwhites, whites should have a higher incidence of mandatory retirement. Similarly, if males enjoy longer job tenure than females, they will experience more mandatory retirement. Similarly, union workers, who have longer job tenure than nonunion workers (see Medoff 1976), should be more likely to experience mandatory retirement. It should be noted that these implications are the opposite of those derived from a queue or discrimination theory. If mandatory retirement were a way to reduce the labor force and make room for the younger, more desirable workers, one would expect that blacks, females, and the poorly educated would be the most affected. (They are the workers who suffer most from layoffs – the phenomenon that queue theory was formulated to explain.) The hypothesis in this chapter, where mandatory retirement is viewed as the result of optimal lifetime contracting, suggests that it is the more favored rather than least favored workers who face mandatory retirement.[17]

Pensions are one way to compensate the worker at T. It was argued above that if there is a progressive tax structure which taxes lump-sum payments at a higher rate than it does pensions, or if cheating is detected with a lag, pensions will be part of the optimal path. Thus, pensions should be positively correlated with mandatory retirement since they both are manifestations of the same contractual arrangement. Also important is that it is necessary to have some type of severance pay in order to avoid the inefficiencies of a long-term contract. As argued above, paying higher pensions to those who retire before T is one such arrangement. Burkhauser (1976) finds that workers who leave the firm before the normal retirement date receive a pension, the actuarial value of which is a monotonic increasing function of the years to normal retirement. This is strong support for the long-term contract view.

This model reinforces the implication of many firm-specific labor models that older workers, if laid off, will have a difficult time finding another job at the same wage. If wage exceeds VMP for older workers, a new firm will be unwilling to pick this worker up at his previous wage.

An additional implication comes from considering types of compensation. Since the steep wage path which necessitates mandatory retirement is seen as the result of an agency problem, piece-rate workers are unlikely to experience mandatory retirement. Mandatory retirement was the necessary consequence of a payment scheme which induced workers to perform optimally. A piece-rate compensation scheme is a substitute. Under this type of payment scheme, workers always have an incentive to reveal their true ability or effort.[18]

The explanation of mandatory retirement provided in this chapter also suggests a particular life-cycle pattern of preference for mandatory retirement. In this scheme workers at $t = 0$ prefer the payment arrangement that implies mandatory retirement. Firms prefer this arrangement as well. At time T, however, given that the worker and firm have followed the mandatory-retirement plan, firms favor mandatory retirement for the old worker, but the worker may oppose it vehemently, even though he favored it when he was young. That is, his lifetime wealth is higher with the mandatory-retirement scheme than without it, but given the wage path, his wealth would be even higher if he could continue to work at $W^*(T)$ beyond T. Thus, firms will oppose laws that restrict the use of mandatory-retirement contracts (explicit or implicit). Labor, in general, will also oppose these laws. Old workers, however, will push for legislation that makes mandatory retirement illegal since they can increase their wealth levels by doing so, given that they enjoyed wage paths $W^*(t)$ from $t = 0$ to $t = T$. This closely parallels the demographic breakdown of support of revisions to the Age Discrimination in Employment Act. Both business and organized labor opposed raising the age of exemption to 70. Major support, however, came from lobbying groups which represent the interests of the elderly.[19]

1.3. An Empirical Model

In this section, the implications discussed above will be given specific functional form and will be tested empirically. Let MR be a dummy which equals one if the individual in question has a mandatory retirement provision on his current job, and zero otherwise.[20] Let E be the number of years that the worker has been employed with his current firm. Let AWG be the average level of wage growth over the individual's lifetime. Then the theory above predicts that

$$(9) \qquad \text{prob}(\text{MR} = 1) = \frac{1}{1 + \exp\{-[\alpha_0 + \alpha_1 E + \alpha_2(\text{AWG} - \widehat{\text{AWG}})]\}},$$

where $\widehat{\text{AWG}}$ is the predicted level of wage growth from a wage growth regression. Further, there will be equations for the determination of E and AWG as well:

$$(10) \qquad \begin{aligned} \text{E} = {}& \beta_0 + \beta_1 \text{ Male} + \beta_2 \text{ White} + \beta_3 \text{ Ed} \\ &+ \beta_4 \text{ Urban} + \beta_5 \text{ Married} + \beta_6 \text{ AFJ}, \end{aligned}$$

where Male, White, Urban, and Married are zero-one dummies, and Ed is the years of schooling completed; AFJ is the age of first job. (This corrects for vintage and inflation effects.)

$$(11) \qquad \begin{aligned} \text{AWG} = {}& \gamma_0 + \gamma_1 \text{ Male} + \gamma_2 \text{ White} + \gamma_3 \text{ Ed} \\ &+ \gamma_4 \text{ Urban} + \gamma_5 \text{Married} + \gamma_6 \text{ AFJ}. \end{aligned}$$

Alternatively, one can specify the following reduced-form equation:

$$(12) \qquad \begin{aligned} \text{prob}(\text{MR} = 1) = 1/\{1 + \exp[-{}&(\eta_0 + \eta_1 \text{ Male} + \eta_2 \text{ White} \\ &+ \eta_3 \text{ Ed} + \eta_4 \text{ Urban} + \eta_5 \text{ Married} + \eta_6 \text{ AFJ})]\}. \end{aligned}$$

The signs of the coefficients in (14) should be the same as the product of the sign on the corresponding variable in (12). This is because α_1 is positive and because $\text{AWG} - \widehat{\text{AWG}}$ should not vary with any of these variables if (13) is specified correctly.

The same set of equations can be estimated with MR replaced by PP, where PP is a dummy equal to one if there is a pension plan. Thus,

$$(13) \qquad \text{prob}(\text{PP} = 1) = \frac{1}{1 + \exp\{-[\delta_0 + \delta_1\text{Ed} + \delta_2(\text{AWG} - \widehat{\text{AWG}})]\}}.$$

If δ_1, and δ_2 have the same signs as α_1, and α_2, we might expect a positive simple correlation between PP and MR.

The data used in this analysis came from the Longitudinal Retirement History Survey, 1969–71. This is a panel study of about 11,000 individuals who were 58-63 years old in 1969. A follow-up survey was done in 1971, and the data used in this analysis are derived from that wave. Only those working in 1971 were used so that data on wages could be obtained.

All were asked whether or not their firm had a mandatory-retirement provision which applied to them. An affirmative answer to this question was coded as $\text{MR} = 1$. The wage rate, W, is the hourly (actual or derived) wage rate on the current job. The measure of job tenure used, E, is the difference between the question date and the date at which the individual reports to have started his current job. Average wage growth, AWG, is constructed as follows: Individuals were asked what their wage rates were on their first full-time jobs. (The starting wage on their current job was not reported.) They also reported the age at which they took this job. Thus, define

$$(14) \qquad\qquad\qquad \text{AWG} \equiv \frac{W_t - W_{t_0}}{t - t_0}$$

where t_0 is the age of first job and t is the individual's current age. All other variables were defined above.

1.4. Results

First and most important, it should be noted that both job tenure and wage growth affect mandatory retirement positively. This is seen in equation (9) in Table 1.1. Individuals who have longer job tenure and more rapid unanticipated wage growth are the ones who are most likely to face mandatory retirement. This finding, although consistent with the theory of this paper, is hard to reconcile in terms of queue or discrimination theories of mandatory retirement. Note that the effect of $AWG - \widehat{AWG}$ is positive and substantial. This is consistent with the incentives or agency view of mandatory retirement. Second, note that the reduced-form coefficients in equation (12) go in the direction predicted by this theory but seem inconsistent with theories of discrimination. Note in particular that males and highly educated workers are the ones most likely to have mandatory retirement.[21]

It is interesting that the pension-plan equation (13) and the mandatory-retirement equation (9) are very similar and that the reduced-form versions are not very different. The theory related to lifetime labor force contracts predicts that this would be the case (note that the mean value of MR is .35 and the mean value of PP is .49). The exogenous variables seem to have virtually the same effect on the existence of mandatory retirement as they do on the existence of pension plans. Furthermore, the correlation between mandatory retirement and pension plans in a simple sense is extremely high. In this sample, 62 percent of those with a pension plan have mandatory retirement. Further, 86 percent of those who have mandatory retirement also have a pension plan. This finding is important. It is strong support for the coupling of mandatory retirement and pensions. The theory above suggests that they should be linked directly as each is the outcome of the same optimal contract. That is, in a world where the tax rate is higher on a lump-sum payment than on a smooth flow of income with the same present value, or in a world where cheating is detected with a lag, all wage paths that have mandatory retirement will also have pensions.

As mentioned above, there may be reporting bias associated with the MR variables. New workers, for example, may be less aware of the rules of the firm and less likely to report the existence of mandatory retirement. To treat this, individuals with tenure levels in the twentieth percentile were separated from the rest of the sample, and the estimation contained in Table 1.1 was repeated for each group separately. (The low-tenure group had $0 \leq E \leq 4.3$; the high-tenure group had $4.3 \leq E \leq 59.0$.) The results, only summarized here for the sake of brevity, reveal the same basic story as Table 1.1. Deletion of the low-tenure individuals leaves the results for the top 80 percent essentially unchanged. In addition, the results for the low-tenure group were simi-

Table 1.1

Logit and OLS Results

	Eq. (9): MR			Eq. (10): E	Eq. (11): AWG	Eq. (12): MR			Eq. (13): PP			PP		
	Logit	$\frac{\partial MR}{\partial X_i}\,\frac{X_i}{MR}$	$\frac{\partial MR}{\partial X_i}$	OLS	OLS	Logit	$\frac{\partial MR}{\partial X_i}\,\frac{X_i}{MP}$	$\frac{\partial MR}{\partial X_i}$	Logit	$\frac{\partial PP}{\partial X_i}\,\frac{X_i}{PP}$	$\frac{\partial MR}{\partial X_i}$	Logit	$\frac{\partial PP}{\partial X_i}\,\frac{X_i}{PP}$	$\frac{\partial PP}{\partial X_i}$
E	.02727 (.00249)	.31	.006						.02958 (.00249)	.28	.007			
AWG − ĀWG	.28992 (.502)	*	.661						5.8557 (.5791)	*	1.46			
Male				2.25 (.87)	.0640 (.0135)	.2268 (.1398)	†	.051				.3451 (.1345)	†	.086
White				1.00 (.77)	.0118 (.0119)	.0757 (.1299)	†	.017				.2650 (.1231)	†	.066
Ed				.153 (.062)	.0084 (.0009)	.0963 (.0100)	655	.021				.0945 (.0097)	.51	.023
Urban				-.289 (.423)	.0183 (.0065)	.2254 (.0672)	†	.051				.3492 (.0652)	†	.087
Married				1.015 (.769)	-.0201 (.0118)	-.0244 (.1230)	†	-.007				.0221 (.1185)	†	.006
AFJ				-.174 (.030)	.0014 (.0004)	.0011 (.0049)	.014	.0002				-.0129 (.0048)	-.14	-.003
DMR														
Constant	-1.1067 (.057)			16.1 (1.2)	-.0833 (.0194)	-1.9852 (.2105)			-.5582 (.0545)			-1.4727 (.200)		
SEE				13.27	.205									
N	4,123			4,123	4,123	4,123			4,123			4,123		
-2 log λ	128.7					119.9			324.9			180.7		
R²				.025	.029									

Notes: Standard errors are in parantheses.

*ĀWG − AWG = 0 by construction; ĀWG = .088.

†Dummy variables; MR = .352, PP = .485.

lar to those for the high-tenure group. The only notable difference is that for this group, married workers were less likely to face mandatory retirement than unmarried ones.

Some empirical evidence can be obtained on variations in T, the age of mandatory retirement, across individuals. Earlier it was suggested that more highly educated individuals would have optimal dates of retirement later in their lifetimes. If the skills which they acquired in school were relatively more useful in the labor market, then they would have an incentive to continue working longer than less educated workers. It follows, then, that if mandatory retirement is a manifestation of an optimal long-term contract, more educated workers should have older ages of mandatory retirement.

Table 1.2

Regression and Logit Results

	MR Age OLS
Male	-.093
	(.256)
White	-.387
	(.246)
Ed	.118
	(.017)
Urban	-.133
	(.120)
Married	.198
	(.225)
AFJ	-.005
	(.009)
E	-.032
	(.004)
Constant	66.4
	(.4)
R^2	.006
N	.429
SEE	2.25

Notes: Standard errors are in parantheses.

In Table 1.2, a regression is presented in which the age of mandatory retirement is regressed on demographic variables, education, and job tenure. Our sample contains only those who face mandatory retirement. The first point is that education has an important (in size and precision of estimate) effect on the age of mandatory retirement. It appears as though more educated workers make contracts which end at a later point in their life cycles. This is consistent with the notion that they choose to retire later voluntarily as well.

Second, note that job tenure has a negative effect on the age of mandatory retirement. In the context of this sample of old workers, all of whom are about the same age, job tenure is a proxy for the date at which the employment contract was made. Holding age about constant, those workers with fewer years of job tenure also have more recently made a "contract" with the employer than those with longer tenure. The results suggest that more recent contracts specify a later age of mandatory retirement. Individuals who have made more recent contracts may have done so either because the value of their leisure did not rise as rapidly as they expected ($\widetilde{W}[t]$ is flatter than had been anticipated) or because they ended up being more productive in the labor force than expected ($V^*[t]$ is higher than anticipated). In either case, it is optimal for them to be "bought out" of their previous contract (through severance pay or early pensions) and to negotiate a new one. The new one will have a later date of mandatory retirement because, as equation (6) shows, the higher is $V^*(t)$ or the flatter is $\widetilde{W}(t)$, the later will be the date of mandatory retirement.

Third, the coefficient on White is negative. Other things constant, whites have earlier ages of mandatory retirement than blacks. Although the explanation of this phenomenon is not obvious, let us conjecture. Even holding education and urbanization constant, whites have substantially higher income than blacks. This is especially true of nonwage income. Thus, if the education effect captures most of the wage variation, the white variable may well proxy higher property income. Since the income effect on leisure is positive, holding education constant yields an increase in the demand for leisure via income effects, so whites are richer individuals with the same wage rate. As such, whites prefer to work less and therefore set up contracts with earlier retirement dates.

1.5. Summary and Conclusions

This chapter provides an explanation of the institution of mandatory retirement that is derived from optimizing behavior on the part of both workers and firms. The theory, simply stated, is that it pays both parties to agree to a long-term wage stream which pays workers less than their VMPs when young and more than their VMPs when old. By using this payment schedule, the worker's lifetime VMP is higher than it would be in the absence of that scheme because this provides valuable incentives to the worker which would otherwise be lost to moral hazard. A necessary consequence of this payment schedule is mandatory retirement, that is, a date at which the contract is terminated and the worker is no longer entitled to receive a wage greater than his VMP. Its mandatory nature is illusory, however. The date of mandatory retirement is the social and private optimum date of retirement.

This theory has some perhaps counterintuitive implications. It suggests that the long-tenured and most able workers will face mandatory retirement rather than the least tenured. It predicts that the highly educated, white, male workers are the ones most likely to be mandatorily retired. These predictions are borne out in the empirical section.

The most important implication of this theory is that workers and firms all benefit from the existence of mandatory retirement. Although older workers may be unhappy about this provision when the retirement day draws near, their lifetime wealth levels are increased as the result of being able to enter into these kinds of contracts. What they lose by being mandatorily retired is more than offset by what they have gained during working years as the result. As mandatory retirement is made illegal before age 70 and the social security payment age is not raised accordingly, there will be an efficiency loss as voluntary and mandatory retirement ages diverge. If the ability to enter into mandatory-retirement contracts is eliminated through legislation, this analysis argues that current older workers will enjoy a small once-and-for-all gain at the expense of a much larger and continuing efficiency loss that affects all workers and firms adversely.

2

Pensions as Severance Pay

When wages equal marginal product and workers are risk neutral, severance pay is not merely superfluous – it is harmful. However, when either of these conditions is violated severance pay becomes an important part of an optimal compensation scheme. For example, if the contemporaneous wage exceeds marginal product then workers prefer to remain with the firm even when it is inefficient to do so. Severance pay causes the worker to leave the job more frequently, and a judiciously chosen combination of wage and severance pay can induce efficient quitting behavior.

Pensions which vary with the date of retirement can be thought of as a form of severance pay. If the expected present value of the pension declines with later retirement, then the worker sacrifices some benefits to remain on the job. Stated conversely, firms appear to be willing to pay a larger pension value (stock, not flow, of course) to workers who retire early. These larger pensions can be interpreted as severance pay because they induce the worker to leave the job more frequently than he would in the absence of such a structure.

This view of pensions is quite different from the one that holds that pensions are a way to save at before-tax rather than after-tax rates of interest. Although there must be some truth to the notion that pensions function as a tax-free savings account, this view alone is inconsistent with the finding (presented below) that the expected value of the pension stream declines with increased age

The original version of this chapter was published as: Lazear, E. P. (1983). Pensions as Severance Pay, in: Zvi Bodie/John B. Shoven (Eds.), Financial Aspects of the United States Pension System. Chicago, 57-90. University of Chicago Press. © 1983 by the National Bureau of Economic Research. Helpful comments by David Wise are gratefully acknowledged.

of retirement. Since nothing is withdrawn explicitly from the account until retirement, the value of pension benefits should be strictly increasing with age of retirement under the savings account interpretation of pensions. The widespread existence of pensions which decline with age of retirement is evidence for the notion that pensions act as a form of severance pay to ensure efficient labor mobility.

Below, a theory of severance pay is presented and specific implications of that theory to pensions are derived. The theory is tested using data which I generated using the 1980 Bankers' Trust Study of Corporate Pension Plans. The results are then compared to those obtained using a similar data set for 1975 which was analyzed in a previous study (Lazear 1982).

The major findings are:

1. Although severance pay does not always guarantee efficient labor mobility, appropriately chosen severance pay moves the economy in the direction of the perfect information optimum under almost all circumstances.

2. Most major pension plans in both 1975 and 1980 paid a larger expected present value of pension benefits for early retirement. This is consistent with the view that pensions act as severance pay but inconsistent with the notion that pensions are merely a tax-deferred savings account.

3. The structure of pensions between 1975 and 1980 does not appear to have changed dramatically. Either ERISA's (1974) effect was almost fully captured by the 1975 data or it did not have a significant effect on pension values.

4. There was about a 50% increase in the average nominal value of pensions across the board between 1975 and 1980. Additionally, there was over a 100% increase in the value of pensions taken 10 years before the date of normal retirement for pattern skews. This may have been a reaction to changes in the Age Discrimination in Employment Act which restricted mandatory retirement clauses.

2.1. The Model

The first task is to derive a simple model of severance pay.[1] To begin, consider a two-period world in which workers are risk neutral. The terms of trade between the worker and firm are set in period 0 and work, if it occurs at all, takes place during period 1. For the moment, we do not elaborate the reasons for setting up a contractual arrangement when a spot market might appear to perform as well or better. Simply take the two-period construct as given.

Define the wage at which trade occurs in period 1 as W, the worker's value to the firm as V, and the value of his alternative use of time as A. If work takes place, the worker receives W, but work does not occur in the event of a "quit" or "layoff," each of which is determined unilaterally. A worker quits if and only if $A > W$ and the firm lays the worker off if and only if $V < W$.

Work is efficient whenever $A < V$. Under these circumstances, appropriate transfers could make all parties better off if work occurs. But if W equals neither A nor V, work will not always occur when it is efficient. To see this, consider Figure 2.1. Work is efficient whenever the realization of V, A lies to the southeast of the $A = V$ line. Suppose that the wage which is negotiated is W. The worker quits whenever $A > W$ or whenever the realization of A is above the horizontal line at W. Some of these quits are efficient since the worker quits when $A > W > V$ and when $A > V > W$, both of which imply that $A > V$ so that the separation should occur. But some of those quits are inefficient since the worker also quits when $V > A > W$. These points are shown in the triangle labeled "inefficient quits." The problem is that the worker can unilaterally determine a separation and he has no incentive to take into account the fact that although his alternatives are relatively good, he is worth even more to society at his current job.

The converse is also true. The firm unilaterally determines that a layoff occurs whenever $V < W$. In the diagram, layoffs occur whenever the realization of V is to the left of the vertical line at $V = W$. Some of these layoffs are efficient because the firm lays the worker off when $W > A > V$ and when $A > W > V$, both of which imply that $A > V$. Thus a separation should occur. But some are inefficient because the firm also lays workers off when $W > V > A$, shown in the triangle labeled "inefficient layoffs." The problem here is that the firm can unilaterally determine a separation, and it has no incentive to take into account the fact that although the worker is worth little to the firm his alternative use of time is even lower.

Labor market situations seem to resemble this simple set-up. Workers have better information about their alternatives than firms and firms have better information about the worker's worth to the firm than the worker. Wages or wage profiles are somewhat rigidly fixed in advance so that the bilateral monopoly situation which arises after the value of A and V are known does not lead to costly negotiation about how rent is to be split.

Figure 2.1

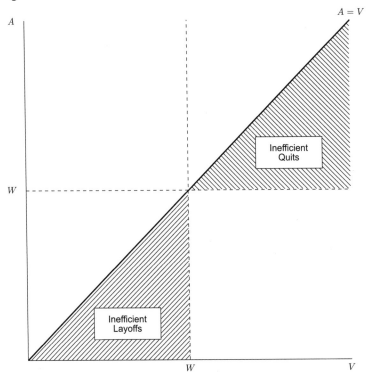

Now consider the role of severance pay. Suppose that the agreement which is negotiated at time zero includes the provision that work takes place at wage W, but that a payment S is made from firm to worker if a separation occurs.[2] The worker quits if and only if $A + S > W$ or if and only if $A > W - S$. The firm lays the worker off if and only if $W - V > S$ or if and only if $V > W - S$.

If both W and S are free to vary, severance pay adds nothing to the analysis. We can simply define $W^* = W - S$ and the previous discussion carries over perfectly to this case as well.

Severance pay is interesting when W or S is not free to vary so that the wage that minimizes the loss due to inefficient separation either is not feasible or is undesirable by some other criterion. In the static context, the division of rent provides a motivation for a separate wage and severance pay. Since $V > A$ automatically implies that rent is generated as the result of trade, that rent must be split up. It is desirable that the way in which rent is shared should not affect the allocation of resources. A two-part wage is sufficient to bring this about. The worker receives S even if no work occurs, so $W - S$ is the marginal payment for work and it is this value that affects behavior.

For example, suppose that $V = \overline{V}$ were known with certainty by all parties. Then if $g(A)$ is the density of A, the expected rent associated with the activity is $\overline{V} - \int_{-\infty}^{\overline{V}} Ag(A)dA$ if no inefficient separation occurs. This value can be realized only if work occurs whenever $A < \overline{V}$. If the marginal payment to work is set equal to $\overline{V}$, a layoff never occurs and quits occur if and only if $A > \overline{V}$. Thus, $W - S = \overline{V}$ is efficient. The split of the rent is a bargaining problem, but it is clear that any level of S chosen is consistent with $W - S = \overline{V}$ because W is free to vary. Thus, the rent-sharing arrangement pays S and the additional degree of freedom provided by W ensures separation efficiency.

A pension can be thought of as this most simple form of severance pay. After signing the contract (becoming vested, perhaps), the worker can quit and receive the pension S, or he can continue to work in which case he receives $W - S$ for work plus a pension of S upon retirement. Below, we enrich the definition of severance pay to encompass the more elaborate forms that pensions take, but the simple notion that a pension may function as a form of severance pay remains.

In this static context, the timing of S is inconsequential. It can be paid during period zero or after period one so that the term "severance pay" may be somewhat misleading. In the dynamic context, the timing of the payment may be crucial. The fact that contracts are not costlessly enforced seems to be a major part of the story and it is this aspect of the problem that makes it necessary that the lump sum part of payment, the severance pay, be paid after employment ceases.

One situation in which it is important that severance pay follow employment arises when effort cannot be monitored costlessly. As has been argued elsewhere (Becker and Stigler 1974; Lazear 1979, see Chapter 1; Lazear 1981), deferred compensation can act as an incentive device to bring about an efficient amount of effort on the job. A pension given on retirement may be regarded as a reward for service well done, and the existence of such a reward induces workers to avoid shirking over their work lives. But a pension awarded only on retirement is not, in general, the best way to produce this result. I have shown that under a number of circumstances it is preferable to combine some pension on retirement with an age-earnings profile which rises more rapidly than worker productivity.

The difficulty associated with steeply rising age-earnings profiles is that they distort the labor supply/separation decision. Mandatory retirement is one institutional adaptation which has arisen to alleviate the harmful effects of that distortion. But the problem is one which affects the worker and firm in all periods of their partnership and is not specific to retirement. In the vocabulary of the earlier discussion, if W exceeds V, then the worker will not leave the job when it is efficient for him to do so. The firm, on the other hand, is too anxious to rid itself of the worker. If V is known to both worker and firm, then it is easy to set up an arrangement that will guarantee both optimal effort and efficient separation. That scheme involves the use of an upward-sloping age-earnings profile with some pension after retirement at the normal age. All separations are initiated by workers except in the case of effort below the required level. Under that circumstance, the worker is fired and loses the right to draw high future salary and perhaps some pension device since the expected present value of the pension, and therefore of the severance pay, varies with age of retirement. Let us formalize the approach.

We broaden our model to consider a situation in which workers remain with a particular firm for a number of periods. Define T as the period of "normal" retirement. (As will be argued below, "normal" retirement is nothing more than the modal age of retirement because, with efficient severance pay, workers leave the firm appropriately.) A typical profile with wage not equal to marginal product is shown in Figure 2.2. Here wage, labeled W, starts out below worker's marginal product, V, and then rises above it. The distortion occurs because the worker reacts to the relationship between his alternative, A, and W, rather than to the relationship between his alternative, A, and marginal product, V. Severance pay can eliminate the distortion.

Figure 2.2

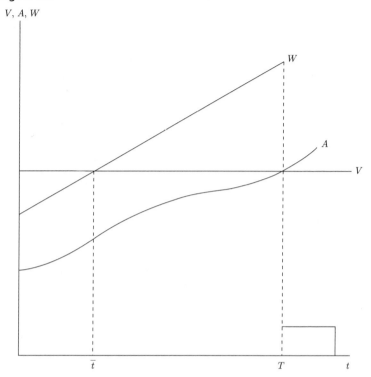

Utility maximization implies that a worker quits and accepts severance pay if two conditions hold: (1) the present value of severance pay plus the alternative stream exceeds the present value of the wage stream in the current firm, and (2) the worker cannot do even better by delaying his retirement to some time in the future.[3] In period $T - 1$, the worker retires if

$$(1) \qquad A_{T-1} + S_{T-1} \sum_{\tau=0}^{K+1} \frac{1}{(1 + r)^\tau} > W_{T-1} + \left(\frac{1}{1 + r}\right)S_T \sum_{\tau=0}^{K} \frac{1}{(1 + r)^\tau}$$

where K is the number of years beyond normal retirement age that the individual lives, S_t is the annual pension payment received from t until death if the worker retires at t, and r is the discount rate.

To induce efficient quitting behavior, it is necessary that the l.h.s. of (1) exceeds the r.h.s. of (1) if and only if $A_{T-1} > V_{T-1}$. If $P_{T-1} \equiv S_{T-1}$

$\sum_{\tau=0}^{K+1} 1/(1 + r)^{\tau}$ and $P_T \equiv S_T \sum_{\tau=0}^{K} 1/(1 + r)^{\tau}$, then choose P_T and P_{T-1}
so that

(2) $$P_{T-1} - \left(\frac{1}{1 + r}\right) P_T = W_{T-1} - V_{T-1}.$$

Substitution of (2) into (1) yields the necessary and sufficient condition that the worker quits if

$$A_{T-1} + W_{T-1} - V_{T-1} > W_{T-1}$$

or

(3) $$A_{T-1} > V_{T-1}.$$

Since this is the efficiency condition, the severance pay arrangement results in efficient turnover.

Now consider that decision at $T - 2$. The worker resigns at $T - 2$ if and only if two conditions hold: First, the present value of retiring at $T - 2$ and receiving severance pay must exceed the present value of continuing to work until $T - 1$ and retiring then, taking the $T - 1$ severance pay. Second, the present value of retiring at $T - 2$ with severance pay must exceed the present value of working until T and taking the normal pension. If we make the assumption that $A_t > V_t$, implies $A_{t'} > V_{t'}$ for $t' > t$, then the second condition becomes redundant (demonstrated below).

Consider the first condition: A worker retires at $T - 2$ rather than at $T - 1$ if and only if

(4) $$A_{T-2} + \frac{E_{T-2}(A_{T-1})}{1 + r} + S_{T-2} \sum_{\tau=0}^{K+2} \frac{1}{(1 + r)^{\tau}} > W_{T-2} + \frac{E_{T-2}(A_{T-1})}{1 + r}$$
$$+ \frac{S_{T-1}}{1 + r} \sum_{\tau=0}^{K+1} \frac{1}{(1 + r)^{\tau}},$$

where $E_{T-1}(A_{T-1})$ is the expectation of the alternative wage offer at $T - 1$ given the information at $T - 2$.

For efficiency, it is necessary that the l.h.s. of (4) exceed the r.h.s. if and only if $A_{T-2} > V_{T-2}$ (which by assumption, implies $A_{T-1} > V_{T-1}$).

An efficient pension plan sets

$$P_{T-2} - \frac{1}{(1+r)} \, P_{T-1} = W_{T-2} - V_{T-2},$$

or

(5) $$S_{T-2} \sum_{\tau=0}^{K+2} \left(\frac{1}{1+r} \right)^{\tau} - \frac{S_{T-1}}{1+r} \sum_{\tau=0}^{K+1} \left(\frac{1}{1+r} \right)^{\tau} = W_{T-2} - V_{T-2}.$$

To see this, substitute (5) into (4). The worker opts to leave if and only if

(6) $$A_{T-2} + W_{T-2} - V_{T-2} > W_{T-2}$$

or if $A_{T-2} > V_{T-2}$, which is the efficiency condition.

Note also that if $A_{T-2} > V_{T-2}$, the worker chooses retirement at $T-2$ over retirement at T. The second condition is redundant. Since $A_{T-2} > V_{T-2}$ implies $A_{T-1} > V_{T-1}$, the efficient pension plan already ensures that inequality (3) holds as well. Since the efficient pension at $T-1$ induced retirement at $T-1$ whenever $A_{T-1} > V_{T-1}$, it is clear that retirement at $T-2$ dominates retirement at $T-1$.

This provides a general statement of the efficient pension:

(7) $$P_{T-i} - \frac{P_{T-i+1}}{1+r} = W_{T-i} - V_{T-i}$$

or

(7') $$S_{T-i} \sum_{\tau=0}^{K+i} \left(\frac{1}{1+r} \right)^{\tau} - \frac{1}{1+r} \, S_{T-i+1} \sum_{\tau=0}^{K+i-1} \left(\frac{1}{1+r} \right)^{\tau} = W_{T-i} - V_{T-i}$$

so

(8) $$P_{T-i} = \sum_{\tau=1}^{i} (W_{T-\tau} - V_{T-\tau}) \left(\frac{1}{1+r} \right)^{i-\tau} + \frac{P_T}{(1+r)^i}.$$

The terminal value, P_T, is exogenous to this problem. It might be the optimal pension to prevent shirking in the final period before retirement or simply a rent-sharing parameter.

It is through equations (7) and (8) that we derive our results. If the wages of old workers exceed their marginal products, then the present value of the pension falls as the age of retirement rises (equation (7)) . Similarly, equation (7) provides us with an estimate of the difference between W and V at each point in time because P_{T-i}, and P_{T-i+1} are observed.

The case of postponed retirement is equivalent. Normal retirement is not special once we allow pension benefits to vary with the date of retirement. The date of "normal retirement" is likely to be the date of modal retirement. In almost all cases that age is 65 and corresponds to the start of social security payments because the social security earnings test causes the $A(t)$ function to take a discrete jump upward at age 65. Except for this detail, the analysis of postponed retirement is similar. The worker's choice is still reflected by (1) so all holds as above with a replacement of subscripts. If j is the number of years after normal retirement, then retirement occurs if and only if

$$(1') \qquad A_{T+j} + S_{T+j} \sum_{\tau=0}^{K-j}\left(\frac{1}{1+r}\right)^{\tau} > W_{T+j} + \frac{S_{T+j+1}}{1+r} \sum_{\tau=0}^{K-(j+1)} \left(\frac{1}{1+r}\right)^{\tau}.$$

Equations (7), (7'), and (8) follow correspondingly, so that an estimate of $W - V$ can be obtained for those years after T as well by examining the way in which pension benefits decline in late retirement.

Let us summarize this section. The pension which acts as severance pay reduces the true wage to V when we take into account the way that the pension value falls with experience. Since the pension is not paid if the separation is punishment for too little effort, incentives are maintained while efficient turnover is produced. Employers are willing to buy out of a long term contract if the wage rate exceeds VMP. The amount that employers are willing to pay reveals something about the difference between W and V. Pensions may act as a buyout. If the value of the pension declines with the age of retirement, this suggests that the pension plays the role of severance pay.

2.1.1. *Less Than Perfect Separation Efficiency*

The model discussed earlier allowed V to be random and unknown by both parties. Under these circumstances, one instrument – in this case the pension stream $P(t)$ – is not sufficient to eliminate all inefficient separation. The reason is that when the firm uniquely knows the value of the worker to the firm, the only way to make that information useful is to give the firm some discretion over when work occurs. But to do this immediately creates a problem, because the firm is anxious to sever the worker whenever $V < W - S$. This leads to situations where $A < V < W - S$, so that a layoff occurs when a separation is inefficient.

The introduction of a second instrument can alleviate some of this difficulty. If different amounts of severance pay are paid depending upon who initiates the separation, some inefficient layoffs and quits can be eliminated. This raises two difficulties. First, it creates a situation where each side tries to induce the other to initiate the separation. Second, it generates inefficient retention as a biproduct. This occurs when $W - L < V < A < W - Q$, where Q is what is paid to the worker as severance pay if the worker initiates the separation and L is what is paid to the worker if the firm initiates the separation. If $L = Q$ this condition can never hold, but for $L > Q$, inefficient retention occurs. This is discussed in depth in Hall and Lazear (1984). It is also shown that it is never optimal to select $L < Q$ because this results in needless inefficient separations. Perhaps because of these difficulties and those associated with determining who actually initiated the separation, pensions rarely vary with the identity of the initiating party.

2.1.2. Vesting

Vesting is an issue that always arises when pensions are discussed. This seems especially relevant when one of the arguments for incorporating a pension into the generalized compensation plan relates to incentives for increased effort or reduced turnover. It is sometimes suggested that nonvested pensions can reduce worker turnover whereas vested pensions cannot. The model in the previous section should make clear that "vesting" in and of itself has little meaning.

Vesting guarantees that a worker is entitled to receive currently accrued benefits. But currently accrued benefits may be small indeed until the last few years before retirement. There are a number of reasons which all derive from the large number of degrees of freedom inherent in setting up a benefit formula. First, many benefit formulas depend upon final salary or an average of salaries earned in the last few years before retirement. Because salary grows with age and, in an inflationary period, with chronological time, the benefits received by a worker who leaves the firm at age 30 may be much smaller than those received by the same worker if he leaves at age 65. Second, because length of service affects benefits, formulas can be specified to make the accrual rate a convex function of years of service, placing a premium on long tenure. Third, as Bulow points out, a worker who is vested but below the age at which early retirement benefits can be received earns a promise of a pension at normal retirement age, not the benefits themselves. Because of the higher value of pensions taken on early retirement, remaining with the firm at least until the age of early retirement election is generally lucrative.

In the same vein, the tendency of many plans to gear pension benefits to final salary is evidence for the incentive role of pensions. Most other rationalizations for pensions (discussed below) at best gear pensions to a lifetime average rather than to an average of final salaries. Since final salary can be adjusted to reflect worker effort, hours worked, and productivity, the multiplier effect on the pension value may provide significant incentives for workers to maintain effort and a high level of hours worked during those final years.

2.2. Empirical Analysis

2.2.1. Data

The data for this analysis were constructed using two sources: the Bankers' Trust Study of Corporate Pension Plans 1975 and the Bankers' Trust Study Corporate Pension Plans 1980. Each of these studies consists of a detailed verbal description of the pension plans of over 200 of the nation's largest corporations. The data sets apply to approximately 8-10 million workers, and this comprises about one-fourth of the entire covered population.

Firms are not identified by name in the descriptions. However, enough detail is given about each firm so that it is possible to match up firms in the 1975 and 1980 samples. For example, the descriptions report the industry in which the firm produces, the date at which the pension plan was adopted and amended, and the number and types of employees covered by the plan. Screening on the basis of these and other criteria resulted in a longitudinal data set of 70 matched firms for the two years in addition to the two cross sections of 200+ firms for each year.

The major empirical task was to convert the verbal descriptions into machine-readable data. This required setting up a coding system that was specific enough to capture all of the essential detail associated with each plan. It was then necessary to write a program which calculates the present value of pension benefits at each age of retirement. A brief summary of that approach follows.

Pension benefit formulas assume three different types. The two most common fall under the rubric of defined-benefit plans. A defined-benefit plan specifies the pension flow as a fixed payment determined by some formula. The pattern plan awards a flat dollar amount per year worked to the recipient on retirement. The conventional plan calculates the pension benefit flow from a formula which depends on years of service and some average salary. In contrast to the defined-benefit plans are the defined-contribution plans in which the employer (or employee) contributes a specified amount each year during the work life to a pension fund. The flow of pension benefits that the worker receives upon retirement is then a function of the market value of that fund. The defined-contribution plan is much less frequently used than is either the pattern plan or the conventional plan.

In order to test the theory exposited above, it is necessary to obtain estimates of the expected present value of pension benefits for each potential year of retirement. Specifically, the way in which pension values vary with age of retirement must be calculated. Some plans do not permit the individual to receive early retirement benefits or only permit early retirement up to a given number of years before the normal date. This means that in order to perform the necessary comparisons, sometimes plans had to be deleted from the relevant sample so that the entire series of retirement values would be valid.

It is important to realize that there are no real individuals in this sample. Since the data sets discussed above are descriptions of pension plans, the "individuals" below are hypothetical ones, created to perform the necessary simulation exercises. For each plan, for each of the two years, 12 "typical" employees were created, having all combinations of salary on normal retirement of $9,000, $15,000, $25,000 and $50,000 and of tenure of 10,20, and 30 years in 1975 and 20,30, and 40 years in 1980. Much of the analysis below relates to these 2,928 "individuals" from 244 plans in 1975 and to the 2,712 "individuals" from the 226 plans in 1980. Because this simulation exercise was computationally expensive, a representative group was selected having salary of $25,000 and tenure of 30 years on normal retirement. Many of the comparative statics results below are derived from an examination of the individuals in this representative sample.

In order to calculate the expected present value of retirement at each age, two steps must be taken. First, for any hypothetical employee, the pension flow that he receives on retirement in any given year must be calculated. Second, that flow must be converted into an expected present value by discounting it appropriately and by taking into account the age-specific death rates. Even the first step is far from straightforward.

Most plans have many restrictions on the maximum amount which can be accrued, and many provide for minimum benefits. Additionally, a number reduce pension benefits by some fraction of the social security benefits to which some basic class is entitled. Moreover, a number of plans provide supplements for retirement before the social security eligibility age. Sometimes these supplements relate directly to social security payments; at other times they depend on the individual's salary or benefit level.

Other restrictions have to do with vesting requirements, with the maximum age at which the individual begins employment, and with the minimum number of years served before the basic accrual or particular supplements are applicable. The accrual rate, or flat dollar amount per year to which the individual is entitled, is often a nonlinear function of tenure and salary, and these kinks had to be programmed into the calculations.

In calculating retirement benefits, assumptions about wage growth for older workers are crucial. All plans which are based on salary compute some average of annual earnings over some relevant period. Therefore, it is nominal earnings growth that will affect the pension values. Elsewhere (Lazear 1981) I estimated earnings growth and found something that is well known among labor economists: earnings growth is often negative in final years because hours of work decline (primarily for health reasons) in the final years before retirement. In the sample I examined, based on CPS data from the mid 1970s, the estimate of earnings growth for a particular synthetic cohort was anywhere from -2%

to -13% depending on how the sample was selected. Because more rapid wage growth will tend to make pension values increase with the age of retirement, selecting higher rates of wage growth tends to push the results against the theory of this chapter. To be conservative, I selected a wage growth rate of zero for most of the analysis and also recalculated pension benefits with a growth rate of positive 5%, well above that actually observed in the data.

Since all values are nominal, the nominal interest rate should be used as the discount factor. For most of the analysis 10% was used, but 15% and 5% were also tried in order to ascertain the sensitivity of the results to the choice of discount rate. Although varying the rates had some effects, it did not alter the qualitative conclusions.

Finally, in performing the actuarial correction, it was necessary to choose a life table. The 1975 life table for Americans was used for the 1975 sample and the 1978 table was used for the 1980 sample. Both were obtained from the U.S. Vital Statistics. The choice of table turns out to be the least crucial part of the analysis. Values do not vary greatly from year to year and discounting makes what small differences there are unimportant. What is important, however, is the possibility that early retirees do not have the same life expectancy of normal retirees. It is likely that many individuals retire early as the result of poor health and consequently have higher age-specific death rates. If this is true, then ignoring those differences will tend to bias the results in the direction of higher pension values for early retirees than is actually the case.

2.2.2. Findings

We start by discussing the data from the 1980 sample. Table 2.1 contains some descriptive statistics. Notice that there is a tremendous amount of variation in the present value of pension benefits even within each salary-tenure group. For all "workers" taken together the standard deviation is as large as the mean. Within each salary-tenure group, the standard deviation is around half of the mean. A simple rule of thumb suggests that the mean pension value is about one-thirteenth of the product of final salary and tenure at retirement. It is somewhat more than this for very low-salary workers and slightly less than this for high-salary workers. This reflects the provisions for both maximum and minimum pension values which make the benefit structure progressive.

Table 2.1

1980 Data: Moments of the Expected Present Value of Normal Retirement
Benefits (sample selection criterion: $\text{EPV} - 0$ valid)

Salary ($)	Tenure (Years)	Mean	Standard Deviation	N
9,000	20	17,102	8,063	218
9,000	30	25,209	11,144	220
9,000	40	32,676	14,610	221
15,000	20	23,054	10,597	220
15,000	30	34,167	14,100	220
15,000	40	44,020	18,027	221
25,000	20	37,367	19,140	221
25,000	30	55,353	26,110	221
25,000	40	70,779	32,897	221
50,000	20	75,730	44,270	221
50,000	30	111,368	61,755	221
50,000	40	140,551	71,253	221

Before going further, it is interesting to compare this to the cross section from 1975. Those data are presented in Table 2.2. Although the average pension value is smaller in 1975 than in 1980, this is the result of differences across groups. The 1975 data are constructed using hypothetical workers with 10, 20, and 30 years of tenure, whereas the 1980 data are constructed using hypothetical workers with 20, 30, and 40 years of tenure. In fact, within each comparable salary-tenure group, the values for 1975 are significantly higher than those for 1980.

Table 2.2

1975 Data: Moments of the Expected Present Value of Normal Retirement
Benefits (sample criterion: $\text{EPV} - 0$ valid)

Salary ($)	Tenure (Years)	Mean	Standard Deviation	N
9,000	10	10,624	3,921	192
9,000	20	20,864	7,700	194
9,000	30	30,403	11,411	183
15,000	10	16,416	7,008	194
15,000	20	31,359	14,116	204
15,000	30	47,369	20,118	186
25,000	10	26,125	13,869	199
25,000	20	51,337	26,328	206
25,000	30	76,989	39,165	188
50,000	10	50,931	31,338	205
50,000	20	101,462	60,683	206
50,000	30	151,337	90,222	188

Table 2.3

1980 Expected Present Value of Pension Benefits: Defined-Benefit Conventional Plans (sample: valid $EPV - 10$ ... $EPV - 0$)

	Final Salary $9,000			Final Salary $15,000		
	20-Year	30-Year	40-Year	20-Year	30-Year	40-Year
Variable	Tenure	Tenure	Tenure	Tenure	Tenure	Tenure
$EPV - 10$	27,225	50,845	73,959	35,384	66,875	97,232
$EPV - 9$	26,911	48,451	69,381	35,391	64,506	92,318
$EPV - 8$	26,392	45,905	64,904	35,116	61,886	87,459
$EPV - 7$	25,684	43,266	60,506	34,603	59,074	83,620
$EPV - 6$	24,856	40,687	56,288	33,945	56,211	77,814
$EPV - 5$	23,868	38,216	52,277	33,162	53,484	73,241
$EPV - 4$	22,752	35,594	48,218	32,058	50,344	68,345
$EPV - 3$	21,496	32,993	44,277	30,634	47,113	63,512
$EPV - 2$	20,089	30,311	40,347	28,890	43,598	58,377
$EPV - 1$	18,699	27,785	36,690	27,146	40,278	53,594
$EPV - 0$	17,032	24,839	31,624	24,846	36,166	45,962
$ERAT - 10$	1.617	2.131	2.517	1.550	2.122	2.542
$ERAT - 9$	1.609	2.038	2.372	1.553	2.041	2.407
$ERAT - 8$	1.587	1.939	2.228	1.541	1.955	2.274
$ERAT - 7$	1.552	1.835	2.085	1.519	1.865	2.143
$ERAT - 6$	1.509	1.733	1.946	1.490	1.773	2.013
$ERAT - 5$	1.453	1.636	1.815	1.456	1.686	1.891
$ERAT - 4$	1.389	1.528	1.679	1.409	1.587	1.762
$ERAT - 3$	1.317	1.421	1.547	1.349	1.485	1.636
$ERAT - 2$	1.234	1.307	1.412	1.274	1.373	1.502
$ERAT - 1$	1.151	1.201	1.287	1.198	1.268	1.377
$ERAT - 0$	1.000	1.000	1.000	1.000	1.000	1.000
$WVDIFF - 10$	121	922	1,764	-2	913	1,894
$WVDIFF - 9$	220	1,079	1,898	116	1,111	2,060
$WVDIFF - 8$	330	1,231	2,051	238	1,311	2,257
$WVDIFF - 7$	424	1,323	2,164	337	1,469	2,466
$WVDIFF - 6$	557	1,394	2,264	441	1,539	2,581
$WVDIFF - 5$	693	1,628	2,519	685	1,949	3,040
$WVDIFF - 4$	857	1,776	2,691	972	2,206	3,300
$WVDIFF - 3$	1,056	2,015	2,952	1,310	2,640	3,857
$WVDIFF - 2$	1,148	2,087	3,022	1,441	2,743	3,952
$WVDIFF - 1$	1,515	2,678	4,605	2,090	3,738	6,938
Normal	2,911	4,267	5,282	4,759	6,994	8,679
N	133	133	134	140	141	144

We defer until later discussion of the reasons for this pattern. Another interesting difference is that the pattern is significantly less progressive in 1975 than in 1980. In 1975, the rule that the pension value equals about one-tenth of the product of final salary and tenure seems to hold across all salary levels with only slight traces of progressivity.

These findings do not suggest that pensions were larger in 1975 than in 1980. There are two main reasons: First, firms are not matched across years in these tables, so that some of the difference may simply reflect random sample variations. Second, final salaries were substantially higher in 1980 than in 1975, so the relevant comparison is not necessarily the one that holds salary level constant.

Table 2.3 (continued)

1980 Expected Present Value of Pension Benefits: Defined-Benefit Conventional Plans (sample: valid $EPV - 10 \dots EPV - 0$)

Final Salary $25,000			Final Salary $50,000		
20-Year Tenure	30-Year Tenure	40-Year Tenure	20-Year Tenure	30-Year Tenure	40-Year Tenure
55,958	107,585	158,225	115,633	226,685	332,604
56,822	105,111	151,713	118,342	222,374	319,890
57,200	101,951	144,918	119,778	216,465	306,211
57,081	98,212	137,902	120,120	209,160	291,814
56,522	94,213	130,778	119,398	201,062	276,943
55,604	90,176	123,844	117,706	192,441	261,907
54,142	85,524	116,234	114,845	182,598	245,945
52,165	80,656	108,553	110,988	172,413	229,942
49,549	75,143	100,236	105,770	160,908	212,544
46,903	69,863	92,429	100,288	149,675	195,920
43,244	63,165	79,476	92,555	135,577	168,913
1.601	2.285	2.836	1.972	2.993	3.816
1.619	2.212	2.694	1.996	2.887	3.609
1.623	2.129	2.550	2.000	2.770	3.401
1.612	2.039	2.406	1.985	2.644	3.194
1.590	1.944	2.263	1.953	2.512	2.989
1.557	1.850	2.126	1.908	2.378	2.789
1.512	1.747	1.982	1.847	2.236	2.590
1.456	1.641	1.840	1.776	2.094	2.395
1.380	1.522	1.689	1.680	1.936	2.192
1.303	1.408	1.549	1.581	1.784	2.000
1.000	1.000	1.000	1.000	1.000	1.000
-332	953	2,510	-1,044	1,661	4,901
-160	1,340	2,881	-609	2,506	5,801
55	1,744	3,272	-159	3,408	6,716
286	2,052	3,655	370	4,155	7,641
518	2,278	3,914	955	4,866	8,476
908	2,888	4,725	1,776	6,112	9,910
1,350	3,324	5,245	2,634	6,956	10,930
1,964	4,141	6,249	3,920	8,644	13,071
2,187	4,363	6,451	4,531	9,282	13,738
3,326	6,089	11,775	7,029	12,816	24,551
7,885	11,608	14,363	15,783	23,258	28,787
141	144	144	143	144	144

In the context of the model, the most important results relate to the way in which pension values vary with the age of retirement. Tables 2.3 - 2.5 select those "individuals" in the 1980 sample who were permitted to retire at least 10 years before the normal age and trace the mean present value of pensions for that group. $EPV - 10$ refers to the expected present value of retiring 10 years before the normal age, and similarly for $EPV - 9 \dots EPV - 1$. $EPV - 0$ is the present value of retiring at normal age. The tables are broken down by pension benefit formula type and then by salary and tenure level.

First examine Table 2.3, which relates to conventional plans. Note that for all tenure-salary groups, the value of early retirement exceeds that of normal retirement (EPV − 10 > EPV − 9 > ... > EPR − 1 > EPV − 0). For ease of reading, ERAT(t) is defined as EPV(t)/EPRO, so that ERAT > 1 for all $t < 0$. This evidence supports the major prediction of the model: The expected present value of pension benefits declines as the age of retirement increases. Firms actually do "buy out" workers who retire early with higher pensions. As such, the interpretation that pensions act as severance pay is consistent with these results.

Table 2.4

1980 Expected Value of Pension Benefits: Defined-Contribution Pattern Plans (Benefits are independent of final salary.)

Variable	20-Year Tenure	30-Year Tenure	40-Year Tenure
EPV − 10	20,450	40,651	64,349
EPV − 9	21,085	40,103	61,913
EPV − 8	21,513	39,296	59,276
EPV − 7	21,704	38,262	56,477
EPV − 6	21,667	37,031	53,554
EPV − 5	21,454	36,164	51,868
EPV − 4	21,053	34,485	48,489
EPV − 3	20,498	32,716	45,117
EPV − 2	19,730	30,752	41,577
EPV − 1	18,863	28,767	38,430
EPV − 0	17,982	26,876	35,361
ERAT − 10	1.113	1.491	1.810
ERAT − 9	1.150	1.473	1.743
ERAT − 8	1.176	1.446	1.670
ERAT − 7	1.189	1.410	1.592
ERAT − 6	1.190	1.367	1.510
ERAT − 5	1.180	1.334	1.461
ERAT − 4	1.161	1.274	1.367
ERAT − 3	1.132	1.210	1.272
ERAT − 2	1.092	1.140	1.173
ERAT − 1	1.047	1.068	1.085
ERAT − 0	1.000	1.000	1.000
WVDIFF − 10	-244	211	939
WVDIFF − 9	-181	342	1,118
WVDIFF − 8	-89	482	1,305
WVDIFF − 7	13	631	1,500
WVDIFF − 6	126	489	951
WVDIFF − 5	249	1,042	2,098
WVDIFF − 4	378	1,208	2,303
WVDIFF − 3	577	1,475	2,659
WVDIFF − 2	716	1,640	2,600
WVDIFF − 1	801	1,718	2,789
Normal	2,766	4,123	5,421
N	38	38	38

Further, ERAT − 10 increases with tenure and salary. The buy-out is larger, not only in absolute terms, but also in relative terms for employees of longer service and of higher salaries. This is consistent with the interpretation that an upward-sloping age-earnings profile acts as an incentive device.

This is most easily seen by examining WVDIFF− 10 ... WVDIFF − 1. WVDIFF(t) is defined as $W_{T-t} − V_{T-t}$ and is calculated using the relationship shown in equation (7). WVDIFF > 0 implies that the worker is being paid more than his marginal product, and it results whenever $P_{T-i} > P_{T-i+1}$. WVDIFF − 1/SALARY is the ratio of over-payment during the final year before retirement. That ratio goes from 1/6 for workers in the group with salary = 9,000, tenure = 20 to 1/2 for workers in the group with salary = 50,000, tenure = 40. This result has a nice interpretation.

First consider tenure: Individuals with shorter tenure are those who initiated their employment with the firm more recently. In the context of Figure 2.2, those workers are less likely to have wages which exceed their marginal products. As the result, the buy-out should be smaller. In fact, for individuals whose tenure is below $\bar{t}$ in Figure 2.2, the buy-out should actually be negative. (Although this occurs in a significant number of cases, it docs not occur frequently enough to make the means display an increasing pattern.)

Second, high-salary workers are those most likely to be performing jobs where wage incentive schemes are useful. Since those may be the jobs which are most difficult to monitor, a large penalty in the form of lost earnings is likely to be an integral part of the optimal compensation profile for these workers.

These points are also supported by consideration of Table 2.4, which relates to pattern plan workers. It is also true that the general tendency is for the pension value to decline with age of retirement. But the decline does not seem to be as pronounced for these employees as for those with conventional plans. In fact, for those with only 20 years of experience at normal retirement, the means of WVDIFF − 10, WVDIFF − 9, and WVDIFF − 8 are actually positive, reflecting location in terms of Figure 2.2 before $\bar{t}$. Since most of these workers are blue-collar workers where more direct monitoring is possible, it is not surprising that the wages conform more to marginal product for these workers than for their higher-level counterparts.

Table 2.5

1980 Expected Present Value of Pension Benefits: Defined-Benefit Conventional Plans (sample: valid $EPV - 10 \ldots EPV - 0$)

	Final Salary $9,000			Final Salary $15,000		
Variable	20-Year Tenure	30-Year Tenure	40-Year Tenure	20-Year Tenure	30-Year Tenure	40-Year Tenure
$EPV - 10$	12,673	25,346	38,019	18,342	36,685	55,028
$EPV - 9$	14,915	28,475	42,035	21,588	41,214	60,840
$EPV - 8$	17,256	31,636	46,016	24,975	45,789	66,602
$EPV - 7$	19,670	34,800	49,931	28,469	50,369	72,269
$EPV - 6$	22,131	37,940	53,749	32,033	54,913	77,794
$EPV - 5$	24,615	41,025	57,435	35,627	59,379	83,130
$EPV - 4$	26,280	42,705	59,130	38,037	61,810	85,584
$EPV - 3$	27,865	44,257	60,649	40,332	64,056	87,781
$EPV - 2$	28,500	44,334	60,168	41,251	64,168	87,086
$EPV - 1$	28,995	44,255	59,516	41,966	64,054	86,142
$EPV - 0$	29,344	44,016	58,689	42,472	63,708	84,944
$ERAT - 10$	0.431	0.575	0.647	0.431	0.575	0.647
$ERAT - 9$	0.508	0.646	0.716	0.508	0.646	0.716
$ERAT - 8$	0.588	0.718	0.784	0.588	0.718	0.784
$ERAT - 7$	0.670	0.790	0.850	0.670	0.790	0.850
$ERAT - 6$	0.754	0.861	0.915	0.754	0.861	0.915
$ERAT - 5$	0.838	0.932	0.978	0.838	0.932	0.978
$ERAT - 4$	0.895	0.970	1.007	0.895	0.970	1.007
$ERAT - 3$	0.949	1.005	1.033	0.949	1.005	1.033
$ERAT - 2$	0.971	1.007	1.025	0.971	1.007	1.025
$ERAT - 1$	0.988	1.005	1.014	0.988	1.005	1.014
$ERAT - 0$	1.000	1.000	1.000	1.000	1.000	1.000
$WVDIFF - 10$	-864	-1,206	-1,548	-1,251	-1,745	-2,240
$WVDIFF - 9$	-992	-1,340	-1,688	-1,436	-1,940	-2,443
$WVDIFF - 8$	-1,126	-1,476	-1,826	-1,629	-2,136	-2,643
$WVDIFF - 7$	-1,263	-1,611	-1,958	-1,828	-2,331	-2,835
$WVDIFF - 6$	-1,401	-1,741	-2,081	-2,028	-2,520	-3,012
$WVDIFF - 5$	-1,033	-1,043	-1,052	-1,496	-1,509	-1,523
$WVDIFF - 4$	-1,082	-1,059	-1,036	-1,567	-1,534	-1,500
$WVDIFF - 3$	-477	-58	360	-690	-84	522
$WVDIFF - 2$	-408	65	539	-591	94	780
$WVDIFF - 1$	-317	217	752	-567	314	1,088
Normal	4,560	6,840	9,120	6,600	9,900	13,200
N	1	1	1	1	1	1

Finally, Table 2.5 reports defined-contribution plans. We hesitate to draw any significant conclusions from this table for two reasons. First, there are so few observations. Second, the Bankers' Trust studies do not really report the appropriate information for defined-contribution plans, so these calculations are more likely to be a function of interpretations made by them and by me. The one obvious feature is that definitionally a defined-contribution plan cannot decline in present value with age of retirement because the worker is always entitled to the present value of his contributions. Since contributions are never negative, that value must grow with age of retirement (although not necessarily at the same rate).

Table 2.5 (*continued*)

1980 Expected Present Value of Pension Benefits: Defined-Benefit Conventional Plans (sample: valid $EPV - 10 \ldots EPV - 0$)

Final Salary $25,000			Final Salary $50,000		
20-Year Tenure	30-Year Tenure	40-Year Tenure	20-Year Tenure	30-Year Tenure	40-Year Tenure
79,855	92,130	104,405	110,490	130,873	151,256
74,546	87,680	103,924	104,846	127,313	150,007
70,081	84,009	112,287	100,447	124,857	156,816
66,364	83,964	120,471	97,148	123,350	170,478
63,310	90,640	128,407	94,808	129,091	183,789
60,836	97,162	136,028	93,295	139,642	196,637
62,885	102,189	141,492	91,610	148,476	206,947
67,321	106,923	146,524	98,781	156,887	216,587
70,731	110,026	149,322	105,018	163,361	223,525
73,865	112,742	151,618	110,929	169,314	229,722
76,686	115,029	153,372	116,434	174,652	235,071
0.916	0.754	0.673	0.760	0.654	0.597
0.876	0.738	0.685	0.747	0.661	0.614
0.846	0.727	0.742	0.744	0.673	0.655
0.825	0.742	0.798	0.748	0.689	0.717
0.810	0.803	0.853	0.759	0.734	0.777
0.802	0.862	0.905	0.775	0.798	0.835
0.835	0.905	0.940	0.786	0.850	0.880
0.892	0.945	0.971	0.849	0.899	0.923
0.932	0.966	0.984	0.902	0.936	0.952
0.968	0.985	0.993	0.953	0.969	0.977
1.000	1.000	1.000	1.000	1.000	1.000
2,046	1,715	185	2,175	1,372	481
1,893	1,557	-3,546	1,865	1,041	-2,887
1,733	20	-3,817	1,539	702	-6,373
1,567	-3,425	-4,072	1,200	-2,945	-6,830
1,396	-3,681	-4,301	853	-5,956	-7,252
-1,272	-3,121	-3,393	1,046	-5,484	-6,401
-3,030	-3,233	-3,436	-4,897	-5,745	-6,583
-2,561	-2,331	-2,101	-4,686	-4,864	-5,213
-2,590	-2,244	-1,898	-4,885	-4,919	-5,121
-2,564	-2,079	-1,594	-5,004	-4,852	-4,863
11,916	17,875	23,833	18,777	28,166	37,555
2	2	2	3	3	3

It is also true that pensions associated with retirement after the normal age should follow the same pattern of decline with age. Most of the sample was subject to mandatory retirement, but 13 conventional plans did allow the worker to elect to remain beyond the date of normal retirement. Table 2.6 presents information on those individuals. Since the pattern is similar across salary and tenure groups, we only report those calculations for a representative group with salary = 25,000 and tenure = 30. The pattern of declining pension values is the same and smooth both before and after normal retirement.

It is interesting that this group for which there is no mandatory retirement has more steeply declining pensions than the group which does not distinguish on the basis of mandatory retirement. Compare ERAT(t) in Table 2.6 with that for the corresponding group (salary = 30,000, tenure = 30) in Tables 2.3–2.5 and it is clear that pensions decline more rapidly in Table 2.6. This suggests that reductions in pensions are an alternative to mandatory retirement.[4]

Table 2.6

1980 Expected Present Value of Pension Benefits: Defined-Benefit Conventional Plans (sample: valid EPV − 10 through EPV + 10)

Salary = \$25,000, Tenure = 30 Years			
Variable	Value	Variable	Value
EPV − 10	172,152	ERAT− 10	1.837
EPV − 9	164,207	ERAT − 9	1.755
EPV − 8	155,953	ERAT − 8	1.670
EPV − 7	147,497	ERAT − 7	1.583
EPV − 6	139,459	ERAT − 6	1.499
EPV − 5	131,337	ERAT − 5	1.415
EPV − 4	123,435	ERAT − 4	1.335
EPV − 3	115,517	ERAT − 3	1.253
EPV − 2	107,090	ERAT − 2	1.167
EPV − 1	98,892	ERAT − 1	1.083
EPV − 0	90,864	ERAT − 0	1.000
EPV + 1	81,761	ERAT + 1	0.899
EPV + 2	73,155	ERAT + 2	0.805
EPV + 3	65,256	ERAT + 3	0.719
EPV + 4	57,955	ERAT + 4	0.639
EPV + 5	51,232	ERAT + 5	0.565
EPV + 6	45,070	ERAT + 6	0.497
EPV + 7	39,446	ERAT + 7	0.435
EPV + 8	34,337	ERAT + 8	0.379
EPV + 9	29,718	ERAT + 9	0.328
EPV + 10	25,562	ERAT + 10	0.282
$N = 13$			

The 1975 cross section provides a basis for comparison. Results for the representative group are reported in Table 2.7. In comparing these values with those for the appropriate groups in Tables 2.3 – 2.5 two things stand out. First, for pattern plans, the pensions are higher in the 1980 cross section than in the 1975 cross section, while the reverse is true for conventional plans. Second, the decline in pension value with age of retirement is sharper in 1975 than in 1980 for pattern plans while the reverse is true for conventional plans. We defer attempts to explain these findings until after discussion of the matched sample because these differences may simply reflect random sampling variation across firms rather than trends over time.

The one obvious feature is again that the expected present value of pension benefits declines with increases in the age of retirement. Both years provide strong support of that conclusion. Again, this is consistent with the idea that pensions function as severance pay in an efficient compensation scheme.

There are some obvious institutional differences between the 1980 period and 1975. The most obvious is that the primary social security benefit, against which many benefit formulas are offset, increased between 1975 and 1980. In order to determine the effect of social security on the calculations, the 1980 analysis was repeated, plugging in the 1975 primary social security formula. Since that value was lower than the 1980 value, pensions increased. That is, some benefit formulas usually subtract some fraction of social security benefits from pension payments. Over time the amount subtracted has increased. Table 2.8 (Column 2) presents the results for the representative group (salary = 25,000, tenure = 30).

Table 2.7

1975 Expected Present Value of Pension Benefits
(sample: valid EPV − 10 ... EPV − 0)

| | Group | | |
| | Defined Benefits | | Defined |
Variable	Conventional	Pattern	Contribution
EPV − 10	125,113	33,779	62,454
EPV − 9	120,062	32,585	62,016
EPV − 8	114,846	31,215	62,273
EPV − 7	109,373	29,698	64,556
EPV − 6	103,770	28,059	67,358
EPV − 5	98,161	26,831	70,045
EPV − 4	92,247	25,215	72,904
EPV − 3	86,338	23,692	75,589
EPV − 2	80,283	22,017	77,623
EPV − 1	74,422	20,478	79,395
EPV − 0	65,962	19,007	80,441
ERAT− 10	2.052	1.764	0.782
ERAT − 9	1.990	1.703	0.779
ERAT − 8	1.922	1.633	0.785
ERAT − 7	1.848	1.555	0.812
ERAT − 6	1.768	1.471	0.846
ERAT − 5	1.686	1.407	0.878
ERAT − 4	1.596	1.323	0.913
ERAT − 3	1.505	1.244	0.945
ERAT − 2	1.409	1.157	0.969
ERAT − 1	1.314	1.077	0.989
N	127	42	11

Table 2.8

1980 Expected Present Value of Pensions: Comparative Analysis (sample: valid $EPV - 10 \ldots EPV - 0$)

| | Salary = $25,000, Tenure = 30 Years | | | |
| | Defined-Benefit Conventional Plan | | | |
Variable	Wage Growth = 0 $r = .1$ Social Security = 1980 (1)	Wage Growth = 0 $r = .1$ Social Security = 1975 (2)	Wage Growth = 5% $r = .15$ Social Security = 1980 (3)	Wage Growth = 0 $r = .05$ Social Security = 1980 (4)
EPV − 10	107,585	115,384	75,317	98,194
EPV − 9	104,511	112,624	72,110	99,791
EPV − 8	101,951	109,222	68,908	100,673
EPV − 7	98,212	105,190	65,751	100,866
EPV − 6	94,213	100,945	62,739	100,629
EPV − 5	90,176	96,537	60,051	100,129
EPV − 4	85,524	91,512	56,973	98,769
EPV − 3	80,656	86,313	53,779	96,880
EPV − 2	75,143	80,482	50,347	93,876
EPV − 1	69,863	74,810	47,206	90,727
EPV − 0	63,165	67,749	43,452	85,261
ERAT − 10	2.285	2.297	2.197	1.548
ERAT − 9	2.212	2.221	2.070	1.558
ERAT − 8	2.129	2.197	1.949	1.559
ERAT − 7	2.039	2.045	1.835	1.553
ERAT − 6	1.944	1.949	1.728	1.540
ERAT − 5	1.850	1.852	1.632	1.523
ERAT − 4	1.747	1.748	1.531	1.496
ERAT − 3	1.641	1.641	1.431	1.461
ERAT − 2	1.522	1.523	1.326	1.409
ERAT − 1	1.408	1.408	1.231	1.355
ERAT − 0	1.000	1.000	1.000	1.000
N	144	144	137	144

Table 2.9

1980 Expected Present Value of Pensions: Comparative Analysis (sample: valid EPV – 10 … EPV – 0)

| | Salary = $25,000, Tenure = 30 Years | | | |
| | Defined-Benefit Pattern Plan | | | |
Variable	Wage Growth = 0 $r = .1$ Social Security = 1980 (1)	Wage Growth = 0 $r = .1$ Social Security = 1975 (2)	Wage Growth = 5% $r = .15$ Social Security = 1980 (3)	Wage Growth = 0 $r = .05$ Social Security = 1980 (4)
EPV – 10	40,651	40,651	48,189	37,328
EPV – 9	40,103	40,103	45,650	38,291
EPV – 8	39,296	39,296	42,961	39,011
EPV – 7	38,262	38,262	40,178	39,489
EPV – 6	37,031	37,031	37,353	39,728
EPV – 5	36,164	36,164	35,134	40,201
EPV – 4	34,485	34,485	32,180	39,859
EPV – 3	32,716	32,716	29,326	39,314
EPV – 2	30,752	30,752	26,481	37,447
EPV – 1	28,767	28,767	23,797	37,358
EPV – 0	26,876	26,876	21,379	36,247
ERAT – 10	1.491	1.491	2.222	1.015
ERAT – 9	1.473	1.473	2.109	1.043
ERAT – 8	1.446	1.446	1.988	1.064
ERAT – 7	1.410	1.410	1.862	1.079
ERAT – 6	1.367	1.367	1.733	1.087
ERAT – 5	1.334	1.334	1.629	1.100
ERAT – 4	1.274	1.274	1.494	1.092
ERAT – 3	1.210	1.210	1.364	1.079
ERAT – 2	1.140	1.140	1.234	1.056
ERAT – 1	1.068	1.068	1.111	1.028
ERAT – 0	1.000	1.000	1.000	1.000

$N = 38$

Pension benefits for 1980 in Column 2 with the 1975 social security formula are about 7% higher than those using the 1980 formula for conventional plans. Although it is difficult to state the increase in primary social security benefits as a scalar, for the average worker that increase amounted to 68%. Thus the "elasticity" of the mean of pension benefits with respect to social security benefits is 0.1. It is less than one primarily for two reasons: First, not all plans offset social security payments. Second, even those that do offset benefits do not do so fully. No pattern plans had social security offset provisions.

A general point is that, because of the way that benefits are offset against social security primary benefits, any change in those benefits has major impacts on pensions and therefore on retirement and tax revenues. We do not explore those implications here.

The rate of inflation, wage growth, and nominal interest rates were different in 1980 than they were in 1975. In fact, one could argue that earnings growth of 5% per year for old workers and a nominal rate of interest of 15% are more reasonable. Column 3 of Table 2.8 reports the results on the 1980 data using these assumptions.

Although the values change somewhat, the qualitative conclusions remain essentially unchanged. Pension values decline significantly with age. Incidentally, the reason that values are so much lower for conventional plans under the revised assumptions is that wage growth of 5% implies that an individual who retires 10 years early has a salary of $15,348 rather than $25,000. Since conventional plans are contingent on final salary, benefits fall. At normal retirement, values are lower because of higher discount rates. Only the latter consideration affects pattern plans, causing their decline to be steepened substantially. The reasoning is not quite so straightforward, however, since these are means of highly nonlinear functions.[5]

Finally, as a last check on the robustness of the results, the analysis was repeated under the assumption that the nominal interest rate was only 5%. Column 4 of Table 2.8 contains those results.

With a nominal interest rate of 5%, the decline in pension value does not occur until about 6 years before normal retirement for the representative group. However, for groups with longer tenure (=40) the decline occurs throughout the period for conventional plans and during the last 9 years for pattern plans. Moreover, in 1980 a nominal discount rate of 5% is surely well below the feasible range since short rates were above 20% and 30-year mortgage rates were around 16%. It is difficult to believe that 5% was the anticipated discount rate.

2.2.3.   The Matched Sample

Any of the differences noted above may have been the result of random differences in the cross section rather than true time variations. To eliminate that source of confusion, 70 plans have been matched across the two years. This section reports findings based on that sample. The results are presented in Table 2.10.

The major changes occured for pattern plans. In the matched sample, there was an increase in pension values of about 50% for normal retirement and over 100% for retirement 10 years early. Since pattern plans are independent of final salary, it is not surprising that their values should increase in nominal terms over the period. However, two points are interesting. First, certainly for early retirement, but even for normal retirement the increase probably exceeds the increase in prices so that some of the gain is real, not nominal. Second, the decline in pension benefits with early retirement seems to have steepened sharply over the 5-year period, reflected in the 100+% gain for early and only 50+% gain for normal retirement.

Again, this may reflect a substitution of pension reductions for mandatory retirement in light of changes in the Age Discrimination in Employment Act. Of course, if pensions acted perfectly as an efficient severance pay device there would be no need for mandatory retirement at all. The inability to induce both efficient layoffs and quitting simultaneously provides a role for mandatory retirement and its restriction works in the direction of inducing more worker-initiated separations.

The results for conventional plans suggest a different pattern. Although differences are small, the benefits have, if anything, declined over time. This should not be taken at face value. More than this decline can be attributed to changes in social security. The maximum decline here is less than 5% and the mean decline due to social security was estimated at 7%. But more important is that conventional plans depend on final salary which increases over time with inflation. This table makes comparisons based on equality of salary in nominal terms. But using the information in Tables 2.3 – 2.5 we can adjust the pension benefits to take this into account.

At tenure = 30, an increase in salary from $25,000 to $50,000 increases normal retirement value by (135,577 - 63,165)/63,165, or 114%. Therefore we can estimate that each dollar increase in final salary at tenure = 30 increases normal retirement pension value by $1.14. If the average final salary in these firms grew say 30% over the

5-year period, normal pension value would be expected to increase from \$61,907 in 1975 to $(61,232)(1.30)(1.14) = \$90,745$ in 1980. This would be an increase of 47%. This increase is about the same as that for pattern plans over the same period.

Table 2.10

Matched Data: Pension Values (sample: valid $\text{EPV} - 10 \ldots \text{EPV} - 0$)

Years before Normal Retirement	EPV80	EPV75	EPV80 − EPV75
	Salary = \$25,000, Tenure = 30 Years		
	Conventional plans		
$\text{EPV} - 10$	99,981	102,380	-2,399
$\text{EPV} - 9$	97,554	98,815	-1,261
$\text{EPV} - 8$	94,583	94,874	-290
$\text{EPV} - 7$	91,241	92,823	-1,581
$\text{EPV} - 6$	87,617	88,272	-654
$\text{EPV} - 5$	84,049	86,952	-2,902
$\text{EPV} - 4$	79,727	82,376	-2,649
$\text{EPV} - 3$	75,201	79,034	-3,832
$\text{EPV} - 2$	70,260	73,616	-3,355
$\text{EPV} - 1$	65,715	68,334	-2,618
$\text{EPV} - 0$	61,232	61,907	-675
$N = 19$			
	Pattern plans		
$\text{EPV} - 10$	43,097	20,199	22,898
$\text{EPV} - 9$	42,476	20,179	22,296
$\text{EPV} - 8$	41,583	23,283	18,300
$\text{EPV} - 7$	40,451	22,842	17,609
$\text{EPV} - 6$	39,112	22,261	16,851
$\text{EPV} - 5$	38,660	25,111	13,548
$\text{EPV} - 4$	36,737	23,818	12,918
$\text{EPV} - 3$	34,729	22,724	12,005
$\text{EPV} - 2$	32,505	21,272	11,233
$\text{EPV} - 1$	30,274	19,925	10,349
$\text{EPV} - 0$			

A similar exercise can be performed to correct the present value of retirement 10 years early. Under the same assumptions, this results in an estimated pension value of 143,886 in 1980 based on the 1975 salary of \$25,000. This is an increase of 40%, so the steepening of the decline in pension values for pattern plans does not seem to be duplicated for conventional plans.[6]

Summarizing, pattern plans on average pay 50% more at normal retirement and 100% more on retirement 10 years early than they did in 1975. In both years and under any reasonable assumptions, the expected present value of pensions tends to decline with increases in the age of retirement.

2.3. An Alternative Explanation and Other Issues

Throughout the model it was assumed that workers were risk neutral. However, if workers are risk averse, then another explanation for the decline in pension value with age of retirement is available. When a worker begins employment, he may not know whether or not he will become ill and be forced to retire before the normal age. Because illness is a bad event, workers may wish to insure against that contingency by paying higher pensions to early retirees.

At some levels, this story is not inconsistent with the model. Equations $(1)-(7)$ would have to be modified to take utility rather than alternative use of time into account. But the pension still acts as severance pay and induces workers to leave when appropriate. "Appropriate" carries a different meaning, however. Now, workers cannot be induced to leave if and only if the alternative use of time exceeds the value of the worker to the firm. To do so destroys the role of severance pay as an insurance device. This well-known result appears in many places,[7] but its point carries with it two implications for this analysis. First, severance pay does not induce efficient separation in the sense of a first best, perfect information optimum. Second, and as the result, the decline in pension value with retirement age is not an accurate measure of the difference between wage and marginal product. In fact, it overstates that value because some of the payment for early retirement is insurance.

There are a number of arguments which suggest that the insurance story is somewhat less plausible. First, there are other forms of insurance, some provided by the firm and others by a third party, which seem to be set up explicitly to handle these contingencies. Health insurance and, more to the point, disability insurance perform exactly those functions. It is not clear why a declining pension value should be required to play the same role.

Second, if pensions act as insurance, one would think that there would be no reason to prevent workers from taking them early. But most pension plans severely limit the age of early retirement. This is not true in general for health insurance and disability insurance. If pensions are an incentive device, it is easier to rationalize the unwillingness to pay pensions to early retirees.

Third, most pensions that are based on salary use the final few years' salary as the basis of computation. If insurance were the motive, a lifetime average which more closely reflects expected permanent income would be appropriate. In fact, with insurance a case could be made for a negative relationship between final salary and pension, given lifetime income, because of the inability of the older disabled worker to adjust to the fall in income.

Fourth, the decline in pension values is steepest for high-income, white-collar workers who have conventional rather than pattern plans. Yet one might argue that it is the blue-collar workers who have both riskier jobs and fewer alternative forms of insurance. Although insurance may be a partial motive for pension values which decline with age of retirement, it seems difficult to believe that this is a major factor in the explanation.

2.4. Summary and Conclusions

The expected present value of pension benefits generally declines with the age of retirement. This phenomenon is easily explained if one views the pensions as a form of severance pay rather than as a tax-deferred savings account. Further, the real value of pension benefits has remained constant or increased in real terms over the period between 1975 and 1980 even though the same is probably not true for older workers' real earnings. Finally, there is some evidence to suggest that higher pensions for early retirement are being used as a substitute for mandatory retirement clauses in labor contracts.

3

Job Security Provisions and Employment

Many European countries restrict an employer's ability to terminate workers at will. Although such restrictions are formally absent from the American labor scene, courts and other institutions, such as experience-rated unemployment insurance, have eroded the employer's ability to dismiss workers without cost. The standard argument in favor of job security laws is that the laws protect workers from unjust termination by employers, which imposes significant mobility costs on workers. Opponents of job security rules argue that unemployment will result because employers become more reluctant to hire new workers.

I have discussed elsewhere the theoretical arguments for and against job security rules.[1] Part of that analysis is repeated here, but this chapter is primarily empirical. When all is said and done, the question is one that can only be answered by examining the data. The data used come from 22 developed countries over 29 years. The most significant results of the analysis follow.

First, at the theoretical level any state-mandated severance pay can be undone in a perfect market by a properly designed labor contract. Thus, without some frictions, severance pay can have no effect. The reason is that any government-ordered transfer from A to B can be offset by a "voluntary" transfer of the same size from B to A.

Second, the evidence suggests that there are significant effects of severance pay on the labor market. Increases in severance pay substantial-

The original version of this chapter was published as: Lazear, E. P. (1990). Job Security Provisions and Employment, in: Quarterly Journal of Economics, 105(3), 699-726. MIT Press. © 1990 by the President and Fellows of Harvard College and the Massachusetts Institute of Technology. Financial support from the National Science Foundation is gratefully acknowledged.

ly lower the number of jobs in an economy. Severance pay also reduces the size of the labor force, but not by enough to leave unemployment rates unaltered. In fact, unemployment rates rise with severance pay.

Third, severance pay can account for varying amounts of the increase in unemployment between 1956 and 1984. For example, in France 59 percent can be explained by changes in severance pay. Other countries did not change severance pay requirements, so the severance pay law can account for none of the changes in these countries.

3.1. A Theoretical Point

Consider a two-period labor market without any government-mandated or voluntary severance pay.[2] The contract is signed in period 1, and work occurs only in period 2. Severance pay must be given to any worker who signs a contract in period 1, but is not offered work in period 2. In the absence of severance pay, supply and demand for labor determines an equilibrium wage W^*a, at which work takes place in period 2. All workers with reservation wages $A < W^*$ choose to work, and firms want to hire all workers with $M > W^*$. The marginal worker is the one that has $A^* = W^*$. Similarly, the marginal employer is the one for which $M^* = W^*$.

Now, suppose that the government imposes a requirement that all workers who signed the contract in period 1 be paid Q as severance pay if they are not employed in period 2. The market offsets the severance pay completely if the equilibrium is such that the marginal worker and marginal firm remain A^* and M^*, respectively. That would guarantee that the same workers work and the same firms employ labor as without state-mandated severance pay.

With severance pay workers work in period 2 iff

$$A + Q < W',$$

and the firm employs labor iff

$$M + Q > W',$$

where W' is the market wage for work in period 2, given the existence of severance pay. To ensure that the same workers work, it is necessary that

$$W' = A^* + Q$$

and

$$W' = M^* + Q$$

or that

$$(1) \qquad W' = W^* + Q,$$

since $A^* = M^* = W^*$. Equation (1) can be solved for arbitrary Q. Thus, in period 2 wages are increased simply by the amount of severance pay, and all is restored.

Of course, the higher wage makes signing the contract more attractive to labor and less attractive to the firm. To offset this, it is necessary that workers pay the firm a fee to sign, such that the expected compensation on signing the contract for any given worker is the same as it was before, namely, PW^*, where P is the probability that work occurs in period 2. (The fee may take the form of a wage that is less than marginal product in period 1.) Thus, it is necessary that

$$(2) \qquad PW^* = -\text{Fee} + PW' + (1 - P)Q.$$

Substituting (1) into (2), one obtains

$$\text{Fee} = Q.$$

The worker must transfer the amount of the severance pay to the firm on signing the contract because he is certain to receive it in period 2. If he works, he gets it in the higher wage W', which exceeds W^* exactly by Q. If he does not work, he gets it as severance pay.

There is nothing that limits the argument to two periods. In a multiperiod context[3] we need only subscript W', W^*, A, M, and Q with t representing the period. It is clear that since only the difference $W'_t - Q_t$ affects labor supply and labor demand in each t, and since $A_t^* = W_t^*$, the wage can be adjusted in every period so as to leave the labor allocation unaffected. Naturally, this implies that the fee must be adjusted to reflect the value of the stream of Q_t. Specifically if $\widetilde{P}_t$ is the probability that a separation occurs in (and only in) period t, then (2) becomes

$$\text{Fee} = Q + (1 - \widetilde{P}_2)Q + (1 - \widetilde{P}_2 - \widetilde{P}_3) + \ldots + (1 - \widetilde{P}_2 - \widetilde{P}_3$$
$$(2') \qquad - \ldots - \widetilde{P}_{T-1})\, Q.$$

The worker is certain to collect Q in period 2. He gets it either by being laid off or by working and collecting W'_2, which, for efficiency, exceeds W^* by Q. With probability $(1 - \widetilde{P}_2)$ the worker is employed through period 3, either by being laid off or by working and collecting W'_3, which, for efficiency, exceeds W^* by Q. This accounts for the second term on the right-hand side. The series continues through period T, which is reached with probability $(1 - \widetilde{P}_2 - \widetilde{P}_3 - \ldots - \widetilde{P}_{T-1})$

The government-mandated transfer is completely offset by a private transfer of the fee from the worker to the firm. Any severance pay arrangement can be offset by an optimal contract that should evolve in a competitive labor market. Of course, in order for the mandatory severance pay to be undone, the worker must be willing to pay the fee on signing the contract. So long as there are no constraints on borrowing and lending, all is well. But any inability or apprehension by workers on this score causes some serious problems.

This is not a technical detail. Without the ability to extract a payment from workers before the job even begins, it is impossible to maintain profit at its previous level and also achieve efficiency. But for a number of reasons listed below, workers may have cause to resist making up-front payments to the firm. If a payment is not made, then firms cannot offer a sufficiently high wage in subsequent periods to achieve efficiency. Thus, the effects of severance pay are offset completely only if there are no limitations on buying the job.

It is also true that severance pay effects are neutral only when the payment made by the firm is received by the worker. There can be no third-party intermediary that receives any of the payment. If this occurs, then incentives are necessarily distorted. Thus, an unemployment insurance system that does not have perfect experience rating will induce inefficiencies. This is shown rigorously, again in the two-period context.

Define Q as the amount of severance pay received by the worker and Q' as the amount paid by the firm. An imperfect experience-rated system has $Q' < Q$. (It may be true that the system as a whole is solvent by charging firms a fixed fee, independent of layoff experience or size of the workforce. But this independence guarantees that those components of cost do not affect the firm's marginal calculation.)

For efficiency in period 2, the same firm and same worker must view the work/no work decision as a marginal one. Thus, it is necessary that

(3)
$$W' = A^* + Q$$

(4)
$$W' = M^* + Q',$$

or substituting, one obtains

$$W_2^* + Q' = W_2^* + Q$$

or

$$Q = Q'.$$

Unless $Q = Q'$, inefficiency must result. The inefficiency takes the form of underemployment. For $Q > 0$, the supply price for any given worker rises by Q. For $Q' > 0$, the demand price for any given worker rises by Q'. Since $Q > Q'$, the supply price rises by more than the demand price so the equilibrium wage is too high to induce efficiency in period 2.

The results of this section are somewhat surprising when put in the context of international comparisons. Consider a European country that has strict severance pay laws, but no state unemployment compensation system. Payments are made directly from firms to workers at termination. Under this system, so long as up-front payments can be made, there are no inefficiencies introduced by this European deviation from employment at will. Neither underemployment in good times nor overemployment in bad times results because wages adjust to offset any detrimental effects. Contrast this situation with the one in the United States. Even though many believe employment at will to be the law of the land, state-run unemployment compensation is pervasive. As Topel (1983) has shown, the experience rating is far from perfect for many firms in many states. As a result, $Q > Q'$, so that overemployment in good times and underemployment in bad times is the result. If these are the facts, and if impediments to perfect offsets are ignored, then the conclusion is not that Europe has too few layoffs during downturns, but that the United States has too many.

Still, one has the sense that European employment constraints are tighter than those that bind American firms. This is likely to result because of the inability to undo completely what the government has done. The usual arguments against such up-front payments are the ones that apply here. Imperfections in capital markets that prevent complete smoothing of consumption limit the amount that workers will pay up front. Worker trust of the firm may be incomplete so that workers fear that the firm may "take the money and run," say, by declaring bankruptcy. Other strategic considerations may apply.

3.2. Implications

Suppose that the world is somewhat imperfect so that man dated transfers cannot be undone by efficient labor contracts. What is expected to occur in the labor market? Unfortunately, theory yields ambiguous predictions on the amount of labor employed. We consider two examples to illustrate the point. Consider Figure 3.1. Here, demand is perfectly elastic in each period, but demand in period 2 lies below that in period 1. The two-period constrained demand curve is D, which lies halfway between D_1 and D_2. (D gives the per period marginal product when workers must be hired for the two periods.) With employment at will L_1 are employed in period 1, and L_2 in period 2. If high enough severance pay is mandated, then $\overline{L}$ are employed. Depending on the shape of the supply curve, $\overline{L}$ can be more or less than the average of L_1 and L_2. Also, once the direction of the effect is determined, the size of the effect depends on the elasticity of labor supply. If the supply curve were perfectly inelastic, for example, then no shift in demand would affect employment. The wage rate would change, of course, but employment would remain constant. Since employment can rise or fall, the size of the labor force can go either way as well. But things are somewhat clearer with respect to average hours worked. Most severance pay rules do not apply to part-time workers, the effect of which is the substitution of part-time (and temporary) workers for full-time ones. This is likely to reduce the average number of hours worked.

Figure 3.1

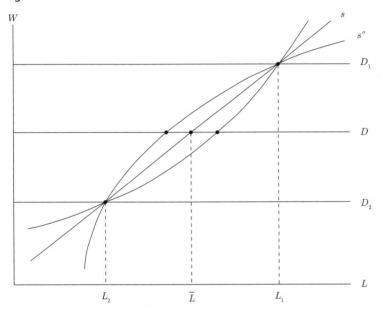

The movement of employment in response to severance pay legislation is investigated by Gavin (1986). He points out, as the last example showed, that the effect of the laws on employment depends on the state of demand. Employment is increased when demand is low, but decreased when demand is high. Kaufman (1979) finds that given changes in GDP generate smaller changes in heads, but larger changes in hours in Europe than in the United States. Nickell (1979) looks at employment and hours data for the United Kingdom and finds that hours fluctuations were greater and employment fluctuations less after the Redundancy Payments Act was passed.

Timing is important in the analysis, especially in its empirical implementation. If the initial effect is to retain incumbents, employment reductions operate through new hires. Thus, the effect of an increase in severance pay should vary with time that has passed since the change. Even when the effect is going to be negative in the long run, the short-run observed effect may well be positive. Unfortunately, there were not enough changes in the data to tease out the specifics of the timing pattern. As is discussed below, the growth variable captures some of the effect of timing.

While timing may not be investigated empirically, there are some theoretical issues that are relevant. In particular, the insider-outsider frameworks, most notably Lindbeck and Snower (1986) and Blanchard and Summers (1986), bear directly on the question. In Lindbeck and Snower an increase in firing costs raises the power of the insiders to extract high wages. This reduces their layoff rate and also has a negative effect on hiring. In Blanchard and Summers wages are negotiated to cater to the incumbents only. Declining demand means a smaller pool of incumbents who then raise wages and keep employment low.

It is not necessary, however, to rely on the incumbent workforce to generate hysteresis. Since severance pay increases the cost of both hiring and laying off workers, firms are slower to respond to given changes in demand for their product. This implies that firms are unresponsive; employment behavior exhibits hysteresis relative to the pre-severance pay regime. Indeed, this is the point made by Figure 3.1. Although the average number of workers employed in any period may rise or fall, it is clear that flexibility is lost by imposing binding severance pay penalties. In Figure 3.1 the unrestricted economy would employ L_1 workers in period 1 and L_2 workers in period 2. The restricted economy employs the same level of workers in both periods. The additional rigidity shows up as more heads in period 1 and fewer in period 2.

The insider-outsider framework is particularly relevant to this analysis because it emphasizes the distinction between incumbents and new hires. It is less than fully satisfying, however, because it implies an inefficiency that should be eliminated by job sale. If insiders (say, union workers) have the property rights to a job, they should be willing to sell those efficiently to new entrants. Indeed, it has been the traditional view that the UMW allows retired miners to vote in union elections so that they can extract rent due them from the current younger workforce. Their pension benefits, which are implicitly paid by current and younger workers, are the fee they collect for "selling" their jobs to the next generation. But this criticism is akin to the one that severance pay can be undone by an efficient contract, which requires very small transaction costs. While it is impossible to distinguish insiders from outsiders in the data used below, some other evidence does bear on the issue. In particular, Nickell (1982) finds that an increase in unfair dismissal actions and increases in relief benefits reduce the flow of workers back into employment. Although this does not speak directly to the incumbent/new-hire question, it is consistent with insider-outsider models.

3.3. Empirical Analysis

Although it is not clear whether severance pay can be offset in ways described in the previous subsection, one thing is clear. If severance pay has an effect, it is most likely to affect the employment-population ratio. Unemployment, being comprised of labor force minus employment, can go up or down as a result of an employment restriction. Even if the effect of severance pay is to reduce the number of workers hired, unemployment could easily fall if workers are discouraged out of the labor force in sufficient numbers. But if employment effects are negative, then labor force participation rates will fall, employment-population ratios will fall, and hours per worker will rise. Unemployment effects are ambiguous.

Modern governments have selected a sufficiently varied set of rules, both over time and across countries, to estimate the effects of these rules on labor force variables. A dataset has been constructed that has measures of the relevant variables for 22 countries over 29 years. This section makes use of those data to estimate the relation of severance pay and the requirement that a firm give worker notice of termination to labor market variables. Of course, rules are not exogenous, and any analysis that follows is subject to the criticism that the labor market phenomena may have caused the rule, rather than the rule having caused the behavior. Also, international comparisons suffer from the problem that many unmeasured factors differ among countries, some of which may be correlated with the presence of severance pay. Even within one country different time periods may see different conditions, some of which may be correlated in subtle ways with the institution of severance pay. Still, a look at data that relate severance pay to employment variables seems useful.

3.4. The Data

The initial data consist of 667 observations made up of 22 countries times 29 years of experience between 1956 and 1984. The variables collected are civilian labor force, employment, population, average hours worked, and gross domestic product.[4] The 22 countries include the United States, Canada, most of Europe, Israel, Japan, Australia, and New Zealand. These numbers are augmented by information on the severance pay rules that a given country uses, as well as its requirements for notice to terminated workers (for example, "Dismissal", 1959). Those rules may vary over time within a given country, and the data have been updated on an annual basis to take rule changes into account. Specifically, what was documented was the number of months of severance pay or notice a blue collar worker with ten years of service received upon termination without "cause." Cause is defined differently by country, but it generally means for reasons having to do with the worker's own shortcomings, and it must be extreme. A reading of the rules suggests that in most countries, dismissal with cause requires the kind of evidence necessary to withdraw an American academic's tenure. In fact, a plant closing in response to poor business conditions often is not regarded as valid cause to avoid paying severance pay. For the most part, rules change once or twice during the period per country, so much of the mileage is cross–sectional, rather than time series.

The severance pay and notice variables have some obvious problems. First, the variable is a measure of severance pay due workers at ten years of service. This is a proxy for the entire system. Since different countries have different formulas, this variable misses some of the subtleties that vary across countries. Second, some countries have policies that vary within. Canada, for example, was dropped because the province sets the policy, but the employment statistics are national. Third, some have gone to almost absolute prohibition of termination without cause. Sometimes the observation was dropped; in other cases where an estimate of the amount of severance pay involved could be made (e.g., France), that estimate was used. Fourth, some severance pay is negotiated ex post rather than stated ex ante. The Netherlands fits this situation, and the corresponding data were dropped. The United States is similar. Although there is no formal severance pay stated ex ante, a worker is free to sue an employer for wrongful dismissal to obtain back pay and damages. Since these suits are infrequent and generally unsuccessful, the United States was included, and SEV and NOTICE are both coded as zero.

Despite the shortcomings, the SEV and NOTICE variables do seem to pick up something, as will be shown below. Means for the variables are reported by country and years in Table 3.1. Definitions are

$$LF = \text{Civilian labor force (in millions)}$$
$$EMP = \text{Employment (in millions)}$$
$$HOURS = \text{Average hours worked per week by production workers}$$
$$POP = \text{Population (in millions)}$$
$$SEV = \text{Number of months of salary given to workers as severance pay upon dismissal after ten years of service}$$
$$NOTICE = \text{Number of months' notice required before termination to workers with ten years of service}$$
$$GDP = \text{Gross Domestic Product (in units of local currency)}$$
$$UNEMP = LF - EMP$$
$$UNRATE = UNEMP/LF$$
$$EMPPOP = EMP/POP$$
$$LFPR = LF/POP$$

$$GROWTH = \frac{GDP_t \backslash POP_t - GDP_{t-1} \backslash POP_{t-1}}{GDP_{t-1} \backslash POP_{t-1}}$$

Most obvious from the tables is that the level of government-mandated severance pay has generally risen over time, although the 1980s experienced a decline from the levels of the late 1970s. A monotonic increase in the amount of notice required occurred from 1955 to 1984. Italy, Spain, Israel, and France have the most stringent severance pay requirements, while Greece and Denmark have the longest amount of required notice before termination.

There are ambiguous expectations about the effects of severance pay and notice requirements on the variables of interest. There are two reasons: first, the theoretical section showed that if capital markets work perfectly, then contracts can be written that can undo any effects of government-mandated severance pay. Second, without perfect offsets the effect on employment and unemployment is ambiguous.

Table 3.1

Means

	LF	EMP	HOURS	POP	EMPPOP	UNRATE	SEV	NOTICE	GDP	GDP/POP	GROWTH	WRKAGE	LFPR
All	13.23	12.45	39.45	30.29	0.4	0.0400	3.48	2.1	1,296	142.42	0.0300	0.630	
(Original sample had 667 observations.)													
By country:													
Austria	3.27	3.20	38.02	7.37	0.43	.0210	0.83	3.00	700	94.20	0.0346	0.638	0.44375
Australia	5.48	5.27	40.02	12.78	0.41	.0442	0.00	0.00	95	7.39	0.0226	0.637	0.42635
Belgium	3.77	3.59	37.35	9.55	0.38	.0506	1.24	1.00	2,474	256.88	0.0293	0.643	0.39478
Canada	8.75	8.16	39.70	21.07	0.38	.0650			211	9.76	0.0230	0.627	0.40967
Denmark	2.34	2.24	35.49	4.88	0.46	.0447	0.48	6.00	289	58.75	0.0233	0.647	0.47868
Finland	2.24	2.17	39.08	4.63	0.47	.0326			135	29.34	0.0379	0.659	0.48456
France	20.86	20.11	43.51	50.25	0.40	.0354	5.24	1.86	1,907	37.14	0.0320	0.629	0.41503
Germany	26.38	25.69	43.15	59.27	0.43	.0265	1.00	1.66	1,064	12.72	0.0278	0.658	0.44602
Greece	3.44	3.29	42.43	8.89	0.37	.0402	1.00	10.00	1,090	119.99	0.0398	0.645	0.38807
Ireland	1.16	1.07	43.03	3.07	0.35	.0712	0.00	0.00	6,139	1954.80	0.0273	0.582	0.37716
Israel	1.04	0.98	40.97	2.95	0.33	.0441	8.41		73	22.63	0.0322	0.593	0.34504
Italy	21.13	19.75	7.84	53.42	0.37	.0631	15.86		230	4.23	0.0324	0.540	0.39624
Japan	50.94	50.06	43.40	104.68	0.48	.0170	0.00		148	1.36	0.0568	0.670	0.48657
Netherlands	4.73	4.54	44.38	12.89	0.35	.0149	12.00	2.00	236	17.90	0.0214	0.634	0.36681
Norway	1.64	1.61	37.28	3.85	0.42	.0157	0.00	3.00	193	49.45	0.0316	0.631	0.42342
New Zealand	1.13	1.11	39.97	2.89	0.38	.0121	0.00		20	7.28	0.0145	0.608	0.38865
Portugal	3.65	3.48	42.74	9.29	0.37	.0408	3.36	2.59	809	85.84	0.0430	0.628	0.39126
Spain	12.43	11.72	42.59	33.87	0.35	.0711	13.56		10,548	303.75	0.0299	0.629	0.36802
Switzerland	2.99	2.98	44.95	6.04	0.49	.00174	0.00	1.00	137	22.49	0.0176	0.659	0.49438
Sweden	3.93	3.84	37.05	7.93	0.48	.0203	0.00	0.76	408	50.99	0.0250	0.652	0.49418
United Kingdom	25.23	24.29	42.58	54.86	0.44	.0401		0.90	189	3.42	0.0181	0.639	0.45991
United States	86.03	80.75	40.20	204.49	0.39	.0600	0.00	0.00	1,985	9.56	0.0183	0.627	0.41758

Table 3.1 (continued)

Means

	LF	EMP	HOURS	POP	EMPPOP	UNRATE	SEV	NOTICE	GDP	GDP/POP	GROWTH	WRKAGE	LFPR
By year:													
1956	12.909	12.501	42.044	29.974	0.411	0.032	1.889	1.687	600.568	72.836		0.484	0.424
1957	12.060	11.693	41.850	28.132	0.410	0.031	1.889	1.687	620.013	67.627	0.028	0.483	0.423
1958	12.125	11.660	41.642	28.458	0.407	0.034	1.889	1.812	632.695	67.768	0.010	0.556	0.421
1959	12.757	11.777	41.662	28.792	0.406	0.030	1.889	1.812	633.566	67.572	0.054	0.632	0.422
1960	11.803	11.450	41.292	27.905	0.406	0.026	2.167	1.812	761.048	97.760	0.126	0.631	0.416
1961	11.928	11.537	41.277	28.266	0.409	0.024	2.167	1.812	815.404	103.227	0.043	0.629	0.419
1962	11.994	11.651	41.090	28.615	0.408	0.023	2.167	1.812	865.291	107.165	0.037	0.630	0.418
1963	12.093	11.743	41.305	28.946	0.406	0.023	2.722	1.812	918.373	111.893	0.040	0.632	0.416
1964	12.230	11.900	40.965	29.271	0.407	0.021	2.722	1.812	972.372	116.845	0.050	0.631	0.416
1965	12.366	12.049	40.741	29.585	0.407	0.021	2.778	1.812	1,019.742	119.903	0.037	0.631	0.415
1966	12.498	12.195	40.572	29.874	0.406	0.023	3.333	1.812	1,066.651	122.107	0.030	0.631	0.415
1967	12.619	12.274	40.092	30.149	0.402	0.028	3.481	1.812	1,112.254	127.107	0.029	0.631	0.413
1968	12.743	12.395	40.042	30.411	0.401	0.027	3.481	1.812	1,182.030	135.462	0.047	0.631	0.412
1969	12.895	12.565	39.924	30.695	0.403	0.025	3.481	2.000	1,265.391	143.448	0.053	0.630	0.412
1970	13.076	12.688	39.550	30.996	0.404	0.024	3.620	2.313	1,321.050	148.543	0.041	0.631	0.414
1971	13.211	12.760	39.420	31.305	0.404	0.026	3.675	2.313	1,378.597	153.107	0.033	0.631	0.415
1972	13.368	12.900	39.199	31.644	0.404	0.027	3.675	2.438	1,471.289	161.052	0.044	0.632	0.417
1973	13.631	13.204	38.730	31.920	0.407	0.025	4.398	2.625	1,565.739	167.707	0.047	0.634	0.420
1974	13.821	13.342	38.317	32.188	0.410	0.026	4.656	2.750	1,623.410	171.775	0.013	0.635	0.422
1975	13.961	13.243	37.672	32.436	0.405	0.042	4.656	2.750	1,640.604	173.524	-0.006	0.637	0.424
1976	14.145	13.405	37.712	32.656	0.406	0.044	4.656	2.750	1,698.513	175.808	0.032	0.638	0.426
1977	14.372	13.615	37.932	32.873	0.407	0.047	5.098	2.750	1,768.324	184.251	0.017	0.641	0.429
1978	14.612	13.859	37.610	33.110	0.412	0.050	5.098	2.750	1,833.286	192.468	0.025	0.643	0.432
1979	14.854	14.100	37.693	33.343	0.414	0.048	5.333	2.750	1,872.871	195.805	0.028	0.646	0.436
1980	15.060	14.197	37.324	33.590	0.412	0.052	4.842	2.750	1,911.784	199.905	0.016	0.649	0.439
1981	15.236	14.220	37.143	33.822	0.409	0.064	4.842	2.750	1,929.345	201.123	0.004	0.652	0.441
1982	15.390	14.146	36.986	34.033	0.407	0.075	4.842	2.750	1,942.462	201.210	-0.001	0.655	0.444
1983	15.557	14.215	36.762	34.228	0.412	0.085	4.842	2.750	1,966.508	200.977	0.014	0.587	0.444
1984	15.724	14.438	38.316	35.857	0.412	0.086	4.842	2.750	2,113.53	215.198	0.025	0.587	0.449

3.5. Results

To give an initial idea of what is going on in the data, Table 3.2 presents results of regressions of the variables of interest on SEV, YEAR, and $YEAR^2$. Only 468 observations had valid data for all the relevant variables. First, note that the coefficients on SEV are negative and significant in both the EMPPOP and LFPR equations. If these results are taken to be causal, then the effect of severance pay is to decrease employment and more importantly, to decrease the number of jobs per head. The effects are not small. If all those workers were to become unemployed, the result would be a substantial increase in the unemployment rate. Of course, some of those lost jobs would likely show up as withdrawals from the labor force. In fact, the negative coefficient on SEV in the LF equation bears this out. Because of these countervailing forces, the effect of SEV on unemployment rate cannot be directly ascertained ex ante, but Table 3.2 suggests that it is positive.

Information is also present on notice requirements. While SEV and NOTICE only have a 0.15 correlation in the pooled data, there is a major difficulty associated with combining SEV and NOTICE into the same regression. Only about half of the observations have valid information on both NOTICE and SEV, so the sample used for comparison with Table 3.2 consists of only a subset of the 468 observations. Still, the results are informative and are reported in Table 3.3.

The coefficients on NOTICE are of the same sign as the SEV coefficients. But the NOTICE coefficients are larger than those on SEV in a couple of cases, which is surprising. At worst, the employer could treat notice requirements as severance pay, simply by telling the worker not to report during the notice period and paying him anyway. That NOTICE affects employment and labor force participation rates more than SEV suggests that something else may be going on.

Of course, there are many reasons why the raw numbers of Table 3.2 are not compelling evidence of any causal relationship. First, much of the variation that drives the results is cross-country comparisons, rather than comparisons for a given country over time. Further, since errors for a given country are not independent over time, the cross-country comparisons yield standard errors that are biased so that hypothesis tests in Tables 3.2 and 3.3 are invalid.

Table 3.2

Basic Regressions – No Country Dummies

Independent variable	Dependent variable			
	EMPPOP	UNRATE	LFPR	HOURS
Intercept	0.54	0.85	0.97	28.2
	(0.18)	(0.1)	(0.17)	(27.8)
SEV	-0.0034	0.00096	-0.0031	-0.795
	(0.0004)	(0.00021)	(0.0004)	(0.06)
YEAR	-0.0036	-0.025	-0.015	0.699
	(0.0053)	(0.003)	(0.005)	(0.796)
YEAR^2	0.00025	0.00019	0.00011	-0.0054
	(0.00003)	(0.00002)	(0.00003)	(0.0056)
R^2	0.15	0.34	0.16	0.29
N	468	468	468	468

Notes: Standard errors are in parantheses.

Second, the obvious problem of causality and endogeneity of the law creates difficulties of interpretation. Third, demographic characteristics may differ across countries or within a country over time and this may account for some of the variation. Fourth, functional form may affect the results. Finally, there are some other econometric issues that weakens the validity of the results. These issues are dealt with below.

Table 3.3

Regression with NOTICE

Independent variable	Dependent variable			
	EMPPOP	UNRATE	LFPR	HOURS
Intercept	0.53	0.82	0.91	83
	(0.19)	(0.11)	(0.18)	(14.4)
SEV	-0.00140	-0.00033	-0.00153	-0.159
	(0.00067)	(0.00038)	(0.00061)	(0.069)
NOTICE	-0.0031	-0.00019	-0.00322	-0.035
	(0.0009)	(0.00054)	(0.00087)	(0.069)
YEAR	-0.0031	-0.0246	-0.0146	-1.00
	(0.0057)	(0.0032)	(0.0052)	(0.41)
YEAR^2	0.000022	0.00019	0.00011	0.0057
	(0.000004)	(0.00002)	(0.00003)	(0.0029)
R^2	0.04	0.35	0.09	0.22
N	373	373	373	373

Notes: Standard errors are in parantheses.

The variation that produces the results in Table 3.2 is a combination of cross-section and time-series variation. As a first test of robustness, it is useful to separate out the two kinds of effects. To do this, first regressions are run on the country means over the entire period for SEV and the relevant dependent variables. Since the number of valid observations varies slightly by country, the regression was run both weighted and unweighted by the number of observations. The results of the two sets of regressions are essentially the same, and Table 3.4 reports the weighted results. The coefficients in Table 3.4 are very close to the corresponding coefficients in Table 3.2. Also, since standard errors are correct in the means regressions, it is somewhat reassuring that the coefficients on SEV, except in the UNRATE regression, remain significant.

Table 3.4

Weighted Regressions on Country Means

Independent variable	Dependent variable			
	EMPPOP	UNRATE	LFPR	HOURS
Constant	0.419	0.0326	0.432	42.0
	(0.013)	(0.0055)	(0.012)	(2.0)
SEV	-0.0041	0.00114	-0.0038	-0.87
	(0.0020)	(0.00087)	(0.0019)	(0.33)
R^2	0.20	0.10	0.15	0.31
N	18	18	18	18

Within-country changes provide the other source of variation that is picked up in Table 3.2. Because within-country analysis takes out country effects, there is some virtue in examining results based on within-country changes over time. Unfortunately, changes in severance pay laws are quite rare, so the variation necessary to estimate within-country effects with great precision is not likely to be present in these data. Nevertheless, it is useful to examine the within-country estimates. Table 3.5 presents the results of regressions of the dependent variables on SEV with country dummies.

Table 3.5

Regressions with Country Dummies

Independent variable	Dependent variable			
	EMPPOP	UNRATE	LFPR	HOURS
SEV	-0.00041	0.0010	0.00007	-0.232
	(0.00033)	(0.0004)	(0.00036)	(0.039)
R^2	0.87	0.41	0.82	0.94
N	468	468	468	468

Not surprisingly, Table 3.5 neither contradicts nor confirms the evidence of the cross section. Only the coefficients in the UNRATE and HOURS equations are significant, and they are of the same sign as those in Table 3.2. The SEV coefficient in the UNRATE equation is identical to the one in Table 3.2, but the within-country SEV coefficient in the HOURS equation is significantly smaller than the one found in Table 3.2. Thus, much of the mileage that is obtained derives from cross-country comparisons.

The standard errors in the means equations (Table 3.4) are correct, but those in Table 3.2 are likely to be biased because the errors are almost certain to contain country effects and therefore are not distributed as a scalar times an identity matrix. In particular, the within-country, off-diagonal elements will contain the country fixed effect. Corrected standard errors were obtained as follows: first, let us postulate that

$$e_{it} = \delta_i + \nu_{it},$$

where e_{it} it is the error in the relevant regression for country i in year t. Then δ_i is the country-specific effect, assumed to be a random variable, and ν_{it} is classical error distributed $\sigma_\nu^2 I$.

Under these assumptions, the covariance matrix for e_i is

$$\sum_i \equiv \sigma_\delta^2 \, j_i j_i' + \sigma_\nu^2 I_i,$$

where

$$j_i = \begin{bmatrix} 1 \\ 1 \\ \cdot \\ \cdot \\ \cdot \\ 1 \end{bmatrix} \quad (T_i \times 1)$$

$$I_i = \begin{bmatrix} 1 & 0 & 0 & \cdots & 0 \\ 0 & \cdot & & & \cdot \\ 0 & & \cdot & & \cdot \\ \cdot & & & \cdot & \cdot \\ \cdot & & & & \cdot \\ 0 & 0 & 0 & \cdots & 1 \end{bmatrix} \quad (T_i \times T_i)$$

and where T_i is the number of years of good data for country i. Then the covariance matrix of e_{it} is

$$
\Omega =
\begin{bmatrix}
\Sigma_1 & 0 & 0 & \cdot & \cdot & \cdot & 0 \\
0 & \Sigma_2 & 0 & \cdot & \cdot & \cdot & 0 \\
0 & 0 & \Sigma_3 & \cdot & \cdot & \cdot & 0 \\
\cdot & \cdot & \cdot & & \cdot & & \cdot \\
\cdot & \cdot & \cdot & & \cdot & & \cdot \\
\cdot & \cdot & \cdot & & \cdot & & \cdot \\
\cdot & \cdot & \cdot & & \cdot & & \cdot \\
0 & 0 & 0 & \cdot & \cdot & \cdot & \Sigma_N
\end{bmatrix};
$$

Table 3.6

Corrected t-Ratios for Table 3.2

	EMPPOP	UNRATE	LFPR	HOURS
Constant	3.38	9.34	6.07	1.18
SEV	-2.05	1.35	-2.04	-2.99
YEAR	-0.82	-10.00	-3.66	1.08
YEAR^2	8.45	9.50	3.67	-1.26

i.e., $I_N \otimes \sum_i$. The expected GLS estimator of the variance-covariance matrix of the coefficients is

$$
(X'X)^{-1}X'\hat{\Omega}X(X'X)^{-1},
$$

where X is the data matrix of independent variables and $\hat{\Omega}$ is obtained from first-stage OLS estimates.

The t-ratios, based on coefficients from Table 3.2 divided by the corrected standard errors, are reported in Table 3.4. The most important result is that, as expected, t's fall in general when nonindependence of observations is taken into account. But the SEV coefficients remain significant in three of the four equations. The larger standard error does render the SEV coefficient in the unemployment equation insignificantly different from zero. It must be pointed out that things are not quite so clean. The same GLS approach can be used to obtain estimates of the coefficients in Table 3.2. When this was done, most retained the same signs, but the magnitudes changed, most in the direction of weaker effects. The only exception is the coefficient on SEV in the UNEMP equation, which becomes -0.00023. The most important coefficient, on SEV in the EMPPOP equation, drops to -0.00034. The coefficients are quite close to those obtained in Table 3.5. Whether these coefficients or the OLS estimates should be believed is an issue that relates to small sample properties. Both estimates are consistent, but if the random effects model is specified correctly, then the GLS estimates are more efficient asymptotically. If that model is misspecified, however, the OLS estimates may well be better and perhaps more robust. The reader may draw his or her own conclusions.[5]

One other approach was tried. Some countries did experience severance pay changes over the period. Those countries were selected, and this resulted in from 183 to 224 valid observations, depending on the dependent variable. A first stage was estimated to obtain by-country serial correlation coefficients. These tended to be in the range of from 0.2 to 0.6. The data (including the intercept) were then ρ-differenced, and the regressions of Table 3.2 were run in their differenced form on this smaller sample. In the interest of space the results are not reported, but merely summarized. The main conclusion is that in three of the four equations, coefficients on SEV and standard errors were not very different from those in Table 3.2. For example, in the EMPPOP equation the coefficient was 0.0044 with a standard error of 0.0005 as opposed to 0.0034 in Table 3.2 with a standard error of 0.0004. The one exception was in the hours equation, where the coefficient on SEV actually became significantly positive.

The picture that comes from Tables 3.2 – 3.6 is that if cross-section results are to be believed, SEV does have a depressing effect on employment rates, labor force participation rates, and hours of work. There is weaker evidence that unemployment rates rise with increased severance pay. While the within-country results certainly do not contradict these findings, they lend support only to the argument that severance pay increases unemployment rates and decreases hours of work.

3.6. Some Details

The force of severance pay may be nonlinear. It can be argued that, for a given firm, once severance pay gets large enough, no firing occurs, which implies a nonlinear SEV effect. Even without correcting standard errors, the quadratic SEV term does not enter significantly. Consequently, all subsequent analyses are performed with only the linear SEV term.

Countries have varying demographic structures. Some countries have a larger proportion of young individuals than others. What is most important is the proportion of the population that is of working age. Thus, define a variable WRKAGE as the proportion of the population that is 25 to 65 years old. Of course, other ages could be used, but data are readily available for that age group and not for others. The variable takes on values that are in the neighborhood of 0.65 for most of the countries.

Table 3.7

Other Variables Included

Independent variable	Dependent variable			
	EMPPOP	UNRATE	LFPR	HOURS
Constant	0.63	0.85	1.009	22.9
	(0.20)	(0.11)	(0.187)	(29.9)
SEV	-0.0037	0.001	-0.0034	-0.68
	(0.0005)	(0.0003)	(0.0005)	(0.08)
YEAR	-0.007	-0.025	-0.0181	0.42
	(0.006)	(0.003)	(0.0053)	(0.86)
YEAR^2	0.000049	0.00019	0.00013	-0.0037
	(0.000004)	(0.00002)	(0.00004)	(0.006)
GSEV	0.0106	-0.0038	0.0103	-2.86
	(0.0112)	(0.0060)	(0.0104)	(1.66)
WRKAGE	0.068	-0.0282	0.057	13.1
	(0.020)	(0.0109)	(0.019)	(3.0)
R^2	0.17	0.35	0.18	0.33
N	455	455	455	455

One final issue is addressed before reporting additional results. The theoretical section suggests that a country's growth rate interacts with the effect of severance pay and notice requirements. The reason is that incumbents are different from new hires. To the extent that severance pay has negative effects on employment, it works by reducing the new hire rate. The reduction is bounded because new hires cannot be negative. Thus, countries that have higher new-hire rates are most likely to rapidly see the negative effects of severance pay on employment. If new-hire rates are low generally, it will take a few years before increased employment due to retention of incumbents is swamped by decreased employment due to reduction in the number of new workers.[6] On the other hand, a severance pay constraint may not be as burdensome in a growing economy, since its cost depends on the expected layoff rate in the future. Two measures of growth were constructed: the first is actual growth in per capita GDP, defined as

$$(GDPP_t - GDPP_{t-1})/GDPP_{t-1}.$$

The second is the same, but replaces GDPP with actual employment EMP. Both were tried in the empirical analysis, and the results were virtually identical.

The results of including WRKAGE and GSEV, defined as the first definition of the growth rate times SEV, are reported in Table 3.7. (An alternative specification that included the growth rate also did not differ, and the linear growth term never entered any of the equations significantly.)

The WRKAGE variable significantly enters all the equations so long as standard errors are not corrected to take account of interdependence within countries. With the exception of the hours equation, GSEV does not enter significantly. The key message is that inclusion of WRKAGE and GSEV does not alter the earlier conclusions about the effects of SEV on the dependent variables. The coefficients on SEV are almost identical to those obtained in Table 3.2.

The effect of SEV on EMPPOP is significant and of reasonable magnitude. Using the coefficients in Table 3.7, in a country with a 1 percent growth rate, a three-month increase in severance pay would decrease the employment-population ratio by about 1.08 percent. In the United States that would cost just over a million jobs. Of course, a move from zero to three months of severance pay is a substantial increase, but it is below the average for the sample as reported in Table 3.1 and is in line with the current change to 60 days of notice to all workers in anticipation of plant closings.

SEV has negative effects on the size of the civilian labor force. If increases in severance pay make jobs harder to obtain, then some workers are expected to leave the labor force exhibiting the "discouraged worker effect." The coefficient in the LFPR equation is of the same magnitude as the coefficient in the EMPPOP and dependent variables run in the same range as well. This would mean that most of the effect of severance pay works through displacement of workers from the labor force. But the coefficient in the unemployment equation is positive and significant. It is substantially smaller than the other two coefficients, but it does imply that some of the effect works through a larger unemployment rate and not merely through a reduction in the size of the labor force. In fact, if the Table 3.7 coefficient in the unemployment equation is accurate, a three-month increase in severance pay in the United States would increase the unemployment rate by about 0.3 points, or by about 5.5 percent.

Finally, SEV has a negative effect on average hours worked. In the United States moving from zero to three months of required severance pay would reduce average hours worked from 40.2 to 38.2, based on the coefficient in Table 3.7. Much of this would probably reflect a shift of work from full-time to part-time jobs. Suppose that the law exempts those who work 20 or fewer hours. Suppose further that all jobs are either 20 hours or 42.5 hours per week. (The number must exceed 40 hours since the average exceeds 40.) Under these assumptions a reduction in average hours from 40.2 to 38.2 implies that over 9 million jobs would change from full-time to part-time, as employers attempt to evade the law by hiring uncovered workers.[7]

Perhaps the most interesting exercise that can be undertaken with these data is to ask, "How much of the changes in unemployment rates over time are explained by changes in the severance pay law?" For example, France had 1 percent unemployment in 1956 and 10 percent unemployment in 1984. During that period France increased the severance pay requirements dramatically. Do the increases account for the change in unemployment that was recorded over the period?

The following approach is used to answer that question. The average unemployment rate from 1956-1959 was computed for each country and subtracted from the average rate from 1981-1984. This was compared with the change in average severance pay requirements over the two periods, multiplied by 0.0037, which is the estimated effect of severance pay on unemployment. (Countries are deleted when data are missing for either unemployment rates or severance pay over the relevant years.) Table 3.8 contains the results.

The results are mixed. In some countries severance pay can go a long way toward explaining the changes in unemployment over time. Those that have had the largest changes in severance pay are the best candidates. For example, France, which experienced a 7.5 point increase in the unemployment rate between the early period and later period also has a predicted change due to severance pay of 4.4 points, that is, 59 percent of the entire change. France also instituted major increases in mandated severance pay between the early period and later period. In Italy, which also instituted major changes, severance pay accounts for 206 percent of the total change in unemployment over the period. A similar statement holds for Portugal and Israel. In other countries, where there was no change in SEV, the proportion of the unemployment rate explained by SEV is necessarily zero. At the extreme is Austria, which actually experienced a trivial decline in unemployment rates. Since severance pay increased somewhat, the predicted change in percentage terms is negative and 4.93 times as large as the actual change in unemployment. Although Table 3.8 is not conclusive in any sense, it does suggest the possibility of a role for severance pay in explaining changes in unemployment when changes in severance pay are substantial.

Table 3.8

Amount of Unemployment Explained by Severance Pay

Country	Δ UNRATE	Δ SEV	% Explained
Austria	-0.003	4	-493.3
Belgium	0.090	2	8.22
Denmark	0.058	1	6.38
France	0.075	12	59.2
Germany	0.042	0	0
Greece	0.003	0	0
Ireland	0.067	0.66	3.64
Italy	0.027	15	205.6
Japan	0.005	0	0
Norway	0.014	0	0
Portugal	0.052	10	71.15
Spain	0.175	0.175	0.37
Switzerland	0.006	0	0
United States	0.034	0	0

3.7. Causality

Perhaps the most troublesome part of the analysis relates to causality. Does the correlation between unemployment rates and severance pay reflect the effect of severance pay on unemployment or the reverse? It is possible, after all, that countries or periods with high unemployment spawn legislation to deal with the rates. But even at a theoretical level the argument is far from clear. For example, in the United States groups that are most likely to be helped by minimum wage legislation (e.g, youth and those who work in retailing) are generally exempted from it. Rather than low wages causing a cry for a minimum, the reverse occurs. Those whom the minimum is most likely to affect seek exemptions because of fears of resulting unemployment. Still, the best evidence is empirical. No instruments are readily available to estimate the propensity to pass severance pay and notice legislation. But timing can be used to shed some light on the issue. Since much of the variation is cross-country, perhaps the within-country variation will provide some information on causality. If causation runs from, say, unemployment rates to severance pay, one would expect that previous levels of unemployment rates would have an effect on the likelihood that a law is changed within countries. That proposition is tested as follows.

Table 3.9

Causality

Independent variable	Dependent variable	
	$SEV_{t+1} - SEV_t$	$NOTICE_{t+1} - NOTICE_t$
Intercept	0.40	0.22
	(0.75)	(0.41)
EMPPOP	2.6	2.5
	(36.7)	(20.2)
UNRATE	0.96	1.3
	(16.0)	(8.8)
LFPR	-3.5	-2.9
	(35.5)	(19.6)
N	387	387
R^2	0.002	0.003

Notes: The number of observations differs from Table 3.2 because complete information on hours is unnecessary here.

Define DSEV as $SEV_{t+1} - SEV_t$ and DNOTICE as $NOTICE_{t+1} - NOTICE_t$. Then if causation runs from, say, unemployment rates to SEV, it is reasonable to expect that DSEV will be related to unemployment in period t. Table 3.9 reports the regressions of DSEV and DNOTICE on some UNRATE, EMPPOP and LFPR. None of the coefficients is significant. There does not appear to be any effect of past employment or unemployment rates on a change in severance pay or notice requirement legislation.

Another way to see this is to examine each change in the severance pay or notice requirement law. To get a sense of whether a change in employment or unemployment precipitated the change in the law, employment and unemployment rates in the two years before the change were compared with corresponding rates after the change. If low employment and high unemployment caused the country to change the law and if the law then had the effects seen in Tables 3.2 – 3.7, the difference between the employment rate after and before should be positive while that between the unemployment rate after and before should be negative. In fact, an examination of the data reveals that there are as many negative differences in employment rates as positive and likewise for unemployment rates. While this evidence does not prove that simultaneity bias does not exist, it lends no support to that hypothesis.

Finally, the Legislative Series were examined to see whether labor laws were changed at or near the same date, perhaps reflecting a general move toward a more restrictive labor environment. The most attention was paid to minimum wage legislation. No obvious pattern of concomitant labor law change was present, at least from this reader's view of the Series. While this lack of intertemporal variation is comforting, it does not dismiss the issue. Since much of the variation is cross-sectional, it can still be argued that countries with high levels of required severance pay also are characterized by an interventionist labor policy. The government might play an active role in wage determination, for example, and may constrain employers to pay wages that are not commensurate with productivity. This is a real possibility, but it is a problem that is common to all empirical analyses. Unless the entire environment can be measured, it is always possible that the measured variable picks up omitted factors. The regressions in Table 3.5 that include country dummies take out any country-specific omitted effects that are constant over time.

3.8. Subpopulations

To the extent that SEV and NOTICE affect the various groups, one expects that new entrants are more likely to be hurt than existing workers, who may benefit from the law. Young workers are disproportionately new entrants so if SEV has effects, they should be more pronounced on young workers. To test this, information was collected on the population of individuals 16-25 years old within each country and time period. Data were not available for all countries, so the sample is somewhat different. The United States, Spain, Norway, and Sweden have data on a slightly different age group as do Israel and Italy, but the differences are time invariant so country dummies are used to pick up these differences. Table 3.10 contains the results of regressing the ratio of EMPPOP and UNRATE for the young group to that for the old group on countries dummies and SEV, holding WRKAGE constant. Old is defined as the population that is not 16-25 years old. HOURS equations are deleted because data were not available for hours worked by age. None of the SEV coefficients is significant by itself, although when GSEV is deleted, SEV is significant and negative on the EMPPOP ratio equation.

Table 3.10

Young/Old Comparison

Independent variable	Dependent variable		
	$EMPPOP_{young}/$ $EMPPOP_{old}$	$UNRATE_{young}/$ $UNRATE_{old}$	$LFPR_{young}/$ $LFPR_{old}$
SEV	-0.000033	0.000052	0.000048
	(0.000028)	(0.000048)	(0.000032)
WRKAGE	0.0063	0.0135	0.0135
	(0.0031)	(0.0052)	(0.0036)
GSE	-0.00021	0.00043	0.00023
	(0.00018)	(0.00036)	(0.00024)
$N = 113$			
R^2	0.84	0.89	0.90

Notes: Country dummies are included.

The effect on UNRATE is positive so that from EMPPOP and UNRATE it appears that the young bear a disproportionate share of the costs imposed by severance pay. The coefficient on SEV in the LFPR ratio equation has the wrong sign. More data are needed to answer this subtle question of whether the young bear a larger share of the cost.

3.9. Summary and Conclusions

There is an irony in this analysis. Those who believe that state intervention in labor markets is harmful and is likely to cause unemployment and other distortions tend to believe that markets function quite well. But in a perfect world any mandated transfer from employer to worker can be undone by an efficient contract. The result is that severance pay legislation and requirements that employers give notice have no effects in a perfect economy. While this may be an interesting theoretical point, few believe that government intervention into labor markets has no effects. The question usually relates to signs or magnitudes. As a result, the empirical analysis is of particular interest.

Data were drawn from 22 countries over a 29-year period. Information on labor force variables were combined with data on levels of mandated severance pay. The results, although not completely consistent, are interesting. The best estimates suggest that moving from no required severance pay to three months of required severance pay to employees with ten years of service would reduce the employment-population ratio by about 1 percent. In the United States that would mean over a million jobs. The young might bear a disproportionate amount of the burden.

Theory gives no guidance on the effects of severance pay on unemployment rates. Since workers who cannot obtain jobs quickly may be discouraged out of the labor force, it is conceivable that a law that reduces the employment-population ratio could also reduce the unemployment rate. As it turns out, mandated severance pay seems to increase unemployment rates. Estimates suggest that an increase from zero to three months of severance pay would raise the unemployment rate by 5.5 percent in the United States.

The estimates suggest that severance pay turns full-time jobs into part-time ones. If the United States were to move from zero to three months of severance pay, over 9 million jobs would change from full-time to part-time. Part-timers and temps are generally exempted from severance pay coverage so employers can partially evade the law by substitution of part-timers and temps for full-time permanent workers. Of course, the substitution can be eliminated by removing the exemption. But then employment effects are likely to be more adverse since employers will have no option other than labor force reduction. Caution must be exercised in using these estimates. First, the statistical model employed was a parsimonious, reduced-form specification.

Causation, although addressed in the analysis, remains an issue. Coefficients are not especially robust to specification, which is troubling. It is hoped that these initial estimates provide a departure point for more refined models and data.

4

An Economic Analysis
of Works Councils

"Students of councils ... have leagues to travel before producing
parsimonious predictive models of council behavior."
– J. Rogers and W. Streeck

Although works councils are an important labor institution in Western Europe and were introduced by many large firms in the United States in the 1920s, economists have rarely studied their operation. The most recent article on councils in a major economics journal was Paul Douglas's 1921 piece in the Journal of Political Economy (Douglas 1921). In part, the neglect of councils reflects economists' traditional unwillingness to look inside the black box of the firm and lack of adequate theoretic tools to treat organizational issues. In part also, it reflects the absence of empirical studies or observations that are needed for parsimonious theorizing. Such neglect of works councils can no longer be justified. The precipitous fall in private sector unionism in the United States, declining unionism in the United Kingdom, and concerns about how different labor relations systems fare in a global marketplace have renewed interest in councils as a workplace institution. Economic theorists have developed tools and models suited to analyzing how councils affect the internal operation of enterprises and to determining the environments more or less conducive to them.

The original version of this chapter was published as: Lazear, E. P. / Freeman, R. B. (1995).
An Economic Analysis of Works Councils, in: J. Rogers/W. Streeck (Eds.), Works Councils:
Consultation, Representation, and Cooperation in Industrial Relations, Chicago: University
of Chicago Press, 27–50. © 1995 by the National Bureau of Economic Research. This work was
supported by the National Science Foundation and the Ford Foundation. The authors benefit
ed from comments at the NBER conference on works councils, in particular from Robert Boyer.

Do councils require external institutional mandating, as in most of Western Europe, or can they be expected to arise from voluntary managerial decision making? When will councils communicate productivity-improving information between workers and firms? What are the benefits and costs of giving councils co-determination rights over some decisions? What can go wrong in a council setting and what arrangements might minimize the risk of poorly functioning councils?

To answer these questions, we model what works councils do inside firms.[1] Since councils are complex institutions, we develop a set of related models, each stressing a particular facet of councils, rather than try to encapsulate the entire institution into a single model.

The main results of our analysis are:

1. Neither employers nor workers have incentives to create voluntarily councils with the power to maximize social value.

2. Councils with rights to information reduce economic inefficiencies by moderating worker demands during tough times. Conversely, by assuring that firms use worker-provided information to benefit labor as well as the firm, councils increase the willingness of workers to communicate to management, raising social surplus.

3. Councils with consultation rights can produce new solutions to the problems facing the firm. This is more likely when both workers and management have relevant information that is unavailable to the other side. Its effectiveness depends on the amount of delay caused by the process.

4. Co-determination rights that increase job security should lead workers to take a longer-run perspective on firm decisions and thus invest more in firm-specific skills and give workplace concessions that enhance enterprise investment in capital.

5. The specific rules for selecting works councils affect their representativeness. Increasing council size raises the likelihood the council will reflect workers' views when there is a strong but not overwhelming majority on an issue but not when workers are evenly divided.

6. Workers with minority views and those who dislike their jobs are likely to run for council office, raising the specter of "maverick" councils dominated by small cliques. One way to reduce the first risk is to choose council members by jury-style random selection. A way to reduce the second is to limit the release time of workers for council work.

This chapter has five sections. Section 4.1. gives our argument why councils must be mandated from outside. Section 4.2. examines the conditions under which council-induced communication from management to workers improves social well-being. Section 4.3. examines communication from workers to management and the voting rules needed for councils to be representative of the workforce. Section 4.4. examines the consultation and co-determination powers of councils. We conclude with some comments on the problems councils might face in a decentralized American or British labor system.

4.1. Works Councils: Mandated or Voluntary?

Most Western European countries mandate elected works councils in enterprises above some size and give the councils rights to information and consultation about labor and personnel decisions. Germany gives councils co-determination over some decisions as well. In contrast to plant-level unions, councils cannot call strikes nor negotiate wages, though they invariably use their power to improve the position of workers within the firm.[2] Their function, often specified in legislation, is to foster labor and management cooperation with the goal of increasing the size of the enterprise "pie." Most observers and participants believe that councils succeed in doing this, and most managers in the Freeman-Rogers interviews endorsed councils as a valuable part of the internal structure of the enterprise.

If works councils increase the joint surplus of the firm–worker relationship, why do countries mandate them instead of relying on firms to institute councils voluntarily?

Our answer is based on the proposition that institutions that give workers power in enterprises affect the distribution as well as amount of joint surplus. The greater the power of works councils, the greater will be workers' share of the economic rent. If councils increase the rent going to workers more than they increase total rent, firms will oppose them. It is better to have a quarter slice of a 12-inch pie than an eighth slice of a 16-inch pie. Formally, we show:

Proposition 1. Employers will give worker institutions within the firm less power than is socially optimal and will fail to establish productivity-enhancing councils when there are high fixed costs to the councils. Analogously, workers will prefer more power than is socially optimal.

The argument is based on two relations. First, let x denote the amount of power or discretion given to the works council. The rent of the organization, R, depends on x. If workers are given no discretion, then $R = R_0$. With some worker discretion, decisions improve and R rises. If too much worker discretion is given, then rent falls because management does not have enough control over decisions. The detailed rationale behind these arguments is explored in Sections 4.2. – 4.4. of the chapter; the result is an $R(x)$ function that has an inverted U-shape. This is shown in Figure 4.1a.

Figure 4.1a

Firm Establishes Weak Council

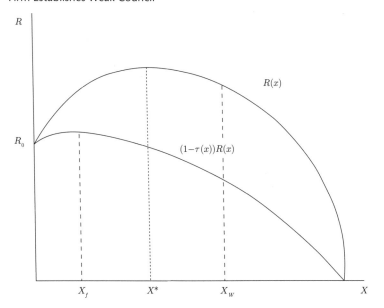

Figure 4.1b

Firm Establishes No Council

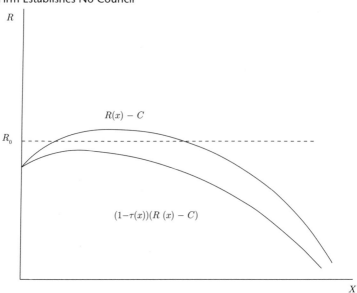

Denote the share of total rent that goes to workers as τ. The share τ also depends on x. It is a standard result of bargaining models (both Nash and Rubinstein)[3] that the share rises with bargaining strength. Thus, $\tau(x)$ is monotonically increasing in x. To start, then,

$$(1a) \qquad\qquad R = R(x)$$

$$(1b) \qquad\qquad \tau = \tau(x).$$

Will the firm voluntarily establish councils with the socially optimal level of worker power? For a profit-seeking firm, analysis of optimizing behavior says "no." The firm will give less than x^* power to the council, where x^* is defined as the level of worker power that maximizes joint surplus. Formally, the profit-seeking firm will maximize

$$(2) \qquad\qquad [1 - \tau(x)] \, R(x),$$

which has the first-order condition

$$-\tau'(x)R(x) + [1 - \tau(X)]R'(x) = 0,$$

so that

(3)
$$R' = \frac{\tau'(x)R(x)}{1 - \tau(x)}.$$

Since τ is increasing in x, the right-hand side of equation (3) is positive, which implies that $R' > 0$ at the firm's optimum point. The firm will choose a level of power for the council on the rising part of the rent-producing curve and will voluntarily give workers less power than x^*.[4] This is shown in Figure 4.1a, where x_f, the optimum point on the firm's profit curve, lies to the left of the social optimum x^*. Given fixed costs to works councils – time and preparations for elections, meetings, reduction in work activity by elected councillors, and so forth – the firm may lose money at x_f so that it will not establish councils at all, even though they raise the social product. This is shown by the curves $R - C$ and $(1 - \tau)(R - C)$ in Figure 4.1b, which lie below the surplus in Figure 4.1a by the fixed amount C. In this case the rent to the firm from establishing the council that maximizes its profits, $[1 - \tau(x_f)][R(x_f) - C]$, is less than R_0, the profit from no works council. Note that a council is socially preferred because $R - C > R_0$ for some values of x.

What about workers? If they could choose the amount of power for the works council, would they choose the socially optimal level? Workers who seek to maximize their share of the total surplus ($\tau(x)R(x)$) will, by symmetry with the analysis of the firm, fail to select the socially optimal point. Workers will choose a level of power that exceeds x^*. They choose x_w in Figure 4.1a, shortchanging the interests of capital.

The preceding analysis has implications for the existence and viability of works councils. It shows that management, on its own, will either fail to institute socially productive councils or give them less power than is socially desirable. If the government knew the R function, it could enact laws giving works councils x^* power. Absent such knowledge, the fact that the optimum level of power lies between the preferred levels of labor and management suggests that some average of the two sides' desires will move toward the social optimum. Whether the political bargaining mechanism institutes rules that are superior to the outcome of industrial bargaining remains an open question.

Mandating councils does not, however, necessarily mean that they will be developed at particular workplaces. Even in Germany, many (small) companies do not have councils. The condition for a company to introduce a council is that either the workforce or the firm sees a potential benefit. If each believes that instituting a council will cost it more than the benefits accruing to it, neither will go to the effort of introducing the council. Thus, there will be no council when the sum of worker and firm costs exceeds the total surplus created. This shows that a council will only be established when the benefits from the council exceed its total costs.

If it were possible to decouple the factors that affect the division of the surplus from those that affect the surplus, there would be an obvious way to establish the optimum division of power: the state (or some other outside party) could determine a rent-sharing coefficient and then allow firms and workers to choose the power to be given the council. With the division of rents fixed, the division of power that maximizes total profits also maximizes the amount each side receives. Such a decoupling of production and distribution of surplus is, however, unlikely. In most bargaining models, the division of rent depends on threat or reservation points that would be affected by changes in the authority given to works councils. In practice, managers in the Freeman-Rogers interviews took it as fact that councils used their power strategically to gain greater surplus for workers.[5] Still, this "solution" suggests that councils fit better in labor relations systems where pay and other basic components of compensation are determined outside the enterprise (essentially bounding divisions of the rent) than in systems where firms set pay, and may help explain why councils are found largely in economies with relatively centralized collective bargaining.[6]

Figure 4.1 can also be used to show why unions may oppose works councils. Reinterpret "joint surplus" to be the surplus that goes to workers, councillors, and union leaders, and think of τ as the share of rent that goes to the works council and workers and $1 - \tau$ as the share that goes to union leaders. Then, assuming the function that relates this joint surplus to x is also an inverted U, the result in equation (3) applies. Union leaders would choose a level of power for works councils that falls short of that maximizing overall labor surplus. Giving the council more power would benefit labor but would reduce the wellbeing of union leaders. This resonates with the fear German unionists had when they first opposed strong works councils, and with American unionists' worry that councils may substitute for unions – the issue Douglas addressed in his article. The possibility that councils benefit workers but not unions means that one cannot take unions as speaking for "labor" on this issue.

The analysis in Proposition 1 illuminates the failure of employer-initiated councils in the United States in the 1920s. In that decade, many "progressive" firms instituted workers' councils or shop committees, to which they gave consultative rights but not access to company financial records. At their peak employer-instituted councils covered some 10 percent of the workforce in manufacturing, mining, transportation, and public utilities (Freeman 1990). While some firms introduced councils solely to prevent unionization, many believed councils were an efficient tool of management. Douglas, who supported unionism, reported favorably on councils in the JPE. The effort to "sell" councils by the Chamber of Commerce (1927), National Industrial Conference Board (1920, 1922), and other management groups also shows genuine commitment. But despite the enthusiasm with which firms formed councils, most abandoned them in the ensuing decade, as our analysis would lead one to expect. Some managements complained that workers did not truly cooperate, while workers complained that councils gave them no real power to affect decisions. Many firms withdrew the limited powers they had given councils and imposed unilateral wage and employment reductions when economic times worsened. These patterns highlight the problem of any employer-established council. As long as the firm is the ultimate authority, workers risk being caught in a "cooperate, defect" prisoner's dilemma solution when the firm sees the relation potentially ending. If the gains from councils, like other cooperative arrangements, are based on long-term benefits, economic changes that shorten horizons can readily undo a voluntarily established council. Finally, when the Wagner Act strengthened the chance for genuine unionism, some councils transformed themselves into unions, raising additional questions about the viability of council arrangements on the labor side.

107

4.2. Communication from Management to Workers

"The works council is for management a very important tool to inform employees of what is happening in the company. You cannot talk every day with 10,000 people."
– manager in Freeman-Rogers interviews

Economic theory recognizes that asymmetries in information between labor and management can produce inefficient social outcomes. Different levels of a firm's hierarchy can use private information opportunistically, possibly through coalitions against other levels of the hierarchy (Tirole 1986). Management may misinform workers about the situation of the enterprise when it sees workers' gains as owners' losses. Knowing that management can use information strategically, workers may disregard what management says even when it is truthful. Workers may fail to inform supervisors about ways to improve conditions for fear that the firm will use that information against them, say by reducing piece rates or speeding up assembly lines. Legal requirements that management disclose information to elected works councils raises the possibility that councils may help resolve the communication problem and raise rents. With access to information that will verify or disprove management's claims, a council can make those claims credible to the rank and file. In Western Europe management provides councils with detailed information about enterprises' financial and business plans and discusses with the council the substantive issues raised by this information.[7] While we know of no statistical study showing that council-facilitated information flows raise the joint surplus, many managers in the Freeman-Rogers interviews believed this, and econometric analysis of Japan's "joint consultation committees," which operate much like councils, shows a positive relation between committee effectiveness and enterprise profitability (Morishima 1991).[8]

We model the economic value of the council as a communicator from management to workers with the following simple situation. A firm and its workers decide on one workplace variable: the speed of work, which can either be fast (F) or normal (N). Workers view speed as bad and prefer a normal pace. They obtain utility U_N working at a normal pace and U_F working at a fast pace, with $U_N > U_F$. In addition, we assume that workers prefer to remain with the firm even at the fast pace, so that $U_F > U_0$, where U_0 is the utility from leaving the firm. In

108

contrast to workers, firms view speed as good because their profits are higher when workers work at the fast pace.

Assume that the environment consists of two states: good and bad, with known probabilities p and $1 - p$. In the good state, firm profits are π_F when the workers work at the fast pace and π_N when they work at the normal pace, with $\pi_F > \pi_N$. In the bad state, profits are $\pi_B > 0$ when workers work at the fast pace but are negative when workers work at the normal pace, forcing the firm to shut down. Total surplus is larger in the good state than in the bad state and is larger in the bad state when work is fast than when the firm goes out of business. This highlights the fact that the major social loss occurs when the firm closes because workers do not accede to management's desire to work at the fast pace.

The problem for workers is that while they prefer to work at the fast speed in the bad state, they lack credible information about the state of the firm. They distrust what management says because management can lie about the state, getting them to work at the fast speed even in the good state and thus garnering more of the joint surplus. Assuming that management finds it profitable to act opportunistically (of which more in a moment) workers will ignore management claims and work at normal speed in all periods or at the fast speed in all periods.[9] Holding out for the normal speed when the firm is in trouble means the firm closes and workers receive utility U_0 instead of U_F. Acceding to fast speeds when the firm does well means that workers get less utility than otherwise. If workers hold out for U_N, p percent of the time they will be right, but $1 - p$ percent of the time they will be wrong and receive utility U_0. The expected utility from working at the normal speed at all times is

(4) $$EU_N = pU_N + (1 - p)U_0.$$

Alternatively, if workers work fast at all times, their expected utility is just U_F. Workers will choose between working at a fast or normal speed depending on the probability of the states and the expected utility of the alternatives. If they think the good state always prevails, they choose N. If they think the bad state always prevails, they choose F. Define p^* as the probability at which workers are indifferent between N and F: $p^*U_N + (1 - p^*)U_0 = U_F$, which yields

(5) $$p^* = (U_F - U_0)/(U_N - U_0).$$

The solution, p^*, lies between 0 and 1 since $U_0 < U_F < U_N$. Since p^* depends on utility levels, it reflects the situation and attitudes of workers, not the likely state of the firm. When p^* is low, workers can be viewed as being more "aggressive" in insisting on working at a normal pace rather than acceding to requests to work fast. When p exceeds p^*, workers will work at a normal pace; when p is less than p^*, they will work at a fast pace.

Differentiating p^* with respect to U_N, U_F, and U_0 shows that increases in U_N and U_0 reduce p^* while increases in U_F raise p^*. This implies that workers are more aggressive the greater the utility of working at a normal pace, the greater the utility of alternative opportunities (they do not mind losing their jobs if the alternative offers nearly the same utility as their job), and the lower the utility of working at a fast pace. Put differently, big differences between U_N and U_F and small differences between U_0 and U_F produce aggressive workers. Since differences between earnings inside the firm and outside will depend on specific human capital, seniority rules, and the like, (younger) workers with less specific training and seniority are likely to be more aggressive than older workers.

Table 4.1 analyzes the surplus going to workers and firms when workers know the actual state versus when they only know the probability. Panel A shows the surplus when they only know p. Here workers must choose a strategy of working at normal or fast speed in both states. By definition of p^*, if $p > p^*$ they choose N, whereas if $p < p^*$ they choose F. This yields one solution when $p > p^*$ and another solution when $p < p^*$. Panel B gives the surplus when workers have full information. In this case they work at normal speed during good times and at fast speed during bad times. This is the socially optimal situation, which produces average utility for workers of $pU_N + (1 - p)U_F$ and average profits for firms of $p\pi_N + (1 - p)\pi_B$. Panel C shows the change in surplus for workers, firms, and society between the two situations. If $p > p^*$ so that absent full information workers choose N in all states, the benefit to workers of full information is $U_F - U_0$ in the $1 - p$ of the time when the firm is in a bad state, the benefit to firms is π_B, and the social benefit is the sum of the two. In bad states information improves the well-being of all parties. If $p < p^*$ so that workers choose strategy F in all states, they lose $U_F - U_N$ in p of the time, while firms gain $\pi_F - \pi_N$.

The social benefit of information from management to labor is that it eliminates the danger that workers choose the N strategy in a bad state. The condition that $p > p^*$ shows that this is most likely to occur when a firm generally does well and workers are "aggressive." Since the firm does well, workers distrust the claim that it is in trouble, and if they are sufficiently aggressive, they will refuse to work at a fast pace in the bad state. Full information allows workers to respond flexibly, working at a fast pace in the bad state and at a normal pace in good states.

Table 4.1

Surplus Produced and Distributed under Alternative Information and Gains from Full Information

A. Workers Not Informed about State		
Utility to:	Choose N $(p > p^*)$	Choose F $(p < p^*)$
Workers	$pU_N + (1 - p)U_0$	U_F
Firm	$p\pi_N$	$p\pi_F + (1 - p)\pi_B$

B. Full Information	
Utility to:	N in Good Times /F in Bad Times
Workers	$pU_N + (1 - p)U_0$
Firm	$p\pi_F + (1 - p)\pi_B$

C. Change in Well-Being from Information		
		With Information
Utility to:	Would Have Chosen N	Would have Chosen F
Workers	$(1 - p)(U_F - U_0)$	$p(U_N - U_F)$
Firm	$(1 - p)\pi_B$	$p(\pi_N - \pi_F) < 0$
Society	$(1 - p)(U_F - U_0 + \pi_B)$	$p(U_N - U_F + \pi_N - \pi_F)$

Since management as well as workers gain when work is fast in the bad state, we would expect management to endorse councils as a valuable tool for conveying "bad" news to workers. In fact, in the Freeman-Rogers interviews several managers volunteered worker responses to potential plant closings as examples of the benefits of councils to the firm. One manager said, "Councils are a very good communication channel, especially with regard to bad news. They are more credible than management." By contrast, in good times the information given the council benefits workers at the expense of management, and no manager cited the virtues of such redistribution as examples of useful councils.

Figure 4.2a

Gains from Information Disclosure as a Function of p – Social Gains

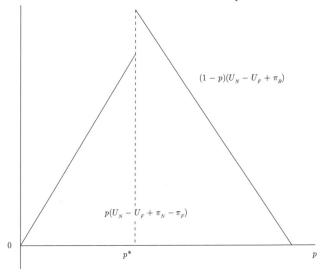

$(1 - p)(U_N - U_F + \pi_B)$

$p(U_N - U_F + \pi_N - \pi_F)$

0

p^*

p

Figure 4.2b

Gains from Information Disclosure as a Function of p – Employer Gains

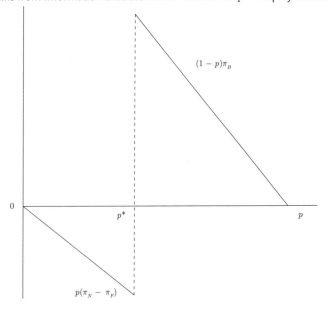

$(1 - p)\pi_B$

0

p^*

p

$p(\pi_N - \pi_F)$

How will the benefits of full information vary with economic uncertainty? In our model uncertainty is measured by p; it is highest at $p = .5$ and lowest at $p = 0$ or $p = 1$. Figure 4.2a graphs the social surplus created by full information as a function of p. When p is 0 or 1, there is no information problem, and the social value of council-provided information is nil. When p is 0, the workers know that the bad state always occurs, so there is no benefit to additional information: $p < p^*$ and workers will always work fast. When p is 1, workers know that the firm is always in the good state so that the plant will not close. Note that the value of information peaks when p is just a bit above (or possibly just below) p^*, not when uncertainty is highest.

One further refinement is needed to complete our analysis. If by opening its books to workers in bad times management can convince workers to work at a fast pace, the firm might be expected to do so, obviating the need for mandatory disclosure of information. But opening the books in the bad state tells workers that the firm is in the good state at all other times, which loses the firm the option of inducing workers to work at a fast pace in good times. The firm will disclose its state voluntarily only when the expected benefits from keeping the enterprise alive in bad times exceeds the gains from inducing workers to work at a fast pace in good times. If the firm knows p but not p^* (a worker characteristic), it will estimate the probability a that $p > p^*$ and will open its books voluntarily when

$$(6) \qquad \alpha(1 - p)\pi_B + (1 - \alpha)p(\pi_N - \pi_F) > 0$$

as derived from firm net benefits in panel C of Table 4.1.

The social value of opening the books is

$$(7) \qquad \alpha(1 - p)(U_F - U_0 + \pi_B) + (1 - a)p(U_N - U_F + \pi_N - \pi_F),$$

derived from the last row of Table 4.1. The difference between equations (7) and (6) is the worker returns to the information, $\alpha(1 - p)(U_F - U_0) + (1 - \alpha)p(U_N - U_F)$, which is necessarily positive. Since the firms' gains are less than the social gains, the firm will voluntarily show workers their books less frequently than is socially desirable.[10] This leads to

Proposition 2. Requiring firms to disclose profit information has social value when firms will not voluntarily provide the information.

Finally, since the social gains of full information depend on the differences in utility and in profits between maintenance and closure of the firm, which will reflect the extent of firm-specific investments in human and physical capital, council-created communication between management and workers will be especially valuable in firms with large firm-specific complementary investments. The prediction that full information will induce workers to be "less aggressive" in bad times also suggests that councils increase effort flexibility.

4.3. Communication from Workers to Management

"Councils give management a better idea of what employees are willing to accept. Things come up in discussion that management didn't know."
– manager in Freeman-Rogers interviews

Councils affect communication from workers to management by improving the incentives for workers to provide information to management and by filtering the information through the subset of workers on councils.

4.3.1. Incentives to Communicate

To see how works councils can increase the incentive for workers to communicate truthfully to management, consider how workers will respond to a management request for information about the compensation package: "How much wage would you give up for various amounts of a fringe benefit?" Assume that workers are divided between those who love the fringe, and who will accept a large wage reduction for it, and those who only like the fringe, and who will accept only a small wage reduction for it.

In Figure 4.3, two sets of indifference curves are shown, corresponding to two types of workers. The convex solid curve, labeled $K0$, shows the points that provide the minimum level of utility to keep a worker who likes the fringe working at the firm. The convex dotted curve labeled $V0$ shows the points that provide the minimum level of utility to keep a worker who loves the fringe working at the firm. The bold, concave curves show the firm's isoprofit contours where movements to the southwest reflect higher profits.

Figure 4.3

Wages versus Fringes

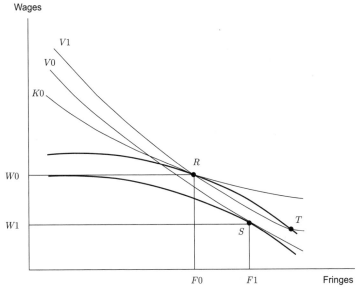

If the firm knew that a worker loved the fringe, it would offer point S with wage $W1$ and fringe level $F1$ since this yields higher profits than any other feasible point. If the firm knew that a worker liked the fringe, it would offer point R with wage $W0$ and fringe level $F0$. Offering S to fringe-likers causes those workers to quit. The problem is that a fringe-lover can gain by telling the firm that he is only a fringe-liker since he prefers point R to point S. The result is that while the fringe-likers tell the employer their true preferences, the fringe-lovers do not, and the firm gets no information from what workers say. Surplus is lost because there are fringe/wage combinations preferred to R by both management and fringe-lovers. In the diagram, all points in the area bounded by points R and T and curve $V1$ and the corresponding isoprofit curve are Pareto improving. For workers to communicate truthfully with management, they need a say over how the firm uses worker-provided information – that is, a guarantee that management will not extract the full surplus. This establishes

Proposition 3. Works councils that give workers some control over the use of information can enhance information flows from workers to management.

4.3.2. *Representative Councils*

Works councils are forms of representative government, giving rise to the question that faces any representative institution, "How well does the subset of the population (works councillors) reflect preferences of the population (workforce)?"

The following situation provides a way of analyzing this question. Suppose management chooses to paint an office blue or red and wants to pick the color preferred by the workforce. A majority, q, of the workforce prefers red, but management does not know this and relies on the council to convey worker sentiment. Assume, in the first instance, that councillors are a randomly selected subset of an odd number n of workers and that councillors give their own preferences in discussion with management. The probability that the council will fail to represent the majority is the probability that $(n - 1)/2$ or fewer prefer red. Let $f(x; n, q)$ be the binomial density function where there are n trials. Let q be the probability of a success defined as vote for red, and x be the number of successes in n trials. The probability that x will vote red is

$$f(x; n, q) = \binom{n}{x} q^x (1 - q)^{n-x}$$

and the probability that the council misrepresents workers is

$$\sum_{x=0}^{(n-1)/2} f(x; n, q),$$

that is, the probability that 0 vote red, plus the probability that 1 votes red, ... , plus the probability that exactly $(n - 1)/2$ vote red.

The probability that the council misrepresents workers decreases as n rises and increases as q approaches .5. A large council is more representative and will communicate preferences more accurately when there is a large majority on an issue. A near-even split of workers raises the danger that the council will favor the minority. If a near-even split means that workers do not feel strongly about the issue, erring in favor of the minority may be relatively harmless. If workers feel strongly, however, a correct decision requires an assessment of the strength of preferences rather than a simple count.

To model the strength of preferences, let ΔU^* be the utility of red (versus blue) to red-lovers and ΔU be the utility of blue (versus red) to blue-lovers. The value of choosing red over blue is then $q\ \Delta U^* - (1 - q)\Delta U$. If this is negative, it would be better to choose blue despite the red majority. If blue fans can convey the strength of their preferences in council meetings, they may be able to sway management and the council to choose blue. If q is near 1, so that there is a large majority, or if red-lovers are nearly as committed as blue-lovers, the average weighted preference is unlikely to favor blue. Discussion is more valuable when the majority is a bare majority, and when the majority has weak preferences and the minority strong preferences.

At first blush, one might expect the optimal size of the council to be highest when the workforce is nearly evenly divided. If 51 percent prefer red and 49 percent prefer blue, a large sample is needed to assure that the minority does not hold the majority on the council. But the value of adding additional randomly selected councillors is actually smallest when q is near .5 or 1. To see this, consider the two extremes. If $q = 1$ every worker prefers red, so the probability of getting a blue fan on a one-person council equals the probability of getting a blue fan on a 1000-person council-zero. Similarly, if $q = .5$, the probability of a blue fan on a one-person council is .5. But the chance that any additional randomly selected worker prefers blue is also .5, so that the probability of blue is .5, independent of the size of the council. Table 4.2 illustrates the point. Column (1) gives the proportion of the workforce that likes red. Columns (2)-(4) give the probabilities that councils with one, three, and five members, respectively, will erroneously consist of a blue majority. Column (5) gives the decline in the probability of an error when council size is increased from one to three persons (the difference between Columns 3 and 2). Column (6) gives the decline in the probability of an error when council size is increased from three to five persons (the difference between Columns 4 and 3). At $q = .5$ or $q = 1$, a council of one is as good as a council of five: the decline in the probability of error is zero. When the proportion preferring red gets near .75, the value of a larger council reaches a peak: in Columns (5) and (6) the incremental reduction in the error is largest when the proportion who favor red is between .70 and .80. Note further that the gain from going from one to three members is larger than the gain from going from three to five members. There are diminishing returns to adding council members.[12]

Table 4.2

Probability of Blue Majority on Council Given that q Prefer Red

q (1)	Prob. of Error $n = 1$ (2)	Prob. of Error $n = 3$ (3)	Prob. of Error $n = 5$ (4)	Error Difference $n = 3$ and 1 (5)	Error Difference $n = 5$ and 3 (6)
0.500	0.500	0.500	0.500	0.000	0.000
0.520	0.480	0.470	0.463	-0.010	-0.007
0.540	0.460	0.440	0.425	-0.020	-0.015
0.560	0.440	0.410	0.389	-0.030	-0.022
0.580	0.420	0.381	0.353	-0.039	-0.028
0.600	0.400	0.352	0.317	-0.048	-0.035
0.620	0.380	0.323	0.283	-0.057	-0.040
0.640	0.360	0.295	0.251	-0.065	-0.045
0.660	0.340	0.268	0.220	-0.072	-0.048
0.680	0.320	0.242	0.191	-0.078	-0.051
0.700	0.300	0.216	0.163	-0.084	-0.053
0.720	0.280	0.191	0.138	-0.089	-0.054
0.740	0.260	0.168	0.114	-0.092	-0.053
0.760	0.240	0.145	0.093	-0.095	-0.052
0.780	0.220	0.124	0.074	-0.096	-0.049
0.800	0.200	0.104	0.058	-0.096	-0.046
0.820	0.180	0.086	0.044	-0.094	-0.042
0.840	0.160	0.069	0.032	-0.091	-0.037
0.860	0.140	0.053	0.022	-0.087	-0.031
0.880	0.120	0.040	0.014	-0.080	-0.025
0.900	0.100	0.028	0.009	-0.072	-0.019
0.920	0.080	0.018	0.005	-0.062	-0.014
0.940	0.060	0.010	0.002	-0.050	-0.008
0.960	0.040	0.005	0.001	-0.035	-0.004
0.980	0.020	0.001	0.000	-0.019	-0.001
1.000	0.000	0.000	0.000	0.000	0.000

Notes: Council size is given by n.

The logic is that information is very valuable when q is close to .5 but almost impossible to obtain by adding council members. At $q = 1$, the value of additional information is zero. In the area around $q = .75$, these two effects balance out: information is valuable and adding a new member contributes information. This demonstrates

Proposition 4. Increasing council size improves the accuracy of information from workers when there is a strong but not overwhelming majority. Size adds little accuracy when the workforce is nearly evenly divided or unanimous over an issue.

Note finally that if, as many models of politics suggest, candidates' positions are close to the preferences of the median voter, majorities will generally be extremely small. For example, if 95 percent prefer red over green but workers are more ambivalent about red versus blue, then the final ballot is likely to be between red and blue, not between red and green. This equilibrating force, coupled with Proposition 4, implies the surprising result that increasing the size of works councils may generally do little to ensure that the right decision is made.

4.3.3. *Elected Councils and Minority Representation*

Counsellors are not, of course, randomly selected from the workforce, but are, rather, elected according to rules that differ across settings. Some countries mandate separate election districts for plant and office workers. Some allow blue-collar workers to elect white-collar workers to represent them. In countries with multiple-union federations, different unions run slates under various proportional representation rules. Belgium restricts counsellors to workers on union election slates. Without analyzing actual voting rules, we show next how specific rules can affect the representativeness of councils.

At one extreme, consider the election of members chosen by workers at large. Suppose the rule is that workers vote for n persons from a ballot of z candidates and that the leading n candidates are elected. As before, q of workers favor red. If the z names were randomly chosen, then an expected qz individuals would, on average, prefer red, and the remaining counsellors would prefer blue. Workers favoring red would vote the "red slate," and as long as there are at least n candidates who favor red the council would be stacked with red-lovers: the minority gets no representation. The usual way to avoid such an outcome is proportional representation, based on ex ante criteria such as occupation, age, income, location, and sex, which may not reflect attitudes on the color question. Proportional representation is a partial but imperfect cure to the problem of guaranteeing minority representation on specific issues. If women and young workers have different preferences on some issues than older men in the same jobs, proportional representation along traditional factory/office or supervisory/nonsupervisory lines may not mirror those differences, suggesting the possible value of grouping by gender, age, and perhaps race in some countries.

An alternative way to obtain minority representation is to select councilors jury style. When councillors are selected randomly from the population, the minority is more likely to be represented in proportion to its numbers than when councillors are elected at large, or when the criteria for proportional representation are unrelated to attitudes. While a jury system produces minority representation, it has a disadvantage as well. When councillors are elected (and may run again), they are accountable to the workforce and thus may make a greater effort to find out what their peers want than a jury-style councillor.[13] And elected councillors may be more able than those chosen by a jury system.[14]

4.4. Consultation and Co-determination

> *"In the press shop the works council ... made many concrete proposals ... making sure there are sufficient racks ... ensuring that a foreman is available to train new workers ... (for) movement of personnel ... to compensate for a faster-moving press line whose parts are in higher demand."*
> – manager in Freeman-Rogers interviews

All works council laws give councils consultation rights over some decisions. For example, management may be required to consider council suggestions about plant closing before proceeding with any action, although final authority still resides with management. In Germany councils have additional co-determination rights over some issues which require agreement by both sides before any action can be taken. (Compulsory arbitration is used on impasses.) Even when management has the final say, however, consultation rights give the council an influence on the firm's behavior. For one thing, consultation is costly: Management must spend time to prepare for and participate in council meetings. The potentially more important indirect cost is delaying decisions until consultation is completed. Nearly every manager in the Freeman-Rogers interviews cited the time delay as a major drawback of consultations. The need for consultation may, in fact, eliminate some profitable options for firms that depend upon rapid responses to market opportunities.

When might consultation increase the enterprise surplus? How will co-determination, particularly over employment security issues, affect the social surplus and the firm's returns? There are four issues involved in co-determination. They are: the overlap of each party's information set, the relevance of nonoverlapping information, the delay caused by consultation, and the creativity that occurs during discussion. We model all four but deal least well with the last.

4.4.1. Council-facilitated Consultation

Consultation can increase enterprise surplus when workers offer solutions to firm problems that management fails to see (vide the quotation at the outset of this section) and when management and labor together discover solutions to company problems that neither would have conceived separately. One necessary condition for either situation is that workers have some information that management does not have that is not conveyed freely when management simply asks. Workers must be able to suggest a better solution than that proposed by management.

For specificity, consider again the choice of color when management plans to paint the office red or blue and workers prefer red. The works council might suggest green, which (for whatever reason) maximizes enterprise surplus. This situation has the flavor of Koike's (1989) and Aoki's (1986) analyses of plantlevel operations in which "unusual circumstances" or shocks occur at workplaces. Occurrences such as daily or weekly breakdowns of machines provide workers with opportunities to alter activities in ways that affect productivity. Key is that these occurrences cannot be foreseen or observed by management but can be exploited by workers.[15]

The essence of co-determination is teamwork. Management has information or thoughts that workers lack, and workers have information or thoughts that management lacks. By combining information and effort, new ideas are spawned and joint surplus is increased. Since teamwork is key, we model co-determination as analogous to playing a team sport. The metaphor we use is American football.

Suppose that only 30 seconds remain in the game and the team with the ball must score a touchdown to win. The best strategy is to throw a pass, but the probability that the pass is completed depends on knowledge of whether the passer and receiver are right- or left-handed. It also depends on the type and distance of the pass thrown. Neither player knows the other player's hand preference and communicating this information to one another requires a huddle. The huddle communicates information and also allows passer and receiver to combine their thoughts on the type of pass that is best.

The huddle takes time, analogous to delay caused by the co-determination process. Suppose that if players stop to huddle, they have time for only one play in the remaining 30 seconds. If they do not stop to huddle, they will have $1 + j$ plays, so j is a measure of the time cost of co-determination.

If they huddle, the probability of completing a touchdown pass is β. There are two potential gains from the huddle. One is that players learn each other's hand preference. The other is that they may select a better play. If they do not huddle, each must guess the other player's hand preference and go with a traditional pass. If they both guess correctly, the probability of completing the pass is $\beta' \leq \beta$. The difference between β and β' is that without a huddle, there is no possibility of inventing a new play for the current situation. Thus, β exceeds β'. If passer or receiver guesses wrong about the other's hand preference, the probability of completing the pass is only ρ, with $\rho < \beta'$. Suppose that the world has γ right-handers with $\gamma > .5$. Then the best guess is that the other player is right handed. Thus, γ^2 of the time, both guesses are correct and the probability of a completed pass is β'. But $1 - \gamma^2$ of the time, they guess wrong, and the probability of a completed pass is only ρ.

The trade-off is that co-determination provides better information, creativity, and thereby expected output. The cost is delay. Delay in this case takes the form of sacrificing some plays. If they huddle, the probability of a touchdown is simply β because only one play is run. If they do not huddle, the probability of a touchdown is

$$\gamma^2 \left[1 - (1 - \beta')^{1+j}\right] + (1 - \gamma^2) \left[1 - (1 - \rho)^{1+j}\right].$$

The first term is the probability, given that players guess correctly, of scoring a touchdown on at least one of the $1 + j$ plays (i.e., one minus the probability of failing on all $1 + j$ plays) times the probability that they guess correctly. The second term is the probability, given that they guess incorrectly, of scoring a touchdown on at least one of the $1 + j$ plays times the probability that they guess incorrectly.

It pays to huddle if and only if

$$\beta > \gamma^2 \left[1 - (1 - \beta')^{1+j}\right] + (1 - \gamma^2)[1 - (1 - \rho)^{1+j}],$$

or if and only if

(11) $\qquad \beta - \gamma^2 \left[1 - (1 - \beta')^{1+j}\right] - (1 - \gamma^2) \left[1 - (1 - \rho)^{1+j}\right] > 0.$

Initially, let us abstract from creativity and focus on coordination by assuming that $\beta' = \beta$, so that the huddle only serves to communicate hand preference. It is obvious that whether condition (11) holds depends on the values of the parameters. For example, if $\beta = 1$, $\rho < 1$, and $\gamma < 1$, the condition holds with certainty since the sum of the last two terms is always less than 1. If a huddle brings certain victory on one play, the strategy should be followed no matter how many plays are sacrificed.

However, if $\rho = \beta$, then condition (11) becomes

$$(1 - \beta)[(1 - \beta)^j - 1] < 0.$$

This situation is one in which there is no gain to communication because the information is useless. (Recall that we have temporarily assumed that there is no creativity, in that $\beta' = \beta$.) Knowing whether the passer or receiver is right or left handed has no effect on the probability that the pass is completed. A huddle only serves to reduce the number of plays that can be attempted, which decreases the probability of a touchdown.

There is no value to co-determination when the knowledge to be transferred has no effect on joint surplus. When $\beta' = \rho = \beta$, there is no relevant information communicated in a huddle, so there is no value to it. There is no point in having works councils meetings to discuss management and workers' taste in wine if wine is never served at work. So the first point is that the information sets must not only be different, but the union of the sets must yield higher joint surplus than the disjoint sets. Sharing information must be valuable, or it never pays to have co-determination.

Second, and related, note that

$$\partial/\partial\rho = -(1 - \gamma^2)(1 - \rho)^j(1 + j),$$

which is negative. As ρ falls, the expression in condition (11) rises. For a given probability of completion given full information, the value of the huddle increases as ρ falls. When ρ falls, the gains to communication rise because joint surplus is increased more by sharing knowledge.

The value of coordination is measured most directly by γ. Recall that γ is the proportion of the population that is right handed. Note that when $\gamma = 1$, equation (11) becomes

$$-[(1 - \beta) - (1 - \beta)^{j+1}] < 0$$

and

$$\partial/\partial\gamma = 2\gamma[(1 - \beta)^{1+j} - (1 - \rho)^{1+j}] < 0.$$

As γ increases, the assumption that passer and receiver are right handed is correct, and there is less need to coordinate. At the extreme, when $\gamma = 1$, there is no role for communication. Coordination of information is redundant. Independent analysis by passer and receiver results in the correct solution and avoids the delay of the huddle.

Discussion and co-determination are valuable when the information sets do not overlap and when that information is relevant. If γ were 1, information would be completely overlapping. If $\beta = \rho$ and $\gamma < 1$, information would not be common, but it would be irrelevant, having no effect on the probability of success.

In the workplace, the more different the relevant experiences of workers and management, the more likely that co-determination will be valuable. Sharing information is most likely to affect the probability that the job gets done when each side has independent, but relevant, information. If ex ante guesses are generally correct, there is little reason to waste time meeting. Further, even if inferences about the other side's characteristics are wrong, meetings are still valuable only when the information is relevant.

The Freeman-Rogers interviews provide examples in which worker suggestions produced more profitable outcomes for the firm and in which the interplay between management and labor proved useful. In one major enterprise, management told the works council that the enterprise had to save a certain amount of money to maintain an engineering facility. Devising a plan to provide the savings was left to the workers. Schemes that management thought were infeasible turned out to be feasible, presumably because management did not have an accurate reading of what could be done or of the sacrifice workers would make to save the facility.

These considerations do not mean, of course, that consultation is always useful. Benefits must be weighed against costs. Thus, we present the third formal result: As the costs of delay rise, co-determination becomes less valuable. Specifically,

$$\partial/\partial j = \gamma^2(1 - \beta)^{1+j} \ln(1 - \beta) + (1 - \gamma^2)(1 - \rho)^{1+j} \ln(1 - \rho),$$

which is negative since $1 - \beta$ and $1 - \rho$ are both less than 1. The extreme cases are informative.

If $j = 0$, then no time is sacrificed by a huddle. In this case, equation (11) becomes

$$(1 - \gamma^2)(\beta - \rho) > 0.$$

It always pays to huddle if there is no cost and some potential benefit.

Also, evaluating equation (11) as j gets large,

$$\lim_{j \to \infty} \beta - \gamma^2[1 - (1 - \beta)^{1+j}] - (1 - \gamma^2)[1 - (1 - \rho)^{1+j}] = -(1 - \beta) < 0.$$

As the delay cost becomes infinitely large, it never pays to huddle.

This may be one reason why it is important to have councillors who speak the same language as managers. If it takes too much time for an accountant to communicate with a machinist, it might be better to have the machinists elect an accountant as their representative. (Of course, this begs the question of how machinists communicate to their representative.) It also suggests a role for training councillors. American managers who do not spend time consulting with their workers or staff can make decisions faster than European or Japanese managers. But they lose the benefits of information from those below them in the organization and may find implementation of decisions more difficult.

Let us return then to the issue of creativity and abstract from coordination. We replace the assumption that $\beta' = \beta$ with the assumption that $\beta' < \beta$, the difference reflecting creativity that occurs in the huddle. To eliminate coordination difficulties, assume that all players are right handed. With $\gamma = 1$, equation (11) now becomes

(11′) $$-(1 - \beta) + (1 - \beta')^{1+j}.$$

If $\beta = \beta'$, then equation (11') is clearly negative for $j > 0$. A huddle does not pay. But with $\beta < \beta'$, it is quite possible that the creativity generated in the huddle outweighs the delay cost. If $\beta' = 0$, the condition clearly holds and it pays to huddle; as β' goes to β, it does not. Define

$$\beta^* = 1 - (1 - \beta)^{1/(1+j)}.$$

Then for $\beta' < \beta^*$, it pays to huddle because the creativity effect outweighs the delay effect. For $\beta' > \beta^*$, a no-huddle offense dominates because the creativity gains do not outweigh the delay costs.

It can be shown as a general proposition, that

$$\beta^* > \beta/(1 + j).$$

The creativity effect is more important than the time effect. For example, if $j = 1$, the council meeting costs half of the firm's time. Even if the probability of success on a given try did not quite double with a huddle, it could still pay to huddle. For example, if $j = 1$, $\beta = .5$, and $\beta' = .29$, a huddle is worthwhile even though it increases the probability of success by less than 100 percent.

4.4.2. Co-determination, Worker Loyalty, and Investment in Skills

Few, if any, managements want to give workers co-determination over important decisions, particularly those relating to employment, conditions of work, and the like. Co-determination can greatly increase worker power. If workers have veto rights over hours worked, as in Germany, they possess a potentially powerful chip in bargaining over the division of rents. Indeed, outside of Germany, works council legislation accords co-determination rights only to decisions on which management is presumably neutral, such as the French-mandated expenditures on benefits that fall under the social fund. When does adopting the German model, which gives works councils rights over employment levels, employment patterns, and work conditions, improve worker surplus?

The German-style works council has the ability to enhance worker job security. The most important positive feature of additional job security is that it induces workers to take a longer-run view of the prospects of the firm. A consequence is that worker interests are brought more in line with those of owners. The easiest way to model this is to add additional periods to our Section 4.2. model (where workers choose how quickly to work) and to make the rewards to the worker in later periods depend on company well-being in earlier periods. Without a formal analysis, the logic is clear: workers who have job security place value on company profits because the profits are reflected in worker compensation in the future. Thus, one would expect workers in enterprises with strong councils to have greater loyalty to their firm and to be more eager to invest in firm-specific skills than workers in other firms. To the extent that there is under-investment in firm-specific human capital (because no one side captures 100 percent of the returns), providing additional job security helps to alleviate the problem.[16]

4.5. Summary and Conclusions

Our analysis has shown that works councils are most likely to improve enterprise surplus when they have limited but definite power in the enterprise. We have attempted to illuminate situations in which the mandated information sharing and consultation can improve social well-being. Further, we have discussed the implications of choosing specific rules for electing councils. We have stressed that the social-welfare-maximizing council power lies between the amount of power management will voluntarily give the councils and the amount of power labor desires.

European countries with works councils give councils limited legal power but also restrict conflict over the division of rents through centralized wagesetting systems. By setting the bulk of pay packages at the industry level, leaving only modest potential increments for bargaining by firms, and by forbidding councils from using labor's main weapon, the strike, European labor relations systems limit councils' ability to increase labor's rents at the expense of the total surplus. On the other side, by setting pay in industry negotiations, unions and employer federations create a wage floor for workers that serves a similar function. The risk that lack of local bargaining power will allow employers to garner the bulk of enterprise surplus is reduced. Industry unions help, of course, to maintain this dual system by influencing the behavior of councils. When centralized wage setting precludes councils from spending time and effort on wage negotiations, they must focus their attention on other aspects of the work environment.

Would mandated councils work in a different labor relations system, for instance the decentralized wage-setting system of the United States or the United Kingdom? Because we have assumed that the internal operation of councils is determined outside the enterprise, our analysis does not adequately address this critical question about the potential portability of institutions across labor relations systems. In a U.S. or British labor relations system, with decentralized wage setting, would councils, once established, turn into aggressive plant-level unions? Or might they become company-dominated quality-of-work circles and wither on the vine, as did the company-initiated U.S. councils of the 1920s? While our analysis does not answer these important questions even in the abstract, it does suggest the value of paying serious attention to the design of council-type arrangements that might best fit decentralized labor systems. There are potential net social gains from works councils. But to work best and gain those potential benefits, the rules governing councils must be carefully written to bound the power of labor and management and "fit" the broader labor system in which councils must function.

5

The Peter Principle:
A Theory of Decline

The Peter principle states that workers are promoted to their level of incompetence (Peter and Hull 1969). One interpretation is that firms systematically make mistakes in their promotion decisions. Another, favored here, is that the decline in ability that is seen after promotion is the natural outcome of a statistical process that displays regression to the mean. Workers are promoted on the basis of having met some standard. To the extent that ability is the sum of both permanent and transitory components, those who meet the standard have expected transitory components that are positive. The expectation of the post-promotion transitory component is zero, implying a reduction in expected ability. Firms that understand the statistical process take this phenomenon into account by adjusting the promotion standard, but the result remains: Expected ability for those promoted is lower after promotion than before.[1]

There is substantial evidence of the Peter principle.[2] In addition to papers from the marketing and organizational behavior literature (see e.g. Anderson, Dubinsky and Mehta 1999), there are a number of findings in empirical labor economics that support the claim. In an early paper that used subjective performance evaluation, Medoff and

The original version of this chapter was published as: Lazear, E. P. (2004). The Peter Principle: A Theory of Decline, in: Journal of Political Economy, 112(1), pt. 2 (2004): S141-S163. University of Chicago Press. © 2004 by the University of Chicago. Sherwin Rosen was my most important teacher, my valued colleague, and dear friend. Sherwin served on my thesis committee and taught me much of what I know. Throughout the 30 years that we were friends, Sherwin was a constant source of inspiration, wisdom, and kindness. A deep thinker who opened up a number of areas of research, Sherwin was interested in hierarchies and promotion, so this paper is very much in keeping with his research agenda and derives from it. This research was supported in part by the National Science Foundation. Useful comments were provided by many. Po-Han Fong, Thomas P. Gherig, Kevin J. Murphy, Torsten Persson, Paul Pfleiderer, Kathryn Shaw, Eskil Wadensjo, and Michael Waldman were particularly helpful.

Abraham (1980) reported that workers' subjective evaluation scores fell the longer they were on the job. In Lazear (1992a, see Chapter 9), it was found that the coefficient of job tenure in a wage regression was actually negative. The longer a worker was in a particular job, given his tenure in the firm, the lower his wage. The reason presumably is that the better workers are promoted out of the job, so those with a given number of years of firm experience who have fewer years in a job are less likely to have gotten stuck in that job. Baker, Gibbs, and Holmström (1994) replicate this finding in their data, and Gibbs and Hendricks (2004) find that raises and bonuses fall with tenure.

The tone of the literature outside of economics is that there is something wrong with promotion dynamics, and this anomaly shows up as the Peter principle. (Indeed, the book written by Peter and Hull is entitled "The Peter Principle: Why Things Always Go Wrong".) The approach taken here is different. The Peter principle results from optimal adjustment to decision making under uncertainty. It is argued that even when firms use exactly the right promotion rule, the Peter principle effect will be observed. The fact that reversals of promotion decisions are rare is more compatible with the view that they were correct in the first place than that something went wrong.

More often, the Peter principle is interpreted in a multifactor context. Individuals who are good in one job are not necessarily good in the job into which they are promoted. As a result, individuals appear incompetent in the job in which they settle. To obtain this result, it is merely necessary to make a slight modification in the regression to the mean structure. Here, general ability is combined with a job-specific ability to produce output. Regression to the mean results because positive readings on the job-specific component prior to promotion are uncorrelated with the job-specific component after promotion.[3]

The fact that promoted individuals are less able than their apparent prepromotion ability induces firms to adjust in two respects. First, firms select their promotion rule with the understanding that the prepromotion ability is a biased estimate of true ability for those who exceed some standard. Second, as the variance in the transitory component of ability rises relative to the variance in the permanent component, the adjustment factor becomes greater. In the typical case, the standard that one must exceed to obtain a promotion increases with the relative importance of the transitory component because the regression effect is larger when the variance of the transitory component is large.

The model presented below yields the following results:

1. Promoted individuals' performance falls, on average, relative to their prepromotion performance.

2. Firms that take the decline into account adjust their promotion rule accordingly, but this does not negate the observation that ability declines after promotion.

3. The importance of the Peter principle depends on the amount of variation in the transitory component relative to the permanent. The Peter principle is most pronounced when the transitory component is large.

4. The length of the prepromotion period depends on the ratio of transitory variation to permanent variation. As the transitory component becomes more important, firms lengthen the prepromotion period.

5. Movie sequels are systematically worse than the original on which they are based.

6. Follow-up visits to good restaurants provide poorer meals than the first sampling.

7. In the absence of learning effects, second-term elected officials are less effective than they were during the first term.

5.1. The Model

Let there be two periods. Each worker has a time-invariant component of ability, denoted $A \sim f(A)$, and a time-varying component of ability, denoted ε_1 for period 1 and ε_2 for period 2. Let the time-varying components be independently and identically distributed with density $g(\varepsilon)$. The firm can observe $A + \varepsilon_t$ in each period but cannot disentangle the time-varying component of ability from the permanent component. There are a variety of interpretations that are consistent with this specification. One can think of the ε_t as being a true transitory aspect of ability or just measurement error. Later, the interpretation of different jobs will be considered.

The Peter Principle: A Theory of Decline

There are two jobs (two are sufficient), which we denote difficult and easy. An individual's productivity in the easy job is given by

$$\alpha + \beta(A + \varepsilon_t)$$

and in the difficult job is given by

$$\gamma + \delta(A + \varepsilon_t),$$

where $\alpha > \gamma$ and $\delta > \beta$. Thus it pays to assign a worker to the difficult job if and only if

$$A + \varepsilon_t > x,$$

where $x \equiv (\alpha - \gamma)/(\delta - \beta)$. The situation and the crossing point that correspond to x are shown in Figure 5.1.[4] The setup seeks to capture the idea that the most able have a comparative advantage in the difficult job.

Figure 5.1

Output

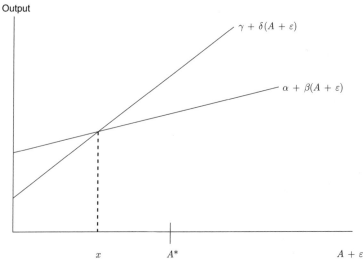

132

Assume that individual ability $f(A)$ is such that, in the absence of information, it pays to assign everyone to the easy job in period 1.[5] Intuitively, this assumption amounts to saying that most people are not well suited to the difficult job and that, in the absence of countervailing information, individuals are assigned to the easy job. With one exception, noted in the appendix, it is sufficient to assume symmetric ignorance, so that workers are no better informed about their abilities than firms.

After the first period, firms obtain an estimate of A, namely $\hat{A} = A + \varepsilon_1$. Since ε_1 is the period 1 transitory component (either measurement error or transitory ability), it is A and not $\hat{A}$ on which a promotion decision should be made. But A is not observed, so firms are forced to base their decision on $\hat{A}$.

5.1.1.   Workers Perform Worse after Being Promoted

Firms must select some criterion level, A^*, such that if $\hat{A} > A^*$, the worker is promoted to the difficult job. If $\hat{A} > A$, the worker remains in his current job. It is now shown that workers who are promoted have levels of ability in period 1 that are higher, on average, than their ability in period 2.

First, note that the expectation of ε_1 given that an individual is promoted is

$$\mathrm{E}(\varepsilon_1 \mid A + \varepsilon_1 > A^*) = \int_{-\infty}^{\infty} \int_{A^*-A}^{\infty} \frac{1}{1 - G(A^* - A)} \, \varepsilon g(\varepsilon) f(A) d\varepsilon dA$$

$$= \int_{-\infty}^{\infty} \mathrm{E}(\varepsilon \mid \varepsilon > A^* - A) f(A) dA,$$

which is positive since $f(A)$ is positive and the conditional expectation of ε given ε greater than any number is positive (because the unconditional expectation of ε is zero). Thus the conditional expectation of ε_1 is positive among those who are promoted.

Now, in period 2, the expectation of the transitory component is

$$\mathrm{E}(\varepsilon_2 \mid A + \varepsilon_1 > A^*) = 0$$

because ε_2 is independent of A and of ε_1. As a result, for any promoted individual with ability A,

$$A + \mathrm{E}(\varepsilon_1 | \ A + \varepsilon_1 > A^*) > A + \mathrm{E}(\varepsilon_2 | \ A + \varepsilon_1 \ > A^*).$$

Thus expected ability falls for promoted individuals from period 1 to period 2.

Individuals who are promoted are promoted in part because they are likely to have high permanent ability,[6] but also because the transitory component of their ability is high. One of the reasons that academics tend to write better papers before they receive tenure is that they would not have received tenure had they not written the better-than-average papers. The point is obvious but is made graphic by the following example. Suppose that a firm promotes all individuals who can obtain three heads on three consecutive coin tosses. Only one in eight will be promoted. But when the firm asks the promoted individuals to repeat the feat, only one in eight will measure up. Seven out of eight will do worse than they did before being promoted. The reason is that all of the "performance" on the coin toss is transitory since tosses are independent.

As a general matter, the larger the transitory component is relative to the permanent component, the more important the Peter principle effect. If there were no transitory component, there would be no regression to the mean. Thus the importance of "luck" is positively associated with the force of the Peter principle.

5.1.2. The Promotion Rule

Firms know in advance that there will be some expected fall in productivity among those promoted and adjust their promotion standard accordingly. Below, the general optimization problem for the firm is presented. Then, the way in which the rule operates is demonstrated by an example.

The firm's problem is to maximize profits (or worker utility) by selecting the job for each candidate with the highest expected value. Recall that individuals who have period 2 ability greater than x, defined above, would be assigned to job 2 were second-period ability known. The firm does not see A, but only $\hat{A}$, and must choose some criterion, A^*, such that it promotes workers whose observed ability in period 1 is greater than it. This is equivalent to promoting individuals when $A > A^* - \varepsilon_1$. Thus the firm wants to choose A^* so as to maximize

$$
(1) \quad \max_{A^*} \int_{-\infty}^{\infty} \int_{A^*-\varepsilon_1}^{\infty} \int_{-\infty}^{\infty} [\gamma + \delta(A + \varepsilon_2)] f(A) g(\varepsilon_1) g(\varepsilon_2) d\varepsilon_2 dA d\varepsilon_1
$$

$$
+ \int_{-\infty}^{\infty} \int_{-\infty}^{A^*-\varepsilon_1} \int_{-\infty}^{\infty} [\alpha + \beta(A + \varepsilon_2)] f(A) g(\varepsilon_1) g(\varepsilon_2) d\varepsilon_2 dA d\varepsilon_1.
$$

Because the expectation of ε_2 is zero, (1) can be written as

$$
(2) \quad \max_{A^*} \int_{-\infty}^{\infty} \int_{A^*-\varepsilon_1}^{\infty} (\gamma + \delta A) dFdG + \int_{-\infty}^{\infty} \int_{\infty}^{A^*-\varepsilon_1} (\alpha + \beta A) dFdG.
$$

The choice of A^* depends on the distribution. However, two examples reveal that A^* does not equal x as a general rule. Instead, in typical cases, firms adjust A^* upward. Knowing that worker ability in period 2 will differ from worker ability in period 1, firms usually set the bar higher than they would, where ability observed in period 1 carried over directly to period 2.

Actual solutions that provide intuition are available for given distributions. Consider, for example, the case in which A, ε_1, and ε_2 are all distributed normally, with mean zero and variance equal to one. Let $\alpha = 1$, $\beta = 0.5$, $\gamma = 0$, and $\delta = 1$. Then x, the ability level at which jobs produce equal value, is two since

$$
\alpha + b(A + \varepsilon) = \gamma + \delta(A + \varepsilon)
$$

for $A + \varepsilon = 2$. However, $A^* = 4.01$. The firm sets its promotion standard more than two standard deviations higher than the crossing point in Figure 5.1 because it understands that the worker's ability in period 2 is likely to be lower than it was in period 1 for the promoted group. As a result, the firm insists on a very high level of observed ability in period 1 in order to warrant promotion. Statements such as "tenure requires that the faculty member be the best in his or her field, having produced outstanding research" is a manifestation of the upward adjustment.

Consider the same example with a twist. Let the distribution of A remain the same, namely, normal with mean zero and a standard deviation of one, but let the standard deviation of ε_1 fall to 0.1. Then A^* drops from 4.01 to 2.08. Although the firm still adjusts its promotion criterion upward from x, the adjustment is much smaller because the importance of the transitory component has been diminished. There is regression to the mean, but the regression that takes place is small relative to the amount in the prior example. When the standard deviation of ε is zero, the promotion standard is two, which is exactly x as expected. Then the distribution of ε_1 is degenerate, so that all observed ability in period 1 is permanent ability. The problem in (2) becomes

$$\max_{A^*} \int_{A^*}^{\infty} (\gamma + \delta A)f(A)dA + \int_{-\infty}^{A^*} (\alpha + \beta A)f(A)dA,$$

which has first-order condition

$$\frac{\partial}{\partial A^*} = -(\gamma + \delta A^*)f(A^*) + (\alpha + \beta A^*)f(A^*) = 0.$$

The solution is

$$\gamma + \delta A^* = \alpha + \beta A^*,$$

which is the crossing point, that is, x, in Figure 5.1. When there is no transitory component, the firm simply promotes those whose permanent ability places them better in the difficult job than in the easy job.

It is possible to derive the relation between A^* and x in more general terms.[7] The first-order condition to (2) is

$$(\gamma + \delta A^* - \alpha - \beta A^*) \int_{-\infty}^{\infty} f(A^* - \varepsilon_1)g(\varepsilon_1)d\varepsilon_1$$
$$= (\delta - \beta) \int_{-\infty}^{\infty} \varepsilon_1 f(A^* - \varepsilon_1)g(\varepsilon_1)d\varepsilon_1.$$

The integral on the left-hand side is always positive, so whether A^* exceeds x or not depends on the sign of the integral on the right-hand side. Assume that both $f(\cdot)$ and $g(\cdot)$ are symmetric densities, and let $g(\cdot)$ be symmetric around zero and $f(\cdot)$ be symmetric around $\overline{A}$. Write the integral on the right side as

$$\int_{-\infty}^{0} \varepsilon_1 f(A^* - \varepsilon_1)g(\varepsilon_1)d\varepsilon_1 + \int_{0}^{\infty} \varepsilon_1 f(A^* - \varepsilon_1)g(\varepsilon_1)d\varepsilon_1.$$

Use a change of variable in the first integral of $u = -\varepsilon_1$, and in the second, allow $u = \varepsilon_1$. Because of symmetry, $g(u) = g(-u)$, so one can write the two integrals as one:

$$\int_0^\infty u[f(A^* - u) - f(A^* + u)]g(u)du.$$

Suppose that the firm wants to promote fewer than 50 percent of the people, that is, that $x > \overline{A}$. (Recall that x is the value such that $\alpha + \beta x = \gamma + \delta x$. If $x = \overline{A}$, then because of symmetry of the density functions, half of the population would have $A > x$ and half would have $A < x$.) Under such circumstances, $f(x - u) > f(x - u)$ (because f is unimodal around $\overline{A}$). Thus the right-hand side of the first-order condition is positive for $A^* = x$, which implies that

$$\alpha + \beta A^* > \gamma + \delta A^*$$

or that $A^* > x$. Thus the firm adjusts the cutoff level upward when fewer than 50 percent of the workers are better suited to the difficult job than to the easy job.

The same reasoning applies in reverse. If more than 50 percent are to be promoted, then $x < \overline{A}$, which means that $f(x - u) < f(x + u)$. As a result, the right-hand side of the first-order condition is negative at x, which means A^* that must be less than x to satisfy optimality. Thus, when more than 50 percent are better suited to the difficult job than to the easy job, the firm reduces the promotion cutoff below the one that would be optimal were there no error in period 1. (Actually, under such circumstances, workers would initially be assigned to the difficult job, and the standard would be one such that workers who fell below it would be demoted after the first period.)

The intuition is this. Although there is always regression to the mean, adjusting the promotion level upward reduces the probability that the firm will make a bad promotion decision. However, at the same time, the adjustment increases the probability that it will fail to promote a qualified worker; that is, it reduces the false positive while increasing the false negative error. Conversely, lowering the promotion cutoff reduces the probability that someone who erroneously was observed to be a poor worker is not promoted but increases the probability that the firm promotes too many bad workers. Thus there is a trade-off. When fewer than 50 percent are to be promoted, the expected cost of making a false positive error exceeds that of making a false negative error so that the criterion must be adjusted upward. To the extent that most hierarchies are narrower at the top than at the bottom, $A^* > x$ is probably the more typical case. Standards are adjusted upward.

5.1.3. *Another Interpretation of the Peter Principle*

Rosen (1986) presents a model of sequential promotions in which individuals are sorted by ability at each stage such that members of the entering class at each round of a tournament have equal (ex ante) ability. Rosen uses the model to determine the optimal compensation at each level to motivate workers. Sorting is also an issue because the pool of workers at successive rounds have higher ability than those at earlier rounds. The Rosen model is in some ways more general than the one described here because it allows for effort as well as ability differences. The focus is quite different, however, because neither the optimal promotion rule nor the worker's output over time is an important part of the analysis. It is likely that many of the Peter principle results that come out of this paper could have been derived in that important paper on sequential promotions.[8]

Still, the Rosen model does not fit one of the most common interpretations of the Peter principle, which is that workers are promoted to their level of incompetence because a worker who is good in one job is not necessarily good in a job one level up. Fine professors do not necessarily make good deans (although not all would interpret moving to the dean's job as a promotion).[9] A slight modification of the definitions above and some of the formulas permits this interpretation.

To see this, allow ε_1 to be defined as the job-specific component of ability associated with the easy job and ε_2 as the job-specific component of ability associated with the difficult job. Individuals are assigned to the easy job in period 1 for the reason given before: Most are better at the easy job, and in the absence of information, the easy job is the right assignment. After evaluation, $\widehat{A}$ is observed and the worker is promoted or not. If he is not promoted, then his ability after promotion is $A + \varepsilon_1$. If he is promoted, then his ability after promotion is $A + \varepsilon_2$.

Under this interpretation, workers who are not promoted have output that remains constant over time and equal to $\alpha + \beta(A + \varepsilon_1)$. Those who are promoted have output equal to $\gamma + \delta(A + \varepsilon_2)$. The argument of Section 5.1.1. holds:

$$E(\varepsilon_1|\ A + \varepsilon_1 > A^*) = \int_{-\infty}^{\infty}\int_{A^*-A}^{\infty} \frac{1}{1 - G(A^* - A)}\ \varepsilon g(\varepsilon)f(A)d\varepsilon dA$$
$$= \int_{-\infty}^{\infty} E(\varepsilon|\ \varepsilon > A^* - A)f(A)dA,$$

which is positive since $f(A)$ is positive and the conditional expectation of ε given ε greater than any number is positive (because the unconditional expectation of ε is zero). But the expectation of ε_2 is zero for promoted workers because ε_1 and ε_2 are uncorrelated. As a result, expected ability is higher before promotion than for promoted workers after promotion.

This does not necessarily imply that output is lower after promotion because workers are in different jobs. On the contrary, if A^* is chosen optimally, it must be the case that expected output for the promoted workers is higher in the difficult job than in the easy job. If it were not, it would be better to raise A^* until expected output were higher. Rather the point is that after promotion, the average promoted worker is not as able in the difficult job as he was in the easy job, that is,

$$E(A + \varepsilon_2|\ \text{promoted}) < E(A + \varepsilon_1|\ \text{promoted}).$$

Also true is that within any job, those left behind and not promoted have lower average ability than those of their cohorts entering into that job. If there were a series of promotion rounds, then at every level, those who were not promoted would have a job-specific component that is negative. This can be seen simply by examining the first round, which can be thought of as a "promotion" from being out of the firm to being hired as a worker. (Individuals must exceed some standard in order to be hired.) Since it has already been shown that

$$E(\varepsilon_1|\ A + \varepsilon_1 > A^*) > 0$$

and since $E(\varepsilon_1) = 0$, it must be true that

$$E(\varepsilon_1|\ A + \varepsilon_1 \leq A^*) < 0.$$

They appear "incompetent" because, within any given job, the actual ability of those who are not promoted out of the job is lower than the unconditional expectation of ability for that job. Those who are left behind and become the long-termers are worse than those who come into the job. They are incompetent relative to the entry pool because the competent workers are promoted out of the job. In a tournament with enough steps, each competent worker would continue to be promoted until he too was incompetent, that is, until $E(\varepsilon_t) < 0$ for those whose highest job attained is job t. This is the Peter principle: Workers are promoted to their level of incompetence. Those who are "competent" are promoted again.[10]

5.1.4.   Mistake or Optimal Adjustment?

The original book was entitled The Peter Principle: Why Things Always Go Wrong. The implications of the view that promotion decisions are biased are different from those of this model. The view in this model is that if A^* is chosen optimally, most of the time firms will not want to undo their decision. Even though ability is below that predicted by a naïve use of the first-period estimate, the promoted worker's ability is still above x, at least on average. If it were not, then the choice of A^* would have been suboptimal. Ability falls but does not fall below x in most cases, so the firm does not want to reverse its decision. The behavioral view that "things go wrong" is different. If the firm really made a mistake, then it would want to demote or fire workers in most cases, which leads to the inevitable question, "Why are demotions so rare?" This analysis provides an answer. The promotion rule is chosen optimally so that ability is not as high as it was before promotion, but it is still high enough to justify the promotion.

5.2. Strategic Behavior by Workers

So far, worker effort has been assumed to be given. In this section, I relax the assumption that effort is given in order to determine how workers may game the system to alter their promotion possibilities. Whether workers overproduce during the probationary period depends crucially on the compensation scheme.

5.2.1.   Efficient Effort with Worker Job Choice

The first result is that if workers are paid piece rates and allowed to choose their own jobs, all is efficient, even if workers know their ability and firms do not. In order to examine incentives, it is necessary to define more terms: let μ_e be the amount of effort that an individual chooses if he is in the easy job and μ_d be the amount of effort he chooses if he is in the difficult job. Let $C(\mu)$ be the cost incurred for any given level of effort μ. Then if A is known but ε is not, individuals for whom

$$
\begin{aligned}
(3) \quad \int_{-\infty}^{\infty} [\gamma + \delta(A + \varepsilon + \mu_d)]g(\varepsilon)d\varepsilon &- C(\mu_d) \\
&> \int_{-\infty}^{\infty} [\alpha + \beta(A + \varepsilon + \mu_e)]g(\varepsilon)d\varepsilon - C(\mu_e)
\end{aligned}
$$

choose the difficult job. Those for whom the condition in (3) does not hold choose the easy job. Effort levels in (3) are merely the optimal levels, given the job chosen.

Because the expectation of ε is zero, (3) can be rewritten as

$$
(4) \qquad \alpha + \beta(A + \mu_e) - C(\mu_e) < \gamma + \delta(A + \mu_d) - C(\mu_d).
$$

If the condition in (4) holds, a worker prefers the difficult job. If it does not, the easy job is selected.[11] This is the same as the efficiency condition, so workers choose jobs and effort efficiently under these conditions. There is no distortion in effort choice. The worker internalizes everything. This is a simple problem of occupational choice with effort. By contrast, were the firm to choose the job for the worker, then effort would be distorted, although the surprising result is that the distortion is as likely to take the form of underwork as it is of overwork. This is shown in the appendix.

5.2.2.   Tournaments

The usual intuition that most have about promotions inducing atypically high effort in period 1 comes from a tournament-like payment structure.[12] When period 2 wages depend on the job rather than on the output in the job, all workers put forth more effort than they would in the absence of period 2 promotion concerns.

The intuition holds whether the tournament is against another player or against a standard. For the purposes here, there is little difference between competing against another player and competing against a standard. In the Lazear-Rosen tournament structure, any level of effort can be implemented for any standard simply by choosing the wage spread appropriately. In the case of a standard, wages in period 2 are fixed in advance and depend only on promotion. Even if workers receive no wage prior to promotion, workers who are ignorant of A put forth effort in order to maximize

$$\max_{\mu_1} \int \{W_d \text{prob}(A + \mu_1 + \varepsilon_1 > A^*) + W_e[1 - \text{prob}(A + \mu_1 + \varepsilon_1 > A^*)]$$
$$- C(\mu_1)\} g(A) dA,$$

where W_d is the difficult job's wage and W_e is the easy job's wage.

The first-order condition is

$$\int \left[(W_d - W_e) \frac{\partial \text{prob}(A + \mu_1 + \varepsilon_1 > A^*)}{\partial \mu_1} - C'(\mu_1) \right] dG = 0$$

or

$$(W_d - W_e)g(A^* - \mu_1 - A) = C'(\mu_1).$$

The firm can obtain any level of effort, μ_1, simply by setting the spread between the difficult job wage and easy job wage appropriately. Then it is necessary only to set the expected wage sufficiently high to attract the marginal worker.

What is clear, however, is that effort in period 1 exceeds that in period 2. The tournament structure induces individuals to work at some positive level in period 1 but to reduce effort in period 2. In this stylized model, since there is no contingent reward in period 2, effort falls to zero. But the general point is that the tournament against a standard creates incentives to perform better in the pre-promotion period than in the post promotion period.

Firms understand that their compensation schemes induce strategic behavior by workers and set A^* accordingly. Although this may mitigate the effects of the behavior, it in no way changes the results of this section. Since all derivations hold for any given A^*, they hold for the A^* chosen to take these effects into account.

As is the case of the tournament against a standard, workers put forth more effort before the promotion decision than after the promotion decision in a tournament against another player. This follows directly from Lazear and Rosen (1981, see Chapter 6), where effort during the contest period exceeds effort after the contest period. Worker effort during the contest period is monotonically increasing in the spread between the winner's wage and the loser's wage. After the contest has been decided, effort falls off.

In both the tournament story and the regression to the mean story, worker output declines after the promotion decision. In the tournament context, the reason is that effort declines. In the regression to the mean version, output declines because of the statistical proposition that ensures that winners do worse after promotion. There is a difference, however. In tournaments, even losers reduce effort after the promotion has been decided, so expected output for all workers falls over time. In the statistical version, winners' output falls and losers' output rises above their prepromotion levels on average.

To amplify this point, just as those who are promoted have higher-than-average prepromotion transitory error, ε_1, so do those who fail to be promoted have lower-than-expected transitory components. Other things equal, this implies that those who do not get a promotion should do better after being turned down than they did before. Thus faculty who are denied tenure and move to other schools should do better, on average, at those other schools than they did when they were assistant professors at the first institution.

Observing this effect may be difficult for a number of reasons. For example, a worker's output might depend on the individuals with whom he works. In an up-or-out context (Kahn and Huberman 1988), those who fail to be promoted may find that the complementary factors in the new job are not as productivity-enhancing as those in the first job. Furthermore, motivation is an issue. To the extent that an individual believes that he is in the running for promotion, tournament effects are present, inducing effort. After the promotion has been denied, the incentives vanish, reducing effort and output.

5.3. Other Examples of the Principle

The regression to the mean phenomenon that is observed as the Peter principle in the labor market has other manifestations. For example, it is often observed that sequels are rarely as good as the original movie on which the sequel is based.[13] If each movie is thought of as having a theme-constant component, A, and a transitory component, ε_t (e.g., actors, specific story, or direction), associated with each particular film, then the same analysis holds. In order for a sequel to be made, the value of the original film, $A + \varepsilon_t$, must be estimated to be greater than A^*. But given that the value exceeds the threshold level, A^*, the expectation of the value of the sequel will be less than that of the original simply because

$$\mathrm{E}(\varepsilon_1 |\ \text{sequel is made}) > 0,$$

but

$$\mathrm{E}(\varepsilon_2 |\ \text{sequel is made}) = 0.$$

As a result, an original film must be sufficiently good to generate a sequel because studios, knowing that the second film is likely to be inferior to the first, adjust upward their cutoff levels.

It is straightforward to test this proposition. Among other things, it implies that measures of film quality such as academy awards or ticket sales should be higher on the original film than on the sequels.[14]

The fact that sequels do worse than originals is not evidence that the studio made a mistake. Once again, if A^* is chosen optimally, then the average sequel is profitable, even if not as profitable as the original. A decline in profitability does not imply that something went wrong in decision making.

Similarly, the first meal in a good restaurant is often the best, followed by less satisfying repeat visits. Just as above, think of A as the restaurant component of the first meal (recipes, management) and ε_1 as the transitory component associated with the meal itself (that night's chef, specific ingredients, dinner companion). A second visit to the restaurant is made only if $A + \varepsilon_1 > A^*$. Once again, the expected value of the second meal lies below that of the first, conditional on the decision to make a second visit to the restaurant. The larger the transitory component, the larger the discrepancy between the first and second meals and the higher the standard set to merit a second visit. As before, the fact that the second visit is not as good as the first does not imply that a mistake was made. The second meal, on average, is good enough to justify a repeat visit to the restaurant, even if it is not as good as the first. The point can also be used to explain why favorite restaurants go out of fashion. A restaurant becomes a favorite in part because of the permanent component (e.g., good recipes and an insightful owner) and in part because of potentially transitory components (e.g., the current chef and the service of the staff). A favored restaurant can be thought of as one that has gotten a draw of $A + \varepsilon_1 > A^*$. It is favored precisely because the value of the output exceeds some standard. Over time, ε_1 is replaced by transitory effects, the expectation of which is zero. The quality falls and the restaurant goes out of fashion.

The same logic can be applied to the "Sports Illustrated effect." It is claimed that it is a curse to be on the cover of Sports Illustrated because athletes' performance falls thereafter. Again this reflects regression to the mean, but it does not imply that Sports Illustrated chose the wrong athlete for the cover.

In the political arena, reelections of elected officials occur when constituents view performance as having exceeded some standard. The postelection performance should be worse without learning and seniority effects. If the learning effect is not too strong, second-term presidents will do less well than they did during their first term. But this does not imply that voters made a mistake. Even when voters know that there is regression, voting for the incumbent is rational if he exceeds a sufficiently high standard.

Finally, there is a close relation of this analysis to that of the winner's curse (Wilson 1969).[15] If a bidder submits a bid based on a naive estimate, the winner will lose money because, on average, the winner has obtained a higher-than-average error. As a result, he shades his bid, so in equilibrium he adopts the rent-maximizing strategy. The same is true here. By adjusting the cutoff criterion, A^*, the decision maker maximizes rent.

5.4. Length of Probationary Period and Relative Importance of the Transitory Component

The longer a firm waits to make a promotion decision, the better the information. One would expect that transitory components that bias a decision could be reduced or eliminated if the firm waited long enough to make a promotion decision. The cost of waiting, however, is that workers are in the wrong job for more of their lifetimes. For example, suppose that it were possible to get a perfect reading on A by waiting until the date of retirement. The information would have no value because the worker would have spent his entire working career in the easy job, even if he were better suited to the difficult job. The trade-off is modeled. The conclusion is that as the variance of ε_1 rises, it becomes more valuable to wait on a promotion decision.

To see this, let us add one period to the previous model (without effort). Now, ε_1, ε_2, and ε_3 refer to the transitory component in periods 1, 2, and 3, and assume that they are distributed independently and identically and, to reduce notation, that $E(A) = 0$. Suppose that by waiting two periods, an employer can obtain a perfect reading of A. Under those circumstances, the optimum is simply to promote those for whom $A > x$. The cost is that when the firm delays its promotion decision to the end of period 2, all workers are in the easy job during period 2 even though it might be better to place some in the difficult job in period 2. Expected output over the lifetime is then

$$
\begin{aligned}
\text{expected output if wait} &= 2[\alpha + \beta E(A + \varepsilon_1)] + \int_x^\infty (\gamma + \delta A)d \\
&\quad + \int_{-\infty}^x (\alpha + \beta A)dFF \\
&= 2\alpha + \int_x^\infty (\gamma + \delta A)dF + \int_{-\infty}^x (\alpha + \beta A)dF.
\end{aligned}
$$

(5)

The alternative is to make a decision after one period, using imperfect information and recognizing that sorting will be imperfect. To make things simple, assume that a firm that makes a promotion decision at the end of period 1 cannot reevaluate at the end of period 2. The gain is that workers are sorted early so that very able people can be put in the difficult job more quickly. The cost is that more errors are made in assigning workers to jobs. Then expected output over the three periods is

$$
\begin{aligned}
\text{expected output early} &= [\alpha + \beta E(A + \varepsilon_1)] + 2\int_{-\infty}^{\infty}\int_{A^*-\varepsilon}^{\infty}(\gamma + \delta A)dFdG \\
&\quad + 2\int_{-\infty}^{\infty}\int_{-\infty}^{A^*-\varepsilon}(\alpha + \beta A)dFdG \\
&= \alpha + 2\int_{-\infty}^{\infty}\int_{A^*-\varepsilon}^{-\infty}(\gamma + \delta A)dFd \\
&\quad + 2\int_{-\infty}^{\infty}\int_{-\infty}^{A^*-\varepsilon}(\alpha + \beta A)dFdG.
\end{aligned}
$$

(6)

In an extreme case, it is clear that it pays to decide early. If the distribution of ε is degenerate so that there is no error, then (6) becomes

(7) $\text{expected output early} = \alpha + 2\int_{x}^{\infty}(\gamma + \delta A)dFdG + 2\int_{-\infty}^{x}(\alpha + \beta A)dF.$

The right-hand side of the expression in (7) must exceed the right-hand side of (5) because

$$
\gamma + \delta A > \alpha + \beta A \quad \text{for } A > x
$$

since that is how x is defined. Thus, when the variance in ε shrinks to zero, it always pays to promote early.

The example used earlier shows that it sometimes pays to defer the promotion decision until the end of period 2. As before, let $\alpha = 1$, $\beta = 0.5$, $\gamma = 0$, and $\delta = 1$, where the distributions of A and ε_t are normal with variance equal to one. As shown earlier, the optimal cut point is $A^* = 4.01$. Then the right-hand side of (5) equals 3.004. The right hand side of (6) is 3.000. Thus deferring the promotion decision until the second period pays when the variance in ε is one. Other numerical examples show that the advantage of deferring the promotion decision becomes larger for higher variances in ε.

The general point is that when the distribution of ε is sufficiently tight, it pays to make the promotion decision early. When it is sufficiently diffuse, it pays to make the promotion decision later. Later promotion decisions are more accurate but result in workers' spending a longer proportion of their work life in the wrong job.

5.5. Summary and Conclusions

Workers who are promoted have been observed to have exceeded some standard. Part of the observation is based on lasting ability, but part is based on transitory components that may reflect measurement difficulties, short-term luck, or skills that are job-specific. As a result, there is regression to the mean, creating a "Peter principle." Workers who are promoted do not appear to be as able as they were before the promotion.

Firms take this phenomenon into account in setting up their promotion rule. Under general conditions, when fewer than 50 percent of the workers are better suited to the high-level job, the firm adjusts the promotion standard upward to compensate for the regression to the mean. The amount of the adjustment depends on the tightness of the error distribution. When the prepromotion error has high dispersion, promotion standards are inflated by more than they are when the error dispersion is low.

The statistical argument has been contrasted with incentive arguments. Whether workers overproduce because they are gaming the system depends on the payment structure. If, for example, output were observable so that workers could be paid on the basis of output both before and after the promotion decision, then it would be optimal to allow workers to make their own job choice. Under these circumstances, there is no distortion in effort; all is efficient. When a tournament structure is chosen because of inability to observe output, workers produce more before promotion than they do after promotion. Although tournaments result in declining output after promotion, the implications of tournaments for losers and winners are different from those of the statistical argument. In particular, in tournaments, the output of both losers and winners falls after promotion. The statistical argument implies that losers' output rises and winners' output falls after promotion.

The Peter principle can be interpreted to mean that workers are not as able as perceived before promotion or that they were better in their prior job relative to their peers than they are in their current one. In a multilevel firm, the typical worker who remains at a given level is "incompetent" in that he is not as good as the average worker coming into the job, nor is he as good as he was in his previous assignment relative to the comparison set.

One way to offset the Peter principle is to wait for a longer time before making a promotion decision. The advantage is that the job assignment is better than it would have been had the decision been made earlier. The disadvantage is that able workers remain in the wrong job for a longer period of time.

The logic of the Peter principle applies in other contexts as well. The regression to the mean phenomenon implies that movie sequels are lower-quality than the original films on which they are based and that excellent restaurant meals are followed by ones that are closer to mediocre.

Appendix

Effort Is Distorted When Firms Assign Jobs but Workers Know Ability

Assume asymmetric information in which workers know their abilities, A, but firms do not. Define μ_1 as effort in period 1, μ_{2e} as effort in period 2 if the worker is not promoted, and μ_{2d} as effort in period 2 if the worker is promoted. Note that effort in period 1 is determined before the promotion decision is made, so period 1 effort is independent of promotion. The cost of effort is given by $C(\mu)$. For simplicity, $C(\mu)$ is assumed to be independent of ability and the same across periods.

The worker is paid a piece rate, so in period 2, a worker who has not been promoted chooses effort μ_{2e} so as to solve

$$\max_{\mu_{2e}} \alpha + \beta E(A + \mu_{2e} + \varepsilon_2) - C(\mu_{2e})$$

or

$$\max_{\mu_{2e}} \alpha + \beta(A + \mu_{2e}) - C(\mu_{2e}).$$

The first-order condition is

(A1) $$C'(\mu_{2e}) = \beta.$$

An analogous problem can be solved for those who are promoted. Their problem is

$$\max_{\mu_{2d}} \gamma + \delta(A_2 + \mu_{2d}) - C(\mu_{2d}),$$

which has first-order condition

(A2) $$C'(\mu_{2d}) = \delta.$$

Equations (A1) and (A2) define μ_{2e} and μ_{2d}. Promoted workers put forth more effort in period 2 because the marginal return to effort is higher in the difficult job than in the easy job, that is, $\delta > \beta$. Given this, the worker solves a two-period problem in period 1, knowing that he will choose μ_{2e} and μ_{2d} depending on whether or not he is promoted.

The worker who knows his own ability has a first-period problem given by[16]

$$\max_{\mu_1} \alpha + \beta E(\mu_1 + A + \varepsilon_1) - C(\mu_1)$$

$$+ \text{prob}(A + \mu_1 + \varepsilon_1 > A^*)E[\gamma + \delta(A + \mu_{2d} + \varepsilon_2) - C(\mu_{2d})]$$

$$+ \text{prob}(A + \varepsilon_1 + \mu_1 \le A^*)E[\alpha + \beta(A + \mu_{2e} + \varepsilon_2) - C(\mu_{2e})]$$

or

(A3)
$$\max_{\mu_1} \alpha + \beta(\mu_1 + A) - C(\mu_1)$$

$$+ [1 - G(A^* - \mu_1 - A)][\gamma + \delta(A + \mu_{2d}) - C(\mu_{2d})]$$

$$+ G(A^* - \mu_1 - A)[\alpha + \beta(A + \mu_{2e}) - C(\mu_{2e})].$$

The first-order condition is

(A4)
$$\beta - C'(\mu_1) + g(A^* - \mu_1 - A)\{[\gamma + \delta(A + \mu_{2d}) - C(\mu_{2d})]$$

$$- [\alpha + \beta(A + \mu_{2e}) - C(\mu_{2e})]\} = 0.$$

Efficient effort is supplied when workers set $C'(\mu_1) = \beta$. According to the first-order condition in (A4), this occurs only when the last term on the left-hand side is equal to zero. In general, it will not be zero. In fact, the last term is positive, implying overinvestment, when

$$\gamma + \delta(A + \mu_{2d}) - C(\mu_{2d}) > \alpha + \beta(A + \mu_{2e}) - C(\mu_{2e}).$$

Sufficiently high-ability workers prefer job 1 because they earn more in job 1. As a result, they overwork in period 1 to enhance the probability that they will be promoted. Because the firm cannot distinguish effort from ability, workers who want to be promoted have an incentive to work too hard in order to fool the firm into believing that their ability levels are higher than they actually are.

Less intuitive, the converse is also true. Low-ability workers, that is, those for whom A is sufficiently low so that

$$\gamma + \delta(A + \mu_{2d}) - C(\mu_{2d}) < \alpha + \beta(A + \mu_{2e}) - C(\mu_{2e}),$$

underwork.[17] These workers underachieve because they do not want to take the chance of being promoted. From their point of view, a promotion is bad because they are likely to earn less in the difficult job than in the easy job.

The workers who are most likely to distort their effort in period 1 are those for whom $g(A^* - \mu_1 - A)$ is high (see Equation (A4)) and for whom

$$|[\gamma + \delta(A + \mu_{2d}) - C(\mu_{2d})] - [\alpha + \beta(A + \mu_{2e}) - C(\mu_{2e})]|$$

is high. Under standard assumptions about the distribution of ε, in particular that

$$\lim_{\varepsilon \to -\infty, \infty} g(\varepsilon) = 0,$$

very high- and very low-ability workers choose the efficient level of effort in period 1. They have little to fear in terms of incorrect promotion decisions. The extremely able are almost certain to be promoted, so that extra effort has very little effect on the probability of promotion. Conversely, the totally inept are almost certain to avoid promotion, so that reducing effort has almost no effect on lowering the probability of promotion.

Also true is that those whose underlying ability is very near the efficient job switch point (x in Figure 5.1) do not distort effort much. Even if they are misclassified, they have little to lose. Define A_0 such that

$$\gamma + \delta(A_0 + \mu_{2d}) - C(\mu_{2d}) = \alpha + \beta(A_0 + \mu_{2e}) - C(\mu_{2e}).$$

Then excess effort is zero at both extremes and also at A_0, which is likely to be close to x. The pattern of distortion is shown in Figure A5.1. Those at A_0 do not distort at all. Those at the ability extremes do not distort. Those with ability less than the switch point underwork and those with ability more than the switch point overwork.

Figure A5.1

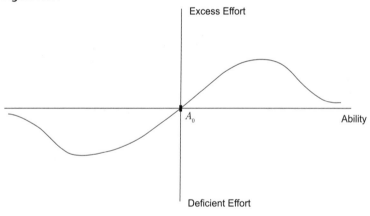

IV Compensation Structures

Introduction

Some topics are natural for economists to think about, whereas others are less obvious. Among the more natural topics for personnel economics is the study of compensation methods and practices. In many respects, compensation analysis formed the bread-and-butter of early personnel economics. Economists are used thinking about prices, and wages are the key price of the labor market. What distinguishes personnel economics from the more traditional labor economics analysis of wages is the focus on form and structure of compensation, rather than the mere level of it.

"Rank-Order Tournaments as Optimum Labor Contracts" (Chapter 6), with Sherwin Rosen, modeled raises and promotions. Although the model is a single period structure, the notion that was behind it was that workers experience a wage jump at the time of promotion. This seems inconsistent with standard human capital models of wage determination because there is no obvious reason why human capital accumulation should occur in a discontinuous fashion and especially later in life when some promotions occur. Furthermore, to the point when the chapter originally was written, and actually since then as well, there was no coherent model of wage structures within the firm. This chapter gave rise to what is now called "tournament theory." The notion in it is completely intuitive. Workers compete with one another for promotion. The intensity of competition depends on the nature of prizes. We use the metaphor of a tennis tournament, but it is strictly a metaphor for the corporate hierarchy. There are three points. First, prizes are determined in advance and depend on workers' relative performance, not on absolute performance. In the corporate world, the salary structure is approximately fixed in advance and whether a worker gets a promotion to a particular job depends on his relative performance. The better worker is promoted. Not all good workers are promoted. Second, the spread between the winner's and loser's prize affects effort. In a tennis match, competition is more energetic in a winner-take-all contest than in one where the prize money is split evenly between winner and loser. Analogously, in a corporation or partnership, young workers work long hours and exert more effort when the wage gain associated with promotion is large. If pay is highly compressed, then workers are less motivated to sweat early in their careers. Third, there is an optimal amount of effort, given by an efficiency condition. More effort is not necessarily better. As a result, the optimal spread is nailed down. Too small a spread results in too little effort. Too large a spread results in more effort and output but also requires higher levels of compensation to attract players to the tournament. Analogously, in a firm if the equilibrium level of effort is too high, the firm will have to pay high (average) salaries to attract workers and the higher average salary may be larger than the additional productivity that results from the additional effort. Tournament theory has led to a large number of testable implications, many of which have been analyzed both with data from the real world as well as those from experiments.

Some workers are paid what appear to be fixed wages, whereas others are paid on the basis of output. For example, most salespeople receive a significant fraction of their compensation on the basis of output, whereas most service workers are paid fixed salaries. Chapter 7, "Salaries and Piece Rates", was the first paper to model this choice and to discuss the implications for pay types across occupations. The distinction in this chapter is pay based on input versus pay based on output. Salaries are pay based on input, usually some time-based unit, such as an hour (hourly wages), a month (monthly earnings), or a year (annual salary). Piece rates are paid on some measure of output, like units sold or the revenues derived therefrom. The choice between the two depends primarily on monitoring costs, heterogeneity across workers, risk preferences, and effort elasticity. Like tournament theory, this chapter provides a rich set of implications for compensation methods and structures that can be and have been tested across industries. Although this work did not receive as much attention as some of the other chapters in this volume (in part because it appeared in a journal that is not as well known to labor economists), it is probably as central to my thinking in personnel economics as any paper that I have written.

An outgrowth of the methodology that is exposited in Chapter 7 is the application to real world data in "Performance Pay and Productivity" (Chapter 8). Primarily by luck, I obtained data from a windshield installation company that had information on individual worker productivity under two regimes: hourly wages (salaries) and performance pay (piece rates). These data were ideally suited to examining the incentive effects associated with piece rate pay. But perhaps equally important, they permitted incentive effects to be separated from sorting effects. In the equilibrium derived in Chapter 7, productivity can be high at piece rate firms, not only because piece rates motivate workers, but also because piece rate firms attract the higher productivity workers. In Chapter 8, I use that logic to show that the introduction of a piece-rate regime should induce a given worker to work harder and should cause the firm to attract over time more able workers. Both effects are found to hold empirically. Furthermore, the effects are very large. Productivity rises by about 40% after the introduction of piece rates, half due to incentives and half due to sorting. About half the increase in productivity was passed on to workers in higher wages. Note that this does not imply that all firms should use piece rates. The windshield case was one that fit the "pay by output" criteria derived in Chapter 7. There was significant heterogeneity among workers and output was easily observed. Since that work, there has been a large literature that relates output to pay method, using data from firms where output can be observed and measured.

The final chapter in this part of the book, entitled "The Job as a Concept," is significant for two reasons. First, it is among the first to make use of company based data to analyze within-firm wage structures, separation, promotion, demotion, raises, and a variety of other phenomena. It was followed by a large literature that examines these questions in more depth, using other data sets, including Baker, Gibbs and Holmström (1994), Gibbons and Waldman (2004), and by industry studies that match worker and firm data to examine wage structures and mobility within and between firms. A recent volume, edited by Kathryn Shaw and myself, reports similar results across a number of developed countries (Lazear and Shaw 2008a). Second, in addition to examining the internal structure of the firm and mobility within it, the chapter asked the basic question, "What is a job?". The concept of a job is absent from economics. Indeed, most of the theory of human capital assumes it away, because wages are determined by a homogeneous skill, multiplied by its rental value. This chapter documents the empirical relevance of the job in determining wages. It then examines various definitions of the job, including that from tournament theory, hedonic wage analysis, and other notions. The "job" as defined in this chapter, explains a large proportion of wage variation. Subsequent work no longer ignores the job as a unit or concept of analysis, and the work is significant in part for that reason. Because the chapter originally appeared in a conference volume primarily on managerial economics, it is relatively unknown. I include it in this volume because many readers will not have seen it and I hope that it will generate renewed interest in this line of inquiry.

6

Rank-Order Tournaments as Optimum Labor Contracts

It is a familiar proposition that under competitive conditions workers are paid the value of their marginal products. In this chapter we show that competitive lotteries are often efficient and sometimes superior to more familiar compensation schemes. For example, the large salaries of executives may provide incentives for all individuals in the firm who, with hard labor, may win one of the coveted top positions.

This chapter addresses the relation between compensation and incentives in the presence of costly monitoring of workers' efforts and output. A wide variety of incentive payment schemes are used in practice. Simple piece rates, which have been extensively analyzed (see e.g. Cheung 1969; Stiglitz 1975; Mirrlees 1976), gear payment to output. We consider a rank-order payment scheme which has not been analyzed but which seems to be prevalent in many labor contracts. This scheme pays prizes to the winners and losers of labor market contests. The main difference between prizes and other incentive schemes is that in a contest earnings depend on the rank order of contestants and not on "distance." That is, salaries are not contingent upon the output level of a particular game, because prizes are fixed in advance. Performance incentives are set by attempts to win the contest. We argue that in many circumstances it is optimal to set up

The original version of this chapter was published as: Lazear, E. P./Rosen, S. (1981). Rank-Order Tournaments as Optimum Labor Contracts, in: Journal of Political Economy, 89(5), 841-864. University of Chicago Press. © 1981 by the University of Chicago. We are indebted to Jerry Green, Merton Miller, James Mirrlees, George Stigler, Joseph Stiglitz, and Earl Thompson for helpful comments. The research was supported in part by the National Science Foundation. The research reported here is part of the NBER's research program in Labor Studies. Any opinions expressed are those of the authors and not those of the National Bureau of Economic Research.

executive compensation along these lines and that certain puzzling features of that market are easily explained in these terms.

Central to this discussion are the conditions under which mechanisms exist for monitoring productivity (Alchian and Demsetz 1972). If inexpensive and reliable monitors of effort are available, then the best compensation scheme is a periodic wage based on input. However, when monitoring is difficult, so that workers can alter their input with less than perfect detection, input-wage schemes invite shirking. The situation often can be improved if compensation is related to a more easily measured output level. In general, input-based pay is preferable because it changes the risk borne by workers in a favorable way. But when monitoring costs are so high that moral hazard is a serious problem, the gain in efficiency from using output-based pay may outweigh the risk-sharing losses. Paying workers on the basis of rank order alters costs of measurement as well as the nature of the risk borne by workers. It is for these reasons that it is sometimes a superior way to bring about an efficient incentive structure.

In the development below we start with the simplest case of risk neutrality to illustrate the basic issues. Then the more general case of risk aversion is treated in Section 6.2. Section 6.3. considers issues of sorting and self-selection when workers are heterogeneous.

6.1. Piece Rates and Tournaments with Risk Neutrality

To keep things simple and to avoid sequential and dynamic aspects of the problem, we confine attention to a single period in all that follows. Therefore, the reader should think of the incentive problem in terms of career development and lifetime productivity of workers. The worker's (lifetime) output is a random variable whose distribution is controlled by the worker himself. In particular, the worker is allowed to control the mean of the distribution by investing in costly skills prior to entering the market. However, a given productivity realization also depends on a random factor which is beyond anyone's control. Employers may observe output but cannot ascertain the extent to which it is due to investment expenditure or to good fortune or to both, though workers know their input as well as output. Worker j produces lifetime output q_j according to

$$(1) \qquad\qquad q_j = \mu_j + \varepsilon_j,$$

where μ_j is the level of investment, a measure of skill or average output, chosen by the worker when young and prior to a realization of the random or luck component, ε_j. Average skill, μ_j, is produced at cost $C(\mu)$, with C', $C'' > 0$. The random variable ε_j is drawn out of a known distribution with zero mean and variance σ^2.[1] Here ε is lifetime luck such as life-persistent person-effects or an ability factor, which is revealed very slowly over the worker's lifetime. The crucial assumption is that productivity risk is nondiversifiable by the worker himself. That is another reason for choosing a long period for the analysis. For example, if the period were very short and the random factor was independently distributed across periods, the worker could diversify per period risk by repetition and a savings account to balance off good and bad years. Evidently a persistent person or ability effect cannot be so diversified when it is undiscoverable quickly, as appears true of managerial talent, for example. It is assumed, however, that ε is independent and identically distributed (i.i.d.) across individuals, so that owners of firms can diversify risk either by pooling workers together in one firm or by holding a portfolio.

To concentrate on incentive aspects of various contractual arrangements, we adopt the simplest technology for firms. Production requires only labor and is additively separable across workers. By virtue of the independence assumptions, managers act as expected value maximizers or as if they were risk neutral. Free entry and a competitive output market set the value of the product at V per unit. Again, these assumptions are adopted to illustrate basic issues in the simplest way. The analysis also applies when there are complementarities among workers in production, which is more realistic but more difficult to exposit.

6.1.1. Piece Rates

The piece rate is very simple to analyze when workers are risk neutral. It involves paying the worker the value of his product. Let r be the piece rate. Ignoring discounting, the worker's net income is $rq - C(\mu)$. Risk-neutral workers choose μ to maximize expected net return

$$E[rq - C(\mu)] = r\mu - C(\mu).$$

The necessary condition is $r = C'(\mu)$ or the familiar requirement that investment equates marginal cost and return. On the other hand, the expected profit of a firm is

$$E(Vq - rq) = (V - r)\mu,$$

so free entry and competition for workers imply $r = V$. Consequently

$$V = C'(\mu).$$

The marginal cost of investment equals its social return, yielding the standard result that piece rates are efficient.

6.1.2.   Rank-Order Tournaments

We shall consider two-player tournaments in which the rules of the game specify a fixed prize W_1 to the winner and a fixed prize W_2 to the loser. All essential aspects of the problem readily generalize to any number of contestants. A worker's production follows (1), and the winner of the contest is determined by the largest drawing of q. The contest is rank order because the margin of winning does not affect earnings. Contestants precommit their investments early in life, knowing the prizes and the rules of the game, but do not communicate with each other or collude. Notice that even though there are two players in a given match the market is competitive and not oligopolistic, because investment is precommitted and a given player does not know who his opponent will be at the time all decisions are made. Each person plays against the "field."

We seek to determine the competitive prize structure (W_1, W_2). The method proceeds in two steps. First, the prizes W_1 and W_2 are fixed arbitrarily and workers' investment strategies are analyzed. Given these strategies, we then find the pair (W_1, W_2) that maximizes a worker's expected utility, subject to a zero-profit constraint by firms. It will be seen that a worker's incentives to invest increase with the spread between winning and losing prizes, $W_1 - W_2$. Each wants to improve the probability of winning because the return to winning varies with the spread. The firm would always like to increase the spread, ceteris paribus, to induce greater investment and higher productivity, because its output and revenue are increased. But as contestants invest more, their costs also rise. That is what limits the spread in equilibrium: Firms offering too large a spread induce excessive investment. A competing firm can attract all of these workers by decreasing the spread because investment costs fall by more than expected product, raising expected net earnings. Increasing marginal cost of skill implies a unique equilibrium spread between the prizes that maximizes expected utility.

More precisely, consider the contestant's problem, assuming that both have the same costs of investment $C(\mu)$, so that their behavior is identical. A contestant's expected utility (wealth) is

$$(2) \quad P[W_1 - C(\mu)] + (1 - P)[W_2 - C(\mu)] = PW_1 + (1 - P)W_2 - C(\mu),$$

where P is the probability of winning. The probability that j wins is

$$(3) \quad \begin{aligned} P &= \text{prob}(q_j > q_k) = \text{prob}(\mu_j - \mu_k > \varepsilon_k - \varepsilon_j) \\ &= \text{prob}(\mu_j - \mu_k > \xi) = G(\mu_j - \mu_k), \end{aligned}$$

where $\xi \equiv \varepsilon_k - \varepsilon_j$, $\xi \sim g(\xi)$, $G(\cdot)$ is the cdf of ξ, $E(\xi) = 0$, and $E(\xi^2) = 2\sigma^2$ (because ε_j and ε_k are i.i.d.). Each player chooses μ_i to maximize (2). Assuming interior solutions, this implies

$$(W_1 - W_2) \frac{\partial P}{\partial \mu_i} - C'(\mu_i) = 0$$

and

$$(4) \quad (W_1 - W_2) \frac{\partial^2 P}{\partial \mu_i^2} - C''(\mu_i) < 0, \; i = j, \; k.$$

We adopt the Nash-Cournot assumptions that each player optimizes against the optimum investment of his opponent, since he plays against the market over which he has no influence. Therefore, j takes μ_k as given in determining his investment and conversely for k. It then follows from (3) that, for player j

$$\partial P / \partial \mu_j = \partial G(\mu_j - \mu_k) / \partial \mu_j = g(\mu_j - \mu_k),$$

which upon substitution into (4) yields j's reaction function

$$(5) \qquad (W_1 - W_2)g(\mu_j - \mu_k) - C'(\mu_j) = 0.$$

Player k's reaction function is symmetrical with (5).

Symmetry implies that when the Nash solution exists, $\mu_j = \mu_k$ and $P = G(0) = \frac{1}{2}$, so the outcome is purely random in equilibrium. Ex ante, each player affects his probability of winning by investing.[2]

Substituting $\mu_j = \mu_k$ at the Nash equilibrium, equation (5) reduces to

$$(6) \qquad C'(\mu_i) = (W_1 - W_2)g(0), \; i = j, \, k,$$

verifying the point above that players' investments depend on the spread between winning and losing prizes. Levels of the prizes only influence the decision to enter the game, which requires nonnegativity of expected wealth.

The risk-neutral firm's realized gross receipts are $(q_j + q_k)V$, and its costs are the total prize money offered, $W_1 + W_2$. Competition for labor bids up the purse to the point where expected total receipts equal costs, $W_1 + W_2 = (\mu_j + \mu_k)V$. But since $\mu_j = \mu_k = \mu$ in equilibrium, the zero-profit condition reduces to

$$(7) \qquad V\mu = (W_1 + W_2)/2.$$

The expected value of product equals the expected prize in equilibrium. Substitute (7) into the worker's utility function (2). Noting that $P = \frac{1}{2}$ in equilibrium, the worker's expected utility at the optimum investment strategy is

$$(8) \qquad V\mu = C(\mu).$$

The equilibrium prize structure selects W_1 and W_2 to maximize (8), or

$$(9) \qquad [V - C'(\mu)](\partial\mu/\partial W_i) = 0, \quad i = 1, 2.$$

The marginal cost of investment equals its marginal social return, $V = C'(\mu)$, in the tournament as well as the piece rate. Therefore, competitive tournaments, like piece rates, are efficient and both result in exactly the same allocation of resources.

Some further manipulation of the equilibrium conditions yields an interesting interpretation in terms of the theory of agency (Ross 1973; Becker and Stigler 1974; Harris and Raviv 1978; Lazear 1979, see Chapter 1):

$$W_1 = V\mu + C'(\mu)/2g(0) = V\mu + V/2g(0)$$

(10)

$$W_2 = V\mu - C'(\mu)/2g(0) = V\mu - V/2g(0).$$

The second equality follows from $V = C'(\mu)$. Now think of the term $C'(\mu)/2g(0) = V/2g(0)$ in (10) as an entrance fee or bond that is posted by each player. The winning and losing prizes pay off the expected marginal value product plus or minus the entrance fee. That is, the players receive their expected product combined with a fair winner-take-all gamble over the total entrance fees or bonds. The appropriate social investment incentives are given by each contestant's attempt to win the gamble. This contrasts with the main agency result, where the bond is returned to each worker after a satisfactory performance has been observed. There the incentive mechanism works through the employee's attempts to work hard enough to recoup his own bond. Here it works through the attempts to win the gamble.

Comparative statics for this problem all follow from (9) and (10) once a distribution is specified. For example, if ε is normal with variance σ^2, then $g(0) = \frac{1}{2}\sigma\sqrt{\pi}$. It follows from (10) that the optimal spread varies directly with V and σ^2. While several other interesting observations can be made of this sort, we note a somewhat different but important practical implication of this general scheme. Even though the optimal prize structure determines expected marginal product through its effect on worker choice of μ and the zero-profit condition (7) implies that expected prizes equal expected productivity, nevertheless actual realized earnings definitely do not equal productivity in either an ex ante or ex post sense. Consider ex ante first. Since $\mu_j = \mu_k = \mu$, expected products are equal. Since $W_1 > W_2$ is required to induce any investment, the payment that j receives never equals the payment that k receives. It is impossible that the prize is equal to ex ante product, because ex ante products are equal. Nor do wages equal ex post products. Actual product is Vq rather than $V\mu$. But q is a random variable, the value of which is not known until after the game is played, while W_1 and W_2 are fixed in advance. Only under the rarest coincidence would $W_1 = Vq_j$ and $W_2 = Vq_k$.

Consider the salary structure for executives. It appears as though the salary of, say, the vice-president of a particular corporation is substantially below that of the president of the same corporation. Yet presidents are often chosen from the ranks of vice-presidents. On the day that a given individual is promoted from vice-president to president, his salary may triple. It is difficult to argue that his skills have tripled in that 1-day period, presenting difficulties for standard theory where supply factors should keep wages in those two occupations approximately equal. It is not a puzzle, however, when interpreted in the context of a prize. The president of a corporation is viewed as the winner of a contest in which he receives the higher prize, W_1. His wage is settled on not necessarily because it reflects his current productivity as president, but rather because it induces that individual and all other individuals to perform appropriately when they are in more junior positions. This interpretation suggests that presidents of large corporations do not necessarily earn high wages because they are more productive as presidents but because this particular type of payment structure makes them more productive over their entire working lives. A contest provides the proper incentives for skill acquisition prior to coming into the position.[3]

6.1.3. Comparisons

Though tournaments and piece rates are substantially different institutions for creating incentives, we have demonstrated the surprising result that both achieve the Pareto optimal allocation of resources when workers are risk neutral. In fact other schemes also achieve this allocation. For example, instead of playing against an opponent, a worker might be compared with a fixed standard $\bar{q}$, with one payment awarded if output falls anywhere below $\bar{q}$ and another, higher, payment awarded if output falls anywhere above standard. Attempting to beat the standard has the same incentive effects as attempting to beat another player. Using the same methods as above, it is not difficult to show that there are spread-standard combinations that induce Pareto optimum investments. Since all these schemes involve the same investment policy, and since average payout by the firm equals average product for all of them, they all yield the same expected rewards and, therefore, the same expected utility to workers.[4]

In spite of the apparent equality of these schemes in terms of the preferences of risk-neutral workers, considerations of differential costs of information and measurement may serve to break these ties in practical situations. The essential point follows from the theory of measurement (Stevens 1968) that a cardinal scale is based on an underlying ordering of objects or an ordinal scale. In that sense, an ordinal scale is "weaker" and has fewer requirements than a cardinal scale. If it is less costly to observe rank than an individual's level of output, then tournaments dominate piece rates and standards. On the other hand, occupations for which output is easily observed save resources by using the piece rate or standard, or some combination, and avoid the necessity of making direct comparisons with others as the tournament requires. Salesmen, whose output level is easily observed, typically are paid by piece rates, whereas corporate executives, whose output is more difficult to observe, engage in contests.

In a modern, complex business organization, a person's productivity as chief executive officer is measured by his effect on the profitability of the whole enterprise. Yet the costs of measurement for each conceivable candidate are prohibitively expensive. Instead, it might be said that those in the running are "tested" by assessments of performance at lower positions. Realizations from such tests are sample statistics in these assessments, in much the same way that grades are assigned in a college classroom and IQ scores are determined. The point is that such tests are inherently ordinal in nature, even though the profitability of the enterprise is metered by a well-defined, cardinal ratio scale. It is in situations such as this that the conditions seem ripe for tournaments to be the dominant incentive contract institution.

Notice in this connection that the basic prize and piece-rate structures survive a broad class of revenue functions other than summable ones. Even if the production function of the firm includes complicated interactions involving complementarity or substitution among individual outputs, there exists the possibility of paying workers either on the basis of individual performance or by rank order. The revenue function itself can even involve rank-order considerations, and both possibilities still exist. For example, spectators at a horse race generally are interested in the speed of the winning horse and the closeness of the contest. Then the firm's (track) revenue function depends on the first few order statistics; yet the horses could be paid on the basis of their speed rather than on the basis of win, place, and show positions. Both methods would induce them to run fast.[5]

There has been very little treatment of the problem of tournament prize structure and incentives in the literature. Little else but the well-known paper by Friedman (1953) based on Friedman-Savage preferences for lotteries exists in economics. In the statistics literature there is an early paper by Galton (1902) that is worthy of brief discussion. Galton inquired into the ratio of first- and second-place prize money in a race of n contestants, assuming the prizes were divided in the following ratio:

$$W_1/W_2 = (Q_1 - Q_3)/(Q_2 - Q_3).$$

Here Q_1 is the expected value of the first- (fastest) order statistic, etc. While a moment's reflection suggests this criterion to be roughly related to marginal productivity, Galton proposed it on strictly a priori grounds. He went on to show the remarkable result that the ratio above is approximately 3 when the parent distribution of speed is normal. Hence, this criterion results in a highly skewed prize structure. From what we know today about the characteristic skew of extreme value distributions, a skewed reward structure based on order statistics is less surprising for virtually any parent distribution. In the more modern statistical literature, the method of paired comparisons has tournament-like features. Samples from different populations are compared pairwise, and the object is to choose the one with the largest mean. Comparing all samples to each other is like a round-robin tournament. An alternative design is a knockout tournament with single or double elimination. The latter requires fewer samples and is therefore cheaper, but does not generate as much information as the round-robin (David 1963; Gibbons, Olkin, and Sobel 1977).

Galton's original work and the more modern developments it has given rise to are not helpful to us; they deal with samples from fixed populations, so the reward structure is irrelevant for resource allocation. The problem we have treated here is that of choosing the reward structure to provide the proper incentive and elicit the socially proper distributions.

6.2. Optimal Compensation with Risk Aversion

All compensation systems can be viewed as schemes which transform the distribution of productivity to a distribution of earnings. A piece rate is a linear transformation of output, so the distribution of income is the same apart from a change in location and scale. A tournament is a highly nonlinear transformation: It converts the continuous distribution of productivity into a discrete, binomial distribution of income. When workers are risk neutral, both schemes yield identical investments and expected utility because their first moments are the same. In this section, it is shown that with risk aversion one method or the other usually yields higher expected utility, because the interaction between insurance and action implies substantially different first and second moments of the income distribution in the two cases.[6]

We have been unable to completely characterize the conditions under which piece rates dominate rank-order tournaments and vice versa, but we show some examples here. Truncation offered by prizes implies more control of extreme values than piece rates but less control of the middle of the distribution. Different utility functions weight one aspect more than the other so that tournaments can actually dominate piece rates.

6.2.1. Optimum Linear Piece Rate[7]

The piece-rate scheme analyzed pays workers a guarantee, I, plus an incentive, rq, where r is the piece rate per unit of output. The problem for the firm is to pick an r, I combination that maximizes workers' expected utility

(11) $$\max_{I,r} [E(U) = \max \int U(\gamma)\theta(\gamma)d\gamma],$$

where

(12)
$$\gamma \equiv I + rq - C(\mu)$$
$$= I + r\mu + r\varepsilon - C(\mu)$$

and $\theta(\gamma)$ is the pdf of γ.

The worker's problem is to choose μ to maximize expected utility given I and r. If $\varepsilon \sim f(\varepsilon)$, the worker's problem is

$$\max_{\mu} E(U) = \int U[I + r\mu + r\varepsilon - C(\mu)]f(\varepsilon)d\varepsilon.$$

The first-order condition is

$$\frac{\partial E(U)}{\partial \mu} = \int [U'(\gamma)][r - C'(\mu)]f(\varepsilon)d\varepsilon = 0,$$

which conveniently factors so that

$$(13) \qquad\qquad r = C'(\mu).$$

Condition (13) is identical to the risk-neutral case, because ε is independent of investment effort, μ.

Assuming risk-neutral employers, $V\mu$ is expected revenue from a worker and $I + r\mu$ is expected wage payments. Therefore, the zero-profit market constraint is

$$(14) \qquad\qquad V\mu = I + r\mu.$$

Solving (14) for I and substituting into (12), the optimum contract maximizes

$$\int U\{V\mu(r) + r\varepsilon - C[\mu(r)]\}f(\varepsilon)d\varepsilon$$

with respect to r, where $\mu = \mu(r)$ satisfies (13). After simplification the marginal condition is

$$(15) \qquad\qquad [V - C'(\mu)]\frac{d\mu}{dr}EU' + EU'\varepsilon = 0.$$

Since risk aversion implies $EU'\varepsilon < 0$, (15) shows that $V > C'(\mu)$ in the optimum contract for risk-averse workers. This underinvestment is the moral hazard resulting from insurance $I > 0$ and $r < V$ implied by (15).

Using familiar Taylor series approximations to the utility function and a normal density for ε, the optimum is approximated by

(16) $$\mu \doteq C'^{-1}\left(\frac{V}{1 + sC''\sigma^2}\right).$$

and

(17) $$\sigma_y^2 \doteq \frac{V^2\sigma^2}{\left(1 + sC''\sigma^2\right)^2},$$

where $s \equiv -U''/U'$ evaluated at mean income is the measure of absolute risk aversion. Investment increases (see (16)) in V and decreases in s, C'', and σ^2, because all these changes imply similar changes in the marginal piece rate r which influences investment through condition (13). The same changes in V, s, and C'' have corresponding effects on the variance of income, see (17), but an increase in σ^2 actually reduces variance, if σ^2 is large, because it reduces r and increases I.[8]

6.2.2. Optimum Prize Structure

The worker's expected utility in a two-player game is

(18) $$E(U) = P\{U[W_1 - C(\mu^*)]\} + (1 - P)\{U[W_2 - C(\mu^*)]\},$$

where * denotes the outcome of the contest rather than the piece-rate scheme. The optimum prize structure is the solution to

(19) $$\max_{W_1, W_2}\left(E(U^*) = \max_{\mu^*}\{PU[W_1 - C(\mu^*)] + (1 - P)U[W_2 - C(\mu^*)]\}\right)$$

subject to the zero-profit constraint

(20) $$V\mu^* = PW_1 + (1 - P)W_2.$$

The worker selects μ^* to satisfy $\partial E(U)/\partial\mu^* = 0$. Since cost functions are the same and ε_j and ε_k are i.i.d., the Nash solution implies

$\mu_j = \mu_k$ and $P = \frac{1}{2}$ as before. Then the worker's investment behavior simplifies to

$$(21) \qquad C'(\mu^*) = \frac{2[U(1) - U(2)]g(0)}{U'(1) + U'(2)} ,$$

where $U(\tau) \equiv U[W_\tau - C(\mu^*)]$ and $U'(\tau) \equiv U'[W_\tau - C(\mu^*)]$ for $\tau = 1,\ 2$. Equation (21) implies

$$(22) \qquad \mu^* = \mu^*(W_1, W_2),$$

and the optimum contract (W_1, W_2) maximizes

$$(23) \qquad E(U^*) = \frac{1}{2}\, U[W_1 - C(\mu^*)] + \frac{1}{2}\, U[W_2 - C(\mu^*)]$$

subject to (20), with $P = \frac{1}{2}$, and (22). Increasing marginal cost of investment and risk aversion guarantees a unique maximum to (23) when a Nash solution exists. Again, assuming anormal density for ε, second-order approximations yield

$$(24) \qquad \mu^* \doteq C'^{-1} \left(\frac{V}{1 + sC''\sigma^2\pi} \right)$$

and

$$(25) \qquad \sigma^2_{y^*} \doteq \frac{\pi V^2 \sigma^2}{\left(1 + \pi sC''\sigma^2\right)^2} ,$$

where

$$y^* = \begin{cases} W_1 - C(\mu^*) & \text{if } q_j > q_k \\ W_2 - C(\mu^*) & \text{if } q_j < q_k \end{cases}$$

and $\varepsilon_j \sim N(0,\ \sigma^2)$, $\varepsilon_k \sim N(0,\sigma^2)$, and cov $(\varepsilon_j,\ \varepsilon_k) = 0$.[9] The comparative statics of (24) and (25) are similar to the piece rate (16) and (17) and need not be repeated.

6.2.3. Comparisons

Equations (16) and (24) indicate that investment and expected income[10] are lower for the contest than for the piece rate at given values of s. Moreover, for values of σ^2 in excess of $1/sC''\sqrt{\pi}$, the variance of income in the tournament is smaller than for the piece rate. This would seem to suggest that contests provide a crude form of insurance when the variance of chance is large enough, but the problem is significantly more complicated than that because there is no separation between tastes and opportunities in this problem: The optimum mean and variance themselves depend on utility-function parameters. Thus, far example, for the constant, absolute risk-aversion utility function $U = -e^{-sy}/s$, the insurance provided by the contest is insufficient to compensate for its smaller mean: It can be shown that the expected indirect utility of the optimal piece rate exceeds that of the optimal tournament for all values of σ^2, at least with normal distributions and quadratic investment-cost functions. However, when there is declining absolute risk aversion, we have examples where the contest dominates the piece rate.

Illustrative calculations are shown in Table 6.1 using the utility function $U = a\gamma^\alpha$, which exhibits constant relative but declining absolute risk aversion, $s(\gamma) = (1-\alpha)/\gamma$. Again quadratic costs and normal errors are assumed. However, this utility function is defined for positive incomes only, so an amount of nonlabor income γ_0 is assigned to the worker to avoid a major approximation error of the normal, which admits negative incomes (i.e., the possibility of losses).

Table 6.1

Constant Relative Risk Aversion

σ^2	μ	$^*\mu$	$E(U)$	$E(U^*)$
		$\gamma_0 = 10; s(\gamma_0) = .005$		
.1	.9995	.9984	5.012155	5.012465
.5	.9975	.9922	5.012150	5.012445
1	.9950	.9846	5.012100	5.012295
3	.9852	.9552	5.011940	5.011925
6	.9710	.9142	5.011800	5.011415
12	.9436	.8420	5.011420	5.010515
		$\gamma_0 = 25; s(y_0) = .020$		
.1	.9980	.9938	2.524665	2.524725
.2	.9960	.9878	2.524616	2.524575
1	.9807	.9419	2.524237	2.523437
12	.8094	.5741	2.519930	2.514282

Notes: $-U = a\gamma^\alpha$; $\gamma = \gamma_0 + I + rq - C(\mu)$ for piece rate; $\gamma = \gamma_0 + W_i - C(\mu)$ for contest $(i = 1, 2)$; $\alpha = .5$, $V = 1$, $C(\mu) = \mu^2/2$: σ^2.

Table 6.1 shows that when $\gamma_0 = 100$ so that $s = .005$, the contest is preferred until $\sigma^2 \geq 3$. However, if $\gamma_0 = 25$ so that $s = .020$, the contest is only preferred for $\sigma^2 < .2$. The intuition is that piece rates concentrate the mass of the income distribution near the mean, while contests place 50 percent of the weight at one value significantly below the mean and the other value significantly above. Strongly risk-averse workers seem to dislike the binomial nature of this distribution when σ^2 is high because it concentrates too much of the mass at low levels of utility. However, when σ^2 is small, the contest which truncates the tails of the income distribution associated with a linear piece rate has higher value.

6.2.4. *Income Distributions*

While it is not possible to make a general argument based on an example, Table 6.1 suggests that persons with more endowed income and smaller absolute risk aversion are more likely to prefer contests, and those with low levels of endowed wealth and larger absolute risk aversion are more likely to prefer piece rates. Consider a situation in which all persons have the same utility function, such as the one in Table 6.1, and face the same costs and luck distribution, the only difference being the fact that some workers have larger endowed incomes than others. If this difference is large enough, it can be optimal to pay piece rates to those with small values of endowed income and to pay prizes to those with large values. Individuals will self-select the payment scheme in accordance with their wealth. The distribution of earnings among those selecting the piece-rate jobs is normal with mean $V\mu$ and variance $r^2\sigma^2$. It is binomial with mean $V\mu^*$ and variance $(\Delta W)^2/4$ for those who enter tournaments. Note that μ and μ^* depend upon $s(\gamma)$, which is smaller for workers who select contests, and it can turn out as it does in Table 6.1 that expected income is larger in the contest than in the piece rate; for example, if $\sigma^2 = 1$ then the rich prefer contests ($5.012295 > 5.012100$) and the poor prefer piece rates ($2.524237 > 2.523437$), but $\mu^* = .9846$ exceeds $\mu = .9807$. This situation is shown in Figure 6.1.

The overall distribution is the sum of a binomial and a normal with lower mean, weighted by the number of individuals in each occupation (see Figure 6.1). It is positively skewed because $V\mu^* > V\mu$. Note also that the distribution of wage income will be less skewed than that of total income. The reason is that γ_0 and mean-wage income are positively correlated because the likelihood of choosing a contest increases with γ_0. These implications conform to the standard findings on the distribution of income in an economy.

This example is interesting because it is very closely related to some early results of Friedman (1953), who studied how alternative social arrangements can produce income distributions that cater to workers' risk preferences. He showed that the Friedman-Savage utility function leads to a two-class distribution. Persons in the risk-averse region are assigned to occupations in which income follows productivity, while persons in the risk-preferring region buy lottery tickets in very risky occupations in which few win very large prizes. The overall distribution is the sum of these two and exhibits characteristic skew. The Friedman-Savage utility function implies that a person's risk preferences depend on the part of his wealth that is not at risk.

Figure 6.1

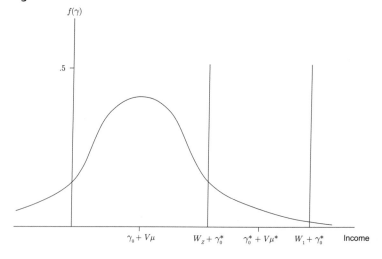

Therefore, Friedman's assignment of people to jobs really follows endowed wealth (γ_0), just as in our example. However, our framework offers two improvements. First, the problem of incentives is directly incorporated into the formulation of the optimum policy. Second, workers in this model are risk averse for all values of incomes, but even so gambles can be the optimal policy.

6.2.5. Error Structure

Relative costs of measurement are still important in choosing among incentive schemes, but the error structure plays additional roles when workers are risk averse. Suppose the output estimator for worker i in activity τ is $\hat{q}_{i\tau} = q_{i\tau} + \rho_\tau + \nu_{i\tau}$ where $\nu_{i\tau}$ is random error and ρ_τ is an error that is specific to activity τ but common to all workers within that activity. In the piece rate the common error ρ adds noise which risk-averse workers dislike, while the common noise drops out of a rank-order comparison because it affects both contestants similarly. That is, the relevant variance for the contest is $2\sigma_\nu^2$, while that for the piece rate is $\sigma_\rho^2 + \sigma_\nu^2$. It is evident that this can tip the balance in favor of tournaments if σ_ρ^2 is large enough and/or workers are sufficiently risk averse.

The common error ρ bears two interesting interpretations. One is activity-specific measurement error. For example, j and k may have the same supervisor whose biased assessments affect all workers similarly. This is similar to monitoring all workers by a mechanical counting device that might run too fast or too slow in any given trial. The other interpretation of ρ is true random variation that affects the enterprise as a whole. For example, suppose all firms produce with the same technology, but that in a given period some firms do better or worse than others. Then risk-averse workers prefer not to have their incomes vary with conditions facing the firm as a whole, and wages based on a contest eliminate this kind of variation. Without its elimination there would be excessive losses due to moral hazard.

It must be pointed out that, in the absence of measurement error, using a contest against a fixed standard $\bar{q}$ discussed above has lower variance than playing against an opponent. As shown in Section 6.2., the relevant variance in a contest is that of $\xi = \varepsilon_k - \varepsilon_j$, which has variance $2\sigma^2$ against an opponent and only σ^2 against a standard (since the standard is invariant, $\varepsilon_k \equiv 0$). Consequently, we might expect risk-averse workers to prefer absolute standards.[11] Again, however, the crucial issue is the costs of measurement and the error structure. For the complex attributes required for managerial positions, it is difficult to observe output and therefore difficult to compare to an absolute standard. In so far as samples and tests are necessary, it bears repeating that these are inherently ordinal in nature. But this leads us back to the problem of common error, where it is often impossible to know whether a person's output is satisfactory without comparisons to other persons. Further, when there are changing production circumstances in the firm as a whole, it is difficult to know whether the person failed to meet the standard because of insufficient investment or because the firm was generally experiencing bad times, a problem of measuring "value added." Risk-averse workers increase utility by competing against an opponent and eliminating this kind of firm effect.

6.3. Heterogeneous Contestants

Workers are not sprinkled randomly among firms but rather seem to be sorted by ability levels. One explanation for this has to do with complementarities in production. But even in the absence of complementarities, sorting may be an integral part of optimal labor contract arrangements. Informational considerations imply that compensation methods may affect the allocation of worker types to firms. Therefore, this section returns to the case of risk neutrality and analyzes tournament structures when investment costs differ among persons. Two types of persons are assumed, a's and b's, with marginal costs of the a's being smaller than those of the b's: $C'_a(\mu) < C'_b(\mu)$ for all μ. The distribution of disturbances $f(\varepsilon)$ is assumed to be the same for both groups. Many of the following results continue to hold, with usually obvious modification of the arguments, if the a's and b's draw from different distributions. The following section addresses the question of self-selection when workers know their identities but firms do not. The next section discusses handicapping schemes when all cost-function differences can be observed by all parties.

6.3.1.   Adverse Selection

Suppose that each person knows to which class he belongs but that this information is not available to anyone else. The principal result is that the a's and b's do not self-sort into their own "leagues." Instead, all workers prefer to work in firms with the best workers (the major leagues). Furthermore, there is no pure price-rationing mechanism that induces Pareto optimal self-selection. But mixed play is inefficient because it cannot sustain the proper investment strategies. Therefore, tournament structures naturally require credentials and other nonprice signals to differentiate people and assign them to the appropriate contest. Firms select their employees based on such information as past performances, and some are not permitted to compete.

The proof of adverse selection consists of two parts. First we show that players do not self-sort into a leagues and b leagues. Second, we show that the resulting mixed leagues are inefficient.

1. Players do not self-sort. Assume leagues are separated and consider the expected revenue R_i generated by playing in league $i = a, b$ with an arbitrary investment level μ. Then

$$(26) \qquad R_i(\mu) = W_2^i + (W_1^i - W_2^i)P^i, \quad i = a,b,$$

where (W_1^i, W_2^i) is the prize money, and P^i is the probability of winning in league i. Recall that P^i depends on the individual's level of investment and that of his rivals. Therefore, $P^a = G(\mu - \mu_a^*)$ and $P^b = G(\mu - \mu_b^*)$, where μ_a^* is the existing players' investments in the a league, where $V = C_a'(\mu_a^*)$, and similarly for μ_b^*. Recalling from (6) and (9) that $W_1^i - W_2^i = V/g(0)$ and from (10) that $W_2^i = V\mu_i^* - V/2g(0)$, equation (26) becomes

$$(27) \qquad R_i(\mu) = V\mu_i^* - \frac{V}{g(0)} [\tfrac{1}{2} - G(\mu - \mu_i^*)]$$

Note that $R_i(\mu) = V\mu_i^*$ when $\mu = \mu_i^*$ and that $dR_i/d\mu \equiv R_i'(\mu) = Vg(\mu - \mu_i^*)/g(0) > 0$. Since $C_a'(\mu_a^*) = V$ and $C_b'(\mu_b^*) = V$, then $\mu_b^* < \mu_a^*$ so that $R_i(\mu_b^*) > R_i(\mu_a^*)$. Furthermore, $R_b'[\mu - (\mu_a^* - \mu_b^*)] = R_a'(\mu)$. Therefore, $R_b(\mu)$ is a pure displacement of $R_a(\mu)$. Since $R_i'(\mu) = V$ for $\mu = \mu_i^*$ and $R_i'(\mu) < V$ elsewhere, and since $R_i(\mu)$ is increasing, the revenue functions never cross. So $R_b(\mu)$ lies to the southwest of $R_a(\mu)$ (see Figure 6.2). Therefore, independent of cost curves, it is always better to play in the a league than the b league: Workers will not self-select.

2. Mixed contests are inefficient. Suppose the proportions of a's and b's in the population are α and $(1 - \alpha)$, respectively. If pairings among a's and b's are random, then expected utility of a player of type i is

$$\overline{W}_2 + [\alpha P_a^i + (1 - \alpha)P_b^i](W_1 - W_2) - C_i(\mu_i),$$

where $(\overline{W}_1, \overline{W}_2)$ is the prize money in mixed play and P^i_j is the probability that a player of type i defeats a player of type j. The first-order condition for investment of type i in this game is

$$\left[\alpha \frac{\partial P^i_a}{\partial \mu_i} + (1 - \alpha) \frac{\partial P^i_b}{\partial \mu_i} \right] (\overline{W}_1 - \overline{W}_2) = C'_i(\overline{\mu}_i).$$

A development similar to Section 6.1. implies equilibrium reaction functions

$$[\alpha g(0) + (1 - \alpha) g(\overline{\mu}_a - \overline{\mu}_b)](W_1 - W_2) = C'_a(\overline{\mu}_a)$$

Figure 6.2

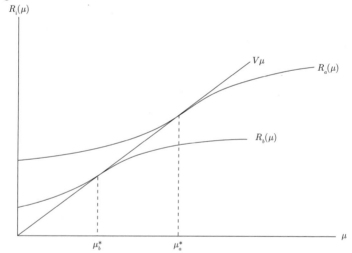

for a's and

$$[\alpha g(\overline{\mu}_b - \overline{\mu}_a) + (1 - \alpha) g(0)](W_1 - W_2) = C'_b(\overline{\mu}_b)$$

for b's. If the solution is efficient, then $C'_b(\mu_b) = V = C'_a(\mu_a)$, which implies

$$\alpha g(0) + (1 - \alpha) g(\overline{\mu}_a - \overline{\mu}_b) = \alpha g(\overline{\mu}_b - \overline{\mu}_a) + (1 - \alpha) g(0).$$

178

Since g is symmetric and nonuniform, this condition can hold only if $\alpha = \frac{1}{2}$. Therefore, except in that very special case, mixed contests yield inefficient investment: One type of player overinvests and the other underinvests depending upon whether or not $\alpha \gtrless \frac{1}{2}$.

We conclude that a pure price system cannot sustain an efficient competitive equilibrium in the presence of population heterogeneity with asymmetric information. Markets can be separated, but only at a cost. Consider, for example, the case where a's want to prevent b's from contaminating their league. By making the spread, $W_1^a - W_2^a$, sufficiently large, $R_a(\mu)$ becomes steeper than $R_b(\mu)$ in Figure 6.2 and crosses it so that the envelope covers $R_b(\mu)$ at low values of μ and $R_a(\mu)$ at high values. Then, for some high levels of μ, it is more profitable to play in the a league and, for low levels of μ, the b league is preferable. Individuals may self-sort, but the cost is that a's overinvest. The result is akin to that of Akerlof (1976) and to those of Spence (1973), Riley (1975), Rothschild and Stiglitz (1976), and Wilson (1977). As they show, a separating equilibrium need not exist, but, even if it does, that equilibrium may be inferior to a nonseparating equilibrium.

The obvious practical resolution of these difficulties is the use of nonprice rationing and certification to sort people into the appropriate leagues based on past performance. Similarly, firms use nonprice factors to allocate jobs among applicants. The rules for allocating those jobs may be important for at least two reasons that we can only briefly describe here.

First, sorting workers of different skill levels into appropriate positions within a hierarchy may be beneficial. In this chapter, production is additive, so it does not matter who works with whom. To the extent that the production technology is somewhat more complicated, sorting may well be crucial. A series of pairwise, sequential contests may efficiently perform that function. Suppose that $q_{it} = \mu_i + \delta_i + \eta_{it}$, where δ_i is an unobserved ability component for player i and η is white noise. Suppose it is efficient for the individual with the highest δ to be the chief executive. There will be a tendency to have winners play winners because

$$E(\delta_j|\ q_{j1} > q_{k1}) > E(\delta_k|\ q_{j1} > q_{k1})$$

in the first round. A sequential elimination tournament may be a cost-efficient way to select the best person.

Second, workers may not know precisely their own abilities or cost functions. A worker who is ignorant about his cost function values information before selecting a level of investment expenditure. Therefore, firms may offer "tryouts" to provide information about optimal investment strategies. In fact, one can imagine the existence of firms which specialize in running contests among young workers – the minor leagues – which provide information to be used when and if the workers opt to increase the stakes and enter a bigger league.

These issues point up an important difference between piece rates and contests. In the pure heterogeneous case, where information is asymmetric and workers are risk neutral, a piece rate always yields an efficient solution, namely, $V = C_a'(\mu_a) = C_b'(\mu_b)$. However, once slotting of workers is important because of complementarities in production, or if it is desirable for workers to gain information about their type, it is no longer obvious that a series of sequential contests does not result in a superior allocation of resources.

6.3.2. Handicap Systems

This section moves to the opposite extreme of the previous discussion and assumes that the identities of each type of player are known to everyone. Competitive handicaps yield efficient mixed contests.

Consider again two types a and b now known to everyone. Prize structures in $a - a$ and $b - b$ tournaments satisfying (11) and (12) are efficient, but those conditions are not optimal in mixed $a - b$ play. Denote the socially optimal levels of investment by μ_a^* and μ_b^*, their difference by $\Delta\mu$, and the prizes in a mixed league by $\widetilde{W}_1$, and $\widetilde{W}_2$. Let h be the handicap awarded to the inferior player b. Then the Nash solution in the $a - b$ tournament satisfies

$$(28) \qquad g(\mu_a - \mu_b - h)\Delta\widetilde{W} = C_a'(\mu_a)$$

and

$$g(\mu_a - \mu_b - h)\Delta\widetilde{W} = C_b'(\mu_b).$$

(The second condition in (28) follows from symmetry of $g[\xi]$.) Since the efficient investment criterion is $V = C'_a(\mu^*_a) = C'_b(\mu^*_b)$, independent of pairings, the optimum spread in a mixed match must be

$$(29) \qquad\qquad \Delta\widetilde{W} = V/g(\Delta\mu - h).$$

From (28), condition (29) insures the proper investments by both contestants. The spread is larger in mixed than pure contests unless a gives b the full handicap $h = \mu^*_a - \mu^*_b$. Otherwise, the appropriate spread is a decreasing function of h. Prizes $\widetilde{W}_1$ and $\widetilde{W}_2$ must also satisfy the zero-profit constraint $\widetilde{W}_1 + \widetilde{W}_2 = V \cdot (\mu^*_a + \mu^*_b)$ independent of h since the spread is always adjusted to induce investments μ^*_a and μ^*_b.

The gain to an a from playing a b with handicap h, rather than another a with no handicap, is the difference in expected prizes:

$$
\begin{aligned}
(30) \quad \gamma_a(h) &= \overline{P}\widetilde{W}_1 + (1 - \overline{P})\widetilde{W}_2 - C_a(\mu^*_a) - [(W^a_1 + W^a_2)/2 - C_a(\mu^*_a)] \\
&= \overline{P}\widetilde{W}_1 + (1 - \overline{P})\widetilde{W}_2 - (W^a_1 + W^a_2)/2,
\end{aligned}
$$

where $\gamma_a(h)$ is the gain to a and $\overline{P} = G(\Delta\mu - h)$ is the probability that a wins the mixed match. The corresponding expression for b is

$$(31) \qquad \gamma_b(h) = (1 - \overline{P})\widetilde{W}_1 - \overline{P}\widetilde{W}_2 - (W^b_1 + W^b_2)/2.$$

The zero-profit constraints in $a - a$, $a - b$, and $b - b$ require that $\gamma_a(h) + \gamma_b(h) = 0$ for all admissible h. The gain of playing mixed matches to a is completely offset by the loss to b and vice versa.

If $C_a(\mu)$ is not greatly different from $C_b(\mu)$, then $\Delta\mu = \mu^*_a - \mu^*_b$ is small and $\overline{P} \doteq \frac{1}{2} + [g(\Delta\mu - h)](\Delta\mu - h)$. This approximation and the zero-profit constraint reduce (30) to

$$(32) \qquad\qquad \gamma_a(h) \doteq V\left(\frac{\Delta\mu}{2} - h\right).$$

The expression for $\gamma_b(h)$ is the same, except its sign is reversed, so the gain to a decreases in h, and the gain to b increases in h. Therefore, $h^* =$

$\Delta\mu/2$ is the competitive handicap, since it implies $\gamma_a(h^*) = \gamma_b(h^*) = 0$. If the actual handicap is less than h^*, then γ_a is positive and a's prefer to play in mixed contests rather than with their own type, while b's prefer to play with b's only. The opposite is true if $h > h^*$.

A two-player game is said to be fair when the players are handicapped to equalize the medians. The competitive handicap does not result in a fair game, since $h^* = \Delta\mu/2 < \Delta\mu$. The a's are given a competitive edge in equilibrium, because they contribute more to total output in mixed matches than the b's do. This same result holds if ε_a has a different variance than ε_b, but it may be sensitive to the assumption of statistical independence and output additivity.

Alternatively, h can be constrained to be zero. In this case, different wage schedules would clear the market. Since $\gamma_a(0) = -\gamma_b(0) \equiv \beta$, paying $\widetilde{W}_1 - \beta$ and $\widetilde{W}_2 - \beta$ to a's, while paying $\widetilde{W}_1 - \beta$, $\widetilde{W}_2 - \beta$ to b's, leaves the spread and, therefore, the investments unaltered. It is easy to verify that a's and b's are still indifferent between mixed and pure contests, because expected returns are equal between segregated and integrated contests for each type of player. With no handicaps, the market-clearing prizes available to a's in the mixed contest are lower than those faced by b's. Still, expected wages are higher for a's than b's in the mixed contest, because their probability of winning is larger. The b's are given a superior schedule in the mixed contest as an equalizing difference for having to compete against superior opponents. This yields the surprising conclusion that reverse discrimination, where the less able are given a head start or rewarded more lucratively if they happen to accomplish the unlikely and win the contest, can be consistent with efficient incentive mechanisms and might be observed in a competitive labor market.

6.4. Summary and Conclusions

This chapter analyzes an alternative to compensation based on the level of individual output. Under certain conditions, a scheme which rewards rank yields an allocation of resources identical to that generated by the efficient piece rate. Compensating workers on the basis of their relative position in the firm can produce the same incentive structure for risk-neutral workers as does the optimal piece rate. It might be less costly, however, to observe relative position than to measure the level of each worker's output directly. This results in paying salaries which resemble prizes: wages which differ from realized marginal products.

When risk aversion is introduced, the prize salary scheme no longer duplicates the allocation of resources induced by the optimal piece rate. Depending on the utility function and on the amount of luck involved, one scheme is preferred to the other. An advantage of a contest is that it eliminates income variation which is caused by factors common to workers of a given firm.

Finally, we allow workers to be heterogeneous. This complication adds an important result: Competitive contests do not automatically sort workers in ways that yield an efficient allocation of resources when information is asymmetric. In particular, low-quality workers attempt to contaminate firms composed of high-quality workers, even if there are no complementarities in production. Contamination results in a general breakdown of the efficient solution if low-quality workers are not prevented from entering. However, when player types are known to all, there exists a competitive handicapping scheme which allows all types to work efficiently within the same firm.

7

Salaries and Piece Rates

Compensation can take many forms. Remuneration can come as pecuniary payments, as fringes such as health and pension benefits, or
as a non-pecuniary reward such as plush office furniture that costs
the firm less than it benefits the worker. Pioneered by Rosen (1974), a
significant literature has examined the trade-offs between pecuniary
and nonpecuniary compensation.

Another body of literature has examined the selection of method
of total compensation, ignoring the distinction between pecuniary
and nonpecuniary payment. This work has focused on risk and incentive factors. It has resulted in comparisons of compensation based
on absolute output levels to that based on relative performance.[1] It
has also led to explorations of the relation of compensation to experience over the work life.[2]

Little attention has been paid to what may be among the most important and obvious distinction in methods of compensation, namely, the
choice between a fixed salary for some period of time, that is, paying on
the basis of input and paying a piece compensation that is specifically
geared to output.[3] Two extreme examples are illustrative. Unskilled
farm labor often is paid in the classic piece-rate fashion: an amount of
payment per pound or piece harvested is specified in advance.

Near the other extreme are middle managers of major corporations
whose annual salaries are specified in advance, and who are then paid
exactly that amount, independent of output. The qualifier is that, if
effort falls below some specified level (e.g., he does not come to work
regularly), the manager may be terminated.

The original version of this chapter was published as: Lazear, E. P. (1986). Salaries and Price
Rates, in: University of Chicago Press, 59(3), 405-431. University of Chicago Press. © 1986 by
the University of Chicago. Helpful comments by Victoria Lazear and Yoram Weiss are gratefully acknowledged. Support was provided by the Department of Labor and the National Science Foundation.

Why are some workers paid piece rates based on output while others are paid salaries for their input? There are a number of common explanations, most of which center around monitoring costs. When it is costly to measure output, it is sometimes argued, workers are paid salaries. When monitoring costs are low, piece-rate payment is appropriate. Although there surely is much truth to this, it leaves a number of issues unresolved. Given the lack of clarity, it seems useful to pursue these points in greater depth. This chapter focuses on a number of issues that affect the choice between salaries and piece rates. The most important are concerned with sorting workers across jobs, inducing appropriate effort levels, and selecting quantity versus quality of output. Additionally, intertemporal strategic behavior is considered. I begin with an attempt to define more concretely what is meant by "salary" and "piece rate."

There is, of course, a large body of literature on compensation schemes. This chapter uses those theories as well as some new analysis and combines it with other work on information and incentives to derive a number of concrete predictions. In particular, the goal is to provide a positive analysis of factors that determine the choice of payment by input over payment by output. I conclude with a sketch of an empirical methodology. Results are summarized in the last section.

7.1. Definitions

The important feature that distinguishes a piece rate from a salary is that, with a piece rate, the worker's payment in a given period is related to output in that period. If the worker is paid a piece rate, then

$$(1) \qquad\qquad w_t = f(q_t),$$

where w_t, is compensation in period t, and q_t, is worker output in period t.

In its purest sense, salary is defined as compensation that depends on input in the current period. Thus salaried workers receive

$$(2) \qquad\qquad w_t = g(E_t),$$

where E_t is (some measure of) effort in period t. Payment is contemporaneous with output for piece-rate workers. Salaried workers receive compensation that is not contemporaneous with output but that is contemporaneous with effort. The measure of effort might be hours worked. For the most part, this chapter ignores compensation that is based on some relative comparison (Lazear and Rosen 1981, see Chapter 6; Holmström 1982) since the focus is on payment by input versus payment by output.

Some examples are useful. Salesmen who are paid on a strict commission basis are piece-rate workers. Magazine, encyclopedia, and cosmetic salesmen often receive no fixed payment but are compensated as a direct and usually linear function of sales. They may choose the number of hours that they work and the effort that they associate with each hour.

Government employees fit the salary classification well. Compensation is independent of output this period and depends strictly on time worked. Certain tasks are required, and dismissal results only when effort falls below some specified standard. Screening through civil-service exams and by monitoring performance during a probationary period is important and allows the government to determine whether workers meet the specified standard.

Most jobs fit somewhere in the middle. For example, many managers in major corporations receive a large proportion of their compensation as a fixed amount specified in advance and independent of that period's output. But at the same time they may often receive a bonus, the size of which is geared directly to this period's output. The bonus component is synchronized to output, is flexible, and is essentially a piece rate. At the top of the corporate hierarchy, senior executives often receive a large proportion of their compensation as bonus and are, in many respects, piece-rate workers.

In what follows, piece rate most often is used to denote the synchronization between output and compensation. Salary implies that workers' pay is independent of this period's output.

7.2. Sorting

The first issue relates to sorting workers across jobs. The major cost of using a piece rate is that output must be monitored, at least periodically, to determine the worker's salary. The extreme version of a salary requires no monitoring of output. To draw out the differences, let us begin by ignoring all effort considerations. Instead, assume that the worker's lifetime output, q, is given and is not subject to the worker's choice. Two cases are worthy of consideration, namely, symmetric and asymmetric information.

7.2.1. Symmetric Information

The first assumes that workers and firms are equally uninformed of q but that both know the distribution of q. Let $q \sim f(q)$ with the distribution function $F(q)$. Assume that the worker can work at an alternative job (or consume leisure) at value $\overline{w}$. One possibility is to pay every worker a salary, S, independent of output level. Another possibility is to pay some piece rate, R, for each unit of q that is produced minus some constant amount to cover monitoring costs. Under the piece-rate scheme, the worker's compensation is

$$(3) \qquad\qquad w = Rq - \theta,$$

where θ is the per-worker monitoring cost.

The goal is the standard one, namely, to maximize worker's expected wealth subject to a zero-profit constraint. Assume risk neutrality so that wealth is the relevant consideration.

If a salary is paid, then no monitoring costs are borne. Zero profits require that

$$S = E(q).$$

As long as the expectation of q exceeds $\overline{w}$ and there are no piece-rate firms, all workers agree to work at this firm.

The problem with this scheme is that it is inefficient to have all workers work at this firm. Those workers for whom $q < \overline{w}$ should take the alternative job, and all can be made better off. Since $F(\overline{w})$ workers have $q < \overline{w}$, separating them from the others causes expected wealth to rise. This is obvious since

$$\text{Expected compensation} \atop \text{with sorting} = \overline{w}F(\overline{w}) + \int_{\overline{w}}^{\infty} qf(q)dq > \int_{0}^{\infty} qf(q)dq$$

$$> E(q)$$

$$> S.$$

This inefficiency can be eliminated if the worker's first day is monitored so that q is revealed. The worker can be induced to leave by paying him a piece rate equal to Rq. Since zero profits are required, in competition $R = 1$ induces both zero profit and efficient separation. But paying a piece rate requires that a monitoring cost, θ, be borne for each worker. The perfect piece rate results in an expected output at the current firm of

$$(4) \qquad w = tE(q) + (1 - t) \int_{\overline{w}}^{\infty} qf(q)dq - \theta,$$

where t is the proportion of the work life spent in the initial monitoring period. (With no noise, it is optimal to push t arbitrarily close to zero.) In the first t of the workers' careers, all work at the piece-rate firm. After they learn q, only those with $Rq > w$ remain. Setting $R = 1$ and reducing all workers' compensation by θ during the first t of the career results in zero profits and efficient separation. Thus the worker's wage profile is

$$(5) \qquad \begin{aligned} w_t &= tq - \theta && \text{during the first } t \text{ of the career;} \\ w_{1-t} &= (1 - t)q, \quad \text{for stayers} \Big\} && \text{during the last } 1 - t \\ &= (1 - t)\overline{w}, \quad \text{for leavers} && \text{of the career.} \end{aligned}$$

So expected lifetime wealth if the worker starts at the piece-rate job and has the option to move when $w_1 - t < (1 - t)\overline{w}$ is

$$(6) \qquad W = tE(q) - \theta + \left[\overline{w}F(\overline{w}) + \int_{\overline{w}}^{\infty} qf(q)dq\right](1 - t).$$

If a straight salary is paid, expected wealth equals $E(q)$.[4]

The condition for selecting a piece rate over a salary is

$$tE(q) - \theta + \left[\overline{w}F(\overline{w}) + \int_{\overline{w}}^{\infty} qf(q)dq\right](1 - t) > E(q)$$

or

$$\overline{w}F(\overline{w}) + \int_{\overline{w}}^{\infty} qf(q)dq - \frac{\theta}{1 - t} > E(q)$$

or

(7)
$$\overline{w}F(\overline{w}) - \frac{\theta}{1-t} > \int_0^{\overline{w}} qf(q)dq.$$

From (7) it is obvious that the piece-rate firm maximizes worker wealth by keeping t as small as possible. Other results are equally intuitive.

First, as θ rises, the likelihood falls that a piece rate will dominate a straight salary. Salaries do not require monitoring; what is lost is the ability to sort workers to their highest valued use. As the cost of sorting rises, it becomes less worthwhile.

For a similar reason, as $\overline{w}$, the alternative use of time, rises, the value of using a piece rate rises. This is true because (7) can be rewritten as

$$\overline{w}F(\overline{w}) - \int_0^{\overline{w}} qf(q)dq > \frac{\theta}{1-t}.$$

Differentiating the left-hand side with respect to $\overline{w}$ yields

$$F(\overline{w}) + \overline{w}f(\overline{w}) - \overline{w}f(\overline{w}) = F(\overline{w})$$

and

$$F(\overline{w}) > 0.$$

Thus piece rates are more valuable when $\overline{w}$ is large. The intuition is clear in that the better are the alternative opportunities relative to those here, the more is lost by failing to sort workers to their most valued use.

That point can be stated in a slightly different manner. For a given $\overline{w}$, the lower is $E(q| \ q < w)$, the more valuable is the piece-rate scheme that sorts workers. If that part of the distribution with $q < \overline{w}$ is very much below $\overline{w}$, then it is valuable to separate them from the firm. A skewed distribution of output with a long left tail is a good candidate for piece-rate pay. If some individuals are extremely bad at performing the task, monitoring and piece rates are more useful. Similarly, the greater the proportion of workers with $q < \overline{w}$, the more valuable is the piece-rate relative to the salary scheme.

The basic idea can be restated. The more heterogeneous workers are, the better it is to use a piece rate with monitoring. But as montoring costs rise, workers become less willing to foot the bill through reduced salaries. If all workers were of similar abilities, a firm would have a difficult time hiring workers on a piece-rate basis because a firm that paid straight salary could offer a higher average wage. Monitoring costs increases the value of a salary relative to piece rates, and heterogeneity across workers decreases the value of a salary relative to piece rates.[5]

To add realism, let us recognize that estimates of workers' output do not perfectly reflect ability. In particular, there is some error associated with measurement and some random variation that results because of factors beyond the worker's control. This complicates the problem somewhat. The most important result is that noise reduces the value of the piece-rate scheme relative to a straight salary.

To see this, let

$$(8) \qquad \hat{q}_t = tq + \varepsilon_t,$$

where t is the period during which monitoring occurs, $\hat{q}_t$ is the observed output during that period, and ε_t is random error. A more general formulation would allow t to be endogenous, trading off quicker sorting against more measurement error. We ignore that and assume that t is set at its optimal level.

Given (8), if ε_t has the classical properties and if errors are not serially correlated, then the efficient and unbiased estimate of q is

$$(9) \qquad \hat{q} \equiv \frac{\hat{q}_t}{t}$$

Now, from (8) and (9),

$$\hat{q} = q + \frac{\varepsilon_t}{t}$$

$$(10) \qquad \hat{q} = q + \xi,$$

where $\xi \equiv \varepsilon_t/t$. Let the density function of ξ be denoted by $g(\xi)$.

The issue is whether piece rates are less likely to be used when the measurement of output is noisy. The worker is given some reading of his output level, $\hat{q}$, and he must decide whether to leave to accept wage $\overline{w}$ or to stay. This amounts to selecting some critical level, q^*, such that, if $\hat{q} < q^*$, the worker leaves and takes the job that pays $\overline{w}$, whereas if $\hat{q} > q^*$, the worker stays.

Piece rates are less likely to be chosen when the estimate of q is noisy. To see this, what needs to be shown is that nondegenerate densities of ξ result in lower expected wages in the piece-rate firm than does the density $g(\xi) = 0$ for all $\xi \neq 0$. If so, then the piece-rate scheme is less advantageous when q is measured with error and is less likely to be chosen over the strict salary (because the strict salary pays $S = E[q]$ to all workers, and this is independent of any measurement error). The proof is tedious and is relegated to the appendix. The intuition, however, is straightforward. The addition of measurement error causes some workers to remain at the piece-rate firm even though $q < \overline{w}$ because a positive ξ is drawn. The worker does not quit because his measured output is abnormally high during the period, so he is deceived into staying. Additionally, it causes some to leave even when $q > \overline{w}$ because a negative ξ makes $\hat{q} < \overline{w}$. Both types of error produce incorrect sorting and reduce the value of using a piece rate. The salary scheme performs no sorting but saves the monitoring cost, θ, so it is more likely to dominate when the variance in ξ is large.[6]

7.2.2. *Asymmetric Information*

The previous section discussed optimality when firms and workers are symmetrically uninformed about ability. But what if workers have better information than have firms about their output potential? Under these circumstances, as long as monitoring costs, θ, are positive, some workers can always be attracted to a salary firm. The reason is that it costs the worker θ to distinguish himself from his peers. For small differences in ability, it does not pay to bear that cost. There is always some group of least able workers that can be made better off by sorting into firms that do not waste resources on measuring output differences. Those firms assume instead that they have attracted low-ability workers, and they pay accordingly. This is straightforward and shown below.

All workers with $q - \theta < S$ work at the salary firm that pays S since they earn only $q - \theta$ at the piece-rate firm. What is required is that the salary firm can pay some S such that workers with $q < q^*$ select the salary firm and that zero profits can be achieved.

For any given S, workers with $q > S + \theta \equiv q_0$ choose the piece-rate firm. It is necessary to show that there exists an S such that

(11)
$$S = \frac{1}{F(S + \theta)} \int_0^{S+\theta} qf(q)dq$$

since the right-hand side is the expected output of a worker at the salary firm. Equation (11) is merely the salary firm's zero-profit condition. Alternatively, (11) can be rewritten as

(12)
$$q_0 - \frac{1}{F(q_0)} \int_0^{q_0} qf(q)dq - \theta = 0,$$

where $q_0 \equiv S + \theta$. Define the left-hand side of (12) as $H(q_0)$. Then, to show that a salary firm can always compete away some workers from the piece-rate firm, it is necessary only to find a fixed point, $q_0 = q^*$, such that $H(q^*) = 0$ (i.e., to find $q^* - H[q^*] = q^*$). But

$$\lim_{q_0 \to q_{min}} H(q_0) = q_{min} - q_{min} - \theta = -\theta < 0$$

and

$$\lim_{q_0 \to q_{max}} H(q_0) = q_{max} - \bar{q} - \theta.$$

If $q_{max} - \bar{q} > \theta$, then $H(q_{max}) > 0$. Since $H(q_0)$ is continuous, there exists a q^* such that $H(q^*) = 0$ so that some workers choose the salary firm. If $q_{max} - q < \theta$, then all workers choose the salary firm because even the most able worker who receives only $\bar{q}$ at the salary firm finds $\bar{q} > q - 0$. The existence of an equilibrium where at least some workers go to the salary firm is proved. (If $\theta = 0$, then a salary firm could exist with only the least able worker at that firm. That worker would be indifferent between employment at piece-rate or salary firms. All others prefer the piece-rate firm.)[7].

The equilibrium value of S is

$$S^* = \frac{1}{F(q^* + \theta)} \int_0^{q^*+\theta} qf(q)dq,$$

and all workers with $q < S^* - \theta$ choose to work at the salary firm, whereas those with $q > S^* - \theta$ work at the piece-rate firm.

The obvious implication is that, for a given occupation, firms that pay workers a straight salary have a lower-quality workforce than have firms that pay piece rates. The best workers select firms where performance has a payoff. The worst ones go to firms where ability has no effect on salary. Firms know this, and salaries are adjusted accordingly. Pencavel (1977) presents some evidence that piece-rate workers earn about 7% more than similar time-rate workers. Similarly, Seiler (1984) finds earnings 14% higher for "incentive" workers.

Productivity in piece-rate firms is higher than productivity in salary firms, but this does not imply that, if all salary firms were to pay piece rates, output would rise; the opposite is true. Switching all piece-rate worker to salary by fiat would save measurement costs θ on each worker and would have no effect on output. This is the classic screening result.

Contrast the result when information is asymmetric with that when information is lacking symmetrically. When information is asymmetric, it is always possible to pick off some workers by paying a straight salary. It is certain then that at least some of the firms will be salary firms. Whether there are piece-rate firms as well depends on the costs of monitoring relative to the value to the most able of being sorted from the least able. When information is lacking on both sides, a corner solution is always achieved; that is, either it pays to sort workers, or it does not. Since workers do not know their abilities ex ante, all choose one type of firm or the other.

7.2.3. Capital

The previous discussion ignores effort considerations and complementarities. It may well pay to place the most able workers in some firms and the least able ones in others for efficiency reasons. Ignoring effort effects for now, consider a production process where capital is important. If capital is important, then it is optimal to separate out low-ability workers. In general, this requires that the piece-rate firm use a two-part wage system,

$$(13) \qquad\qquad W(q) = a + bq,$$

193

rather than simply paying $W(q) = Rq$. A possible alternative is to use one-part piece rate, Rq, combined with a standard, $\underline{q}$. If output falls below $\underline{q}$, then the employee is terminated (without compensation). Even when effort is not an issue, this scheme breaks down. However, a fixed salary coupled with a standard is efficient and sustainable but results in workers of only one ability level applying for employment. The scheme in equation (13) looks identical to the piece rate described in the earlier section with $a = -\theta$ and $b = 1$. The difference, and it is a crucial one, is that, there, there is no problem with observability of output or ability. In this section, the focus is on fixed costs with perfect information. It differs from earlier sections, in which both sides were assumed to lack information or in which only one side was assumed to lack information.

First, let us show that a one-part piece rate without a standard is not efficient in general. To focus on this assume that measurement costs are zero. Suppose that the production technology requires that each worker use a machine to produce output and that the rental price of the machine is γ. Then net output at this firm from worker with ability q is $q - \gamma$. For efficiency, it is necessary that only and all workers whose net output levels, $q - \gamma$, exceed the alternative use of time, $\overline{w}$, work at the current firm or one identical to it. In order to induce this to occur it is necessary that $w(q) < \overline{w}$ for $q < \overline{w} + \gamma$ and $w(q) > \overline{w}$ for $q > \overline{w} + \gamma$. If $w(q)$ is continuous, this implies that $w(\overline{w} + \gamma) = \overline{w}$.

A one-part piece rate has the form $w(q) = Rq$. Since $w(\overline{w} + \gamma) = \overline{w}$ this implies that

$$R = \frac{\overline{w}}{\overline{w} + \gamma}.$$

But for this to be an equilibrium it must be true that the firm earns zero profits or that compensation equals output. Required is that

$$\int_{\overline{w}+\gamma}^{\infty} Rqf(q)dq = \int_{\overline{w}+\gamma}^{\infty} (q - \gamma)f(q)dq.$$

After making the substitutions, this implies that

(14) $$1 - \left(\frac{\overline{w}}{\overline{w} + \gamma}\right) \int_{\overline{w}+\gamma}^{\infty} qf(q)dq = \gamma[1 - F(\overline{w} + \gamma)].$$

Equation (14) cannot hold in general because $\overline{w}$, γ, and $f(q)$ are all exogenous. There is one equation but no unknowns. This proves that a one-part piece rate without a standard is not generally efficient.

(A special case is when there is no capital requirement or when capital is free. In that case, $\gamma = 0$, so (14) holds: $R = 1$, and all workers with $q < \overline{w}$ work elsewhere; the rest are employed here.)

It is a trivial extension, however, to show that a two-part piece rate is efficient. If $w(q) = -\gamma + q$, then profit equals zero since each worker is paid his net output. Further, for those with $q - \gamma < \overline{w}$, $w(q) < \overline{w}$, and for those with $q - \gamma > \overline{w}$, $w(q) > \overline{w}$. So worker sorting is perfect.

An alternative is to pay a one-part piece rate Rq (R not necessarily equal to one) and simply to terminate all workers with $q < \overline{w} + \gamma$. This will not work because of adverse selection. For zero profits, it is necessary that

$$\int_{\overline{w}+\gamma}^{\infty} Rqf(q)dq = \int_{\overline{w}+\gamma}^{\infty} (q - \gamma)f(q)dq$$

or that

$$R = 1 - \frac{\gamma[1 - F(\overline{w} + \gamma)]}{\int_{\overline{w}+\gamma}^{\infty} qf(q)dq}$$

so that $R < 1$.

But if $R < 1$ at this firm, workers at the top of the distributional ways prefer a firm that pays $w(q) = q - \gamma$. Figure 7.1 illustrates this. Only workers with $q < q^*$ work at the firm that pays Rq with $R < 1$, so they are all paid more than their net contribution. The firm cannot break even, and there is no readjustment of R that will allow zero profit so long as $R < 1$.

In the absence of monitoring cost, a salary firm that pays $S = \overline{w}$ and requires that the worker have $q \geq \overline{w} + \gamma$ can stay in business, but it attracts only those workers with $q = \overline{w} + \gamma$. All others do better at the piece-rate firm. Any higher S with the same standard results in losses, but it is always possible to select a standard consistent with any $S > \overline{w}$ that does not result in losses. All that is necessary is that the required level of performance be equal to $S + \gamma$. The only workers that apply are those with $q = S + \gamma$, which is likely to be a costly way to recruit.

Figure 7.1

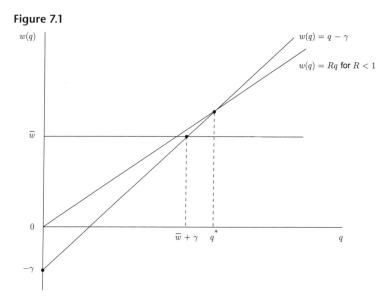

Recapping, a piece rate with a fixed component (in this case $-\gamma$) has salary attributes. The amount $-\gamma$ is paid to input rather than to output. That is, it is a fixed fee that is levied for coming to work and is independent of output. As capital costs go up, γ rises, so the importance of the payment (or fee) by input grows relative to payment by output. In that sense it can be said that the existence of physical capital pushes in the direction of payment by input.

7.3. Effort

It is commonly argued that piece-rate pay is an incentive device whereas straight salary provides no incentives. To determine the validity of this statement, it is first necessary to distinguish the characteristics that may or may not be attributed to salaries. The first is the invariability of the salary with the current effort level. The second is the invariability of salary with the past effort level. If effort level is observed perfectly and contemporaneously, then there is no reason to expect the salary defined as payment by input to be invariant to the current effort level. An example is a situation in which effort per hour is fixed but hours are variable. Paying the appropriate hourly wage would provide exactly the right incentives.

In this case, and in all cases in which output and input are observed perfectly, the choice of payment by input or output is irrelevant. When everything is observed, a payment by either criterion can be efficient. This is obvious. If E is effort, the cost of effort function is given by $C = C(E)$, and the production function is given by $q = E$,[8] then the efficient level of effort, E^*, is given by

$$E^* = \arg \max_E q - C(E)$$

or

$$= \arg \max_E E - C(E).$$

So E^* solves

$$C'(E^*) = 1.$$

If the worker were paid $S(E) = E$, then he would choose E so as to maximize

(15) $$S(E) - C(E) = E - C(E)$$

and would set $C'(E^*) = 1$, achieving efficiency. Alternatively, if the worker were paid a piece rate on output such that $P(q) = q$, then he would choose E to maximize

$$P(q) - C(E) = q - C(E) = E - C(E),$$

so again E^* is chosen, which ensures that $C'(E^*) = 1$.

Still, it is commonly alleged that salaries do not provide the same incentives as do piece rates. What is meant by this statement? The definition of salary implicitit in it includes some invariability of payment with effort. For some reason the salary does not respond to effort appropriately. Clearly, at the extreme, if $S(E) = \overline{S}$, then the worker's choice in (15) is to choose E so as to minimize $C(E)$, hardly consistent with efficiency.

The question then becomes, What is it that makes $S(E)$ deviate from $S(E) = E$? The most straightforward answer relates to the inability to observe E. If E were unobservable, but if q were perfectly observable, then the choice would be clear: payment function $P(q) = q$ results in perfect efficiency whereas $S(E) = \overline{S}$ does not.

But this is extreme. The choice between payment by input and payment by output may be characterized more appropriately by the notion that it may be cheap to observe that minimal effort, $E \geq \overline{E}$ (the worker comes to work and goes through the motions of doing the job), but more expensive to measure his actual level of output (and it may be impossible to measure his exact level of effort). Thus suppose that the firm can determine output exactly if it bears cost θ_1 but can know that effort exceeds some minimum, E, at cost $\theta_2 < \theta_1$. The issue is when the firm should bear the larger monitoring cost and pay on the basis of output.

As shown earlier, the piece rate that pays $q - \theta_1$ induces efficient effort E^* such that $C'(E^*) = 1$. If the low-monitoring strategy is used, it is clear that the worker supplies exactly $\overline{E}$ of effort. (Note that $\overline{E}$ may be less than or may exceed E^*.) If E is the level of effort, then all low-monitoring workers receive a salary, $S = \overline{E} - \theta_2$. The choice of whether to use a salary or a piece rate then implies that a salary is paid if and only if

$$(16) \qquad \overline{E} - \theta_2 - C(\overline{E}) > E^* - \theta_1 - C(E^*)$$

since the worker receives $\overline{E} - \theta_2$ if he is on a salary and $E^* - \theta_1$ if he is on a piece rate. Equation (16) can be approximated as

$$(17) \qquad \theta_1 - \theta_2 \gtrsim (\overline{E} - E^*)^2 \left[\frac{C''(E^*)}{2} \right],$$

where the right-hand side uses second-order Taylor series expansion around E^* since $C'(E^*) = 1$.

Equation (17) has a number of straightforward implications. First and most obvious is that as $\theta_1 - \theta_2$ increases, the salary tends to be preferred. As the cost of the more precise type of monitoring rises, a salary that

depends only on satisfying some minimal level of performance dominates. Note again that this does not imply that effort is lower with a salary than with a piece rate, for $\overline{E}$ is exogenous and may well exceed E^*.

Second, as $|E^* - \overline{E}|$ increases, the value of the piece-rate scheme
rises relative to a salary. At one extreme, if $\overline{E} = E^*$, then it is clear that
the salary is always preferred because effort is the same and monitoring costs are lower. (Indeed, the firm should set $\overline{E}$ as close to E^* as
possible, to the extent that $\overline{E}$ is subject to choice.)

Third, for a given $\overline{E}$, the more elastic is the marginal cost function
(i.e., the lower is $C''[\overline{E}]$), the larger is the deviation between $\overline{E}$ and E^*.
Then it is necessarily true that the more elastic is the $C'(E)$ function
(i.e., the closer to zero is $C''[E]$), the poorer the salary performs. Figure
7.2 makes this clear.

Figure 7.2

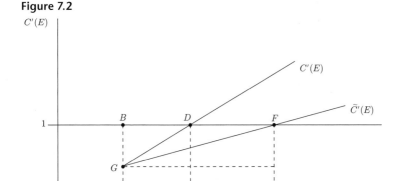

Suppose $\overline{E} < E^*$. Then $C'(\overline{E}) < 1$. Consider $C'(E)$ and $\widetilde{C}'(E)$ such
that $C'(\overline{E}) = \widetilde{C}'(\overline{E})$ but $\widetilde{C}''(\overline{E}) < C''(\overline{E})$. Then $\widetilde{C}'(E)$ is a more elastic
marginal cost-of-effort function than is $C'(E)$. If the worker faced
$C'(E)$, then a piece rate induces him to supply E^* of effort. If he faced
$C'(E)$, he would supply $\widetilde{E}^*$ of effort. The salary induces him to supply
$\overline{E}$ of effort with either function.

What does the worker lose by stopping at $\overline{E}$ rather than at E^*? The
lost output is $E^* - \overline{E}$, which equals the area of rectangle $\overline{E}BDE^*$
(since the height equals one). But in return the worker bears smaller
cost. The incremental cost of moving from $\overline{E}$ to E^* is the area of trap-

ezoid $\overline{E}GDE^*$. So the net loss in stopping short of E^* is triangle BDG. Similarly, if the cost function were $\widetilde{C}'(E)$, the net loss from stopping at $\overline{E}$ would be triangle BFG. Since $BFG > BDG$, the salary is less likely to be preferred to the piece rate when $C'(E)$ is more elastic.[9]

Summarizing, when effort is endogenous, both piece rates and salaries can act as incentive devices. An alternative to a piece rate is a salary that is contingent on exceeding some performance standard. This may be a cheaper, but less efficient, incentive device. It tends to be preferred to a piece rate when the differences in costs of the two kinds of monitoring are large and when, for a given observable standard level, the marginal cost of effort function is steep, that is, effort is supplied inelastically.

7.3.1. Quantity versus Quality

It is sometimes alleged that piece rates induce the worker to produce too many low-quality goods and that salaries avoid the problem. Under what conditions is this a correct statement?

The piece rate can be made contingent on the output quality characteristics as well as on the quantity characteristics. More formally, suppose that the firm's revenue function is

$$\text{Revenue} = P(q, Q),$$

where q is the number of units sold, and Q is their quality (arbitrarily defined). Suppose further that the worker can convert effort into output as

$$f(q, Q, E) = 0.$$

Then the efficient competitive firm that maximizes workers' expected wealth subject to zero profits wants to induce q, Q, and E as

(18) $$\max_{q,Q,E} P(q, Q) - C(E)$$

subject to

$$f(q, Q, E) = 0.$$

The worker faces some announced piece-rate schedule, $R(q, Q)$, and seeks to maximize

$$R(q, Q) - C(E)$$

subject to

$$f(q, Q, E) = 0.$$

The firm that sets $R(q, Q) \equiv P(q, Q)$ guarantees that the worker's problem becomes identical to (18) and so yields an efficient allocation of resources. This maximizes worker wealth, consistent with zero profits.

When $R(q, Q) \equiv P(q, Q)$, the piece-rate worker does not emphasize quantity to the exclusion of quality. Real-world examples of piece-rate workers who are paid for quality as well as for quantity exist. Executives' bonuses depend on profits, not on the number of units sold, and profit is the measure that weights quantity and quality in exactly the appropriate fashion. Salesmen's commissions depend on sales revenues, not on units sold. Sales revenues weight "big-ticket" high-quality items more heavily. Even agricultural workers may be penalized for turning in bruised fruit.

Of course, it is possible to induce piece-rate workers to favor quantity to the exclusion of quality. All that is required is that $\partial R / \partial Q \leq 0$. But this payment scheme would never be sensible.

Although a salary does not automatically solve the problem, there is an important sense in which salary emphasizes quality relative to the piece rate. Since the standard on which the salary is based is an effort standard rather than an output standard, the worker is indifferent to allocations of q, Q, so long as they satisfy $f(q, Q, \overline{E}) = 0$, where $\overline{E}$ is the required level of effort. A mere request that the worker produce $(\overline{q}, \overline{Q})$ should be met with compliance if $f(\overline{q}, \overline{Q}, \overline{E}) = 0$, given that $\overline{E}$ is required anyway.

For salaried workers, one proxy for effort is hours worked. If that were the only dimension of effort, then paying an hourly wage would be equivalent to paying for effort. These workers would be instructed to produce the right combination of q, Q. No monitoring of output would be necessary since there would be no incentive to deviate from the optimum, so long as it required no more than $\overline{E}$ of effort.

When effort is less costly to monitor than both quantity and quality of output, then a salary based on effort may be preferable. An example is an hourly wage, where weekly compensation depends on time worked. Hours are easily measured, and the worker is indifferent between quantity and quality, given hours worked, so that the firm's priorities are likely to be realized.

7.4. Risk

There are two sources of income variation associated with a piece rate. The first is variation over time that results because of factors beyond the worker's control, which affect output. The state of the market, exogenous factors of production, and other sources of luck cause the worker's output to vary even if his effort does not. The second kind of variation results from unobserved differences in worker ability. If workers and firms are unaware of each worker's ability, then lifetime output is nondeterministic.[10]

A salary that is not contingent on last period's output tends to smooth out intertemporal variations in income induced by a piece rate. But this kind of risk does not seem to be a major problem. Borrowing and lending in capital markets can smooth much of it. The time period over which output is measured can be lengthened to make compensation per period vary by a smaller amount (see Weiss 1984).

The more important kind of risk that the worker faces is risk in his lifetime wealth. In its purest form, the salary, which is totally independent of output, offers complete insurance against lifetime risk. Since no attempt is made to measure individual's output, there is no difficulty in keeping high-quality workers. Those workers who sign on with the salary firm accept the average salary because they are ignorant about their ability levels or are averse to risk. The implication is that salaries are more likely to be paid when workers have a high degree of risk aversion relative to owners.

7.5. Intertemporal Strategic Behavior

Often, piece rates are negatively related to past output. One problem that arises is that workers artificially depress this period's output because of the effect on next period's compensation. For example, workers pressure peers who show management that the task can be done more rapidly than believed in order to increase their own current salaries. Similarly, salesmen are wary of doing too well today, lest their quotas be raised tomorrow.

Salaries that are contingent on meeting some standard suffer from the same drawback when the standard is adjusted as a function of last period's output. But these effects can be offset if they are anticipated properly.[11]

Consider the piece rate. If workers know that tomorrow's rate is a function of today's output, it would seem that too little effort would be exerted in the current period. But this kind of strategic behavior can be undone by the appropriate piece-rate structure.

In order for the firm to be able to gear next period's rate to this period's output, the firm must enjoy some ex post monopsony power. Otherwise a competitive firm can attract all workers who are poorly treated.[12] The problem arises when specific capital or mobility costs lock the worker into the firm such that there is a wedge between what the worker can receive elsewhere and what he receives here. The firm, knowing this, exploits the worker in an ex post sense. Of course, when workers begin employment with the firm, they are aware of this situation, and total lifetime compensation must be set so as to leave the firm with zero profits. But there still is no way to prevent the firm from behaving opportunistically in the second period.

To formalize this, the worker lives two periods and produces $q_1 = E_1$ and $q_2 = E_2$ in periods 1 and 2, where E_t is effort in period t. Workers have an alternative use of time (say, leisure) at zero effort with value $\overline{w}$ for each period. Further, workers differ in their cost-of-effort functions. Some view effort as less distasteful than others, so

$$\text{Cost} = \widetilde{C}(E_t),$$

where $\widetilde{C}$ is a stochastic function that is known to workers but not to firms.

Firms exploit workers ex post by learning the cost-of-effort function from actions taken in period 1. Low-cost workers find that their piece rates are lower in period 2 than high-cost workers, and they behave strategically as a result, attempting to prevent the firm from learning $\widetilde{C}(E)$.[13] Ex post monopsony power implies that the firm need only pay the worker a wage in period 2 that makes him indifferent between work here and work elsewhere:

$$(19) \qquad w_2 - \widetilde{C}(E_2) = \overline{w}.$$

It is obvious from (19) that the firm sets w_2 lower for workers with low realizations of $\widetilde{C}(E_2)$ if the firm can discover that value.

In period 1, the worker receives w_1, and the ex ante zero-profit constraint implies that $w_1 + w_2 = q_1 + q_2$ for every worker (because markets are assumed to be competitive). The question is, Does there exist a $w_1(q_1)$ and $w_2(q_1, q_2)$ such that the worker can be induced to behave efficiently in both periods even though he knows that the firm has ex post monopsony power and that the firm will lower his wage if it finds him to be a low $\widetilde{C}(E)$ worker? The answer is a definite yes. Even though the worker behaves strategically in period 1, his strategic behavior can be offset by an appropriate piece-rate schedule.

Let us conjecture that the functional form of that compensation scheme is given by

$$(20a) \qquad w_1 = R_1(q_1) + K_1,$$

$$(20b) \qquad w_2 = R_2(q_2) + K_2(q_1).$$

To derive the efficient scheme that maximizes ex post exploitation but is consistent with zero profits, start by noting that the worker optimizes by selecting $E_1(= q_1)$ and $E_2(= q_2)$ such that

$$(21a) \qquad \widetilde{C}'(E_1) = \frac{\partial w_1}{\partial q_1}\frac{\partial q_1}{\partial E_1} + \frac{\partial w_2}{\partial q_2}\frac{\partial q_1}{\partial E_1} = R_1' + K_2',$$

$$(21b) \qquad \widetilde{C}'(E_2) = R_2'.$$

For efficiency in period 2, it is necessary that $R_2' = 1$. For efficiency in period 1, it is necessary that

$$(22) \qquad R_1' + K_2' = 1$$

or that

$$R_1' = 1 - K_2'.$$

For full ex post exploitation, it is necessary that

(23) $$R_2(q_2) + K_2(q_1) - \widetilde{C}(E_2) = \overline{w}.$$

For any $K_2(q_1)$, selecting $R_1'(q_1) = 1 - K_2'(q_1)$ guarantees efficiency in the first period since substitution into (21a) implies that the worker sets $\widetilde{C}'(E_1) = 1$. Letting $R_2(q_2) = q_2$ guarantees efficiency in period 2. The ability of the firm to act as an ex post monopsonist in period 2 depends on its knowledge of the functional form of $\widetilde{C}(E)$. Since the firm chooses $R_1' = 1 - K_2'$, it knows that the worker chooses E_1 such that $\widetilde{C}'(E_1) = 1$. If the firm knows the functional form of $\widetilde{C}(E)$, under some circumstances this allows perfect identification of the worker's actual $C(E)$. But even if the firm cannot perfectly identify $C(E)$, the worker still behaves appropriately. All that happens is that the firm loses some quasi rent because of its inability to act as an ex post monopsonist. (Because of competition, this does not affect the firm's profits, which are zero anyway. Nor can the firm trade off quasi rent in period 2 for inefficiency. Doing so would result in lower lifetime worker wealth and would result in a failure to attract workers in the first place.)

To see this, suppose that the firm forms some estimate of $C(E)$ based on its observation of q_1, and denote this estimate as $\widehat{C}(E; q_1)$. (It is not necessary that $\widehat{C}$ be unbiased or have any other property.)

Now let the firm define

$$K_2'(q_1) \equiv \frac{\partial \widehat{C}}{\partial q_1}(q_1; q_1).$$

Let the firm simply announce that

$$R_1'(q_1) \equiv 1 - \frac{\partial \widehat{C}}{\partial q_1}(q_1; q_1)(= 1 - K_2').$$

Equation (22) is satisfied, so efficiency in period 1 is guaranteed. Again, $R_2(q_2) \equiv q_2$ so that period-2 efficiency is guaranteed and K_1 is set so as to guarantee ex ante zero profits.

The intuition is straightforward. Because the worker takes into account the effect of this period's output on next period's rate, he tends to underproduce this period. But this can be offset by increasing the payment per piece during the first period.

An example is useful. Let $\widetilde{C}(E) = \lambda E^2$, where λ is a random variable unknown to the firm. If

$$w_1 = \frac{3}{2} \cdot q_1 - \overline{w}$$

and

$$w_2 = q_2 - \frac{q_1}{2} + \overline{w},$$

then all is fully efficient, zero profits are earned ex ante, and the firm fully exploits the worker ex post. The worker chooses E_1 such that

$$C'(E_1) = \frac{3}{2} - \frac{1}{2} = 1$$

so E_1 is efficient. He chooses E_2 such that

$$C'(E_2) = 1,$$

so E_2 is efficient. Further, full ex post exploitation is achieved because (23) holds. Required is that

$$R_2(q_2) + K_2(q_1) - \widetilde{C}(E_2) = \overline{w}$$

or that

$$q_2 - \frac{q_1}{2} + \overline{w} - \lambda(E_2)^2 = \overline{w}$$

or that

$$q_2 - \frac{q_1}{2} = \lambda(q_2)^2.$$

Since $q_2 = q_1$, this reduces to

$$\frac{q_2}{2} = \lambda q_2^2.$$

But $C'(E_2) = 1$ implies that $q_2 = \frac{1}{2\lambda}$, so this becomes

$$\frac{1}{4\lambda} = \lambda\left(\frac{1}{2\lambda}\right)^2 = \frac{1}{4\lambda},$$

so the necessary condition for full exploitation is met. Finally, ex ante profits equal zero since $w_1 + w_2 = q_1 + q_2$.

The conclusion is that intertemporal strategic behavior does not render the piece rate inefficient. Even though workers select effort levels with effects on future rates in mind, all is efficient in equilibrium. This does not negate that workers worry about the effects of today's output on future rates. It merely implies that this worry can be offset with an inflated piece rate in the first period.[14]

7.6. Empirical Issues

The preceding analysis presents a number of testable implications about when piece rates and salaries are most likely to be used. Additionally, it offers predictions on the distribution of output within piece-rate jobs as compared to salary jobs.

In order to test these implications, it is necessary to have data, the unit of analysis of which is the job rather than the worker. It is useful to sketch out briefly the empirical issues to be addressed.

First, recall that the definition of a piece rate involved the relation between this period's pay and this period's output. To classify jobs into piece-rate or into salary categories, one would like to examine a time series of output and compensation. A regression equation could be specified of the form

(24) $$\gamma_t = a + bt + c_0 q_t + c_1 q_{t-1} + \ldots + c_i q_{t-i} + dH_t,$$

where γ_t is compensation in t, q_t is output, and H_t is hours worked in t. A pure piece rate implies that $c_0 = 1$ and that $c_1, \ldots, c_1 = 0$, $d = 0$. A pure salary implies that $c_0,...,c_i = 0$. A salary that is contingent on past performance implies that $c_1,...,c_i \geq 0$, $c_0 = 0$.

The estimated coefficients then become data for successive stages of the empirical analysis. What one would like to predict is the size of $c_0,...,c_i$ across jobs, and the theory presented above provides a structure. Although it is unlikely that reliable data on output could ever be obtained, let us proceed as if that were not a problem to outline the possibilities.

First, heterogeneity in worker abilities implies that piece rates are more likely to be used. This implies that there should be a positive correlation between c_0 and between the variance in q_t across workers. (Seiler, 1984, already has found higher variance in the earnings (γ_t) of piece-rate workers, but this follows even if the variance in output is higher in salary firms because salaries ignore differences in output.)

Second, costs of monitoring output should be negatively related to c_0. To the extent that a measure of the monitoring costs could be obtained, the implication is testable.[15]

Third, if piece rates act as a sorting device, then there should be a positive correlation between c_0 and turnover rates.

Fourth, if information is asymmetric, then the least able workers work at the salary firms. This implies that, within a given job (whatever that means), there should be a positive correlation between c_0 and the average level of output. For the same reason, c_0 should be positively correlated with the wage rate.

Fifth, the cost of measuring output quality should be negatively correlated with c_0. Additionally, as costs of measuring quality relative to effort rise, $a + b + dH$ should rise as well.

7.7. Summary and Conclusions

Some traditional and not so traditional factors that are associated with piece rates are analyzed. Piece-rate workers are distinguished from salary workers in that piece rates depend on current output whereas salaries do not. Salaries are closer to payment by input, broadly defined.

Because salaries are independent of this period's output, it is not necessary to measure output. Although monitoring costs are saved, workers are not sorted as efficiently. Salaries suffer from the drawback that some low-output workers who could do better else-where are not induced to leave. The efficient piece rate induces all workers to leave appropriately but carries with it a monitoring cost. These considerations imply that piece rates are likely to be used over salaries when the following conditions hold: (a) the cost of measuring output is low; (b) the value of the alternative wage is high relative to average output at the current firm; (c) workers are heterogeneous in ability levels; and (d) output is measured without too much error.

If workers know their ability levels and firms do not, then it is al-ways true that at least some of the firms will pay a straight salary. Piece-rate firms may or may not coexist, depending on the strength of the considerations above. More important is that the least able workers are always in the salary firm. They are the ones who are un-willing to bear the monitoring costs necessary to distinguish abili-ties. Symmetric ignorance, on the other hand, pushes the solution to a corner; that is, either all workers work in piece-rate firms, or all work in salary firms.

When capital is an important factor of production, firms are not indifferent about which workers are employed by the firm. Fixed costs increase the value of high-ability relative to low-ability work-ers. Two-part piece rates are efficient and dominate one-part piece rates, which are never efficient when capital is a factor. Salaries, with output requirements, are efficient but tolerate workers of only one ability level. This is yet another reason why piece-rate firms are characterized by a more heterogeneous workforce. When effort is less costly to measure than is output quality, a salary based on effort is likely to dominate a piece rate.

Intertemporal strategic behavior is a sometimes noted problem with piece rates. Workers slack off because next period's rate de-pends on this period's output. This problem is not unique to piece rates. More important, it can always be efficiently offset by the ap-propriate reward in the early periods. Effects are summarized in Figure 7.3.

Figure 7.3

Pay by Output (Piece Rate)		Pay by Input (Salary)

	Output Monitoring Costs	
Low		High

	Alternative Use of Time $(\overline{w})$	
High		Low

	Worker Heterogeneity (σ^2_q)	
High		Low

	Measurement Error (σ^2_ϵ)	
Low		High

	Elasticity of Effort $[1/C'(E)]$	
High		Low

	Costs of Monitoring Effort	
High		Low

	Costs of Monitoring Quality	
Low		High

Appendix

Proof that Noise Reduces the Value of the Piece Rate

We desire to show that

(A1)
$$
t\int_{-\infty}^{\infty}\int_{0}^{q^*-\xi} qf(q)g(\xi)dqd\xi + (1-t)\overline{w}\int_{-\infty}^{\infty}\int_{0}^{q^*-\xi} f(q)g(\xi)dqd\xi
$$
$$
+ \int_{-\infty}^{\infty}\int_{q^*-\xi}^{0} qf(q)g(\xi)dqd\xi - \theta < t\int_{0}^{w} qf(q)dq
$$
$$
+ (1-t)\overline{w}F(\overline{w}) + \int_{\overline{w}}^{\infty} qf(q)dq - \theta.
$$

The θ drops out. Then, taking t of the last term on the left-hand side and adding it to the first term on the left-hand side allows us to rewrite the left-hand side as

$$
t\overline{q} + (1-t)\left[\overline{w}\int_{-\infty}^{\infty}\int_{0}^{q^*-\xi} f(q)g(\xi)dqd\xi + \int_{-\infty}^{\infty}\int_{q^*-\xi}^{\infty} qf(q)g(\xi)dqd\xi\right],
$$

where $\overline{q} \equiv E(q)$. Similarly, the right-hand side can be rewritten as

$$
t\overline{q} + (1-t)\left[\overline{w}F(\overline{w}) + \int_{\overline{w}}^{\infty} qf(q)dq\right].
$$

After canceling terms, the problem reduces to showing that

(A2)
$$
\overline{w}F(\overline{w}) + \int_{\overline{w}}^{\infty} qf(q)dq > \overline{w}\int_{-\infty}^{\infty}\int_{0}^{q^*-\xi} f(q)g(\xi)dqd\xi
$$
$$
+ \int_{-\infty}^{\infty}\int_{q^*-\xi}^{\infty} qf(q)g(\xi)dqd\xi.
$$

Define $\mu \equiv \xi$. Then the right-hand side of (A2) can be written as

(A3)
$$
\int_{-\infty}^{\infty}\left[\overline{w}\int_{0}^{\mu} f(q)dq + \int_{\mu}^{\infty} qf(q)dq\right]g(\xi)d\xi.
$$

Taking the derivative of the inside of (A3) with respect to μ yields:

(A4)
$$
\frac{d}{d\mu} = \overline{w}f(\mu) - \mu f(\mu).
$$

Setting this equal to zero implies that $\mu = \overline{w}$. Since the integral of the maximum is never exceeded by the maximum of the integral, setting $\mu = \overline{w}$ yields an upper bound to the right-hand side. But when $\mu = \overline{w}$, the right-hand side and left-hand side of (A2) are identical. Thus, for any nondegenerate distribution of ξ, the right-hand side exceeds the left-hand side of (A2). QED.

The worker's choice of a cutoff, q^*, is derived as follows. The problem for the worker is to choose some q^* such that, if $\hat{q} < q^*$, the worker quits. The worker's problem is to use the information given by $\hat{q}$ optimally to infer q and then to make a decision about his work location. The worker can earn $\overline{w}$ elsewhere and quits if

$$\hat{q} < q^*$$

or if

$$q < q^* - \xi.$$

The risk-neutral worker wants to choose q^* to solve

(A5) $$\max_{q^*} \left[\overline{w} \int_{-\infty}^{\infty} \int_0^{q^*-\xi} f(q)g(\xi)dqd\xi \ + \ \int_{-\infty}^{\infty} \int_{q^*-\xi}^{\infty} qf(q)g(\xi)dqd\xi \right] (1 - t).$$

The first term reflects that he earns $\overline{w}$ at the alternative job, and the double integral is the probability of observing $\hat{q} < q^*$. The second term is the expected output at the firm conditional on staying when $\hat{q} > q^*$. Differentiating (A5) with respect to q^* yields

$$\frac{d}{dq^*} = \overline{w} \int_{-\infty}^{\infty} f(q^* - \xi)g(\xi)d\xi - \int_{-\infty}^{\infty} (q^* - \xi)f(q^* - \xi)g(\xi)d\xi$$

or

(A6) $$\frac{d}{dq^*} = (\overline{w} - q^*) \int_{-\infty}^{\infty} f(q^* - \xi)g(\xi)d\xi - \int_{-\infty}^{\infty} \xi f(q^* - \xi)g(\xi)d\xi.$$

Although (A6) does not appear to be easily interpreted, a simple example proves this false. Suppose that ξ is distributed symmetrically around zero and that q is uniform between q_0 and q_1. When should the criterion level be set so that $q^* = \overline{w}$? Doing so would appear to provide first-best decision making.

For $q^* = \overline{w}$ to be an optimum, equation (A6) must equal zero. Rewrite (A6) as

$$\frac{d}{dq^*} = (\overline{w} - q^*)\int_{-\infty}^{\infty} f(q^* - \xi)g(\xi)d\xi + \int_{-\infty}^{q^*-q_1} \xi f(q^* - \xi)g(\xi)d\xi$$
$$+ \int_{q^*-q_1}^{q^*-q_0} \xi f(q^* - \xi)g(\xi)d\xi + \int_{q^*-q_0}^{\infty} \xi g(\xi)d\xi.$$

If $f(q)$ is a constant between q_0 and q_1, then this reduces to

(A7) $$\frac{d}{dq^*} = \frac{\overline{w} - q^*}{q_1 - q_0}\int_{q^*-q_1}^{q^*-q_0} g(\xi)d\xi + \frac{1}{q_1 - q_0}\int_{q^*-q_0}^{q^*-q_0} \xi g(\xi)d\xi.$$

In order for (A7) to equal zero at $q^* = \overline{w}$, it is sufficient that

$$q^* - q_1 = -(q^* - q_0)$$

(since ξ is distributed symmetrically around zero) or that

$$2\overline{w} = q_1 + q_0.$$

When $\overline{w} = 0$ and $q_0 = -q_1$, this holds. But, in general, the condition is not satisfied. In particular, suppose that $q_0, q_1 > 0$ and that $\overline{w} < E(q)$. Then from (A7) it can be shown that $q^* < \overline{w}$. This is intuitive. At the extreme, $w < q_0$. Then there is never any situation in which it is efficient to leave for the alternative job: q^* should be set at minus infinity so there is no possibility of $\hat{q} < q^*$. At the other extreme, $\overline{w} > q_1$. Then there is no efficient work at the piece-rate firm: q^* should be set to plus infinity so that no possibility of $\hat{q} > q^*$ exists.

The addition of noise, ξ, to the problem makes the criterion deviate from $\hat{q} \gtrless \overline{w}$. It also results in inefficient separation and inefficient retention.

8

Performance Pay and Productivity

A cornerstone of the theory in personnel economics is that workers respond to incentives. Specifically, it is a given that paying on the basis of output will induce workers to supply more output. Many sophisticated models have been offered, but they have gone largely untested because of a lack of data. Of course, there are some difficulties associated with performance pay schemes that have been pointed out in the literature.[1] There is a literature that examines the choice of payment schemes and its effects on profits and/or earnings.[2] But overall, there have been few attempts to examine the choice of payment scheme and its effect on output.[3] How sensitive is worker behavior to incentives and what specific changes in behavior are elicited? A newly available data set allows these questions to be answered.

The analysis in this chapter is based on data from Safelite Glass Corporation, a large auto glass company. During 1994 and 1995, after the introduction of new management, the company gradually changed the compensation method for its workforce, moving them from hourly wages to piece-rate pay. The effects, which are documented by examining the behavior of about 3,000 different workers over a 19-month period, are dramatic and completely in line with economic theory.

In what follows, the theory of piece-rate compensation is sketched with particular emphasis on the predictions that pertain to changes in the compensation method used by Safelite. The theory is backed up by the empirical results, the most important of which are:

1. A switch to piece-rate pay has a significant effect on average levels of output per worker. This is in the range of a 44-percent gain.

The original version of this chapter was published as: Lazear, E. P. (2000). Performance Pay and Productivity, in: American Economic Review, 90(5), 1346-1361.

2. The gain can be split into two components. About half of the increase in productivity results from the average worker producing more because of incentive effects. Some of the increase results from an ability to hire the most productive workers and possibly from a reduction in quits among the highest output workers. None reflects the "Hawthorne effect".

3. The firm shares the gains in productivity with its workforce. A given worker receives about a 10-percent increase in pay as a result of the switch to piece rates.

4. Moving to piece-rate pay increases the variance in output. More ambitious workers have less incentive to differentiate themselves when hourly wages are paid than when piece-rate pay is used.

The evidence implies that the choice of compensation method has important incentive effects, not that piece-rate schemes are more profitable. In equilibrium, firms choose a compensation method based on the costs and benefits of the various schemes. Firms that continue to pay hourly wages in equilibrium are those for which the benefits of paying an hourly wage, such as low monitoring costs and perhaps higher quality output, outweigh the costs in the form of lower output.

Some conclusions are unambiguous. Workers respond to prices just as economic theory predicts. Claims by sociologists[4] and others that monetizing incentives may actually reduce output are unambiguously refuted by the data. Not only do the effects back up economic predictions, but the effects are extremely large and precisely in line with theory.

The evidence allows somewhat broader interpretation. It is often difficult to obtain actual data on consumers and their reactions to changes in prices. Tests of even the most basic tenets of economic theory are difficult to perform, at least at a micro level. These data are well suited to that purpose. While experiments bear out the basic response of economic agents to prices, the data used in this chapter come from the real world rather than a laboratory setting. Compensation, which reflects the most important price that a consumer faces, truly matters to the workers in this setting, and they respond accordingly.

8.1. Modeling Choice of Pay Scheme: Hourly Wages versus Piece Rates

The primary motivation behind instituting a piece-rate scheme is to increase worker effort. While it may seem obvious that moving from hourly wages to piece rates would increase effort, it is not. When a firm institutes an hourly wage schedule, it usually couples the payment with some minimum level of output that is acceptable. It is possible, therefore, that the minimum acceptable output chosen for hourly wage workers exceeds the level of output that workers voluntarily choose under a piece rate. Further, it may be that the minimum level chosen under hourly wages is so high that only the most able workers can make the cut. When piece rates are instituted, more heterogeneity might be tolerated, resulting in lower average levels of output.

This suggests that the term "performance pay" is not very useful. Even if we restrict performance pay to refer to pay based on output (rather than input), a broad set of compensation schemes are included. Hourly wages that are coupled with some minimum standard could be called performance pay because an output-based performance standard must be met to retain employment. In fact, were workers homogeneous, an hourly wage structure with a minimum number of units tolerated per hour could achieve the efficient outcome.[5]

The conditions of the job determine which workers choose to accept employment. If standards are too strict, only the most able will find the job suitable, even at a high wage. A rough sketch of a framework that permits an analysis of the choice of standards and ability is given here.[6]

Define e to be the output level chosen by a worker, which is a function of underlying ability, A, and of effort choice. Suppose that the firm can observe e.

The firm that pays an hourly wage can specify some minimally acceptable level of output per hour e_0. The firm fires workers whose output falls consistently below e_0. Commensurate with that level of required output is some wage, W, that the firm offers. The worker's utility function is given by

$$(1) \qquad\qquad \text{Utility} = U(Y, X)$$

where Y is income and X is effort. Naturally, $U_1 > 0$ and $U_2 < 0$.

Let A denote ability. Then output, e, depends on ability and effort according to

$$(2) \qquad\qquad e = f(X, A)$$

with f_1, $f_2 > 0$. For any given required level of output e, and ability level, A, there is a unique level of effort X that satisfies (2). Denote by $X_0(A)$ the level of effort necessary to satisfy

$$(3) \qquad\qquad e_0 = f(X_0(A), A)$$

for the required level of effort e_0. It is clear that given (2),

$$\frac{\partial X}{\partial A} = \frac{f_2}{f_1},$$

which is negative. Higher-ability individuals need exert less effort to achieve a given level of output.

For any given pair of required output and wage, (e_0, W), there is a group of workers who will accept the job. The minimum-ability individual who will accept a job in lieu of leisure that requires e_0 of output to be produced is A_0 such that

$$(4) \qquad\qquad U(W, X_0(A_0)) = U(0, 0)$$

where $U(0, 0)$ is interpreted as the utility associated with leisure.

All workers with ability levels that exceed A_0 earn rents from employment because they are required only to produce e_0 of output, and the pain associated with producing it is lower than the pain for individuals with ability A_0, who are just indifferent between working and not. However, because there is competition from other firms, a worker must compare the rents earned at this firm with those offered elsewhere.

Those willing to work at the firm must not have work alternatives that are preferred to those here. The utility that a worker of ability A can get at another firm that does not necessary pay workers of all types the same amount is given by $U(\hat{W}(A), \hat{X}(A))$ where $\hat{W}$, $\hat{X}$ refer to the wage and effort levels on the best alternative job for a worker of ability A. Higher-ability workers are likely to find that the straight hourly wage job is not as attractive as an alternative that demands more, but pays more, even if the less able workers would find such a job onerous. Thus, there may exist an upper cutoff, A_h, such that

$$(5) \qquad U(W, X_0(A_h)) = U(\widehat{W}(A_h), \widehat{X}(A_h)).$$

Those who choose to work at the current firm have ability greater than A_0, but less than A_h.[7]

A linear piece rate takes the form $(be - K)$ where K is the implicit charge for the job. The utility that a risk-neutral worker receives can be written

$$\text{Utility under piece rate} = U(bf(X^*(A), A) - K, X^*(A))$$

where $X^*(A)$ is the effort that an individual with ability A chooses when faced with the piece rate b.

Figure 8.1

Compensation before and after at Safelite

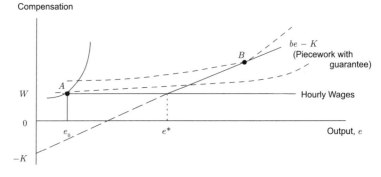

In order to fit the Safelite situation analyzed in the empirical section below, it is useful to model the effects of switching from an hourly wage with minimum standard to a piece rate with a minimum guarantee. As part of Safelite's plan, it offered a guarantee at approximately the former wage. The guarantee was coupled, presumably, with the same minimum standard of e_0 as before. Thus, the plan paid W to anyone who would have earned less than W under the piece rate, but paid the piece rate to all of those whose compensation by the piece-rate formula would have exceeded W. The scheme used is

$$\text{Compensation} = \max[W, be - K].$$

The situation is shown in Figure 8.1.

This scheme is typical of many salespersons' plans. A draw, in this case equal to W, is paid to workers whose output exceeds e_0 up to some level of output, e^*. At output greater than e^*, the worker begins to receive additional compensation for increases in output. As long as the worker produces $e > e^*$, his compensation is given by $be - K$. At most firms, workers who continually dip into their draw by producing $e < e^*$ are likely to find their employment terminated after some period of time.

Low-ability workers have steep indifference curves because additional effort must be compensated by large increases in income. The solid indifference curve through A is that of a relatively low-ability worker. The dotted indifference curve through A reflects the preferences of a higher-ability worker since it takes less income to induce him to provide a given amount of effort.[8]

The hourly wage schedule is shown by the step function that starts at zero, becomes vertical at e_0 and then horizontal at point A. The piece-rate schedule with guarantee is the same, except that compensation rises with output above e^*, as shown by the upward-sloping segment. When workers are offered hourly wages, all, even the most able, choose point A. When offered the piece-rate schedule with a guarantee, the less able worker (solid) still chooses A, but the more able worker (dotted) chooses B. This can be stated more formally in three propositions, which are proved in the Appendix.

Proposition 1. Effort does not decrease when the firm switches from hourly wages to piece rates, and as long as there is some ability type for which output rises, average effort increases.

Because the guarantee binds for some workers, but not for all, effort does not increase for all workers. Workers whose optimal level of effort lies to the left of e^* in Figure 8.1 gain nothing by increasing effort. But those whose optimal level of effort is sufficiently high may choose to work enough to be on the upward-sloping portion of the compensation function.

Another proposition can be stated, given two conditions:[9]

Condition 1: If a worker with ability A chooses to work at an effort level in the piece-rate range, then any worker with ability greater than A also chooses to work at an effort level in the piece-rate range.

Condition 2: If a worker with ability A chooses to work at an effort level in the wage-guarantee range, then any worker with ability less than A also chooses to work at an effort level in the wage-guarantee range.

Then,

Proposition 2. A sufficient condition for the average ability of the workforce to be non-decreasing, and more generally, to rise after the switch to piece rates is that some workers accept the guaranteed wage and some workers choose to work enough to be in the piece-rate range.

Average ability rises because the ability of the lowest-quality worker does not change as a result of the switch in compensation scheme, but the ability of the highest-quality worker rises. Because a piece rate allows the more able to work harder and receive more from the job, and because the hourly wage does not, more able workers prefer piece rates. The least-able worker is indifferent between the two schemes. Switching to piece rates has the effect of changing the pool of applicants to Safelite. Those who prefer to work at high levels of effort favor Safelite over other firms in the industry after the switch.

Finally,

Proposition 3. A sufficient condition for the range of worker ability and output to rise after the switch to piece rates is that some workers choose to work enough to be in the piece-rate range.

Even if underlying ability levels did not change, variance in productivity would rise because workers choose the same level of output under an hourly wage, but type-specific levels of output under piece rates. When it is recognized that the maximum ability level increases under a piece rate, the change in output variance becomes even greater.[10]

8.2. The Data

Safelite Glass Corporation is located in Columbus, Ohio, and is the country's largest installer of automobile glass. In 1994, Safelite, under the direction of CEO Garen Staglin and President John Barlow, implemented a new compensation scheme for the auto glass installers. Until January 1994, glass installers were paid an hourly wage rate, which did not vary in any direct way with the number of windows that were installed. During 1994 and 1995, installers were shifted from an hourly wage schedule to performance pay – specifically, to a piece-rate schedule. Rather than being paid for the number of hours that they worked, installers were paid for the number of glass units that they installed. The rates varied somewhat. On average installers were paid about $20 per unit installed. At the time that the piece rates were instituted, the workers were also given a guarantee of approximately $11 per hour. If their weekly pay came out to less than the guarantee, they would be paid the guaranteed amount. Many workers ended up in the guarantee range.

Staglin and Barlow changed the compensation scheme because they felt that productivity was below where it should have been. Productivity could have been raised by requiring a higher minimum level of output under a time-rate system. If all workers had identical preferences, this would have worked well. Given differences in work preferences, a uniform increase in required output, coupled with a wage increase, would not be received in the same way by all workers. In particular, the lower-output workers would find this more burdensome than the higher-output workers. In order to avoid massive turnover, the firm adopted a piece-rate schedule, which allowed those who wanted to work more to earn more, but also allowed those who would accept lower pay to put forth less effort.

Safelite has a very sophisticated computerized information system, which keeps track of how many units of each kind each installer in the company installs in a given week. Safelite provided monthly data. Since PPP (Performance Pay Plan) was phased in over a 19-month period, many workers were employed under both regimes. Thus, data on individual output are available for most installers both during the hourly wage period and during the PPP period. This before-and-after comparison with person-specific data provides a very clean body of information on which to base an analysis of performance pay incentives.

Performance Pay and Productivity

Table 8.1

Data Description

Variable	Definition	Mean	Standard Deviation
PPP dummy	A dummy variable equal to 1 if the worker is on PPP during that month	0.53	
Base pay	Hourly wage	$11.48	$2.94
Units-per-worker-per-day	Average number of units of glass installed by the given worker during the month in question	2.98	1.53
Regular hours	Regular hours worked during the given month	153	41
Overtime hours	Overtime hours worked that month	19	19
Pay	Pay actually received in a given month	$2,254	$882
Pay-per-day	Actual pay per eight hours worked; this differs from PPP pay in that the wage guarantee and other payments are included in the total	$107	$36
Cost-per-unit	Actual pay for a given worker, divided by the number of units installed by that worker in a given month	$40	$62
Log of pay-per-day	Log of actual pay per eight hours worked	4.62	0.29
Seperation dummy	A dummy equal to 1 if the employee quit during this month	0.047	

Notes: There were 2,755 individuals who worked as installers over the 19-month period covered by the data. The unit of analysis is a person-month. There are 29,837 person-months of good data. Pay-per-day is calculated only for workers whose total hours in a month exceeded 10 and cost-per-unit only for workers whose monthly units installed exceeded 3.

Some basic characteristics of the sample are reported in Table 8.1. The data are organized as follows. Each month provides an independent unit of observation. There are 38,764 person-months of data covering a 19-month period. Over the 19-month period, there was a total of 3,707 different individuals who worked for Safelite as installers. The number of "good" observations is 29,837 when partial months and observations with incomplete data are dropped from the data set.

There are a number of possible productivity measures. The one that most Safelite managers look to is units-per-worker-per-day. This is the total number of glass units per eight-hour day that are installed by a given worker. The units-per-worker-per-day number for each individual observation relates to a given worker in a given month. Thus, units-per-worker-per-day is the average number of units per eight-hour period installed by the given worker during the given month.

The average number of glass units installed per day over the entire period is 2.98, with a standard deviation of 1.53. The average actual pay was $2,254, which is above the amount that would be paid had the worker received exactly the amount to which he was entitled based on a straight piece rate. The difference reflects vacation, holiday, and sick pay, as well as two other factors. First, not all workers are on PPP during the period. When on hourly wages, some received higher compensation than they would have had they been on PPP, given the number of units installed. Of course, when a given worker switches to PPP, incentives change and his output may go up enough to cover the deficit. Second, even when workers are on PPP, a substantial fraction of person-weeks calculated on the basis of the PPP formula comes in below the guaranteed weekly compensation. The guarantee binds for those worker weeks, and actual pay then exceeds PPP pay. In all months after the introduction of PPP, at least some workers received the guaranteed pay and some earned more than the guarantee. Thus, the sufficient conditions for Propositions 2 and 3 are met throughout the period.

Table 8.2

Mean and Standard Deviations of Key Variables by Pay Structure

	Hourly wages		Piece rates	
N	13,106		15,246	
Variable	Mean	Standard deviation	Mean	Hourly wages
Units-per-worker-per-day	2.70	1.42	3.24	1.59
Actual pay	$2,228	$794	$2,283	$950
PPP pay	$1,587	$823	$1,852	$997
Cost-per-unit	$44.43	$75.55	$35.24	$49.00

Note: 1,485 observations were dropped because the individual spent part of the month on PPP and part on hourly wages.

Means for actual and PPP pay reveal almost nothing about the effects of PPP on performance and sorting. A more direct approach is needed. Table 8.2 presents some means of the key variables and breaks them down by the PPP dummy, which is set equal to one if the worker in question is on PPP during the given month.[11]

The story that will be told in more detail below shows up in the simple means. The average level of units-per-worker-per-day is about 0.54 units, or 20 percent higher in the piece-rate regime than in the hourly wage regime. Also, the variance in output goes up when switching from hourly wages to piece rates, as can be seen by comparing the standard deviations of 1.59 to 1.42.[12]

Thus, Propositions 1, 2, and 3, which state that both mean and variance in output rise when switching from hourly wages to piece rates, are borne out by the simple statistics. Further, note that there is good indication that profitability went up significantly with the switch. The cost per unit is considerably lower in the piece-rate regime than it is with hourly wages.[13]

The simple statistics do not take other factors into account. In particular, auto glass demand is closely related to miles driven, which varies with weather. Major storms, especially hail, also cause glass damage. Month effects and year effects matter. Perhaps more important, the management change that took place before PPP was instituted had other direct effects on the company that may have changed output during the sample period, irrespective of the switch to PPP. To deal with these factors, month and year dummies are included. The simplest specification in the first row of Table 3 yields a coefficient on the PPP dummy of 0.368. Evaluated at the mean of the log of units-per-worker-per-day, this coefficient implies that there is a 44-percent gain in productivity with a move to PPP.

Table 8.3

Regression Results

Regression number	Dummy for PPP person-month observation	Tenure	Time since PPP	New regime	R^2	Description
1	0.368 (0.013)				0.04	Dummies for month and year included
2	0.197 (0.009)				0.73	Dummies for month and year; worker-specific dummies included (2,755
3	0.313 (0.014)	0.343 (0.017)	0.107 (0.024)		0.05	Dummies for month and year included
4	0.202 (0.009)	0.224 (0.058)	0.273 (0.018)		0.76	Dummies for month and year; worker-specific dummies included (2,755 individual workers)
5	0.309 (0.014)	0.424 (0.019)	0.130 (0.024)	0.243 (0.025)	0.06	Dummies for month and year included

Notes: Standard errors are reported in parentheses below the coefficients. Dependent variable: ln output-per-worker-per-day. N: 29,837.

There are three possible interpretations of this extremely large and statistically precise effect. First, the gain in productivity may result from incentive effects associated with the program. Second, the gain may result from sorting. A different group of workers may be present after the switch to piece rates. Third, the pattern of implementation may cause a spurious positive effect. Suppose that Safelite picked its best workers to put on piece rates first. The PPP dummy coefficient would pick up an ability effect because high-ability workers would have more PPP months than low-ability workers. Unless ability is correlated with region in a particular way, the third explanation can be ruled out because Safelite switched its stores to PPP on a regional basis, starting with Columbus, Ohio, where the headquarters is located, and moving out. The other two effects can all be identified by using the data in a variety of ways.

When worker dummies are included in the regression, the coefficient drops to 0.197 from 0.368. The 0.197 is the pure incentive effect that results from switching from hourly wages to piece rates. Evaluated at the means, it implies that a given worker installs 22 percent more units after the switch to PPP than he did before the switch to PPP. This estimate controls for month and year effects. Individual ability is held constant as is shop location by including the person dummies. Approximately half of the 44-percent difference in productivity attributed to the PPP program reflects an incentive effect.

Nor does this gain appear to be a Hawthorne effect.[14] This can be seen by examining regression 3 in Table 8.3. The regression includes a variable for tenure and also one for time that the worker has been on the PPP program. It is zero for all months before the individual is on piece rates. It is the number of years that the individual has been on piece rates in the current person-month observation. For example, a worker who started 1994 on hourly wages and was switched to PPP on July 1, 1994 would have time since PPP equal to zero for the June 1994 observation, to 0.5 for the January 1995 observation, and to 1.0 for the June 1995 observation.

Consider the estimates with fixed effects in regression 4. The coefficient of 0.273 on time since tenure coupled with a PPP dummy coefficient of 0.202, means that the initial effect of switching from hourly wage to piece rate is to increase log productivity by 0.202. After one year on the program, the increase in log productivity has grown to 0.475. The Hawthorne effect would imply a negative coefficient on time since PPP. If the Hawthorne effect held, then the longer the worker were on the program, the smaller would be the effect of piece rates on productivity. The reverse happens here. After workers are switched to piece rates, they seem to learn ways to work faster or harder as time progresses.

8.3. Sorting

Tenure effects are large and significant. Using regression 3 of Table 8.3, it is estimated that one year of tenure raises log productivity by about 0.34. As is true of all tenure estimates, there are two interpretations. The first is learning. Turnover rates are over $4\frac{1}{2}$ percent per month, and the mean level of tenure is only about two-thirds of a year. It would not be surprising to see a worker increase his windshield installation rate dramatically during the first few months on the job. The second interpretation is one of sorting. Those who are not making it get fired or quit early. Regression 4 of the table assists in interpretation.

Regression 4 reports the estimates of the regression in regression 3, including fixed effects for individuals. Thus, the tenure coefficient reflects the effect of tenure for a given worker, averaged across individuals. The estimate of 0.20 on log productivity can be interpreted as the average effect of learning within the sample.[15] Thus, the effect of learning appears substantial.

The theory stated in Propositions 2 and 3 suggests that the optimal piece rate is implemented such that both mean and range of worker ability should rise after the switch to piece rates. The theory implies specifically that there should be no change in the number of low-ability workers who are willing to work with the firm, but that piece rates would allow high-ability workers to use their talents more lucratively. Thus, the top tail of the distribution should thicken.

Underlying ability is difficult to measure, but actual output can be observed. The fifth regression of Table 8.3 provides evidence on this point. "New regime" is a dummy set equal to one if the individual was hired after January 1, 1995, by which point almost the entire firm had switched to piecework. The theory predicts that workers hired under the new regime should produce more output than the previously hired employees.[16] Indeed, workers hired under the new regime have log productivity that is 0.24 greater than those hired under the old regime, given tenure.

Separations can also be examined. Suppose that workers must try the job for a while to discover their ability levels. Workers who find the job unsuitable leave. Then, looking at the relation of ability to separation rates (quits plus layoffs) before and after the switch to piece rates will provide evidence on the validity of Propositions 2 and 3.

A separation is defined as an observation in which the worker in question did not work during the subsequent month. Thus, a dummy is set equal to one in the last month of employment. Those workers who work through July 1995 (the last month for which data are available) have this dummy set equal to zero for every month in which they worked. A worker who was employed, say from January 1994 through February 1995, would have the dummy equal to zero in every month of employment, except for February 1995, when it would equal one.

Table 8.4 reports a breakdown of separation rates by PPP regime and by worker output deciles where output is defined as units-per-worker-per-day during the previous month.[17]

First note that the simple effect of a move to PPP increases turnover from 3.3 percent per month to 3.6 percent per month, but the difference is not statistically significant.[18] The direction of the change is not surprising since a major change in the pay system may make some of the incumbents unhappy enough to leave or may signal that the firm has become less tolerant of low productivity.

Table 8.4

Seperation Rates by Regime and Decile

Decile	Hourly regime			PPP regime			Difference between PPP and hourly separation rates	
	Separation rate	Number of observations	Standard error	Separation rate	Number of observations	Standard error	Difference	Standard error
Lowest								
0	0.041	1,641	0.005	0.039	1,285	0.005	-0.002	0.007
1	0.043	1,465	0.005	0.038	1,491	0.005	-0.006	0.007
2	0.042	1,358	0.005	0.037	1,625	0.005	-0.005	0.007
3	0.039	1,245	0.005	0.037	1,691	0.005	-0.002	0.007
4	0.037	1,282	0.005	0.034	1,693	0.004	-0.003	0.007
5	0.038	1,279	0.005	0.04	1,792	0.005	0.002	0.007
6	0.025	1,223	0.004	0.03	1,777	0.004	0.005	0.006
7	0.029	1,135	0.005	0.03	1,879	0.004	0.001	0.006
8	0.03	880	0.006	0.022	2,169	0.003	-0.008	0.007
9	0.033	2,437	0.004	0.027	339	0.009	-0.007	0.009
Highest								
Overall	0.033	13,945	0.002	0.036	15,741	0.002	0.003	0.002

Second, theory predicts that those at the higher end of the ability spectrum should see turnover rates that decline. Although the highest output deciles are the ones that experience the largest declines in separation rates, the differences are not statistically significant.

8.4. Fixed Effects

Some of the theoretical predictions can be tested by estimating person-specific fixed effects. Since the data set consists of multiple observations on a given individual over time and under different regimes, person-specific effects can be estimated. Fixed effects are estimated from a regression of the log of output-per-worker-per-day on tenure and time dummies. Should this be done using data from both regimes combined or from one or the other? Some workers were employed in both hourly wage and piece-rate regimes whereas some worked in only one regime. The theory implies that incentives are muted during the hourly wage period, so it is not clear that fixed effects based on output during the hourly wage period are good proxies for ability. This might suggest using the fixed effects estimated during the piece-rate regime for those who worked in both regimes. But then separation behavior over the two regimes cannot be examined since no one who worked in both hourly wage and piece-rate regimes left the firm during the hourly wage regime.

An alternative is to use the hourly wage regime estimated fixed effects, based on the argument that fixed effects are highly correlated across periods. Indeed, there is evidence of strong correlation. Figure 8.2 shows the scatter plot, which reveals the pattern. The correlation between the fixed effect from the hourly wage period and that from the piece-rate period is 0.72 with 1,519 observations. This correlation is high, but not perfect. There are some workers who performed relatively better under the hourly wage system than under the piece-rate system and vice versa. A regression of the fixed effect from the piece-rate regime on the same individual's fixed effect from the hourly wage regime yields a coefficient of 0.700 with a standard error of 0.017. The constant term is -0.04 with a standard error of 0.01. The effect of ability on effort is attenuated during the hourly wage period because there is less incentive to put forth effort. If the fixed effect of output in the piece-rate period measures true ability, whereas the fixed effect during the hourly wage period measures ability only imperfectly, then the coefficient in the regression of piece-rate fixed effects on hourly wage fixed effects is biased toward zero.[19] The fact that it equals 0.700 suggests that workers do reveal their abilities to a large extent even during the hourly wage period.[20]

This evidence provides a rationale for using the hourly wage-period fixed effects to examine turnover. The median level of fixed effect for those who leave no later than two months after the start of the piece-rate system (the leavers) is 0.15 with an upper bound of the 95-percent confidence interval of 0. 19. The median level of fixed effect for those who stay beyond the initial two months (the stayers) is 0.22 with a standard error of lower bound of the 95-percent confidence interval at 0.21. The medians are significantly different, with the more able, as measured by pre-period fixed effects, being more likely to stay.[21]

Figure 8.2

Scatterplot of Fixed Effects from the Two Regimes

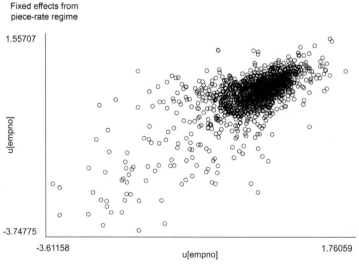

Fixed effects from hourly wage regime

Table 8.5

Variation in Fixed Effects

Regime	Number of individuals	Standard deviation in fixed effects	Difference between 90th and 10th percentile in fixed effects
Hourly wage	1,519	0.65	1.28
Piece rate	1,519	0.64	1.12

There is no evidence that the stayers have higher variance in ability than the leavers. The standard deviation of the fixed effects for the stayers is 0.68 and that for the leavers is 0.89, with number of observations equaling 1,511 and 659, respectively. More evidence on this point is presented in Table 8.5, where fixed effects estimated on hourly wage-regime data are computed for those individuals who worked in both regimes.

Again, the results of Table 8.5 suggest that the prediction about variance in ability finds no support in the fixed effects results.[22] The standard deviation in fixed effects among piece-rate workers is virtually identical during the piece-rate and hourly wage regime. The 90-10 percentile is higher during the hourly wage regime. Although Table 8.2 reveals an increase in the variance in output when the firm switches from hourly wages to piecework, the increase in variance does not reflect an obvious change in the dispersion of underlying ability.

Figure 8.3

Kernel Densities in the Two Regimes

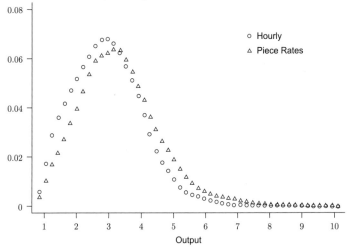

Table 8.6

Regression Results

Regression number	PPP dummy	R^2	Description
1	0.068	0.06	Dummies for month
	(0.005)		and year included
2	0.099	0.76	Dummies for month
	(0.004)		and year; worker-specific dummies included (2,755 individual workers)

Notes: Standard errors are reported in parentheses below the coefficients. Dependent variable: ln pay-per-day. Number of observations: 29,837.

Summarizing, it is clear that person-specific effects are important. They play a significant role in the interpretation of the results of Table 8.3, and their pattern is consistent with the theory in that their mean levels tend to rise as the firm goes from time rates to piece rates. They provide no support for the hypothesis that variance in underlying ability increases when the firm switches from time rates to piece rates. Ability is higher among those who work at the end of the sample period than among workers present at the beginning of the sample period. Most of the increase in ability is a result of selection through the hiring process that occurs after piece rates are adopted.

The effect of differential changes in turnover rates, hiring policy, and incentives can be summarized by the kernel densities of output shown in Figure 8.3. The two distributions look rather similar, but it is clear that the piece-rate distribution lies to the right of the hourly wage distribution. Further, the peak value of the density function during the piecework regime is lower than that of the hourly wage regime. There is less concentration of output around the modal value under piece rates than there is under hourly wages.[23]

8.5. Pay and Profitability

The effect of the program on pay can be traced also. Table 8.6 reports the effects of the switch to the PPP regime.

The log of pay-per-worker went up by 0.068, implying about a 7-percent increase in compensation. Recall that the increase in productivity for the firm as a whole was 44 percent. Regression 2 of Table 8.6 implies that the log of pay for a given worker rose by 0.099, implying a 10.6-percent gain in earnings. This is just under half the increase in per-worker productivity. Thus, the firm passes along some of the benefits of the gain in productivity to its existing workforce. The effect without worker dummies is smaller than that with worker dummies because the newer workers are paid less than the more senior workers whom they replace. Further, 92 percent of workers experienced a pay increase, with a quarter of the workers receiving increases at least as large as 28 percent.

Did profits rise? This depends on the increase in productivity relative to the increase in labor and other costs. Given the numbers (44-percent increase in productivity, 7-percent increase in wages), it is unlikely that other variable costs of production ate up the margin still given to the firm. The piece-rate plan seems to have been implemented in a way that likely made both capital and labor better off.[24]

There is one cost that has been ignored throughout. Piecework requires measurement of output. In Safelite's case, the measurement comes about through a very sophisticated information system. But the system involves people and machines that are costly. Indeed, in equilibrium, firms that pay hourly wages or monthly salaries are probably those for whom measurement costs exceed the benefits from switching to output-based pay.

In this case, the gains in productivity were very large. Further, the information systems were initially put in place for reasons other than monitoring worker productivity, having to do with inventory control and reduced installation lags. The economies of scope in information technology, coupled with the labor productivity gains, are probably large enough to cover whatever additional cost of monitoring was involved.[25]

8.6. Quality

One defect of paying piece rates is that quality may suffer.[26] In the Safelite case, most quality problems show up rather quickly in the form of broken windshields. Since the guilty installer can be easily identified, there is an efficient solution to the quality problem: The installer is required to reinstall the windshield on his own time and must pay the company for the replacement glass before any paying jobs are assigned to him. This induces the installer to take the appropriate amount of care when installing the glass in the first place. [27]

Initially, Safelite used another system that relied on peer pressure.[28] When a customer reported a defect, the job was randomly assigned to a some worker in the shop that was responsible for the problem.[29] The worker assigned to do the re-do was not necessarily the worker who did the original installation and the worker was not paid for doing the repair work. But workers knew the identity of the initial installer. If one installer caused his peers to engage in too many re-dos, his coworkers pressured him to improve or resign. More recently, the system was changed to assign re-do work to the worker who did the initial installation. Workers are not paid for the re-do, but they are not charged for the wasted glass or for other costs associated with the re-do, as a fully efficient system would require. The outcome has been that quality has gone up after the switch to PPP, rather than down. The firm surveys its customers on their satisfaction with the job. The customer satisfaction index rose from slightly under 90 percent at the beginning of the sample period to around 94 percent by the end of the sample period. Because re-dos are costly to the worker, he is motivated to get it right the first time around.

8.7. Piecework Is Not Always Profitable

It is interesting that the productivity gains are so large for this particular firm. Of course, this is only one data point and it is one where the case for piece rates seems especially strong. Output is easily measured, quality problems are readily detected, and blame is assignable.

Managerial and professional jobs may not be as well suited to piecework. The fact that the productivity gains are so large in this case is worthy of attention, but these results do not imply that all firms should switch to piece-rate pay.

Piece-rate pay, defined narrowly, is used sparingly in the United States. Although it is difficult to obtain data on the distribution of piece-rate work, one national survey, the National Longitudinal Survey of Youth,[30] asked whether a worker was on piece rates up through 1990. Results from this survey are shown in Table 8.7.

In a subsample of 7,438 workers, 3.3 percent reported being on piece rates. The number varies significantly by occupation. As expected, managers, whose output is difficult to measure, are least likely to be on piece rates. At the other extreme, about 14 percent of laborers are paid piece rates. The use of incentive pay, broadly defined, is more widespread. Pencavel (1977 p. 228, Table 2) reports a peak of 30 percent of workers in manufacturing who received incentive pay in the United States in 1945-1946, with a downward trend afterward.

The relative paucity of piece-rate pay in the United States is not particularly disturbing for this study. For one thing, piece rates remain more prevalent in other countries. For example, using a data set on manufacturing in Sweden (which accounts for 20 percent of the workforce), it is found that 22 percent of workers received piece-rate pay as late as 1990. But even were this not the case, the experiment would be relevant. As far as the workers are concerned, the effect of a change in compensation was exogenous, and the data consist of about 3,000 independent worker responses to that common change. The implication of the study is not that firms should switch to piece-work, but rather that when workers faced a new compensation scheme, they responded by altering effort, turnover, and labor-supply behavior in the way predicted by theory.

Table 8.7

Piece-Rate Proportions in the National Longitudinal Survey of Youth

Occupation	Number in occupation in NLSY	Percent piece rate
Professional/technical	1,848	1.4
Managers/officials/proprietors	468	0.9
Sales	477	1.3
Clerical	1,522	1.3
Craftsmen	2,278	3.6
Operatives	296	9.8
Nonfarm labor	543	13.8
Farm labor	6	16.7
TOTAL	7,438	3.3

8.8. Summary and Conclusions

The results imply that productivity effects associated with the switch from hourly wages to piece rates are quite large. The theory implies that a switch should bring about an increase in average levels of output and in its variance. These predictions are borne out. The theory does not imply that profits must rise. Market equilibrium is characterized by firms that choose a variety of compensation methods. Firms choose the compensation scheme by comparing the costs and benefits of each scheme. The benefit is a productivity gain. Costs may be associated with measurement difficulties, undesirable risk transfers, or quality declines.

The theory above implies that average output per worker and average worker ability should rise when a firm switches from hourly wages to piece rates. The minimum level of ability does not change, but more able workers, who shunned the firm under hourly wages, are attracted by piece rates. As a result of incentive effects, average output per worker rises. Thus, average ability and output, as well as variance in output and range of ability, should rise when a firm switches from hourly wages to piece rates.

The effects of changing the compensation method were estimated using worker-level monthly output data from Safelite Glass Corporation. The primary predictions of the theory are borne out. Moving to a piece-rate regime is associated with a 44-percent increase in productivity for the company as a whole. Part of the gain reflects sorting, part reflects incentives, and some may reflect the pattern in which the scheme was implemented. The incentive effect of the piece-rate scheme accounts for an increase in productivity of about 22 percent. The rest of the 44-percent increase in productivity is a result of sorting toward more able workers or possibly some other factors. Sorting occurs primarily through the hiring process, where a disproportionate share of new hires come from higher ability groups after the switch to piece rates. There is no strong evidence that the change to piece rates increases separations relatively more among lower-output workers. Nor is there evidence of an increase in range or variance in underlying ability after the switch to piecework.

Since the data measure actual productivity, tenure effects on productivity (rather than wages) can be estimated. Tenure effects on productivity are found to be large. Part reflects learning on the job, but a significant fraction reflects sorting that induces the least productive workers to leave first. Also, time since the introduction of the piecework scheme is positively associated with productivity.

Workers captured some of the return from moving to piece rates. The average incumbent worker's wages rose by just over 10 percent as a result of the switch. Over 90 percent of the workers had higher pay during the piece-rate period than they did during the hourly wage period.

Appendix

Proof of Proposition 1:

Output cannot fall below e_0 because of the firm-imposed constraint at e_0. But output may exceed e_0 if for some A, $A_0 \leq A \leq A_h$,

(A1) $$U(W, X_0(A)) < U(bf(X^*(A), A) - K, X^*(A))$$

where $X^*(A)$ is the effort level chosen by worker of type A given piece rate b. As long as there is some type A for whom output rises, average output must rise.

Proof of Proposition 2:

If any choose to work in the piece-rate range, then surely the worker with the highest ability chooses to work in this range. But the highest-ability worker cannot, except in the rarest coincidence, be A_h. If A_h chooses to work in the piece-rate range, then A_h, who was indifferent to working under hourly wages, is at worst indifferent to working under piece rates, but more generally, strictly prefers the piece rate. If A_h earns rents under the new plan, then A_h is no longer the marginal worker. There exists an A_h^* with $A_h^* > A_h$ who would now be the marginal worker, i.e., the worker for whom

$$U(bf(X^*(A_h^*), A_h^*) - K, A_h^* = U(\widehat{W}(A), \widehat{X}(A))$$

where $X^*(A_h^*)$ is defined as the effort for type A_h^* under piece rates b and where $\widehat{W}$, $\widehat{X}$ are the wage and effort on the alternative job.

Also, if any accept the wage guarantee, then surely A_0 accepts the guarantee. We know that A_0 is willing to work for W at effort e_0 because A_0 worked under these terms before. Furthermore, since the guarantee has not been made any more attractive, no one with $A < A_0$ is willing to work for the guaranteed wage. Since the lower bound on ability remains the same and the upper bound does not fall and generally rises, average ability does not decrease and generally increases after the switch to piecework.

Proof of Proposition 3:

From the Proof to Proposition 2, $A_h^* \geq A_h$. But A_0 cannot rise because the wage guarantee is still available so A_0 remains willing to work. This is sufficient to imply that range or variance in ability rises. Also, since all workers choose to produce e_0 under the hourly wage, but some produce in the piece-rate range with the new scheme, positive variance in A implies positive variance in e under piece rates.

9

The Job as a Concept

Few managers would deny that slots or jobs are well defined concepts fundamental to the organization of a firm. And yet standard production theory has provided no technological role for the job. Indeed, it has ignored jobs altogether.

In this analysis I seek to enlarge our knowledge of jobs in two ways. First, I review the labor literature, pointing out the place the various theories assign to the job as a concept. Second, I apply a panel data set derived from studying a large organization to determine whether the job concept has any significance. Specifically, I ask whether assignment to a job affects real variables such as wages and turnover rates.

The key empirical findings are:

1. Changing jobs is the key to increasing wages. Individuals who change jobs are the ones who experience growth in wages.

2. Within-job heterogeneity is important. Individuals who remain on the job longer do worse than those who are promoted out early. Wages actually decline with job tenure, probably reflecting the fall in the average worker's quality with length of time in the job.

3. The pattern of job-to-job turnover within the firm mimics the pattern often observed for movement between firms: turnover occurs most frequently at the beginning of the job and dies out with additional experience.

The original version of this chapter was published as: Lazear, E. P. (1990). The Job as a Concept, in: Performance Measurement, Evaluation, and Incentives, William J. Bruns, (Eds.), Boston: Harvard Business School Press, 1992. Copyright © 1992 by Harvard Business Publishing; all rights reserved. This work was supported in part by the National Science Foundation. I am grateful to Edward Glaeser for excellent research assistance.

4. In almost all jobs significant hiring from the outside occurs. Although some jobs are more likely to be entry points into the firm than others, this firm has no strict ports of entry.

9.1. The Theory of Jobs and Its Historical Relevance

The concept of a "job" is an important one. Does the person define the job or does the job define the person? This question lies at the heart of modern theories of the labor market. The traditional, institutional view emphasizes the job as the unit of analysis. Although some recognize that skills affect an employee's placement in a specific slot, this view tends to assert that workers can be substituted for one another and that individuals' allocation to jobs generally reflects luck or other factors.[1] The literature that most forcefully advances this view deals with internal labor markets.[2]

The other view, dominant since the 1960s, derives from the theory of human capital.[3] This view focuses on the supply-side approach, arguing that workers invest in productivity-enhancing skills, which they bring into the labor market. The job is unimportant. Wages and lifetime wealth are determined primarily by the individual's stock of human capital, although it is admitted that psychic aspects of the job (such as danger, dirtiness, and undesirable hours) also affect monetary compensation. Occupation and industry variables are secondary in this theory. In fact, jobs are never even mentioned.

The concept of a job has no place in standard production theory. Labor and capital are defined as continuous variables. Slots and other integer problems are ignored. When labor differentiation is discussed, it is generally about the skills or quality of the workforce, rather than the tasks to which the labor is assigned. The view reflected in this literature deviates significantly from the businessperson's concept of labor markets. Personnel managers and department heads are usually aware of their slot allocations. But some evidence suggests that jobs are often tailored to the individual at high levels in the firm's hierarchy. A job is created, for example, to accommodate a former CEO when a new person steps into the job.[4]

9.1.1. Tournaments

A growing body of analytic literature emphasizes jobs or slots. The most obvious example, and the one with which I am most closely associated, is the tournament model.[5] In this model, workers compete with one another for a limited number of slots. By beating his or her competitors, the winner obtains a coveted job and the higher earnings that go with it. In this theory, jobs are another name for wage categories, but with two key provisions.

First, assignment to the job is based on relative rather than absolute performance. The individual who gets to be boss is not the one who is good, but rather the one who is best (even if both are excellent).

A second and related provision is that the number of slots is fixed in advance. Wages are assigned to the slots, not to the individuals. The reason for this arrangement is that appropriate incentive effects are generated by relative comparisons.

The attachment of wages to slots means that employers are less able to renege on promises to pay high wages if a standard is met. In this case, because someone must receive the high wage, employers gain little by lying.[6]

Indeed, it is the fixed slots that distinguish tournament incentive structures from others based on relative performance. One reason for using a tournament is to difference out random factors or common noise. Workers who are risk averse do not like their compensation to vary with market conditions, over which they have no control. A tournament eliminates the effect of common external forces on compensation. If the economy is in a slump, it affects all salespersons equally. Rewarding salespeople on their performance relative to that of their peers thus eliminates the common noise of a recessionary economy.

Tournaments are not the only way to eliminate the effects of common noise. For example, paying workers on the basis of their performance relative to the group mean eliminates common noise. This scheme differs from the tournament, however, in that tournaments imply slots, whereas relative pay by itself does not. With tournaments, only one individual gets the first prize or top job. One and only one gets the second prize or second-best job, and so forth. With relative compensation, the structure of wages and positions evolves ex post, rather than ex ante. Tournament models emphasize relative performance, but also rely on jobs themselves.

9.1.2.   *Insurance*

Tournament models are not the only reason to be concerned about the concept of jobs. Jobs are at the center of any discussion of insurance and worksharing. Firms may reduce hours during downturns without eliminating jobs (if only by variations in overtime), but layoffs are still an accepted part of the American work environment. Thus, a job may be defined as the right to work in a specified state of the economy. Cutting employment by reducing the number of heads means that there must be a fixed cost, either in production or in leisure, that makes it preferable to set up jobs of fixed length and vary the number of them according to the state of the economy. Fixed costs in production are easy to imagine. Setup time in the office or shop is required for many production processes. Transportation time to work is an obvious fixed cost that it pays to amortize. Similarly, leisure may have fixed costs. Few individuals go on four-hour ski trips because travel time, packing time, and time merely to switch gears are required. Although the number of slots varies with economic conditions, slots have a well-defined meaning.

The insurance literature places a great deal of weight on who holds a job.[7] Here, workers are regarded as interchangeable. Little emphasis is assigned to level of skill or other characteristics in determining order of layoff. The individual who is laid off is drawn randomly from some distribution, and the investigation relates to the compensation of the two groups over the cycle. This approach resembles the institutional analyses, which treat workers as interchangeable and focus on jobs as the unit of analysis.

9.1.3.   *Hierarchies*

The literature on hierarchies and on the structure of control in organizations is inherently cast in terms of jobs.[8] The hierarchy analyses are explicit in their use of jobs. Most assume that each position has a span of control over a fixed number of other positions. Thus, the shape of the pyramid is determined ex ante, although the size of the firm, the number of levels, and the quality of the workforce are endogenous.

Contemporary theories of control in organizations also assume that slots are crucial. Here the question is whether projects should be evaluated vertically or horizontally. In a vertical organization, only projects accepted at lower levels are evaluated by more senior individuals. But seniority implies that the job, rather than the incumbent, defines the activity. The individual who is supervisor is assigned responsibility for making decisions on approved projects. Someone is always in that role. The human capital approach would assign authority to individuals based on the skills that they possessed. Rather than assigning all authority in advance to one supervisor, authority would be determined only after the incumbent's qualifications were known.

9.1.4. *Hedonics*

Hedonic wage analysis also dignifies the concept of jobs. Proponents of this school of thought have emphasized the characteristics of the job. The focus is not on the individual's skills or attributes but rather on the attributes of the position itself. For example, some jobs have more variable employment schedules than others. It is well known that durables manufacturing is more procyclic than health care. Researchers have found as much as a 25% wage premium for working in the most cyclically sensitive industries.[9] The layoff pattern attaches to the job, not to the individual who holds it. Layoffs are not high in manufacturing because the individuals who work there enjoy losing their jobs. Layoff rates are high as a result of demand conditions which pertain to the industry and which consequently dictate the duration of jobs in the industry.

Similarly, jobs with significant safety hazards tend to pay higher wages as a compensation differential.[10] The higher wages are attached to the jobs because the jobs themselves are risky, not because the workers who hold them are clumsy. The hedonic wage literature is thus the best example of empirical analysis that focuses on the characteristics of jobs rather than workers.

This approach has permeated the business community as well. Consulting firms such as Hay Associates place a great deal of emphasis on jobs and their characteristics. Their surveys and resulting salary recommendations adjust for the skill requirements, technical know-how, accountability, and pleasantness of work associated with a job. Although the incumbent may help to define the job, such analyses are targeted on deciding the salary appropriate to the position rather than to the individual who holds it.

9.1.5.   Investment

Even human capital theory offers a role for the concept of a job. Some jobs offer more opportunity for advancement than others. In some fields, young workers spend a great deal of time and effort acquiring human capital, which makes them more productive in later work years. In other fields, human capital is less important. One way to define jobs is by the opportunities for technological investment available to workers. Different career paths are available, but the opportunity for investment is fixed in advance, with the workers assigned to those paths determined in some maximizing fashion.[11] Unlike other theories that deal with job structures, human capital theory does not assert that the number of slots must be fixed in advance. If more investors show up at the door during a period, this theory assumes that the firm can accommodate them by creating more positions of the investment type. Jobs dictate, ex ante, the amount of investment that the incumbent undertakes. Individuals can choose the amount that they invest only by choosing the appropriate job.

One interpretation is that the opportunity for human capital investment is one of the characteristics of the job that enter the hedonic wage function. An alternative view is that jobs are unimportant in determining how much investment occurs. Workers simply alter the amount of time that they spend investing and working to suit their optimal investment profile, irrespective of job assignment.

9.1.6.   Collection of Tasks

The final interpretation of a job is the most traditional one. A job can be defined as a collection of tasks. The tasks need not be hierarchic, nor need they be compensated in any specific way. In this sense, a job is defined as a partition of the firm's technology.

9.2. Some Specific Questions

It is somewhat of an overstatement to dichotomize theories into those which look at jobs and those which look at workers, but previous work in labor economics, especially empirical work, has paid little attention to jobs. This chapter is an attempt to remedy that oversight. The general questions are, "Do jobs matter?" and "Do firms behave as if they have some reasonably well-defined idea of slots in mind when they make decisions?" Because most empirical work follows from human capital models, such questions have been all but ignored in previous years. In the empirical section of this chapter, I address these general questions. But more specific questions can be asked as well.

9.2.1. Jobs and Wages

How does a worker's placement in a job affect his or her wages and lifetime wealth? Suppose that two otherwise identical individuals end up working different jobs in the same firm, purely by chance. Will their lifetime wealth levels differ? Does the job path matter, or does one's stock of human capital dominate the determination of wages? That is, do jobs determine wages or do the individual's characteristics determine wages? It has been argued that once occupation and industry are held constant, male-female wage differential is slight.[12] Is the same true for other human capital variables, such as education and prior experience?

A related question is important. Wages in one job may be higher than wages in another, but the job path of which the lower-wage job is a part may provide higher expected lifetime wealth than the typical path of which the higher-wage job is part. This result would be expected if human capital were important and if wages reflected the different levels of productivity associated with the investment period. Alternatively, steeper profiles that start lower could reflect an incentive mechanism, which underpays young workers and overpays old workers as an instrument of motivation.[13]

9.2.2. Jobs and Turnover

It is well known that the varying turnover rates of workers are a function of demographic characteristics and of tenure with the firm.[14] But jobs may have different turnover rates, independent of the incumbents. In fact, it may be argued that the job determines the turnover rate and that once this rate is held constant, no demographic effects remain. Demographic characteristics may be important in placing individuals in jobs, but demographics may have no independent effect on anything real.

9.2.3. Movers versus Stayers

Differences in job assignment may reflect heterogeneity in the population. One possibility is that individuals who start out in high-wage positions tend to remain in high-wage positions throughout their tenure with the firm, an example of a fixed unobserved effect. Some individuals may have higher levels of ability that are not held constant by the variables included in the regression. Alternatively, ability may be constant but some workers may be favored for varied reasons. It is quite possible that a worker once favored would tend to remain that way. Unfortunately, the data used here will not distinguish between unobserved heterogeneity, either in ability or treatment, and actual productivity-based reasons for different wages.[15]

9.2.4. Classification into Jobs

Comparing differences in job assignments raises the question of how those assignments are determined. A basic question is whether it is possible to explain job assignments systematically. Demographics, seniority, or past job assignments may be good predictors of future job assignments, but it is also possible that nothing predicts job assignments very well. If the latter description fits, it gives more credence to the hypothesis that individuals are alike and job assignments are gained by sheer luck. Of course, one can always argue that unobservables must make up for differences in observed ability, or individuals would not be assigned to the jobs. But if they did, one would still expect the measured ability variables to matter.

9.2.5. Careers

Another question is whether an interesting pattern of background variables affects assignment of jobs. Aside from the issues of whether race and sex matter (which are not our focus in this study), it is interesting to know whether "careers" occur within firms. An individual may move from assembly-line worker to foreman to supervisor and dead end there. Another may move from secretary to administrative assistant to manager I to general manager. It may be that production workers rarely become managers, whereas clericals have a higher probability of moving into the managerial track. These career paths would be interesting to document. As far as I am aware, they have not been studied.

9.2.6.   Ports of Entry

One's casual impression is that very little hiring occurs at upper levels in management. Most individuals are promoted from within, implying that the firm has entry-level jobs. More concretely, the probability of having held another job in the company is expected to be positively related to the position of the job in the firm's hierarchy. But the exact relation is an empirical question. A weak result implies that the firm has no real "ports of entry." A stronger one implies that some jobs are prerequisites for others, a premise that is worth documenting.[16]

9.2.7.   The Data

The data used in the analysis come from the personnel files of one large corporation. Data cover a thirteen-year period from the late 1970s through the 1980s. Because the data are from only one company, this analysis is closer to an econometric case study than to an empirical study claiming to represent the bigger picture. Still, the corporation is a large one, and we have no reason to believe it is idiosyncratic. Higher-level managerial employees are not included in the data set, and so all information about promotions and job mobility relates to individuals in jobs paying less than $100,000 a year in 1989.

About 100,000 people worked for the company at some time during the thirteen-year period. We have slightly fewer than .5 million records, each record consisting of an observation for an individual during one year. If all the employees in the data set had worked during all thirteen years, we would find about 1. 3 million records. That as many as .5 million remain suggests that a significant number of individuals had relatively lasting careers with the corporation.

The sample is restricted to full-time employees. Some individuals are hourly employees and some are on monthly salary. When conversion was necessary, a monthly salary was computed for hourly workers by multiplying the hourly wage by 173.93.[17] The variables, definitions, and sample statistics are reported in Table 9.1.

For confidentiality, descriptions of industry and occupation are deleted or disguised. As far as I can tell, they are not relevant to any of the statistical tests or conclusions. It is convenient to think of this firm as a manufacturer of durable goods. The firm is mature, having been in business for about fifty years. Management changed hands about halfway through that period. Output is somewhat sensitive to business cycles in this industry.

Table 9.1

Means and Standard Deviations

Variable	Description	Mean	Standard Deviation
SAL	Salary per month	2,182.22	1,137.32
ED	Years of education		
	(12 = high school completed)	12.35	1.73
COTEN	Yaers in company	17.13	8.77
JOBTEN	Years in job	12.34	8.28
CHG	Average number of job changes for		
	each individual, 1977 - 1990	0.15	0.50
PROM	Average number of promotions for		
	each individual, 1977 - 1990	0.08	0.30

Workers are separated into hourly and salary categories. These correspond roughly to production workers and clericals, the latter including managers as well.

We find a number of advantages in using data on one company.

First, national panel data sets do not permit extensive analysis at the firm level. Thus, questions on subjects such as promotion paths or ports of entry simply cannot be answered using a panel data set.

Second, even when data sets include significant detail on individual firms, the results tend to average within-firm and between-firm effects. Unless we had many observations from each company, we would not be able to ascertain whether a positive correlation between promotions and wage growth meant that individuals who were promoted received larger raises or that companies in which promotions were common had steeper age-earnings profiles.

Third, most national data sets do not carry detailed information on job assignments within firms. For example, in the Panel Study of Income Dynamics, within-firm job changes were followed only in the data collected during the 1980s.[18] Significant career paths cannot be traced in national data sets of this kind.

9.3. Empirical Analysis

The distinction between human capital-based theories and job-based theories of the labor market is useful from the conceptual point of view. But distinguishing between the two theories is quite difficult empirically. Although my argument touches on human capital issues, the primary goal in our empirical analysis is to study issues in which jobs are the important explanatory variables. This area has been neglected in favor of traditional analyses of human capital and earnings.

Furthermore, most work on job mobility has been focused on changes between firms rather than within firms, perhaps because the data bases available lent themselves to this type of analysis. It is time to give movement from job to job within the firm at least some of the attention that has been paid to movement between firms, and to ask questions about the causes and effects of job movement among firms. The rate of interfirm job turnover sharply declines with experience on the job. Is this reduction observed for job changes within firms as well?

9.3.1. *Jobs and Variation in Wages*

We must determine the correlation between jobs and wage variation if we are to determine the role of jobs within the firm. One possibility is that jobs are simply another name for wages. If a different job were defined for each grade and step combination in the federal GS system, the result would be one wage for each job, for grade and step uniquely determine the compensation that the worker receives. Skill and experience probably matter in determining grade and step, but no salary variation appears within the grade-step category. Probably it is more accurate, however, to classify the job as a grade rather than a gradestep. Thus within each job we find as much variation as the different steps allow.

Job classifications such as these may be somewhat arbitrary, but they are useful tools for analyzing the individual and the firm. Choosing a meaningful definition of jobs within the firm is a crucial first step in analyzing my data set. The definition must help explain wage variation within the firm, and it must form a basis for considering issues of mobility, especially promotion and entry into the firm.

In the subject firm, jobs are assigned five-digit codes. As specificity increases, the job becomes synonymous with wage. This parallel is easily documented by looking at Table 9.2, row 1. The R^2 that is reported comes from an analysis of variance; that is, a regression of individual monthly earnings levels on a series of job dummies. In the first row, each of the five-digit codes is considered as defining a different job, for a total of 791 jobs in the firm. At this level, the job is almost synonymous with wage. As the ANOVA results show, 95% of the variation in monthly earnings can be accounted for by the job dummies.

Table 9.2

Monthly Earnings Variations (ANOVA). Within Jobs versus between Jobs

Level of Job Definition	R^2	Number of Jobs
5 digit	.958	791
4 digit	.923	371
3 digit	.814	134
2 digit	.791	45
1 digit	.373	5

Number of employees = 19,023.

Notes: The analysis of variance reports the proportion of total variance removed by a regression of salaries on job dummies; that is, it shows the deviations from within-job salary means as a proportion of total deviations from the salary grand mean.

Thus, most of the variation in earnings is between jobs, not within jobs, when the job is defined by its five-digit classification.

At the other extreme, if the job is defined as the one-digit classification, with the other four digits possibly signifying level, location, or specific task or seniority within the job, then only five "jobs" are found within the firm and those five explain only 37% of the variation in wages. At the one-digit level, then, most of the job variation is within rather than between jobs. Of course, we could define job at the zero-digit level, leaving only one job in the firm! Then all the variation would be within the job and none between.

I have chosen the two-digit definition of the job for several reasons. First, moving from the two- to the three-digit definition does little to increase our power to explain variation in earnings. Second, what is gained comes at the cost of tripling the number of jobs. Because this condition would reflect many parallel jobs at the same levels, the two-digit analysis is a more reasonable choice. Furthermore, when mobility is considered, the two-digit level offers the advantage of larger cell sizes. Though admittedly arbitrary, the results shown below suggest that the two-digit job classification is a meaningful one.[19]

9.3.2. Wage Growth

A more direct way to examine the importance of jobs is to use the panel aspect of the data. This approach shows that job changes in a given year occur for some workers, but not for others. Yet all workers receive raises. In Table 9.3, we examine the effects of job changes on earnings growth over the worker's entire career with the firm.[20]

Table 9.3

Job Changes, Promotions, and Wage Growth (Dependent variable = average annual percentage of change in real wages)

	1	2
Intercept	0.082	.0084
	(.0003)	(.0003)
Number of job changes	-.0114	.0044
	(.0006)	(.0003)
Number of promotions	.029	
	(.001)	
Number of years in	-.00129	-.00131
sample	(.00003)	(.00004)
R^2	.06	.04
N	33,290	33,290

Notes: The sample size is larger than that of Table 9.2 because it includes any individual who worked during the thirteen-year period.

In Table 9.3, we look at average wage growth over an individual's career as a function of job changes. The results reveal that promotions positively affect wages, as we'd expect, for promotion is defined as a move from one job to another having a higher mean wage. Any job change other than a promotion is lateral or a demotion, and so the coefficient on such internal job changes is negative. Finally, the coefficient on the years in the sample is negative as well. The reason is best understood by considering the second specification, which suppresses the distinction between promotions and other job changes. For a specified number of job changes, an individual with more years in the sample has spent longer on each job. Such individuals are likely to be the losers – workers who have not been promoted. Thus, remaining in a job for a long time has adverse implications for salary growth.[21]

The results explain why the two-digit job definition is meaningful for this analysis. First, a significant amount of switching occurs. The average number of job changes is .17 per worker year. Second, most job changes are promotions. About two-thirds of the job changes in the sample are promotions. This proportion can also be observed when we see that the coefficient on job changes goes from negative to positive when we omit promotions from the regression. The result implies a positive (partial) correlation between promotions and job changes.

The Job as a Concept

Table 9.4

Annual Wage Growth (Dependent variable: percentage of real wage change between $t - 1$ and t)

Variable	
Intercept	.012
	(.002)
Company tenure	-.0011
	(.0001)
Promotion	.191
	(.011)
Job change	.021
	(.009)
R^2	.005
N	228,000

Notes: Exact N not available.

Finally, job change is the key to the story of wage growth in this firm. Without job change, even at the two-digit level, Column 2 of Table 9.3 reveals that real wages would fall after about seven years of experience. (At seven years, the negative experience effect is larger than the intercept.) More accurately, individuals who are in the sample for more than seven years and who experience no job change are expected to see a decline in real wages each year. The most reasonable explanation for this decline is that these workers are not valuable enough to earn promotions. The longer an individual has been in the job without a promotion, the lower his or her expected quality as a worker. Table 9.5 presents more evidence on this subject.

Another way to examine the same issue is by looking at annual changes in wages as a function of job change. In Table 9.4, each two-year interval is treated as an observation. The form of the dependent variable is

(1)
$$\frac{W_{it} - W_{it-1}}{W_{it-1}}$$

where W_{it} is the wage for person i in period t.

Table 9.4 confirms the findings shown in Table 9.3. Individuals who won promotions got 21% (.19 + .02) higher average raises in that year than individuals who did not. (Remember that growth in Table 9.3 refers to average wage growth over the entire career, whereas Table 9.4 treats each year separately.) Individuals who experience job changes other than promotions still experience wage growth, but by an order of magnitude less.

250

Table 9.5

Earnings Functions for Movers versus Stayers

	Movers	Stayers
Constant	7.239	7.063
	(0.042)	(0.014)
Education	.0085	.0088
	(.0030)	(.0010)
Tenure	.0117	.0152
	(.0006)	(.0002)
R^2	.10	.28
N	2,928	16,044

Notes: Dependent variable in ln (monthly salary in 1989).

The average individual in the sample received .02 promotion per year. At worst, an individual might never receive a promotion. At best he or she may be promoted repeatedly until reaching the top job.

The problem with the analyses in Tables 9.3 and 9.4 is that they treat promotions as annual events independent of the past and future. The specification in Table 9.4 ignores, for example, the effect of promotions on subsequent wages. This reading neglects the entire concept of a career path. It may be that future growth in wages, and indeed future promotions, are functions of past promotion. In the next section we investigate these issues.

9.3.3. Careers

One way to think about careers is to imagine two basic groups of workers – movers and stayers. Movers get promoted and move up the corporate ladder. Stayers never get promoted, but remain in their first job throughout their entire career with the firm.

We have various sensible ways of defining movers and stayers. I have chosen to define stayers as the group of workers who never changed jobs and movers as the group who changed jobs at least once during their career. Earnings functions are estimated separately for each group. Those regressions are reported in Table 9.5.

From the earnings regressions in Table 9.5 and 9.6, it is possible to predict the lifetime wealth of movers versus stayers. Of course, turnover behavior may differ across groups, as I document below. The wealth simulations are conditional on the assumption that the careers of workers last thirteen years. (The number thirteen is selected so that earnings can be estimated without extrapolating outside the period of the sample.)

Table 9.6

Starting Log Wages

Year	Movers' Log Wage	Standard Error	Stayers' Log Wage	Standard Error	Diff. (M - S)	Standard Error
1979	12.05	0.033	11.97	0.009	0.08	0.035
1980	12.10	0.027	12.03	0.009	0.07	0.029
1981	12.18	0.021	12.14	0.008	0.04	0.023
1982	12.14	0.018	12.23	0.009	-0.09	0.021
1983	12.21	0.017	12.28	0.008	-0.07	0.018
1984	12.25	0.024	12.43	0.010	-0.18	0.026
1985	12.26	0.014	12.37	0.008	-0.11	0.016
1986	12.35	0.019	12.43	0.007	-0.08	0.021
1987	12.19	0.017	12.21	0.012	-0.02	0.021
1988	12.21	0.021	12.15	0.011	0.06	0.024
1989	12.27	0.025	12.15	0.013	0.12	0.029
Unweighted Average Difference					-0.016	0.080

N	Movers	Stayers
	7,729	20,675

Using the estimates from Table 9.5, and assuming a 2% real interest rate, we can calculate wealth:

$$(2) \qquad \text{Wealth} = \sum_{i=1}^{13} \frac{\hat{W}_{it}}{(1 + .02)^{t-1}}$$

where $\hat{W}_{it}$ is predicted from the appropriate Table 9.5 regression and year 13 is taken to be 1989. The individual is assumed to have fourteen years of education and to have started in 1977.

The simulations reveal that movers have a thirteen-year wealth level of $235,875. The corresponding number for stayers is $203,675. Thus the wealth level of movers is about 16% greater than that of stayers. The difference in initial wages of movers and stayers is about 13%. Thus much of the difference in wealth is reflected in wages on the first job.

To get a sense of how important promotions are in the firm, it is useful to compare an individual who was promoted three times over a thirteen-year career with one who was never promoted. The estimates of wage growth and of the effect of job change on wage growth are taken from Table 9.4. The calculation algorithm follows equation (2). The first promotion is assumed to occur at year 3, the second at year 6, and the third at year 9. The initial wage is assumed to be $1,500 per month.

Under these circumstances, the wealth for those promoted totals about $337,000, whereas for those not promoted it totals only $225,000. This is an enormous difference, equal to almost 50% of total wealth, and it suggests that tournaments may have had a large role in this firm's incentive structure. Of course, other explanations may be correct as well. Heterogeneity is the most obvious alternative.

We can find some evidence for heterogeneity. A strong test of heterogeneity implies that individuals are different when they join the firm, and these differences show up then and throughout. The first piece of evidence against this hypothesis is that even observable attributes such as education do little to predict starting wages in the firm. Education never enters regressions of log wage starting on year dummies, even when the initial job is not held constant.

In Table 9.6, workers are separated into movers and stayers according to the definition given above. Starting log wage is computed separately for each group. In some years, the starting wage of movers is significantly higher than that of stayers, but in others the reverse is true. On average, over the full period, no significant difference appears between the starting wages of movers and stayers. If heterogeneity is an important determinant, it is nevertheless not clearly detected among workers at the outset and it is not reflected in wages.

This result is not especially surprising. Even if firms could identify the better workers at the time they were hired, selective offering of general human capital would tend to depress the starting wage of the ablest, so that no strong observable differences would at first be perceived. Interestingly, however, Table 9.5 shows that the experience effect by itself is no larger for movers than for stayers. It is the move itself that captures the wage difference. This is consistent with the tournament view of promotions.

9.3.4. *Turnover*

External turnover can be defined as mobility between firms. Internal turnover refers to job changes within the firm. Although much work has been done on external turnover, very little attention has been focused on internal turnover and on the relation between internal and external turnover.

In this section, I merely report hazard rates for internal turnover. Figure 9.1 and 9.2 plot the probability of changing jobs within the firm by years of tenure.[22] In Figure 9.1, the absolute number of job changes is plotted against years of tenure. In Figure 9.2, the hazard rates of job changes are plotted.

From panel B, we can conclude that individuals with less than a year of tenure have about a 25% chance of changing jobs during their first year. By the time their tenure with the firm has reached approximately eleven years, the hazard rate for job change is less than 2%. This pattern of internal job change looks very similar to the pattern of job change between firms.

9.4. Job Paths

Let us now return to our main focus in this analysis. The key question is whether we can gain insight by looking at firm-based data and using the job as a unit of analysis that we could not gain from cross-section or panel data on individuals. Perhaps the most important issues relate to job paths. Are some jobs necessary transit points to higher levels of success? This question can be asked in two ways: Are individuals more likely to be promoted out of some jobs than others? And are the individuals who hold the top jobs more likely to have come from some jobs than from others? The first question is answered by export analysis and the second by import analysis.

Figure 9.1

Intrafirm Job Exit Rate: Levels

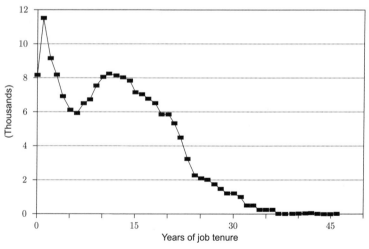

Figure 9.2

Intrafirm Job Exit Rates: Hazard

9.4.1. Export Analysis

At any time, each job category includes a set of incumbents, who may or may not be promoted to new jobs during the year. For this analysis, all the years in the sample are pooled and the number of individuals who were promoted out of their job category during each year is calculated. Jobs are ranked by the proportion of individuals who were exported. To prevent contamination by movement out of jobs that were eliminated, only promotions are considered. Individuals who separated during the year are dropped from the sample.

Table 9.7

Promotion Export Analysis, Summary Statistics

Highest promotion export rate	1
Lowest promotion export rate	0
Mean	.13
Median	.03
90th percentile	.40
25th percentile	0
10th percentile	0
Number of jobs in analysis	44

Notes: One job was lost because no one in it met criterion of this sample.

Table 9.7 gives some summary statistics on the distribution of exports by jobs. It reveals that some jobs are true dead ends as expected. For example, CEO is a dead-end job, for no promotions are possible from there. Although CEO and other top-level jobs are not included in the sample, others at high levels might also be expected to be dead-end jobs. Another possible explanation is that some jobs have very few incumbents and that the zero promotion rate results from random bad luck that hits only a few individuals.

Table 9.8

Regression of Job Export Rates on Job Characteristics

Independent Variable	1	2
Intercept	-.94	.18
	(.55)	(.07)
Average salary	-.00076	-.00043
	(.000037)	(.00028)
Average tenure	.0105	.0034
	(.0061)	(.0044)
Production	.1084	
	(.0773)	
Education	.0792	
	(.0412)	
R^2	.09	.05
Number of jobs in sample	44	44

Notes: Dependent variable = Promotion export rate.

Still, it is surprising that more than 25% of the job categories export no one. The jobs in those categories, however, are only a few of those in the firm. Only 700 of 218,073 worker years were spent in these zero-export jobs. Thus, almost all jobs that account for significant numbers of workers export to other jobs.

Another way of throwing light on job exports is to examine whether the high-export jobs have characteristics in common. We do so by regressing the job's export rate on some job characteristics. Among the independent variables are average salary, average tenure of incumbents, hourly dummy, and production worker dummy. The results, reported in Table 9.8, reveal that low-salary production jobs tend to have the highest export rates. If tenure with the firm enters at all, it enters positively. Jobs with experienced workers are more likely to export workers than jobs with inexperienced workers.

Note further that the education variable does affect the rate of promotion. Jobs with more highly educated workers tend to export more than those with less-educated workers. This result is consistent with most human capital analyses. But more interesting is that the other variables matter as much and perhaps more. This preponderance does not imply that human capital is less important than job assignment. It is plausibly argued that individuals who are assigned to the same job have the same human capital; those with low levels of education make it up in higher experience or unobserved ability. It is noteworthy, however, that job paths matter in a way that is not explained well by human capital variables. That some jobs and some job characteristics are more likely to lead to promotions than others does not surprise us. But it is important because it suggests that useful ways of thinking about wage determination, namely by job selection, may have been unduly ignored in the past.

Table 9.9

Feeder and Dead-End Jobs

Means	Feeder Jobs	Dead-End Jobs
Company tenure	17.3	16.8
	(.02)	(.02)
Job tenure	13.0	14.3
	(.02)	(.02)
Paid hourly	.61	.51
	(.001)	(.001)
Production	.92	.93
	(.001)	(.001)
Education	12.3	12.1
	(.004)	(.004)
Salary	2,214	2,136
	(2)	(2)
N	216,877	261,429

Notes: The standard errors of the mean are given in parantheses.

9.4.2. Import Analysis

It is possible to perform an import analysis that is symmetric with the export analysis shown above. Jobs could be ranked by the probability that the incumbent was in a lesser job during the previous year. It is more useful, however, to focus on selected jobs within the firm. Specifically, I want to consider the top jobs in the firm, as determined by a mean salary in the firm's top 2%, and to find out which jobs feed into those.

Let us now divide all jobs into feeder jobs and dead-end jobs. A feeder job is defined as a job included in the set that leads to top jobs. The dead-end jobs are other jobs in the current sample that have zero probability of being feeder jobs.

The characteristics of both jobs can be described. The means of some of the relevant variables are presented in Table 9.9 by feeder or dead-end group. Because of the large sample sizes, the differences in characteristics of feeder and nonfeeder jobs are all significant but not very great. One might expect that production jobs would have fewer opportunities for promotion than clerical jobs. But the dead-end jobs are only a bit more likely to be held by production workers.

As might be expected, levels of education are higher in feeder jobs than in dead-end jobs. Similarly, salaries are higher in feeder jobs. It is counterintuitive that the feeder jobs have a higher proportion of hourly workers and dead-end jobs have a higher proportion of salaried workers.

Of course, this approach may not capture the actual job path of the typical high-level worker. But it does seem to illustrate that mobility is quite even within this firm.

Although the characteristics of feeder and nonfeeder jobs seem to vary little, this characteristic does not imply that job assignment is unimportant. Recall that Table 9.7 showed that some jobs have extremely high export rates, and others export almost no one. These differences may reflect the unobserved characteristics of workers assigned to the jobs. They do not, however, appear to greatly or consistently reflect the observable characteristics.[23]

9.4.3.   Ports of Entry

It is natural to believe that hiring into some jobs is more likely than hiring into others. If firm-specific human capital were important, then individuals would be hired into low-level jobs and very few would be hired into the upper-echelon jobs. Beyond any theoretical significance of hiring patterns, it is interesting to determine whether hiring focuses on lower-level jobs. That is, are ports of entry important phenomena in the American corporation?

Here again, firm-based data are necessary, because the question cannot be answered by using national cross-section or even panel data sets. The current data set is ideal for addressing the issue. The approach used here is similar to that in earlier sections.

First, for each job category, we record the proportion of incumbents for whom the job is their first in the firm. They are the individuals who were hired from the outside. All jobs are ranked by those proportions. The numbers are reported in Table 9.10. Only 1989 is used for this analysis.

Significant variation appears in the outside hiring rates among the different jobs. More than 10% of the jobs hire exclusively from the outside. Even the median job selects only 13% of its employees from among other insiders. This imbalance gives the impression that ports of entry may be relatively unimportant. Indeed, 6,789 of 8,147 workers in 1989 worked in jobs with high outside hiring rates (exceeding .87). Of course, this proportion may merely reflect the fact that low-level jobs account for most of the workforce.

Table 9.10

Port-of-Entry Analysis, Summary Statistics

Highest outside hiring rate	1
Lowest outside hiring rate	0
Mean	.78
Median	.87
90th percentile	1
10th percentile	.35
Number of jobs in analysis	38

This issue can be investigated more fully. Again, it is possible to describe the characteristics of the jobs with the highest outside hiring rates by regressing the job-hiring rate on the mean level of various characteristics. The job is the unit of analysis. The results are reported in Table 9.11.

Table 9.11

Regression of Outside Hiring Rates on Job Characteristics (Dependent variable: job outside hiring rate)

Independent Variable	1	2
Intercept	1.40	.963
	(.70)	(.108)
Average salary	.000028	-.000102
	(.000076)	(.000056)
Average education	-.0449	
	(.0512)	
Average tenure	-.0222	
	(.0123)	
Production	.165	
	(.089)	
R^2	.23	.08
Number of jobs in sample	38	38

Notes: The number of jobs falls short of 45 because jobs were deleted if they were not held in 1989 by workers who had been with the firm since 1977.

Although variation in hiring rates occurs across jobs, the variation is not adequately explained by the job's measurable characteristics. The only important variable in explaining differences in hiring rates is a dummy for whether the job is a production job. Production jobs are somewhat more likely to hire from the outside than other jobs.

An almost automatic relation also appears between average tenure and the likelihood that the job is a port of entry. Jobs that have many entrants from the outside are likely to have many individuals with less tenure, for they did not come from other jobs within the firm. Similarly, some weak evidence shows that lower-salary jobs have a higher outside hiring rate when other variables are not included in the regression. But the type of job, rather than its compensation level, is more important in explaining the outside hiring rate.

These findings seem consistent with the notion that the ports of entry concentrate among low-paying production jobs. But we must remember that even high-paying nonproduction jobs hire a substantial proportion of workers from outside. Table 9.10 reveals that 90% of the jobs hire more than 35% of their workers from outside, which means plenty of chance for entry at high levels in this firm.

9.4.4.   Equalizing Differences

Differences in salary among jobs reflect workers' characteristics such as education and experience. They also reflect nonpecuniary attributes of the job itself. Although no data on the nonpecuniary attributes are available, one implication can be tested. If residual variance reflects nonpecuniary differences, then the path taken in getting to the job should be irrelevant in determining its compensation level. If, on the other hand, most of that residual variance reflects either differences in ability or internal labor market considerations of the tournament variety, for instance – then the path to the job might well be important. The proposition is testable.

One easy test is to determine whether the number of jobs that each worker has held within the firm prior to his or her current job affects compensation. The test requires us to hold the job constant and then ask whether or not past history matters. Table 9.12 reports the results of including job dummies in the earnings regression along with education, company tenure, job tenure, and number of previous changes.

Two results are of particular interest. First, the longer an individual remains in the job, given company tenure, the lower the salary. This relation suggests that the best workers are promoted out of the job and that stayers are likely to be of lower quality.

Table 9.12

Effect of Job Path on Earnings; Job Dummies Included in the Regression (Regression dependent variable: ln [real monthly salary])

ldependent Variable	
Constant	7.3
	(0.09)
Education	.0031
	(.0002)
Tenure	.00736
	(.00006)
Number of job changes	-.0252
	(.0007)
Job tenure	-.00372
	(.00006)
R^2	.66
N	219,674

Second, the number of previous job changes affects salary on the present job. This relation implies that nonpecuniary characteristics do not solely determine the definition of a job, because there would be no reason for these characteristics to vary with the number of prior job changes. An individual who gets to a level without many intervening jobs makes more money than an individual who moves through many jobs to get to the current job.[24]

9.4.5. Matching

By providing evidence on the importance of matching, we can further illuminate the subject of job paths. Matching models were designed primarily to explain mobility and wages among firms.[25] But the concept of matching can also be applied to movement within firms.[26] It can be argued that people who are good matches to jobs are more likely to remain in those jobs, in the same way as people who are good matches to firms are more likely to remain in the firm. The problem is that one expects individuals with high ability to be promoted out of low-level jobs and into higher-level jobs. But the same could be true among firms, for high-ability workers might tend to move from low-ability to high-ability firms. The question is how much of performance is based on firm-specific capital and how much on general ability. The same question can be asked of internal job switches. If most ability is job-specific, rather than general to the firm, then individuals who are good matches should tend to stay in their jobs.[27] If, instead, the most important variation among individuals is in their ability to do all jobs well, then the higher-ability workers should be in the more important jobs. An ability-learning model would then better describe the dynamics of internal mobility and wage determination than would a model that emphasizes job-specific components.

One implication of internal matching is that individuals who have been in the job for a long time are better at their work. As a result, they should receive higher wages. In other words, the implication is that job tenure should be positively related to wages.

In addition to matching, institutional features would lead one to expect a positive relation of wages to job tenure. Some jobs in this firm are unionized, and unions usually codify a wage-seniority relation within jobs. Thus, any finding to the contrary is even more surprising.

The regression in Table 9.12 illustrates this issue: the effect of job tenure on earnings is significantly negative. Other factors being equal, individuals who have been in the job longer have lower earnings, suggesting that job matching is not important within the firm, unless the concept of matching is broadened to include general ability sorting.

Once again, heterogeneous ability is probably the dominant factor. Within a job, the best people are promoted out more rapidly. Those who are left for a longer time are likely to be of lower quality. The evidence suggests that this firm follows the practice of promoting out the best people.

9.4.6.   *Shape of the Pyramid*

We can estimate the shape of the hierarchic pyramid from these data. Figure 9.3 plots the number of workers in each job by salary.

This is not a smooth pyramid. The numerically largest jobs seem to be in the midrange of salary, although we find some very low-salary jobs as well. The highest-paid jobs are the smallest ones in the firm.

9.4.7. Shortcomings

Before concluding, let us consider a few limitations in the preceding analysis. First, and most important, that jobs help explain the data cannot be taken to refute human capital analysis. Obviously, job title may be a proxy for human capital levels. Further, the measures of human capital used in this analysis – education and experience – are hardly comprehensive. But probably more compelling is that the firm is able to set standards and exercise discretion when individuals are hired. Individuals with low levels of measured human capital must make up for the lack by having higher levels of unmeasured characteristics.

The most reasonable interpretation for this analysis is that it focuses on internal rather than external mobility and determination of wages. It can thus use the notion of the job to help classify the information in the data. The questions asked in this analysis differ from those generally asked when human capital

are performed because answers can be obtained only with a firm-based data set, and because focusing on jobs rather than supply characteristics allows us to draw fresh conclusions.

Figure 9.3

Job Pyramid by Salary

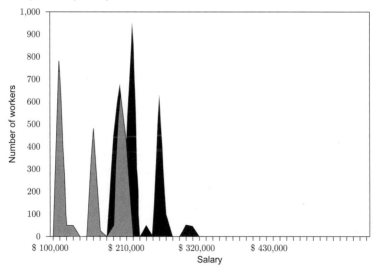

Further, even though we pay attention to the job, jobs are taken to be exogenous. We make no attempt, for example, to explain the tasks that are assigned to each job, nor do we try to explain how jobs evolved.[28] To get inside the job definition requires detail that goes beyond intrafirm data. The current data set permits no investigation of these issues, but the data can be augmented with specific job descriptions, which change with time, in the future.

9.5. Summary and Conclusions

The notion of the job has been given too little attention in the literature on labor. In part, this omission has resulted from the failure to clearly define job. Jobs can be defined in a number of ways.

In tournament models, which emphasize incentives, and in insurance models, which emphasize risk sharing, a job is a name for a wage level or profile. A job has no technological attributes. The holder of the job is entitled to a specified compensation scheme.

In hierarchic theories, the job describes a control relationship: the boss makes the decisions and allocates work assignments.

Hedonic wage analysis defines a job as a series of attributes about which workers care; cleanliness, status, and security are all part of the definition.

Even human capital theory has a role for a job, which can be thought of as an investment opportunity.

Finally, a job can be described as a collection of tasks, thus emphasizing its technological features.

The importance of the job as a concept depends on its empirical relevance. The major reason jobs have been ignored in the past is that available data – primarily large individual-based micro data sets – do not permit analysis by the job. To examine the job, firm-based data are necessary.

Using panel data from a major American corporation, I have been able to answer a number of job-related questions. These are among the more interesting findings:

1. Changing jobs is the key to increasing wages. Changes occur relatively often and result in significant raises.

2. Internal turnover patterns are similar to external patterns previously examined in labor literature. Turnover is most frequent during the first few years on the job. By the time the worker has been with the firm several years, job switches within the firm are very unlikely.

3. Some jobs in the firm are much more likely than others to lead to promotions. This firm has feeder jobs and dead-end jobs. The low-wage jobs are the ones most likely to produce a promotion.

4. For most jobs a significant amount of hiring is done from outside. Although internal promotion is a common way to fill jobs, hiring from outside is frequent enough to suggest that this firm gives plenty of chance for entry at high levels. The firm seems to have no ports of entry throughout, but it is true that production jobs have somewhat higher outside hiring rates than other jobs.

5. Within-firm job matching does not seem an important phenomenon in this firm. Heterogeneous ability appears to matter more, for individuals who remain in the job for a long time do worse than those who are transferred out.

V   Social Interactions and
Personnel Economics

Introduction

Most of personnel economics, and especially the earlier work, was focused on the individual. Even tournament theory, which pairs one individual against another in a contest environment, places minimal emphasis on the interaction between the two parties. Indeed, each contestant plays against an anonymous opponent and all that is relevant is the rival's equilibrium level of effort.

In a true business environment, workers interact with each other, and the behavior of their co-workers can affect their own actions. Forces may work through a variety of different mechanisms and the factors at play often go in opposite directions. One type of peer effect has workers mimicking their colleagues in ways that multiply up the effect of effort on output. When one worker puts forth additional effort, it may induce another worker to strive to meet the standard set by his co-worker. Conversely, shirking by one might cause others to slack off as well. Things are more complex in a competitive world, where workers may actually take actions to undermine their colleagues because of the competitive nature of the environment. Then, the additional effort by one worker may actually lead to lower output, because the effort is of a negative sort in two ways. First, it offsets the productive activity of another worker and second, it robs that second worker of some incentives to put forth effort because he knows that some of it will be in vain, as his rival will destroy some of the benefits that derive from it.

Two following chapters explore these possibilities. In "Peer Pressure and Partnerships" (see Chapter 10) the direct and indirect interactions between workers are explored. Consider a partnership, for example. The compensation rule inevitably divides output among the partners in a way that mutes incentives. Because the pie is shared in some fashion, each worker does not capture the full returns to his or her effort. The problem becomes more pronounced as the size of the partnership increases. Small partnerships may be able to avert most of the adverse incentives because one partner can more easily monitor the actions of other partners. The threat of dissolution of the partnership can be an effective force in staying close to the efficient level of effort. In larger partnerships, mutual monitoring becomes more difficult and the incentives to engage in it become diluted.

Forces such as shame or guilt can help to establish norms, where a norm is defined merely as the equilibrium level of effort, given the direct and indirect interaction of the players. Shame involves observability, where a worker suffers when another observes that he has put forth lower levels of effort. Guilt works even in the absence of observability. It is a motivator when individuals get disutility from shirking even if the lower level of effort is unobserved. Organizations may invest in creating shame or guilt by trying to alter the utility function. The military is well-known for effectively creating bonds among soldiers so that individuals will act outside self-interest to protect the group because of guilt that comes from letting one's friends down. The distinction between observable and unobservable actions is crucial. It explains why partnerships tend to be formed among substitutes rather than complements. Although there are clear production reasons why it would be more likely to pair with a complementary factor of production, the ability to judge someone who is more like oneself creates a force that works toward similar rather than different skills held in the same firm.

Competition between workers creates a different kind of social interaction. When reward is relative rather than absolute, individuals have incentives not only to do well themselves, but also to make their rivals do poorly. At the extreme, this results in sabotage and outright malfeasance. Chapter 11, "Pay Equality and Industrial Politics," examines these forces in depth. Because individuals may have different preferences or aversions to hurting their neighbors, sorting the workforce by type can improve productivity. Some firms will have a concentration of aggressive individuals. In those firms, incentives must be muted to prevent workers from engaging in active sabotage. In other firms that are comprised of more cooperative types, incentives can be strong. Implications for wage levels and wage differences by job

267

and hierarchical level are thereby derived. Specifically, cooperative firms have less compressed salary structures than those consisting of aggressive types. Additionally, because the top of the firm's hierarchy has a disproportionate number of aggressive individuals, motivation at the top should be based more on absolute performance and less on relative performance. At very high levels, piece rates, say, as reflected in stock or stock options, dominate promotion as a motivating factor.

It is for these reasons that firms pay so much attention to personality and fit. Firms often emphasize that group dynamics and culture are important components in their hiring decisions. This is particularly true among firms that have cooperative cultures. This factor justifies the sometimes significant expenditures that firms make to screen individuals on the basis of personality and potential cohesiveness with the existing group.

Finally, the political interaction between workers within the firm provides a motivation for having particular paths of promotion. It makes sense to have workers compete against individuals with whom cooperation is unimportant rather than having competition among members of the same team. Thus, a firm should set up promotion tournaments such that an individual from division A competes against someone from division B, where A and B have only limited interaction, rather than having one person from A compete against another from A and one from B compete against another from B.

The last chapter in this part of the book examines a topic that lies outside of personnel economics, namely assimilation of individuals into a culture. The focus of "Culture and Language" (Chapter 12) is on immigrants and how rapidly they acquire the culture and/or language of the native population in their new country. Although the topic is very different from the others considered in this book, the model and mechanism that is emphasized is one that comes directly from personnel economics, namely incentives to undertake effort.

The model focuses on trade, broadly defined, among individuals in a society. Trade between individuals is facilitated when all traders share a common culture and language. A common culture allows individuals to trade with one another without intermediaries. In the case of language, this is most clear. If two agents speak the same language, they can negotiate a contract without the use of a translator. A common culture allows the traders to have common expectations and customs, which enhances trust. The incentive to learn a language or culture depends on the difference between the amount of trade that can be accomplished without learning a language and that enjoyed when the new language is learned. This in turn depends directly on the proportion of individuals who speak one's native language. This simple idea provides a number of testable implications, the most important of which is that individuals from a minority group are more likely to become assimilated into the majority when the minority comprises a small part of the total population. Put starkly, an individual who is the only one in his community who speaks his native tongue must learn the community's language or suffer grave consequences. Data from the 1900 and 1990 U.S. Census shows that immigrants are most likely to be fluent in English when they live in communities with small numbers of individuals from their native lands. Further, voluntary concentration of minority members into neighborhoods is a natural consequence of the desire to trade and to avoid the costs associated with learning new cultures or languages. The structure also implies that immigrants are more likely to come from countries or cultures that are already well represented in the receiving country's population. The model also provides a rationale for chauvinism, where a majority culture is vigorously protected. Chauvinism is an attempt to prevent a new equilibrium, in which natives are forced to bear the costs of learning the culture or language of a new group.

The lessons of this chapter can be directly extended to the firm and to its desire to acquire new employees who are like those currently in the firm. This is an area that is ripe for future work and the "Culture and Language" model and results should apply directly.[1]

10

Peer Pressure and Partnerships

Many firms that use profit-sharing plans claim that such plans have beneficial incentive effects. Partnerships, which share profits, not necessarily equally among partners, are thought by their owners to have some incentive features that are lacking in an employer/employee relationship. Indeed, the idea has even made its way down Madison Avenue into television advertising. Witness, for example, an advertisement for Avis Corporation that boast that the employees are owners and therefore will work harder to serve the customer. But the idea that joint ownership can do much for incentives when the number of workers is large seems wrong on the face of it. After all, each worker bears the full cost of his or her own effort but reaps at most $1/N$ of the benefit in an N-worker firm. The prevalence of partnerships and profit sharing, even when risk allocation is not central, is difficult to explain in the standard principal-agent framework.

The introduction of a third party may make the team incentive problem more manageable. If every member of the team can be punished when output falls below some target level, then sufficient incentives may be provided. When central authorities cannot cheaply monitor the actions of their citizens, they may rely on mutual monitoring. Many Moslem societies can punish an entire family for the actions of one of its members. The logic is that the family is in the best position to discipline and control its members, so family punishment provides motivation to those who have the power to prevent crimes.[1]

We concentrate on schemes that use only internal motivation. Partnerships and, to a lesser extent, corporations that make worker com-

The original version of this chapter was published as: Lazear, E. P. (1992). Peer Pressure and Partnerships, in: Journal of Political Economy, 100(4), 801-817. University of Chicago Press. © 1992 by the University of Chicago. We thank Eugene Fama, Peter Mueser, Kevin J. Murphy, and Sherwin Rosen for helpful comments. Financial support was provided by the National Science Foundation.

pensation contingent on company profits are the central focus of this chapter. Partnerships are different from hierarchical organizations in that the members of the team are all residual claimants: the members share in the fortunes and misfortunes of the firm and do not pass the risk to another party.

Much has been said about the role of team spirit in motivating workers. For example, it is alleged that Japanese firms have been successful because of the team atmosphere that prevails, perhaps because compensation is based in large part on firm output (see Freeman and Weitzman 1987). But the discussion on team motivation has, with few exceptions,[2] been loose and nonrigorous. In what follows, the discussion is formalized. Only in this way can issues be clarified so that the true role of mutual monitoring, team compensation, corporate culture, and norms can be assessed. In many respects, this chapter is a progress report. There are some loose ends, but there are some definitive results as well. In theoretical research, one gets out what one puts in, as is apparent in what follows.

The goal is to investigate the conditions under which peer pressure is operative rather than to show that partnership or profit sharing is the solution to all agency problems. The following questions are considered: (1) Does profit sharing foster peer pressure? (2) How are "norms" established and how do they affect motivation within the firm? (3) Are incentives always weakened as firm size increases? (4) Is the firm, department, or some other unit's size key in determining effort? (5) When do workers have incentives to engage in mutual monitoring? (6) Why do partnerships form among individuals in the same occupation?

The analysis deviates from standard incentive theory because it focuses on preferences. Most economic analysis concentrates on behavioral variations that result from changes in prices for a given set of preferences; the discussion of preferences is generally in the domain of other social sciences. We trespass in hopes that the discussion can be made more precise.

10.1. Free-Rider Effects and Peer Pressure

Let us begin with the most basic situation. Suppose that output from a group of identical workers is some function of each worker's effort, e_i, given by $f(e)$, where e is an N-dimensional vector of workers' effort levels and N is the number of workers. To provide a reason for partnerships, assume that $f(\mathbf{e})$ is nonseparable in e_i. Separability permits self-employment, which eliminates incentive problems. Define a partnership as a work situation in which each worker's compensation is determined as $f(\mathbf{e})/N$. For now, ignore considerations of other possible compensation schemes. It is painful to put forth effort, and the pain that a worker feels is given by $C(e_i)$, where $C' > 0$ and $C'' > 0$.

The free-rider problem is easily seen in the following algebra. The worker wants to maximize

$$(1) \qquad \max_{e_i} \frac{f(\mathbf{e})}{N} - C(e_i)$$

with first-order conditions

$$(2) \qquad \frac{f_i(\mathbf{e})}{N} - C'(e_i) = 0.$$

Efficiency requires that total surplus be maximized or that

$$(3) \qquad \max_{e_1, e_2, \dots, e_N} f(\mathbf{e}) - \sum_{i=1}^{N} C(e_i)$$

with first-order conditions

$$(4) \qquad f_i(\mathbf{e}) - C'(e_i) = 0 \quad \forall i.$$

Since $C'' > 0$, $\mathbf{e}^*$, defined as the solution to (4), exceeds $\mathbf{e}'$, defined as the solution to (2) for $N > 1$. The chosen level of effort in a partnership falls short of the efficient level.

If effort were observable, first-best would be achieved by paying $a + be$, where $b = f_i(\mathbf{e}^*)$. But observability of effort is the heart of the problem. Thus we rule out payment on the basis of effort and ask how peer pressure might operate.

To motivate the analysis, we introduce a "peer pressure" function:

$$(5) \qquad \text{peer pressure} = P(e_i; e_j, \dots, e_N, a_i, a_j, \dots, a_N).$$

The pressure that worker i feels depends generally on his own effort, e_i; on the effort of his peers, $e_j,...,e_N$; and on other actions that he and his peers may take, $a_i,...,a_N$. The actions a_i have no direct effect on firm output. Since these actions may require effort, the cost to i of taking action a_i is shown by redefining cost as $C(e_i, a_i)$.[3]

Under this formulation, the general maximization problem for partner i is

$$(6) \qquad \max_{e_i, a_i} \frac{f(e)}{N} - C(e_i, a_i) - P(e_i; e_j,...,e_N, a_i,...,a_N).$$

In many respects, the pressure function is the same as the cost of effort, but there are differences. One is that the nature of P is social; that is, it depends on others' effort and actions. Another difference, crucial below, is that $P(\ )$ may be subject to manipulation by the group, whereas $C(e)$ is not. The function $C(e)$ is the part of the utility of effort that is exogenous and $P(\ )$ is the part that is cultural and endogenous. The peer pressure function is an attempt to formalize the discussion of tastes. By making explicit assumptions about $P(\ )$, we clarify the exact nature of the tastes required to explain a particular behavior.

To illustrate the basic mechanism, suppose that an extreme Cournot-Nash assumption holds so that each worker takes others' effort and actions as given. Now consider a pure partnership of fixed size N, where each worker receives $f(e)/N$. Assume further that a's have no effect on P. Under these conditions, the worker's problem is

$$(7) \qquad \max_{e_i, a_i} \frac{f(e)}{N} - C(e_i, a_i) - P(e_i,...)$$

with first-order condition

$$(8) \qquad \frac{\partial f / \partial e_i}{N} - C_1 - \frac{\partial P}{\partial e_i} = 0$$

since a_i is set to zero.

Peer pressure here means that $\partial P / \partial e_i < 0$. Since $\partial P / \partial e_i < 0$, the level of effort that solves (8) exceeds the level that solves (2). The proof follows.

Denote $\hat{e}$ as the solution to (8) and e' as the solution to (2). Then

$$\frac{f_i(\hat{e})}{N} - C_1(\hat{e}_1,...) - \frac{\partial P}{\partial e_i} = \frac{f_i(e')}{N} - C_1(e'_1,...).$$

To show that $\hat{e}_i > e'_i$, assume the opposite. Then since $C'' > 0$,

$$\frac{f_i(\hat{e})}{N} - \frac{\partial P}{\partial \hat{e}_i} < \frac{f_i(e')}{N}.$$

Also, since $\partial P/\partial e < 0$, this means that $f_i(\hat{e}) < f(e')$, which violates concavity of $f(e)$.[4] QED.

With peer pressure, equilibrium effort is higher than it would be without peer pressure. While this is the essence of our argument, we have done little more than to assume it. The $P(\ )$ function can be interpreted as implying that workers get utility from effort. As such, it is not surprising that more effort is the outcome.

Less obvious is that workers in a firm with peer pressure may be worse off than those in one without it. While pressure guarantees higher effort, it does not guarantee higher utility because the pressure itself is a cost borne by all members of the firm. It may produce higher effort levels, but workers may feel badly about working in an environment that has rampant peer pressure. To make clear statements about the two states, it is necessary to compare utility functions, one with and one without $P(\ )$. Such comparisons present deep philosophical problems. Of course, different equilibria for the same $P(\ )$ can be compared.

10.2. Creating Peer Pressure

How is peer pressure generated, and what is the role of profit sharing? These questions are addressed through attempts to tie specific actions taken by organizations to the peer pressure function defined in the previous section.

Any form of peer pressure function must rely on two components to be effective as a motivational device. First, member i's effort must affect the well-being of the rest of the team for them to have incentive to exert pressure on him. Second, in addition to the desire to exert pressure, the team members must have the ability to affect the choices of i. The first component requires some form of profit sharing, because if workers are paid straight salaries, the choice of a worker's effort has an effect on shareholders but not on his peers. Peers have no incentive to exert pressure because they do not care what action he chooses.

Profit sharing is necessary but not sufficient to create incentives beyond those present in (2). If co-workers do not have the means to exert pressure, then by default the peer pressure function cannot provide incentives. We assume that both components can be created and manipulated by the firm to some extent. This section analyzes the possible ways to accomplish this task.

It is useful to classify pressure as either internal or external. Internal pressure exists when an individual gets disutility from hurting others, even if others cannot identify the offender. External pressure is created when the disutility depends specifically on identification by others.

Sociologists sometimes distinguish guilt from shame. Guilt is internal pressure, whereas shame is external pressure. In the context of the firm, the important issue is observability. A worker feels shame when others can observe his actions. Without observability, only guilt can be an effective form of pressure. Shame requires that $a_j > 0$. If others do not take the time to watch, then a worker feels no shame. Formally, let a_j be defined to be monitoring of worker i by worker j. Shame requires external observation so that

$$\frac{\partial P(e_i;\ e_j,...,e_N,\ a_i,\ a_j,...,a_N)}{\partial e_i} < 0$$

only if some $a_j > 0$. Guilt is internal, implying that $\partial P/\partial e_i < 0$ even if $a_j,...,a_N = 0$.

Guilt may require a greater amount of past investment than shame. Past investment may be necessary to ensure that an individual loses utility when he shirks, even in the absence of observability by others. Physical punishment by peers is an alternative to making past investments. In this respect, it is similar to shame, which requires that others be aware of effort reduction. Since guilt functions even in the absence of observability, it is a valuable force in production environments in which individuals work on their own but total output depends on the team.

The military provides an example of one such situation.[5] A fighter pilot may be alone on a mission in which bravery or cowardice is difficult to observe by others. Still, the safety of his squadron may depend on his success. Guilt, in the form of loyalty to his comrades, provides incentives that operate even in the absence of observability. Thus the military spends much time and money creating loyalty and team spirit. The up-front investment has a large payoff because shame, which may be cheaper to create, cannot be used when actions are unobservable.

If peer pressure and guilt can be manipulated, why doesn't the firm instill in workers a sense of guilt toward cheating shareholders? Empathy may be the answer. A worker may empathize more with co-workers than with shareholders or managers.[6] If the group with which the individual empathizes or the group that is able to do peer monitoring is not the same as the group within which profits are shared, incentives will not be well served. A worker who cares only about the opinions of the nearest 10 workers will not behave efficiently when profits are shared among the larger group of 100,000. If nothing else, the group of 10 should free-ride on the other 99,990 workers.

Define N^* as the number of profit sharers about whom the individual cares. Let $P(e_i,..., 0) = 0$ so that if there are no relevant peers, there is no relevant pressure. The maximization problem is then

$$\max_{e_i} \frac{f(e)}{N} - C(e_1,...) - P(e_i,...,N^*),$$

where N remains the number sharing the profit. If there is no profit sharing among workers, then N consists of shareholders only. If there is no empathy with shareholders, then N^* is zero, which means $P = 0$. Peer pressure would not be an effective motivator. Maximum motivation for any given number of profit sharers is achieved by allowing only individuals about whom workers care to be profit sharers. Then the free-riding that occurs as a result of profit sharing is offset maximally by P.[7]

Partnerships are often formed among friends or family members. Despite the free-rider problems inherent in the partnership structure, partners often put in long hours and exert substantial effort. One explanation is that when partners are friends or relatives, empathy is strong, so shirking results in significant guilt or shame. It is frequently suggested that trust is greater within small ethnic or religious groups than between groups. If individuals feel guiltier about cheating "their own kind" than about cheating others, we would expect to see partnerships among individuals from the same cultures.[8]

Similarly, it is possible that little of substance occurs in quality circles used by Japanese firms or their American copies. The motivation behind "team" meetings may be no different from that behind an intercompany softball league, company picnics, or even a company song. Once $P(\ )$ is endogenous, it is worthwhile to invest some resources in altering $P(\ )$ to provide better incentives for the employees. Since profit sharing is complementary with team spirit, partnerships should be more likely than wage and salary firms to invest in spirit-building activities.

Not only may the firm instill guilt by affecting work attributes, but it may also operate on the individual's alternatives. This can work in two ways. First, the firm may bring the worker's family into the organization, for example, by having a child care center on the premises or by having organizations to which spouses belong. When a worker shirks, he imposes costs not only on his co-workers but also on his family. Second, as in Iannaccone (1992), the firm may ruin a worker's alternatives so that he substitutes his time away from leisure and toward work. Academia selects people whose hobbies are their primary disciplines.

The environment in which initial investments in loyalty are most important is characterized by two features. Already mentioned is the inability (even by peers) to observe the worker's effort. But also required is complementarity in production. An empirical investigation of this point would require information on three components: a measure of complementarity in production, a measure of costs of observability, and a measure of expenditures on "indoctrination." While not easy to come by, as more firm-specific data become available, proxies may present themselves.

10.3. Norms

Sociologists often think of peer pressure as arising when individuals deviate from a well-established group norm. One possible specification is that individuals are penalized for working less than the group norm. Suppose

$$(9) \qquad\qquad P(\cdot) = P(\bar{e} - e_i),$$

where $\bar{e} \equiv 1/(N - 1) \sum_{i \neq j} e_j$.

Start with a firm of identical individuals. Each player maximizes

$$(10) \qquad\qquad \frac{f(\mathbf{e})}{N} - C(e_i) - P(\bar{e} - e_i)$$

with first-order condition

$$(11) \qquad\qquad \frac{f_i(\mathbf{e})}{N} - C'(e_i) + P' = 0.$$

(Since a_i has no effect on output or P, it is set to zero at the optimum.) With this formulation of peer pressure, there is a unique and symmetric equilibrium as long as cost and production functions have the standard properties. For example, if P is linear in $\bar{e} - e_i$, P' is just a constant and (11) has a clear and unique solution.[9]

It is also possible (although not likely) that peer pressure results in the efficient equilibrium, where efficient is defined as the level of effort, e^*, that a social planner would choose. To see this, let $P = (\bar{e} - e_i)\gamma$, with $\gamma > 0$. The interpretation is that $\bar{e}$ is the norm and γ is a measure of the penalty associated with falling below it. Then the worker's first-order condition is

$$(12) \qquad \frac{f_i(e)}{N} - C'(e_i) + \gamma = 0.$$

To achieve efficiency, it is necessary that the solution to (12) be identical to the solution to (4). Thus

$$\frac{f_i(e^*)}{N} - C'(e^*) + \gamma = f_i(e^*) - C'(e^*) = 0$$

or

$$(13) \qquad \frac{f_i(e^*)}{N} + \gamma = f_i(e^*),$$

which generally has a solution (see Figure 10.1). Earlier, it was suggested that P could be manipulated. To the extent that manipulation is possible, setting γ to solve (13) maximizes joint surplus.[10]

An implication is that the effort norm should be higher when deviations are more heavily punished. Finding actual measures of punishment may be very difficult to obtain in practice.

In some work environments, workers may be chastised by their peers for exceeding the norm.[11] Mechanically, this merely requires $\gamma < 0$ in (12). While this is feasible, it is unlikely to be true in a partnership. Here, individuals like their partners to put forth more effort because it implies higher income. "Rate-busters" are ostracized in hierarchical firms, not partnerships. There, working too hard tips off the supervisor that the quota is too low.[12] Ratchet effects are required for this story to work.

Figure 10.1

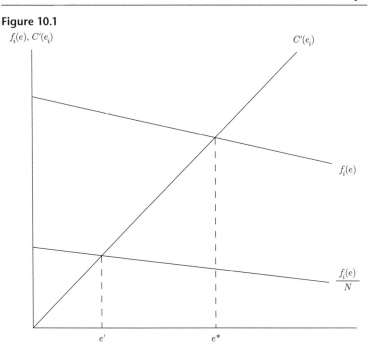

More reasonable in a partnership may be that deviations from the norm, in either direction, are punished. Reduced effort means lower income for each of the other partners, but effort above their own levels may shame them. If $P(\ )$ were quadratic in effort, so that $P(e_i) = (\bar{e} - e_i)^2$, then deviations from $\bar{e}$ in either direction bring the same disutility. In equilibrium, $e_i = \bar{e}$, so the level of effort chosen equals the level that would be chosen in the absence of peer pressure; that is, (8) becomes identical to (2).

10.4. Mutual Monitoring

The popular press frequently attributes Japanese productivity to mutual monitoring by workers. The *kanban* system or just-in-time inventory approach is mentioned as a facilitator of team monitoring. In this section, we analyze that claim rigorously.

Suppose that, in addition to exerting effort, workers can monitor each other, at a cost. Workers who are caught shirking can be penalized by their partners. The penalty for now is best thought of as a nonpecuniary one, such as mental or physical harassment. Of course, if monitoring implies that effort is observable with error, why should a partnership be used at all? A better scheme would reward workers for their own effort, irrespective of firm output. If workers are not efficient risk bearers, then there is a cost to making pay completely responsive to variations in measured effort. Peer pressure provides another instrument and thereby makes the compensation strategy richer.[13]

The actions, a, defined above can now be thought of as peer monitoring. Let the expected penalty associated with being caught shirking now be $P(e_i; a_j,...,a_n, N)$. More specifically, since all workers are ex ante identical, the choice of monitoring level by k will be identical to that by j, so that we write $P(\ )$ as $P(e_i, (N-1)a_j)$. Additionally, with symmetry of f, i's maximization problem is

$$(14) \qquad \max \frac{f(\mathbf{e})}{N} - C(e_i, a_i) - P(e_i, (N-1)a_j)$$

with first-order conditions

$$(15a) \qquad \frac{f_i(\mathbf{e})}{N} - C_1 - P_1 = 0$$

and

$$(15b) \qquad \frac{N-1}{N} f_i \frac{\partial e_j}{\partial a_i} - C_2 = 0.$$

Each worker's choice of monitoring level a must satisfy (15b), in which other workers respond to i's choice of a. The worker puts forth monitoring effort because he believes that other workers will increase their effort as a response. To derive j's response to i's choice of a_i, differentiate (15a) with respect to a_j since the problem is symmetric over all workers:

$$(16) \qquad \left. \frac{\partial e_j}{\partial a_j} \right|_{(15a)} = \frac{-P_{12}}{(f_{ii}/N) - C_{11} - P_{11}}.$$

The denominator is unambiguously negative. The sign of the expression is therefore opposite the sign of P_{12}. In the context of P being the expected punishment, P_{12} is related to accuracy of detection. As monitoring increases, presumably the reading on whether a worker is shirking or not becomes more accurate. It is now clear why it is necessary that $P_{12} < 0$. If additional monitoring is to increase the level of effort, there must be a gain to increasing effort when monitoring increases. The P_2 term does not enter. Increasing the penalty without altering effort's effectiveness in forestalling it will have no effect on effort. It is the interaction between monitoring and effort in altering the probability or effect of being caught that causes effort to increase when other workers monitor more.

The free-rider effect appears in (15a) in the term $1/N$. As N increases, the direct incentive to put forth effort falls. Effort may increase, however, because other workers' monitoring, a_j, may increase in N. Whether effort is actually increasing or decreasing in N depends on the shapes of the production function and the peer pressure function.

10.5. Group Size and Mutual Monitoring

Consider the large Japanese firm. It may consist of 100,000 employees, most of whom work at different plants. The N that is relevant in (16) is the size of the entire firm, since profits are shared among all workers of the corporation and are not tied to individual (or even small group) performance. But in such a large firm, P_{12} is likely to be very close to zero. Monitoring by a worker in Osaka of a worker in Tokyo is likely to have little effect on the accuracy of the Tokyo worker's effort reading. As such, the Tokyo worker's effort should be affected primarily by the free-rider effect, not by the monitoring effect.[14]

Put differently, any given worker can observe maybe 100 of his peers. But the fruits of the monitoring and peer pressure that he doles out are shared with 99,999 other workers. This implies that there is little incentive to engage in mutual monitoring, even with profit sharing. The monitoring story has some appeal in smaller groups, but as the firm gets very large, the ability of workers to monitor or even inform on each other is somewhat reduced. If mutual monitoring is a force in Japanese firms, it is not a result of profit sharing.

10.6. Committing to Punish

Is the threat to punish peers credible? If $P(\ )$ is self-imposed guilt, then credibility is not an issue. But if $P(\ )$ reflects a sanction imposed after a team has observed shirking, then would peers carry through on the threat? Sufficient to ensure punishment is that revenge, but not random penalties, provides positive utility.

A system of "norms" might provide another mechanism. Suppose that the norm is that shirkers must be punished. An individual who permits a shirker to go unpunished must be punished himself by an increased amount, and so forth. If each believes that punishment will be doled out, it will be. But multiple equilibria may exist because the amount of punishment that individuals undertake depends on their beliefs about others' actions. Additionally, the norm may unravel. If there is an end to the chain so that someone believes that he will not be punished for not disciplining another who let another go without punishment, then there is no reason for anyone to discipline anyone. But the firm can be thought of as a circle. As long as a worker is told only that he is to punish the neighbor on his right or suffer punishment from the one on his left, he will carry out the punishment.

10.7. Homogeneous Workers

Partnerships tend to occur among individuals of similar type and quality. There are partnerships of lawyers, accountants, and physicians, but it is rare to find a partnership between a physician and an accountant.

The grouping of partners by occupation is a direct implication of the mutual monitoring analysis. The effectiveness of peer pressure is directly related to $|P_{12}|$ in (16). If $P_{12} = 0$, peer monitoring has no effect on worker effort. But P_{12} is accuracy, so $|P_{12}|$ is likely to be larger when the monitor knows the job of the individual who is being observed. Sometimes partnerships use specialization. One partner sells and the other manages. But even in those cases, the partners were frequently drawn from the same field so that each can evaluate the other's work. Partnerships should be less prevalent in firms in which workers specialize in nonoverlapping tasks.

It is also possible to explain the grouping of individuals by appealing to technology. For example, it may be advantageous for a tax lawyer to work with a labor lawyer because cases may involve both disciplines. But working together does not imply sharing the profit. The tax lawyer could own the firm and hire the labor lawyer. The fact that they form a profit-sharing partnership probably says more about peer pressure and incentives than it does about technology.

10.8. Infiltration

Suppose that the world consisted of two types of workers: the social, for whom $P_1 < 0$, and the independent, for whom $P = 0$ for all e_i, a_j, and N.[15] If one's type is known only by the individual himself, does a separating equilibrium exist in which each type of worker prefers firms of his own kind? If P depends only on e_i and N, then the answer is no. The independents would never prefer to join a firm with their own kind. Rather, they would benefit by infiltrating a partnership of social individuals, where output is higher.

To see this, assume that a separating equilibrium exists. Denote e**, N** as the effort-firm size pair that exists in the firm that attracts social types and e″, N″ as the pair that exists in the firm that attracts independents. Then separating equilibrium implies that the social do not want to join the independents' firm, so

$$\frac{f(e^{**})}{N^{**}} - C(e^{**}) - P(e^{**}, N^{**}) > \frac{f(e'')}{N''} - C(e'') - P(e'', N'').$$

There are two possibilities: If $P(e^{**}, N^{**}) > P(e'', N'')$, then

$$\frac{f(e^{**})}{N^{**}} - C(e^{**}) > \frac{f(e'')}{N''} - C(e''),$$

which implies that independents would prefer the social firm to their own even if they worked at e**, so there would be no separating equilibrium. If independents chose their own optimal level of effort in the social firms, they would do even better. (An independent's utility is $[f(\cdot)/N] - C(\cdot)$.)

Alternatively, $P(e^{**}, N^{**}) < P(e'', N'')$. Now, since $P_1 < 0$ and $P_2 > 0$, either e″ < e** or $N'' > N^{**}$ or both. This means that

$$\frac{f(e'')}{N''} - C(e'') < \frac{f(e^{**})}{N^{**}} - C(e^{**}),$$

since $[f(e)/N] - C(e)$ is increasing in e for e less than the optimum. But that implies that e″, $N″$ is not optimum for the independents' firm. Thus no separating equilibrium exists.

10.9. Does Effort Fall as Firm Size Rises?

The standard argument, as illustrated by (2), is that effort falls as firm size increases because of free-riding. Is it possible that peer pressure can reverse the standard intuition? The answer is a qualified yes.

The first-order condition for $N = N_0$ is the solution to

$$\frac{f_i}{N_0} - C' - P_1^0(e_i,...; a_j) = 0,$$

where P^0 denotes P for $N = N_0$. Let $N_1 > N_0$. Then the first-order condition is the solution to

$$\frac{f_i}{N_1} - C' - P_1^1(e_i,...; a_j) = 0.$$

Effort can increase in N only if the P_1 function becomes much larger for each e_i as N increases. This requires that as N increases, the effect of effort on peer pressure must be greater.

It is possible that this might hold, at least up to some point. If more workers can observe an individual, then sanctions (implicit or explicit) imposed by the group may be greater. For example, in a firm of 10, a worker must deal with nine discontented peers. In a firm of two, he has only one to contend with. After some point, however, adding workers may serve only to make the relationships more impersonal or sanctions more difficult to enforce.

Of course, even if effort rises with N, it is not necessary that utility rise with N. As always, there is an optimal level of effort: a compensation scheme that induces higher effort does not imply higher utility.[16]

The conclusion is that an appropriate, and not unreasonable, form of peer pressure can mean that effort is greater in large firms than in small ones. It is well known that wages and firm size are positively correlated (see Brown and Medoff 1989). But this probably reflects worker sorting and rent sharing more than differential effort.

10.10. Summary and Conclusions

The notion that peer pressure can be an effective motivator is not new. This analysis has attempted to clarify the conditions under which peer pressure operates in an industrial environment. Some of the more significant points follow.

1. Peer pressure and partnerships (or some other form of profit sharing) go hand in hand. Incentives are generated when an individual empathizes with those whose income he affects. Thus peer pressure is expected to be a more effective force in firms in which profits are shared among those in similar circumstances.

2. In the absence of peer pressure, larger partnerships have greater free-rider problems and less effort. But peer pressure can reverse this conclusion under reasonable assumptions.

3. The sociologists' distinction between shame and guilt as effective motivators hinges on observability. Shame requires observability whereas guilt does not. The logic implies that indoctrination designed to instill guilt is more important when workers' actions are unobservable.

4. Norms develop in firms to establish an expected level of effort. A norm is an equilibrium phenomenon that results because deviations from the norm bring disutility.

5. Mutual monitoring is a specific application of peer pressure. Mutual monitoring can affect effort but is likely to be effective only when profits are shared by a very small group.

6. Partnerships tend to be formed among individuals who perform similar tasks because mutual monitoring is more effective.

7. Incentives are improved when the group relevant for profit sharing is the peer group, where peer group means the individuals about whom a worker cares or by whom a worker is monitored.

11

Pay Equality
and Industrial Politics

The politics of the workplace are of great importance to businessmen. Few aspiring young executives ignore the individuals with whom they work, and competition between workers who are attempting to climb the job ladder may be fierce. Even at lower levels, workers are cognizant of their peers. Perhaps the most important interactions between workers relate to relative pay. It is common for both management and worker groups such as labor unions to express a desire for homogeneous wage treatment.[1] The desire for similar treatment is frequently articulated as an attempt to preserve worker unity, to maintain good morale, and to create a cooperative work environment. But it is far from obvious that pay equality has these effects. The morale of high-quality workers is likely to be adversely affected by pay that regresses toward the mean. That the morale of the rest of the workforce is sufficiently improved to offset does not follow automatically. The problem is exacerbated by competitive forces that bring about adverse selection in turnover (see e.g. Lazear 1986a).

Cooperation and comparison between workers mean that the reference group is crucial. In order to talk about homogeneous treatment of workers, it is essential to define the relevant group. For example, it is not considered inappropriate to treat vice-presidents differently from salespeople, although it may be considered un-

The original version of this chapter was published as: Lazear, E. P. (1989). Pay Equality and Industrial Politics, in: Journal of Political Economy, 97(3), 561-580. University of Chicago Press. © 1989 by the University of Chicago. Barry Nalebuff made important suggestions that dramatically improved the paper. Helpful comments were also provided by Debra Aron, Jeremy Bulow, David Kreps, Paul Milgrom, Kevin M. Murphy, James Patell, John Roberts, Sherwin Rosen, Myron Scholes, Robert Wilson, and Mark Wolfson. This work was supported in part by the National Science Foundation.

desirable to pay a vice-president of human resources more than a vice-president of marketing. All vice-presidents may be in the same group, but that group probably does not include salespeople. At the center of this is who works with whom. It is not sensible to create rivalry by setting up implicit promotion contests between workers whose cooperation is important to the firm. Similarly, it may be important to sort workers into different groups depending on their personality types.

Political interaction between workers is a significant aspect of the work environment, but it has been all but ignored by economists who analyze labor markets. This chapter is an attempt to fill some of the void. In particular, since workers can affect the productivity of their co-workers, organization of the firm and the structure of relative compensation must be considered. There are two thoughts that can be summarized.

Relative comparisons imply that individuals can increase their wealth in two ways. Competition encourages increased effort, which has a positive effect on output. This is the idea of Lazear and Rosen (1981, see Chapter 6). But competition also discourages cooperation among contestants and can lead to outright sabotage. The larger is the spread between the compensation that the winner and loser receive, the more important is each of these effects. This is much like an arms race: as the value of winning the war increases, each country devotes more resources to fighting. Those additional resources are unproductive. They reduce the other country's output without changing the outcome of the war. If the winning and losing countries fared equally in the postwar situation, fewer resources would be devoted to defense. Similarly, in the labor market, pay equality discourages uncooperative behavior and is one reason why both workers and firms may push for equal treatment.

The second point is that the organization of the workforce, that is, the definition of the reference group, affects cooperation and competition. Worker personalities are crucial in this respect because pairing two passive workers may dilute some incentives that might be realized by putting an aggressor with a passive individual. Folklore has it that tuna fishermen sometimes throw a shark into the holding tank with live tuna to keep them active until the ship reaches the cannery. A price is paid in that the shark takes its share of tuna, but the benefit is the increased freshness of the rest of the catch. There is no direct complementarity between tuna and sharks (tuna that associate with sharks do not taste better). It is merely an incentive effect that is at work here. Since personalities are not distributed randomly throughout the workforce, different policies are appropriate for different levels of the hierarchy. Those policies are examined below.

The most important theme is that equality is desirable on efficiency grounds. The compression of wages suppresses unwanted uncooperative behavior. Profit-maximizing firms choose more equitable wage structures even in the absence of worker risk aversion or other fairness considerations. Thus an efficiency argument for equality is at the heart of the analysis. Some of the more important results are the following: (1) Pay is more equitable when workers have the ability to affect each other's output. (2) Other things equal, predatory behavior is always output reducing. Incentive effects do not offset the lost output that results from uncooperative behavior. (3) "Personality counts." Aggressors do not self-sort, so firms are rational in using personality as a hiring criterion. (4) Wage compression and organization by product (rather than function) are likely to be positively related.

11.1. The Competitive Structure

To begin, consider the basic model of relative competition. Whether payment should be relative or absolute is not questioned here. I simply assume that relative payment is more efficient in some contexts. This results if it is cheaper to obtain an unbiased estimate of rank than of level (as is the case when one grades on a curve).[2]

To make it simple, games consist of two players, j and k, with output q_j, and q_k. Let output be given as

$$(1) \qquad Q = Q(q_j, q_k),$$

where $q_j = f(\mu_j, \theta_k) + \varepsilon_j$; $q_k = f(\mu_k, \theta_j) + \varepsilon_k$; μ_j, μ_k is effort by j, k; θ_k is k's "sabotage" inflicted on player j; θ_j is j's "sabotage" inflicted on player k; and ε_j and ε_k are random terms such that $E(\varepsilon) = 0$. The term "sabotage" is used as shorthand for any (costly) actions that one worker takes that adversely affect output of another. For example, erecting barriers so that co-workers cannot obtain useful information falls under this definition. The random component, ε, can be thought of as production luck, unobserved and uncontrollable market forces, or measurement error (unknown in advance). The production function $f(\ )$ is general. To capture the idea that μ is effort and θ is counterproductive activity, let $f_1 > 0$ and $f_2 < 0$. Further, it is not necessary that the errors be additive. All that is required is that it is possible to solve out for ε in the production function. Nothing is lost, however, by using the additive form. (A multiplicative structure is equally simple.) Separability of some form is needed in production, or it makes no sense to assume that j's output can be observed, even in a relative sense, distinct from k's. Also, since the identities of the players should not matter, Q must be of a symmetric form such that $Q(q_0, q_1) = Q(q_1, q_0)$.

Each player has the ability to inflict injury on or, more realistically, to block cooperation with the other. It is immediately obvious from the production technology that aggressive behavior ($\theta > 0$) has the direct effect of output reduction. It is not clear, however, that the final effect is output reduction. The outcome of a game based on relative performance is affected by choices of θ_j, and θ_k, so it is possible that μ_j, and μ_k are sufficiently larger to make up for the lost output through sabotage. As it turns out, output always decreases when the cost of sabotage falls. This result can be derived, along with a number of others, in a more general context.

Suppose that there are two types of workers, "hawks" and "doves." Hawks produce μ and θ according to (2a), whereas doves produce μ and θ according to (2b):

$$(2a) \qquad \qquad \text{cost} = C^H(\mu, \theta),$$

$$(2b) \qquad \qquad \text{cost} = C^D(\mu, \theta),$$

where $C_2^H(\mu_0, \theta_0) < C_2^D(\mu_0, \theta_0)$ for any μ_0, θ_0. That is, the marginal cost of sabotage is always lower to hawks than to doves. All workers are risk neutral.

When only relative performance matters, what is crucial is the difference between the reward that the winner receives, W_1, and the one that the loser receives, W_2. To see this, let us take W_1 and W_2 as parametric and allow the worker to optimize against his or her opponent, given the prizes.

11.1.1.   The Worker's Problem: Symmetric Players

Suppose that two hawks are paired in one contest. Then hawk j wants to solve the following problem:

(3) $$\max_{\mu_j, \theta_j} W_1 P(\mu_j, \theta_j; \mu_k, \theta_k) + W_2[1 - P(\ )] - C^H(\mu_j, \theta_j),$$

where $P(\mu_j, \theta_j; \mu_k, \theta_k)$ is the probability that j wins, conditional on his choice of μ_j and θ_j. The equilibrium is Nash, so μ_k and θ_k are taken to be parametric by j.

Player j wins if $q_j > q_k$. Thus

$$P(\mu_j, \theta_j; \mu_k, \theta_k) = \text{prob}(q_j > q_k)$$

$$= \text{prob}[f(\mu_j, \theta_k) - f(\mu_k, \theta_j) > \varepsilon_k - \varepsilon_j]$$

$$= G[f(\mu_j, \theta_k) - f(\mu_k, \theta_j)],$$

where $G(\ )$ is the distribution function of the random variable $\varepsilon_k - \varepsilon_j$.
The first-order conditions to (3) are

$$(W_1 - W_2) \frac{\partial P}{\partial \mu_j} = C_1^H(\mu_j, \theta_j),$$

$$(W_1 - W_2) \frac{\partial P}{\partial \theta_j} = C_2^H(\mu_j, \theta_j),$$

or

$$(W_1 - W_2)g[f(\mu_j, \theta_k) - f(\mu_k, \theta_j)] = \frac{C_1^H(\mu_j, \theta_j)}{f_1(\mu_j, \theta_k)},$$

$$(W_1 - W_2)g[f(\mu_j, \theta_k) - f(\mu_k, \theta_j)] = \frac{-C_2^H(\mu_j, \theta_j)}{f_2(\mu_k, \theta_j)}.$$

Player k solves the corresponding problem. Since players are identical, in equilibrium, $\mu_j = \mu_k$ and $\theta_j = \theta_k$.

Thus the solution is characterized by the solution to the first-order conditions:[3]

$$(4a) \qquad (W_1 - W_2)g(0) = \frac{C_1^H(\mu_j, \theta_j)}{f_1(\mu_j, \theta_k)},$$

$$(4b) \qquad (W_1 - W_2)g(0) = \frac{-C_2^H(\mu_j, \theta_j)}{f_2(\mu_k, \theta_j)},$$

$$(4c) \qquad (W_1 - W_2)g(0) = \frac{C_1^H(\mu_k, \theta_k)}{f_1(\mu_k, \theta_j)},$$

$$(4d) \qquad (W_1 - W_2)g(0) = \frac{-C_2^H(\mu_k, \theta_k)}{f_2(\mu_j, \theta_k)}.$$

Equations $(4a)$ – $(4d)$ reveal some useful information. Since costs are increasing in θ, $(4b)$ and $(4d)$ imply that as long as C_{12} is not sufficiently negative, increasing the wage spread increases the level of sabotage. Thus pay equality implies less sabotage. Of course, pay equality also implies less effort by the same argument, and by $(4a)$ and $(4c)$. Whether firms and workers desire more equitable pay structures when sabotage is possible depends on the firm's optimization as well. That pay equality is desirable is shown below, but the basic ingredients to the argument are $(4b)$ and $(4d)$.

As long as C_{12} is not sufficiently negative, sabotage lowers expected net output per worker, defined as $E(Q/2) - C(\mu, \theta)$.

11.1.2. The Firm's Problem: Symmetric Players

To derive this result, it is useful to turn to the firm's optimization problem. The competitive firm must maximize workers' expected rent subject to a zero-profit constraint by choosing W_1 and W_2, given worker behavior described in $(4a)$ – $(4d)$. Thus the firm solves

$$(5) \qquad \max_{W_1, W_2} W_1 + W_2 - C(\mu_j, \theta_j) - C(\mu_k, \theta_k)$$

subject to zero expected profits:

$$W_1 + W_2 = E[Q(q_j, q_k)].$$

When the zero-profit constraint is inserted, (5) becomes

$$\max_{W_1, W_2} E\{Q[f(\mu_j, \theta_k) + \varepsilon_j, f(\mu_k, \theta_j) + \varepsilon_k] - C(\mu_j, \theta_j) - C(\mu_k, \theta_k)\}.$$

Now from $(4a) - (4d)$, it is clear that μ and θ depend only on the spread, $W_1 - W_2 \equiv \Delta$. The levels of W_1 and W_2 are tied down by the zero-profit condition. Thus rewrite the maximization problem as

(6)
$$\max_\Delta E\{Q[f(\mu_j(\Delta), \theta_k(\Delta)) + \varepsilon_j, f(\mu_k(\Delta), \theta_j(\Delta)) + \varepsilon_k] \\ - C(\mu_j(\Delta), \theta_j(\Delta)) - C(\mu_k(\Delta), \theta_k(\Delta))\}.$$

The first-order condition can be written as

(6′)
$$E[(f_1\mu' + f_2\theta')Q_1 - C_1\mu' - C_2\theta'] = 0$$

because Q is symmetric and the game has ex ante identical players. (Thus identity subscripts are suppressed.)

If sabotage were not possible, (6′) would reduce to

(7)
$$E(Q_1 f_1 \mu' - C_1 \mu') = 0.$$

Equation (7) implies that $C_1 = E(Q_1 f_1)$, whereas (6′) implies that

$$C_1 = E\left(Q_1 f_1 + \frac{Q_1 f_2 \theta'}{\mu'} - \frac{C_2 \theta'}{\mu'}\right).$$

Now $Q_1 f_2 \theta'/\mu' < 0$, as is $-C_2 \theta'/\mu'$. If C is separable in μ and θ ($C_{12} = 0$), then it is clear that effort is lower when the possibility for sabotage exists (since C_1 increases in μ). In fact, only if C_{12} were sufficiently negative could effort be higher when sabotage is a possibility.

If we ignore the pathological case in which C_{12} is extremely negative, it follows that net output is lower when sabotage is a possibility than when it is not. Since effort, μ, is lower and θ is higher, q is lower with sabotage. Since $C_2 > 0$, when $C_{12} = 0$, $C(\mu, \theta) > C(\mu, 0)$ for all μ. Therefore, costs are higher for any given μ. Even extreme doves, who are incapable of sabotage, could always implement $\hat{\mu}_D$ defined as the effort that generates the optimum expected output in the hawks' contest. But $f(\mu_H^*, \theta_H^*) - C(\hat{\mu}_D, 0) > f(\mu_H^*, \theta_H^*) - C(\mu_H^*, \theta_H^*)$ since $\mu_H^* > \hat{\mu}_D$ and $C_2 > 0$. Thus even at the hawks' optimum output, extreme doves have higher net revenue. But if that is true, then profits are even higher without sabotage at the nonsabotage optimum by the definition of an optimum. Thus net output, $Q(q_j, q_k) - 2C(\mu, \theta)$, is lower when sabotage exists.[4]

11.1.3. Pay Equality

The optimal wage spread is larger when sabotage is not possible. The intuition is that hawks are so aggressive that they kill each other in pursuit of the high reward. As such, firms select more equal wages for hawks to reduce their sabotage of one another. The cost is that effort falls as well.

For simplicity, let us continue to think of doves as extreme, where $\theta_D = 0$. That wages are more equal in hawklike firms is easily seen. It has already been shown that $\mu_D^* > \mu_H^*$ (from the comparison of (6′) with (7)). But with $C_{12} = 0$, the worker's first-order condition, (4a), implies that in order to induce the lower level of effort, $W_1 - W_2$ must be smaller (since μ is monotonic in $W_1 - W_2$). As a result, $W_1^D - W_2^D > W_1^H - W_2^H$. There is more equality in hawklike environments.

There is another way to make the point. There are really two kinds of effort in this model. Suppose that $f(\ )$ is additive so that $q_j = \mu_j - \theta_k + \varepsilon_j$ and $q_k = \mu_k - \theta_j + \varepsilon_k$. Workers would like to minimize the cost of producing this generalized effort, $\sigma \equiv \mu + \theta$, for any choice of σ. Firms prefer that for any choice of σ, all of it takes the form of μ rather than of θ. The problem is that the firm has only one instrument and can affect only the sum. Consider the wage differential that induces μ^*, the optimal level of effort when sabotage is fixed at zero. At that differential, workers who can engage in sabotage set $\theta > 0$. Now, by the envelope theorem, a small change in μ has no first-order effect, while there is a first-order gain from lowering θ. As a result, the wage differential should be reduced.[5] The result implies that personnel managers may push for internal equality because they recognize that an unequal reward structure creates incentives for uncooperative behavior.

The argument in favor of pay equality is based strictly on efficiency. Wage differentials are smaller than those that would prevail in the absence of sabotage because compression raises the average net output of the firm, and workers' expected utility rises as a result. Risk neutrality has been assumed throughout, and no exogenous demand for equality has been introduced. The equality is necessary to reduce worker incentives to destroy each other. This may not be too different from what personnel managers (and deans?) claim to be the justification for pay equality.[6]

Senior management often forces its supervisors to make relative comparisons by limiting the size of the bonus pool that may be distributed to subordinates. In this zero-sum framework, sabotage becomes an issue, which may explain why supervisors tend to equalize bonuses awarded to their subordinates. In addition to maintaining good supervisor/worker relations, bonus compression discourages uncooperative behavior.

11.1.4. Sainthood

One variant of the reasoning above permits analysis of saintlike behavior. Although the rhetoric has implied that $\theta > 0$, nothing formally constrains $\theta > 0$. In fact, it is possible that $C_2(\mu, \theta)$ is low, even zero, for negative values of θ. Figure 11.1 illustrates a case. A person with such a cost function could be called a "saint." That individual would be willing to increase the other worker's output, even though it lowers his chance of winning because it gives him utility of fellowship.

Figure 11.1

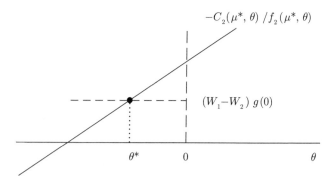

$$-C_2(\mu^*, \theta) / f_2(\mu^*, \theta)$$

$$(W_1 - W_2)\, g(0)$$

θ^* 0 θ

Nothing in the previous mathematics required that θ exceed zero, so the implication that wages are compressed for saints must hold. The intuition is that increasing the wage differential tempts even a saint. As $W_1 - W_2$ increases, the value of sabotage rises, so sainthood falls. What is important, of course, is the effect of altering the spread on changes in θ. Neither the level nor the sign of θ has any bearing on the firm's decision to select a particular wage differential.

11.2. Personality Counts

Some firms and academic departments pride themselves on ignoring personality attributes when hiring new workers. Others place considerable emphasis on the recruit's personality. "Old-boy" networks may serve to certify these less easily observed traits and often play an important role in the determination of which candidate gets the position. This section seeks to predict which firms use personality as a hiring criterion and which firms do not.

The question can be stated in terms of the familiar concept of separating equilibria (see e.g. Rothschild and Stiglitz, 1976). There are two questions. First, is it better to match or to mix types? If it is better to match, then personality need not be a factor if workers voluntarily sort to the appropriate firm. The second question then is, Do workers self-sort? The answer is that hawks generally prefer to work with doves. Thus firms must attempt to assess the personality (hawkishness) of workers.

It is not necessarily true that it is better to match than to mix types. However, sufficient (although not necessary) conditions for matching to dominate are that workers are risk neutral, that production, $f(\mu, \theta)$, is linear, that workers cannot be awarded handicaps, and that type-contingent compensation is not paid. To see this formally, consider the first-order conditions that workers face when they are paired against workers of their own type:

(8a)
$$(W_1^D - W_2^D)g(0) = C_1^D,$$

(8b)
$$(W_1^D - W_2^D)g(0) = C_2^D,$$

(8c)
$$(W_1^H - W_2^H)g(0) = C_1^H,$$

(8d)
$$(W_1^H - W_2^H)g(0) = C_2^H.$$

The wage structure in dovish firms may (in fact, will) differ from that in hawkish firms.

If instead workers are paired against the opposite type, the first-order conditions become[7]

(9a)
$$(W_1 - W_2)g(\mu^D - \mu^H + \theta^D - \theta^H) = C_1^D,$$

(9b)
$$(W_1 - W_2)g(\mu^D - \mu^H + \theta^D - \theta^H) = C_2^D,$$

(9c)
$$(W_1 - W_2)g(\mu^H - \mu^D + \theta^H - \theta^D) = C_1^H,$$

(9d)
$$(W_1 - W_2)g(\mu^H - \mu^D + \theta^H - \theta^D) = C_2^H.$$

Since all firms now consist of one hawk and one dove, there is only one wage structure. Also, since $g(\ )$ is symmetric around zero, $g(x) = g(-x)$, which implies that the left-hand sides of (9a) − (9d) all have the same value. Thus system (8a) − (8d) weakly dominates system (9a) − (9d).[8] The optimal values from (9a) − (9d) can always be obtained in the matched contest by selecting the appropriate W_1^D, W_2^D, W_1^H, and W_2^H. The reverse is not true. Thus under these conditions, firms should segregate aggressors from nonaggressors. The dominance of matched over mixed contests is based on linear technology with risk-neutral workers. Wages are not permitted to be type contingent, which is considered explicitly below.

Now it is shown that workers do not self-sort. Suppose that a firm of doves exists. Denote the equilibrium level of effort as μ_D^*. It has already been shown that as long as C_{12} is not sufficiently negative, hawks' output, q_H^*, is lower than doves', q_D^*. In competition, workers receive the full surplus so

$$\left(\frac{W_1 + W_2}{2}\right)^D > \left(\frac{W_1 + W_2}{2}\right)^H.$$

Hawks prefer to work at the dovish firm: net output is higher there and so are their chances of winning since their costs of choosing any $[\mu, \theta]$ can never exceed those of the doves; that is, $C^H(\mu, \theta) \leq C^D(\mu, \theta)$ for all θ. Thus hawks want to work in the doves' firm.[9] The reverse is not true: wages are lower in the hawks' firm and doves are at a cost disadvantage. Thus doves prefer to work with other doves.

This implies that dovish firms should use personality as a hiring criterion. Hawks will attempt to pass themselves off as doves, feigning a noncompetitive personality. It is rational for dovish firms to limit the workforce to genuine doves.

The same argument does not apply to hawkish firms. First, no doves would attempt to sneak in. Second, all incumbents are made better off when a dove enters. He raises average output and raises the probability above 1/2 that a hawk wins. It is no surprise that hawkish firms ignore personality attributes in hiring decisions. If the firm is already 100 percent hawk, it can do no worse. In fact, under these circumstances, all firms, including hawkish ones, attempt to convince new applicants of their dovishness.

Below, some assumptions are altered that change the results of this section somewhat. But even under the alternative assumptions, it is not generally the case that workers will self-sort. Sometimes doves prefer to pass themselves off as hawks because hawks are sufficiently lower-cost effort producers.

11.2.1. Segregation or Personality-Contingent Wages?

There is an alternative to segregation. If applicants' personalities can be identified, then contingent wages can be used instead of segregation. That is, hawks and doves can compete against one another, but the prize that a victorious hawk receives can differ from (and is lower than) that received by a victorious dove. Similarly, losing prizes are contingent on personality as well.

With linear production, in equations $(9a)$ and $(9b)$ $W_1 - W_2$ is replaced by $W_1^D - W_2^D$. Similarly, in $(9c)$ and $(9d)$, $W_1 - W_2$ is replaced by $W_1^H - W_2^H$ as follows:

$$(10a) \qquad (W_1^D - W_2^D)g(\mu^D - \mu^H + \theta^D - \theta^H) = C_1^D,$$

(10b) $$(W_1^D - W_2^D)g(\mu^D - \mu^H + \theta^D - \theta^H) = C_2^D,$$

(10c) $$(W_1^H - W_2^H)g(\mu^H - \mu^D + \theta^H - \theta^D) = C_1^H,$$

(10d) $$(W_1^H - W_2^H)g(\mu^H - \mu^D + \theta^H - \theta^D) = C_2^H.$$

Now, equations $(10a) - (10d)$ differ from $(8a) - (8d)$ only in that equilibrium in segregated firms has equal levels of μ and θ among contestants. That $g(\ )$ is not evaluated at zero has no consequence. It can be offset by changing wage spreads appropriately. In integrated firms, μ and θ depend on personality.

Which is better? The answer is that if equilibrium exists, it does not matter. Any (μ^*, θ^*) allocation that was achievable through $(8a)$ $- (8d)$ is also achievable through $(10a) - (10d)$. The converse is also true: any allocation achievable through $(10a) - (10d)$ is also achievable through $(8a) - (8d)$.

An implication is that wage inequality is greater in integrated firms. Since $g(X)$ attains a maximum for $X = 0$, the wage inequality between winners and losers is higher in integrated firms than in segregated ones. Additionally, all winners are not rewarded equally in integrated firms, but they are within each segregated firm.

When production is not linear or when workers are not risk neutral, personality-contingent wages are not equivalent to segregation. Unfortunately, there is no generalization that describes when one dominates the other. In particular, the spreads are different and win probabilities are type specific when workers are mixed and are paid type-specific wages. Risk-averse workers care about these distinctions. They cannot be offset in the simple way that applied for risk-neutral workers.

There is one consideration outside the model that is worthy of mention. Integrated firms create a situation in which disparate treatment is required. This means that management must tell some workers that they receive lower salaries, win or lose, because of their personality problems ("poor attitude"?). As a result, morale problems and labor unrest might result. With segregation, under the appropriate conditions, nothing is lost and hawks are not around to complain. Additionally, all hawks are treated ex ante equally in the hawkish firm. Of course, considerations of this sort are outside the formal structure because it has been assumed explicitly that worker types are observable.

11.2.2. Handicapping

These issues are related to handicapping. Segregation weakly dominates type-contingent compensation when workers are risk neutral and technology is linear, and may dominate or be dominated by type-contingent compensation when workers are risk averse. But there is an alternative. If types can be identified, workers can be "handicapped" as in Lazear and Rosen (1981, see Chapter 6). In fact, since effort plus sabotage can be thought of as generalized effort where hawks and doves have different technologies of production, all the results of Lazear and Rosen apply.[10] There, it was shown that giving the high-cost type a handicap (in the additive case equal to half the difference between optimal effort levels for the two types) results in efficient effort choice when cost functions have similar forms. The same can be achieved here. For any given level of σ, defined above, workers choose the most efficient method of production. That boils down to meeting the first-order conditions in (4). Thus a handicap system can achieve the same levels of μ and θ in an integrated environment that would be achieved by segregation. Further, it is accomplished without resorting to type-specific wages. The wages that must be used, however, generally imply larger spreads than necessary in the segregated matches. But since the handicap is not equalizing, the hawk's probability of winning exceeds $\frac{1}{2}$, whereas the dove's probability of winning falls short of $\frac{1}{2}$. Again, risk-averse workers may prefer one scheme to another, depending on the distribution of errors.

11.3. Multiworker Firms

The results of the two-person game generalize readily to games with more than two. To see that nothing is changed, the three-person firm is examined briefly.

Consider three players j, k, and L. Sabotage is modeled as a "public bad," so that θ_j reduces k's and L's output simultaneously, but this is not crucial. Thus the production function is now

$$q_j = f(\mu_j, \theta_k, \theta_L) + \varepsilon_j,$$
(1')
$$q_k = f(\mu_k, \theta_j, \theta_L) + \varepsilon_k,$$
$$q_L = f(\mu_L, \theta_j, \theta_k) + \varepsilon_L,$$

with $f_2, f_3 < 0, f_1 > 0$.

Assume that $\varepsilon_j - \varepsilon_L \sim g(\varepsilon_j - \varepsilon_L)$ is the same density as $\varepsilon_j - \varepsilon_k \sim g(\varepsilon_j - \varepsilon_k)$, and similarly for $\varepsilon_k - \varepsilon_L$.

The worker's problem is now

$$(3') \qquad \max_{\mu_j, \theta_j} P_1 W_1 + (1 - P_1 - P_3)W_2 + P_3 W_3 - C(\mu_j, \theta_j),$$

where P_1 is the probability of winning, P_3 is the probability of losing, and $1 - P_1 - P_3$ is the probability of finishing second.

The first-order conditions are

$$W_1 \frac{\partial P_1}{\partial \mu_j} - W_2 \frac{\partial P_1}{\partial \mu_j} - W_2 \frac{\partial P_3}{\partial \mu_j} - W_3 \frac{\partial P_3}{\partial \mu_j} - C_1(\mu_j, \theta_j) = 0$$

and

$$W_1 \frac{\partial P_1}{\partial \theta_j} - W_2 \frac{\partial P_1}{\partial \theta_j} - W_2 \frac{\partial P_3}{\partial \theta_j} - W_3 \frac{\partial P_3}{\partial \theta_j} - C_2(\mu_j, \theta_j) = 0.$$

Now

$$P_1 = \text{prob}[f(\mu_j, \theta_j) - f(\mu_k, \theta_k) > \varepsilon_k - \varepsilon_j \text{ and } f(\mu_j, \theta_j) - f(\mu_L, \theta_L) > \varepsilon_L - \varepsilon_j]$$

and

$$P_3 = \text{prob}[f(\mu_k, \theta_k) - f(\mu_j, \theta_j) > \varepsilon_j - \varepsilon_k \text{ and } f(\mu_L, \theta_L) - f(\mu_j, \theta_j) > \varepsilon_j - \varepsilon_L].$$

Since the density of $\varepsilon_m - \varepsilon_n$, $m \neq n$, is identical and symmetric irrespective of the choice or order of m and n, at the point of symmetric equilibrium[11] $\partial P_1/\partial \mu_i = -\partial P_3/\partial \mu_i$ and $\partial P_1/\partial \theta_i = -\partial P_3/\partial \theta_i$, for all i.

Thus the first-order conditions can be written as

$$(W_1 - W_3) \frac{\partial P_1}{\partial \mu_j} = C_1(\mu_j, \theta_j)$$

and

$$(W_1 - W_3) \frac{\partial P_1}{\partial \theta_j} = C_2(\mu_j, \theta_j).$$

With the exception of the replacement of W_2 by W_3, these are identical to the first-order conditions in the two-player game. In essence, this says that when workers are risk neutral, only one spread matters. The other wage can be set arbitrarily. The firm's problem is identical except that there is a redundant degree of freedom in the zero-profit condition. Thus all other results hold. An extension of the argument applies to four or more players as well since extra wage choices simply provide redundant degrees of freedom.

11.4. Other Issues

11.4.1. Complementarities

It is useful to explore how relationships are altered when complementarities are present. Workers who have low marginal costs of sabotage may also have low marginal costs of effort. Complementarities are easily treated. Only the sorting results of an earlier section are affected. Then it was necessary to argue that total output for hawks was less than that for doves. That assumption implied that hawks would try to pass themselves off as doves. But if cost advantages are correlated across types, then it is possible that things may be turned around. Doves may want to feign hawkish personalities to obtain a job in the high-output, hawkish firm. Applicants are sometimes aggressive in interviews, attempting to convince recruiters that they have low costs of effort, not low costs of sabotage. Only a positive correlation between the costs explains this behavior.

11.4.2. Inference

It has already been demonstrated that hawks will not show their true colors voluntarily. Suppose that hawks and doves cannot be distinguished perfectly at the outset. Victory over other contestants may tip management off about their type. (Pool sharks let their opponents win every so often to avoid having their true ability discovered.) This implies that firms should adjust their treatment of winners to take into account that they are likely to be dealing with low-cost individuals. Low cost can arise in two ways. A worker can be good at producing effort because he is effective at producing the positive output, μ, or he can be good because he is effective at sabotage. If the firm cannot distinguish (or cannot distinguish perfectly) between worker types at the time of hiring, some individuals who win contests are likely to be good at sabotage.

More formally, suppose that α of the population consists of individuals with low cost of effort functions, Quicks, and $1 - \alpha$ with high cost of effort functions, Slows, such that $C^Q(\sigma) < C^S(\sigma)$ for all σ, where Q denotes Quick and S denotes Slow, and $\sigma \equiv \mu + \theta$, as above. It can be shown using Bayes's theorem that

$$\text{prob}(\text{Quick}|\text{win}) = \alpha[2(1 - \alpha)G^* + \alpha],$$

where G^* is defined as the (endogenous) probability that a Quick wins in a contest in which he knows that he is paired against a Slow (and the Slow knows it as well). Since $G^* > \frac{1}{2}$,

$$\text{prob}(\text{Quick}|\text{win}) > \alpha.$$

Thus a victory implies that the posterior moves toward the conclusion that the winning player is a Quick.

The change in language to Quick and Slow is intentional. The firm does not want to promote good saboteurs, but only good (low-cost) producers. The problem is that there is no easy way for the firm to distinguish the two. An individual is more likely to win when he is a low cost of effort type, but this can arise either because he is an effective producer or because he is an effective saboteur. Unless the correlation between being productive and being a good saboteur is negative, there will be more hawks in the population of winners than in the population as a whole. If winning is necessary for a promotion, then higher levels in the hierarchy will tend to be somewhat hawk intensive. Thus relative payment is particularly dangerous at higher levels in the hierarchy because the upper echelons have more than their share of hawks. Bonuses, based on individual or firm output, may be better for high-level management because they do not carry with them the disadvantage that they encourage sabotage.

Keeping arm's length relations between opposing contestants is another way for the firm to mitigate hawks' predatory behavior. If relative comparisons are to be used, they should be between individuals from different branches or between individuals with responsibilities that are quite separate from one another. For example, before the breakup of American Telephone and Telegraph, the president of the parent company was usually chosen from the ranks of presidents of the operating companies. These individuals were not in positions to sabotage their rivals easily.[12]

An extension of this kind of argument may help explain why some firms are organized by function and others by product. For example, General Motors could have an accounting department, a marketing department, and a production department for all its cars. Alternatively, it could organize by products, namely Chevrolet, Oldsmobile, and so forth and have smaller groups within each. The president of General Motors can be chosen from among the heads of each car line. Chevy's chief has an incentive to avoid cooperation with Pontiac's, but the effects may not be as bad as when Chevy's marketing group works against Chevy's sales force. The disadvantage of grouping by product line is that such a grouping does not take full advantage of positive interactions between, say, accountants at Chevy and those at Olds. The point is that a system of relative compensation discourages cooperation between rivals for the same salary. As such, the lines along which rivalries are set up are far from arbitrary. In one real-world example, the Dow Chemical Corporation makes it a policy to move people from field to home office and back at each promotion. Although there are a number of possible explanations for this phenomenon,[13] the policy is consistent with avoiding rivalry within units in which cooperation is important. Since the next vice-president at the home office is chosen from among assistant vice-presidents at different field sites, there is little chance for the assistants to affect one another adversely.

11.5. Empirical Implications

The main point of this analysis is that wage compression is optimal under competitive circumstances. Further, average productivity is lower in a firm of competitive individuals. These two points give rise to an immediate implication: The average wage is lower in firms that have more compressed wage structures. Other things equal, compression is a reaction to having a hawkish group of workers. Thus compression and hawkish behavior should be correlated across firms. As such, average productivity and average wages should be lower in firms with more equal wages. The implication on compression and average wage takes a specific form. Consider the following earnings regression: wage $= X\beta + \varepsilon$, where X is a vector of productivity characteristics (such as schooling and experience). The model assumes that within a group all workers are ex ante identical. Thus it is not compression evidenced by small β's that is relevant. All the X's are observable, and wages and rivalries should already be conditioned on them. Rather, it is the standard error of the estimate that matters. Given a group of ex ante identical workers, hawks should end up with more compressed wages than doves. Thus there should be a positive relation of mean wage to standard error of the estimate by firm.[14]

To the extent that wage compression is a measure of hawkishness, a couple of implications follow. First, since hawkish firms are unconcerned about attracting the wrong type, personality screening should be unimportant in firms in which wages are compressed. Second, since the value of organizing a firm by product line increases with the hawkishness of the workers, wage compression and organization by product (rather than function) should be positively related.

11.6. Summary and Conclusions

It is often useful to pay workers on the basis of their relative performance. This means that workers benefit not only by their own successes but also by their rivals' failures. Incentives exist, therefore, to devote some resources to making opponents look bad. When one worker makes a good point, it is often followed by another worker's attempt to discredit it. In large corporations, in which promotions depend on relative performance, workers are reluctant to share their secrets with other workers, even at the expense of reduced output. Visibility and credit are coveted attributes of most jobs for the obvious reason that they increase the chances of promotion and the resulting higher wealth.

Perhaps the most important result is that some pay compression is efficient. The argument by union leaders and personnel managers that pay dispersion leads to disharmony is correct. If harmony is important, pay compression is optimal on strict efficiency grounds. Thus the ability to sabotage one's rival provides an efficiency argument for equitable treatment within a firm.

Other results are the following: (1) Firms rationally take personality into account when deciding which workers to hire. Ignoring personality may result in excessively competitive behavior. (2) Pay by relative performance is more of a problem at the higher levels of the job hierarchy. Those jobs tend to have an abnormally high proportion of competitive individuals, so pay may be closer to piece rates. Alternatively, rivals can be separated so that they do not damage one another.

12

Culture and Language

Culture is defined by anthropologists in a variety of ways. The definition usually includes some notion of shared values, beliefs, expectations, customs, jargon, and rituals. Language is the set of common sounds and symbols by which individuals communicate.[1] Societies may include a number of cultures and languages. For example, while the majority of Americans speak English, a significant proportion are Spanish-speaking. Even among the English speakers, accents and vocabularies differ by region of the country.

Multiculturalism, or the tolerance by a society of many different cultures and languages, seems to be on the rise in the United States. This shows up in a number of ways. One of the most tangible of these is the recent growth of bilingual education.[2] In the past, most immigrants insisted that their children be taught in English so that they could become "Americans." The growth of multiculturalism, for good or bad, takes the view that Americans speak many languages and have many different cultures.[3]

The original version of this chapter was published as: Lazear, E. P. (1999). Culture and Language, in: Journal of Political Economy, 107(6), 95-126. University of Chicago Press. © 1999 by the University of Chicago. This essay is in honor of Gary Becker, who influenced my thinking enormously. During my almost 20 years at Chicago, Gary, as a senior colleague and friend, was a source of constant inspiration. I believe that the analysis in this paper is very much in the spirit of Gary's work. It is probably closest to his Economics of Discrimination (1957), and its goal is to take an economic framework and use it to explain a phenomenon that would have been viewed as essentially sociological. In this case, the parallels with his work on discrimination are quite close. Prices drive the model, and the question relates to how different ethnic groups interact with one another. I hope that the analysis will bolster the argument, made most convincingly by Becker, that economics is a very powerful discipline that can be used to shed light on almost all aspects of behavior. This work was supported in part by the National Science Foundation. I thank Michael Schwarz for research assistance. I also acknowledge the useful comments of Richard Adelstein, Annelise Anderson, Gary Becker, David Card, Nicholas Economides, Henry Farber, Eugene Fama, Robert Gibbons, Edward Glaeser, Matthew Jackson, Andrew John, Ken Judd, Jacob Mincer, Casey Mulligan, Paul Romer, Sherwin Rosen, George Shultz, Karen Van Nuys, Michael Waldman, Kei-Mu Yi, and participants of seminars at the Stanford Graduate School of Business, Hoover, Princeton, the University of Chicago, and the University of Rochester.

In 1900, 85 percent of immigrants were fluent in English. Surprisingly, in 1990, the fluency rate among immigrants was only 68 percent, despite dramatic improvements in communication during the century. What accounts for the change over time? When do immigrants hold on to their native cultures and languages? Under which circumstances is assimilation most likely to occur? Given that society exists at a point in time with more than one culture, do the benefits from moving to a common culture outweigh the costs of the transition? How do government transfer policies affect assimilation? Is the localization of minorities into neighborhoods a natural outgrowth of maximizing behavior and is subsidized integration welfare enhancing? Is chauvinistic behavior by some societies socially beneficial or merely an emotional response without any social value? These questions are addressed below. The theory is confirmed by an empirical analysis based on U.S. census data from 1900 and 1990.

12.1. A Model of Culture

Trade between individuals is facilitated when all traders share a common culture and language. A common culture allows individuals to trade with one another without intermediaries. In the case of language, this is most clear. If two agents speak the same language, they can negotiate a contract without the use of a translator. A common culture allows the traders to have common expectations and customs, which enhances trust.[4]

The model presented here focuses on common culture and the facilitation of trade, defined broadly to include nonmarket interaction as well.[5] Let us begin by assuming that an individual randomly encounters one and only one other individual in each period.[6] Suppose that the expected value to one party of meeting another individual with whom one can trade is normalized to be one. Initially, suppose that there are only two cultures in a country, labeled A and B. Define p_a as the proportion of individuals who belong to culture A in equilibrium and p_b as the proportion of individuals who belong to culture B in equilibrium. The majority culture is A, which means that $p_a > p_b$. It is possible that $p_a + p_b > 1$ since one individual can belong to two cultures, as, for example, in the case of bilingual persons. In order for trade to occur, an individual must encounter another individual with his own culture. If the value per trader of a trade is one, then the expected gains from trade that accrue to A's and B's are

$$(1a) \qquad\qquad R_a = p_a$$

and

$$(1b) \qquad\qquad R_b = p_b.$$

Since $p_a > p_b$, $R_a > R_b$. Individuals from the majority are richer than those from the minority.

Either type of individual can acquire the culture of the other group. When B's acquire the A culture, they become "assimilated" into the A group. They may still retain some or all of their old culture, but they now have the ability to trade with the majority group. In the case of language, this can be thought of as becoming fluent in the majority language while retaining the ability to speak the native tongue. Similarly, A's might acquire the B culture or learn the B language. Individuals make choices atomistically. The model is one of competition. Neither A's nor B's can collude as a group to choose a strategy.

In reality, trade can occur between individuals with different cultures or languages. In the case of language, a translator can be used. In the case of culture, mistrust and misunderstandings can be avoided by hiring individuals who are bicultural to act as liaisons. But such activity is costly, and it is best to think of the value of a trade as the net gain associated with being able to conduct the trade without engaging the services of an intermediary.

Resources must be expended to acquire the new culture or to learn the new language. Define t_j as an individual-specific cost parameter that measures (inversely) the efficiency with which individual j acquires the new culture. The density and distribution functions for t_j are denoted $g(t_j)$ and $G(t_j)$, respectively.

It is now straightforward to determine whether an individual will become bicultural. A B who is monocultural expects to receive income p_b. If the minority member becomes bicultural, every encounter results in a trade, but t_j is spent learning the ways of the majority.

Thus the B acquires the A culture if and only if $1 - t_j > p_b$ or if and only if

$$(2) \qquad\qquad t_j < 1 - p_b.$$

It follows that the proportion of B's who learn A is

$$(3) \qquad\qquad \text{prob}(t_j < 1 - p_b) = G(1 - p_b).$$

A proportion $G(1 - p_b)$ of the B's are sufficiently efficient at acquiring the new culture to make it worthwhile.

Analogously, an individual of culture A acquires culture B if and only if

$$(4) \qquad\qquad t_j - 1 - p_a,$$

so that the proportion of A's who learn B is

$$(5) \qquad\qquad G(1 - p_a).$$

(This assumes that the distribution of costs of learning B is the same as the distribution of the costs of learning A. This assumption is made so that behavioral differences are not a result of differences in distributional assumptions across groups.)

Since $G(1 - p_b)$ is decreasing in p_b, the proportion of a minority group that becomes assimilated into the majority culture is decreasing in the proportion of the population comprising the minority group. Analogously, because $\partial G(1 - p_a)/\partial p_a < 0$, the proportion of the majority group that learns the minority language is decreasing in the proportion of the population that speaks the majority language. Further, $p_a > p_b$ guarantees that the proportion of majority members who learn the minority language is smaller than the proportion of minority members who learn the majority language.

As p_b decreases, the minority group becomes smaller relative to the majority, which means that random contact with another is less likely to result in a trade. When p_b is very small, minority members must be assimilated in order to survive in the society. Conversely, if the majority holds only a slight population advantage over the minority, the likelihood that the majority learns the minority culture is almost as great as the likelihood that the minority learns the majority culture.

A member of the majority might learn the minority culture. Individuals who are particularly adept at learning languages or cultural traditions have low values of t_j. Consequently, some majority members will learn the minority language even though encounters with minority members are relatively rare.

Encounters with other members of society are hardly random. Individuals tend to cluster with others from their own culture, in large part because doing so enhances trade. Formally, this is handled by defining the relevant group for analysis as that set of individuals with whom random encounters are equally (and most) likely. An individual's circle of encounters depends on the amount of specialization in the economy. In a society with no specialization in which each individual produces everything that he or she consumes, there is little reason to encounter individuals outside a very narrow group of family and neighbors. Indeed, as countries have increased their levels of specialization and trade with other countries, they have found it valuable to learn a common language, which in the current world is English. Air traffic control provides an example. Were all flights domestic ones, there would be no need to communicate in a common language. But with increased international travel, it becomes necessary to use one language for air traffic control. Historically, the choice has been English.

12.2. Some Evidence

The theory presented above implies that individuals who locate in areas that are highly concentrated are less likely to be assimilated into the majority culture. That hypothesis can be examined using data from the 1900 census and from the 1990 census for the United States. To get at this question, some measure of concentration must be adopted. Define

CNTYPCT = 100 (number of persons in the county who were born in the given immigrant's native country ÷ number of persons in the county).

The variable CNTYPCT is defined for every immigrant in the surveys. Two immigrants who live in the same county would have different values of CNTYPCT if they were immigrants from different countries. For example, a native of Germany living in Chicago in 1900 would have a higher value of CNTYPCT than a native of New Zealand living in Chicago because there were more people living in Chicago in 1900 who were born in Germany than were born in New Zealand.

For the purposes of analysis here, culture is proxied by the ability to speak English. Unfortunately, cross-year comparisons are somewhat limited by the differences in questionnaires between 1900 and 1990. In 1990, English-speaking ability was categorized as speaks English (1) very well, (2) well, (3) not well, or (4) not at all. In 1900, speaks English was simply coded as (1) yes or (2) no. As a result, another variable, FLUENT, was defined as follows:

$$\text{FLUENT} = \begin{cases} 1 & \text{if year is 1990 and English takes on values 1 or 2,} \\ & \text{or if year is 1900 and English takes on value 1} \\ 0 & \text{otherwise.} \end{cases}$$

Two other variables are used in the analysis. They are the age of the individual, AGE, and YEARS−US, which measures the number of years that the individual has been in the United States. SPANISH, CHINESE, GERMAN, and SWEDISH are dummy variables equal to one if the individual's language in the home country matches the name of the variable. Table 12.1 reports the mean values of some key variables by year.

Table 12.1

Means of Key Variables among Immigrants, 1900 and 1990

Variable	1990 Data	1900 Data
FLUENT	.68	.85
CNTYPCT	5,40	9,00
AGE	38,80	40,00
YEARS−US	14,80	20,20
CNTYSQ	121,30	181,30
SPANISH	.48	
CHINESE	.07	
GERMAN		.33
SWEDISH		.06
N	70,782	11,171

Table 12.2

Means of CNTYPCT by Fluency, 1900 and 1990

Variable	1990 Data	1900 Data
Overall	5.4%	9.0%
FLUENT = 0	8.3%	12.5%
FLUENT = 1	4.0%	8.4%

To see the effects of concentration, it is easiest to look at the mean level of concentration, that is, CNTYPCT among the fluent and non-fluent. Table 12.2 presents the findings.

In both 1900 and 1990, the pattern is the same. Individuals who are fluent in English tend to live in communities in which a smaller percentage of residents are from their native lands than those who are not fluent in English. In 1900, persons who were not fluent in English lived, on average, in counties in which 12.5 percent of the residents of the county were born in their native land. In the same year, persons who were fluent in English lived in counties in which only 8.4 percent of the county residents were from their native land. The same pattern prevails in 1990. Those who were fluent in English lived in counties that had about half the proportion of residents from the immigrant's native land as those who were not fluent.[7]

Table 12.1 implies significant clustering. In 1900, the largest group of immigrants were Germans, who accounted for about one-third of the immigrant population, or about 4 percent of U.S. residents. If all counties were the same size and German-born immigrants were spread randomly across the United States, the average level of CNTYPCT in 1900 would be 4 percent among Germans. For all other groups it would be much smaller. If each immigrant lived in a county that was composed entirely of immigrants from his or her native land, then the mean of CNTYPCT would be 100 percent because the sample consists only of immigrants. The fact that the mean of CNTYPCT overall is 9 percent implies clustering among immigrants. Further, while the observed pattern implies clustering, those who cluster are less likely to know or learn English.

The figures in Table 12.2 are simply raw numbers that do not correct for other factors. For example, the average immigrant in 1900 was in the United States for a longer period of time than the average 1990 immigrant. Differences in these variables might explain some differences between residency patterns among those fluent and those not fluent. Thus logits were run specifying FLUENT as the dependent variable and positing CNTYPCT, YEARS–US, and AGE as explanatory variables.[8]

Table 12.3 reports logits with different nonlinear specifications for 1900 and 1990.[9] All nonlinear variables were permitted to enter each logit in each year. In 1900, the squared term did not enter significantly, and its point estimate was virtually zero. In 1990, the squared term is important. The reverse is true for CNTYPCT × YEARS–US. In 1900, the interaction term enters significantly. In 1990, it never entered significantly, despite the fact that there are over 70,000 observations. The coefficient is almost certainly close to zero.

From the coefficients in Table 12.3, in 1900 the effect of a one-standard-deviation increase in CNTYPCT, evaluated at the mean of YEARS–US, implies a reduction in the probability of being fluent by 5.3 percentage points. For 1990, the effects are extremely large. The effect of a one-standard-deviation increase in CNTYPCT is to lower fluency in 1990 by .23 or by about one-third of the total level of fluency for the country. Data from both years support the contention that concentration and fluency are negatively correlated. But the nature of the effect is quite different, as will be discussed in the next section.

Table 12.3

Logit Estimates: FLUENT as Dependent Variable and with Nonlinearities, 1990 and 1900

Variable	Coefficient	Standard Error	z
	1990 (Mean of FLUENT = .68; N = 70,782)		
CNTYPCT	-.157	.0027	-57.7
CNTYPCT^2	.0026	.000057	45.7
YEARS–US	.137	.0026	53.4
(YEARS–US)^2	-.001	.00006	-17.9
CNTYPCT × YEARS–US	-.00004	.00008	-.462
AGE	-.054	.0007	-76.6
Constant	1.88	.0285	66
Log likelihood	-36,791		
	1900 (Mean of FLUENT = . 85; N = 11,171)		
CNTYPCT	-.0143	.0072	-1.99
CNTYPCT^2	.00002	.0001	.175
YEARS–US	.239	.008	29.6
(YEARS–US)^2	-.0022	.00138	-16.1
CNTYPCT × YEARS–US	-.0014	.00023	-5.876
AGE	-.0596	.00254	-23.4
Constant	1.54	.097	15.8
Log likelihood	-3,718		

12.2.1. Sorting versus Learning

There are two interpretations of the results of Table 12.3, both of which are consistent with the model. The first interpretation is that English is learned more rapidly by immigrants who are in integrated communities. This takes residential location as exogenous. It is a direct implication of the model because those who are in communities in which the majority language dominates have greater incentives to become assimilated and to learn the language.[10]

The second interpretation is one of sorting. Individuals who are not fluent in English are probably more likely to move to areas in which there are many others who speak their own language. The sorting explanation is clearly possible but surely reflects the same mechanism described in this chapter. Individuals who are not fluent in English move to areas that are dominated by individuals who speak their native language precisely because they cannot interact with others unless they do. If it were unnecessary to be with individuals who share language to interact, the locational pattern of immigrants would be uncorrelated with English fluency. Immigrants might still cluster just because different areas settle at different times and immigrant waves are time dependent. But there would be no reason to expect that those who did not live in neighborhoods with high concentrations of immigrants would be more likely to attain English fluency.[11]

The two interpretations are more a question of timing than of substance. Immigrants who know English had to make a decision to learn it at some point in the past. That decision was likely influenced by their desire to trade with other English speakers. Those who learn English after coming to the United States perform the same calculation, but do so at a later stage. Thus the sorting story differs from the learning story primarily in the timing at which English was learned, not on the motives for learning English.

The coefficients in Table 12.3 allow these effects to be disentangled. If learning in the United States is the primary mechanism, then one would expect the effect of clustering to operate through the YEARS–US variable. Those who live in highly concentrated communities would have lower rates of learning and therefore lower effects of YEARS–US. The negative interaction term found for 1900 in Table 12.3 is exactly this effect. For example, in 1900, 2 percent of the immigrants from Germany lived in communities in which at least 40 percent of the population was born in Germany. In these communities, the estimated effect of an additional year in the United States is[12]

$$40(-.0014) + .239 - (.0022)(2)(20.2) - .059 = .035.$$

If the individual lived in a community with no other Germans, the estimated effect would be .094. Thus those who live in the majority community are about two and a half times more likely to learn English in any given year than those who live in a county that is 40 percent German.

Table 12.4

Regressions of Fluency Rates on Group Numbers ($N = 193$)

Variable	Degrees of Freedom	Parameter Estimate	Standard Error	T for H_0: Parameter = 0
	Dependent Variable: FLUENT Unweighted ($R^2 = .03$)			
Intercept	1	.858126	.01525142	56.265
N	1	-.000026155	.00000969	-2.698
	Dependent Variable: FLUENT Weighted by $N^{1/2}$ ($R^2 = .03$)			
Intercept	1	.811211	.01124277	72.154
N	1	-.000016750	.00000213	-7.847

In 1990, no significant interaction effects were found. This favors the sorting interpretation for 1990. Those who locate in areas in which the majority language dominates are more likely to have learned English before coming here. From the numbers in Table 12.3, it does not appear that concentration has any effect on the rate of learning once the individual is in the United States.[13]

It is not unreasonable that clustering would have a bigger impact on the rate of learning in the United States in 1900 than in 1990. To the extent that television and other improvements in communication over time have made information more integrated, individuals who live in highly segregated areas still have contact with other cultures and languages through the media. This is interpreted as a leftward shift in the distribution of t_j over time. The direction of the change is not surprising, but it is somewhat surprising that the within-United States learning effect vanishes almost completely by 1990.

Not surprisingly, older immigrants are less likely to be fluent in English than younger ones. This is a direct prediction of Becker's

(1975) human capital theory. Since learning a language is an investment that has a payback over time, the older the individual, the fewer years over which to recoup the investment and the smaller the return. Additionally, it may be true that it is more difficult for older individuals to learn a new language, which would show up formally as a rightward shift in the distribution of t_j.

12.2.2. Additional Evidence

The data from 1990 were grouped by country of origin. For each country of origin, a fluency rate was computed. Table 12.4 reports the results of regressing the fluency rate on the number of individuals in the particular group, of which there are 193.

There are two regressions reported. One is unweighted; the other weights by $\sqrt{N}$. Both show the negative relation between country of origin and fluency. Those groups that make up large proportions of the immigrant population are also less likely to be fluent in English.

The group regressions are not compelling for the 1900 data. The Table 12.4 analysis done for 1900 yields, if anything, positive coefficients on N. Why? A deeper investigation (Lazear 1996a), beyond the scope of this chapter, reveals that Germans, who were a very large group in 1900, are more fluent than expected, given their large numbers in the population. This reflects two factors. First, German immigrants had been in the United States considerably longer than other immigrant groups. Second, they had a pattern of clustering different from that of current immigrants, which tended to cause a larger proportion to be in touch with English speakers.

There are sufficient numbers of Spanish and Chinese speakers in 1990 and of German speakers in 1900 to perform the analysis of Table 12.3 on each of these groups separately. All three logits produce similar negative effects of CNTYPCT on FLUENT, even within groups. Those Germans who lived in heavily German neighborhoods in 1900 were less likely to be fluent in English. The same is true of Spanish and Chinese speakers today.

Finally, there is other evidence on these points. In a series of papers, Chiswick (1991) and Chiswick and Miller (1995, 1996) have documented similar results for a number of countries. Using an Australian data set, Chiswick and Miller find that the acquisition of destination language skills is inhibited by living in an area in which many others speak the same minority language. Chiswick finds that English fluency increases with the duration of time the immigrant has been in the United States.

12.2.3. Reconciling the Two Periods

Fluency rates in 1900 are substantially higher than they are in 1990, perhaps because of differences in the characteristics of the immigrant pool or a different underlying structure of the economy. It is possible to parcel out these effects. If the structure of the economy remained unchanged but the immigrants were different, then most of the difference between 1900 and 1990 should be explained by changes in the explanatory variables, not in the coefficients. Thus, define $\hat{p}_{90}$ as the mean value of the predicted level of p when the logit from 1900 and the actual characteristics of the individuals in the 1990 sample are used. Conversely, define $\hat{p}_{00}$ as the mean value of the predicted level of p when the logit from 1990 and the actual characteristics of the individuals in the 1900 sample are used. The logit model fitted for 1900 is $p_{00} = \exp(x_{00}\beta_{00})/[1 - \exp(x_{00}\beta_{00})]$ and that for 1990 is $p_{90} = \exp(x_{90}\beta_{90})/[1 - \exp(x_{90}\beta_{90})]$. If the structure were unchanged, then $\beta_{90} = \beta_{00}$, and we can write

$$p_{90} - p_{00} = \frac{\exp(x_{90}\beta_{00})}{1 + \exp(x_{90}\beta_{00})} - \frac{\exp(x_{00}\beta_{00})}{1 + \exp(x_{00}\beta_{00})}.$$

Taking expectations, we get

$$\overline{p}_{90} - \overline{p}_{00} = \hat{p}_{90} - \overline{p}_{00}.$$

Thus one estimate of the proportion of the change between 1900 and 1990 that is accounted for by changes in the explanatory variables is $(\hat{p}_{90} - \overline{p}_{00})/(\overline{p}_{90} - \overline{p}_{00})$.

Alternatively, instead of using 1900 as the base year, we can use 1990. Then, if the structure is unchanged, we can write

$$p_{90} - p_{00} = \frac{\exp(x_{90}\beta_{90})}{1 + \exp(x_{90}\beta_{90})} - \frac{\exp(x_{00}\beta_{90})}{1 + \exp(x_{00}\beta_{90})}.$$

Another estimate of the amount of the change accounted for by changes in the explanatory variables is then $(\overline{p}_{90} - \hat{p}_{00})/(\overline{p}_{90} - \overline{p}_{00})$. Now, $\overline{p}_{90} = .68$, $\hat{p}_{00} = .68$, $\hat{p}_{90} = .78$, and $\overline{p}_{00} = .85$. Thus the estimates of the proportion explained by changes in the variables are bounded by $(.68 - .68)/-.17 = 0$ and by $(.78 - .85)/-.17 = 41$ percent. By any interpretation, most of the change over time is a result of a change in the structure rather than a change in the values of the explanatory variables.

It is common to find that cross-sectional analyses do not go far to explain differences over time. The same is true here. In this case, there is no obvious explanation. The largest group of immigrants in 1900 spoke German; the largest group in 1990 speaks Spanish. The model does well in explaining differences in fluency within each of the groups in any given time period but does much worse in explaining why Spanish-speaking immigrants today learn English at different rates than German-speaking immigrants of 1900.

One possible explanation is that the individuals are drawn from different parts of the donor population. If the costs of migration are lower today than they were in 1900, particularly for less educated or lower-ability individuals, then the level of human capital among the pool of immigrants could well be lower today than it was in 1900. This is the point of Borjas (1985).

The conclusion from this section is that the model does well to explain fluency for any given group or all groups taken together at any point in time. The model does less well in accounting for variations over time in fluency rates and assimilation.

12.3. Extensions

12.3.1. Fragmentation, Neutral Cultures, and Critical Mass

Some countries have no significant majority, but instead are fragmented into a large number of small minorities. India and some African countries come to mind. Is acquisition of another culture more likely or less likely in such an environment? The answer is not obvious. While the gains to learning any other single language are few, the alternatives are also poor. Since each minority is very small, the number of trading partners for a monocultural individual is small.

The model allows the question to be answered. Instead of having one minority B having p_b members, consider the situation in which the entire population consists of minority individuals split into N groups, each of which has $1/N$ members. As before, allow the cost of learning each culture to be t_j. Given constant costs, an individual who learns one culture learns every culture. Thus the choice is to learn all other $N - 1$ cultures at a cost of $(N - 1)t_j$ or to trade only with $1/N$ individuals in the economy.[14] The individual learns other cultures if and only if $1 - (N - 1)t_j > 1/N$ or if and only if

(6) $$t_j < \frac{1}{N - 1}\left(1 - \frac{1}{N}\right).$$

When (6) is compared to (2), individuals in a fragmented society are less likely to learn other cultures if

(7) $$\frac{1}{N - 1}\left(1 - \frac{1}{N}\right) < 1 - p_b.$$

Now, p_b is the proportion of minority members in a bicultural society. "Minority" implies that they make up less than half of the population. Thus, to show that learning other cultures is less likely in a fragmented society, it is sufficient to show that the left-hand side of (7) is less than one-half for $N > 2$. This follows directly: When $N = 2$, the left-hand side equals one-half. Also, $\partial/\partial N = -(1/N^2)$, which implies that the left-hand side is less than one-half for $N > 2$.

Thus, while not obvious, it is true that societies that begin fragmented are more likely to remain fragmented. The incentive for any given individual to become multicultural is smaller when no other culture accounts for much of the population.

Under fragmented circumstances, a "neutral" culture is sometimes chosen. If all others in a society speak the neutral language, an individual learns it whenever $1 - t_j > 1/N$ or when $t_j < 1 - (1/N)$. The right-hand side of this expression exceeds the right-hand side of (6) for $N > 2$, which means that an individual in a fragmented society is more likely to learn a neutral language than other minority languages.

Under which conditions will a neutral culture be established? Suppose that we begin with N equally powerful cultures in a given country. Resources would be saved if one of the N cultures was chosen as the dominant one, rather than a neutral culture that is not already present in the society. Then only $N - 1$ rather than N groups would have to learn a new culture. Of course, the group whose culture is chosen to be dominant gains relative to other cultures. This can be dealt with through side payments but would necessitate a tax or subsidy structure that based treatment on culture (e.g., affirmative action). The chosen minority would be taxed at a higher rate than other minorities. If this is done correctly, every group would be indifferent between being the chosen culture and being one that receives a transfer.[15]

In the absence of transfers, the catalyst for moving to a neutral culture is likely to be imperialism. The "choices" of English for India and of Russian for Eastern Europe were brought about by the intervention of a foreign power. Still, in countries such as India, where there are a very large number of languages spoken, individuals learn English (or Hindi) so that they can communicate with the vast majority of others in the society who do not speak their language. Israel made a conscious decision to use Hebrew as its language and to set up programs to teach the vast majority of immigrants this language. Since the immigrants came from many different countries and spoke different languages, (e.g., German, Yiddish, Russian, Romanian, Hungarian, Polish, French, Arabic, and English), it was natural to seek a common language. As a result, Israel was successful in inducing its population to use a language that was not spoken by any group of people for 2,000 years.[16] The choice of Hebrew over, say, Yiddish carried costs. Had Yiddish been adopted, Yiddish speakers would not have had to learn another language, and this benefit could have been shared. But again, a tax and subsidy structure that could implement such transfers was probably politically infeasible.[17]

When a "critical mass" forms, adoption of a neutral language may slow. A modification of (2) shows that a minority that accounts for p_x of the population learns the neutral language when $t_j < 1 - p_x$. If $p_x > 1/N$, the minority member has less incentive to learn the neutral language than a member of the representative group in the fragmented society. If p_x, is sufficiently large, the failure by group x relative to smaller minority groups to acquire the neutral culture may be significant.

Indeed, many Israelis now fear that the huge wave of Russian immigrants who have entered Israel in recent years may have reached a critical mass. Rather than becoming assimilated into Israeli culture, the new Russian Israelis may continue to speak Russian and subscribe to Russian culture.[18]

This point has been made before in another context. McNeill (1989, p. 57) writes that

"From the 1830s and especially after 1850, rapid urban growth together with the ravages of a new disease, cholera, disrupted cultural patterns of long standing in the Hapsburg monarchy. Peasant migrants into the towns of Bohemia and Hungary had long been accustomed to learn German, and in a few generations, their descendants became German in sentiment as well as in language. This process began to falter in the nineteenth century. When the number of Slav- and Magyar-speaking migrants living in the cities of the monarchy passed a certain point, newcomers no longer had to learn German for everyday life. Presently nationalist ideals took root and made a German identity seem unpatriotic. The result was that Prague became a Czech- and Budapest a Magyar-speaking city within half a century."

It is possible for a society to "tip" from one language to another in one generation, but migration would have to be massive for it to occur. A more typical scenario involves a change that occurs over time as subsequent generations learn a language different from the language of their parents. Usually, the children of immigrants learn the language of the majority, but in cases like the one described above, it is possible that children of the majority might learn the language of the minority.

To understand the dynamics, it is useful to consider briefly the decision by parents to teach their children a language. First, consider the B's. As before, it costs t_j for a B to learn A. It is likely to be easier to teach a child one's own language than a foreign one, so let the cost of learning B by a B child be λt_j. Then a family must choose to raise its children as monolingual B's or monolingual A's or as bilingual. This depends on choosing the maximum of the following: (a) The rent to a B child who is raised bilingual is $1 - (1 + \lambda)t_j$, (b) the rent to a B child who is raised a B is $P_B - \lambda t_j$, and (c) the rent to a B child who is raised an A is $P_A - t_j$.

Even if there are fewer B's than A's, a B family might choose to raise its child as a monolingual B because the cost of doing so is lower. But an A family would never choose to raise its children as B's unless $P_B > P_A$. A B family might choose to raise its children as A's, however, because P_B exceeds P_A. The dynamics are as follows.

Start out initially with only A's. In each period t, beginning with zero, β_t of the population are new B immigrants. They teach their children a language and die out at the end of the period. Their children survive into the next period. Further, define q as the proportion of immigrant children who learn B and define s as the proportion of children of the native-born who learn B. Thus, in period 0, proportion $P_{B0} = \beta_0$ are B speakers. In period 1, proportion

$$P_{B1} = \beta_1 + \beta_0 q + (1 - \beta_0)s$$

are B speakers.

The concept of critical mass can be given a more precise meaning. In order for B's to grow as a proportion of the new country, it is necessary that $P_{B1} > P_{B0}$ or that[19]

(8) $$\beta_0 q + (1 - \beta_0)s > \beta_0 - \beta_1.$$

In the situations described above, β_0 exceeds β_1 because this reflects an immigration wave associated with some exogenous event (e.g., a plague) that will not be repeated in the future. In order for B to take over as a culture within the new country, the proportion of children who learn B must exceed the drop-off in the immigration rate. It is most typical for new cultures to die out, but sometimes (8) holds and B grows in strength over time. When does a majority of the society speak B? Definitionally, this occurs when $P_{Bt} > \frac{1}{2}$.

Even when migration rates are constant, it is difficult to tip a society from one language to another. If a generation is 25 years, then to tip a society from all one language to all of a new language in 50 years, it would be necessary for some stringent conditions to hold. To understand how rare this must be, consider a recent example. Suppose that political events in Russia caused a massive migration of Russians to Israel, accounting for approximately 20 percent of the Israeli population. Suppose that every Russian immigrant taught his children Russian and that those children never learned Hebrew. Suppose further that for the next generation, migration of Russians to Israel fell to a number that represents, say, 10 percent of the Israeli population. Even a level this high is unlikely since most of the Russian Jews who wanted out will have left during the first generation's migration wave. Finally, suppose that 5 percent of the Israeli-born population learns Russian. Given these extreme circumstances,

$$P_{B1} = .1 + (.2)(1) + (.8)(.05) = .34.$$

After 50 years of migration, two-thirds of the country would speak exclusively Hebrew. The country does not tip to Russian. Migration waves of this magnitude are rare in history, which makes clear why cultures and languages are so stable over time. Societies may evolve, but they rarely switch from one culture to another.

More likely than tipping is the formation of subsocieties, where P_B reaches some stable upper bound. For example, suppose that $\lambda = 0$, that $\beta_t = \beta_0/(1 + t)$, and that $\min(t_j) > \frac{1}{2}$, so that no children,[20] grandchildren, and so forth of the initial native-born population learn B until $P_B > \frac{1}{2}$. Since $\lambda = 0$, all children learn to speak their parents' native tongue. A generalization of the formulation above reveals that under such circumstances,

$$P_B(t) = \beta_0 + \frac{\beta_0}{1 + t} \sum_{i=0}^{t-1} \beta_i \prod_{j=0}^{t-1-i} q_{t-1-j} \ .$$

This function increases without limit, but its rate of increase is very slow. If $\beta_0 = .05$, then after one generation, the proportion who speak B is 9.9 percent, and after 10 generations (i.e., 250 years), it is 15 percent. There is a stable minority group of B's in country A, which resembles the situation in Canada or Belgium.

Thus tipping is unlikely. When migration rates are sufficiently high and when the children of immigrants learn their parents' native language rather than that of their new country, subcultures form within societies. Probably more typical is that minorities die out, in the sense that the children of immigrants adopt the language and culture of the new country, thereby reducing the proportion of B's in a population to the immigration rate.

12.3.2. Optimal Assimilation

Members of small minorities are more likely to acquire the culture and language of the majority than members of large minorities. This implies that balanced immigration leads to more rapid assimilation since, to the extent that rapid assimilation is socially worthwhile, a policy that promotes balanced immigration improves welfare. This subsection discusses optimal rates of assimilation.

The existence of more than one culture or language imposes a cost on a society. The expected surplus per person in a purely monocultural society (where no one is bicultural) is $p_a^2 + p_b^2$ since an individual of type i encounters another type i p_i^2 of the time. Each encounter yields a surplus of one to each side. Surplus is maximized when $p_a = 1$ and $p_b = 0$. Monocultural societies allow the most trade to occur because all encounters are matches. In a multicultural society, individuals suffer when they cannot deal with differently cultured individuals.

This result may be offset if different cultures bring enriched trading opportunities that would be absent in a single-culture society. To take a somewhat trivial example, the United States has a wide variety of cuisines because of its underlying cultural diversity. Being able to choose among many different kinds of restaurants provides more social value than would be present were only English food available. Formally, this amounts to saying that the value of a trade is higher in multicultural societies than in single-culture societies. If this effect is sufficiently large, it can swamp the reduced surplus that comes about from the failure to match types as frequently.[21]

Even without the introduction of gains to diversity, there is a transition problem that affects the optimal amount of assimilation and cultural homogeneity. Societies have initial conditions, and it is most useful to respect the initial conditions when defining optimal assimilation. One vivid example involves Quebec, where the majority culture and language are French and the minority culture and language are English. Suppose that, initially, p of the population is French-Canadian and $1 - p$ of the population is English-Canadian. For simplicity, it is assumed that all individuals are monocultural and monolingual in the initial population. As before, p_a denotes the equilibrium proportion of those who know culture A and p_b denotes the equilibrium proportion who know culture B. Initially, consider social welfare under two extreme regimes. In the first regime, all minority members, in this case English-Canadians, are required to adopt the majority culture and speak French. In the second regime, individuals are free to choose their cultures and languages.

The main advantage of the monocultural regime is that all encounters result in trades. Another advantage is that no members of the majority, who, by definition, constitute the larger number of individuals, need to learn the minority culture. The disadvantage is that those minority members who are particularly poor at learning new cultures are forced to bear very high learning costs. It may be better to allow some members of the majority, who are efficient at learning cultures, to learn the minority culture rather than forcing the most inefficient of the minority members to learn the majority culture. The issue here is one of adopting a common standard. When this is done, some in society bear costs to increase the overall social benefit.

Consider the problem of maximizing social per capita surplus by dictating that A's with $t_j < t_a$ learn B and that B's with $t_j < t_b$ learn A, where t_a and t_b are chosen in the maximization problem. Thus

$$\max_{t_a, t_b} \text{ social surplus} = \{pG(t_a) + (1-p)G(t_b) + p[1 - G(t_a)][p + (1-p)G(t_b)]$$

$$(9) \qquad + (1-p)[1 - G(t_b)][1 - p + pG(t_a)]\}$$

$$- p\int_0^{t_a} tg(t)dt - (1-p)\int_0^{t_b} tg(t)dt.$$

The first term, enclosed in braces, is the probability that a match results in a trade (which has a per capita value of one). It is the sum of the probability that a bicultural individual meets anyone, plus the probability that someone who knows only A meets someone who knows A, plus the probability that someone who knows only B meets someone who knows B. The last two terms are the costs borne by A's and B's, respectively, of learning the other culture. A monocultural society is a special case of (9), where $t_a = 0$ and $t_b = \infty$ (no A's learn B and all B's learn A).

Differentiating (9) and using the first-order conditions yields the solutions to the maximization problem:

$$(10a) \qquad\qquad t_a = 2(1-p)[1 - G(t_b)]$$

and

$$(10b) \qquad\qquad t_b = 2p[1 - G(t_a)].$$

The 2 reflects the fact that a trade has a total value of two to society since the per capita return to trade is one.

Recall from (2) and (4) that A's voluntarily choose to learn B when $t_j < 1 - p_b$ and B's choose to learn A when $t_j < 1 - p_a$. Both A's and B's voluntarily assimilate at rates that are socially optimal only when

$t_a = 1 - p_a$ and when $t_b = 1 - p_b$, which cannot be true as a general matter, given (10a) and (10b).

There is a tax (or subsidy) policy that can achieve the optimal amount of assimilation without having to know any individual's cost of assimilation. The B's should be charged $k_b = t_b - 1 + p_b$ if they fail to learn culture A and A's should be charged $k_a = t_a - 1 + p_a$ if they fail to learn culture B. Then a B will learn A whenever $1 - t_j > p_b - k_b$ or whenever $t_j < t_b$, which is the efficiency condition. Analogously, an A will learn B whenever $1 - t_j > p_a - k_a$ or when $t_j < t_a$, which is the efficiency condition for A's.

A monocultural society can emerge as the optimum. For example, suppose that t_j is distributed uniformly on the interval $[0,1]$. Then $t_a = 0$ and $t_b = 1$, so no A's should learn culture B and all B's should learn culture A.[22] From the definitions of k_a and k_b above, the B's should be taxed p_b if they do not learn A. This guarantees that every B opts to learn A, which is the efficient solution. Conversely, A's should be taxed $p_a - 1$ for not learning B. This is a negative number, which means that A's are subsidized not to learn B. The size of the subsidy is just large enough to prevent any A from learning B, which is the efficient outcome in this particular case.

If B's are sufficiently averse to learning A, the optimum t_b will be relatively low, reflecting the large costs imposed on B's who must learn culture A. For example, if all of society's members viewed the costs of becoming bicultural as equal to two (the full value of trade when all encounters are matches), the optimum would be to leave things as they are. There would never be any learning that is socially worthwhile, and both t_a and t_b would be zero. The monocultural society is a special case and need not be optimal.

12.3.3. Chauvinism

The deviation between private and social rates of assimilation may have led some societies to adopt policies that encourage minorities to become assimilated more quickly into the majority. Again, Quebec comes to mind. The Quebecois fear that, left unchecked, society may become largely bilingual or even completely English-speaking.[23] In the process, each individual has had to bear cost t_j to make the switch. The new equilibrium may be no better than the old; communication in French may be as effective as communication in English. The change has come about only at a social cost to the current generation.[24]

Most of the time, chauvinism takes the form of quantity constraints rather than price incentives. It is possible to use a tax system as an alternative. In Quebec, children must (with few exceptions) be educated in French-speaking schools. An alternative would be to tax English-speaking schools or those who attend them. In the United States, higher tax rates for noncitizen residents coupled with a tough English language requirement for citizenship would penalize minority members for slow assimilation rates.

In societies in which the majority is very large, such policies are probably unnecessary and likely do more harm than good. In the 1990 U.S. census data, 98 percent of the population reports fluency in English. Given this number, the problem of majority overinvestment in minority culture and language and minority underinvestment in majority culture and language as a result of free choice is likely to be minimal. It is straightforward to show that $\lim_{p \to 1} t_a = 0$ and that $\lim_{p \to 1} t_b = 1$ when $G(1) = 1$. Equations (2) and (4) are equal to one and zero as well when $p = 1$. Thus social and private incentives are almost the same when the majority is very large.

Further, when the costs of learning the majority culture are very high to some individuals, either because they are slow learners or because they place a very high value on retaining their own culture, the socially optimal level of change is smaller. Perhaps a greater problem is the over- and underinvestment in culture and language that occur because of government programs, which may reflect special interests of politicians or their constituents.

The argument against chauvinism depends on whether current residents or only new immigrants are affected. If only new immigrants are affected, then the model of buying into a club seems appropriate. A country selects a "standard," and outsiders, who have the option of staying in their native land or going elsewhere, make a voluntary migration choice. As long as there is competition among countries, there is no obvious problem.[25] For residents, a change in a government's position may be viewed as a breach of an earlier contract. Of course, the costs associated with that breach are taken into account explicitly by the optimum computed in (9).

12.3.4. *Voluntary Migration*

Individuals have some choice over the country to which they migrate. Before an individual decides to move to another country, he takes into account that the culture that he will encounter is different from the one with which he is familiar. The more foreign the new culture, the less likely an individual is to migrate.

Consider the decision of a B who lives in country B and receives surplus R. He will move to country A if

$$(11) \qquad \max\{p_b, 1 - t_j\} - \text{moving costs} > R.$$

The first term in (11) reflects the fact that the migrant can move and remain monocultural, in which case, he receives p_b, or he can move and learn the majority culture and receive $1 - t_j$.

Inefficient learners (i.e., those with high t_j) are most likely to migrate to a country with high concentrations of individuals from their native land. A very inefficient learner will move only if $p_b -$ moving costs $> R$, which is most likely to be true when p_b is high. Borjas (1985, 1995) has argued that more recent waves of Hispanic immigrants have been less able than earlier-waves. As the proportion of Spanish-speaking individuals in the United States rises, the Spanish speakers who previously were unwilling to come to the United States because their language-switching costs were too high now find it worthwhile to come and simply not switch languages. To the extent that ability to learn English is positively correlated with other learning skills or ability, Borjas's finding is predicted.[26]

The general point is that pioneers are among the most able of the donor population. Because the returns to migration are lowest for individuals with high learning costs when there are many others who have gone before, the slow learners wait until others have blazed the path. Those who migrate early are likely to be the most able.

Do countries with large or small proportions of a given minority type place the highest value on an immigrant? The value of a trade with an immigrant from country B to a country in which the majority consists of A's is

$$\text{value} = p_a G(1 - p_b) + p_b$$

since p_a of the population can interact with the immigrant only if she learns A and p_b can interact with her whether she learns A or not.

Differentiating with respect to p_b yields

(12) $$\frac{\partial \text{value}}{\partial p_b} = -p_a g(1 - p_b) + 1.$$

The sign of the derivative is ambiguous. The negative term reveals that the probability that a B learns A declines as p_b grows. The positive term reflects that the larger the proportion of B's in the receiving country, the larger the proportion of individuals who can interact with the monocultural immigrant.

The empirical analysis on U.S. data provides some guidance on the size of the two terms. The first term is $p_a[\partial G(1 - p_b)/\partial p_b]$, which can be estimated from Table 12.3. With the data from 1990, the estimate of $\partial G(1 - p_b)/\partial p_b$ that comes from the logit equation is 2.4 evaluated at the point of means. Even though immigrants are not spread randomly throughout the country, those communities in which they locate have, on average, 9 percent of immigrants from a given land. Thus a lower-bound estimate of p_a that corresponds to the data used for the logit in Table 12.3 is $1 - .09 = .91$. (This is a lower bound to p_a because many of the immigrants speak English.) The first term is therefore -2.2, so the expression in (12) is -1.2, which is negative.

Countries with larger groups of immigrants receive less value from an incremental immigrant than countries with smaller groups.[27] In the United States, the reason is that most U.S. residents are fluent in English. Since there are so few who are limited to speaking the language of the largest immigrant group's country, in this case Spanish, the gains from obtaining another Spanish speaker are outweighed by the effects of obtaining immigrants who are more likely to learn English. When p_b is small, immigrants are more likely to learn English.

Immigrants, especially those who do not plan on rapid assimilation, want to go to countries with the largest groups of current residents from their native land. Countries with large groups of minority members may be the least interested in having new immigrants from that same country. Since each country is free to set its own immigration policy, there is nothing to prevent those countries that are least anxious to have immigrants from being more stringent.

Restrictions on immigration may take the form of quotas or prices, where immigration slots are auctioned off. One advantage to using explicit fees is that the native population can collect a larger proportion of the rent associated with immigration than is the case with quotas. Further, anti-immigrant sentiment may be reduced when a fee is paid by the immigrant on entry. Finally, fees allocate scarce immigration slots to those with the highest willingness to pay. They are likely to be younger and more able than the population as a whole for the standard human capital reasons.

12.3.5. Regionalization and Ghettos

Concentration of minority populations into localities reduces minority incentives to become assimilated into the majority culture. Formally, p is defined in terms of the others with whom an individual comes into contact. If an individual travels only within local circles, the relevant population proportions may be very different from those of the country as a whole. Thus, while Polish may be spoken by a very small minority of Americans, there is a large and concentrated Polish community in Chicago. A native Pole who migrates to the Polish neighborhood in Chicago can function much better without a knowledge of English than he could were he to move to, say, San Francisco.

Ghettos are an extreme form of concentration and are a natural consequence of the desire to trade. Individuals can increase the probability that trade occurs by living in areas in which they will encounter only individuals who share their culture. Economists tend to spend a large proportion of their time in close proximity with other economists in order to enhance the likelihood of productive interaction. One can think of some homogeneous countries as large ghettos, where language and culture are sufficiently homogeneous to allow trade among all individuals.

Limiting primary contact to those with whom one can communicate has a cost only when there remain unexploited economies of scale. If the ghetto is too small and if it has insufficient contact with outsiders, there may be opportunities to become richer by enlarging the circle of trade. Sometimes this can be accomplished at small cost through translators who deal in product markets. When the typical American driver pulls up to the gasoline pump, he need not speak Arabic to complete a purchase, even if the oil comes from Saudi Arabia. But sometimes a group's transactions are limited by its isolation, and members of the group may prefer to live outside the community.

In order for a minority member to want to live outside the ghetto, it is necessary that a trade outside the ghetto be worth more than a trade inside. Suppose that as a result of economies of scale, specialization, or access to wider international markets, trades that take place outside the ghetto are worth potentially more than those inside. Let trades outside be worth one, as before, and let those inside be worth θ, with $\theta \leq 1$. For simplicity, consider the special case in which there are only two distinct cultures, A and B. If communities are segregated, then every encounter by minority members and by majority members results in a match. The expected social value per person is then

$$(13) \qquad\qquad V_G \equiv p_a + (1 - p_a)\theta$$

because p_a belong to the majority and $1 - p_a$ to the minority. If ghettos are destroyed and minority and majority individuals encounter each other randomly, then the expected social value per person is

$$(14) \qquad\qquad V_{NG} \equiv p_a^2 + (1 - p_a)^2.$$

It can be shown that $V_G > V_{NG}$ for all values of $\theta < 1$.[28] Thus the clustering and segregation that may result naturally when people voluntarily choose their residences increase social welfare over that associated with forced integration.[29]

The value calculated in (14) assumes that economies of scale for the majority have been exhausted. Moving individuals from the ghetto to the outside does not increase the average value of a trade outside. The value of a trade remains one whether individuals from the ghetto move into the majority or not.[30] This ignores any value of diversity.[31]

Much of the discussion surrounding the impacts of ghettos involves subsequent generations. It is possible that children who are raised in the ghetto are less likely to be assimilated into the majority culture than those raised outside. The analysis changes somewhat when subsequent generations are considered.

Two periods are sufficient to illuminate the issues. In period 1, there are adults and children. In period 2, the children become adults. Each adult has one child. Only adults trade. Suppose that a minority child raised in a ghetto has a probability λ of being assimilated into the majority culture, whereas a child raised outside the ghetto is certain to become assimilated. This means that $p_a + \lambda(1 - p_a)$ of the population will know the majority culture in the second period. Let δ be the discount factor. Then the two-period version of (13) and (14) is

$$(13') \; V_G = p_a + (1 - p_a)\theta + \delta\{[p_a + \lambda(1 - p_a)] + [(1 - p_a) - \lambda(1 - p_a)]\theta\}$$

and

$$(14') \qquad\qquad V_{NG} = [p_a^2 + (1 - p_a)^2] + \delta.$$

Now, whether V_G exceeds V_{NG} or not depends on the parameters. If $\delta = 0$ so that no weight is placed on the next generation, then (13') becomes (13) and (14') becomes (14), and the previous proof that $V_G > V_{NG}$ holds. But at the other extreme, suppose that $\delta = 1$ (no discounting of the future), $\lambda = 0$ (children raised in the ghetto never become assimilated), and $\theta = 0$ (within-ghetto trades have zero value). Then (13') becomes $V_G = 2p_a$ and (14') becomes $V_{NG} = [p_a^2 + (1 - p_a)^2] + 1$. It is easily shown that under these assumptions, V_{NG} exceeds V_G for all p_a.[32] If $V_{NG} > V_G$, then the integrated economy produces higher welfare than the segregated one. Whether parents voluntarily undertake the costs of integration so that their children may benefit depends on the extent to which they internalize effects on their offspring.[33]

12.3.6. Government Transfers

In the same way that local neighborhoods can offer support to minority individuals who are not members of the majority culture, so too can a government reduce the incentives to become assimilated. When an individual can obtain government support, the value of assimilation is reduced. Formally, a government transfer program places a floor on the amount that an individual earns. In the absence of government transfers, the condition for acquiring the majority culture is $1 - t_j > p_b$. A government transfer program can be thought of as guaranteeing some average level of surplus, S. If $S > 1 - t_j > p_b$, then an individual who would have become assimilated in the absence of the government transfer will remain monocultural and will merely accept the transfer. Reducing the size of government transfers would increase the rate of assimilation in the society.

12.3.7. Superior Cultures

It has been assumed that an equilibrium in which 100 percent speak English is no better nor any worse than one in which 100 percent speak Spanish. But there may be factors that cause one language or culture to be more efficient. For example, English has many irregular cases and is less consistent phonetically than Spanish. As a result, the distribution of costs in going from Spanish to English may lie to the right of that in going from English to Spanish. This could cause a society to favor a Spanish-only policy, even if the majority speaks English.

It could also be the case that some languages and cultures are simply more efficient than others. If it were easier to communicate using an alphabet than Chinese characters, then the value of trades conducted in a European language might be higher than for those in Chinese or Japanese. Contracts might be easier to write and communication might be richer in one language than in another. Again, this could lead to favoring one language over another, even if the language were not spoken by the majority.

12.3.8. Persecuted Emigrants

In some situations, individuals fled their native lands under extreme persecution. Russian Jews who fled the pogroms at the turn of the century, South Vietnamese who escaped in the early 1970s before the communists took over, and the earliest settlers of the American colonies are some obvious examples of individuals who left their former lands under duress. Persecuted peoples may have been less attached to their former cultures than those who were not persecuted. It seems reasonable that persecuted individuals are more likely to become assimilated than those who were not. Formally, this can be interpreted as the distribution of costs among the persecuted being stochastically dominated by other immigrants. As a result, those who emigrate under duress are more likely to adopt the new culture.

12.3.9. Optimal Number of Cultures

How many cultures are optimal? Ignored in most of the preceding analysis are gains from specialization and diversity. The case is clearest in the context of language. There is value to having everyone know and communicate in one language, in the same way that there is value to having one standard. But one standard may be suitable for some purposes and not for others. For example, economists have their own jargon and vocabulary as auto mechanics do. Communication between economists and auto mechanics would be smoother if all terms were shared. But it is costly to learn additional vocabulary, and it is socially wasteful to do so if the words are rarely, if ever, used. Worse, the words can be confusing. The word "differential" means one thing to an auto mechanic and something quite different to an economist. Forcing both groups to share language would require more words and add costs to the system. The trade-off can be modeled. The analysis bears some relation to the literature on optimal currency areas or country borders, but is left for subsequent work.

12.4. Summary and Conclusions

Individuals from minority groups are more likely to adopt the culture and language of the majority when the minority group accounts for a small proportion of the total population. The incentives are greater for any individual to learn the majority language when only a few persons in the country speak his or her native language. Thus slow and balanced immigration, where the flow of individuals from any one culture is small, results in more rapid assimilation than immigration that favors any one particular group. Individuals from the majority may learn the language or culture of one of the minorities. But it is less likely that the majority will learn a minority language than that a minority will learn the majority language.

Empirical evidence from the 1900 and 1990 U.S. censuses demonstrates conclusively that immigrants are most likely to be fluent in English when they live in communities that have small proportions of individuals from their own native country. Individuals who are from poorly represented groups learn English quickly. Those from groups with large proportions in the local population learn English more slowly. This is a rational response to the differences in the value of learning English across groups. The finding holds up within cultural groups as well as across groups.

Some additional points are summarized below.

1. Government transfers, which place a floor on consumption, reduce the incentives to adopt the majority culture and learn the majority language.

2. The optimal pattern of assimilation trades off the costs borne by majority members against those of minority members. The gain to a common culture and language is that all encounters result in viable interaction. The cost is that some members of society must learn another culture or language during the transition period.

3. Immigrants to a given country are more likely to emigrate from countries whose cultures are well represented in the population of the new country.

4. Country-specific immigration policies, and especially fees, can improve the allocation of individuals across societies.

5. Self-induced concentration of minority members into neighborhoods is a natural consequence of the desire to trade. Integration is most rapid when parents take into account the adverse effects of segregation on their offspring.

6. Chauvinism, where a particular majority culture is tenaciously protected, may be rational and welfare increasing. The introduction of minority cultures can bring about a new equilibrium that is no better than the old. In the process of moving from the old equilibrium to the new one, transition costs are incurred.

VI Skill Acquisition and Personnel Economics

Introduction

Human capital theory is the primary engine of the analytics of wage determination. In one of the most important papers ever written in labor economics, Gary Becker (1962) lays out the formal theory of human capital, discussing formal education and on-the-job training, as well as the distinction between general and firm-specific training and the implications of each for wage profiles.

The acquisition of skills, both before entry into the labor market and during work, is central to personnel economics because it interacts directly with wages, worker selection, sorting and mobility, promotion, occupational choice, as well as hierarchical considerations that are central to personnel economics.

This part of the book contains four chapters. Two deal directly with education, one examines firm-specific skills and presents a new interpretation of the theory of firm specific human capital. The final chapter focuses on occupational choice and, in particular, the choice to become an entrepreneur.

Chapter 13 recasts firm-specific human capital in a different light. Recall the definitions of general and firm-specific human capital. General human capital makes workers more productive at multiple firms; firm-specific human capital raises the productivity of the worker only at the current firm. In the former case, workers' wages are determined by competition, in the latter case by bilateral monopoly. Examples of firm-specific human capital include learning techniques that are idiosyncratic to a particular firm, knowing the identities of the relevant players within an organization and other details of a particular firm's layout and location that pertain to that firm only. Because skills are specific to one firm, that firm must share in the cost of training. A more general view of specific human capital is offered in Chapter 13, entitled "Firm-Specific Human Capital: A Skill-Weights Approach". Firm-specific human capital is actually a form of general human capital. Most specific human capital is actually general human capital, where the uses are specific to the firm. There are a variety of general skills used on each job, but the weighting of these skills differs across firms.

The theory has some different implications from the original view of human capital. In addition to the point about firms financing of general skills, thickness of markets plays a crucial role in the skill-weights view. For example, the wage gain from quitting goes to zero in thick markets and the wage loss associated with involuntary turnover also is smaller. This is not an implication of standard specific human capital stories. Firm idiosyncracy is also important in the skill-weights view. The more idiosyncratic is the worker's initial firm, the less balanced is the investment profile and the lower is the probability of a quit. Additionally, workers' post-training wages are higher and wage loss on involuntary layoff is greater in firms that have lower ex ante probabilities of an exogenous layoff. When workers are more secure in their current position, they invest more idiosyncratically in the skills that suit the initial firm. This implies that the wages of stayers are higher in idiosyncratic firms and that when a layoff does occur, the wage loss is greater for workers from those firms. The value of the new approach, outlined in Chapter 13, lies in the richness of implications. A literature has already begun to test some of the implications that have not previously been documented. This is another area for further investigation.

A very large literature exists on the economics of education. Surprisingly, given the amount of time and attention devoted to its study, little remains known about the educational production function. Indeed, if we knew how to best use the educational establishment to produce skills, many of the problems that plague the education industry and its output, namely its past students, would be lessened. Chapter 14, "Educational Production," is an attempt to model the educational production process, using economic theory. Key to understanding learning is that most of it occurs in a public setting, where students affect the ability of one another to learn. In particular by asking questions, acting up, or causing other disruptions, one student can take learning time away from the rest of the class. As a consequence, schools should and do adjust class size to take into account the different likelihoods of disruptions by its students. Not only does this explain why it is difficult to find class size effects in the data, it also explains class size and composition across different groups. At the most basic level, it explains why classes for young children and those with learning problems are smaller than those for older students. It also explains why better students are placed in larger classes, and further, that educational output is higher in these larger classes, despite the increased student/teacher ratio. In equilibrium, class size matters very little but matters more for lower grades than for higher ones. As in the personnel literature, and in particular, as in Chapter 7, sorting by type, in this case academic ability, enhances output.

The importance of this work for personnel economics is that skills are a key input into the workplace environment. They affect promotion, help determine wages, and generate interaction among workers at the firm. But additionally, understanding the production of skills in the formal education setting also helps understand how skills may be formed at the workplace.

Chapter 15, "Speeding, Terrorism, and Teaching to the Test", is a straight application of the methodology of incentives and personnel economics to motivating skill formation. It has much in common with models that discourage workers from shirking or engaging in malfeasant behavior. In Chapter 15, the application is to motivating individuals to learn skills, either in formal education or conceivably on the job or elsewhere. The approach is to use the same analysis one would use to deter drivers from speeding. It is demonstrated that it is better to concentrate incentives for testing and detection when skill formation is costly, and to use more diffuse incentives when skill formation is inexpensive. As such, highly motivated students should not be given very specific tests guidelines, but instead should be encouraged to learn a broad array of skills. Less motivated individuals will not react well to such diffuse incentives and must be told precisely what it is, at school or on the job, that they are responsible for knowing. The approach can be extended to a number of different areas, including approaches to detecting tax evaders, catching and deterring terrorists, and other criminal activities.

To understand motivating skill acquisition, the analysis in Chapter 15 begins by modeling the formally equivalent problem of deterring drivers from speeding. The question is whether to announce where the police are posted or let the drivers guess. Most people's first reaction is that the answer is the obvious one: keep their locations secret. If the locations of the police are announced, then motorists will obey the law only at those locations, and will speed at all other locations. But if police are very few and their locations are unknown, drivers are likely to speed everywhere because the probability of being caught is very low. If the alternative of announcing police locations is adopted, there is a better chance that speeding will be deterred at least in those places where police are posted. The total amount of speeding could actually be lower when locations are announced. Tax fraud is virtually identical. The tax authority can announce the items to be audited or just let taxpayers know that there will be random audits. When auditors are expensive or few, it is better to announce the audit rules. When auditors are cheap and abundant, it is better to use a random audit algorithm.

All of these phenomena are examples of a similar kind of incentive problem. When individuals become aware of the rules, they obey them within a narrow range and disregard them elsewhere. But that may be better than having them disregard the rules everywhere. Extensions of this analysis could be to rules on the job. The question how specific instructions to workers should be is a direct, but not yet spelled out, implication of this thinking. The model in Chapter 15 could be used directly to derive testable implications for rules and behavior in the workplace.

Chapter 16 concentrates on one specific area of occupational choice, namely the decision to become an entrepreneur or to work for someone else in a wage and salary relationship. The insight of "Entrepreneurship" is that entrepreneurs are generalists, whereas wage and salary workers can be specialists. Entrepreneurs need not be excellent at anything, but they must be good at everything. The theory, which has already received significant attention and empirical support, has been dubbed the "jack-of-all-trades" approach to entrepreneurship. The earliest tests and confirmations came from using American data and German data.[1]

The idea explored in Chapter 16 is that entrepreneurs differ from specialists. Entrepreneurs have a comparative disadvantage in a single skill but have more balanced talents that span a number of different skills. Specialists can work for others who have the talent to spot and combine a variety of skills, but an entrepreneur must possess precisely this talent. Although entrepreneurs can hire others, the entrepreneur must be sufficiently well-versed in a variety of fields to judge the quality of applicants. Thus, an individual can decide to become an entrepreneur using a variety of skills, or to specialize using only one. The market pays a premium to those who have more balanced talents and this is what induces them to move away from concentrating on their best skill.

Using data from Stanford business school alumni, it is found that those who have more varied careers, as evidenced by having performed more roles as part of their work experience, are more likely to be entrepreneurs. Additionally, it is found that the pattern of investment that occurs prior to entering the labor market is also consistent with the generalist view of entrepreneurship. The Stanford MBA data reveal that those students who study a more varied curriculum are more likely to be entrepreneurs and to start a larger number of businesses over their careers.

13

Firm-Specific Human Capital: A Skill-Weights Approach

Becker (1962) proposed a distinction between two types of human capital. General human capital helps productivity not only at the current firm but also at other firms, creating competition for a worker's services. Firm-specific human capital raises the productivity of the worker at the current firm, but not elsewhere, setting up a bilateral monopoly structure between the worker and firm. Examples of firm-specific human capital include learning techniques that are idiosyncratic to a particular firm, knowing the identities of the relevant players within an organization, and other details of a particular firm's layout and location that pertain to that firm only. As a result, Becker argues, the firm bears part of the cost of investment in specific human capital, but the worker bears the full cost of investing in general human capital. Many of the predictions of the original model have been borne out, but some have received more mixed support, such as the willingness of firms to pay in some cases for what appears to be general capital.

A more general view of specific human capital is offered here. The word "general" is used in two senses. First, most specific human capital is actually general human capital, where the uses are specific to the firm. The approach is this. Suppose that there are a variety of

The original version of this chapter was published as: Lazear, E. P. (2009). Firm-Specific Human Capital: A Skill-Weights Approach, 117(5), 914-940. University of Chicago Press. © 2009 by the University of Chicago. I am grateful to my Stanford colleagues who have provided many insightful comments that are incorporated in the paper. Susan Athey, David Kreps, Steve Levitt, Ulrike Malmendier, John McMillan, Derek Neal, Paul Oyer, Paul Pfleiderer, Peter Reiss, Michael Schwarz, Kathryn Shaw, Steve Tadelis, Justin Wolfers, and Jeffery Zwiebel made important suggestions. Kevin Lang and Derek Neal gave useful input and references. Ben Ho, Korok Ray, and Ron Siegel provided able research assistance. Ray, and Siegel supplied substantial assistance on some of the proofs. I also thank participants of the NBER Personnel Economics for helpful comments.

skills used on each job, and suppose that each of these skills is general in the sense that it is used at other firms as well. The difference, however, is that firms vary in their weighting of the different skills. A real-world example of which I have some personal knowledge may be helpful. A small Silicon Valley firm provides enterprise software that does tax optimization. The typical managerial employee in this firm must know something about tax laws, something about economics, and something about software and computer programming. In order to enhance communication and innovation, it is important that individuals do not merely specialize in one of the three. Most employees must have at least some knowledge of each. None of these skills, taken alone, is firm-specific. There are many other firms in the economy that make use of knowledge on taxes. Other firms use economic reasoning to produce their products. Computer programming is used throughout the modern world. But the combination of these skills, especially in the quantities used at the start-up in question, are unlikely to be replicated in many, if any, other firms. A manager who leaves the start-up will have a difficult time finding a firm that can make use of all the skills he acquired at the first firm. The second job might use some of the economics and some of the tax, but little of the programming expertise. Or it might use tax and programming, but little economics. As a consequence, these seemingly general skills are firm-specific in the combination demanded and the worker may be unwilling to bear the full cost of learning them because he will not be able to transfer them with the same value to another firm.

Second, the theory has more and some different implications from the original view of human capital. In addition to the point about firm financing of general skills, thickness of markets play a crucial role in the skill-weights view. For example, the wage gain from quitting goes to zero in thick markets and the wage loss associated with involuntary turnover also is smaller. This is not an implication of standard specific human capital stories. For example, in the traditional view, the value of knowing the identity of the relevant players in the initial firm is independent of market thickness.[1]

Firm idiosyncrasy is also important in the skill-weights view. The more idiosyncratic the worker's initial firm, the less balanced the investment profile and the lower the probability of a quit.

Additionally, workers' post-training wages are higher and wage loss on involuntary layoff is greater in firms that have lower ex ante probabilities of an exogenous layoff. When workers are more secure in their current position, they invest more idiosyncratically in the skills that suit the initial firm. This implies that the wages of stayers is higher in idiosyncratic firms and that, when a layoff does occur, the wage loss is greater for workers from those firms.

Why bother with another story for specific human capital? The traditional view seems to have generated many validated predictions. The advantage of this new skill-weights view of human capital is that it provides a tangible story, and a single model that is consistent with a number of empirical results, rather than invoking one model for one result and another for other results. Finally, the theory provides an endogenous definition of specific human capital, where whether human capital is labeled specific or general depends on observable market parameters.

Because the skill-weights view, like the original view, involves some bilateral monopoly, it is impossible to avoid discussing bargaining. Both the post-training wage and initial wage depend on bargaining outcomes. The paper borrows insights from the vast literature on bargaining in the labor context, particularly when firm specificity is involved. Perhaps most relevant to the approach used below are the papers by MacLeod and Malcomson (1993), which examines wage profiles and resulting specific investments, and Stole and Zwiebel (1996), which analyzes firm and worker decisions in an employment-at-will context.[2]

13.1. The Model

Let there be two skills, A and B, which the individual can acquire at cost $C(A, B)$ with C_A, $C_B > 0$ and C_{AA}, $C_{BB} > 0$. There are two periods. Investments are made during period 1 and the payoff from work is received in period 2.

A worker with skill set (A, B) has output at firm i given by

$$\lambda_i A + (1 - \lambda_i)B$$

with $0 \leq \lambda_i \leq 1$. The λ_i reflects the fact that each firm i may weight the two skills differently from another firm j. The random variable λ has density $f(\lambda)$.

Define the initial firm, denoted firm 1, as the firm at which the worker is employed during the first period. The worker receives one job offer before starting the initial job, so λ_1 is not a choice variable from the worker's point of view.

After investment, but before the second period begins, the worker obtains an offer from another firm, denoted j, which depends on the skills that he takes into that period. The worker's output at firm j is given by

$$\lambda_j A + (1 - \lambda_j)B.$$

Because the situation is one of ex post bilateral monopoly, the second period wage is determined by the equilibrium to some bargaining game. One extreme is to give all the ex post rents to the firm, paying the worker no more than the alternative wage offer. The other extreme is to give all the ex post rents to the worker, paying exactly the full value of output. All investment increases the alternative wage as well, although not necessarily by the same amount elsewhere as in the current firm.

For sake of conformity with much of the economic literature, it is assumed that the wage during period 2 is determined according to a Nash bargaining framework. Since the worker is worth $\lambda_j A + (1 - \lambda_j)B$ at the alternative firm, the alternative firm would be willing to pay up to $\lambda_j A + (1 - \lambda_j)B$ for the worker's services. The initial firm receives output of $\lambda_1 A + (1 - \lambda_1)B$, so the Nash bargain implies that the wage in period 2 is

(1) $$W_2 = \tfrac{1}{2}\{[\lambda_1 A + (1 - \lambda_1)B] + [\lambda_j A + (1 - \lambda_j)B]\}$$

or

$$W_2 = B + \tfrac{1}{2}(\lambda_1 + \lambda_j)(A - B).$$

This formula holds whether the worker stays or quits to accept the outside offer. In the former case, the threat is determined by output in the new firm. In the latter case, where the outside firm can pay more, the threat is determined by output at the initial firm.

The period 2 wage is stochastic because it depends on the realization of the period 2 outside value. High outside values result in high period 2 wages, even for workers who choose to stay because their alternatives are better, which raises the threat value. Given the ex ante expectation of the period 2 wage, the firm must offer a wage during period 1 (the investment phase) that attracts workers. The period 1 wage is deterministic because it depends only on the expected, not realized, wage for period 2. It is derived in a later section.

Nash bargaining implies that the wage paid exceeds the maximum that the losing firm could pay, which guarantees that labor moves voluntarily to its highest value. Separation is efficient, despite the existence of specific human capital, because the structure allows for bargaining after both inside and outside offers are observed.[3] The worker stays with his initial firm during the second period whenever the inside value exceeds the outside output value.

A voluntary separation occurs whenever

$$\lambda_1 A + (1 - \lambda_1)B > \lambda_j A + (1 - \lambda_j)B$$

or whenever

$$(\lambda_1 - \lambda_j)(A - B) > 0.$$

This condition makes clear that the skill-weights model is a particular kind of matching model, where workers choose jobs that best suit their strengths. It differs from original matching models in that the worker's choice of job depends upon his early unbalanced investment strategy, which itself depends on the technology of the job in which he first lands.

Initially, consider the case where λ_1 is sufficiently high that optimal investment implies $A > B$. Consequently, workers favor high-λ firms. The condition for retention then becomes

$$\lambda_1 > \lambda_j,$$

which happens with probability $F(\lambda_1)$ where $F(\cdot)$ is the cumulative distribution function of λ_j.

Turnover that occurs when $\lambda_j > \lambda_1$ is often, if not always, associated with a quit because firm j can outbid firm 1 for the worker's services. This turnover is called "voluntary." Additionally, let there be some exogenous probability of a layoff, say from a plant shutdown, given by q. Much, if not most, of this turnover shows up as layoffs. The probability of remaining with firm i during the second period is given by

$$F(\lambda_1)(1 - q).$$

This is the probability that a worker is not laid off exogenously, $1 - q$, times the probability that the worker's outside offer is inferior to the one at the current firm, $F(\lambda_1)$. A firm that has very high levels of λ retains its workers more often because it is less likely that outside firms will value the dominant skill more.

When a worker is laid off, he does not have the initial job as an alternative to discipline the wage paid by the new firm. Instead, his fall back position is to accept leisure, which has value

$$\lambda_L A + (1 - \lambda_L)B.$$

The Nash bargaining wage for those laid off exogenously and who have no alternative job is then

$$W_{\text{layoff}} = \begin{cases} \dfrac{\lambda_j A + (1 - \lambda_j)B + \lambda_L A + (1 - \lambda_L)B}{2} & \text{if } \lambda_j > \lambda_L \\[2ex] \dfrac{\lambda_L A + (1 - \lambda_L)B}{2} & \text{if } \lambda_j < \lambda_L. \end{cases}$$

To save on notation, it assumed in what follows that λ_j always exceeds λ_L.[4] Then, the expected value of the wage at layoff is

$$W_{\text{layoff}} = \frac{\lambda_L A + (1 - \lambda_L)B + \bar{\lambda} A + (1 - \bar{\lambda})B}{2}$$

where $\bar{\lambda} \equiv E(\lambda)$.

Similarly, there is a Nash bargaining wage for those who remain with the firm with expected value given by

$$W_{\text{stay}} = \tfrac{1}{2}\{\lambda_1 A + (1 - \lambda_1)B + E(\lambda_j | \lambda_j < \lambda_1)A + [1 - E(\lambda_j \mid \lambda_j < \lambda_1)]B\}$$

or

$$W_{\text{stay}} = B + \frac{[\lambda_1 + E(\lambda_j|\lambda_j < \lambda_1)](A - B)}{2}$$

and one for those who quit with expected value

$$W_{\text{quit}} = \tfrac{1}{2}\{\lambda_1 A + (1 - \lambda_1)B + E(\lambda_j|\lambda_j > \lambda_1)A + [1 - E(\lambda_j|\lambda_j > \lambda_1)]B\}$$

or

$$W_{\text{quit}} = B + \frac{[\lambda_1 + E(\lambda_j|\lambda_j > \lambda_1)](A - B)}{2}.$$

The investment problem is to choose A and B, knowing that the worker may remain at the initial firm, but that there is some chance that he will move to another firm, either because he gets a better outside offer, or because his firm shuts down. The privately efficient choice of A and B maximizes expected net surplus to the combination of the worker and firm:[5]

$$S(\lambda_1) = F(\lambda_1)(1 - q)[\lambda_1 A + (1 - \lambda_1)B] + (1 - q)[1 - F(\lambda_1)]E(W_{\text{quit}})$$

$$+ qE(W_{\text{layoff}}) - C(A, B)$$

or

$$S(\lambda_1) = F(\lambda_1)(1 - q)[\lambda_1 A + (1 - \lambda_1)B]$$

(2)
$$+ [1 - F(\lambda_1)](1 - q)\left\{B + \frac{[\lambda_1 + E(\lambda_j \mid \lambda_j > \lambda_1)](A - B)}{2}\right\}$$

$$+ \tfrac{q}{2}[\lambda_L A + (1 - \lambda_L)B + \overline{\lambda}A + (1 - \overline{\lambda})B] - C(A, B).$$

Note that $S(\lambda_1)$ is firm and worker joint surplus. It is not the socially efficient amount because the second and third terms of the expression ignore the surplus that goes to other firms through the bargaining process in those situations where the worker leaves the firm.[6] The firm has no interest, quite the contrary, in raising the worker's value at another firm. But to the extent that the increased value is reflected in the worker's outside wage, as in (2), side payments to the firm could be made. This is done by adjusting the rent splitting value and shows up in the period one wage, discussed in a later section.

Equation (2) has three terms and captures the skill-weights approach to specific human capital. There are only two skills, A and B, and both are "general" in that they are used by firms other than the current employer. But the wage that the worker receives depends on the firm in which he is employed because weights that firms attach to the two skills are idiosyncratic.

In (2), the first of the three terms reflects output if the worker remains with his current firm, which happens $F(\lambda_1)(1 - q)$ of the time. The second term reflects earnings when he receives a better outside offer than at the current firm and his current firm does not shut down. This occurs whenever $\lambda_j > \lambda_1$, and when no layoff occurs, or $[1 - F(\lambda_1)]$ $(1 - q)$ of the time.[7] Finally, the firm may shut down, in which case he must take the alternative job with earnings shown in the third term. This occurs q of the time. The last two terms ignore the part of output that is captured by other firms.

The first-order conditions are

(3)
$$\frac{\partial}{\partial A} = (1 - q)F(\lambda_1)\lambda_1 + (1 - q)[1 - F(\lambda_1)]\left[\frac{\lambda_1 + E(\lambda_j \mid \lambda_j > \lambda_1)}{2}\right]$$
$$+ \frac{q}{2}(\bar{\lambda} + \lambda_L) - C_A = 0$$

and

(4)
$$\frac{\partial}{\partial B} = (1 - q)F(\lambda_1)(1 - \lambda_1) + (1 - q)[1 - F(\lambda_1)]\left[1 - \frac{\lambda_1 + E(\lambda_j \mid \lambda_j > \lambda_1)}{2}\right]$$
$$+ \frac{q}{2}(1 - \bar{\lambda} + 1 - \lambda_L) - C_B = 0$$

Again, there are three terms in each of the two conditions, reflecting the three possibilities: stay with the current firm, quit, or get laid off.[8]

Equations (3) and (4) hold for workers who find themselves in firms with $\lambda_1 > \lambda^*$ where λ^* is the minimum value of λ such that $A > B$ in (3) and (4). There is another set of initial firms, specifically those with low values of λ, for which workers choose to favor B relative to A. In all that follows, the analysis is firms for which $\lambda_1 \geq \lambda^*$ so that $A > B$. But all results shown for firms and their workers favoring A also hold for firms favoring B except when noted.

The general skills discussed are often learned in schools, not on the job, and the firm has control over this only through its choice of whom to hire. What is most likely is that an individual with one of the skills acquired before starting the job is promised that additional skills will be provided as part of the training process. For example, a computer programmer might be told that he will be taught tax accounting after beginning work. How much of this is credible? Investment may be observable but not contractible. This is explored formally in Appendix A, but relevant for this discussion is that the firm would underinvest in both A and B. There are two reasons. First, the firm captures only a fraction of the return to the investment were the worker to stay because investment raises the value of outside alternatives. Second, the firm has no interest in raising the value of the worker to another firm in the event that the worker chooses to leave. In the context of the example, some of the promised tax training may not be provided were the investment observable but not contractible. Additionally, the firm biases investment toward those skills that favor its own weighting rather than those that are most prevalent in the market.

13.1.1.   Period 1 Wage

The choice of investment strategy is one that maximizes joint surplus of the worker and the current firm. The rent is distributed through the choice of the wage in period 1, W_1. A general formulation simply allows that γ of the rent go to the firm and $1 - \gamma$ of the rent go to the worker.

The total rent is given by $S(\lambda_1)$ defined above. The firm receives output when the worker stays in period 2, pays out the wage that is the result of the bargain, and "writes the check" to cover the training costs. In addition, the firm pays W_1 in period 1. The firm then nets

$$[\text{Output} - W_{\text{stay}}] \, \text{prob(stay)} - W_1 - C(A, B)$$

or

$$(\lambda_1 A + (1 - \lambda_1)B - \{B + \tfrac{1}{2}\,[\lambda_1 + E(\lambda \mid \lambda < \lambda_1)]\})(1 - q)F(\lambda_1)$$
$$- W_1 - C(A, B),$$

and this must equal $\gamma S(\lambda_1)$. After the appropriate substitutions, one obtains

$$W_1 = (\text{Output if Stay})(1 - \gamma)(1 - q)F(\lambda_1) - W_{\text{stay}}(1 - q)F(\lambda_1)$$
$$- (W_{\text{quit}})(1 - q)[1 - F(\lambda_1)] - W_{\text{layoff}}q - (1 - \gamma)C(A, B)$$

or

(5)
$$W_1 = [\lambda_1 A + (1 - \lambda_1)B](1 - \gamma)(1 - q)F(\lambda_1)$$
$$- \left[B + \frac{\lambda_1 + E(\lambda_j \mid \lambda_j < \lambda_1)}{2}(A - B)\right](1 - q)F(\lambda_1)$$
$$- \left[B + \frac{\lambda_1 + E(\lambda_j \mid \lambda_j > \lambda_1)}{2}(A - B)\right](1 - q)(1 - F(\lambda_1))$$
$$- \tfrac{q}{2}\{\lambda_L A + (1 - \lambda_L)B + \bar{\lambda}A + (1 - \bar{\lambda})B\} - (1 - \gamma)C(A, B).$$

The first-period wage is the rent-splitting parameter, which is determined taking into account that the second-period wage will be set by a bargaining process. The outcome of that process affects the wage paid during the first period (as does the bargain over the distribution of total rents). The first-period wage is derived in order to be able to see how it is affected by investment. The goal is to determine the share of investment costs that are borne by the worker and by the firm. This is explored later.

13.1.2. Wage Differences: Stayers and Leavers

One motivation given for the new view of firm-specific human capital provided in this analysis is that workers lose sometimes significant earnings when they suffer an involuntary separation. Wage loss associated with involuntary separation is reflected in the tenure coefficient that is sometimes estimated in standard wage regressions. The model presented above also has implications for wage differences between stayers and leavers and it is instructive to examine the empirical implications of this model for earnings functions.

From the derivations of the wages for stayers and leavers,[9]

$$(6) \qquad W_{\text{quit}} - W_{\text{stay}} = \tfrac{1}{2} \left[E(\lambda_j \mid \lambda_j > \lambda_1) - E(\lambda_j \mid \lambda_j < \lambda_1) \right](A - B).$$

The expression in (6) is positive. Workers only quit when they do better elsewhere.

Similarly, the expected wage change among involuntary leavers is

$$(7) \qquad W_{\text{layoff}} - W_{\text{stay}} = \tfrac{1}{2} \left[\lambda_L + \overline{\lambda} - \lambda_1 \right) - E(\lambda_j \mid \lambda_j < \lambda_1) \right](A - B).$$

Although one would expect (7) to be negative since stayers should do better than those who get laid off, the expression cannot be signed.[10] But were $W_{\text{layoff}} > W_{\text{stay}}$, the firm would only be in the training business. No worker would choose to stay voluntarily during the second period since he does better by taking his chances on the outside market.

13.1.3. *Idiosyncratic Firms and Unbalanced Investment*

The pattern of investment is more unbalanced for workers whose initial job is at a firm with relatively idiosyncratic weights. This is not surprising since a primary reason for investing in skills is to use them in the current firm.

Formally, an idiosyncratic firm is one defined as having λ that is far away from the mean and at the extreme, having $\lambda_1 = 1$. The value of $A - B$ is maximized when $\lambda_1 = 1$, and the amount that individuals lose at layoff increases in the idiosyncrasy (see Appendix B).

Workers at firms that require unusual combinations of skills lose more when they suffer an unexpected layoff. Lawyers at a firm that requires that their lawyers also be medical doctors are likely to suffer larger wage losses on involuntary separation than lawyers at the typical law firm.

In A-favoring firms, a quit occurs only when $\lambda_j > \lambda_1$, which is less likely the closer λ_1 is to one. Conversely, in B-favoring firms, a quit occurs only when $\lambda_j < \lambda_1$, which is less likely the closer λ_1 is to zero. Thus quitting – and therefore turnover – is lower the more idiosyncratic the firm.

Finally, the wages of stayers are higher and wage loss on involuntary layoff is greater in firms that have lower ex ante layoff probabilities.[11] As q rises, investment becomes more balanced, which lowers wages among stayers and raises them among quitters.

13.2. Additional Implications of the Model
13.2.1. Market Thickness

One implication of the skill-weights view of human capital that is less obvious under the traditional view is that wage loss associated with job turnover is greater in very thin markets than in very thick markets. As is made clear in this section, the definition of firm-specific human capital is endogenous. As markets become very thick, investments that would otherwise be viewed as firm-specific become more general. Also, as markets become thick, the individual undertakes investment strategies that are closer to the strategy that would prevail in the absence of any involuntary mobility.

An increase in market thickness is modeled here as allowing more offers. The model above assumes that before the work period begins, the worker gets a new draw of λ. A thicker market is represented as one where the worker gets multiple independent draws of λ before the work period and can select the job that best suits his prior investment strategy. There are two key results in this section. First, as the market gets extremely thick, investment becomes idiosyncratic; that is, $A - B$ increases. Second, and despite this, as the market thickens, the wage loss associated with separation declines.

The probability that the current weight λ_1 exceeds all N draws is $F(\lambda_1)^N$ so expected surplus in (2) is now given by

$$S(\lambda_1) = F(\lambda_1)^N(1 - q)[\lambda_1 A + (1 - \lambda_1)B]$$
$$(2') \quad + [1 - F(\lambda_1)^N](1 - q)E(W_{\text{quit}}) + qE(W_{\text{layoff}}) - C(A, B).$$

As is intuitive, expected joint surplus, equation $(2')$, increases in thickness of the market. The more offers the better even though this results in a higher probability of separation from the original firm. Formally, first note that for a given A and B, an increase in N raises the expected wage of both quitters and those laid off because the set of offers over which to choose increases. Second, differentiate $(2')$ with respect to N to obtain

$$\frac{\partial S}{\partial N} = F(\lambda_1)^N \ln[F(\lambda_1)](1 - q)[\lambda_1 A + (1 - \lambda_1)B - E(W_{\text{quit}})]$$
$$+ [1 - F(\lambda_1)^N](1 - q)\frac{\partial E(W_{\text{quit}})}{\partial N} + \frac{q\partial E(W_{\text{layoff}})}{\partial N},$$

which is positive because $\ln[F(\lambda_1)]$ and $[\lambda_1 A + (1 - \lambda_1)B - E(W_{\text{quit}})]$ are both negative and both W_{quit} and W_{layoff} increase in N (more offers improves the alternatives for a given A, B).[12] Finally, allowing A and B to vary optimally can only increase surplus. Therefore, expected joint surplus increases in market thickness.

Perhaps counterintuitively, the wage gain from quitting declines as market thickness increases to the limit. In the thinnest market, where $N = 1$, the difference between the wages of quitters and stayers is given by (6), which is positive.

At the other extreme, as $N \to \infty$, the worker is certain to get an outside value of λ that not only dominates the current one, but also is the upper support of the distribution. So $\lambda_j = \lambda_{\text{max}}$. The same logic implies that the next best draw of λ is also λ_{max}. Every worker, whether a quit or layoff, leaves the initial firm for another firm that has the highest possible value of λ. The only workers who stay with the firm are those who have drawn maximum values of λ in their initial firm.[13] Thus, wage of both stayers and leavers is given by

$$(\lambda_{\text{max}})A - [1 - \lambda_{\text{max}}]B,$$

so the difference between them is zero.

Because the worker knows that he will be able to obtain $\lambda = \lambda_{\text{max}}$, as shown before, $A - B$ reaches a maximum as N goes to infinity. Yet, despite idiosyncratic investment, the wage loss for movers is necessarily zero because wages are the same for both stayers and leavers, voluntary or involuntary. There is no wage loss on changing firms. The highest order statistic and second-highest order statistic are identical, and the identity of the firms (outsiders or incumbent) is therefore irrelevant.[14]

This effect is reinforced by the fact that market thickness not only is expected to increase wages in period 2 but also results in more offers in period 1. Rather than assuming that the worker receives only one offer in the first period, it is more natural to assume that if N exceeds one in period 2, it exceeds one in period 1 also. Suppose that the number of offers in period 1 equals (or merely increases with) the number of offers in period 2. When markets are thick, they are thick for trained and untrained workers alike.

Surplus, defined in $(2')$, increases as λ_1 (see Appendix C for a proof) moves away from λ^*, the level of λ that induces $A = B$. If N increases, then the worker has more choice of λ_1 in the first period. Other things equal, the worker would choose the firm with the most extreme value of λ. However, multiple offers in period λ mean that firms must now compete for new workers.

Consider the limiting case. As N approaches infinity, the new worker is certain to receive an offer from a firm with $\lambda = \lambda_{max}$ or $\lambda = \lambda_{min}$. Since λ values are technologically determined, market equilibrium requires that wages adjust such that all viable firms are able to attract workers.[15] Second-period wages are determined by a competitive bargaining process, so W_1 must adjust correspondingly. Extreme value λ firms are better for workers in period 2, so firms with λ close to λ^* will have to pay higher first-period wages to attract workers. In the limit, as N goes to infinity, the worker is sure to draw $\lambda = \lambda_{max}$ among the firms making offers in period 1. Also, as N goes to infinity, the second-highest order statistic is also equal to λ_{max}. In the limit, therefore, all firms must pay period 1 wages that make workers indifferent between working in that firm and working in the firm with $\lambda = \lambda_{max}$ (or λ_{min} if that results in higher surplus). The firms with λ closer to λ^* will have to pay higher period 1 wages than those with λ closer to λ_{max}, because period 2 wages rise in λ as well.

In general equilibrium, an increase in N will change the underlying distribution of λ. As N rises, the preference of workers for higher-λ firms in period 1 means that some firms with λ close to λ^* will be unable to survive. The increase in costs associated with the higher wages that they will have to pay will drive them out of business, pushing the underlying distribution of λ toward bimodality. This is an additional factor in creating more idiosyncratic investment patterns as N rises and contributes to the direct partial equilibrium effect that results from moving to more extreme λ firms in period 2 as N rises.

Similarly, and consistent with most search models, as $N \rightarrow \infty$, laid-off workers are also certain to find a job with $\lambda_j = \lambda_{max}$. So $W_{layoff} - W_{stay} = 0$ as well. When thickness of the market increases, investment stay in human capital, although unbalanced, is not firm specific. Each skill taken by itself can always find a use in another firm, and as market thickness increases, the chances of finding a firm that uses skills in a less unfavorable combination also increase. It is in this sense that the definition of specific capital is endogenous. When the market is thin, a skill can be used by only a few firms and thereby becomes firm specific. As the market thickens, the same skill now takes on a general nature, because other firms can use the skill to the same extent as the original firm. This is quite different from the more historical motivation of specific human capital. If specific human capital takes the form of knowledge of the key players or methods that are specific to the firm, then thickness of the market would not make those skills more general.

Another implication follows. As in other matching and search models, the number of offers that a worker receives depends not only on the number of vacancies but also on the number of other workers searching for a job. The analysis in this section has implications for business cycle downturns, when there are many searchers and few vacancies. During downturns, the wage loss associated with an involuntary termination should be greater than during booms because the ability to find a firm with favorable weights is reduced during downturns. More to the point, Jacobson, LaLonde, and Sullivan (1993) find that wage loss associated with mass layoffs is greater than wage loss associated with other displacement. When there are mass layoffs, many workers with the same (or similar) prior investment patterns are looking for jobs in other firms with like skill-weights. The number of offers, N, per worker is lower, markets are thinner for those who are subject to mass layoffs, and the probability of finding a firm with favorable skill-weights is reduced. As such, individual displacement should, on average, be associated with less wage loss than mass layoff, which is consistent with their findings. Also directly related to market thickness, Crossley, Jones, and Kuhn (1994) find that wage loss from displacement is smaller when the population in which the plant was located is greater.

One implication and finding that goes in the opposite direction is in Lazear (1986a) and Gibbons and Katz (1991). Both papers argue that the negative stigma that firms attach to a worker's productivity with layoff is muted when many others are laid off as well. Gibbons and Katz test this and find that wage loss is lower when it is associated with mass layoff. Their finding relates directly to N because one would assume that a larger pool of applicants results in a smaller N. But the strength of the applicant pool effect, as opposed to the stigma effect on which

Gibbons and Katz focus, depends on the size of the market relative to the size of the plant closing. If the market is large, then a single plant closing should not affect the relevant N by very much.

13.2.2. Skill-Weights and Matching

The skill-weights interpretation is also consistent with the matching view of the labor market (Jovanovic 1979a, 1979b). As mentioned earlier, the skill-weights approach is a matching model because in period 2, the worker takes a new job only when he finds a firm where $\lambda_j > \lambda_1$. Most matching models are cast in terms of the worker's underlying (endowed) skills, but that is a minor twist on the model presented so far. To see this, simply think of a worker as being endowed with some vector of skills, (A_0, B_0). Output is

$$\text{Output} = \lambda_1 A_0 + (1 - \lambda_1)B_0,$$

and the derivative with respect to λ_1 is

$$\frac{\partial \text{Output}}{\partial \lambda_1} = A_0 - B_0$$

which carries the sign of $A_0 - B_0$. Matching consists of finding a firm with the highest λ_1 if $A_0 - B_0 > 0$ and finding a firm with the lowest λ_1 if $A_0 - B_0 < 0$.[16] Consequently, the important implications of matching models are also implications of the skill-weights view.[17]

13.2.3. Firms and Jobs

Do skill-weights relate to firms, industries, or jobs? Were skill-weights measurable, a regression to explain them would likely reveal the importance of firm, industry, and occupation effects.

Consider again the motivating example of the Silicon Valley startup. The chief executive officer in this firm must know computer programming, tax, and economics. But a software engineer can get by knowing mostly computer programming and some tax, with very little economics. Even the software engineer knows more about tax than the typical software engineer, but his skills are more specialized in computer programming than those of the CEO.

Thus, one can think of the λ as being not only firm specific but job and perhaps industry specific. For modeling purposes, virtually nothing is changed by expanding the view to include jobs. But at the empirical level, the distinction matters. It suggests, for example, that there may be firm effects that are important in explaining wage loss associated with involuntary turnover, but it also suggests that occupation might matter as well.

Once we begin to think of λ as being tied to jobs, the approach of Gibbons and Waldman (2004) becomes relevant. They model "task specific" human capital and argue that different jobs in the firm use different amounts of it. Promotions are performed in a way to minimize underutilization of task specific skills. This is not unlike selecting a new job in round 2 that has weights that favor the skills already acquired during period 1.

13.2.4.   Who Pays for General Training?

One of the puzzles in the literature has been that some forms of training seem general, yet firms sometimes bear the cost of acquiring them.[18] Under the skill-weights view, it is natural that the firm would pay for at least some of the human capital that appears to be general. Take the example given earlier where a firm requires tax, economics, and computer programming. Because a worker who leaves the firm will almost certainly fail to find another firm that needs the skills in the same proportions, and because this imposes a wage cost on mobile workers, the worker is unwilling to bear the full cost of training. The firm finances some learning about taxes, economics, and computer programming, even though each of these skills, taken separately, is completely general.

Unfortunately, there is no unambiguous analytic result that can be given on the relation of training costs borne by the firm to idiosyncrasy, λ_1. However, that the firm bears some portion of the costs under some circumstances can be demonstrated by the following numerical example.

Let $\gamma = 0.1$ (most rents go to the worker), $q = 0.05$ (the probability of exogenous layoff is low), $\lambda_1 = 0.95$ (the firm weights strongly favor A), the cost of investment is

$$C(A, B) = \frac{(A^2 + B^2)}{2},$$

and the density of λ is uniform on [0,1]. With these values, the cost of investment equals 0.43, and the wage in period 1 is -0.35, which means that the worker pays for most but not all of the training. The firm bears 0.08 of the training costs, which is almost one fifth of the cost. There is a very good chance that the worker will stay with the firm, in which case he receives wage $W_{\text{stay}} = 0.68$ in period 2. But if he gets laid off, his wage will only be 0.5 and the idiosyncratic investment that he made in A ($A = 0.93$; $B = 0.07$) will turn out to have been a poor ex post investment strategy. Even though both A and B have value in the layoff situation (the expected λ in layoff is 0.5), and even though A is, therefore, a general skill, the worker is unwilling to bear the full costs and need not in the bargaining equilibrium.[19]

13.2.5. Other Views of Wage Loss

Firm-specific human capital is not the only reason why wages might fall with involuntary turnover. Lazear (1979, see Chapter 1) provides an incentive motivation for upward sloping age earnings profiles where workers' wages exceed output later in life. Additionally, asymmetric information in labor markets can offer an alternative view.

For example, in Waldman (1990), when insiders have more information about workers than outsiders, up-or-out contracts may be used to reduce the ability of outsiders to use the actions of insiders to gauge worker productivity. Chang and Wang (1996) focus on under-investment in human capital that might occur as a result of asymmetric information. Acemoglu and Pischke (1998) provide an explanation for why firms might pay for general training using asymmetric information. Lazear (1986a) describes the bidding and turnover process when workers have a component of productivity that is general across firms and a component that is specific to each firm and where information about the two components is imperfect and asymmetric. The common thread of these papers is that all involve asymmetric information, where insiders and outsiders do not have the same amount of information about worker productivity. As a result, firms must guess the amount of human capital that the worker possesses, which can result in expected wage loss associated with turnover.

13.3. Empirically Testable Implications

The goal of theory is to provide implications that can be tested and verified or refuted. There are a number of implications of the skill-weights approach that go beyond those of the traditional view of firm-specific human capital and some that can distinguish between the two.

1. Market thickness: The implications regarding market thickness differentiate the skill-weights from traditional view of specific human capital. In the skill-weights approach, wage loss from involuntary turnover should be smaller in very thick markets than in very thin markets. A market is thick when the worker receives many offers for a given amount of search effort. Additionally, and perhaps counterintuitively, the wage gain for quitters goes to zero in very thick markets. Empirical proxies of search costs and offer frequencies might include regional population densities and industry and occupation concentration ratios.

2. Idiosyncratic firms: The more idiosyncratic is a firm's skill-weights, the less balanced is investment and lower is the probability of a quit. Measuring idiosyncracy may be difficult, but proxies might include the age of an industry (new industries may use skill-mixes that differ more from existing ones) and having an unusual combination of observable worker types at the firm. Returning to the motivating example, few firms that hire Java programmers also hire economists and tax specialists. Geel, Mure, and Backes-Gellner (2008) find support for this proposition. They have detailed measures of the skills used within a firm and find that the more unusual is the skill set used in an occupation, the smaller is the probability of an occupational change during an employee's career.

3. Payment for general training: As already mentioned, firms pay for what would otherwise appear to be general training because leaving a firm involuntarily implies wage loss when inferior skill-weights are encountered on the replacement job.

4. Industries and Occupations: A very detailed definition of industry and occupation might be thought to hold constant the skill-weights. That is, one way to define an industry or occupation is such that all individuals in the industry or occupation have identical skill-weights. If so, then holding industry and occupation constant in the wage regression should reduce the magnitude of the tenure effect. Early work by Shaw (1984) supports the implication (see her Table 4). Her wage regressions that include occupational experience have somewhat lower tenure coefficients than those without. Furthermore, the occupational effect itself is about four times as large as the pure tenure effect. To the extent that occupation is a proxy for skill-weights – and it surely cannot reflect firm-specific capital in the traditional sense – then the fact that occupational experience is so important suggests that the skill-weights view has merit.[20]

5. In firms that have low probabilities of exogenous layoff (low q), workers base more of their investment decision on the firm-specific skill-weights. As a result, mature workers' wages are higher and wage loss on involuntary layoff is greater in firms that are ex ante unlikely to lay off their workers.

13.4. Summary and Conclusions

Workers who experience involuntary job changes often have significantly lower wages on their subsequent jobs. One frequent interpretation is that the loss reflects firm-specific human capital. An alternative approach that is based on general human capital with firm-idiosyncratic weights provides all the implications of the traditional story, and provides additional ones, some of which have already been shown to be consistent with the data.

Like the traditional view, the skill-weights approach implies that workers who experience an exogenous change in job lose some earnings associated with their previous tenure. The amount of the loss associated with involuntary turnover tends to be greatest when exogenous separation probabilities are low, inducing a worker to invest idiosyncratically based on the weights at the initial firm. Further, the more idiosyncratic is the initial firm's technology, the more unbalanced is the investment.

There are a number of additional implications that come from the skill-weights view. The firm may bear some or even most of the cost of skills that look general. In the skill-weights version, no skills need be truly "firm-specific" in the sense of there being no other firm at which they have value. On the contrary, the skills appear to be general because in isolation, they are used at a number of firms in the market. But the weights differ by firm. If the skills are acquired in relatively idiosyncratic patterns, e.g., learning medicine and law in the same firm, expected wage loss is great when the worker is involuntarily separated.

Finally, the wage loss should be reduced when industry and occupation effects are taken into account. There is evidence, found in a variety of data sets, that supports this implication.

Appendix A

The socially efficient choices of A and B are compared with the levels that maximize the joint surplus in (2). The socially efficient level of surplus takes into account the rents going to other firms in the economy when a worker quits or is laid off. The joint surplus in (2) ignores the rent to other firms and only focuses on that going to the worker or current firm.

The social surplus is then

$$
\text{Social Surplus} = F(\lambda_1)(1 - q)\{\lambda_1 A + (1 - \lambda_1)B\} + (1 - F(\lambda_1))(1 - q)
$$

$$
(2A) \qquad \cdot \{E(\lambda_j \mid \lambda_j > \lambda_1)A + [1 - E(\lambda_j \mid \lambda_j > \lambda_1)]B\}
$$

$$
+ q\{\overline{\lambda}A + (1 - \overline{\lambda})B\} - C(A, B).
$$

The first-order conditions are

$$
(3A) \qquad \frac{\partial}{\partial A} = (1 - q)F(\lambda_1)\lambda_1 + (1 - q)(1 - F(\lambda_1))E(\lambda_j | \lambda_j > \lambda_1)
$$

$$
+ q\overline{\lambda} - C_A = 0
$$

and

$$\frac{\partial}{\partial B} = (1 - q)F(\lambda_1)(1 - \lambda_1)$$

(4A)
$$+ (1 - q)(1 - F(\lambda_1))(1 - E(\lambda_j|\lambda_j > \lambda_1))$$

$$+ q(1 - \overline{\lambda}) - C_B = 0.$$

Recall that the first order conditions for joint surplus maximization are

$$\frac{\partial}{\partial A} = (1 - q)F(\lambda_1)\lambda_1 + (1 - q)(1 - F(\lambda_1))\left(\frac{\lambda_1 + E(\lambda_j|\lambda_j > \lambda_1)}{2}\right)$$

(3)
$$+ \frac{q}{2}(\overline{\lambda} + \lambda_L) - C_A = 0$$

and

$$\frac{\partial}{\partial B} = (1 - q)F(\lambda_1)(1 - \lambda_1)$$

(4)
$$+ (1 - q)(1 - F(\lambda_1))\left(1 - \frac{\lambda_1 + E(\lambda_j|\lambda_j > \lambda_1)}{2}\right)$$

$$+ \frac{q}{2}(1 - \overline{\lambda} + 1 \lambda_L) - C_B = 0.$$

Compare (3A) to (3). The social optimum is to invest more in A than the firm and worker choose when maximizing their joint surplus. The second term of (3A) is larger than the second term of (3) because the worker and firm do not take into account the rent going to the new firm. The worker does not quit unless $\lambda_j > \lambda_1$ so that firm benefits from more A-intensive investment, but the worker and firm favor their current situation too much relative to the social optimum because the λ_1 affects the portion of the rents that the worker receives in the new firm. Similarly, when the worker is laid off, he receives only half of the difference between the firm weight, λ_j, and his alternative λ_L and so maximization of the surplus going to worker and firm, which ignores the new firm, under-invests in A.[21] The converse is also true for B: The firm and worker over-invest in B because they do not take into account appropriately the lower weight that the new firm places on B in the cases of quits and layoffs.

Were workers allowed to choose A and B and were they required to bear the costs of investment, the maximization problem would be

$$F(\lambda_1)(1 - q)\left\{B + \frac{(\lambda_1 + E(\lambda_j|\lambda_j \leq \lambda_1))(A - B)}{2}\right\}$$

(2A')
$$+ (1 - F(\lambda_1))(1 - q)\left\{B + \frac{(\lambda_1 + E(\lambda_j|\lambda_j > \lambda_1))(A - B)}{2}\right\}$$

$$+ \frac{q}{2}\left\{\lambda_L A + (1 - \lambda_L)B + \bar{\lambda}A + (1 - \bar{\lambda})B\right\} - C(A, B)$$

with first-order conditions

$$\frac{\partial}{\partial A} = (1 - q)F(\lambda_1)\left(\frac{\lambda_1 + E(\lambda_j|\lambda_j \leq \lambda_1)}{2}\right)$$

(3A')
$$+ (1 - q)(1 - F(\lambda_1))\left(\frac{\lambda_1 + E(\lambda_j|\lambda_j > \lambda_1)}{2}\right)$$

$$+ \frac{q}{2}(\bar{\lambda} + \lambda_L) - C_A = 0$$

and

$$\frac{\partial}{\partial B} = (1 - q)F(\lambda_1)\left(1 - \frac{\lambda_1 + E(\lambda_j|\lambda_j \leq \lambda_1)}{2}\right)$$

(4A')
$$+ (1 - q)(1 - F(\lambda_1))\left(1 - \frac{\lambda_1 + E(\lambda_j|\lambda_j > \lambda_1)}{2}\right)$$

$$+ \frac{q}{2}(1 - \bar{\lambda} + 1 - \lambda_L) - C_B = 0.$$

Except for the first-terms, (3A') and (4A') are identical to (3) and (4). It is clear from the comparison of the first-terms that the worker would choose too little A and too much B. This improves the worker's net return when he stays at the firm because he stays when $\lambda_j < \lambda_1$. The worker over-invests in outside options to increase his wage at the current firm.

Alternatively, were the firm to choose A and B and, correspondingly, to bear the costs of training, the maximization problem would be

$$F(\lambda_1)(1 - q)\{\lambda_1 A + (1 - \lambda_1)B - W_{\text{stay}}\} - C(A, B)$$

or

$$F(\lambda_1)(1 - q)\left\{\lambda_1 A + (1 - \lambda_1)B - \left[B + \frac{\lambda_1 + E(\lambda_j|\lambda_j \leq \lambda_1)}{2}(A - B)\right]\right\} - C(A, B).$$

The first-order conditions are

$$(3A'') \qquad F(\lambda_1)(1-q)\left\{\lambda_1 - \frac{\lambda_1 + E(\lambda_j | \lambda_j \le \lambda_1)}{2}\right\} - C_A = 0$$

and

$$(4A'') \quad F(\lambda_1)(1-q)\left\{1 - \lambda_1 - \left(1 - \frac{\lambda_1 + E(\lambda_j | \lambda_j \le \lambda_1)}{2}\right)\right\} - C_A = 0.$$

The first term in each of $(3A'')$ and $(4A'')$ is unambiguously lower than the first term in (3) and (4), respectively. Additionally, the other two positive terms in (3) and (4) are absent from $(3A'')$ and $(4A'')$. The firm would choose to invest less in both A and B because the firm does not want to invest in skills that improve the worker's bargaining power if he stays. In addition, the firm does not does take into account the value of skills if the worker were to go to another firm. Finally, because $(3A'')$ and $(4A'')$ do not contain the terms that reflect quit or layoff, investment is biased toward the skill that is most favored in the current firm.

Appendix B
Proof That $A - B$ Is Maximized When $\lambda_1 = 1$.

Rewriting (3) so as to put C_A on the r.h.s. gives

$$(3') \quad (1-q)F(\lambda_1)\lambda_1 + (1-q)(1-F(\lambda_1))\left(\frac{\lambda_1 + E(\lambda_j | \lambda_j > \lambda_1)}{2}\right)$$
$$+ \frac{q}{2}(\overline{\lambda} + \lambda_L) = C_A.$$

When $\lambda_1 = 1$, $(3')$ becomes

$$(3'') \qquad\qquad (1-q) + \frac{q}{2}(\overline{\lambda} + \lambda_L) = C_A.$$

A sufficient condition for A to reach a maximum when $\lambda_1 = 1$ is that the l.h.s. of $(3'')$ exceeds the l.h.s. of $(3')$ for all values of $\lambda_1 < 1$.

Subtract the l.h.s. of (3') from that of (3'') to obtain

$$(1 - q)\left\{1 - \left[F(\lambda_1)\lambda_1 + (1 - F(\lambda_1))\right]\left(\frac{\lambda_1 + E(\lambda|\lambda > \lambda_1)}{2}\right)\right\}$$

which equals zero when $\lambda_1 = 1$. The second term inside the curled brackets is a convex combination of λ_1 and $\frac{\lambda_1 + E(\lambda|\lambda > \lambda_1)}{2}$, which cannot exceed one since both λ_1 and $E(\lambda|\lambda > \lambda_1)$ are less than one. As a result, the expression is positive for $\lambda_1 < 1$, which implies that C_A is higher when $\lambda_1 = 1$ than it is for any other value. Since C_A is increasing in A, this implies that A reaches a maximum when $\lambda_1 = 1$.

Additionally, note from (3) and (4) that $C_A + C_B = 1$ so that if A increases, B must decrease.[22] Because A reaches a maximum at 1, B reaches a minimum at $\lambda_1 = 1$ so $A - B$ is maximized when $\lambda_1 = 1$.[23]

The amount that individuals lose at layoff increases in the idiosyncracy. Using (7),

$$\frac{\partial W_{\text{layoff}} - W_{\text{stay}}}{\partial \lambda_1} = \frac{1}{2}\left[\lambda_L - \bar{\lambda} - \lambda_1 - E(\lambda_j|\lambda_j < \lambda_1)\right]\frac{\partial(A - B)}{\partial \lambda_1}$$
$$+ (A - B)\left(-1 - \frac{\partial E(\lambda_j|\lambda_j < \lambda_1)}{\partial \lambda_1}\right)$$

which is negative because $\frac{1}{2}\left[\lambda_L - \bar{\lambda} - \lambda_1 - E(\lambda_j|\lambda_j < \lambda_1)\right]$ is negative for there to be any stayers and because $\frac{\partial(A - B)}{\partial \lambda_1} < 0$.

Appendix C
Proof That Surplus Increases in λ_1

Surplus from (2') is defined as

(2'')
$$(1 - q)[\text{prob(stay)}][\lambda_1 A + (1 - \lambda_1)B]$$
$$+ (1 - q)[1 - \text{prob(stay)}](E(W_{\text{quit}}) + qE(W_{\text{layoff}})) - C(A, B).$$

Differentiate $(2'')$ with respect to λ_1, holding A, B, and the probability of staying constant to obtain

$$\frac{\partial}{\partial \lambda_1}\bigg|_{A,B,\text{prob(stay)}} = (1 - q)\text{prob(stay)}(A - B)$$
$$+ (1 - q)[1 - \text{prob(stay)}]\,\frac{\partial(W_{\text{quit}})}{\partial \lambda_1}\bigg|_{A,B,\text{prob(stay)}}\quad \frac{\partial E(W_{\text{layoff}})}{\partial \lambda_1}\bigg|_{A,B,\text{prob(stay)}}.$$

Now

$$E(W_{\text{quit}}) = \left[\frac{\lambda_j^{1(N)} + \lambda_j^{2(N)}}{2}\right]A + \left[1 - \frac{\lambda_j^{1(N)} + \lambda_j^{2(N)}}{2}\right]B,$$

where $\lambda_j^{i(N)}$ is the ith-highest order statistic on λ_j, given N draws, subject to $\lambda_1^{1(N)} > \lambda_1$.[24] Thus,

$$\frac{\partial E(W_{\text{quit}})}{\partial \lambda_1}\,\frac{A - B}{2}\left[\frac{\partial \lambda_j^{1(N)}}{\partial \lambda_1} + \frac{\partial \lambda_j^{2(N)}}{\partial \lambda_1}\right].$$

Because $\lambda_1^{i(N)}$ is defined to be greater than λ_1^{*}, $\lambda_1^{i(N)}/\partial \lambda_1 > 0$. So $E(W_{\text{quit}})$ increases in λ_1. Similarly,

$$E(W_{\text{layoff}}) = \left[\frac{\overline{\lambda}_j^{1(N)} + \overline{\lambda}_j^{2(N)}}{2}\right]A + \left[1 - \frac{\overline{\lambda}_j^{1(N)} + \overline{\lambda}_j^{2(N)}}{2}\right]B,$$

where $\overline{\lambda}_j^{i(N)}$ is the unconditional ith-highest order statistic. Since this is unconditional,

$$\frac{\partial \overline{\lambda}^{i(N)}}{\partial \lambda_1} = 0,$$

so

$$\frac{\partial E(W_{\text{layoff}})}{2\lambda_1}\bigg|_{A,B,\text{prob(stay)}} = 0.$$

Therefore,

$$\frac{\partial}{\partial \lambda_1}\bigg|_{A,B,\text{prob(stay)}} =$$

$$(1-q)\text{prob(stay)}(A-B) + (1-q)[1-\text{prob(stay)}]\ \frac{\partial E(W_{\text{quit}})}{\partial \lambda_1}\bigg|_{A,B,\text{prob(stay)}}$$

which is positive because $A > B$.

Allowing A, B, and the prob(stay) to vary optimally can only increase surplus.[25] So

$$\frac{\partial \text{surplus}}{\partial \lambda_1} > 0.$$

QED.

Appendix D

The numerical example in the text is repeated here, but $\gamma = 0.5$ instead of 0.1 so that rents are split evenly between worker and firm. As before, $q = 0.05$ (the probability of exogenous layoff is low), the cost of investment, $C(A, B) = (A^2 + B^2)/2$, and the density of λ is uniform on $[0,1]$. Then, as can be seen in Table D1, when λ_1 increases from 0.5 to 0.75, W_1 rises, but when λ_1 continues to increase to 0.95, W_1 falls.

Table D1

Effect of λ_1 on A, B, and W_1

λ_1	A	B	W_1
0.5	0.56	0.44	-0.51
0.75	0.75	0.25	-0.49
0.95	0.93	0.07	-0.5
1	0.98	0.03	-0.5

14

Educational Production

There exists an enormous empirical literature on the relation of educational attainment to class size. Results in this literature vary from significant class size effects to no (or sometimes even perverse) class size effects.[1] The inability to find consistent class size effects is most perplexing. At some basic level, the failure to observe class size effects makes no sense because observed class size is generally smaller than the entire number of students at any particular grade level. Why bear the expense of having four kindergarten classes of 30 rather than one class of 120 if class size truly does not matter? Furthermore, observed class size varies with age of the student. Preschool classes are smaller than large lecture classes for college students. How is this to be explained if class size is irrelevant?

Although there is a vast empirical literature on educational production and its determinants, there is a relatively small theoretical literature.[2] In what follows, a theory is presented that addresses the class size puzzle. The basic structure begins with the recognition that education in a classroom environment is a public good. But as with most public goods, classroom learning has congestion effects, which are negative externalities created when one student impedes the learning of all other classmates. There is empirical support for this proposition. Peer effects have long been recognized as crucial in education.[3] While hardly novel, to understand peer interaction effects, it is necessary to embed the spillovers in a framework where changing the size of a class or its composition has a cost. The primary cost takes the form of teacher salary and infrastructure.

The original version of this chapter was published as: Lazear, E. P. (2001). Educational Production, in: Quarterly Journal of Economics, 116(3), 777-803. MIT Press. © 2001 by the President and Fellows of Harvard College and the Massachusetts Institute of Technology. This research was supported in part by the National Science Foundation. I am grateful to Orley Ashenfelter, Julian Betts, Gary Becker, Simon Board, Janet Currie, Williamson Evers, Victor Fuchs, Jeffrey Grogger, Eric Hanushek, James Heckman, Caroline Hoxby, Alan Krueger, and Sherwin Rosen for comments and discussions. I especially thank Michael Schwarz for outstanding research assistance.

The answer to the class size puzzle rests on the realization that class size is a choice variable and the optimal class size varies inversely with the attention span of the students. It is efficient to use fewer teachers and a higher student-teacher ratio when the students are better behaved. But an envelope theorem implies that actual educational output varies directly with the behavior of the student, despite the fact that fewer teacher inputs are used. An implication is that class size matters, but the observed relation of educational output to class size may be small or even positive.[4]

The main purpose of the model presented here is to tie together a wide variety of facts and to integrate the literature on class size and student performance. A further goal is to provide a new empirical strategy for understanding student performance and the determinants of it. The goal is ambitious, but it is hoped that some progress can be made by emphasizing the role that behavior plays in the determination of class size. The primary implications of the theory are the following.

1. Optimal class size varies directly with student behavior and with the value of human capital and varies inversely with the cost of teachers. As a result, educational output per student can be lower in smaller classes.

2. The effect of reducing class size depends on the size of the class and the behavior of the students in it. Class size effects are larger for less well-behaved students.

3. Classes segregated by ability are the outcome of a private educational system and are efficient under a wide variety of circumstances.

4. The trade-off between discipline and class size is modeled and can be estimated empirically. Further, classroom etiquette and class size are determined simultaneously.

5. An exact function relates class size, student behavior, and educational output. The theory permits a new metric of school quality, and data exist that permit estimation of the relation and testing of the model.

14.1. The Model

The driving force is the idea that peer effects are important in classroom education. At some level the point is obvious. A classroom almost defines what is meant by a public good.[5]

In the context of the public goods discussion, the cost of adding additional students can be thought of as congestion effects. In this setting, however, it is better to model the congestion effect more explicitly by thinking in terms of negative externalities that students may convey on one another. In classroom education, the ability of one student to get something out of a moment of class time depends on the behavior of others in the class. This is a clear application of the bad apple principle. If one child is misbehaving, the entire class suffers. Thus, let p be the probability that any given student is not impeding his own or other's learning at any moment in time. Then, the probability that all students in a class of size n are behaving is p^n so that disruption occurs $1 - p^n$ of the time.[6]

The impediment may take a variety of forms. Student disruption provides a concrete example. Neither the student nor his classmates can learn much when the student is misbehaving, causing the teacher to allocate her time to him. Less nefarious, but equally costly is time taken by a student who asks a question to which all other students know the answer. One can think of p as the proportion of time that a given student does not halt the public aspects of the classroom education process. Thus, the assumption made is that one child's disruption destroys the ability of all students (including himself) to learn at that moment.[7] It is expected that p would be relatively high because even having $p = .98$ in a class of 25 students results in disruption 40 percent of the time ($1 - .98^{25} = .40$). Disruptive behavior may be viewed as deviant behavior, but most students are capable of disrupting for at least some fraction, in this case, $1 - p$, of the time, especially when disruption is interpreted to mean asking a question to which others know the answer.

In contrast to negative externalities, students also provide public goods to one another. Although true, it is uninteresting to look to the range of class size values where adding students produces positive rather than negative externalities. Because increasing class size reduces cost per student, the profit-maximizing school will always increase class size to at least the point where additional students have negative effects on others. The optimum must be in the range where externalities are negative, and so the focus is on this part of the story throughout the chapter.

So far, only technology has been discussed; the foregoing says nothing about optimality. To determine the schools' actions under varying conditions, let us begin by asking how much a student would pay to be in a class of size n. Suppose that the value of a unit of learning is given by V, which is determined by the market value human capital and the likelihood that a student is focusing on learning during the given instant.

To determine optimal class size, consider a school of Z students with m teachers and m classes. Let the cost of a teacher and the rental value of the associated capital for her classroom be given by W. For now, W is assumed to be independent of p and other working conditions. Then a private school that wants to maximize profits can sell each moment at the school for ZVp^n, at a total cost of Wm. Maximization of profit would mean choosing m so as to maximize

(1) $$\text{Profit} = ZVp^{Z/m} - Wm$$

or equivalently,

(1a) $$\text{Profit per student} = Vp^n - W/n$$

because each class has $n = Z/m$ students in it.

The first-order condition is then

(2) $$-V\frac{Z^2}{m^2}p^{Z/m}\ln(p) - W = 0$$

or using (1a),

(2a) $$Vp^n\ln(p) + W/n^2 = 0.$$

Variations in V can result either because the market for educated individuals relative to less-educated individuals changes, or because the amount of learning that takes place during an uninterrupted moment of schooling changes. However, as a modeling strategy, little emphasis is placed on variations in V. The goal is to attempt to provide as many testable predictions as possible by focusing on variations in p.

371

Variations in teacher and student quality as well as other differences in the production function can always be thought to enter through V, but they are not the focus of the model.

Market equilibrium is achieved in two ways, given any existence of positive profits. Competitive entry of firms into the education industry drives up W through demand pressure on wages in the teachers market. At the same time, the supply of educated graduates to the labor market drives down V. Equilibrium occurs when maximization of profit results in zero overall profit to the competitive supplier of education.

This is the basic model, and a number of implications can be derived from it.[8]

14.2. Comparative Statics

Using equation (2), a proposition, proved in the appendix, can be derived.

Proposition 1. The optimal class size rises in teacher's wage, falls in the value of a unit of education, and most important, rises in the probability that students behave well. It is optimal to reduce class size when students are less well-behaved.[9]

The main purpose of the model is to provide a framework for discussing class size and how it varies with a number of factors.[10]

To get a feel for this, consider an example. Normalize V to 1. Then W, the price of a teacher's time, must be priced relative to V. In equilibrium, the price of teacher time relative to the productivity of student time must be sufficiently low to make the activity profitable. If it were not, private schools could not exist.

Suppose that the ratio of W to Vp^n is 5. The teacher's time is five times as valuable as what any one student gets out of the class. Then, if $Z = 100$ and $p = .99$ so that 99 percent of the time any given student is not causing enough disruption to interrupt learning in the classroom, the first-order condition (2) yields an optimum m of 3.94, which gives a class size of 25 students.

This example makes clear why it is so difficult to find significant class size effects.[11] Increasing class size from 25 to 27 would reduce educational output per student by only about 2 percent.[12]

The more important point is that class size is a choice variable. Because class size is a choice variable, researchers often observe small, or possibly even positive class size effects in cross-sectional data. The optimal number of teachers declines with p, which means that better-behaved students are in larger classes. The relation of n to p explains why kindergarten classes are smaller than college lectures. Furthermore, the fact that the optimum n depends on p and generally provides an interior solution explains why there are four kindergarten classes of 30, rather than one of 120. If p were .97, learning would occur 40 percent of the time in a class of 30, but only $2\frac{1}{2}$ percent of the time in a class of 120.

Although more disruptive students, who are themselves poorer learners, are found in smaller classes, the effect of reducing class size is not sufficient to overcome their deficiencies. Thus,

Proposition 2. After optimal class-size adjustment, educational output per student is higher in the larger classes with better behaved students than in the smaller classes with less well behaved students. (Proved in the appendix.)

There is substitution, but it is incomplete. Educational output in high p classes is higher. If class size varies primarily because schools are adjusting class size in response to the behavior of the students, then the larger classes will have the better students and higher educational output, providing a positive observed relation between class size and educational output.[13] In the example above, when $p = .99$, optimal class size is 25, and educational output per student is .78. When p falls to .98, the optimal class size is 19, and educational output per student is .68 because the effect of the lower value of p swamps the effect of the reduced class size. This impairs the ability of the researcher to find improved educational output when class size is reduced.[14] The incongruity of educator statements and common sense with the failure to find class size effects is reconciled once it is recognized that class-size, student characteristics, and educational output are related in a particular way.[15]

It is also clear why class size effects are potentially quite important despite the inconsistency of the data. If a given group of students with a given value of p were to be placed in a larger class, educational output would fall. Although the endogeneity of class size is well-understood, the point is not simply that poorer-quality students may be in smaller classes. When class size adjusts optimally, reductions in class size do not offset the effect of slower learning. A natural experiment that leaves p constant and changes class size should induce the expected class-size effect. Even if large classes have more educational output, reducing the size of a given class would increase educational output further.[16] Angrist and Lavy (1999) and Krueger (1999) obtain this result, but Hoxby (2000a), who also uses a natural experiment approach, does not.[17]

The point is that even if class size effects are potentially important, in equilibrium, marginal changes in class size may have small effects on observed educational output. If large gains were available from lowering class size, then those changes would have been made.[18]

Since class size varies inversely with W, large class size effects are most likely to be observed when the cost of teachers is low. Low teacher salaries imply low optimal class sizes. Reducing class size has a larger effect on educational output in small classes than in large ones. The empirical implication is that class size effects are most likely to be observed when teachers are relatively inexpensive. Preschool teachers are less expensive than professors, which generates small class size for preschoolers. Because of the nonlinearities in educational production function, class size effects should be more important in preschool classes than they are at the college level.

14.2.1. Behavior and Class Size

What happens as p, the probability that a student is a nondisruptive learner, changes? There are two obvious applications, one relating to age and the other to underlying social behavior of a student body. Age is the most straightforward. Younger children have shorter attention spans than does the typical college student. In a class of kindergarten children, the probability that a child is behaving is lower than that in a college class.

Even within grade level, class size varies with topic. Some topics require more discussion and tend to have lower class size. If other student time were as valuable as teacher time, there would be no need to have small classes. It would not matter whether another student or the teacher was speaking. Because these effects are negative, at least on the margin, "air time" devoted to other students has negative effects on learning. These lower p classes have smaller optimal class sizes, and lower educational output, other things the same.[19]

Figure 14.1

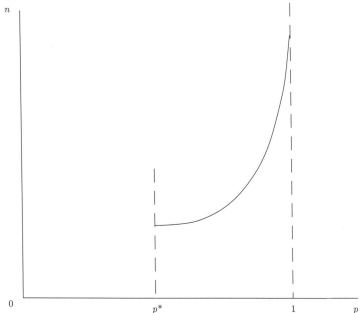

The implication is that if V, the value of a minute of first-grade schooling is the same as the value of a minute of college schooling, then the first-grade class should be smaller than the college class. Although not particularly surprising, it is a direct implication of a model that takes into account the cost of teacher time and trades this off against the gains from having a less frequently disrupted class.

Further, the marginal value of reducing class size is greater for low p students than for high p students. If special needs children have lower p values than other children, then the implication is that special education classes should be smaller than regular education classes. Sufficient for this implication is that the value of a moment of education for special needs children is as high as it is for other children.

Angrist and Lavy (1999) and Krueger and Whitmore (2001) report that the class size effects are more important for disadvantaged students than for others.[20] Suppose that disadvantaged students are also low p students. Then, the proportionate increase in educational output associated with a decrease in class size from nk to n students is

$$(p^n - p^{nk})/p^{nk}.$$

375

Differentiate with respect to p to obtain

$$d/dp = -np^{(n-nk-1)}(k-1) < 0$$

for $k > 1$. This implies that the effect of a class-size reduction is greater for low p students than for high p students.

14.2.2. Private Schools and Severe Behavior Problems

Very poorly behaved children who have sufficiently low values of p cannot be accommodated by a private school that must earn nonnegative profits. This is obvious from (1) since for $p = 0$, profits are negative for any positive value of m and therefore, any finite value of n. Figure 14.1 depicts the relation between the optimal n and p. As p declines, n declines until p reaches p^*, at which point it does not pay to supply any education. The firm provides no teachers and sets $m = 0$. Of course, no one would buy education of this sort in a private market. In the public sector, both schools and students might be forced to attempt to provide education, even to very low p students. There a social planner who took only efficiency considerations into account would be induced to set m, the number of teachers per student, as close to zero as legally possible, creating large classes where there is little pretense of education. This situation might be thought of as a babysitting role of schools.

There exist private schools that cater to very low p students, particularly those whose focus is special education. They exist primarily because society has decided that the value of educating these low p individuals is higher than the private value of V and are subsidized as a result. Subsidies are generally confined to younger low p students. Implicitly, society imputes a high value to early education. But society is generally reluctant to subsidize older low p students. College subsidies are rarely given to disruptive or slow-learning students. The pattern of subsidy is consistent with a view that there is little deviation between the private value of schooling and the social value of schooling for college students.

14.2.3. Differences in the Value of Education by Grade Level

As already mentioned, the approach in this chapter is to ignore differences in educational value across students as a way to explain observed class size, focusing instead on variations in behavior, as proxied by p. Still, it is useful to consider the effects of the value of education on class size. Proposition 1 states that an increase in V implies a decrease in class size. Because elementary education is the foundation for all that follows, the value of knowledge acquired during a year of schooling might be expected to be highest in the earlier grades. ("Everything I need to know, I learned in kindergarten.") The fact that p is lower for young children than for older ones coupled with the observation that wages for elementary school teachers are significantly lower than those for college professors implies that all of the factors push in the direction of smaller class size for younger children.

14.2.4. Special Programs

Schools sometimes set up special programs and allocate slots in these programs on some kind of lottery or first-come-first-served basis. The programs often involve smaller class sizes and sometimes feature a different or extended curriculum. Unless the purpose of such programs is experimentation, it cannot be efficient to set up special programs with random student assignment. When lotteries or other nonattribute-based selection processes are used, the pool of selected students will have the same characteristics as those of the nonselected attributes so p does not differ over students. Since (2) implies a unique optimum for m and therefore n, deviating from the optimum by making some classes smaller and others larger cannot improve allocations. If a deviation in either direction were an improvement, it would be possible to choose every class with that alternative class size and do even better. Therefore, there are no asymmetrically efficient solutions when all students have the same p. Note that nothing in this discussion requires that the material taught in the different classes be the same. The same logic applies to new superior curricula. If it is optimal to provide the new curriculum to some group of the students, then it is optimal to provide it to all students because students are ex ante identical. Special classes allocated randomly fail the test of ex post fairness and are also inefficient. The best argument for asymmetric classes is that of experimentation.

14.3. Sorting

To this point, it has been assumed that all students in a given class have the same behavior pattern. There are two questions that arise: first, is it efficient to integrate students, or should they be segregated into behavior-homogeneous classes? Second, does a market-based system of private education induce students to self-sort? In this section it is shown that segregation is efficient and that a market system does induce self-sorting.

14.3.1. Segregation by Type

Suppose that there are two types of students. Let the A group have a higher value of p than the B group so that $p_a > p_b$. While A and B need not refer to grades earned by such students, the interpretation is not an unnatural one.[21] A direct implication of Proposition 1 is that class size for A students is larger than class size for B students. It is now possible to state Proposition 3.

Proposition 3. Total output is maximized when students are segregated by type.

To prove this proposition, first assume that all classes are of size n. Suppose that the economy consists of α A students and $1 - \alpha$ B students. Then a school with matched classes[22] has output

(3) Output per student with segregated schools $= \alpha p_A^n + (1 - \alpha)p_B^n;$

whereas output per student in an economy with integrated schools is

(4) Output per student with segregated schools $= p_A^{\alpha n} p_B^{(1-\alpha)n}.$

To show that it is always better to match than mix, it is merely necessary to show that the difference between the right-hand side of (3) and (4) is positive. The difference is

(5) $$\text{diff} = \alpha p_A^n + (1 - \alpha)p_B^n - p_A^{\alpha n} p_B^{(1-\alpha)n}.$$

When $p_A = p_B$, diff $= 0$, as it must because then there is only one type, so mixing and matching is irrelevant. Next, differentiate (5) with respect to p_A to obtain

$$\frac{\partial \text{diff}}{\partial p_A} = \alpha n p_A^{n-1} \left(\frac{1 - p_B^{(1-\alpha)n}}{1 - p_A^{(1-\alpha)n}} \right) > 0$$

for $p_A > p_B$. Thus, the difference is zero for $p_A = p_B$ and becomes positive for $p_A > p_B$. Since $p_A > p_B$, school output is maximized by matching rather than mixing student types in classes.

Now, allow the choice of class size to differ. Define n, in (3), (4), and (5) to be the class size that is optimal when student types are mixed. Allowing segregation also allows schools to adjust class size optimally so as to allow different size classes for A's and B's. But segregation dominates even when all classes are constrained to be at the mixed optimum. Segregation must surely dominate if segregated classes can be of different sizes, which completes the derivation of Proposition 3.

Coleman and Hoffer (1987) and Coleman, Kilgore, and Hoffer (1981) report that performance is higher in private schools, and Catholic schools in particular, than in public schools.[23] One possibility is that Catholic schools expel the troublemakers, leaving a population of students who are easier to teach than those in the public schools. However, the facts are that expulsion rates are lower in the Catholic schools than they are in the private schools. It is possible that sorting occurs at admission. Given that public schools are free and that private schools cost, there is a positive difference in price associated with going to a private school.[24]

It is straightforward to show that A's are willing to pay a higher price for admission to an all A school than are B's, although both are willing to pay a positive price. An A receives value p_A^n from an all A school and $p_A^{\alpha n} p_B^{(1-\alpha)n}$ from an integrated school. (V is normalized to 1.) A B receives value $p_A^{n-1} p_b$ from an all A school and $p_A^{\alpha n} p_B^{(1-\alpha)n}$ from an integrated school. The difference between what an A will pay and what a B will pay to move from the integrated school to an all A school is then

$$p_A^n - p_A^{n-1} p_B,$$

379

which is positive. Thus, A's are more likely to pay private school tuition to get into an all A school than are B's, given that the alternative is free public school.[25] The students who will pay the most to go to a private school are students with higher values of p, which is consistent with selection effects on Catholic schools working through admission, rather than expulsion.[26]

The intuition is this: B's benefit from being around A's, but A's also benefit from being around other A's. If there is a group of $n - 1$ A students who will let one more student into the class, all of the current classmates prefer to admit an A. Furthermore, an outside A gets more from entering an all A class than does an outside B. Therefore, matching student types both is efficient and is the outcome of a competitive bidding process.

Public K–12 schools use neither type-specific prices nor admissions criteria to sort students. The implicit price of K–12 public schools does vary through housing prices and local taxes. Furthermore, these indirect price variations appear to sort students, albeit imperfectly.[27] The within-school variation in educational attainment, even in public schools, is small relative to the total variation. Some of this may be a result of the schooling itself, and some is a result of the characteristics of the underlying student bodies.

14.3.2. The Case for Integration

Some educators believe that it is important to have integrated classes, where tracking by ability does not occur early, if at all. There are two arguments for integration of classes, in light of Proposition 3: efficiency and equity.

The efficiency case rests on the ability to transform low p students into high p students as a result of integration. To make the case, it is necessary that B's can be transformed into A's by being around them. If this effect is strong enough, then integrated classes are efficient.[28]

For example, if B's were immediately transformed into A's when integrated with them, and if this imposed no cost on A's, then efficiency would be enhanced by mixing B's with A's.

As a practical matter, transformation of B's into A's is most likely to occur when the ratio of A's to B's is large. If a school of 100 had 99 B's and 1 A, it is unlikely that the one A student would change the behavior of all of the other B students.[29] Clear evidence of the effect of peer group on transforming behavior is presented by Katz, King, and Liebman (1999). They find that children who move from high poverty areas to higher income areas experienced reduced incidence of behavior problems, including those at school. The effect was significant for boys, but not for girls. Equity issues may also be at play. Even if it is more efficient to segregate schools, B's bear the costs and are poorer than A's, even without segregation. Segregating classes exacerbates income inequality because A's benefit from segregation and B's may lose by it.[30] This follows directly from (3) and (4). Note that a B receives p_B^n in an all B class, which can be rewritten as $p_B^{\alpha n} p_B^{(1-\alpha)n}$. Now, $p_B^{\alpha n} p_B^{(1-\alpha)n} < p_A^{\alpha n} p_B^{(1-\alpha)n}$ because $p_A > p_B$. But $p_A^{\alpha n} p_B^{(1-\alpha)n}$ is what B's receive in a mixed class, so B's receive more in a mixed class than in an all B class. Similar logic reveals that A's receive more in mixed classes than in an all A classes. Thus, moving to integrated classes reduces educational inequality.

In addition to the results by Katz, King, and Liebman (2001), Betts and Shkolnik (1999) find that the percent of time spent on instruction rises and that on discipline falls as the class becomes more female. Following the logic above, boys would want to be in all-girl schools, but girls would not want them there.[31]

14.4. Endogenous Discipline, Teacher Quality, and Other Issues

14.4.1. *Endogenous Discipline*

Disruption has been assumed to be given, but it is clear that discipline can affect the level of disruption, for better or worse. Catholic schools are known for strict discipline, and some attribute the success of their educational programs to discipline. Discipline, however, is not without a cost. In addition to stifling potential creativity, the act of disciplining students is time-consuming and unpleasant.

The choice of discipline level can be modeled, and p, the probability of behaving, can be made endogenous. Let

$$p = p(d, t),$$

where d is the amount of discipline and t is the student's type. It is reasonable to assume that more discipline results in less disruption so $p_1 > 0$. Also, t, the student's type is defined such that $p_2 > 0$; that is, higher t students are better-behaved students. Standard concavity assumptions are that $p_{11} < 0$ and $p_{22} < 0$. Finally, assume that better-behaved students are more heavily affected by a given amount of discipline or that $p_{12} > 0$. Discipline occurs only when a disruption is initiated, so total discipline in a class of size n is

$$nd[1 - p(d, t)^n].$$

Now, let there be a cost of imposing discipline on a student given by $c = hc(d)$, with c', $c'' > 0$ where h is a shifter reflecting different costs of discipline. Given that p can be affected by discipline, one can rewrite (1a) as

(1′)
$$V(p(d,t))^n - \frac{W}{n} - \frac{(1 - p(d,t)^n)hc(d)}{n}.$$

The first-order conditions are then

(2′a)
$$\frac{\partial}{\partial n} = Vp^n \ln(p) + \frac{W}{n^2} + \frac{p^n \ln (p)hc(d)}{n} + \frac{(1 - p^n)hc(d)}{n^2} = 0$$

and

(2′b)
$$\frac{\partial}{\partial d} = Vnp^{n-1}p_1 - \frac{(1 - p^n)hc'(d)}{n} + p_1 p^{n-1}hc(d) = 0.$$

Using (2′b),

$$\frac{\partial d}{\partial t}\Big|_{(2'b)} = \frac{[\partial(\partial/\partial d)]/\partial t}{\partial^2/\partial d^2}$$

which equals

$$\frac{\partial d}{\partial t}\Big|_{(2'b)} = -\frac{[(n - 1)p^{n-2}p_1 p_2 + p^{n-1}p_{12}][nV + hc(d)] + p^{n-1}p_2 hc(d)}{\partial^2/\partial d^2}.$$

The numerator is positive, and the denominator negative, so the expression is positive. Better behaved students encounter more discipline per infraction because the positive effects of discipline on their behavior are greater.[32]

Catholic schools may obtain better outcomes for two reasons, both related to discipline.[33] It has already been shown that the pricing structure automatically induces better-behaved, higher t, students to attend Catholic schools. Since $\partial d/\partial t$ is positive, Catholic schools should use more discipline per infraction. Second, the political constraints that public schools face relative to private schools may make it more costly to discipline students in a public school. Formally, this means that h is higher in the public schools. Under usual conditions, the effect of raising h, the cost of discipline, is that the amount of discipline used will fall.[34]

Discipline, learning, and class size have been linked empirically. Betts and Shkolnik (1999) find a significant positive effect of class size on the amount of time spent on discipline and a negative effect of class size on the amount of time spent in instruction. Currie and Thomas (1996) find that discipline has negative effects on test scores, although the results are imprecise.[35] Grogger (1997) finds that an extreme form of disciplinary problem, namely violence at school, has negative effects on high school graduation and college attendance. The model presented gives precise predictions on the relation of disciplinary problems to class size.

Strict discipline is a substitute for small class size, given the production technology postulated. For any given level of educational output per head, X, there is always a trade-off between class size and p. The functional relationship between class size and discipline is very simple. In order to increase class size by a factor of k and keep educational output per student constant, it is necessary to improve discipline such that p rises to $p^{1/k}$.[36] For example, in a class of 25, where $p = .98$, educational activity occurs 60 percent of the time. To double class size and obtain the same level of educational output, it is necessary to raise p from .98 to $\sqrt{.98}$, which equals .99. Thus, each student must behave 1 percent more of the time. Although this may seem like a relatively minor improvement in behavior, the statement can be turned around: the amount of misbehavior must be cut from 2 percent of the time per student to 1 percent of the time per student. This implies that a halving of misbehavior is necessary to effect a constant educational output while doubling class size. Whether this is large or small depends on student responsiveness to disciplinary incentives, and this cannot be stated a priori.

Discipline is one way to produce higher p in the classroom. Another may be to promote a particular classroom etiquette. Although students are generally allowed to ask questions in class in college and graduate courses, questions are generally discouraged in large lecture classes having a few hundred students. Etiquette varies directly with class size. As class size increases to numbers like 500, p needs to approach 1 for there to be any educational output at all. Of course, neither discipline nor etiquette comes without cost. If it were free to produce high levels of p, then all classes would consist of an extremely large group of passive and silent students. At some point, the learning component suffers when questions are prohibited.

14.4.2. Teacher Quality

Classroom behavior, captured by p or p^n, may be as much a function of the teacher as it is of student characteristics. A given student is more attentive and has fewer off-the-mark questions in a good teacher's class than in a poor teacher's class. Just as there is a role for discipline in raising p, there is a role for altering teacher quality. Hanushek, Kain, and Rivkin (2004) argue that teachers are the most important determinants of educational output.

Teacher quality can be raised by paying higher salaries. To the extent that labor supply to the profession is upward-sloping, higher salaries imply a larger pool of applicants, which permits a school to engage in more selective hiring. How much is this worth? The effect of raising teacher quality, even through substantial pay increases can be impressive. To see this, consider the following numerical example.

Consider a school of 100 students, where $p = 0.97$, and teacher's wage, W, =5. Optimal class size is then 16.5 students, learning occurs 61 percent of the time, and the profit (or net social value) in this school is 30.2. Suppose that teacher salary is doubled and that the effect is to raise p from 0.97 to 0.99. Then, optimal class size rises to 25 students, learning occurs 78 percent of the time, and the profit in this school rises to 57.8.

A doubling of teacher salary is quite a dramatic increase. Using 1999 CPS data, this would mean an increase in average teacher salary from $32,300 to $64,600, which would put teachers near the eighty-fifth percentile of college grads, and well above the median college graduate who earns $36,000 per year. Whether this kind of selectivity could bring about an increase in p of at least 2 percent is an empirical question, but the example makes clear the potential power of teacher quality in affecting outcomes.

14.4.3. Movers

Using data from Texas, Hanushek, Kain, and Rivkin (2004) find that children who switch schools perform more poorly than those who do not and that moving imposes costs on other students. Both can be interpreted in the context of the model presented above. Since movers are unaccustomed to their new classroom, their questions are more likely to be disruptive in that they relate to material that the initial class members have already covered. The movers' p is low relative to the nonmovers, which implies that movers' own learning is slower than it would have been if they had not moved. It also implies that because movers lower the average p for the class, learning by others is reduced as well.

14.4.4. An Empirical Strategy

The fraction of the time that a student is not an initiator of disruption, denoted p, is not a mere abstraction, but is observable. One could imagine obtaining information on p by surveying teachers or by actually observing a classroom. Given p, quality of education should vary with p^n. Since n is also observable, p^n can be thought of as a measure of quality that is different from educational expenditures used by others.[37] A year of adjusted schooling could be defined as a year, multiplied by p^n.

The model has very specific predictions about the relation of n to p. The first-order condition in (2) implies that class size should be smaller, the larger is p. This is testable using data such as TIMSS, where the classroom experience is videotaped, reviewed, and graded.[38]

Operationally, it is probably easier to observe p^n than p. An alternative to direct viewing of classrooms is surveying the teachers on the proportion of their class time spent in actual teaching versus discipline or disruption. The Longitudinal Study of American Youth provides information on time spent on learning and discipline as reported by teachers.[39] These data provide an estimate of p^n, which when coupled with information on n, provide an estimate of p. For the purposes of quality adjustment, p^n by itself is all that is of interest. For normative purposes, for example, determining the optimum class size by grade level, p is useful. It might also be of interest to compare student characteristics with p. How does p vary with age, socioeducational background, and parent's income? Understanding variations in p may provide some implications for school reform.

14.5. An Alternative Model of Class Size

The disruption model emphasizes teaching technology as a determinant of class size. There is another possible explanation of why classes are not larger than they are. Class size may be limited by the extent of the market. Consider, for example, a small college that has students in both literature and economics. Suppose that the college has 100 students, half of whom are in each field. On the basis of congestion effects, the condition in (2) might imply an optimal class size of 100, which is infeasible because only 50 want to study each field. Heterogeneous study preferences limit class sizes beyond congestion considerations. It is for this reason that schools do not put high school seniors in the same class with first-graders. Absent other constraints, one would conclude that a school of 100 is too small. Because class sizes must be below the efficient number of students, a merger of two small schools into one larger one could achieve both division of labor and class size efficiency. To the extent that a desire for neighborhood schools or other preferences limit the size of a school, heterogeneous learning preferences limit the size of classes.

That having been said, a limited extent of the market cannot be used to explain a number of facts that are consistent with the congestion hypothesis. First, congestion implies that schools may have four identical classes of 30 students at a particular grade level, whereas heterogeneous preferences would imply one class of 120. Second, heterogeneity would argue for smaller classes among older students, not the reverse. The curriculum for preschool students is more homogeneous across students than is the curriculum for high school students who are following different paths. Preschool classes are smaller than high school classes, not because different courses are being offered, but because things get out of control when there are more than ten preschoolers in the same place. Similarly, special education classes are small not because the course material is so varied, but because p is low for special students.

14.6. Summary and Conclusions

Classroom teaching is a public good. As such, congestion effects can be important. A student who is disruptive or who takes up teacher time in ways that are not useful to other students affects not only his own learning, but that of others in the class. It is for this reason that class size may have important effects on educational output. Much of the empirical evidence, however, suggests otherwise. Class size effects are small or nonexistent in most studies.

A theory of educational production, with particular emphasis on classroom dynamics, has been presented. The model, which offers direct implications about the choice of class size as a function of student characteristics, is consistent with a large variety of findings in the education literature. The empirical literature has wide-ranging findings on the relation of educational output to class size. The model implies that better students are optimally placed in larger classes, and further, that educational output is higher in the large classes, despite the reduced teacher–student ratio. The disruption framework provides a specific model of class-size endogeneity that can be tested, verified, or refuted. There is already a great deal of evidence with which the model is consistent, although there remain some countervailing pieces of evidence. The theory provides implications for class size and its effect on total output. The analysis predicts variations in class size by grade level and by other student and teacher characteristics. In equilibrium, class size matters very little. To the extent that class size matters, it is more likely to matter at lower grade levels than at upper grade levels where class size is smaller.

The technology implies that class size effects are more pronounced in smaller classes and for lower values of p, which implies that class-size reductions provide better results for disadvantaged and special needs children.

Discipline is a substitute for class size. The structure provides an exact relation of disruption to class size. Specifically, educational output per student remains constant when class size is increased by a factor of k as long as the proportion of the time that students behave rises from p to $p^{1/k}$.

Under most circumstances, segregating students by academic ability maximizes total educational output. Self-selection induces the more attentive students to attend private schools. This mechanism implies that students who opt for Catholic schools (at a positive price) are inherently more attentive than those in public schools. It also means that discipline should be more intense in Catholic schools which would lead them to outperform public schools.

Teachers may prefer smaller classes either because wages do not reflect working conditions fully or because teachers as a group can raise the demand for their services by lowering class size. However, in a competitive labor market, where teachers' wages depend on job attributes, there is no tension between teacher preferences and those of students or their parents.

Appendix

Proof of Proposition 1:

Using the implicit function theorem on (2), note that

$$\frac{\partial^2 \text{profit}}{\partial m^2} = VZ^2 p^{Z/m} \ln(p) \frac{2m + Z \ln(p)}{m^4},$$

which is negative for the solution to be an interior one. This implies that

$$2m + Z \ln(p) > 0.$$

Next, because $\partial/\partial W = -1$,

$$\frac{\partial m}{\partial W}\Big|_{f.o.c.} = \frac{1}{\partial^2 \text{profit}/\partial m^2} < 0.$$

Also,

$$\frac{\partial m}{\partial p}\Big|_{f.o.c.} = \frac{-VZ^2 p^{(Z-m)/m}(m + Z \ln(p))/m^3}{\partial^2 \text{profit}/\partial m^2} < 0$$

for interior solutions, which are guaranteed for p near 1. Further,

$$\frac{\partial m}{\partial V}\Big|_{f.o.c.} = \frac{(Z^2/m^2)p^{Z/m} \ln(p)}{\partial^2 \text{profit}/\partial m^2} > 0.$$

Also,

$$\frac{\partial m}{\partial Z}\Big|_{f.o.c.} = \frac{VZp^{Z/m} \ln(p)(2m + Z \ln(p))/m^3}{\partial^2 \text{profit}/\partial m^2} = \frac{m}{Z} > 0$$

and

$$\frac{\partial m}{\partial Z} \frac{Z}{m} = 1$$

which is as expected because no class-size–school-size interactions are built into the model.

Now, since $m = Z/n$, $dn/dm = Z/m^2$, so $\partial n/\partial W > 0$, $\partial n/\partial Z < 0$, $\partial n/\partial V < 0$, and $\partial n/\partial p > 0$.|||

Proof of Proposition 2:

At the optimum m, educational output-per-student decreases in p.[40] First, without loss of generality, normalize Z and V to 1. Then, denote profit as

$$\pi = x(p,m(p)) - Wm(p),$$

where

(A1) $$x(p,m(p)) = p^{1/m(p)}.$$

The first-order condition says that

$$x_2(p,m(p)) = W.$$

Totally differentiating with respect to p gives

(A2) $$x_{12} + x_{22}m'(p) = 0.$$

Now, differentiating $x()$ with respect to p yields

(A3) $$\frac{\partial x}{\partial p} = x_1 + x_2m'(p).$$

Educational Production

Substituting (A2) into (A3) yields

$$\frac{\partial x}{\partial p} = x_1 + x_2 \frac{x_{12}}{x_{22}}.$$

Using the definitions in (A1) and applying them to (A4) yields

$$\frac{\partial x}{\partial p} = \frac{1}{m}p^{1/m-1} + \frac{1}{m^2}p^{1/m}\ln(p)\frac{(-p^{1/m-1}/m^3)[\ln(p)+m]}{(p^{1/m}\ln(p)/m^4)(2m+\ln(p))} = \frac{p^{1/m-1}}{2m+\ln(p)} > 0$$

because $2m + \ln(p) > 0$ by the second-order condition and p is positive. Thus, educational output rises in p.

15

Speeding, Terrorism, and Teaching to the Test

High-stakes testing, where teachers, administrators, or students are punished for failure to pass a particular exam, has become an important policy tool. The "No Child Left Behind" program of the George W. Bush administration makes high-stakes testing a centerpiece of its approach to improving education, especially for the most disadvantaged. Proponents of high-stakes testing argue that testing encourages educators to take proper actions and that testing also identifies those programs that are failing.[1] But critics counter that high-stakes testing induces educators to teach to the test, which has the consequent effect of ignoring important areas of knowledge.[2] Almost every teacher is familiar with the question, "Will it be on the final?" The implication is that if it will not be on the final, the student will not bother to learn it.

Which argument is correct? The main result of the following analysis is that to maximize the efficiency of learning, high-stakes, predictable testing should be used when learning and monitoring learning are very costly, but should not be used when learning and monitoring are easy.

The best way to focus the question is to examine another problem that is formally equivalent, namely that of deterring speeding.[3] Sup-

The original version of this chapter was published as: Lazear, E. P. (2006). Speeding, Terrorism, and Teaching to the Test, in: Quarterly Journal of Economics, 121, 1029-1061. MIT Press. © 2006 by the President and Fellows of Harvard College and the Massachusetts Institute of Technology. This research was supported by CRESST. I am indebted to Edward Glaeser for fundamental suggestions on the framework and for some derivations contained in the paper. In addition, George Akerlof, Gary Becker, Thomas Dohmen, Richard Freeman, Eric Hanushek, Caroline Hoxby, Lawrence Katz, Paul Oyer, Paul Romer, Kathryn Shaw, Andrzej Skrypacz, Michael Spence, and Steven Tadelis were especially helpful in providing comments. Benjamin Ho provided excellent research assistance on the formal analysis, and along with Ron Siegel, provided detailed review and comments.

pose that the city has available to it a given number of police, who patrol the roads. Should the city announce the exact location of the police or simply allow drivers to guess? At first blush, the answer seems obvious. Of course, their locations should be kept secret. If the locations of the police are announced, then motorists will obey the law only at those locations, and will speed at all other locations. But the answer is not obvious. If police are very few and their locations are unknown, drivers might decide to speed everywhere. If police locations are announced, there is a better chance that speeding will be deterred at least in those places where police are posted. The total amount of speeding could actually be lower when locations are announced.

Tax fraud is virtually identical. The tax authority can announce the items to be audited or just let taxpayers know that there will be random audits. In the absence of announcing specific items to be audited, taxpayers may cheat on all tax items, especially when there are few auditors and audits are unlikely. Instead, the authority can announce those items that will be audited with certainty and likely deter cheating on those items, which is better than failing to deter any cheating.

Terrorism presents a third application of the principle. A country's announcement that it has increased its effort to deter terrorism may have no effect on terrorism if those efforts are spread widely throughout the country. But focusing the increased patrols on airports may at least have the effect of making air travel safer.

Teaching to the test is analogous because the body of knowledge is like all of the roads. Announcing the items to be tested is like telling drivers which miles of road will be patrolled. If the test questions are not announced, but instead some random monitoring is done, students will have to decide whether to study a large amount or very little. When they would choose to study very little or nothing, announcing what is on the test may motivate them to learn at least those items. With the exception of definitions and some other formalities, the problems are the same.

The issue is one of concentrating or spreading incentives. Concentrating incentives provides very strong motivation, but over a limited range of activity. Spreading incentives provides weak motivation, but over a broader range. When agents are responsive to incentives, spreading them over a large range encourages more of the desired action. But if agents are insensitive to incentives, then spreading them too thin might provide too little incentive to do anything, which results in a reduction in the amount of desired action.

The decision to concentrate or spread a given amount of incentive can be put generally and more formally. Suppose that we want to encourage some action A, like obeying the law, and that the decision to obey depends on the expected penalty P, according to $A(P)$. There is a broad space over which we can monitor activity, or we can restrict our attention to some fraction q of that space and let the other $1 - q$ be ignored. In the case of speeding, this is like announcing which q of the roads are patrolled and which $1 - q$ of the roads are not. When the full space is subject to stochastic punishment that has expectation P, then the agent takes action $A(P)$. However, if only q of the space is subject to punishment, then the expected penalty over that subset is $P/q > P$ since $q < 1$ and the action taken there is $A(P/q)$.[4]

Incentives are strengthened over that part of the space. However, on the $1 - q$ of the space announced to be ignored, the penalty is 0, so the action is $A(0)$. Incentives are weakened on the part that is clear of patrol. Should incentives be concentrated over some subset q or spread over the entire range? Let there be some social value of the action A, given by $R(A(P))$. Then, it is better to spread the incentives broadly if

$$(1) \qquad R(A(P)) > (1 - q)R(A(0)) + qR(A(P/q)).$$

If the inequality in (1) goes the other way, then it is better to concentrate over some subset q.

Expression (1) can be recognized as Jensen's inequality, which states that the left-hand side exceeds the right-hand side if and only if $R(A(x))$ is concave in x. Thus, incentives should be spread out if the R function is concave and concentrated if the R function is convex. Convexity of the R function relates to the responsiveness to incentives. As will be shown in the applications below, when individuals are responsive to incentives, the R function is concave. When they are less responsive, the R function is convex.

15.1. A Model of Speeding

15.1.1.   Deterring Speeding

There are Z miles of road. A driver can either speed or obey the speed limits. Suppose that the extra utility that is derived from speeding is V per mile and that the fine for speeding, if caught, is K. There is a vast literature on optimal fines, but that is not the point of this example, so the fine is assumed to be given exogenously.[5]

Suppose that there are G police and that each policeman can patrol one mile of road. If police are distributed randomly along the road, then on any given mile the probability of being caught speeding is G/Z, and the expected fine from speeding is KG/Z. Thus, if drivers do not know the location of the police, they will speed if

$$(2) \qquad\qquad KG/Z < V.$$

Since the cost and value of speeding on every mile is the same, if the driver chooses to speed on one mile, he speeds on all.

Now suppose that the location of the police along the roads is announced. A more general approach allows for some miles to be subject to patrol with some probability and others with some different probability, but to get the basic intuition, let us start with the more extreme version of the model. If roads are either patrolled or not, then drivers are certain to be caught if they speed on a patrolled section. As a result, no speeding occurs on the patrolled section as long as $V < K$, but speeding occurs on all nonpatrolled roads because the drivers know that the probability of detection there is zero. The law will be obeyed on G miles of road, and there will be speeding on the other $Z - G$ miles.

If locations are unannounced, there is either no speeding at all or always speeding, depending on whether the expected fine KG/Z exceeds or falls short of the utility value of speeding, V. But when locations are announced, there is speeding on $Z - G$ miles, but not on G miles as long as $K > V$. More speeding is deterred by announcing the location of police whenever

$$KG/Z < V < K.$$

If $KG/Z < V$, drivers would always speed if locations were secret because the probability of detection is sufficiently low, which makes the speeding gamble worthwhile. But announcing the locations deters speeding on G miles (since $V < K$) so this is the better outcome. If instead, $KG/Z > V$, the expected fine is sufficiently high to deter all speeding when locations are secret, and this dominates revealing locations.[6]

The intuition is simple. If police are few, drivers assume it very unlikely that they will be caught speeding and speed everywhere. Announcing locations of the police strengthens incentives on patrolled roads and at least deters speeding at those locations. If police are abundant and the probability of being caught sufficiently high, no one will speed. With many police, revealing their location induces drivers to speed on all roads except the G miles that are patrolled. So when there are many police, it is better to keep their locations secret; with few police it is better to reveal their locations and at least deter speeding on the few roads that are patrolled.[7]

The structure can be generalized easily. Now allow q of the Z roads to be patrolled and $(1 - q)$ to be unpatrolled. The question can be stated in its most extreme form. Is there any q such that it is better to limit patrol to qZ of the miles and announce it, rather than randomly patrolling all Z miles? Reverting to (1), in this extreme case, $R(A)$ can be thought of as a linear function where A is the number of miles over which the law is obeyed and V is also linear in those miles. For example, if there were a social cost to speeding equal to γ, this would simply require that $V < \gamma$ on all miles. In this context, $A(P)$ is the number of miles on which speeding does not occur if the expected penalty is P. The concavity of $R(A(x))$ depends only on concavity of $A(x)$. If only qZ of the miles were patrolled, then the expected penalty on those qZ miles would be P/q, and the expected penalty on the unpatrolled miles would be zero. By (1) it is better to announce a limitation on patrolled roads when the $R(A())$ function is convex. If it requires strong incentives to induce individuals to do anything, then the $R(A())$ function is convex (see Figure 15.1a). When individuals are very responsive to incentives, the $R(A(x))$ function is concave in the relevant range between 0 and P/q (see Figure 15.1b).

In Figure 15.1a individuals speed when punishment is P, but obey if punishment is P/q. In Figure 15.1b individuals obey if punishment is P and obviously continue to obey at punishment P/q. The $A(x)$ function is therefore convex over the relevant range in Figure 15.1a, but concave in Figure 15.1b.

Figure 15.1a

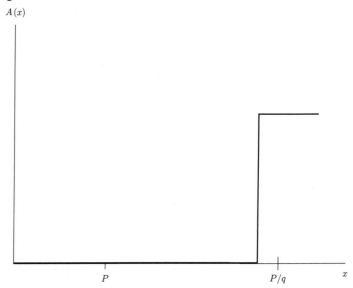

Figure 15.1b

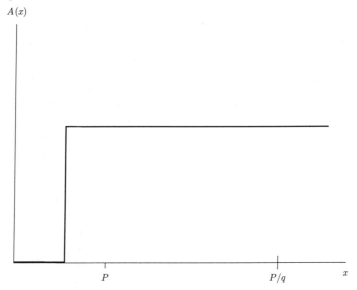

When the costs of detection are high or penalty is low relative to the gains from speeding, Figure 15.1a is relevant. Then, $A(P) = 0$ because P, which equals KG/Z, is less than V so the individual never obeys the law. Since the lower limit of q is zero, there always exists some $q < 1$ for which $KG/qZ > V$, so $A(x)$ equals 1 (obey the law with certainty) over this range. The California Highway Patrol (CHP) uses the strategy of setting $q < 1$ and announcing the roads on which patrolling will occur. For example on the July 4 weekend of 2004, the CHP announced on all TV news stations that the 250 miles of Interstate 80 from San Francisco to the Nevada state line were being singled out to check for intoxicated drivers.

When the cost of detection is low, penalties are high, or benefits to speeding are low, Figure 15.1b is relevant. Then P, which equals KG/Z, exceeds V, and the individual obeys the law even for $q = 1$.

In this simple case, the optimal q can be calculated to set incentives just sufficient to deter speeding, or using (2), set

$$q = KG/ZV.$$

If $q > 1$, then it is unambiguous that the number of police G should be reduced until $q = 1$ because additional police serve no purpose; all speeding is deterred when $KG/ZV = 1$ or when $G = ZV/K$.

15.1.2. Tax Fraud

The extension of the idea to tax fraud is straightforward. The tax authority can do random audits, examining taxpayers and items without advance notice, or they can announce that all deductions of a particular kind will be audited. If they announce the items to be audited, taxpayers will report their expenditures honestly on the audited items. If they do not announce, then taxpayers will either cheat profusely or not cheat at all. So, when the cost of auditing is high perhaps because there are very few auditors, announcing the items that will be audited results in less cheating. Announcing audited items ensures that at least some taxes get paid honestly. However, if the cost of auditing were low and auditors were abundant, then keeping audited items secret would result in more taxes being paid. Because auditing is sufficiently likely, taxpayers are honest on all items.

The model is identical. V can be thought of as tax due on each of the Z items. As such, it is the savings on taxes that results from cheating on one of Z reported items on the tax form. K is the fine associated with being caught, which includes repayment of the V dollars initially saved. Thus, $K > V$. Redefine G as the number of items that can be audited (per return), given the number of tax auditors.

As before, when

$$KG/Z < V < K,$$

filers will cheat on every item if monitoring is stochastic and will pay the penalty on those items on which they are caught. If the goal is to deter cheating, then a better system is to announce all of the items that will be audited and to deter cheating at least on those items that are audited with certainty.

When G is low (auditors are very costly), there is a conflict between deterrence and revenue collection. If G is low, more fraud is deterred by announcing the audit rules than by keeping them secret, but more revenue is collected by keeping rules secret. When G is too low to deter cheating if rules are unannounced, individuals cheat on all items, paying zero taxes, but are caught on G items (on average) and so pay GK in total. With announced auditing rules, individuals pay taxes on the G announced items, and revenues are GV. No fines are ever collected because the items on which the individuals cheat go undetected with certainty. Because $V < K$, revenues are highest in the stochastic monitoring regime, even though no cheating is deterred.

Keeping the rules secret induces everyone to cheat, which is like setting a trap for cheaters. Entrapment can be useful for revenue collection because "tricking" people into cheating results in fine collection, which brings more money into the treasury than the paying of taxes without fines.

The difference between the tax auditing problem and the speeding problem is that in speeding, the assumption is that the social cost of speeding is sufficiently high to swamp any distortions associated with reduced fine collection that might be part of an optimal tax structure.[8] Here, if taxes are not collected through fines by the tax authority, the revenues must be raised in other ways, which may create other distortions. The goal of taxing, at least in large part, is revenue collection.

15.1.3. Terrorism

Speeding and tax fraud are particular forms of crime. Terrorism is another and fits the structure directly. Like speeders, who might speed on a segment of road at an unknown time and place, terrorists can strike randomly at various locations and times. Deterring terrorists from striking targets is conceptually the same problem as deterring drivers from speeding. Let V be the value that terrorists place on hitting a target, γ the social cost of being a victim of terrorism, K is the punishment that the terrorist receives if caught, and Z the total number of potential targets, where each of the G enforcers can patrol one of the Z targets. As before, the size of the expected penalty relative to the terrorist's value of committing the act determines the optimal allocation of enforcers. When terrorists place a very high value on terrorism or the number of enforcers is low relative to the number of potential targets, it is virtually impossible to deter terrorism everywhere, even with very large penalties. (Since many of these individuals make suicide part of the strategy, it is difficult to think of feasible penalties sufficiently large to deter.) This, the most likely situation, corresponds to Figure 15.1a, where the $R(A(x))$ function is convex. It is better to concentrate incentives, deterring terrorism somewhere rather than not at all. For example, airport screening, reinforced cockpit doors, and other measures make it difficult to conduct terrorism using airports or airplanes. Terrorists know this and avoid those targets so at least airports are relatively secure. If there were infrequent screening spread over all possible targets, none would be safe. The expected penalty would be too low anywhere to deter committed terrorists.

This example points up two issues. The first is heterogeneity; the second is substitution. Heterogeneity is particularly important in the context of terrorism. Some targets produce higher value to terrorists than others. Some create more social damage than others. Some are harder to patrol than others. It has already been shown that even when all targets are equal, it sometimes (when $R(A(x))$ is convex) is better to narrow the patrolled targets to some subset of the total possible and to announce those that are patrolled and those that are not. Heterogeneity makes the case stronger, but one can also say something about which targets should be patrolled.

It is obvious that other things equal (V, K, and γ), it is better to patrol the less costly targets. If there are G enforcers, higher cost of patrol can be thought of as more than one enforcer per target. This simply reduces the number of enforcers available for other targets with no additional gain in deterrence. More interesting is whether the most precious targets, i.e., those for which γ is high, warrant more resources. The analysis, contained in Appendix A, shows that there are situations in which it pays to concentrate enforcement on high value targets, but the necessary and sufficient conditions are stringent. The reason is that if a target has strategic value, it is reasonable to assume that it has higher value to terrorists as well as to the citizens, who are the owners of the target. Under general circumstances, unless the precious targets are valued more relative to the less precious by the citizens than they are by the terrorists, concentrating on those targets will not be optimal. If Americans value protecting the White House relative to my house by more than terrorists want to take out the White House relative to my house, then it is optimal to guard the White House over my house. If the relative values are reversed, my house should be guarded over the White House. Of course, if enforcement is sufficiently cheap or if the social damage is sufficiently high, it pays to allocate sufficient resources to protect both targets. The idea also relates to substitution. If terrorists regard most targets as close substitutes for one another (having similar V), but citizens do not view all targets similarly, then citizens prefer to concentrate enforcement on those targets on which the citizens place a higher value.

15.1.4. Announced Inspections

There are many activities in which inspections occur. Government agencies such as the Food and Drug Administration and the Federal Aviation Administration inspect private sector firms that are under their jurisdictions. In the military, drill sergeants inspect the uniforms and gear of their subordinates. Sometimes, inspections are random and unannounced, but at other times they are scheduled. It might seem silly to inform one's charge of the exact time at which an inspection is going to occur, but the logic of previous sections reveals that there are circumstances under which it is better to make the timing known than to keep it secret.

There is nothing in the formalism that distinguishes space from time. Just as Z could reflect geography or items, it can also be thought of as a linear index of time, where a particular Z refers to a point in time. As before, qZ would limit the time during which an inspection would occur to a particular interval; e.g., "an inspection will be held during the week of August 5." Further, just as before, it is better to concentrate incentives and limit inspection possibilities to $q < 1$ when $R(A(x))$ is convex. Convexity is produced by high costs of inspection or by high costs of meeting prescribed requirements.

In the case of checking that shoes are polished, it would seem that drill sergeants could monitor this at relatively low cost and that the benefit from not polishing shoes would be low to soldiers. As a result, $R(A(x))$ is concave, and inspections should be random over time and unannounced. Weak, diffuse incentives are sufficient to motivate.

Consider FAA inspections. There are so many potential parts on an airplane that could be defective that it would be impossible to inspect all on every plane without rebuilding the entire fleet. In the context of the model, Z is interpreted as all the parts that could be inspected at a point in time and G, the number of inspections, is small relative to Z. As a result, $R(A(P))$ is convex, and it is better to concentrate incentives. This appears when the FAA sometimes focuses on a particular part (like a hatch door) and announces that it will inspect all of these. Incentives are thereby concentrated, giving airlines an incentive to increase the attention that they pay to maintenance.

Often, the part that is the subject of attention has been defective on another aircraft, which introduces the kind of heterogeneity discussed in the previous section. Heterogeneity, where one part (target) has higher inspection value than another, reinforces the tendency to concentrate.

15.1.5. Drug Screening in Sports

In the Tour de France, Lance Armstrong visited a tent after completing the various stages to be tested for drug usage (steroids, etc.). Armstrong knew that he would be tested at the end of the stage.

The argument for announcing that the test would be conducted at the end of the stage rather than at some other random time had little to do with concentrating incentives. Instead, it was based on the technological fact that infractions on one Z indicates an infraction on another Z. In the examples given above, independence across Z is assumed, although primarily for simplicity. In the case of drug testing, independence makes no sense. An individual who uses performance-enhancing drugs before the race will test positively for those drugs after the race.

15.1.6. Legislature or Courts?

Detailed legislation and court rulings can be viewed as substitutes. When legislation is very detailed and legitimate behavior is prescribed, the courts have less room for interpretation. When legislation is broad, loose, or nonexistent, justice is ex post and less predictable. The distinction between civil and common law has the same flavor. Civil law lays out more specifics than common law. Civil law is an ex ante system, attempting to specify as clearly as possible what is and is not permitted. Common law focuses on the principles of good behavior and to a greater extent determines deviations from good behavior on an ex post basis. Which system is better?

One interpretation of the current model can be used to examine the choice between detailed legislation or court discretion. Define Z as the number of potential actions that can be legislated and G as the number that is checked. Suppose that Z is small relative to G. Such would be the case in a simpler world that existed 500 years ago, in primarily agrarian societies where the variety of interactions were limited compared with those today. The expected penalty P equal to KG/Z was high relative to the benefits of breaking the law. There are three reasons. First, Z is small because of limited interactions. Second, G is large because in small communities, it is difficult to find anonymity. Every neighbor is an enforcer. Third, penalties were high. Individuals who deviated from the common law or social norm and were ostracized could find few other ways to survive outside their small communities. As a result, the $A(P)$ function is concave (and presumably $R(A(P))$ is concave) in the relevant range which means that loosely specified rules work.

In contrast, a complex society with many possible interactions and much anonymity creates conditions where the logic of common decency is insufficient to deter bad behavior. As a result, a detailed system of laws, specified ex ante by the legislature with limited discretion for the courts, concentrates incentives and prevents infractions of those laws that are announced and monitored. In this situation, $R(A(P))$ is convex, so general or less well-specified ex post strategies are inefficient relative to the more concrete structures offered by precise ex ante legislation and civil law.

15.2. Teaching to the Test

The lesson of the speeding example can be applied in a straightforward way to the issue of high-stakes testing. High-stakes testing as a practical matter places the learning and teaching emphasis on items that are expected to be on the exam. In this sense, it is similar to the idea of announcing where the police are posted. The items on the exam receive special attention, whereas untested items may be neglected by students and teachers. The speeding model can be applied to this problem in an almost direct fashion to obtain some insights. As above, the first result is that high-stakes testing is best used when monitoring is costly or when expenditures on enforcement are low. If expenditures on enforcement are high, then it is better to leave the testing regime more open. Second, high-stakes testing with well-defined exam questions is best used when the distribution is weighted toward high cost learners.[9]

Let us start by defining the knowledge base, which consists of n items. This is analogous to the Z miles of road. Suppose further that there are m questions on a high-stakes exam, analogous to the G policemen. Should the exam questions be announced or not? A more direct way to put the issue is "What comprises a good high-stakes test?" Should it be a test where questions are well-defined and known in advance, or should it be a test where questions are drawn randomly from a larger body of knowledge? Most would say the latter. It will be argued that the former rule is appropriate in some circumstances.

As a policy issue, testing is as much about motivating teachers as it is about motivating students, and the model applies to teachers as well. Initially, however, think of the student as making the choice about learning, and let the teacher be a passive agent. That assumption will be altered below.

To be consistent with the speeding model, the return side is modeled as follows. Think of the test score as an observable signal to employers, or more accurately, to future schools which the student might attend. If a student is asked a question to which he does not know the answer, he bears cost K in the form of lower earnings, most directly reflected as reduced probability of admission into a desirable college. The SAT exam is a high-stakes test with exactly that effect. The "fine" K is taken to be exogenous, but a richer model would allow K to be the solution of an inference problem that colleges or employers make about the individual's ability based on the answers to the exam.

Let us reinterpret V and K from the speeding model as follows: if the student does not learn the item, he does not have to bear cost V of learning the material. The student knows what is on the test, so he opts to avoid learning an item when the extra utility from not learning, V, exceeds the cost of not learning, which is lost earnings K. If the student knows what is on the test, he will choose to learn those items if and only if $V < K$. Since $K = 0$ for items not on the test, he learns nothing that is not to be asked explicitly.

To generalize the earlier framework, allow there to be a distribution of V that reflects the cost of learning on any given item by any given person. Let that distribution be written as $J(V)$ with corresponding density $j(V)$. The unit of analysis is a person-item so that V can vary for a given individual because some items are more difficult to learn than others. Also, V can vary across people because some people learn more easily than others. Then $j(V)$ is the density across all items potentially learnable by all students. Note that a given student might learn some items and not others and some students might learn everything always and others nothing, depending on the distribution of V across items and people. Further note that the assumption is that all items and students characterized by the distribution $J(V)$ are observationally identical. If items or people are observably different, then separate distributions must be written to characterize each. Finally, note that V is assumed to be independent of whether learning of other items occurs. For the sake of simplicity, such complications are ignored.

Suppose that there is some expected penalty X. A given student learns an item if and only if $V < X$. Let the social value of learning be given by γ. Items for which $V < X$ are learned. Those for which $V > X$ are not learned. Thus, the social damage associated with any expected penalty X is

$$(3) \qquad S(X) = \int_X^\infty (\gamma - V)j(V)dV.$$

Also note that

$$(4) \qquad S'(X) = (X - \gamma)j(X),$$

and that

$$(5) \qquad S''(X) = j'(X)(X - \gamma) + j(X),$$

which will be useful later. In what follows, optimal solutions are found in the more general analysis where a rich structure of strategies is considered.

From (4) and (5) it is clear that social damage is minimized when $X = \gamma$. Setting the expected fine equal to the social cost of the infraction induces the appropriate behavior.

The goal is to choose q so as to maximize social benefit from learning or equivalently to minimize the damage associated with the failure to learn. Items in the knowledge set can be made eligible for testing, and others can be declared off limits. At the extremes, when $q = 1$, all items are fair game. When $q = m/n$, $(m/n)n$ or m items are subject to testing. Since there are m questions, each item subject to testing is identified.[10]

The student learns an item when the cost of learning is less than the expected penalty or when

$$V < Km/qn$$

for items subject to testing. On those items, the fine is K, and the probability that any given item will be tested is m/qn for the items subject to test. The expected penalty is a certain zero for those items not subject to test.

Because $S(X)$ is the social damage on a given item when the expected penalty is X, the expected damage as function of q is given by

$$(6) \qquad \text{Full social damage} \equiv FSD(q) = n[qS(X) + (1 - q)S(0)].$$

On the qn eligible items, damage is $S(X)$, and on the $(1 - q)n$ ineligible items, the damage is $S(0)$.

The first-order condition for minimizing (6) is

$$(7) \qquad \frac{\partial}{\partial q} = n\left[S\left(K\tfrac{m}{qn} \right) - S(0) - \left(K\tfrac{m}{qn} \right) S'\left(K\tfrac{m}{qn} \right) \right] = 0.$$

Corner cases are possible where the solutions are $q = m/n$ (reveal the questions) or $q = 1$ (do not reveal anything). Stated formally,

Proposition 1. When $S(X)$ is globally concave, the optimal q is m/n. When $S(X)$ is globally convex, the optimal q is 1.

Proof. See Appendix B.

In the language used earlier, $S(X)$ being globally concave is equivalent to $R(A(P))$ being globally convex. Under those conditions, it is necessary to concentrate incentives because spreading them too thinly results in no effort.

There is no necessity that q be at either corner. It is possible and perhaps likely that the solution is an interior q with $m/n < q < 1$.

Next, consider what occurs when individuals have higher ability. Define ability a, such that individuals choose to learn as long as[11]

$$V + a < X,$$

or equivalently,

$$V < X - a.$$

Ability acts to displace the distribution by the constant a. We can then state the following proposition.

Proposition 2. If an interior solution for q exists such that $m/n < q < 1$, then q is increasing in ability level a.

Proof. See Appendix B.

The range of material that is subject to testing is optimally larger for high ability students than for low ability students. The intuition is that it is more difficult to motivate low ability students because their costs are high. As a result, failure to concentrate incentives produces little or no learning among low ability individuals. But high ability individuals have low costs of learning. Even mild incentives on any given item are sufficient to induce them to learn a subject. Consequently, a larger number of items can be made subject to test for high ability individuals, and they will still opt to learn those items.

The number of questions available may vary because of the cost associated with testing. When it is cheap to test, m is high. This is analogous to having many police when the cost of police is low. How does the optimal q vary with m? The following proposition shows that it is optimal to choose a higher value of q when m is high.

Proposition 3. Given that q is interior such that $m/n < q < 1$, q varies directly with m.

Proof. See Appendix B.

15.3. Discussion, Implications, and Extensions

Proposition 1 provides a result on when it is best to announce the specific questions and when it is best to say nothing at all. The intuition is identical to that given in the speeding model. If the distribution of costs is such that little or nothing will be learned when questions are unannounced because incentives are too diffuse, then the only hope is to limit the number of items subject to test. When costs are truly high and concentrated, corresponding to concavity of the social damage function, $S(x)$, (or equivalently convexity of the $R(A(P))$ function), then announcing the questions concentrates incentives and induces at least some learning. When V is concentrated and high, it is optimal to announce the items that are to be tested. When V is concentrated and low, it is optimal to keep the questions secret. High cost of learning requires that the questions be announced to provide sufficient incentive, whereas low cost of learning allows for secrecy because even low expected penalties induce learning.

Another intuitive result is easily derived. If it is very costly to test, it is better to announce the specific questions. If it is very cheap to test, it is better to keep the questions secret. Costly testing is reflected in a low number of questions. Suppose that m is sufficiently small so that Km/n is too low a number to motivate learning; i.e., the minimum value of V exceeds Km/n. Then $S(Km/n) = S(0)$ because failing to limit items subject to testing is equivalent to setting the penalty equal to zero; both result in no incentives. When m is sufficiently low, the optimum cannot be the policy of keeping questions secret.[12]

When questions are expensive, failure to announce them results in no learning. Announcing the questions induces learning of the announced items.

Conversely, if it is very cheap to test, then the optimum must be to leave vague the items to be tested. Suppose that m is so large that $Km/n > V \; \forall \; V$. Then the optimum is to announce nothing. By announcing nothing, all items in the knowledge base are learned. Any $q < 1$ results in less learning.[13] Questions are so numerous, and the cost of learning is sufficiently low that no student risks leaving any item unlearned.

Interior solutions to q are common throughout education. Study sheets give students strong clues as to the material that will be on the exam without announcing specifically which questions will be asked. "Pop quizzes" on the previous night's reading that are given randomly provide another example of $m/n < q < 1$. If students were told specifically when the exam would be given, then the student could read that night's and only that night's assignment. But the fact that students are told that the quiz will only be on the reading from the previous night limits q to a number much smaller than 1. If nothing else, it rules out material from earlier nights or from future readings.

15.3.1.   What Is a "Good" Test?

One common view is that a good test is one that is not so predictable that students essentially know what is on the exam. It would be possible to create an exam that randomized question selection so as to prevent students from knowing what is on the exam. Educators often view as a goal of testing that test scores generalize to reflect knowledge of material not on the test.[14]

The view that a good test is one that is unpredictable and one where the test score is informative about items not on the test is incorrect as a general proposition. Although it may be optimal to construct a test that draws from a larger body of knowledge, the main theorem of this chapter (Proposition 1) is that sometimes it pays to restrict the relevant required material to a specified subset of the entire knowledge set. A "good" test when students have very high costs of learning is a test that announces the questions and sticks to them. Under those circumstances, students at least learn the material that is on the test. The alternative test, which chooses questions from a broader base of knowledge, results in no learning or very little learning.

For low cost learners, the reverse is true. A test that draws from the entire or a larger knowledge base is a better test because it encourages more learning than one that is well-specified and announced. For these students, a "good" test is one that is not completely predictable because it provides more incentives to learn.

Defining a "good test" captures exactly the intuition of both sides of the argument over high-stakes testing. Most agree that imposing high-stakes testing will induce teaching to the test because the incentives are strong to learn what is on the test and then to teach to it. The disagreement is over whether this is good or bad. The concern by critics of such testing is that a strategy that is tantamount to announcing the exam questions will stifle learning of the more general curriculum. These critics are correct if they have in mind students who would be sufficiently motivated to learn all the material. But for those who are less able, choosing to keep questions secret will result in little or no learning because diffuse incentives are too weak to provide any motivation at all for high cost learners. For them, the policy does not stifle additional learning because those students would not learn that additional material even if the questions were not announced.

Proposition 2 speaks directly to this issue. The optimal q is increasing in ability. As the ability of the students in question rises, it is better to increase the number of items that are subject to testing. High ability students are more easily motivated, so spreading incentives thin, which provides enough incentive to learn, increases the range of items that will be learned. The trade-off between weakening incentives on any given item and increasing the number of items that a student may learn moves in the direction of more items as ability rises.

"No Child Left Behind" emphasizes high-stakes testing only for low performing schools. Although all schools are required to take the test, high performing schools are in little danger of failing to meet the standards. As such, the test provides only weak incentive to those schools. If there is any monitoring incentive at all for upper quality schools, it is provided through more indirect stochastic methods. But failing schools are in the range where the high-stakes test matters. As a result, the NCLB system acts as a bifurcated program, producing high-stakes testing for those who attend problem schools and stochastic monitoring (at best) for those who go to schools that are doing well. The ability variable a in Proposition 2 can be interpreted as reflecting the cost of schooling rather than the ability of the underlying students. Because a is a shifter, which simply displaces the $j(V)$ distribution, a school with higher costs of teaching is one where a is lower. Whether the costs are higher because the students have lower ability or because the schools have fewer resources, poorer teachers, or poor family support is of no consequence to the proposition. The model provides a rationale for the NCLB approach since the regime appropriate for high ability students is stochastic monitoring where q is closer to 1, whereas the regime appropriate for children in poorly performing schools is likely to be high-stakes testing.

15.3.2. Age, Background, Difficulty, and Test Form

Proposition 2 provides intuition on why testing and monitoring methods vary across grades and schools. Consider the learning ability of young children relative to college-age students. It is more costly for young children to learn academic subjects than for older ones, but probably cheaper for them to learn language.[15] As a result, the distribution of learning costs associated with academic subjects is higher for younger children than for older ones. This is parameterized by assigning a lower value of a to younger children than to older ones. Proposition 2 dictates that the optimal q should be lower for younger children. At the extreme, $q = m/n$, so that they are told exactly what is on the test. Spelling tests given to elementary school children generally specify exactly which ten words must be known for Friday's test. By the time students reach graduate school, only the papers and books and sometimes only the general subject area from which the test will be drawn are announced.

Analogously, children who are in honors classes are likely to have lower costs of learning than those in remedial classes. Indeed, tests in honors classes are less predictable, pose questions that are extensions of material learned, and are drawn from a larger body of knowledge than those in remedial classes. In short, q is higher in honors classes than in remedial classes.

15.3.3. Separating Teacher and Student Incentives

The discussion has been put in terms of motivating students, but most of the thought behind specific programs like "No Child Left Behind" is that it is the teacher, not the student who needs motivating. The model as set up can be interpreted to refer to teachers instead of students.

Suppose that teachers have full control over what is learned by the student. Interpret V as the teacher's cost of teaching the student an item of knowledge. Let K be the penalty associated with her student failing to answer a question correctly in the high-stakes environment or as the penalty that the teacher faces if the student is detected to be ignorant of an item of knowledge. Then all of the above analysis holds exactly as written, and nothing is changed.

The problem of interest, though, is how are teachers motivated. Many would argue that the current system of random monitoring does not motivate teachers at all. Teachers are motivated by intrinsic considerations only, and intrinsic motivation is insufficient to induce some teachers to do the right thing. Again, the issue is one of heterogeneity as well as motivation, but let us consider the incentive issue in a world of homogeneous teachers first.

Intrinsic motivation might be thought to serve as the main motivator for tenured teachers whose salaries are fixed and jobs are secure, being virtually independent of performance. Intrinsic motivation is best modeled by assuming that $j(V) > 0$ for $V < 0$. That is, for some values of V, the cost of imparting knowledge is negative. Even if teachers received no compensation for the amount of knowledge their students acquired, they would still choose to provide some knowledge to each student, namely $J(0)$ items would be taught. Teachers with high amounts of intrinsic motivation teach even in the absence of any extrinsic penalty.

Proposition 2 is relevant here also. The more costly or difficult is teaching, or the less able are the teachers, the lower is the optimal q. Good teachers should not be told explicitly what to teach and on which items their students will be tested. Vague descriptions of curriculum requirements (with q close to 1) are more appropriate for intrinsically motivated or able teachers.[16]

The assumption that K is exogenous can be altered. Under the current system, it is unlikely that information about a teacher's ability to raise students' test scores would become public information or part of what determines their compensation. But it is useful to consider what could be done if the school opted to implement an optimal compensation structure. Given that the social value of learning a particular item is γ, the school would simply set $q = 1$ so that all items in the knowledge set are potentially tested and choose

411

K such that the expected penalty equals γ. If the number of questions is given as m, then the teacher would be fined K such that

$$Km/n = \gamma,$$

or

$$K = \gamma n/m,$$

for each question that each of her students misses on the exam. The teacher would teach the item whenever

$$V < \text{expected fine},$$

or

$$V < Km/n,$$

or

$$V < \gamma,$$

which is the efficiency condition.

15.3.4. Monitoring Input or Output?

Formally, the model has been structured in terms of monitoring output not input. Much of the discussion of high-stakes testing views stochastic monitoring as being based on input. For example, in the absence of high-stakes tests, teachers could be monitored by having the principal visit the classroom on either a predicted or random basis. As is shown here, input monitoring is accommodated by the model already presented.

Think of teachers as being in the classroom for n minutes, and let one item of knowledge be conveyed if the teacher bears cost $V \sim j(V)$

as before. The principal announces that he will monitor classes for m minutes (per teacher) and that q of the n minutes of total teaching time are subject to monitoring. If he finds that the teacher has not conveyed the information in the minute during which he is in the room, the teacher will be fined K for that minute in lower salary. (Of course, K may be zero or close to it.) Setting $q = m/n$ is tantamount to telling the teacher exactly when the principal will visit the room. Setting $q = 1$ tells the teacher that all minutes are equally likely to be monitored. Then the expected penalty is Km/qn, just as before and the teacher's decision is to teach if

$$V < Km/qn.$$

Everything in the prior setup applies to monitoring on the basis of input. Both interpretations, monitoring on input or monitoring on output, are consistent with any given level of q. Whether monitoring is done on the basis of input or output relates to the costs of measuring by each method and is not special to teaching. That issue has been analyzed elsewhere.[17]

A high-stakes test creates incentives for teachers and students to find out what will be tested. As such, it is closest to the case of setting $q = m/n$. The current alternative, which is to monitor input and sometimes output in a stochastic fashion, is formally treated at having a $q > m/n$ and in the limit, equal to 1. Because the current situation tends to be coupled with low stakes, i.e., low values of K associated with "infractions," teachers have little incentive to attempt to discover when and how the monitoring will be done. It is for this reason that the typical situation in schools corresponds more closely to high values of q and high-stakes testing to low values of q. But this argument suggests that the choice of K and of q are not independent. When the stakes are raised, there is a natural tendency by those being monitored to learn the specifics of what will be monitored, which induces a positive, endogenous relation of q to K.

15.4. Extensions and Further Discussion

In this section some details, additional implications, and directions for future research are considered.

15.4.1. Interdependence of Learning

As in the speeding structure, independence of V has been assumed. Having learned one item does not affect in a direct way the cost of learning another item. This is unrealistic in three respects. First, a student may have a capacity for learning so that as the amount of studying increases, he is unable to absorb new material at the same cost. Only a limited number of items can be remembered in one sitting. Second, and working in the opposite direction is that learning begets learning. It is easier to learn calculus after algebra has been mastered. Third, because the distribution of V also includes variation across people, interactions between students is ignored. But peer pressure and identity might be important. Coleman (1961) was the first to argue this and found that the group in which an individual classified himself (e.g., bookworm, athlete ...) was a predictor of academic performance. Akerlof and Kranton (2002) summarize and build on this notion to explain why academic performance may vary greatly from school to school, even when resources do not. Building in some form of dependence is possible, but complex and is ignored in this formulation.

15.4.2. Test Design and Learning Incentives

It is possible to ask how test design, and in particular scoring, affects incentives. For example, one very large, high-stakes test could be given or many smaller, low-stakes tests could be required. The incentives to study or teach are very different under the two approaches.

Additionally, exams could be graded pass/fail or in a continuous fashion. The pass/fail structure is more like a tournament against a standard, where the standard is calibrated on the basis of previous classes' performances. A continuous grading structure is like paying a piece rate. It is already known that the incentive effects of the two different structures vary, depending on the nature of the payoff scheme and the heterogeneity of the underlying population.[18]

On a different note, good exams are neither too easy nor too difficult, and this is primarily for statistical reasons, but also because of the effect on incentives. On a very easy exam, a careless mistake can cause a student to fall well below the rest of the class. Such exams have low signal-to-noise ratios. On a very difficult exam, average scores are very low, and it is difficult to distinguish among people because all do so poorly. Again, the signal-to-noise ratio is low. As for incentives, it is a general principle in incentive theory that when noise is high relative to the signal, incentives are diminished. The optimal test difficulty should take this incentive effect as well as statistical issues into account.

Investigation of these issues is left to subsequent work.

15.4.3. *A Theoretical Observation on Optimal Enforcement*

The model used above is a generalization of the usual optimal enforcement literature. Rather than having the probability of detection being the same over all actions, this structure allows for different probabilities of detection. In the case of education, it is that qn items have a probability of detection equal to m/qn and $(1 - q)n$ items have a probability of detection of zero. This generalization can be extended. At the extreme, it is possible to allow for each item (or each mile) to be given a different probability of detection. Eeckhout, Persico, and Todd (2010) show that when potential criminals are homogeneous, it is never optimal to use more than two different enforcement probabilities. In general, enforcement resources could be spread over the entire set of possible crimes so as to minimize social loss.[19]

Different characteristics lead to different strategies. It has already been shown that when detection is expensive or costs of learning or teaching are high, it is best to go to a corner, having the questions announced in advance. Since it is only the difference between social value and social cost, $\gamma - V$, that is relevant, it is possible to turn this around and think of situations where the difference is high because γ is high, not because V is low. For example, it might be optimal to put the police on more congested roads where the social cost of an accident is especially high. Similarly, it might be better to test certain skills like basic literacy over others because they have higher social value. The model can be interpreted to address these issues, but more structure would be needed before specific implications about items tested could be provided.[20]

15.5 Summary and Conclusions

Speeding, terrorism, tax fraud, inspections in the military, and teaching to the test are all symptoms of the same kind of incentive problem. Individuals become aware of the rules, obey them within a narrow range, and disregard them everywhere else.

The analysis has shown that providing well-defined requirements dominates stochastic incentives for individuals for whom compliance costs are high. In the context of education, this means that predictable tests are best used for high cost learners or low ability types and stochastic monitoring, where students are not informed in exact terms what will be required of them, provides better incentives for low cost learners or high ability types.

Put differently, a "good test" is a well-defined concept once incentives are considered. Good tests are not necessarily those that draw evenly from the knowledge base, or those for which scores generalize to predict other aspects of knowledge mastery. Sometimes, especially for high cost learners or for failing teachers, tests that are predictable are best at providing incentives to learn or to teach. For high ability students or successful teachers, somewhat less predictable, more amorphous tests are best.

Additional results are provided.

1. If teachers have low degrees of intrinsic motivation, then well-defined high-stakes tests are best, but for teachers with high intrinsic motivation, a more randomized accountability system is efficient.

2. Number of questions and randomness are complements. When testing is cheap, and more questions can be on the exam, the optimal proportion of items which are subject to testing rises. When testing is expensive and only very few questions can be asked, it is better to announce those questions, or the student will learn almost nothing.

3. Exam specifics are made known to younger children and to students who are assigned difficult material because revealing exam questions provides better incentives.

Appendix A

As before, let there be Z targets where targets 1 through Z_1 have value V_1 to the terrorists and γ_1 to the citizens. For targets between Z_1 and Z, $V = V_2$, and $\gamma = \gamma_2$ with $V_2 > V_1$ and $\gamma_2 > \gamma_1$.

The highest q_1 consistent with deterring terrorism on V_1 targets, is

$$q_1 = KG/V_1 Z$$

since expected penalty is then

$$(A1) \qquad \frac{KG}{q_1 Z} = \frac{KG}{(KG/V_1 Z)Z} = V_1,$$

so expected penalty exactly equals the value of terrorism to the terrorist. Similarly, the highest q_2 consistent with deterring terrorism on V_2 targets, is

$$(A2) \qquad q_2 = KG/V_2 Z.$$

As before, there are G enforcers. If all enforcers are used on the γ_1 value targets, then it is possible to deter

$$q_1 Z = KG/V_1$$

terrorist acts. If all are used on the γ_2 value targets, it is possible to deter

$$q_2 Z = KG/V_2$$

terrorist acts. It is clear that

$$q_2 Z < q_1 Z$$

because $V_2 > V_1$. To make things simple, assume that $q_1 Z < Z_1$ and $q_2 Z < Z - Z_1$ (see Figure 15.2).

Because it is possible to specialize in either high value or low value targets, no mixing ever occurs. If it is better to place enforcement resources on one high value target than on more than one low valued target, it is better to do the same for the second high valued target and so forth since all high valued targets are identical and all low valued targets are identical.

The assumption that there are enough of both high and low valued targets to exhaust all enforcement resources is realistic. There are many more targets of high value (government buildings, hospitals, stadiums, auditoriums, and amusement parks where many people congregate) than there are enforcers. There are innumerable targets of low value consisting of individual homes, small retail stores, automobiles, etc.

Figure 15.2

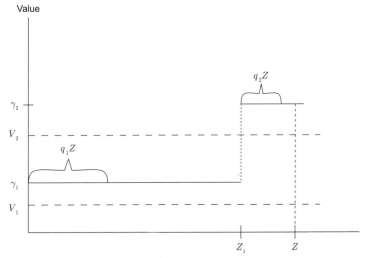

It is possible to specialize in one type of target or another and since the value of all targets within a class is the same, it is best to focus on one type of target only. The trade-off is that it is easier to deter acts against low valued targets (because $V_1 < V_2$) and so more can be protected. Fewer high valued targets can be protected, but each target spared has higher value.

Ignoring the utility value of terrorism to the terrorist (a natural approach) in social value, enforcement should be concentrated on high valued targets if and only if

$$\gamma_2 q_2 Z > \gamma_1 q_1 Z$$

or using (A1) and (A2), if

$$\gamma_2 \frac{KG}{V_2} Z > \frac{KG}{V_1} Z,$$

which is

(A3) $$\gamma_2/\gamma_1 > V_2/V_1.$$

It is better to focus on high valued targets over low valued ones if and only if citizens value those targets relative to low valued ones more than terrorists do.

Appendix B

Proof of Proposition 1

$$FSD(q) = n[qS(X) + (1 - q)S(0)].$$

The expected penalty on the eligible items is

$$X = K\,\frac{m}{qn}$$

so (6) can be written as

(A4) $$FSD(q) = n\Big[qS\Big(K\tfrac{m}{qn}\Big) + (1 - q)S(0)\Big].$$

Differentiate with respect to q to obtain

(A5) $$\tfrac{\partial}{\partial q} = n\Big[S\Big(K\tfrac{m}{qn}\Big) - S(0) - K\tfrac{m}{qn}S'\Big(K\tfrac{m}{qn}\Big)\Big].$$

In order for it to be optimal to state exactly which questions are on the exam, q must be equal to m/n. This happens if $\partial/\partial q$ in $(A5)$ is positive at $q = m/n$. Then, increasing q will only increase social damage so the corner solution is best. The requirement is that

$$S(0) - S(K) < -KS'(K).$$

A sufficient condition for this to hold is that $S(X)$ is concave over the range of X from 0 to K (see Figure 15.3). In order for the $S(X)$ function to be concave between 0 and K, it is necessary that

$$j'(X)(X - \gamma) + j(X) < 0$$

from (5). Since it is likely, especially in the education structure, that the expected penalty will be well below the social damage, γ, necessary is that $j'(X)$ is positive, which means that the density function is increasing over the range 0 to K.

Figure 15.3

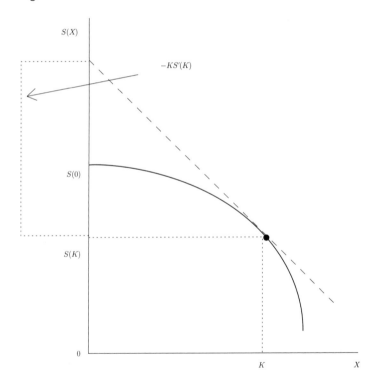

It is also possible that the other corner solution is optimal, where students are told that all items are subject to testing. For $q = 1$ to be optimal, $\partial/\partial q$ in $(A4)$ must be negative when $q = 1$ or

$$\frac{\partial}{\partial q} = n\left[S\left(K\frac{m}{n}\right) - S(0) - K\frac{m}{n}S'\left(K\frac{m}{n}\right)\right] < 0.$$

which requires that

$$S(0) - S\left(K\frac{G}{Z}\right) > -K\frac{G}{Z}S'\left(K\frac{G}{Z}\right).$$

This holds if S is convex throughout the relevant range.

Interior solutions, where $m/n < q < 1$, are also possible. Using $(A5)$, they occur when

$$S\left(K\frac{m}{qn}\right) - S(0) - K\frac{m}{qn}S'K\left(\frac{m}{qn}\right) = 0$$

for $m/n < q < 1$.

Proof of Proposition 2

The student learns an item if $V - a < x$ or if $V < x + a$. Define $c(x, a) = x + a$. Desired is to show, given an interior solution for q, $(m/n < q < 1)$, that

$$\frac{\partial p^*}{\partial a} = -\frac{\partial FOC/\partial a}{\partial FOC/\partial q}\Big|_{q=q^*} > 0.$$

Since q^* is at the minimum, the second-order condition implies that

$$\frac{\partial FOC}{\partial q}\Big|_{q=q^*} > 0.$$

By the chain rule

$(A6)$ $\quad \dfrac{\partial FOC}{\partial q} = \dfrac{\partial FOC}{\partial x}\dfrac{\partial x}{\partial q}\Big|_{x=Km/q^*n} = \dfrac{\partial FOC}{\partial x} - \left(\dfrac{Km}{q^{*2}n}\right)\Big|_{x=Km/q^*n} > 0.$

Given $c(x, a) = x + a$,

$$\frac{\partial S}{\partial x} \equiv (c(x, a) - \gamma)j(c(x, a)) \equiv \frac{\partial S}{\partial a}.$$

Because the FOC is made up of $S()$ and $S'()$ only,

(A7) $$\frac{\partial FOC}{\partial a} \equiv \frac{\partial FOC}{\partial x}.$$

Combining (A6) and (A7),

$$\frac{\partial FOC}{\partial a}\left(-\frac{Km}{q^{*2}n}\right)\Big|_{q=q^*} > 0,$$

which implies that

$$\frac{\partial FOC}{\partial a} < 0\Big|_{q=q^*},$$

so

$$\frac{\partial q^*}{\partial a} = -\frac{\partial FOC/\partial a < 0}{\partial FOC/\partial q > 0}\Big|_{q=q^*} > 0.$$

Proof of Proposition 3

The first-order condition for the optimal q is

$$\frac{\partial}{\partial q} = n\left[S\left(K\frac{m}{qn}\right) - S(0) \; K\frac{m}{qn}S'\left(K\frac{m}{qn}\right)\right] = 0.$$

Using the implicit function theorem on,

$$\partial q/\partial m - \frac{S''(Km/qn)(-K^2m/q^2n)}{S''(Km/qn)(K^2m^2/q^3n)} = q/m > 0.$$

16

Entrepreneurship

What is entrepreneurship? Economic growth may be related to the formation of new businesses, but what is it exactly that entrepreneurs do?[1] The view of entrepreneurship taken here is that it is the process of assembling necessary factors of production consisting of human, physical, and information resources and doing so in an efficient manner. Entrepreneurs put people together in particular ways and combine them with physical capital and ideas to create a new product or to produce an existing one at a lower or competitive cost. Because the entrepreneur must bring together many different resources, he or she must have knowledge, at least at a basic level, of a large number of business areas. An entrepreneur must possess the ability to combine talents and manage those of others. Why do some choose to become entrepreneurs, and what characteristics create successful ones? Most of the past work on entrepreneurship has been empirical,[2] but it is useful to have theory to guide the empirics and to assist in interpretation of the results.[3]

It is tempting to argue that the most talented people become entrepreneurs because they have the skills required to engage in creative activity. Perhaps so, but this flies in the face of some facts. The man who opens up a small dry-cleaning shop with two employees might be termed an entrepreneur, whereas the half-million-dollar-per-year executive whose suit he cleans is someone else's employee. It is unlikely that the shop owner is more able than the typical executive.

The original version of this chapter was published as: Lazear, E. P. (2005). Entrepreneurship, in: Journal of Labor Economics, 23(4), 649. University of Chicago Press. © 2005 by the University of Chicago. I thank first Boyan Jovanovic for a useful derivation that is used in this article. Comments from Anat Admati, Uschi Backes-Gellner, George Baker, Gary Becker, Lanier Benkard, Jennifer Hunt, Andrea Ichino, Stephen Jones, Kenneth Judd, David Kreps, Robert Lucas, John McMillan, Paul Oyer, Canice Prendergast, Korok Ray, John Roberts, Kathryn Shaw, Steven Tadelis, Robert Wilson, Justin Wolfers, and Jeffery Zwiebel are gratefully acknowledged. Able research assistance was provided by Yuliy Sannikov on theoretical issues and Eugene Kwok and Zeynep Emre on data compilation.

The reverse might be true. As necessity is the mother of invention, perhaps entrepreneurs are created when a worker has no alternatives. Rather than coming from the top of the ability distribution, they are what is left over.[4] This argument also flies in the face of some facts. Any ability measure that classifies John D. Rockefeller, Andrew Carnegie, or, more recently, Bill Gates near the bottom of the distribution needs to be questioned.

The idea explored below is that entrepreneurs differ from specialists in that entrepreneurs have a comparative disadvantage in a single skill but have more balanced talents that span a number of different skills. Specialists can work for others who have the talent to spot and combine a variety of skills, but an entrepreneur must possess that talent. Although entrepreneurs can hire others, the entrepreneur must be sufficiently well versed in a variety of fields to judge the quality of applicants.

How shall we define entrepreneur? There are a number of possible definitions. In keeping with the empirical analysis to be performed below, an entrepreneur is defined for this study as someone who responds affirmatively to the question "I am among those who initially established the business." Such individuals, even if they leave the business early, are usually responsible for the conception of the basic product, hiring the initial team, and obtaining at least some early financing. Other definitions are possible. For example, CEOs who "reinvent" a company might also consider themselves entrepreneurs. Conceptually, the model is consistent with including this latter group in the collection of entrepreneurs, but they will be excluded (with one exception) in the empirical analysis. The definition is conceptually distinct from "self-employed." A self-employed person need not have any other employees, and the kinds and combinations of skills that are necessary for real entrepreneurship are less important for, say, a self-employed handyman who works alone. At the empirical level, self-employed individuals are entrepreneurs if they view themselves as having started a business.

The model presented below is one where an individual can decide to become an entrepreneur using a variety of skills or to specialize using only one. The model is tested using data on graduates from the Stanford Graduate School of Business. The data combine information on postgraduate work experience and incomes with courses taken and grades obtained when the individuals were attending the Stanford Graduate School of Business.

The primary theoretical predictions are:

1. Individuals with more balanced skill sets are more likely to become entrepreneurs.

2. The supply of entrepreneurs is smaller for production processes that require a higher number of independent skills.

3. Individuals who become entrepreneurs should have a more balanced human capital investment strategy on average than those who become specialists.

A number of the predictions are tested empirically using data on Stanford alumni and are borne out. Specifically, those who end up being entrepreneurs are more likely to have varied backgrounds, both in school and on the job. The probability of being an entrepreneur in an employment spell is positively related to the number of different roles that an individual has had over his or her career and with the generality of the curriculum followed when at school. Some of this reflects balanced skills that the individual possesses before entering the labor market and some reflects the balance that is acquired after entering the workforce. There is also some evidence that risk tolerance enters into the decision to become an entrepreneur. Specifically, those individuals who have displayed willingness to choose risky occupations in the past are more likely to become entrepreneurs.

16.1 A Model of the Choice to Become an Entrepreneur

Initially, let there be only two skills, denoted x_1 and x_2 with $x_1, x_2 \geq 0$. An individual can be a specialist, in which case he receives income associated with his best skill, or he can be an entrepreneur, in which case he is limited by his weakest attribute. Thus, for specialists,

(1)   Specialist income $= \max[x_1, x_2]$.

Entrepreneurs, however, must be good at many things. Even if they do not do the job themselves, they must know enough about a field to hire specialists intelligently. The jack-of-all-trades aspect of entrepreneurship is captured in the income function

(2)   Entrepreneur income $= \lambda \min[x_1, x_2]$,

where λ is a parameter that is determined by market equilibrium that establishes the value of an entrepreneur. The value of λ, which is called the market value of entrepreneurial talent, will be derived below.

Figure 16.1

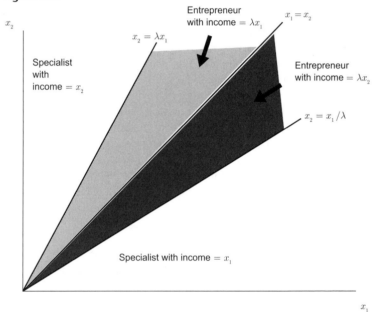

The income-generating functions described in (1) and (2) may seem special, but they are implied by a general production function that exhibits constant returns to scale and ability distributions that are symmetric. This is shown in the appendix, entitled "The Underlying Economy."[5] Creativity and willingness to take risks are two factors that are often mentioned as affecting the decision to become an entrepreneur.[6] Creativity is suppressed in this model because it is unobservable. Formally, more creative individuals can be thought of as those with larger values of λ. They have higher market values for entrepreneurial talent because a given amount of raw skill translates into more entrepreneurial output. Risk preference is simply ignored in this model where everything other than endowment of x_1 and x_2 is deterministic.[7] Risk can be thought of as entering through a stochastic λ.

16.1.1. Who Becomes an Entrepreneur?

Who decides to become an entrepreneur and who decides to become a specialist? The decision is straightforward. Think of individuals as being endowed with a pair of skills (x_1, x_2).[8]

The joint density on x_1 and x_2 is given by $g(x_1, x_2)$. The individual chooses to become an entrepreneur if and only if

$$(3) \qquad \lambda \min[x_1, x_2] > \max[x_1, x_2].$$

It is easiest to see this graphically. A given individual is endowed with x_1 and x_2 shown as a point in Figure 16.1. For all points below the 45° line, $x_1 > x_2$, so that a specialist whose endowment lies below the 45° line would always choose to specialize in x_1 and would have income given by x_1; x_2 is irrelevant to this specialist. In order for that individual to prefer being an entrepreneur to being a specialist, it is necessary that

$$\lambda \min[x_1, x_2] > \max[x_1, x_2],$$

which here requires that

$$\lambda x_2 > x_1$$

because $\min[x_1, x_2] = x_2$ and $\max[x_1, x_2] = x_1$.

Thus, for individuals for points below the 45° line, the condition for entrepreneurship is

$$(4) \qquad x_2 > x_1/\lambda.$$

This is shown as the dark shaded area on the diagram between the lines $x_1 = x_2$ and $x_2 = x_1/\lambda$. The area below the line $x_2 = x_1/\lambda$ corresponds to points where the individual specializes and receives income x_1.

Above the 45° line, the converse is true. Here, $x_2 > x_1$ so the specialist receives income x_2. In these cases, the condition for entrepreneurship, that

$$\lambda \min[x_1, x_2] > \max[x_1, x_2]$$

becomes

$$\lambda x_1 > x_2,$$

so an individual for whom x_2 exceeds x_1 becomes an entrepreneur when

(5) $$x_2 < \lambda x_1.$$

This is shown as the light shaded area in the diagram. The region in the northwest corner corresponds to individuals who have sufficiently high values of x_2 relative to x_1 that it pays for them to specialize in x_2 and to receive income x_2.

The probability of becoming an entrepreneur for any λ is given by the probability that the pair of skills lies in one of the two shaded areas in Figure 16.1 or

(6) $$\text{prob[entrepreneurship]} = \int_0^\infty \int_{x_1/\lambda}^{\lambda x_1} g(x_1, x_2) dx_2 dx_1.$$

It is now possible to derive and explain intuitively how the entrepreneurial decision varies with a number of different parameters. First, consider λ, the market value of entrepreneurial talent. Differentiate (6) with respect to λ to obtain

$$\partial \, \text{prob}/\partial \lambda = \int_0^\infty \left[g(x_1, \lambda x_1) x_1 + g\left(x_1, \frac{x_1}{\lambda}\right)\frac{x_1}{\lambda^2} \right] dx_1,$$

which is positive.

The higher is λ, the more likely is the individual to become an entrepreneur. Diagrammatically, as λ increases, the shaded areas become larger because the borders move toward the axes. If λ were infinity, everyone would become an entrepreneur since for any positive values of x_1 and x_2 entrepreneurial income would be infinite. As λ goes to one, the shaded areas get pinched. When $\lambda = 1$, the borders of the shaded areas are the line $x_1 = x_2$, and there are no entrepreneurs. Obviously, if $\lambda = 1$, it is impossible for condition (3) to hold since the min of something can never exceed the max of that same thing.

This result is important for equilibrium. The market value of entrepreneurial talent, λ, is a parameter that determines the supply of entrepreneurs in an economy. As λ rises, everyone chooses to become an entrepreneur. As λ falls to one, no one opts for entrepreneurship. This will guarantee an interior solution for λ and will ensure that there is a finite number of individuals wanting to enter entrepreneurship.

It is also possible to think of λ as being person specific. Some individuals have a comparative advantage in entrepreneurship. This might relate to creativity or other skills, but it is reflected in high values of λ. Since such talents are generally unobservable, not much more is said about the idiosyncratic variation in λ.[9]

If λ is person specific, it might also be unknown. This would explain why some people try entrepreneurship and then switch back to working for others. Perhaps individuals must try being an entrepreneur before they know whether they have a natural talent for running their own business. There is some evidence of this. There is a significant fraction of individuals who move back to working for others after having been an entrepreneur, but the probability is about 10 times as high that a year as an entrepreneur is succeeded by another year as an entrepreneur than by a year working for someone else.

16.1.2. Balance

In what follows, it is shown that as the correlation between x_1 and x_2 rises, the supply of entrepreneurs increases. Before deriving this formally, we state the intuition. Since entrepreneurial output and income is determined by the weakest link, it does little good to have a high value of x_1 if x_2 is not also high. Under such circumstances, it is necessary that x_2 be high whenever x_1 is high or there is little chance that an individual will become an entrepreneur. Diagrammatically, for any given λ, a larger proportion of the population prefers to be entrepreneurs, the more points lie in the dark shaded area of Figure 16.1. This area consists of points where x_1 and x_2 are close in value. For small values of λ, only points very close to the $x_1 = x_2$ line result in choosing to become an entrepreneur. If most of the mass of the distribution lies close to the axes, then individuals will be inclined to specialize in one or the other skill because they have a strong absolute advantage in one skill. Entrepreneurs are jacks-of-all-trades, which means that they must be relatively good (or relatively bad) at everything.[10]

Formally, let x_2 be defined in terms x_1 of as follows:

$$x_2 = \rho x_1 + (1 - \rho)\nu,$$

where x_1 has density $f(x_1)$ and ν has density $h(\nu)$. When $\rho = 1$, x_1 and x_2 are perfectly correlated. When $\rho = 0$, they are uncorrelated. In fact, ρ is the correlation coefficient between x_1 and x_2. The probability of being an entrepreneur in (6) can be rewritten as

(7) $\qquad \text{prob[entrepreneurship]} = \int_0^\infty \int_{[(x_1/\lambda)-\rho x_1]/1-\rho)}^{(\lambda x_1 - \rho x_1)/1-\rho)} f(x_1)h(\nu)d\ \nu dx_1$

by using a standard change of variables and altering the limits of integration appropriately.

Next, differentiate (7) with respect to ρ to obtain

$$\frac{\partial}{\partial \rho} = \int_0^\infty \left[h(UL)\frac{\partial UL}{\partial \rho} - h(LL)\frac{\partial LL}{\partial \rho} \right] f(x_1)dx_1,$$

where UL and LL stand for upper and lower limits of the inside integral in (7). After substitution, this becomes

$$\frac{\partial}{\partial \rho} = \int_0^\infty \left[h(UL)\frac{x_1(\lambda - 1)}{(1 - \rho)^2} + h(LL)\frac{x_1(1 - 1/\lambda)}{(1 - \rho)^2} \right] f(x_1)dx_1,$$

which is positive since density functions are always positive and since $\lambda < 1$ for there to be any entrepreneurs in the economy at all. Thus, as correlation increases between the two variables, the proportion of entrepreneurs rises.

The idea that balance is important suggests that the supply of entrepreneurship may vary by industry. For example, consider insurance agencies. The ability to understand complex insurance policies is a skill that is likely to be correlated with the accounting and management skills necessary to run a business. As a result, there are many who are well suited to running their own agencies and so the number of agencies should be great and their average size small.

An alternative example involves artists. Because art and business are quite distinct skills, there is no reason to expect strong positive correlation between artistic talent and business skills. As long as both artistic and business skills are relevant for production in the art business, then few will have high enough levels to avoid specializing in one or the other aspect of the business. Thus, the supply of entrepreneurial talent in art would be expected to be low, so most artists must be managed by others. The prediction is that there would be very few artists who run their own studios and publicize their own work.

The empirical statements are verifiable by looking at real world data.[11] In situations where entrepreneurs are rare, a few must run the whole industry, driving up concentration ratios. In situations where many opt to be entrepreneurs, the concentration ratios should be low. Of course, other technological considerations are key here and must be held constant. If scale economies are more important in some industries (e.g., automobiles) than in others (e.g., restaurants), the concentration ratios are likely to be higher in the former than the latter, independent of entrepreneurial supply considerations.

16.1.3. Complexity of Production

Some production processes are very complex, requiring many skills in order to produce output. Others are relatively straightforward. As the world has become complex, a larger variety of skills may be required to be an entrepreneur. In an agrarian society, a farmer did not require too many business skills to run his small farm and get his produce to market. The founders of the modern corporation are a different breed. They are more than competent technicians; they must understand how to create a worldwide business.

What happens to the supply of entrepreneurs as the number of factors increases? Without being more specific about the distribution of the factors, it is impossible to make qualitative statements. However, it is possible to show that the introduction of independent factors always reduces the supply of entrepreneurs.

Entrepreneurship

Consider the original joint density $g(x_1, x_2)$. Now introduce a third factor, x_3, and let the density of the three be denoted $k(x_1, x_2, x_3)$. If x_3 is an independent factor with (marginal) density $m(x_3)$, then it is possible to write

$$k(x_1, x_2, x_3) = \int m(x_3)\left\{\int\int g(x_1, x_2)dx_2 dx_1\right\}dx_3.$$

The condition necessary to ensure an entrepreneur for two variables must still hold. For any given x_3 and for a given λ, if the projection onto the (x_1, x_2) plane does not lie in the entrepreneurial area, the individual will not choose to be an entrepreneur. That is, if

$$\lambda\min[x_1, x_2] < \max[x_1, x_2],$$

the individual becomes a specialist, irrespective of x_3. In addition, there are some potential cutoff values, x_3^* and x_3^{**}, that are also required for entrepreneurship. So the probability of being an entrepreneur cannot exceed

$$\int_{x_3^*}^{x_3^{**}} m(x_3)\left\{\int_0^\infty \int_{x_1/\lambda}^{\lambda x_1} g(x_1, x_2)dx_2 dx_1\right\}dx_3,$$

which can be written as

$$\{M(x_3^{**}) - M(x_3^*)\}\int_0^\infty \int_{x_1/\lambda}^{\lambda x_1} g(x_1, x_2)dx_2 dx_1.$$

Since the first term cannot exceed one, the probability of being an entrepreneur cannot be higher with three factors than with two and, in general, must be lower.

The proof can be repeated, adding one factor at a time. Therefore, the supply of entrepreneurs falls as the production process requires more independent skills. More individuals can run family farms than multinational, multiproduct conglomerates.

There is some relation between correlation of skills and complexity. For example, it is possible to think of being an accountant as requiring only one skill, namely, accounting, which can be used to serve clients or run the business. A skill is necessarily perfectly correlated with itself, so the probability that individuals possess all the skills necessary to run an accounting business, other things equal, might be thought to be higher than that associated with running an art business, where two distinct skills are required.

16.1.4. The Premium to Entrepreneurship

It is now straightforward to show that an equilibrium λ always exists. To make things simple, but without loss of generality, suppose that there are a fixed number of firms in an economy and each firm requires one and only one entrepreneur. Then the demand for entrepreneurs is perfectly inelastic at q^*, where q^* is the number of entrepreneurs demanded. Let the number of individuals in the labor force be given by N. Then, using (6), which defines the probability of being an entrepreneur as a function of λ, the supply of entrepreneurs is simply

$$N \int_0^\infty \int_{x_1/\lambda}^{\lambda x_1} g(x_1,\, x_2) dx_2 dx_1.$$

Market equilibrium occurs when λ is set such that

(8) $$N \int_0^\infty \int_{x_1/\lambda}^{\lambda x_1} g(x_1,\, x_2) dx_2 dx_1 = q^*.$$

Equation (8) is one equation in one unknown, namely λ, which determines the equilibrium value of entrepreneurship. The market value of entrepreneurial talent adjusts to induce enough individuals to become entrepreneurs so that demand is satisfied. When $\lambda = 1$, no one chooses to be an entrepreneur. As $\lambda \to \infty$, all choose to be entrepreneurs so there must be λ that sustains N^* as the equilibrium number of entrepreneurs. This is true for any demand for entrepreneur function. There is always an intersection of demand with supply, although corner solutions are possible.

16.1.5. Investment

So far, x_1 and x_2 have been taken as given. But much of economic activity as it relates to labor markets involves investment in skills. It is important to take investment in skills into account both for the purposes of completing the theory and in order to allow predictions for empirical analysis.

433

Augment the previous model by defining x_1^0 as the initial stock of skill x_1, x_2^0 as the initial stock of skill x_2, and x_1 and x_2 as the (final) attained level. Let a particular individual, with endowed skills (x_1^0, x_2^0), obtain levels of x_1^0, x_2^0, according to the cost function

$$C(x_1, x_2),$$

with $C_1, C_2 > 0, C_{ii} > 0$.

Define x_1 to be the skill with which the individual is endowed the largest amount. This means that a worker who chooses to specialize is likely to specialize in x_1 and will solve

$$\max_{x_1} x_1 - C(x_1, x_2)$$

with first-order condition

$$1 - C_1(x_1, x_2) = 0.$$

Someone who is going to specialize will invest in only one of the two skills. There is no value to augmenting a skill that will not be used. It is possible that C_2 is sufficiently low relative to C_1 that the individual will ignore his higher endowment of x_1 and instead specialize in x_2. This is of little importance. Essential here is that the specialist invests in one or the other, but not both.

Now consider an individual who is going to become an entrepreneur. His constraint is the minimum skill, defined to be x_2. Should the aspiring entrepreneur invest in x_1, in x_2, or in both?

Since the constraint is x_2, there is no point in investing in x_1 unless x_2 is brought up at least to the level of x_1. If there is an interior solution for x_2, then it satisfies

$$\lambda - C_2(x_1, x_2) = 0.$$

There are three possibilities, but they can be dealt with quickly. If $C_2(x_1^0, x_2^0) > \lambda$, then it does not pay for the individual to increase his stock of x_2 and so no investment occurs. (It surely does not pay to increase x_1 since there is already an excess of x_1 at x_1^0.) If $C_2(x_1^0, x_2^0) < \lambda$, but $C_2(x_1^0, x_1^0) > \lambda$, the individual will invest only in x_2 because it does not pay even to bring x_2 up to the endowed level of x_1. (There is no advantage to augmenting x_1 until x_2 has reached the level of x_1.) In this case, the individual specializes in investment in x_2 and behaves identically to a specialist, except that he invests in the skill in which he is weak instead of the skill in which he is strong, which is the more common case for the specialist. Finally, if $C_2(x_1^0, x_1^0) < \lambda$, then it pays for the individual to exceed x_1^0 in attained x_2. But now x_1 becomes the constraint. As long as $C_1(x_1^0, x_1^0) < \lambda$, the individual benefits by increasing his investment in x_1 as well and continues to do so, but the optimum must have $x_1 = x_2$ in this case. What is important, however, is that, in this situation, the individual does not look like a specialist; he invests in more than one skill.

Investment can take a number of forms, the most important of which is formal schooling and on-the-job training. Thus, those who eventually become entrepreneurs should not specialize in skill acquisition, and this might be reflected in taking a wide variety of courses.

Additionally, individuals who will eventually become entrepreneurs should take on a variety of jobs to acquire the skills necessary to become an entrepreneur. Thus, an individual might spend some time working in a financial role, some time in human resources, some time as a manager, some time as a skilled staff worker, and so forth. Having a large variety of roles is a standard way to acquire a variety of skills and is the method used for workers where the intention is to create a multiskilled workforce.

To summarize, those who are going to specialize invest in only one skill. Those who become entrepreneurs may invest in one skill, but if they do so, it will be the skill in which they are weak. But entrepreneurs are the only individuals who may invest in more than one skill. To put this in somewhat less stark terms, individuals who become entrepreneurs should have a more balanced investment strategy on average than those who end up specializing as wage and salary workers.

16.1.6. Innovation

No reference has been made to innovation. When thinking of the truly successful entrepreneurs, individuals who had some new idea usually come to mind. Even in a traditional industry such as retail, a founder like Sam Walton of Walmart used a new business process that allowed his firm to undercut the competition. The generalist view of entrepreneurship deemphasizes innovation, although it is not inconsistent with it. One interpretation of the value of having multiple skills is that it is easier to innovate when the entire situation can be seen. A technical engineer may be superb at creating a new device, but that device may not have any business value. The innovator who succeeds is the one who can come up with something that is not only technically sound but business relevant as well.

16.2. Empirical Analysis

There are a number of implications that have been suggested in the theory section above. Before going to direct tests of the model, it is useful to provide some information on the composition of entrepreneurs.

16.2.1. Who Are the Entrepreneurs?

To examine the issues discussed in the theory section more directly, a unique data set will be used. In the late 1990s, Stanford surveyed its Graduate School of Business alumni (from all prior years). The primary focus of the survey was compiling a job history for each of the graduates, with special emphasis on information about starting businesses.[12] This resulted in a sample of about 5,000 respondents. In addition to the detailed job histories, these data were matched with the student transcripts so that it is possible to see which courses were taken by those who went on to be entrepreneurs and which by those who became specialists. Additionally, the grade obtained in each of the courses taken is reported in the data.

The Stanford MBA data make clear that at least among this population, most entrepreneurs are not in technical fields. In Table 16.1, the industries in which Stanford MBAs are found are dominated by construction and real estate, retail trade, and business consulting of some form. The technical fields are much less important. This finding is less surprising in these data, given that the more technical people would likely be found in engineering rather than MBA programs at Stanford. The Stanford MBA program recruits a significant fraction of engineers and students with technical backgrounds but fewer than would be found in those technical departments themselves. However, a comparison with the March 2002 Current Population Survey displays the same pattern.

Table 16.1

Industrial Breakdown of Entrepreneurs in the Stanford MBA Sample

Industry Code	Percent
Management Consulting	14.51
Construction/Real Estate Development	8.07
Investment Management	5.87
Retail/Wholesale	5.08
Venture Capital	5.08
Hardware/Software/Systems Services	4.86
Investment Banking/Brokerage	4.23
Real Estate Finance	4.01
High Tech – Computers/Software	3.73
Entrepreneurial Services	3.67
Consumer Products	2.65
Entrepreneurial Manufacturing	2.32
Entertainment/Leisure/Sports	2.20
Food/Lodging	2.03
Marketing Services	1.69
Diversified Financial Services	1.58
Diversified Service	1.58
Printing/Publishing	1.58
High Tech – Other	1.36
Health Care Services	1.30
Extractive Mineral/Natural Resources	1.30
Telecommunications Services	1.24
Foundation/Nonprofit Organizations	1.13
Agriculture	1.02
Medical Instruments and Devices	1.02
Accounting	.90
Import/Export/International Trade	.90
Commercial Banking	.85
Education	.79
Radio/TV/Cable/Film	.79
High Tech – Telecommunications Products	.79
Energy	.73
High Tech – Computers/Hardware	.73
Industrial Equipment	.73
Advertising	.68
Insurance	.68
Transportation Services/Shipping	.68
Legal Services	.62
Multimedia Services	.62
High Tech – Multimedia Products	.56
Rubber/Plastics	.56
Biotechnology	.51
Diversified Manufacturing	.45
Public Relations	.34
Chemical	.34
High Tech – Consumer Electronics	.34
High Tech – Semiconductors	.34
Architecture	.28
Arts	.28
Environmental/Waste Management/Recycling	.28
Social Services	.28
Unknown	.28
Aerospace	.28
Automotive/Transportation Equipment	.28
High Tech – Optics	.28
Apparel/Textiles	.23
Government	.17
Pharmaceuticals	.17
Utilities	.06
High Tech – Networking	.06

Notes: 1,771 observations, entrepreneurs only.

Table 16.2

Variables and Descriptive Statistics

Variable	N	Mean	SD	Min	Max
A. Whole sample:					
mbayear	26,901	74.27	14.21	13	97
male	27,283	.83	.37	0	1
age	26,863	50.24	13.59	25	93
white	27,283	.86	.35	0	1
exp	26,778	9.54	9.29	0	63
NPRIOR	27,277	3.26	3.39	0	37
NROLES	4,877	5.23	3.78	0	37
NROLESOTH	4,216	4.73	3.27	1	32
entre	27,283	.07	.25	0	1
numbus	27,283	.39	.79	0	5
avjobten	26,737	2.03	1.70	0	25
specdif	1,996	2.49	1.13	0	9
nafter	27,262	3.76	3.73	0	37
yrleft	26,588	10.74	9.93	0	45
B. Specialists:					
mbayear	25,120	74.34	14.25	13	97
male	25,482	.83	.38	0	1
age	25,081	50.18	13.65	25	93
white	25,482	.86	.35	0	1
exp	25,010	9.14	9.08	0	63
NPRIOR	25,476	3.10	3.26	0	37
NROLES	3,710	4.67	3.39	0	32
NROLESOTH	671	4.60	3.02	1	21
entre	25,482	0	0	0	0
numbus	25,482	.36	.75	0	5
avjobten	24,969	1.97	1.68	0	25
specdif	1,673	2.51	1.14	1	9
nafter	24,457	3.92	3.74	0	37
yrleft	23,879	11.39	10.01	0	45
C. Entrepreneurs:					
mbayear	1,781	73.22	13.62	13	97
male	1,801	.89	.31	0	1
age	1,782	51.12	12.76	26	88
white	1,801	.86	.34	0	1
exp	1,768	15.25	10.21	0	59
NPRIOR	1,801	5.55	4.27	0	35
NROLES	1,167	6.95	4.39	0	37
NROLESOTH	3,545	4.76	3.32	1	32
entre	1,801	1	0	1	1
numbus	1,801	.85	1.19	0	5
avjobten	1,768	2.88	1.75	0	18
specdif	323	2.36	1.05	0	7
nafter	2,805	2.34	3.28	0	25
yrleft	2,709	5.06	7.04	0	41

Among incorporated self-employed (which eliminates most household and other service workers who work alone), the dominant industries are, in order, construction, retail trade, professional services, business services, and real estate. Again, technical fields are minor players.

The basic hypothesis is that entrepreneurs are jacks-of-all-trades. In the "Investment" section above, it was shown that individuals who want to become entrepreneurs invest in a broader range of skills than do those who want to become specialists. Going into any job, individuals with a broader range of skills, acquired either through investment or through endowments, are more likely to be entrepreneurs.[13]

The data allow this hypothesis to be tested. The data set is a job history panel so that each respondent has one row of data corresponding to each employer (including self) that he or she has held. For example, an individual who had six employment spells would have six rows of data, one for each spell. An individual who had four employment spells and one spell of unemployment would have five rows of data. The beginning and ending dates for each job are recorded, as are the beginning and ending salary and size of firm. Additionally, all roles within the employment spell (up to five) are described through a coding system that corresponds to occupational titles. Industry and demographic data are also provided.

16.2.2. Number of Prior Roles

Table 16.2 provides the means and standard deviations of the relevant variables used in subsequent analyses. An entrepreneurial employment spell is defined to be one for which the respondent stated that he or she was "Founder—among those who initially started the business." The standard way to acquire human capital is through formal schooling and on-the-job training. Therefore, individuals who plan to become entrepreneurs are expected to invest in "general" on-the-job training, where "general" here refers to a variety of skills.

Table 16.3

Proportion of Entrepreneurs by Number of Prior Roles

| | A. Roles | | | | |
	≤ 3	3-16	> 16		
Proportion of entrepreneurs	.03	.10	.29		
	B. Experience Level				
	P Low NPRIOR	P High NPRIOR	Difference	SE	N
Roles:					
3 or fewer	.015	.029	.014	.003	8,163
4-8	.034	.073	.039	.005	6,971
9-13	.073	.11	.037	.009	4,597
14-19	.099	.115	.016	.011	3,415
20-29	.102	.138	.036	.012	2,965
30 or more	.145	.187	.042	.022	1,148

Notes: P = proportion.

The unit of observation in Tables 16.2 and 16.3 is the row, which consists of an employment spell for any given individual. The key independent variable, "NPRIOR," is the number of roles in total that the individual has had before the employment spell in question. So if an individual had three previous employers, and held two roles with the first, four roles with the second, and one with the third, then NPRIOR would equal seven. The dependent variable, ENTRE, is a dummy equal to one if the employment spell is one in which the individual founded his or her own business. About 6.6% of all employment spells (rows) are entrepreneurial ones. Taken over the lifetime, however, about 24% of the sample started at least one business.

Table 16.3 provides the initial evidence on the relation of varied background to entrepreneurship. Panel A of Table 16.3 reports the proportion of entrepreneurial employment spells, broken down by number of prior roles. Only 3% of those who have had fewer than three roles are entrepreneurs, whereas 29% of those with over 16 prior roles are entrepreneurs.[14] Although having more than 16 roles is well above the mean, it is far from the maximum number of roles held by individuals (see Table 16.2). The point is that the simplest statistics show that those who undertake many different assignments also have much higher probabilities of becoming entrepreneurs. More detail is given by the plot in Figure 16.2. A clear positive relation of entrepreneurship to number of prior roles is apparent.

Because it may be expected that individuals become entrepreneurs after acquiring some on-the-job experience, it is useful to break the data up by experience level. This is done in Table 16.3, panel B. The column "P Low NPRIOR" is the proportion of entrepreneurial spells in the group of individuals who have the median or fewer than the number of prior roles for this experience group. The column "P High NPRIOR" gives the proportion of entrepreneurial spells in the group of individuals who have more than the median number of roles for that experience group. Thus, the first row of panel B shows that those with the median or fewer prior roles were half as likely to be entrepreneurs as those with more than the median number of roles (.015/.029). Since an individual may enter the data set a number of times at different levels of experience, the rows are not independent tests of the hypothesis.[15] But the pattern is clear. Those who have had more roles in the past are more likely to be entrepreneurs.

Figure 16.2

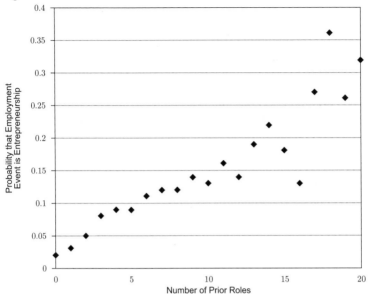

There are two interpretations of the NPRIOR variable, both of which are consistent with the jack-of-all-trades hypothesis. The first is that those who are endowed with high levels of multiple skills (or have acquired them by the time they reach the labor market) are able to perform many roles and NPRIOR proxies a person-specific effect– high NPRIOR are endowed with a balanced skill set. The second interpretation is that those who want to be entrepreneurs intentionally choose to perform a number of roles in order to acquire a balanced skill set. This is the investment route emphasized in the investment section above. Either interpretation is consistent with the model. The point is that a general set of skills is required for entrepreneurship. The existence of multiple roles is evidence for the prior existence or acquisition of the broad skill set. Below, some attempt will be made to distinguish between the two versions.

16.2.3. A Deeper Analysis

Table 16.4 contains the results of a deeper examination of the likelihood of starting a business to varied background. The basic result is contained in Column 1. Each observation is a row in the work history matrix, referring to one employment spell for one individual. The data are stacked. Two spells for one individual count the same as one spell for each of two individuals. Columns 2 and 3 do not assume that same statistical structure, but more on that later.

The key result is that the likelihood that an employment spell is entrepreneurial is positively and strongly associated with the number of prior roles. The partial effect is .0851 in the logit. This translates into a large effect. A one standard deviation increase in the number of prior roles implies an increase in the probability of being an entrepreneur by about .018, which is about one-fourth the probability that an employment spell is an entrepreneurial one. The finding is again consistent with the view that entrepreneurs have more varied backgrounds, at least in terms of the roles that they have played at work, than nonentrepreneurs.

Although not proof of the theory, this evidence can be viewed as consistent with the premise on which the model is based. That premise is that the entrepreneurial production technology is one that exhibits strong complementarity among skills. The extreme formulation used for expository purposes is that entrepreneurial output is proportional to $\min[x_1, x_2]$. Given that technology, the implication is that individuals who possess more varied skills are those most likely to be entrepreneurs. That prediction is borne out by the data in the sense that those with general backgrounds are more likely to start companies.

Table 16.4

Logit Analysis Panel Data

| | Correlation Structure | | | | | Year Basis – | |
Variable	Independent (1)	AR-1 (2)	Unstructured (3)	Independent (4)	Independent (5)	Unstructured (6)	Independent (7)
EXP	0,0452	0,0502	0,0534	0,007	0,0205	0,0341	0,043
	(.0036)	(.0039)	(.0038)	(.0044)	(.0048)	(.0058)	(.0037)
NPRIOR	0,0851	0,0769	0,0706	0,0808	0,1166	0,0875	0,0764
	(.0079)	(.0088)	(.0092)	(.0082)	(.0088)	(.0117)	(.0078)
MALE	0,4757	0,4562	0,4565	0,5266	0,4769	0,6021	0,4605
	(.0843)	(.0950)	(.0998)	(.0865)	(.0846)	(.1376)	(.0867)
MBAYEAR	-0,007	-0,0044	-0,0054	-0,0214	-0,0094	-0,0136	-0,0218
	(.0074)	(.0084)	(.0090)	(.0076)	(.0074)	(.0110)	(.0074)
AGE	-0,0265	-0,025	-0,0256	-0,0117	-0,0281	-0,0299	0,0024
	(.0078)	(.0089)	(.0095)	(.0080)	(.0078)	(.0112)	(.0079)
NAFTER				0,0186			
				(.0119)			
YRLEFT				0,0786			
				(.0060)			
AVJOBTEN					0,1218		
					(.0152)		
SDFIRST							0,0009
							(.00020)
Constant	-2,1085	-2,3626	-2,2253	-0,7957	-1,9849	1,583	-5,499
	(.9397)	(1.0669)	(1.1369)	(.9587)	(.9330)	(1.37)	(.9904)
Wald $\chi 2$	842	706	786	944	876	281	617
N	26819	26663	26819	26163	26779	62229	21956

Notes: Dependent variable: 1 if employment spell is entrepreneurial. Standard errors are in parentheses.

Table 16.5

Multinomial Logit Analysis of C-Levels, Employees, and "True" Entrepreneurs

	1		2		3	
	Other	C-Levels	Other	C-Levels	Other	C-Levels
EXP	-.049	.008	-.025	.028	.049	.008
	(.003)	(.005)	(.004)	(.005)	(.004)	(.005)
NPRIOR	-.090	.0004			-.092	-.001
	(.008)	(.098)			(.008)	(.010)
MALE	-.517	.575	-.480	.602	-.515	.577
	(.090)	(.143)	(.091)	(.143)	(.090)	(.143)
MBAYEAR	-.010	.027	.010	.046	-.013	.024
	(.008)	(.011)	(.008)	(.011)	(.008)	(.011)
AGE	.011	.030	.029	.048	.007	.026
	(.008)	(.011)	(.009)	(.011)	(.008)	(.011)
NROLES			-.175	-.069		
			(.007)	(.009)		
SDFIRST					-.00075	-.00084
					(.00021)	(.00032)
Log likelihood		-10,540		-10,325		10,533
N		20,920		20,920		20,920

Notes: Omitted category: "true" entrepreneurs.

Experience is also important. Five years of additional experience increase the probability of being an entrepreneur by about .014, or about one-fifth the probability that an employment spell is an entrepreneurial one. Men are more likely to start companies than women and younger individuals, for a given amount of experience, start more companies than older ones.

A statistical issue is that the rows are not independent because they belong to the same individual. For example, individuals who have already started one company are more likely than the average individual to start another at the next employment effect. Treating each row (employment spell) as independent may not be appropriate under these circumstances and the standard errors will be inconsistent. To run logit, taking into account correlation between rows due to the panel nature of the data, the approach of generalized estimating equations is used. The results are reported in Table 16.4.

Columns 2 and 3 of Table 16.5 introduce different forms of dependence across observations to allow for the fact that the data consist of a panel in which more than one row of data may belong to one individual. In Column 2, an AR-1 structure is assumed so that the correlation between rows s and t for a given individual is

$$\rho^{|t-s|}.$$

In Column 3, the correlation matrix is unstructured, and each correlation is allowed to be free and is estimated by the data.

The key result is that the coefficient on NPRIOR is not very sensitive to the correlation structure assumed. Even when nonindependence is taken into account, the relation of number of roles on entrepreneurial activity is large and significant.[16]

There is another potential statistical structure. Employment spells vary in duration. To address this, let us define a person-year as the relevant unit of analysis for the purpose of correlation structure. Every year of a person's career constitutes a separate observation during which he or she is an entrepreneur or working for someone else. Thus, someone who has been in the labor force for 15 years contributes 15 observations to the analysis. The within-job, between-year correlation structure is taken into account in estimating the logit so that standard errors are estimated consistently. Results are reported in Column 6 of Table 16.4. It is evident that NPRIOR maintains the same relative importance, has almost identical magnitude, and is statistically significant.

16.2.4. Which Interpretation?

Already mentioned is that there are (at least) two possible versions of the jack-of-all-trades view. One is that people are endowed with skills and that their labor market behavior merely reflects endowed skills or those acquired in school before they enter the labor market. An alternative is that individuals choose to perform a variety of roles as an investment in acquiring the broad skills necessary to become an entrepreneur. To get at this, the panel data are helpful.

If endowed characteristics simply enable a generalist to perform many roles, then the timing of those roles should not matter. That is, roles held after any particular employment spell should have the same "effect" on the likelihood that the spell is an entrepreneurial one as a role held before. However, if performing many labor market roles actually enhances the individual's ability to become an entrepreneur, then roles before any particular employment spell should be more salient than roles held after an employment spell. Therefore, another variable, NAFTER, was created, which counts the number of roles that an individual had in all employment spells following the one in a given row. It is analogous to NPRIOR, but it is defined in reverse. Rather than counting the roles held up to that point, it counts the roles after that point. Also, just as it was necessary to correct for experience, it is also necessary to correct for number of years after or number of roles will pick up life cycle effects. (Those who have a long career in the data after a particular spell will have higher values of NAFTER, irrespective of their general skills.) YRLEFT measures the number of years remaining until the end of the career record at the point at which the employment spell in question occurs.

Results are reported in Column 4 of Table 16.4. Although NAFTER enters positively, it is less than one-fourth as important in magnitude as NPRIOR. This is evidence that multiple roles are actually productive in preparing a person to be an entrepreneur and that they are not merely a proxy for unobserved general skills.[17]

One caveat: NAFTER is defined only for those who have a subsequent employment spell so NAFTER might relate to a preference for changing employers. This is unlikely, because, as discussed below, those who change employers frequently are less likely, rather than more likely, to become entrepreneurs.

16.2.5. Alternative Explanations

Might the results reflect something other than the jack-of-all-trades view? One possibility is that entrepreneurs have more roles when they are entrepreneurs than others and that the results are spurious. Indeed, there is some evidence that this is the case. On average, entrepreneurs have on average 2.4 roles during their entrepreneurial job compared to an average of 1.2 roles for all nonentrepreneurial spells.

To deal with this, a variable like NPRIOR was defined, except that each entrepreneurial spell is allowed to add only one role to NPRIOR, irrespective of the number of roles claimed during the entrepreneurial employment spell. This approach intentionally biases the results against finding a positive relation of entrepreneurial activity to the number of roles because one role is below the mean number of roles per employment spell. The results are qualitatively identical to those reported. The coefficient on the redefined variable is about half that on NPRIOR, but otherwise similar.

It is also possible that those with more roles received more promotions with their previous employer. To check this, the same models were run including a variable that measured the final salary on the last job. This was done only for those with at most one entrepreneurial spell so that the prior salary would be unambiguously defined. Those with higher final salaries do have a slightly higher probability of being entrepreneurs, but the coefficient is not significant in the logits with ENTRE as the dependent variable.

One theory, that entrepreneurs are those who are impatient, want variety, or fall into entrepreneurship accidentally because they are the individuals who change jobs often, is not borne out by the data. To examine this hypothesis, "average employment tenure" defined as experience/number of employment spells was included in the logit. The result, in Column 5 of Table 16.4, is that those who have longer employment spells are more likely to be entrepreneurs. If entrepreneurs were impatient types, the relation of entrepreneurship to average job tenure (AVJOBTEN) should be negative, not positive. There is surely some version of a taste argument that can be made, but the most straightforward ones do not seem to be consistent with the sign on AVJOBTEN.

The most frequently offered explanation of entrepreneurship is that entrepreneurs are those who are willing to take risks. Taste explanations are never particularly appealing unless they can be related to something measurable. There is some hope of doing just that in the data set. Most entrepreneurs work in other jobs before starting their own companies. The jobs that they choose before becoming entrepreneurs can provide some information on their preference for risk. Specifically, the data provide detailed industry/occupation codes that correspond to fields like accounting, education, insurance, chemical manufacturing, and so forth. There are 74 different industry/occupation categories. Some industries/occupations are riskier than others, as can be proxied by examining the wage distribution of individuals within these occupations. To measure this, the standard deviation of income in each of the 74 groups was calculated. Then, each individual was classified according to the industry/occupation of his or her first job choice after graduation from Stanford. The standard deviation of income in that category becomes a variable attached to the individual. The idea is that those who are less risk averse should be willing to enter the higher income variance occupations than the most risk averse, so that the standard deviation of income in the first occupation measures their tolerance for risk

The standard deviation in income of the individual's first industry/occupation, FIRSTSD, is entered as a variable in the entrepreneurship logit. The results are reported in Column 7 of Table 16.4.

Note first that the coefficient on FIRSTSD is positive. Those who enter high income variance industries/occupations are more likely to have later entrepreneurial employment spells. This is consistent with the view that entrepreneurs are less risk averse. Of course, it could also reflect other differences across occupations correlated with wage variance. For example, fields with high wage variance like investment banking might attract people who think they are movers and shakers, and the same people might also be inclined to start their own businesses. This is a taste explanation, and there are surely others that cannot be rejected by these data, but the risk aversion view is consistent with the findings.

Second, even though FIRSTSD enters significantly, the coefficient and standard errors on NPRIOR remain virtually unchanged. Even if risk or other taste factors affect the choice to start a business, the generalist argument still seems to apply and is not weakened by this effect.

16.2.6. Defining "Entrepreneur"

Because the definition of "Entrepreneur" is somewhat arbitrary, another group was defined to be entrepreneurs. They are those who reported their position as high-level general manager, specifically, "I am responsible for the organization's overall direction, including responsibility for major business functions and personnel decisions (examples: CEO, President, COO, Executive Director)." Although individuals in this category may not assume the same risk as those who found a business, they are senior general managers, so the jack-of-all-trades argument should pertain to them as well.

To determine whether general managers are also jacks-of-all-trades, a multinomial logit was estimated. The dependent variable can either be "entrepreneur," which is the left-out group, "C-level manager," or "other." The results (see Table 16.5, Column 1) show a significant negative coefficient on NPRIOR for those who are neither C-level managers nor entrepreneurs relative to "true" entrepreneurs. But the coefficient on NPRIOR for those who are C-levels is zero relative to the true entrepreneurs. Apparently, prior roles do not distinguish between entrepreneurs and C-level managers. The prior skills seem to be the same. So the jack-of-all-trades story applies well to senior-level managers.

It is possible to distinguish senior managers from true entrepreneurs. The theory suggests that those who start their own businesses must perform many tasks as entrepreneurs that are not required of C-level managers. For example, the chief technology officer need not raise funds for the firm since the chief financial officer generally performs that task. As a result, NROLES, which differs from NPRIOR only in that it includes the roles performed in the current job, should be more important for true entrepreneurs than for chief-level managers. Column 2 of Table 16.5 contains the results of a multinomial logit, where the comparisons are relative to true entrepreneurs.

The multinominal logit results are as predicted. As before, NROLES has a strong negative effect on being an employee throughout the career, that is, it has a strong positive effect on being a true entrepreneur. More important, NROLES also has a negative effect on being a chief-level manager relative to being a true entrepreneur. Although having many roles increases the probability of having been a high-level manager, having many roles makes one even more likely to be a true entrepreneur.

One difference between C-levels and true entrepreneurs is the amount of risk that they face. It is likely that being a true entrepreneur is riskier than being a C-level employee because one's own physical capital is often at stake when starting a business. Also, high risk of failure might create riskiness associated with true entrepreneurship. Perhaps risk preferences help distinguish between being a C-level employee and a true entrepreneur.

Using the earlier approach, where risk aversion is proxied by avoidance of industry/occupations with high income variance, Column 3 of Table 16.5 reports the results with SDFIRST included. There is in fact evidence that a difference between C-level managers and entrepreneurs is that true entrepreneurs are more inclined to take risks. The SDFIRST variable enters negatively in both the employee and C-level manager part of the multinomial logit and with almost the same magnitude. Both groups, C-level managers and other employees, are less inclined to start out in high variance industries/occupations than those who become true entrepreneurs.

One interesting aside is that women are more likely to be employees of others than they are to be entrepreneurs, but they are more likely to be entrepreneurs than they are to be high-level managers. Women may have escaped historical discrimination at very high levels of corporations by starting their own businesses.

16.2.7.   General and Specialized Curricula

The data on work histories were matched with data from student transcripts. As a result, we have information on the courses taken while the individual was a student at the Stanford Graduate School of Business. The records begin in the mid-1980s, so the transcript-matched data pertain only to those who graduated during approximately the last 15 years. But almost 2,000 records of alumni work history data have been matched with transcript information, so a significant amount of information is contained in the 15 years of records.

Simple relationships can be seen in the comparison of means in Table 16.2. The variable SPECDIF is the difference between the maximum number of courses taken in one field and the average number of courses taken across fields. This is a measure of lopsidedness in the study curriculum. SPECDIF is lower by about one-fifth of a standard deviation for entrepreneurs than it is for specialists. The difference between the average level of SPECDIF between groups suggests that those who later become entrepreneurs took a more balanced set of courses while at Stanford.

Additionally, the simple correlation between SPECDIF and NROLES for lifetime roles is negative and significant, as is the partial correlation, holding constant MBA year. Those who take more specialized curricula also take on fewer roles when they enter the labor market, which suggests that generalized formal education and generalized on-the-job training are complements.

Table 16.6

Tobit and Logits with Stanford Course Data, Number of Businesses Started (Tobit and Ordered-Probit), and Ever Started a Business (Logit)

Variable	Logit (1)	Tobit (2)	Ordered Probit (3)
EXP	.0259	.0266	.0612
	(.0185)	(.0196)	(.0042)
SPECDIF	-.1458	-.1452	-.0433
	(.0581)	(.0592)	(.0180)
MALE	.6025	.6305	.3857
	(.1511)	(.1531)	(.0482)
MBAYEAR	-.0318	-.0384	.0241
	(.0215)	(.0224)	(.0069)
AGE	.0250	.0264	.0146
	(.0179)	(.1531)	(.0053)
Constant	.0202	.3243	Cut parameters
	(2.4182)	(2.4897)	omitted
Log likelihood	-841	-1,181	
N	1,952	1,950	

Notes: Standard errors are in parantheses.

The first analysis reported in Table 16.6 presents logits, tobits, and ordered probits, analogous to those in Table 16.4, but only pre-labor-market characteristics are allowed to affect the career. The approach is to assume that school prepares an individual for the labor market and then to observe how differences in the educational experience are reflected in the subsequent career. The jack-of-all-trades theory suggests that those who have large values of SPECDIF should be less likely to become entrepreneurs.

The results confirm the hypothesis. The more specialized is the curriculum, as measured by SPECDIF, the fewer businesses the individual starts and the less likely is the individual to start a business. Once again, it is the generalists, as reflected in generalized course curricula, who end up founding a business after they leave school. Those who want to found a business prepare themselves by taking a variety of different courses that they hope will later prove useful when they start businesses. An alternative view is that those who happen to take a varied set of courses start a business later because the spell has given them the general skills necessary to found a business. Both views are consistent with the jack-of-all-trades view of entrepreneurship. Only if entrepreneurs need general skills will a varied course background be correlated with later entrepreneurial activity.[18]

The results of the Stanford course data support the earlier conclusions. Entrepreneurs are jacks-of-all-trades. They have more varied course work while in the MBA program and have many more positions when they are actually in the labor market.

16.3. Summary and Conclusions

Entrepreneurs are individuals who are multifaceted. Although not necessarily superb at anything, entrepreneurs have to be sufficiently skilled in a variety of areas to put together the many ingredients required to create a successful business. As a result, entrepreneurs tend to be more balanced individuals.

Two kinds of evidence are provided. First, those who have more varied careers, as evidenced by having performed more roles as part of their work experience, are more likely to be entrepreneurs. There are two interpretations of this result, both consistent with the jack-of-all-trades view. The first is that the correlation between number of roles and entrepreneurship reflects endowed differences in general skills across people. Those with more general skills can perform more roles. The second is that the correlation reflects conscious investment, where individuals who plan to become entrepreneurs take on many roles so that they can acquire the varied background necessary to start a business. Each version finds some support, but the investment view seems to dominate.

Second, the pattern of investment that occurs prior to entering the labor market is also consistent with the generalist view of entrepreneurship. In the Stanford MBA data, it is found that those students who study a more varied curriculum are more likely to be entrepreneurs and to start a larger number of businesses over their careers.

Much more can be done, especially at the empirical level, given the richness of the data. The prevalence of entrepreneurship by occupation and industry is predicted by the model. Educational systems differ by country in terms of amount of specialization, and this has implications for the proportion of entrepreneurs by country. The model gives quite specific predictions about these relations, but investigation is left to the future.

Appendix
The Underlying Economy

In this section, the income-generating functions shown in (1) and (2) are derived from a more fundamental production function.[19]

Let there be two raw skills, γ_1 and γ_2, for example, verbal and quantitative ability. In any given firm with an entrepreneur who has the ability pair (γ_1, γ_2), output is given by

$$\text{Output} = Q(\min(\gamma_1, \gamma_2))f(Y_1, Y_2),$$

where $Q(\ )$ and $f(\ )$ are parts of the production function and Y_1 and Y_2 are the amounts of skills employed by the firm in efficiency units. Normalize the price of a unit of output to 1 and let wages (determined by the equilibrium) be given by w_1 and w_2. Then profit is given by

(A1) $\quad \pi(\gamma_1, \gamma_2, w_1, w_2) = Q(\min(\gamma_1, \gamma_2))f(Y_1, Y_2) - w_1Y_1 - w_2Y_2.$

To avoid discussion of number of firms in an industry, which is not central to the analysis, simply assume that each entrepreneur is a local monopolist. Thus, the $Q(\ )$ function incorporates the monopoly price into the measure of output.

Maximization of the profit function in (A1) yields the firm's demand curves for Y_1 and Y_2, which are written as

(A2) $\qquad Y_i^d = Y_i^d\left(\min(\gamma_1,\ \gamma_2), w_1, w_2\right)\quad$ for $I = 1,\ 2.$

The underlying density of skills in the overall working population is given by $g(\gamma_1,\ \gamma_2)$. $A_1(w_1,\ w_2)$ is the set of individuals who choose to specialize in supplying skill γ_1. It is given by

(A3) $\qquad A_1(w_1,\ w_2) = \{(\gamma_1,\ \gamma_2)|w_1\gamma_1 > \max[w_2\gamma_2,\ \pi(\gamma_1,\ \gamma_2,\ w_1,\ w_2)]\}.$

Analogously, A_2, the set of individuals who choose to specialize in skill γ_2 is given by

(A4) $\qquad A_2(w_1,\ w_2) = \{(\gamma_1,\ \gamma_2)|w_2\gamma_2 > \max[w_1\gamma_1,\ \pi(\gamma_1,\ \gamma_2,\ w_1,\ w_2)]\}.$

Finally, entrepreneurs are defined as the set

(A5) $\qquad E(w_1,\ w_2) = \{(\gamma_1,\ \gamma_2)|\pi\ (\gamma_1,\ \gamma_2,\ w_1,\ w_2) > \max[w_1\gamma_1,\ w_2\gamma_2]\}.$

Then let $g_i(\gamma_1,\ \gamma_2)$ be the density function of abilities of individuals in set A_i derived from $g(\ )$ and (A3) and (A4) and $g_e(\gamma_1,\ \gamma_2)$ be the corresponding density among entrepreneurs, derived from $g(\ )$ and (A5).

The following two supply-equals-demand equations determine the equilibrium values of w_1 and w_2:

(A6)
$$\int \int \gamma_1 g_1(\gamma_1,\ \gamma_2) d\gamma_1 d\gamma_2$$
$$= \int \int Y_1^d\left(\min(\gamma_1,\ \gamma_2),\ w_1,\ w_2\right) g_e(\gamma_1,\ \gamma_2) d\gamma_1 d\gamma_2$$

and

(A7)
$$\int \int \gamma_2 g_2(\gamma_1, \gamma_2) d\gamma_1 d\gamma_2$$
$$= \int \int Y_2^d (\min(\gamma_1, \gamma_2), w_1, w_2) g_e(\gamma_1, \gamma_2) d\gamma_1 d\gamma_2.$$

Next, define $x_1 = w_1\gamma_1$ and $x_2 = w_2\gamma_2$ where the wages are obtained from the market equilibrium given in (A5) and (A7). Sufficient conditions to derive income-generating functions (1) and (2) are constant returns to scale and symmetry. Specialist income in (1) comes directly from the definition of x_i and the conditions that define sets A_i. This is simply relabeling. Given that specialist income is x_i, it is now shown that entrepreneurial income moves in proportion to $\min(\gamma_1, \gamma_2)$ under the assumptions of constant returns to scale and symmetry. Let production exhibit constant returns to scale such that

(A8) $Q(k\min(\gamma_1, \gamma_2))f(kY_1, kY_2) = kQ(\min(\gamma_1, \gamma_2))f(Y_1, Y_2),$

and symmetry such that $f(\gamma_1, \gamma_2) = f(\gamma_2, \gamma_1)$ and $g(\gamma_1, \gamma_2) = g(\gamma_2, \gamma_1)$.
We want to show that

(A9) $\pi(\gamma_1, \gamma_2, w_1, w_2) = \lambda \min (x_1, x_2).$

Symmetry guarantees that $Y_1^0 = Y_1^0$ and that $w_1 = w_2 = w$. Let $z = \min(\gamma_1^0, \gamma_2^0)$. Constant returns to scale implies that if an entrepreneur of skill z employs y^0 of each type of labor, then an entrepreneur of skill z' employs $(y^0)(z'/z)$ of each type of labor. That, coupled with (A8) implies that profits are equal to $(z'/z)\pi(z, w, w)$. Let $\lambda(z, w, w)/zw$. Then

$$\pi(z', w, w) = (z'/z)\pi(z, w, w)$$
$$= \lambda z'/w$$
$$= (\lambda/w)\min(\gamma_1, \gamma_2)$$
$$= \lambda\min(x_1, x_2),$$

which is (2), the entrepreneurial income function.

453

VII Personnel Economics:
The Past and Future

In this book, I have attempted to lay out the papers which I believe have been among my more significant contributions to the field of personnel economics. But a field is not a true field unless a literature blossoms and continues to flourish, enriching the overall knowledge base. As a result, in this chapter I do not summarize what has come before, but rather discuss the literature that is related to some of my contributions and those of other early researchers in the field of personnel economics.

To restate the prior point made in the introduction, personnel economics is an attempt to add the rigor of mathematics and statistics, with the discipline that those sciences bring to the field to the study of human resources. Within the field of personnel economics, topics such as compensation, turnover and incentives that are inherently economic are considered. But in addition, other topics involving norms, teamwork, worker empowerment, peer relations, and non-monetary compensation are also part of personnel economics. The tools come from advances in information economics, econometrics, game theory, and other areas of the economic literature.

As already discussed, personnel economics is, above all, economics and as such it uses the methodology that is most important for doing economic analysis. That methodology includes three components.

First, personnel economics assumes that both worker and firm are rational maximizing agents, seeking either utility or profits. Of course, the approach allows for imperfections and other constraints such as imperfect information, transaction costs, and other rigidities through legislation that may alter the way in which firms and workers interact. But these can be incorporated into a formal model that uses maximization with constraints as its fundamental building block.

Second, personnel economics requires models that derive an equilibrium. Equilibrium is essential for science because it provides a discipline that requires all the pieces add up to form a consistent picture. Equilibrium which is central to economics is not an important concept in the other social sciences.

Third, efficiency is at the heart of economics and allows us to do welfare analysis. When inefficiencies arise, the economist asks whether there is a way that the market can invent new institutions or trades that will eliminate the inefficiencies. As such, it pushes the frontier both in terms of welfare analysis and also in terms of positive economic thinking.

Personnel economics uses sophisticated econometrics and statistics to identify underlying causal relationships. Like much of labor economics, our ability to use experimental design, both laboratory and field, and to look at real world data to draw inferences, has advanced significantly. As a result, personnel economics, which initially was an almost exclusively theoretical field, has moved into the empirical realm. The most significant and growing parts of the field are in the areas in which data have become available.

Often, the approaches of personnel economics differ significantly from those used in organizational behavior, psychology, and other fields that have been important in analyzing human resources questions. Those fields frequently emphasize intrinsic motivation. While the economist does not reject intrinsic motivation, we argue that it is not the intrinsic part of motivation that is relevant for market behavior. Rather it is the behavior that is not easily motivated that is most important for consideration by personnel economists. The employer does not have to worry so much about the kinds of things that employees like to do, but it is important for firms to address areas where there is a tension between the desires of the employer and those of the worker. Specifically, economists consider how behavior on the margin is affected, not how average behavior is affected because marginal behavior affects equilibrium prices and quantities. This does not mean that intrinsic motivation is not important. Indeed it may determine a significant fraction of behavior in the labor market. But when analyzing incentives, pay, motivation, and other aspects, generally it is marginal behavior not average behavior that is relevant.

Money isn't everything. It is clear that workers care about many aspects of their jobs other than pay. Flexibility of work hours, comfortable working conditions, good colleagues, interesting projects, bosses who are respectful and provide positive feedback are all important components of the job. But economic models, and in particular the hedonic model introduced by Sherwin Rosen (Rosen 1974), allow non-monetary components of the job to be monetized, that is, to be thought of in terms of their monetary equivalents. This is an enormous breakthrough because it means that traditional economic models that put things in terms of pecuniary compensation are relevant even for non-monetary factors. And furthermore it means that non-monetary factors can always be translated into a monetary equivalent.

Finally, personnel economics tends to be more normative than other parts of economics. The primary reason is that personnel economics is used in business schools where training is directed toward individuals who will some day become managers. Consequently, the teacher of personnel economics is not only trying to explain what exists in the world but also to assist individuals in determining what they should do when they participate in that world. So personnel economics, which I believe does a good job at explaining what we observe in the economy, can also be applied to creating new structures and new ways for firms and workers to interact.

The first five chapters of this book were devoted to examining the existence of some puzzling institutions. The theme is that these puzzles can be solved by using an analytic economic framework that follows the methodology described above: the assumption of maximizing, rational behavior, the requirement of equilibrium, and the premise that efficiency is a driving force.

The existence of mandatory retirement was the first among these, but Chapter 1 was probably more important for thinking in terms of lifetime incentives than it was for explaining the existence of mandatory retirement per se. To the extent that there is an important insight in the chapter, it is that competitive labor markets do not require that workers earn their marginal products at each point in time, but instead can have wages that deviate in a systematic way from productivity. In particular, young workers may be paid less than they are worth and old workers may be paid more than they are worth.

Other researchers also provided explanations of wages that deviate from spot productivity using other rationales, but also employing the rigorous models that economics supplies. For example, a few years after the mandatory retirement paper was originally published, Milton Harris and Bengt Holmström (1982) suggested a model where life-cycle considerations could cause a similar upward sloping age-earnings profile because workers who were risk averse would buy insurance from their firms. The profile sloped upward because workers pay a premium in the form of low wages received early in their careers followed by higher wages, in some workers' cases exceeding their marginal products, later in their careers.

Another early contribution to this literature was by Robert Frank (1984) who provided a taste-based motivation for having wages deviate from marginal products. He suggested that workers may care about their pay relative to other workers in the firm. Workers derive utility by being better than others in their firms. As a result, they were willing to give up compensation in order to be the biggest fish in a small pond. Conversely, those at the bottom of the distribution must be compensated for the disutility they suffer from being in a low relative position. In his work, high ability workers are underpaid relative to their productivity and lower productivity workers are overpaid relative to their productivity.

The empirical literature has corroborated many of the early conjectures. In particular, a very early paper by Medoff and Abraham (1980) used subjective performance data and found that wages rose more rapidly than productivity. Although their data have been criticized for being merely a subjective measure of productivity, still their results are informative. Also in early work, Claudia Goldin (1986) argued that, historically, women had shorter attachment to the labor force. Because they were not in jobs for long enough periods of time to be motivated by life time incentive schemes, they had to be paid piece rates. She documented this tendency using historical data in her 1986 paper in the Journal of Labor Economics. In a similar vein, Hutchens (1987) argued that different occupations were more susceptible to lifetime compensation schemes than others, having to do with the degree to which effort could be monitored. Hutchens finds that jobs that are more conducive to monitoring are less likely to have pensions, upward sloping age-earnings profiles, and mandatory retirement, again supporting the idea that these institutions form part of an implicit incentive contract. Later, Janet Spitz (1991) obtained data from a supermarket chain. She found that the productivity of workers rose over their lifetime, but not as rapidly as their wages did. More recently, Lazear and Shaw (2008b) found that during early years on the job productivity rises more rapidly than wages, but in later years wage gains outstrip productivity gains, again breaking the link between wages and productivity over the work life.

The essence of personnel economics is that it focuses on the relation between the employer and the firm and does not examine the labor market as a whole. For example, wage determination is an extremely important part of labor economics. Estimating rates of return to education and wage functions along the lines of the literature that was spawned by Jacob Mincer's work is essential in labor economics. But it is not part of personnel economics because it maps out market equilibria, rather than the specific interaction between the worker and the firm. That said, institutions that affect the way wages are paid and the mobility that results are part of personnel economics because they interact directly with the firm–worker relationship. It is for this reason that job security provisions are so central to personnel economics and employment protection laws have become an important part of the personnel economics literature.

Since my early work and that of others, there has been a very significant literature on employment protection legislation, only a small part of which is mentioned here. Although one of the more important theoretical points of Chapter 3 was that efficient labor markets could undo the negative consequences of firing costs, it was also argued there that, absent complete contracting, firing costs could have substantial employment effects. Indeed, in the empirical section of the chapter significant employment effects were found.

That work has been corroborated by others. In particular, Dertouzos and Karoly (1992), DeLeire (2000), Acemoglu and Angrist (2001) and Autor, Donohue, and Schwab (2006) all show that there is substantial evidence that firing costs increase unemployment. Blanchard and Portugal (2001) compare the performance of U.S. and Portuguese labor markets and suggest that large differences in unemployment durations and flows of workers into and out of unemployment are largely attributable to differences in employment protection between the two countries.

David Autor has a number of papers that document the use of temporary hiring as an alternative to permanent employment. He argues that the growth in temporary employment is at least in part a result of firing restrictions, either explicit through legislation or implicit, associated with potential court action (see e.g. Autor 2003).

Oyer and Schaefer (2000) find that the costs of firing associated with civil rights legislation in the United States have altered the way firms and workers interact and argue that the pattern of termination in hiring is consistent with theoretical propositions from the employment protection literature. Gibbons and Katz (1991) analyze the inferences that can be drawn about terminated employees. The inference depends on the underlying institutional environment, for example, whether others have been laid off at the same time. Firing costs also change the distribution of the individuals who are terminated and those who remain with the firm. This point has been documented and discussed by Kugler and Saint-Paul (2004).

In a different line of work, Falk, Huffman and MacLeod (2008) examine the incentive effects of dismissal barriers and bonus contracts in an experimental environment. They show that employment protection legislation harms worker performance and that the formation of long-term relationships can be altered by such restrictions. They also find that some of this can be undone, again in the spirit of Chapter 3, by allowing firms and workers to contract in richer, more efficient ways.

Finally, works councils and other firm–worker wage setting organizations were discussed in Chapter 4. The key argument was that, while works councils may raise labor productivity, they also have the effect of transferring rents from firms to workers. Cappelli and Neumark (2001) provide evidence that this is in fact the case. They show that work practices that are sometimes labeled "high performance practices" which empower the workers, also raise labor costs per employee. But they also find that these work practices are sometimes associated with increases in productivity. Additionally, Addison, Schnabel and Wagner (2001) show that works councils in Germany are associated with reduced labor fluctuations and higher productivity, but that they do result in lower profitability and higher wages. Again, there is a question as to what the optimal amount of worker empowerment is from a social point of view and whether government institutions that require worker–firm wage setting bring us closer to or further away from the social optimum. The literature has not yet been informative on that point.

The second part of the book dealt with topics that are inherently economic. Central to understanding worker–firm relations are models of compensation structures, and especially models that relate compensation to incentives. Of course there is an enormous literature in personnel economics on incentives. Both the theoretical literature that discusses the design of compensation and the empirical literature that examines compensation practices are quite developed.

The early compensation literature was confined primarily to high level managers and especially to CEOs, primarily because those data were most likely to be available. But the more recent literature has been able to analyze the compensation practices of ordinary workers in manufacturing and services. Besides the work on life-cycle earnings profiles, Chapter 6 reports some of the earliest work on compensation and incentives. The theoretical developments in that chapter were extended by Green and Stokey (1983) to make explicit what was not discussed in the Lazear and Rosen work (Chapter 6). Green and Stokey highlight the importance of tournaments in removing common shocks from risky performance measures. Tournaments are a relative performance system rather than an absolute performance system. As such, noise that is common to both contestants is differenced out by looking at rank rather than looking at level of output. The basic tournament structure was extended by Rosen (1986) who considered tournaments in a multi-stage context. Rosen showed that in order to keep incentives constant across stages, it is necessary to skew the earnings structure. Because early promotions in a career contain two rewards, they have more incentive power, other things equal, than later promotions. When a worker is promoted early in his career, not only does he enjoy the higher salary that is associated with that promotion, but he also gets the option to play in the next round of the tournament which permits some possibility of even higher wages later on. At the last stage of the tournament, however, the option value vanishes. As such, those promoted into the CEO position should experience a larger jump in wages to compensate for the fact that there is only the higher wage and no option value associated with that promotion.

Tournaments have associated with them a number of problems. Ronald Dye (1984) discusses some of those problems and how they can involve collusion or competition. That work was extended in the work reported in Chapter 11.

An additional set of implications comes from the work of Chan (1996). Chan argues that one of the disadvantages of hiring from the outside is that it reduces the incentive for workers inside the firm to perform. As a result, firms should favor inside promotion over hiring from the outside, other things equal. Later, Chan shows that an implication of the 1996 work is that individuals who are hired from the outside should necessarily be better than those who are promoted into the same level from the inside. As a result, subsequent promotions of individuals hired from the outside should be more likely and more rapid than promotions of individuals from the same rank who reach that level from internal promotion (Chan 2006).

There is a significant amount of support for tournament theory that comes from a variety of empirical approaches. Some papers examine the entire structure of wages and promotions within a firm to test general consistency with the theory (see, for example, Eriksson 1999 and DeVaro 2006). More directly, prizes and the prize structures seem to have a direct effect on the level of effort and resources devoted to an activity. The first study of this sort was by Bull, Schotter, and Weigelt (1987). Using laboratory experiments, they found that the Nash equilibrium predicted by the Lazear and Rosen tournament model was replicated in laboratories and was quite robust to methods and specification. Slightly later, Ehrenberg and Bognanno (1990) used data from the Professional Golfers Association to show that scores in golf tournaments were responsive to the structure of prizes in the way that the tournament model predicted. Drago and Garvey (1998) used a sample of Australian firms to show that individuals put more effort into their jobs as measured by absenteeism when incentives are strong. They also found, consistent with the pay-equality-and-industrial-politics analysis (Chapter 11), that high differences in prices within a tournament structure also induced workers to be less cooperative with one another. Similarly, Falk, Fehr and Huffman (2008) demonstrate, using experimental methods, that behavior of subjects is consistent with tournament theory, both with respect to effort and sabotage. Finally, in a series of papers Bandiera, Barankay, and Rasul have analyzed the effects of relative performance and of tournaments and piece rates in a farm environment in the United Kingdom (see Bandiera, Barankay and Rasul 2005, 2007, 2009a).

Gneezy, Niederle, and Rustichini (2003) as well as Niederle and Vesterlund (2007) examine gender differences between piece rates and tournaments and find behavior to differ across these two incentive structures. Of course, it is possible to create piece-rate structures that are more powerful in motivating workers than tournament structures and vice versa, simply by changing the slope of the piece rate or the structure of the tournament. For example, a

461

tournament can be run where prizes are very close together. In that tournament one would expect very low levels of effort. If it is compared with a piece rate where the piece rate is very high it is likely that piece rates would be more powerful than tournaments. Conversely, a piece rate could be set low and the difference between the winning prize and the losing prize in a tournament could be set very high. In that structure, tournaments would dominate piece rates. So it is always possible to alter the structure to get one type of compensation scheme to provide more motivation than the other. It is for that reason that Gneezy et al. attempt to design tournament and piece-rate structures such that, for risk neutral agents, efforts should be the same.

The purpose of the literature on compensation is not to suggest that one compensation structure dominates another. Indeed, Chapter 7 explains how the choice between salaries and piece rates should be determined by factors associated with heterogeneity in monitoring costs and other components. Rather, the point of the compensation literature is that compensation structures vary with the environment in predictable ways. For example, the work by Bandiera, Barankay, and Rasul is informative in showing how these mechanisms may play out in agriculture. Although agriculture is a very small part of most modern economies, the principles learned from those studies are likely to be relevant in other contexts as well.

The second part of this book also discussed more direct incentive methods, namely those where workers are paid piece rates, bonuses or other variants of straight incentive pay. In an early paper, Bengt Holmström (1979) pointed out the important trade-off between risk and incentives. This work built on a literature that dates back to the fifties and had more recent precedent in Steven Ross' paper on agency (Ross 1973). But Holmström was the first to lay out in a clear and concise way how insurance and incentives were opposed to one another. In order to provide insurance to workers, compensation must be insulated from variations in pay that depend on output variations over which workers have no control. The problem is that effort usually cannot be observed directly. Thus, the firm must chose to either dampen the relation of pay to output, which dampens incentives, or to allow pay to vary completely with output, which creates risk for the worker. Pay compression may exist in part to insure against risk when workers are more risk averse than firms.

There is a great deal of literature that documents the effect of incentive pay on performance; one piece of this literature is contained in the compensation section of this book (see Chapter 8). That work was followed by others in a similar vein. Shearer (2004) studies how piece rates affect the productivity of tree planters in British Columbia and finds that workers who are paid a piece rate are approximately 20% more productive than those paid by the hour. Coincidentally, this was the same increase in productivity observed in the "Safelite" study. But that is merely a coincidence. As I pointed out earlier, whether piece rates have a large or small effect on increases in productivity depends on the exact relation of piece rate to output, i.e., the slope of the compensation function. A very flat piece-rate schedule would be expected to have little effect on output. But it is interesting that the 20% figure seems to be an empirical constant or close to it. Bandiera, Barankay, and Rasul (2007) also find that average fruit picker productivity increased by 21%, in this case when managers' pay was related to productivity.

Other studies that document the relation of productivity to piece rate pay include Asch (1990) who finds that Navy Recruiters vary their effort in response to performance based pay, Fernie and Metcalf (1999) who show that incentive contracts generate superior performance than other non-contingent pay systems, Freeman and Kleiner (2005) who find that productivity falls in the shoe industry when firms switch from piece rates to salary, Lo, Ghosh, and Lafontaine (2006) who find that salespeople also respond to piece rate pay; and Parent (1999) who finds that men paid on a piece rate work harder and more efficiently.

Again, to restate the point that I have already made a few times, the fact that productivity increases with piece rate pay does not imply that piece rate pay is efficient. Productivity may increase but measurement costs also increase, and the compensation that is required may be larger than the increase in productivity associated with piece rate pay. Furthermore, there are unintended consequences associated with piece rate pay. One that has been identified frequently is the effect of piece rate pay on the quality of output. There is no necessity that quality falls when firms switch from salary to piece rate pay. But as a practical matter that is a frequent consequence. The reason is that it is generally easier to observe attributes that are usually associated with quantity than it is to observe attributes that are associated with quality. As a result, workers tend to push on the quantity dimension and shirk on the quality dimen-

sion (see, e.g., Holmström and Milgrom 1991). This can be reme-
died, but it requires more sophisticated compensation schemes that
place heavy penalties on quality failures. Because quality defects
are observed only infrequently, it is necessary to punish defects
more heavily than the actual cost associated with it. For example,
if a defect is detected only one in ten times, to a first approximation
the penalty associated with detecting a defect must be ten times the
size of the cost of that defect to the firm.

Other effects that have been observed derive from incentives
associated with non-linear compensation schemes. Oyer (1998) is
among the best examples of work on this topic. He documents that
salespeople and managers move work around to take advantage of
or to mitigate end-of-year effects. Because of quotas and nonlinearities in the bonus structure it sometimes pays for salespeople to attempt to accelerate sales into the current quarter and sometimes to
delay them. Larkin (2007), using data from a large software company, shows that some of the inadvertent effects of piece rate compensation can cost the firm a significant amount, in this case 6–8%
of potential revenue.

In Chapter 7, it was argued that pay can be determined by effort
(salaries) or by output (piece rates). But one concept that was almost
completely missing from economic analysis was the notion of the
"job" per se. There is virtually no role for the "job" in human capital
theory at all. Wage determination occurs simply by taking the total
amount of human capital and multiplying it by its rental price. Jobs
are not only not mentioned, they are irrelevant and anathema to
the theory of human capital. And yet, in the real world workers and
firms tend to think in term of jobs and slots.

The tournament model allows for jobs as a relevant unit of analysis. But even there the job was simply defined as a wage slot. Securing the manager's job simply meant securing the wage that went
with that job, and failing to be promoted meant remaining in a job
that had a low wage. There is nothing in tournament theory that
associates tasks or other characteristics that we normally think of
as being important to a job with a job. But in the work reported in
Chapter 9, I found that jobs were not only important as a conceptual matter, but were important empirically, determining a large
amount of pay variation. The subsequent work by Baker, Gibbs
and Holmström (1994) and other studies that used firm-based data
found very much the same thing. Many have defined jobs in terms

of the tasks associated with them. For example, Prendergast (1995) models jobs as an opportunity to invest in human capital. This work dates back to Rosen (1972) who analyzed job assignment and human capital acquisition. Other theoretical work on jobs and tasks includes that by Zábojník (2002), Olson and Torsvik (2000), Holmström and Milgrom (1991), Itoh (1994), and Schöttner (2007). Additionally, a number of papers by Garicano and coauthors, including Thomas Hubbard and Esteban Rossi-Hansberg, focus on the sorting of workers to specific types of firms and jobs when communication and information costs change (e.g., Garicano 2000, Garicano and Rossi-Hansberg 2006, Garicano and Hubbard 2009).

The Garicano work is based on earlier papers by Sherwin Rosen, in particular Rosen (1982). There are a number of ways to define or conceive of jobs. Jobs can be thought of as a collection of tasks, as a learning opportunity, as a wage slot, as a set of non-monetary attributes, or some combination of the above. Gibbons and Waldman (2006) develop a model where task-specific human capital is key, so that a person's job assignment has important effects on how the career develops.

Finally, efficiency wage models discuss incentives for workers to perform within the firm, and argue that termination is a substitute for more continuous monitoring (see Shapiro and Stiglitz 1984, Akerlof and Yellen 1988). These models derive unemployment equilibria, primarily because the compensation contract is constrained by an inability to "buy the job" or, in some simpler cases, by an inability to use a linear payment scheme that has a non-zero constant term. The macroeconomic implications and their validity or lack thereof are not central to personnel economics, but the literature that grew up around efficiency wages is fundamentally one that uses personnel economic concepts as its primary motivating factor.

It is clear that incentive theory and compensation will continue to receive an enormous amount of attention in the economic literature, whether the studies examine CEO compensation (see Kevin J. Murphy's many papers on CEO compensation, e.g., Murphy 1985, Jensen and Murphy 1990, Murphy 1999) or pay as it relates to lower-level employees, as illustrated by Chapter 8 in this book.

The third part of this book discussed social interactions and personnel economics. The key observation in the chapters contained therein is that successful personnel management is not merely a question of motivating each individual worker and providing appropriate incentives to engage in work in isolation. Were that the case, there would be no reason for firms to exist in the first place. One could argue that the greatest value of the firm is that it provides mechanisms for people to work together and to take advantage of the complementarities in their skills and interests. As such, group incentives and group interaction are central. Chapters 10 and 11 of this book examine the interaction of workers in a social setting and how incentives and the organization of the firm would affect output in contexts where workers work with or against one another.

The literature on insider econometrics that began with Ichniowski, Shaw and Prennushi (1997) focuses on human resource practices and how those practices affect productivity within firms in a particular industry, in this case steel. The human resource practices that were examined often involved team incentives, communication between workers, training, and other aspects of the job that were done not in isolation, but rather with other individuals. Since then, there has been a significant empirical literature that has studied not only human resource practices but also team formation and production.

In one such example, Hamilton, Nickerson, and Owan (2003) study a garment manufacturer that switched the compensation scheme from individual piece rates to group-based incentives. Surprisingly, the most productive workers tended to be the ones who volunteered to join teams, and it was found that collaboration among those workers raised productivity. Again in the steel industry, Boning, Ichniowski and Shaw (2007) analyzed team production and found that productivity was higher at firms that used teams, and especially so in situations where the production process was complicated.

In my 1998 Paish Lecture to the Royal Economic Society (Lazear 1999b), I tried to describe the nature of complementarities within teams and focused on three factors: disjointedness, that is team members having different information sets; relevance, that is the different information that individuals possess must be useful to their teammates; and communication, which enables one team mate to transmit his or her information to the other one. One can envision that these attributes would be more important in more complex work environments and in those where workers tend to be more highly educated. But it is not only educated workers who seem to benefit from team production. Again the work by Bandiera, Barankay and Rasul is relevant here where teams were formed among agriculture workers (Bandiera, Barankay and Rasul 2009, 2010a, 2010b). Creating teams that may even be artificial in terms of productive complementarities can have effects on incentives, sometimes positive and sometimes negative.

The theoretical literature suggests that the effectiveness of team-based systems is likely to vary from firm to firm, as a result of the importance of complementarities. Indeed, several studies have shown that the adoption of progressive work place practices are correlated with one another and with productivity. See for example Black and Lynch (2001), Cappelli and Neumark (2001) and Bloom and Van Reenen (2007).

But team production is not necessary in order for peer interaction to be interesting and important. This has already been demonstrated in a variety of settings, both experimental and empirical. For example, Falk and Ichino (2006) find significant peer effects in an experiment where subjects were given the mundane task of stuffing envelopes under a fixed wage scheme. There are no direct complementarities involved here; production is individual, not team. Still, productivity was higher when individuals worked in the same room with another person than when they worked in isolation, reflecting peer effects. Furthermore, the positive effects of being combined with a fast person outlaid the negative effects of being combined with a slow person. Similarly, Mas and Moretti (2009) demonstrate that supermarket clerks are affected by the productivity of other clerks working at the same time.

Another form of interaction involves relative performance evaluation, either in the context of piece rate pay that is indexed by some metric of common shocks or by tournament pay. I have already discussed empirical and subsequent theoretical literature that relates to the early tournament work. So here I focus primarily on work that discusses relative performance evaluation in a bonus or other context. Perhaps the most prevalent form of compensation that relates to teams is paying workers in stock or in stock options. Because the value of a firm's stock depends not on one single worker's productivity but instead on the output of the entire firm, workers are tied to one another when payment takes the form of stock. But workers own only a very small part of the firm, and that is true in most contexts, even for the highest level employees in the organization. How can it be then that stock is used as a motivator for workers in a team setting? Oyer (2004) discusses this issue. He views stock as a way to vary pay as business cycle and other conditions change that affect the value of work in the firm. If a worker is paid in the form of stock options, those options become relatively less valuable in periods when the firm is worth less, which is also the time during which the firm would be less averse to losing the worker. In good times, when the firm wants to keep the worker, the value of stock options, which are then in or closer to being in the money, is likely to be higher. The greater value of the stock options results in greater incentives to stay with the firm. There are also self-selection reasons for using stock and stock options. The motivation for this dates back to Salop and Salop (1976) and is discussed in a more modern fashion in Lazear (2004c). Oyer and Schaefer (2005) and Bergman and Jenter (2007) examine possible rationales for using stock as a payment method. Oyer and Schaefer, in particular, try to distinguish between different motivations and come down on the side of sorting and retention as opposed to motivation.

Although stock and stock options are of growing importance in compensation, relative performance evaluation and pay based on it is rare. This is somewhat surprising because risk theories of compensation imply that compensation should be based on relative performance when there is common noise. Why is it that workers are not insulated from externally observable shocks over which they have no control? The lack of relative pay (except through tournaments) is documented by a variety of authors. Murphy (1999) summarizes much of the literature on CEO compensation. Bertrand and Mullainathan (2001) detail the lack of relative performance evaluation in setting compensation.

Indeed, it is not only the failure to observe relative performance evaluation that seems to contradict the insurance/incentive models. Those models have a large number of implications specifying where one should and where one should not observe pay that is based on output. In particular, one would not expect to see high levels of output-contingent pay in industries in which there is a great deal of risk. In a series of papers, Prendergast argues that this is contradicted by the facts. He provides a series of theoretical possibilities for why this may be the case. Much of this revolves around observability and the necessity to pay on the basis of performance in highly volatile industries because those are the situations in which the agent has the most local information (see Prendergast 2000, 2002a, 2002b).

It is clear that the literature on peer effects, team work, relative performance evaluation, and other kinds of social interactions will be a lasting part of personnel economics. That literature is likely to blossom over subsequent years as more relevant data becomes available.

The final part of the book discusses skill formation and its implications for personnel economics. In many respects, this is the oldest and also the newest area of personnel economics. Human capital theory precedes personnel economics by about 15 years, and now personnel economics has begun to focus on human capital, its acquisition, incentives in the human capital producing industry, and how all of this affects worker–firm relations.

The chapters of the book devoted to this topic cover a few different ideas. Chapter 14 and 15 discussed the building of skills and incentives in their formation. There have been a large number of papers in the education literature that look at the incentive effects that particular programs create for students and teachers. Victor Lavy is one of the leading figures here and has written a number of papers on the topic of incentives in the education industry and their effects. In one of the more recent ones, Lavy (2009) finds that the introduction of rewards for teachers improves student performance in high school matriculation exams. He also finds that these gains seem real in that there was not any evidence of specific "teaching to the test" as is the concern of Chapter 14. Related work by Angrist and Lavy (2009) finds small effects of the particular incentive program, but significant positive effects for students in a marginal category. This is an important point. It is often the case that tests of incentive effects, or treatment effects in general, focus on the outcomes for the mean of a large group rather than for particular subgroups of the population. Especially in the context of education, it may be more important to examine the progress made by certain groups, for example, disadvantaged students. It is important to identify those who are most affected by educational investments. Indeed, the highest rate of return for investments in education may come from confining attention to particular groups of students, and the personnel economics approach is well-suited to exploring these relationships, both at the theoretical level and to testing it empirically.

Interesting work by Duflo, Hanna and Ryan (2008) analyzes the effects of monitoring and financial incentives on teacher performance and, in particular, teacher labor supply. By examining data from India, Duflo, Hanna and Ryan are able to identify in the context of a structural model the effects of programs that change the reward to being at work for teachers. They find these effects to be significant. In particular, the treatments improve child learning that occurs in the classrooms.

Glewwe, Ilias and Kremer (2008) do a similar analysis for teacher absenteeism and its effects on student performance in Kenya. They find that students who were in programs where schools had attempted to induce teachers to increase their labor supply performed better on exams during the program period. They also are concerned about issues of "teaching to the test" and raise the point that student performance was not persistent. One of the disadvantages of the Kenya programs is that there was reversion to lower levels of performance after the program ended. Finally, work by Muralidharan and Sundararaman (2008) has examined the effect of different kinds of labor on production in the educational environment. In this context, the issue is heterogeneity in labor and how using different kinds of inputs affects the production function. There are many personnel economic issues in this work that involve matching and sorting, as well as incentives.

It is clear that the burgeoning education and personnel literature will be fertile ground for additional research. Not only does it lend itself to testing and clear availability of data but it is among the more important industries in the economy. The production of human capital affects the outcomes of many other production processes.

In Chapter 16, a new theory of entrepreneurship was presented. This theory has already been tested in a number of different countries and contexts. For example, Wagner (2003, 2006) examines the creation of entrepreneurs in German data and finds that the jack-of-all-trades theory holds up. Silva (2007), using data from Italian families, finds similar results, but argues that most of this has to do with innate ability.[1] Still, the specific interpretations of the jack-of-all-trades model are somewhat less important than the basic notion that well-rounded individuals are more likely to become entrepreneurs, whether they become well-rounded because of the skills they acquire or whether they are simply born with a series of well-rounded traits. Astebro and Thompson (2009) examine Canadian data. They also find that diversity in occupational background increases the probability of becoming a successful entrepreneur. Astebro and Thompson focus on the distinction between returns to variety and diversity in skills.[2]

The inference that one draws from this growing new literature is that the jack-of-all-trades model provides a variety of testable implications. The area of entrepreneurship and understanding its contributing factors will likely become increasingly important over the next decade or so. Personnel economics and the methodology therein have helped inform that literature.

Conclusion

This book has attempted to provide an overview of some of my work in the area of personnel economics. Although I was one of the early researchers in the field, I was hardly alone. Many others have been key contributors to our understanding of the way in which firms and workers interact. Personnel economics focuses primarily on interactions between the firm and worker that involve incentives, matching and sorting of workers to firms, compensation, skill development, and the actual organization of work. We have already learned a great deal about these areas that were essentially unexplored two to three decades ago. Personnel economics promises to produce many important new ideas in the years to come.

Notes

Part II

What Is Personnel Economics?

1   Much of this section is taken directly from Lazear, E. P. (2000a). The Future of Personnel Economics, in: Economic Journal, 110(467): F611-39.
2   Early papers in the agency literature include Johnson (1950), Cheung (1969), and Ross (1973). Contract theory grew out of macroeconomic inquiries, reflected in papers by Baily (1977), Azariadis (1975) and Gordon (1974). Finally, Alchian and Demsetz's (1972) important work on monitoring helped frame the discussion.
3   See Rosen (1974).

Part III

Chapter 1

1   See Gordon (1960), Kreps (1961), National Industrial Conference Board (1964), and U.S. Department of Health, Education, and Welfare (1976) for some commonly offered explanations of mandatory retirement.
2   Given this definition, the institution of term contracts with up-or-out employment arrangements (i.e., arrangements where the worker is either promoted or forced to leave the firm) is a form of mandatory-retirement contract. The model to be presented in this chapter could be applied to the analysis of that problem as well. In a theoretical paper by Freeman (1977), retirement and promotion decisions are linked. His model will not, per se, yield mandatory retirement, however. The reason is that in his framework there is no reason to distinguish between lump sums at critical time points and smooth payment streams with the same present value. The former will not yield mandatory retirement as it is commonly used.
3   This assumes that the worker can borrow and lend at rate r. To the extent that this does not hold, a utility-maximizing framework must replace the wealth-maximizing one. The fundamental analysis and its conclusions, although somewhat more complex, remain essentially the same.
4   That is, the worker is "mandatorily retired" at T. This is not the same as saying that the worker leaves the firm at T. He is retired from his old contract, but not necessarily from his old firm. For example, at age 65 many professors are mandatorily retired from their former contracts and renegotiate a new contract frequently called

"emeritus." The wage rate changes, as do the working conditions. In this case, the worker stays with the former firm. In most cases, however, "mandatory retirement" will be coupled with firm-worker separation as well. The reason is that at T when renegotiation occurs, it is no longer necessarily the case that the worker-firm match and corresponding working conditions (hours, flexibility, effort, etc.) that were optimal between 0 and T will also be optimal between T and retirement (or death). For example, older workers may want shorter and more flexible hours with limited responsibility (or they may want zero hours of work, i.e., retirement). This is not necessarily the type of work conditions/wage trade-off that they would choose between 0 and T. If not, T will be characterized by a reshuffling of workers among firms. What is crucial is the termination of the former contract.

5   Papers which have dealt with this issue are Becker and Stigler (1974) and Stiglitz (1975).

6   This is a result rather than an assumption. It is true because any worker who finds it optimal to cheat at $t = t_0$ will cheat with certainty at $t > t_0$. Therefore, the firm gains by replacing him with a worker whose probability of cheating is less than one at that point.

7   "Unintentional" is in quotes because the value of bankruptcy depends upon how much the firm owes workers and so is at least in part endogenous.

8   It is a trivial extension of the model to allow the worker a probability of detection less than one. In the terminology below, $R(t)$ is merely replaced by $R(t)P$, where P is the probability of detection.

9   The $c(t)$ may be zero or positive. One example is the loss suffered when the worker takes customers with him upon his departure.

10 Available from author upon request.

11 The Becker-Stigler (1974) solution is a special case of this general form.

12 Again, available from the author upon request.

13 See Fama (1980) on this point.

14 This suggests that a firm with an unanticipated decrease in its horizon will be more likely to cheat on workers. Thus, one may expect to find that the incidence of pension default and early termination is higher in declining industries.

15 An alternative justification for a wage profile which rises more steeply than VMP is risk aversion coupled with uncertainty about VMP. If some workers will have low VMPs in the future relative to others, but neither workers nor firms can identify these workers initially, workers will prefer to buy "insurance" from the firm. This notion is related to the insurance ideas of Baily (1974), Azariadis (1975), Grossman (1978), and the self-selection analyses of Rothschild and Stiglitz (1976) and Salop and Salop (1976). The empirical evidence, however, is at odds with this view and so I only mention it in passing.

16 What is observable to the economist may be much more limited than that which is observable to the employer. It is the latter that is relevant. We are, unfortunately, restricted to the former.

17 It has been suggested that this view explicitly characterizes the Japanese labor market. Mandatory retirement takes place at age 55 after a long-term contract with the firm has been completed. Often, renegotiation takes place and the worker remains with the firm after 55 (see e.g. Hashimoto 1979).

18 Unfortunately, data on piece-rate vs. time-rate compensation are very difficult to obtain. They are unavailable in the data set used below in this study.

19 It should be pointed out, however, that there are many other models of mandatory retirement which generate the same structure of preferences. On the other hand, Ehrenberg (1980) finds that firefighters and policemen who have mandatory-retirement provisions also obtain higher wages. This is consistent with this model.

20 This variable actually understates the true incidence of mandatory retirement. Some retirement is mandatory as a result of pension schemes which essentially prevent anyone from continuing to work past 65. For example, mandatory retirement is likely to be unnecessary in a firm that offers no pension to individuals who leave the firm after age 65, and a full salary pension to those who leave at 65.

This points out that the mandatory-retirement response is itself a function of price. Some attempt to deal with response bias is made below.

21   The reversal in signs on the urban variable may reflect the fact that information is easier to obtain in small towns and there is, therefore, less need for payment schemes which require mandatory retirement.

Chapter 2

1   This analysis marries the models presented in Lazear (1981) and Hall and Lazear (1984).
2   A more general formulation allows the severance payment to vary with the identity of the party who initiates the separation. Hall and Lazear (1984) consider this case and discuss its drawbacks.
3   That the entire remaining stream must be examined is recognized in Fields and Mitchell (1981). Bulow (1981) also points out (as my calculations implicitly do) that the "true" current wage also includes the value of changing the pension as the result of working that period.
4   See also Burkhauser and Quinn (1983).
5   E.g., for some ages the mean rises even though no one plan ever rose. The nonlinearities make some plans fall by less than others.
6   There was only one matched defined-contribution plan.
7   To name a few, see Azariadis (1983), Arnott and Stiglitz (1981), Green and Kahn (1983), Grossman and Hart (1981, 1983).

Chapter 3

1   See Lazear (1987). Gavin (1986) also looks at the theoretical effects of severance pay legislation, but ignores the ability to contract around the constraint. Emerson (1988) too ignores that possibility, but his work comes closest to the analysis presented here. He uses similar sources of information and categorizes the countries, but provides no estimates of the effects based on his data. Still, his evidence is striking. His Table 1 (p. 781) shows Italy as having the smallest percentage of employees holding jobs for less than two years. The United States has the largest. Italy probably has the most restrictive job security rules, and the United States the least.
2   Much of this material is taken directly from Lazear (1987).
3   A period is defined such that no new information (and therefore decisions about work) becomes available within it.
4   Data were collected from the Annuaire Statistique de la Belgique of the Institut National de Statistique (1985), Annuario Statistico Italiano of the Instituto Centrale di Statistico (1974-1984), Aronstein (1976), Blanpain (various years), Information Canada, Canada Yearbook (various years), Demographic Yearbook of the United Nations (various years), Employment and Unemployment (1986), Handbook of Labor Statistics (1985), Japan Statistical Yearbook (various years), Labor Force Statistics of the OECD (various years), ILO, Legislative Series (various years), National Accounts Statistics of the United Nations (1967, 1983), National Accounts of the OECD (1984, 1986), Norton and Kennedy (1985), Portugal Annuario Estatistico of the Instituto Nacional de Estatistica Servicos Centrais (1978), Statistical Abstract of Israel of the Central Bureau of Statistics (various years), Statistical Yearbook for Asia and the Pacific of the United Nations (various years), Statistical Yearbook of Finland of the Central Statistical Office (various years), Statistical Yearbook of the Netherlands (1979), Statistiches Jahrbuch für die Bundesrepublik Deutschland of the Federal Statistical Office (various years), World

Tables (1980, 1982), and Yearbook of Labor Statistics (various years).

5   A more formal way to test the assumptions that underlie the random effects model is given by Hausman and Taylor (1981). One version of the test uses the information in the within-country regressions (Table 3.5) and compares them with the overall regression (Table 3.2).

6   This argument is complementary with the insider-outsider model, exposited by Lindbeck and Snower (1986). Severance pay and notice requirements provide a reason for distinguishing between insiders and outsiders.

7   Emerson (1988) makes a related, but different point. He says that in Europe, part-timers and full-timers are treated more equally so one would expect more part-timers in United States. He finds this among youth, but also points out some European deviations and large variance among European countries. The estimates in this paper play on the cross-country and intertemporal variations in hours of work.

Chapter 4

1   Our selection of issues is guided by the empirical papers in Rogers and Streeck (1995) and the interviews conducted by Richard Freeman and Joel Rogers in the winter of 1991-92 with management officials at various U.S.-owned subsidiaries and other multinationals having experience with works councils in Europe and with some union officials and works councillors, as well.

2   By our definition Spanish works councils, which can legally call strikes, are de facto local unions rather than works councils.

3   We are grateful to Peter Crampton for pointing this out.

4   The reader will notice that this contradicts the Coase theorem in which two parties to an arrangement are expected to attain the joint surplus through some means or other. By giving the two sides only one tool to produce the joint surplus and divide it, we have ruled out such an arrangement.

5   In Germany, respondents gave cases in which councils would trade off their legal right to codetermine the timing of vacations or the need for them to gain the right to approve a social plan for redundancies for wages or benefits beyond those in the industry agreement.

6   There are several complexities that we do not address. A system that sets the level of compensation outside the firm and has no profit sharing might be viewed as giving councils no way to raise workers' well-being. In fact, in countries with relatively centralized bargaining, firms can pay wages above the central agreement, and stronger councils are likely to make gains in this way. But councils cannot push too far in light of the central agreement. In addition, with pay fixed, workers can still benefit from increasing the surplus if that means faster promotions and the like.

7   The Freeman-Rogers interviews showed that large European firms obey the spirit as well as the letter of information and consultation laws. Note also that councillors receive some information on a confidential basis, so that it does not become known to competitors.

8   In the United States, Kleiner and Bouillon (1988) show that information does not in fact harm profitability.

9   Under the conditions of the model that we describe shortly, firms have an incentive to lie about the state of the world, knowing that workers will choose an F or N strategy.

10   The firm's ability to commit to a nonrevelation strategy is key. Ex post, firms in bad states want to show their books to workers. But doing so makes the absence of a report a signal that the good state must hold. Firms may be able to commit to nonrevelation by hiring a third party to keep the books. Alternatively, separating the human resource department from the accounting department and giving the latter incentives to withhold information from workers may solve the problem.

11   This assumes that the real resource costs of disclosure do not exceed the social gain from disclosure. The real costs are auditing the books to ensure accuracy and training workers to read the books. There is also the risk that information revealed to workers may find its way to rivals who can use it to firms' detriment, which may or may not have social costs.

12   The formal proof of these propositions relies on the monotonicity of the binomial density function. The key ingredient is that the binomial is monotone increasing for $x < (n + 1)p$ and monotone decreasing for $x > (n + 1)p$.

13   What about alternatives to councils, such as votes (referenda) on issues? There are two advantages to using a council instead of general voting. First, as the management quote given at the outset indicates, it should be cheaper to canvas 10 representative workers than to survey an entire workforce. Second, votes do not register strength of preferences very well. Oral communication in the council setting may provide management with a better sense of how strongly each side's views are held.

14   If some randomly selected delegates do not want to serve, they could be given the right to name a substitute from the same group. The substitute would likely have similar views and might be chosen because he or she is a more able spokesperson.

15   The color-green example differs from their cases, however, because the optimal solution when workers face unusual plant-level circumstances is for management to delegate to workers the authority to respond. Consultation rather than on-the-spot treatment of problems requires that management can also contribute to the solution, for instance by bringing other information to bear on the problem or by changing investments or coordinating activities that lie under its control. This is more likely when shocks have a pattern, permitting a general solution to the problem.

16   See e.g. Kennan (1979) and Hall and Lazear (1984).

Chapter 5

1   It is also true that those who are denied promotion do better after they are turned down than they did before the decision was made, for the same reason.

2   Two recent papers on this topic, Faria (2000) and Fairburn and Malcomson (2001), use an approach very different from the one in this chapter and from each other. The Peter principle is a byproduct of using promotion to solve a moral hazard problem in Fairburn and Malcomson. Rather than motivate through money, which induces influence activity, firms choose promotion because then managers must live with the consequences of their decisions. Too many workers are promoted under certain circumstances, resulting in a Peter principle effect. In Faria's paper, workers have two skills. Those who are good at one are necessarily less good at another when on the frontier. Faria argues that this is what is meant by the Peter principle.

3   The structure is a variant of the Jovanovic (1979a, 1979b) model that was modified and used in a context closer to this structure in Lazear (1986a).

4   This production structure is similar to that used in a comprehensive analysis by Gibbons and Waldman (1999b), who also allow for transitory and permanent components with regression. The focus of their paper is earnings and promotion. Neither optimal decision making by firms given the transitory component nor strategic effort in response to promotion rules is central to their discussion.

5   This amounts to assuming that

$$\int_{-\infty}^{\infty}\int_{-\infty}^{\infty}[\alpha + \beta(A + \varepsilon)]dGdF > \int_{-\infty}^{\infty}\int_{-\infty}^{\infty}[\gamma + \delta(A + \varepsilon)]dGdF.$$

6   The notation ε_1 and A could be swapped in the discussion above to show that $E(A|A + \varepsilon_1 > A^*) > E(A)$.

7   I am indebted to Wing Suen for this derivation.

8   Gibbons and Waldman (1999a) and Prendergast (1999) survey the large literature on careers and promotions.

9   Anderson, Dubinsky and Mehta (1999) claim that the data reveal a Peter principle for sales managers because the skills needed by salespeople are generally distinctly different from those needed by sales managers.

10   One difference between this interpretation of the Peter principle and the one used in the rest of this paper is that the output of those not promoted does not rise under the job-specific interpretation. Since ε_1 is a job-specific effect and not a transitory component, those who are not promoted have ability $A + \varepsilon_1$ in both periods.

11   In a competitive market with a rising supply price for workers (because they are distinguished by ability), firms earn zero profit. The marginal worker is the one for whom ability A_0 is low enough that $\alpha + \beta(A_0 + \mu) - C(\mu) = 0$.

12   Here again, Rosen is instrumental. The first paper on the subject is Lazear and Rosen (1981), Chapter 6 in this volume.

13   Data from Teichner and Luehrman (1992) establish clearly that revenues are lower and costs higher on sequels than they are on the original on which they are based. See e.g. their exhibits 4 and 5.

14   A countervailing effect is the notoriety that is created by the first film, which makes it easier to sell tickets on the sequel than on the original. Even if consumers understand that the sequel is worse than the original, more tickets might be sold on the sequel if, say, the actors and director are not well known before the first film is made.

15   Winner's curse usually relates to a reading relative to others' readings rather than the time dimension of taking multiple readings, sometimes in different settings. The transitory vs. permanent component is central to the discussion of this chapter, but not the theme of most of the winner's curse literature. Actually, loser's curse is as important to the assignment problem as winner's curse. In the job context, the goal is to assign a worker to the right job. Workers who do not satisfy the promotion criterion are, on average, undervalued just as those who are promoted are overvalued. The optimal selection of the cutoff point trades off the two kinds of errors.

16   The discount rate is assumed to be zero.

17   Since μ_2 is independent of A, there is always an A sufficiently low to make this condition hold.

Part IV

Chapter 6

1   In this chapter the worker has no choice over σ. This does not affect the risk-neutral solution but does have an effect if workers are risk averse, since they tend to favor overly cautious strategies. Also, virtually all the results of this chapter hold true if the error structure is multiplicative rather than additive.

2   However, it is not necessarily true that there is a solution because with arbitrary density functions the objective function may not be concave in the relevant

range. It is possible to show that a pure strategy solution exists provided that σ^2 is sufficiently large: Contests are feasible only when chance is a significant factor. This result accords with intuition and is in the spirit of the old saying that a (sufficient) difference of opinion is necessary for a horse race. Stated otherwise, since $\partial P/\partial \mu_j = g'(\mu_j - \mu_k)$ and $g(\cdot)$ is a pdf, $\partial^2 P/\partial \mu_j^2 = g'(\mu_j - \mu_k)$ may be positive, and fulfillment of second-order conditions in (4) implies sharp breaks in the reaction function. If σ^2 is small enough the breaks occur at very low levels of investment, and a Nash equilibrium in pure strategies will not exist. Existence of an equilibrium is assumed in all that follows.

3   If ε is a fixed effect, there is additional information from knowing the identity of winners and losers. The expected productivity of a winner is $\mu + E(\varepsilon_j | \, q_j > q_k)$, while that of a loser is $\mu + E(\varepsilon_j | \, q_j < q_k)$. In a one-period contest there is no possibility of taking advantage of this information. However, in a sequential contest with no firm–specific capital, the information would be valuable and would constrain subsequent wage payments in successive rounds through competition from other firms. It is not difficult to show that this does not affect the general nature of the bond-gamble solution. Alternatively, if the investment has firm-specific elements or firms adopt policies that bind workers to it (as in Chapter 1 in this volume), these restrictions do not necessarily apply.

4   The level of the standard is indeterminate, since for any $\bar{q}$ a corresponding spread can be chosen to achieve the optimal investment. This is also true of contests among more than two players. With N contestants, the prizes of $N - 2$ of them are indeterminate. When risk neutrality is dropped, the indeterminacy vanishes in both cases.

5   The reader is reminded that throughout this section and the next workers are identical a priori and differ only ex post through the realization of ε. In the real world, where there is population heterogeneity, market participants are sorted into different contests. There players (and horses, for that matter) who are known to be of higher quality ex ante may play in games with higher stakes. If it can be accomplished, the sorting is by anticipated marginal products. In that sense, pay differences among contestants of known quality resemble the effect of a "piece rate." These issues are more thoroughly discussed below.

6   One might think that risks could be pooled among groups of workers through sharing agreements, but that is false because of moral hazard. A worker would never agree to share prizes since doing so would result in $\mu = 0$, and consequently $E(q_j + q_k) = 0$ and bankruptcy for the firm. As a result, firms offering tournaments or piece rates in the pure sense yield higher expected utility than the sharing arrangement.

7   The following is similar to a problem analyzed by Stiglitz (1975). A linear piece-rate structure is a simplification. A more general structure would allow for nonlinear piece rates (see Mirrlees 1976).

8   Furthermore, $r \doteq V/(1 + sC''\sigma^2)$ and $I \doteq sV^2\sigma^2/(1 + sC''\sigma^2)^2$, so that $r = V$ and $I = 0$ in the case of risk neutrality ($s = 0$). All these approximations use first-order expansions for terms in $U'(\cdot)$ and second-order expansions for terms in $U(\cdot)$. The same is true of the approximations below for the tournament.

9   Futhermore, $C'(\mu^*) \doteq g(0)(W_1 - W_2)$, so the spread is still crucial for investment incentives, as in the risk-neutral case.

10 Since $\gamma = V\mu - C(\mu)$, and since μ is below the wealth-maximizing level of μ when workers are risk averse, lower μ implies lower γ because revenue falls by more than cost.

11 Playing against a standard is like Mirrlees's (1976) notion of an "instruction." It is clear that using standards as well as piece rates must be superior to using one alone. That scheme would allow workers to be paid $\bar{I}$ if $q < \bar{q}$ and $I_0 + rq$ for $q \geq \bar{q}$. This is important because it truncates the possibilities when $Vq < 0$. Given the technology, it is possible that very large negative values of output can occur, and since it is impossible always to tax workers the full extent of this loss, some form of truncation is desirable. A contest is an alternative way to control the tails of this distribution.

Chapter 7

1   See Chapter 6 in this volume, Nalebuff and Stiglitz (1983), Holmström (1982), Green and Stokey (1983).
2   See Chapter 1, Lazear (1981) and Harris and Holmström (1982).
3   Pencavel (1977) discusses some of the same issues that are addressed in this chapter. He also provides some evidence on punch-press operators in Chicago. Seiler (1984) presents empirical evidence based on 100,000 employees in the footwear industry.
4   It is not arbitrary that θ is borne by all workers during the initial period rather than by the stayers alone during the last $1 - t$ of the career. Even if workers are risk neutral, putting the cost θ on the last periods results in inefficient separation, whereas having it borne up front does not. That is, if

$$W_{1-t} = (1 - t)q - \gamma\theta,$$

where γ is chosen to arrive at zero profit, the worker leaves whenever

$$\overline{w} > q - \left(\frac{\gamma}{(1 - t)}\right)\theta.$$

For efficiency, he should leave only if $\overline{w} > q$, so too many leave.
5   Even though θ may only provide private information to the firm, the assumption is that the firm does not renege on the contract, so the promise to pay q if q is observed is kept. Reputation or morale costs associated with violation of the contract may rationalize this assumption.
6   The choice of the optimal sample period is a sequential search problem (see Wald 1947, 1950) and is not addressed here. The idea is that lengthening the number of periods over which the output is sampled before a decision is made provides a more precise estimate of $\hat{q}$ and reduces the amount of incorrect sorting mistakes. The cost is that some workers with very low q work at the piece-rate firm longer than would be necessary. The optimum is likely to take the following form. Examine $\hat{q}$ in the first period. If $q_1 < \hat{q}$, then retain the worker for at least one more period. After the second period, if some function of $\hat{q}$ in period 1 and $\hat{q}$ in period 2 exceeds some q_2, then retain the worker for another period, and so forth. The point is that there will be a tenure-specific standard based on the worker's history of estimated output below which output cannot fall without inducing a termination. See Harris and Weiss (1981) and Weiss (1984).
7   This result is akin to Riley's (1975) argument in the context of screening that the least able worker never signals ability to employers. Thus, salary firms devote zero resources to screening. It may depend on the discrete nature of θ, however. If monitoring can take place α of the time, and a straight salary paid $(1 - \alpha)$ of the time, then, by selecting different α's, firms may be able to upset the equilibrium. If an equilibrium exists with firms other than straight salary payers, the implication is that as α increases, the average quality in the firm rises.
8   Because the form of $C(E)$ is free, any production function can always be reduced to $q = E$ with an appropriate redefinition of $C(E)$.
9   A similar argument holds for $\overline{E} > E^*$.
10 Stiglitz (1975) derives optimal piece rates that trade insurance for efficiency.
11 Rogerson (1988) has treated a similar problem in a slightly different context. The problem is analogous to the problem of a division manager spending too much this year because next year's budget depends positively on this year's expenditure.
12 This ignores the possibility of tilting the entire age-earnings profile such that all workers receive more than the value of their output in the later years (see Chapter 1).
13 Mixed strategies are assumed away.
14 A similar analysis applies for the setting of standards based on last period's output. Its effects, too, can be offset to yield efficiency. This analysis relates very closely to

Notes

the literature on setting quotas in a planned economy. The analysis here is most similar to Weitzman's (1980) analysis of the "ratchet effect." Freixas, Guesnerie, and Tirole (1985) have extended the general theory to consider cases in which the planner does not commit himself to an intertemporal incentive scheme at the start. Earlier papers on the same issue include Yunker (1973), Fan (1975), Bonin (1976), and Weitzman (1976).

15   There is a problem in that those jobs for which output measures are not easily obtainable will, simply because of errors in variables, have c_i coefficients that are biased toward zero.

Chapter 8

1   See Chapter 7 for a detailed discussion of when to pay a piece rate, which is defined to be payment on the basis of output. Also, Fama (1991) discusses other reasons for paying on the basis of some measured time interval. Baker (1992) discusses the difficulties created by pay-for-performance structures when measurement is a problem. A very early discussion of the incentive effects of piece rates can be found in Slichter (1928, Chapter 13).

2   See, for example, Ashenfelter and Pencavel (1976), Seiler (1984), Brown (1992), and Booth and Frank (1996), who look at compensation method and resulting income. Pencavel (1977), Brown and Philips (1986), Goldin (1986), Brown (1990), and Drago and Heywood (1995) examine choice of compensation scheme and changes in pay for performance over time.

3   There are some attempts to examine the effect of incentives on productivity. Sue Fernie and Metcalf (1999) find that when payment is contingent on performance, jockeys perform better than when payment is unrelated to performance. Also, Paarsch and Shearer (1997) find that tree planters in British Columbia produce higher levels of output when paid piece rates, but that they become fatigued more rapidly.

4   The hypothesis was first stated by Deci (1971). Early evidence supporting the claim in the area of child development is presented by Lepper, Greene, and Nisbett (1973).

5   To do this, simply solve for the efficient level of effort per hour, which sets the marginal cost of effort equal to the marginal value of effort. Require that level of effort as the minimum standard for the job. Then, set the hourly wage just high enough to attract workers to the firm.

6   A more complete version of the model is available in Lazear (1996b).

7   Rents are higher on the current job for higher-ability workers in that the more able accomplish the task more easily. But other firms need not constrain all workers to earn the same amount. It is for this reason that some high-ability workers may choose to work elsewhere. If opportunities outside are sufficiently bad, all workers with $A > A_0$ would work at this firm and $A_h = \infty$. It is also possible that there are multiple crossings. These are assumed away for analytic convenience.

8   "Ability" can be read "ambition" in the interpretation of A. Nothing is changed.

9   Define $X = g(e, A)$ as the inverse of (2). Then it can be shown that Condition 1 and Condition 2 hold as long as $\partial g(e, A)/\partial A < 0$, $\partial g(e, A)/\partial e > 0$, and $\partial U(Y, X)\partial X^2 > 0$ all hold.

10   The condition that some workers continue to opt for the guaranteed wage is not superfluous. If all workers opt for the piece rate, then it is possible that even very low ability workers who did not work before now work for the firm. Their addition could actually result in a lowering of average ability.

11   Only observations where workers were on one pay regime or the other for the full month are used. Partial month observations are deleted.

12   This number includes within-worker components as well as between-worker components. The latter is of interest and is investigated in more detail below.

480

13 The fact that actual pay has only risen slightly after the switch to PPP than before reflects the phase-in pattern of the PPP program. Lower-wage areas were brought into the program first, which means that the PPP = 1 data are dominated by lower-wage markets. This pattern also affects the differences between piece-rate and hourly wage output if early switchers to PPP have different average output levels than late switchers to PPP.

14 The Hawthorne effect, named after the Hawthorne Western Electric Plant in Illinois, alleges that any change is likely to bring about short-term gains in productivity.

15 The term "average" is used cautiously. The sample contains different numbers of observations at each tenure level so that the average picks up not only nonlinearities, but different tenure effects for different types of individuals that may be more or less heavily weighted in the sample.

16 Taken literally, the theory implies that none of the low-output incumbents should leave since the guarantee makes them no worse off than before, but some higher-quality workers are now willing to take the job.

17 This is done so that no mechanical connection between low output per week and separation would exist as a result of leaving in the middle of a week.

18 Note that the turnover rates in Table 8.4 are lower than the one reported in Table 8.1. This is because in order to be in the sample for Table 8.4, the worker must have been with the firm during the previous month as well. Thus, those who leave during their first month are included in Table 8.1 but not in Table 8.4.

19 The bias is caused by the standard errors-in-variables problem, where the observed independent variable is not the true effect, but instead the true effect plus measurement error.

20 The relation of ability to output need not be monotonic, especially during the hourly wage period. Since the lowest- and highest-ability workers, A_0 and A_h, earn no rents, they should be least concerned about losing their jobs. Middle-ability workers earn rents and may therefore put forth additional effort to reduce the likelihood of a termination.

21 Part of this difference may reflect pure selection that would occur even in the absence of a regime change. Presumably, the tenure variable included in the output regression controls for most of the regime-independent sorting.

22 The difference between this sample and the previous one is that the former sample included those who left before piece-rate-based fixed effects could be estimated.

23 The model in Figure 8.1, taken literally, implies that there should be holes in the data, which are not found. There are a number of possible explanations. First, workers may try to get into the piece-rate range and fail. Second, since the unit of measurement is a month, there may be some weeks during which the worker hits the piece-rate range and others where he does not, averaging out to some amount between 2.5 and 5 units. Third, the worker may not guess e_0 perfectly, and this creates variance around e_0. Finally, there may be other reasons to exceed the minimum level of output.

24 The firm's earnings are up substantially since the switch to piece rates, but this could reflect other factors as well.

25 This was not always so. Whenever a firm switches from one pay system to another, it is almost certain that one system does not maximize profit.

26 See Chapter 7 and Baker (1992).

27 Asch (1990) examines the effects of compensation schemes on military recruiter performance with a focus on quality dimensions. As recruiters receive incentive pay for signing up recruits, there is a tendency to take lower-quality applicants.

28 See Chapter 10 below for a discussion of the effects of peer pressure and norms in an organization.

29 There are two advantages of assigning the re-work to the shop rather than the individual. First, the customer gets faster service since it is unnecessary to wait for the availability of the original installer. Second, some workers will have already separated from the firm before the defect is noticed. Assigning the work to the shop

deals with this problem. Neither argument provides a rationale for forcing the rework to be done by others without pay.

30 The NLSY is a nationally representative sample of 12,686 young men and young women who were 14 to 22 years of age when they were first surveyed in 1979.

Chapter 9

1 These factors may include race, sex, ethnic background, and family ties.

2 See, for example, Doeringer and Piore (1971), Thurow (1972), and Reder (1955).

3 The major references here are Becker (1962, 1975) and Mincer (1962).

4 See Murphy (1984).

5 See Chapter 6, Nalebuff and Stiglitz (1983), and Green and Stokey (1983) for examples.

6 See Carmichael (1983a).

7 See Baily (1974), Gordon (1974), and Azariadis (1975) as well as Grossman and Hart (1981) and Rosen (1986).

8 See Miller (1982) and Rosen (1982) on hierarchies; see Sah and Stiglitz (1986) on organizations.

9 See Abowd and Ashenfelter (1981).

10 See Antos and Rosen (1975).

11 This is the approach used in Lazear and Rosen (1990) to examine male-female wage differences. There, the investment profiles of jobs are determined ex ante, although the number of individuals assigned to each type is endogenous.

12 See Groshen (1991) and Blau (1984).

13 See Chapter 1 and Lazear (1981).

14 See Mincer and Jovanovic (1981), Gronau (1988), and Hall (1982).

15 The literature on heterogeneity in the labor market is large. One of the early studies in this field is Heckman and Willis (1977).

16 Leonard (1989) has found elsewhere that entry into high-level positions in some major U.S. corporations is quite common. Although related, this observation is somewhat different from the question posed here. Entry may be high, but still much lower at top jobs than at lower-level jobs. Leonard also states that, in his data, entry from outside is commoner at higher levels in the hierarchy. His evidence, however, applies more to turnover rates and tenure than to career paths. He states, "Nine or ten levels down, less than 5% of all managers were hired from 1981 to 1985. But between two and seven levels down, more than 17% of all managers joined the firm in the past five years." This comparison may reflect higher turnover rates at levels two through seven or more new jobs at those levels. The evidence is suggestive but it does not directly apply to the importance of internal labor markets.

17 This formula is derived thus: A year consists of 365.25 days or $365.25/7 = 52.1786$ weeks. Each week has 40 work hours, and so the work year $= 2,087.14$ hours, meaning that an average month has $2,087.14/12 = 173.93$ hours.

18 See McCue (1990). She uses these data to examine the determinants of promotion and the general effects of promotion on wage growth. Hers is among the few studies that even considers the job as an important unit of analysis.

19 Of course, using the wrong cut could actually obscure relevant mobility. For example, if the fifth digit referred to level within a job track, much of the movement might be from one fifth-level job to another fifth-level job within the same fourth-level job. As you will see, this firm has significant job mobility even when jobs are defined at the two-digit level. Furthermore, the mobility has the right properties. Most movement is to higher-wage jobs that appear to be promotions, but some lateral movement occurs as well.

20 For workers who worked with the firm before the sample period began, company tenure is recorded correctly, but the dependent variable refers only to the period of the data. The variable Z refers to the number of years worked during the sample

period for all workers. They are highly collinear, differing only because of integer effects and because some individuals began work with the firm before our analysis. I am unaware of any potential biases introduced by this method. Furthermore, deleting individuals who started before the period had very little effect on the results.

21 See Lazear (1986a).

22 Individuals who leave the firm are dropped from the sample during the year in which they leave, but are valid data points for all years up to that one.

23 It is possible to perform this analysis as a cross-section or as a time series. In a cross-section, the work histories of the current level-2 incumbents would be examined to determine the feeder jobs. In a time series, only individuals in the top 2% would be used. Their entire work histories would be constructed to get the actual paths of these workers. The cross-section approach was followed to prevent idiosyncrasies in a few individuals' careers from dictating the entire path. The disadvantage is that moves from level 3 to level 2 for level-2 incumbents may differ from moves from level 3 to level 2 for present level-1 incumbents. Thus, the path traced is not necessarily representative of any actual individuals. But the time series approach means that very few individuals are examined as we move down to the firm's bottom layers.

24 The worker with fewer job changes also has longer tenure in each job, which means lower wages. But the job tenure variable measures tenure on the current job, not on previous jobs. Job change is really a proxy for average tenure on previous jobs, for company tenure is held constant as well.

25 See Jovanovic (1979a).

26 In Lazear (1986a), the matching story is questioned because of some empirical evidence that contradicts implications of the matching model.

27 See Lazear (1986a) for a theoretical argument on this proposition.

28 See the span of control literature, such as Mayer (1960), F. M, Miller (1982), and Rosen (1982). Holmström and Milgrom (1991) have examined the specific tasks that are assigned to the worker.

Part V

Introduction

1 In other work that preceded "Culture and Language," I considered corporate culture using a related, but somewhat different model. I believe that the model and approach used in the later work is superior to and more informative than that incorporated in the earlier paper, Lazear (1995a).

Chapter 10

1 This is the scheme described in Holmström (1982). That scheme may fail for a number of reasons: The third party may not want to bear all the risk, he may not have the information necessary to implement the scheme, or strategic or opportunistic behavior can create difficulties.

2 See e.g. Holmström (1982), Jones (1984), Kreps (1986), and Varian (1990). See also Alchian and Demsetz (1972), Fama and Jensen (1983a, 1983b), and, Holmström and Milgrom (1990). Some examples in the sociology literature are Hechter (1987), Coleman (1988), Heckathorn (1988), Pfeffer (1990), and Petersen (1992); Farrell and Scotchmer (1988) provide a discussion of information sharing and sorting in

Notes

partnerships. Radner (1986) explores the free-rider problem in static and repeated games, showing that moral hazard can be eliminated if there is no discounting and other conditions hold. Early work by Cheung (1969) discusses the free-rider problem that can occur when agents share profit.

3   A related structure is contained in Hollander (1990). He examines contribution to a public good and motivates contributions by utility that individuals receive through peer approval.

4   Symmetry of the problem for all agents guarantees $e_i = e_j$.

5   Sociologists have been aware of the importance of peer pressure and reference groups for a long time. An early analysis of the implications for pressure in the military is contained in Parsons (1954, esp. pp. 362-65). In the military, the goal is to convince a soldier of two things: first, that his actions affect his colleagues (profit sharing) and, second, that he should care about them. Guilt encompasses both.

6   Burt (1987) shows that "happiness" increases with the size of a person's discussion network but decreases with the number of strangers in the group. Hollander (1990) also discusses the importance of the reference group for motivation.

7   The observed patterns of indoctrination expenditure, profit sharing, turnover, and productivity differ between Japan and the United States. One possible explanation, frequently voiced, is that Japanese management style and organizational structure are very different from the American ones. The other attributes more weight to the cultural differences. Varian (1990) argues that Japanese society traditionally has had very strong clan links. Some have argued that the Japanese educational system is geared toward conformity and building team loyalty. Under these assumptions, it is less costly to instill the company team spirit in a Japanese firm than in an American one, which operates in a much more individualistic society (see Hollander 1990). The cultural differences vs. different management hypothesis can be tested using a cross-sectional comparison of the variables by ownership (management style) vs. by country of operation.

8   Kreps (1986) makes the argument that "corporate culture" may move the situation toward a superior equilibrium. An alternative explanation is that information about others' skills is better within the group. Even without motivation effects, better information means less adverse selection and better sorting, which provides another reason to pair with "one's own kind."

9   If $P(\ )$ is convex and $P'(0) < 0$, then uniqueness is guaranteed.

10   It is possible that P is such that a firm might even provide workers with "pride." If P is negative at the equilibrium value of e, then workers get something for nothing. It implies that the worker derives utility simply from being at work. Hollander's (1990) parameterization of individualism and group belonging is similar to γ.

11   This is close to Jones's (1984, pp. 40-52) idea of conformism.

12   Jones (1984, pp. 28-37) considers two-sided pressure by bringing in asymmetries in the compensation function. Low-effort workers depress the size of the pie but have little effect on the schedule. High-effort workers significantly affect the standard according to which the wage is set.

13   Arnott and Stiglitz (1991) analyze some of the risk-bearing features of a partnership.

14   The interaction between peer pressure and group size is considered by Allen (1982).

15   Alternatively, independents could be defined as those in whom it is more difficult to instill guilt, loyalty, or other social characteristics.

16   An example is the rat race result in Akerlof (1976), also described in Chapter 6.

Chapter 11

1   Indeed, a look at the data reveals that union wages tend to vary less with worker characteristics than nonunion wages (see e.g. Lewis 1983 or Townsend 1985).

2   See Chapter 6, Holmström (1982), Carmichael (1983b), Green and Stokey (1983),

484

and Nalebuff and Stiglitz (1983) also consider the question of when relative payments should be used over absolute payment.

3   The existence of a unique interior solution is not guaranteed. There must be enough dispersion of $\varepsilon_k - \varepsilon_j$, to ensure that adopting a certain losing strategy is not better. This is explored in Chapter 6 and detailed in Nalebuff and Stiglitz (1983). It is also necessary that the second-order conditions hold, namely that $(W_1 - W_2)g(0)$ $f_{11} - C_{11} < 0$ and $W_1 - W_2)g(0)f_{22} - C_{22} < 0$.

4   An important assumption here is that aggressors are not sufficiently lower-cost producers of effort. It is conceivable that such strong complementarities could reverse the results. That possibility is considered later.

5   The argument can be extended to explain actions by trade associations that are designed to counter aggressive advertising. Thus Schneider, Klein, and Murphy (1981) suggest that cigarette manufacturers were behind the ban of cigarette ads from television. But Rogerson (1988) argues that there are beneficial effects of advertising with reference to opticians.

6   Milgrom (1986) has a model of industrial politics that yields some similar results. His mechanism does not focus on relative aspects of work relations. Rather, he argues that a worker can spend time producing or politicking. To reduce the latter, managers ignore some information presented to them by their workers. There is no necessary interaction between workers in his model, and the politics there is closer to that between principal and agent than among workers. The model in this chapter ignores, for the most part, attempts to fool the supervisor. What is common to both analyses is that there are two types of effort in which a worker can engage, and only one is productive.

7   The firm's maximization problem under this situation changes. It can be written as

$$\max_{W_1, W_2, S^H, S^D} W_1 P^D + W_2(1 - P^D) + W_1 P^H$$
$$+ W_2(1 - P^H) - C_D(\mu^D, \theta^D) - C_H (\mu^H, \theta^H) + S^D + S^H,$$

where

$$P^D \equiv G[f(\mu^D, \theta^H) - f(\mu^H, \theta^D)]$$

and

$$P^H \equiv G[f(\mu^H, \theta^D) - f(\mu^D, \theta^H)]$$

The zero-profit constraint is that total payment equals $E(q^H + q^D)$. Note that S^H and S^D are mere rent-splitting parameters so that W_1 and W_2 can be chosen to maximize total output. Then S^H and S^D must be chosen so that

$$W_1 P^H + W_2(1 - P^H) + S^H > \frac{W_1^H + W_2^H}{2}$$

and

$$W_1 P^D + W_2(1 - P^D) + S^D > \frac{W_1^D + W_2^D}{2}.$$

If both these constraints can be satisfied, then a pooling equilibrium can exist and dominates two matched contests.

8   In general, strict dominance of the matched contest holds under these conditions.

9   It may seem somewhat paradoxical that the hawks, who have a dominant cost function, do worse than doves in equilibrium. This is standard when payoffs are like a prisoner's dilemma. All can be made better off, but each player acts in his own interest. Opportunistic behavior results in an equilibrium that is not first-best. Since doves do not have the same options, they actually come out ahead.

10   Others who have examined mixed tournaments are Bhattacharya and Guasch

Notes

(1988) and Rosen (1986). The former considers gains from using tournaments in which workers must beat their opponents or a standard of a certain level. Structuring tournaments among different types in this way can be Pareto improving. Rosen considers sequential tournaments, in which the average type changes at each level because the lower-cost players are more likely to survive.

11 Let $h(\xi_k, \xi_L)$ be the probability density function of $\xi_k \equiv \varepsilon_k - \varepsilon_j$ and $\xi_L \equiv \varepsilon_L - \varepsilon_L$. Define $X_1 \equiv \mu_j - \mu_k + \theta_j - \theta_k$ and $X_2 \equiv \mu_j - \mu_L + \theta_j - \theta_L$. Then

$$P_1 = \int_{-\infty}^{X_1} \int_{-\infty}^{X_1} h(\xi_k, \xi_L) d\xi_k d\xi_L.$$

Some manipulation reveals that

$$\frac{\partial P_1}{\partial X_1} = \int_{-\infty}^{0} h(0, \xi_L) d\xi_L$$

and

$$\frac{\partial P_1}{\partial X_1} = \int_{-\infty}^{0} h(\xi_K, 0) d\xi_K$$

since $X_1 = X_2 = 0$. Thus

$$\frac{\partial P_1}{\partial \mu_1} = \int_{0}^{\infty} h(0, \xi_L) d\xi_L + \int_{0}^{\infty} h(\xi_K, 0) d\xi_K$$

since the density function is symmetric around zero. Now

$$P_3 = \int_{X_2}^{\infty} \int_{X_1}^{\infty} h(\xi_k, \xi_L) d\xi_k d\xi_L$$

so

$$\frac{\partial P_3}{\partial \mu_j} = -\int_{0}^{\infty} h(0, \xi_L) d\xi_L + \int_{0}^{\infty} h(\xi_K, 0) d\xi_K$$

at $X_1 = X_2 = 0$. Thus

$$\frac{\partial P_3}{\partial \mu_j} = \frac{-\partial P_1}{\partial \mu_j}.$$

12 Rosen (1986) has worked out the prize structure for a multi-round contest, taking into account that the population differs at each round.

13 Training and exposure to different areas and people in the organization are the two most obvious alternatives.

14 If certain industries are better suited to hawks and others to doves, then a cut by industry would yield the same correlation. The implication is for wages, not for marginal products as in Frank (1984, 1985). As shown in Lazear (1984), there is no necessity that wages be more or less compressed than output in a tournament-like setting. Frank's argument, that wages are more compressed than marginal product, says nothing about the relation of average wage to spread across firms.

Chapter 12

1 Both terms are somewhat ambiguous. "Culture" is the more amorphous of the two terms, but even "language" lends itself to somewhat blurred distinctions. Within any given language, there are dialects that belong to certain subgroups. Some of the words are sufficiently idiosyncratic that only individuals within that subgroup understand their meanings. Schelling (1960) was perhaps the first to recognize the importance of focal points. Culture and language are among the most general kinds of focal points.

2 Before World War I, there were a number of schools that used German as the

language. But the allocation of a significant amount of public money for education in a student's native tongue is a recent development.

3   A book by Sowell (1994) is a much more ambitious attempt to understand culture. He attempts to define the relation of culture to most aspects of social, economic, and political life on a global scale. The analysis in this chapter shies away from being specific on culture and how it operates.

4   Adelstein (1994) points out that to use a common language, individuals must give up some freedom. They cannot retain the right to attach whatever verbal labels they like. To communicate, individuals must tailor their expressions to meet the expectations of others. Adelstein argues that language is not simply communication, but a way to coordinate behavior. These ideas fit well with the use of the term "language" throughout this chapter.

5   The empirical literature on the economic returns to assimilation began with Chiswick (1978). More to the point of this analysis is the work by McManus, Gould, and Welch (1983), which shows that English-speaking Hispanic-Americans do better in the labor market than non-English-speaking ones. Also, Chiswick (1991) finds that both speaking and reading fluency affect earnings, with reading fluency playing the more important role. Chiswick (1998) studies the acquisition of Hebrew language skills in Israel. Chiswick finds that, as in the United States, the ability to speak the majority language increases earnings in Israel.

6   Lazear (1995a) uses a random encounter model to analyze the choice by businesses of a corporate culture.

7   Chiswick and Miller (1994) find that in Canada, immigrants tend to learn the language that predominates in their region of residence. Chiswick (1998) studies the acquisition of Hebrew language skills in Israel.

8   Fluency rates were higher in 1900 than in 1990. In part, this reflects the fact that immigrants had been in the United States longer in 1900 than in 1990. But even when one corrects for length of time in the United States, the difference in fluency rates remains.

9   Ordered logits, with various levels of English-speaking ability as the dependent variable, were run. Very similar results were obtained. The 1990 regression was run on a 1/200 sample to cut down on computation time.

10   It may also be true that being in a community with more native English speakers makes it easier to learn English. Formally, this means that the distribution of t_j depends on the composition of the community.

11   Incidentally, country of origin, not merely language, is important. Natives of Mexico do not live in the same neighborhoods as natives of Cuba or Puerto Rico.

12   The age coefficient is added because one cannot spend a year in the country without also aging one year.

13   Recall that the CNTYPCT × YEARS−US variable did not enter significantly into the 1990 logits, despite the very large number of observations. Actually, in more refined specifications, negative effects of CNTYPCT × YEARS−US interactions are found in 1990 data. But even when the effects are statistically significant, they are very small.

14   An individual learns a second language if and only if $(2/N) - t_j > 1/N$ or if and only if $t_j < 1/N$. Given that an individual knows two languages, he or she learns the third if $(3/N) - t_j > 2/N$ or if and only if $t_j < 1/N$. This continues for all N languages. Thus anyone who finds it worthwhile to learn one additional language finds it worthwhile to learn all other languages.

15   Randomized schemes are unenforceable. Once a particular culture is selected, the $N - 1$ other cultures have incentives to roll the dice again, excluding the winner of the last round. The winner would then be forced to join, but this problem repeats itself. The same is true of other voting schemes.

16   The former Soviet Union provides another example. Because of the many different languages spoken throughout the USSR and its satellites, Russian was made the official language and the one that Soviet citizens had to learn in school.

17   Additionally, there were emotional reasons for choosing Hebrew over Yiddish.

Notes

18 Chiswick (1998) studies the acquisition of Hebrew language skills in Israel. As in the United States, Chiswick finds that the ability to speak the majority language increases earnings in Israel.

19 This threshold condition is analogous to those in biology describing the initial conditions that are necessary for an epidemic to take off. The classic reference on this is Kermack and McKendrick (1927). More modern analyses are provided by Anderson (1982) and May and Anderson (1987).

20 For simplicity, assume that there is no intermarriage between initial native-born offspring and immigrant offspring.

21 The value of diversity has been modeled formally by Weitzman (1992). The desire for diversity is the opposite of the desire for commonality that is the focus of this analysis. But some (see DiPasquale and Glaeser 1998) have argued that there are direct costs of having a multicultural society. They analyze riots and find that the likelihood of a riot depends on ethnic heterogeneity. Further, O'Reilly, Williams, and Barsade (1998) have found that the gains to diversity outweigh the costs at the workplace. The network externality aspect of language has been noted by Church and King (1993) and the benefits of standardization for trade by Katz and Matsui (2004). John and Yi (1997) study the effect of skewed language endowments on language acquisition. In another related literature, Laitin (1994) treats language as a coordination problem, much like the standards literature in economics. See also the earlier paper by Pool (1991). In another paper, Lazear (2000c) analyzes the impact of the diversity argument on immigration policy.

22 Actually, t_a computes to be less than one and t_b to a number greater than one for $.5 < p < 1$. Since the lower and upper supports of the distribution are zero and one, zero and one are the relevant values.

23 This is related to Schelling's (1978) famous tipping result, where neighborhoods change because of externalities imposed on other residents.

24 A similar point is made by Lang (1986). Robinson (1988) finds that French as the first language is no disadvantage in Canadian earnings, probably because of the higher level of bilingualism among the French-speaking population. Also, since French speakers congregate with other French speakers, the model predicts that there should be no difference in earnings.

25 To the extent that countries are heterogeneous, there may be a thin-markets problem, which results in less than optimal migration patterns.

26 This is not an automatic result of immigration, however. It depends crucially on the rate of immigration. As immigration rates slow, it is possible that the Spanish-speaking proportion of the U.S. population would decline, leading to less incentive for individuals with high switching costs to migrate.

27 This ignores any other country-specific factors, which may be important. Countries that have large numbers of immigrants may be the ones best suited to using immigrant labor.

28 *Proof.* Define $\Delta = V_G - V_{NG}$, and note that Δ is increasing in θ. Therefore, if Δ is positive for all $p_a > \frac{1}{2}$ when $\theta = 0$, it is positive for any θ. For Δ to be positive for $\theta = 0$, it is necessary and sufficient for $p_a - p_a^2 - (1 - p_a)^2 > 0$. The left-hand side equals zero for $p_a = (\frac{1}{2}, 1)$. Taking the derivative of the left-hand side with respect to p, one obtains $1 - 2p_a + 2(1 - p_a)$, which is positive at $p_a = \frac{1}{2}$ and negative at $p = 1$. Thus $\Delta > 0$ for $\frac{1}{2} < P < 1$, so $V_G > V_{NG}$ for all values of θ and $p > \frac{1}{2}$.

29 Diamond and Maskin (1979) have explored the implications of different assumptions about random meeting probabilities for externalities. Specifically, I have assumed that movement of an individual from inside the ghetto to the outside does not increase the probability of an encounter (which is assumed to be one). If changing the number of individuals outside the ghetto were to increase the likelihood of an encounter, the effect of the externality could be diminished.

30 It is not necessary to assume that scale economies within the ghetto have been exhausted. It has already been shown that ghettos are efficient under the previous assumptions. Moving more into the ghetto would only raise V_G relative to V_{NG}.

31 The issue of how many communities a society should be divided into is related to

the question of how many separate markets there should be in an economy. This has been analyzed by Economides and Siow (1988), who argue that externalities may produce too many markets, much like too many languages and distinct communities.

32   It is true that $(1 - p_a)^2 >$ or $1 - 2p_a + p_a^2 > 0$. So $p_a^2 + 1 - p_a > p_a$, which implies that $2p_a^2 + 2 - 2p_a > 2p_a$ or that $p_a^2 + (1 - p_a)^2 + 1 > 2p_a$. Thus $V_{NG} > V_G$.

33   Lazear (1983b) examines whether parents would acquire enough schooling or move to the appropriate community, given the interests of their children. The empirical finding is that the effects on children, both of migration and of parental schooling, are substantial in the nonwhite population.

Part VI

Introduction

1   See Wagner (2003, 2006) and Lazear (2004b).

Chapter 13

1   This implication is consistent with some search and matching models. The skill-weights view has some things in common with those theories, as discussed below.

2   MacLeod and Malcomson's "third case," where one party, in this case the firm, takes actions that benefit both sides, seems closest to the analysis below.

3   Inefficiencies would result were workers and firms to precommit to a second-period wage on the basis of ex ante rather than ex post information. In this model, and compare with MacLeod and Malcomson (1993) where the issue of renegotiation is central, both investment and separation are efficient because investment is observable in period 1, contractible, and assumed to maximize joint surplus and because competitive bidding is permitted in period 2.

The issue of efficient investment with specific human capital has received a great deal of attention. More recently, Carmichael and MacLeod (2003) show that caring about sunk costs can enhance incentives in situations where individual agents would otherwise invest inefficiently. Baker and Voicu (2007) analyze the effects of various linear wage policies on incentives to invest and on overall stability of the firm in equilibrium.

In bargaining models, where renegotiation of the wage is permitted and depends on outside options, workers and firms have distorted and contradictory investment incentives to bring up their wages. There are a number of papers that look at the effects of outside options on behavior. For example, Stole and Zwiebel (1996) show that firms over-employ labor in order to reduce labor's bargaining power in employment-at-will negotiations. Prendergast and Stole (1999) examine situations where using markets for one purpose affects the value of relationships in other non-market transactions. The issue of distorting investment from the social optimum is explored in Appendix A.

4   This is not without loss of generality. Because $A > B$, $\lambda_j > \lambda_L$ implies that the worker never prefers leisure to the alternative job. To guarantee this is true in an ex ante sense, one would have to assume that $\lambda_L = \lambda_{\min}$. Without this assumption, it would be necessary to include branching that allowed for the case where λ_j exceeded and that where it was exceeded by λ_L.

5   It is assumed that investment choices of A and B are observable. Under these conditions, it can be argued that even a firm (or worker) with a great deal of

Notes

6   bargaining power prefers to maximize joint surplus and then to extract a larger share of it through the bargaining process. Another justification is provided by Aghion, Dewatripont, and Rey (1994), who show that efficiency can be obtained when renegotiation is observable. Efficiency in their model corresponds to joint surplus maximization here.

6   The difference between the chosen and socially efficient levels of investment is explored in Appendix A.

7   Actually, even when a layoff occurs, sometimes the worker would have left anyway, i.e., when $\lambda_j > \lambda_1$. This is included in the third term because $\bar{\lambda}$ integrates over these high-λ events.

8   The results do not make use of specific properties of the density function, $f()$, nor of the cost function except that C_A, C_B, C_{AA}, and $C_{BB} > 0$, which hold irrespective of details about A and B. Additionally, $C_{AB} \geq 0$.

9   All derivations are for $\lambda_1 \geq \lambda^*$. Were $\lambda_1 < \lambda^*$, the corresponding expression would reverse those who stay and those who leave so that

$$W_{\text{stay}} = B + \tfrac{1}{2}\,[\lambda_1 + E(\lambda_j \mid \lambda_j > \lambda_1)](A - B)$$

and

$$W_{\text{layoff}} = B + \tfrac{1}{2}\,[\lambda_1 + E(\lambda_j \mid \lambda_j < \lambda_1)](A - B).$$

10   For example, let $\lambda \sim U[0,1]$ and $\lambda_1 = 0.6$ then the $E(\lambda \mid \lambda < \lambda_1) = 0.3$ and $\bar{\lambda} = 0.5$. If $\lambda_L = 0.5$, the right-hand side of the expression is positive so those laid off do better in expectation than the stayers.

11   Using $(3')$ in Appendix B, note that the derivative of the left-hand side with respect to q is

$$-F(\lambda_1)\lambda_1 - [1 - F(\lambda_1)]\left[\frac{\lambda_1 + E(\lambda_j \mid \lambda_j > \lambda_1)}{2}\right] + \tfrac{1}{2}(\bar{\lambda} + \lambda_L).$$

Sufficient for this to be negative is that $\lambda_L < \lambda_1$, which means that wages are expected to fall when an individual is laid off. Again, as long as there are voluntary stayers, expected wages must fall on layoff. This implies that A decreases in q, and since $C_A + C_B = 1$, B increases in q.

12   Recall that quits only occur when efficient and that the wage that the acquiring firm bids must exceed the output at the current firm to steal the worker away.

13   For workers who specialize in B, the logic is identical: workers take the job with the minimum value of λ rather than the maximum.

14   This result is similar to Wasmer (2006), who shows that as markets become more competitive, investment becomes less firm specific. Here, as markets become thick, investment becomes more idiosyncratic. But that is because it comes closer to the outside option, which, at the extreme is to obtain $\lambda_{\max}$ or $\lambda_{\min}$ from another firm.

15   Some firms with λ may go out of buisness as a consequence.

16   Heckman and Sedlacek (1985) and Heckman and Scheinkman (1987) consider a linear multifactor model that has some similarities to the one in this chapter. Heckman and Sedlacek estimate an extended Roy model, where workers have different characteristics and sort to various sectors. They refer to "sector-specific capital." Their emphasis is on sorting and estimating prices across the sectors. Sorting in their model relates closely to that considered in Willis and Rosen (1979). Heckman and Scheinkman also use a model with linear technology and different skills. Their focus is on describing conditions under which characteristics are uniformly priced across sectors and testing the validity of uniform pricing.

17   An in-depth discussion is provided in earlier drafts of this paper; specifically, see the April 2009 version available on request.

18   This issue has attracted a good bit of attention in the literature, especially recently. Best known among recent contributions are Acemoglu and Pischke (1998) and

Booth and Zoega (1999). Cappelli (2004) argues that this helps attract better workers to the firm. Even earlier, Stevens (1994) argued that with imperfect competition, the standard argument that workers bear the full cost of general training and invest optimally breaks down. Acemoglu (1997) showed that some of the costs of general training are borne by the employer in a labor market with search and other frictions. Similarly, Booth and Chatterji (1998) produce a similar result by invoking ex post monopsony power in wage setting.

19   Appendix D uses the same example to show that W_1 does not always fall in λ_1.
20   Neal (1995) and Parent (2000) find that industry effects reduce or even eliminate the firm tenure effects. Neal also holds constant broadly defined occupations (e.g., manager, professional, technician, sales, and other similar titles.)
21   Recall the not-innocuous assumption that leisure is never preferred to work, even in the laid off state.
22   This assumes that C_{AB} is not sufficient negative, but this is likely to be true. If anything, C_{AB} is likely to be positive because using time and effort to invest in A is likely to reduce that available to invest in B.
23   This does not mean that B is zero. Because of convexity in the cost function for $A (C_{AA} > 0)$, even for $\lambda_1 = \lambda_{max}$, B is generally positive.
24   If $\lambda_1^{2(N)} < \lambda_1$, then the second-highest order statistic is replaced by λ_1.
25   Recall that separation occurs only when privately efficient, i.e., when it increases surplus.

Chapter 14

1   See Hanushek (1998) who finds little evidence that anything matters, including class size reductions. Coleman and Hoffer (1987) and Coleman, Kilgore, and Hoffer (1981) report that Catholic schools with large class sizes produce better students than public schools with smaller class sizes. Class size effects are documented by a number of authors. The literature goes back very far. For example, Blake (1954) summarized a literature where 35 studies found smaller class size was better, 18 found larger class size was better, and 32 were inconclusive. More recent are Hanushek (1998), Hoxby (1998, 2000a), and Krueger (1998, 1999). Angrist and Lavy (1999) find that class size matters for elementary school children in fourth and fifth grade in Israel. Lavy (1999), using an experimental design, finds that class size does not matter in OLS regressions, but does when political variables are used, exploiting a discontinuity structure.
2   Some exceptions are Caucutt (1996) and Fernandez and Rogerson (1998). The focus of these studies is somewhat different from the one here, but there is overlap in deriving sorting equilibria. Positive assortative mating, of the kind derived in these studies, goes back at least as far as Becker (1991). Closest to the analysis contained herein is work by Brown and Saks (1975).
3   There is a large literature here. An early empirical paper is Henderson, Mieskowski, and Sauvageau (1978).
4   Hanushek (1998) reports that expenditures per student more than doubled between 1960 and 1990 at a time when there was no steady trend in test scores or other measures of performance. Others to examine the relation between expenditures and class size are Card and Krueger (1992) and Betts (1996a). There is evidence that competition both lowers costs and improves school performance. See Hoxby (1996, 1998), McMillan (2000), and Urquiola (2005).
5   Heckman (1999) and Heckman and Lochner (2000) point out that learning is a lifetime affair and that the emphasis on formal schooling is misplaced, particularly when it is recognized that early success breeds later success. There is one major difference between formal schooling and the learning that occurs from infancy and continues after the cessation of school. Formal classroom schooling has public good attributes and externalities are key, whereas training given by a parent to his

child or by an employer to his employee is essentially a private good.

6   Actually, $1 - p$ is the probability that a given student initiates a disruption. It does not matter, given the technology postulated, that others may or may not follow. Furthermore, it could also be assumed that the individual who asks the question benefits from that time even if others do not. This will change the functional form only slightly as educational output per person rises from p^n to p^{n-1}. All results remain qualitatively identical.

7   This technology is that of perfect complementarity. Kremer (1993) also presents a model using a perfect-complements-style technology.

8   In a very fine unpublished paper, Brown and Saks (1975) constructed a model with an educational production function that has features similar to those in this chapter. First, schools maximize something, in their case, mean and minimum variance of test scores, by choosing resource allocations. They allow for there to be some public goods production of educational services.

9   The model is constructed in a way that ensures that class size is not a function of school size. However, Bedard, Brown, and Helland (1999) have found some school size effects.

10   The model could, in principle, be generalized to consider other kinds of expenditures as well. Focusing on class size is probably the place to start, particularly since Flyer and Rosen (1997) show that almost all of the rise in the cost of schooling over time is a result of reductions in class size.

11   Krueger (1999) is one of the few exceptions.

12   Akerhielm (1995) finds that the poorer-performing students are likely to end up in small classes. She also suggests that this may create bias in estimates of class size effects.

13   Becker and Murphy (1992) show that optimal teacher–student ratio varies with the distance from the final product produced. This, too, provides a relation of equilibrium class size to technological parameters, although their focus is somewhat different from the one of this chapter.

14   Olson and Ackerman (2000) find that wages are positively related to the pupil–teacher ratio of the schools that they attended. They attribute this to differences in teacher quality across districts.

15   Japan has high test scores and large class sizes. The finding is consistent with having a group of high p, well-behaved students.

16   Brown and Saks (1975) also make this point.

17   Betts (1996b) and Betts and Shkolnik (1999) provide evidence on class size effects that vary, depending on what is held constant. The model in this paper provides implications for their data as well.

18   Krueger (1999) finds that the benefit of reducing class size is roughly equal to the costs.

19   An early economics paper on class size by Summers and Wolfe (1977) found different effects for low achievers than for high achievers. Low achievers benefit from smaller class size, but the reverse is true for high achievers. Their results are somewhat consistent with this model because low achievers probably have higher values of p, where the reduction in size effects are greater.

20   Using the STAR data, Rouse (2004) also finds that smaller classes raise performance for inner city and minority students.

21   In the context of two different types, a question by a B student might be viewed as disruption to A students if all the A students already know the answer and B students do not.

22   It is assumed that α and m are such that proportions work out to guarantee an integer number of classes, each of which has n students.

23   See also Evans and Schwab (1995), Neal (1997, 1998), and Sander (1997) for more recent papers.

24   If all schools were private and competitive, A schools would be less costly than B schools, since the latter optimally use more teachers per student.

25   In equilibrium, if all A's go to private schools, then the public schools consist only

of B's. It remains true, however, that A's will pay more than B's to be in an all A school than in an all B school. The difference between what an A will pay and what a B will pay is

$$[Vp_A^n - Vp_B^{n-1} p_A] - [Vp_A^{n-1} p_B - Vp_B^n],$$

which is positive for $p_A > p_B$.

Further, all B private schools charge more than all A private schools because optimal class size is smaller in the all B school, raising costs. If public schools are already exclusively B, private B schools could not compete unless they differed on other dimensions of quality.

Rothschild and White (1995) show that if type-specific prices can be charged, then a competitive equilibrium results in optimality. Becker and Murphy (2000) discuss market-induced sorting in the presence of externalities. Without a sufficient number of prices, there is inefficient allocation. In this context, scholarships allow for enough prices to induce social efficiency. Epple and Romano (1998) derive similar results and simulate some voucher experiments. The results of these studies apply here directly.

26   Private schools with A's should have larger classes and should be cheaper than those with B's. This is surely true, at least at the extremes. Private schools for special needs children have small classes and are very expensive (although they are sometimes subsidized by the state).

27   See Hoxby (1998).

28   Interestingly, there is an increasing trend toward using other factors, one of which is community service, as a criterion for admission to college. Perhaps colleges believe that those A's who engage in community service are also likely to encourage B's to behave like A's.

29   Chapter 12 presents a model of cultural acquisition. There, it is argued that incentives to become assimilated into the majority culture depend on the size of the relevant groups. The smaller is the minority relative to the majority, the greater is the incentive of a minority member to acquire the culture of the majority.

30   This is a somewhat controversial point. It is possible that even B's do better by being in segregated classes. The questions that A students ask may be disruption as far as B's are concerned, if the questions are so far above the B level as to render them time-wasters.

31   Hoxby (2000b) finds that female classes perform better in the lower grades and that gender composition alters classroom conduct. There is a recent push to create girls-only classes in the public schools. It is important to define "disruption" in this context. Males who interrupt their teachers more might be more engaged in the class, raising the value of the educational experience. The optimal amount of student participation is not zero.

32   This does not imply that there is more discipline in classes where students are inherently better behaved. Because p increase in t, total discipline may be higher or lower in classes with better (higher t) students because students encounter discipline $(1 - p)$ of the time.

33   Grogger and Neal (2000) find that Catholic schools raise performance primarily for urban minority students. If urban minority students are in public school environments where discipline is a particular problem, then one would expect effects of shifting to Catholic schools to be largest in such environments.

34   Required is that $(1 - p^n)c'/n > p_1 p^{n-1} c$.

35   Rosen (1987) argues that teaching is a labor-intensive service that does not lend itself to mass production. This can be interpreted in this context as saying that what one student needs to know another does not, which can be interpreted as $p < 1$. When the teacher is addressing the specific needs of one student, the rest of the class is not benefiting, or at least not benefiting by as much as they would if their personal needs were addressed.

36   To see this, let p_1 be initial p, p_2 be the new p. To keep educational output constant

while changing class size by a factor of k, it is necessary that

$$p_1^n = p_2^{nk}$$

or

$$p_2 = p_1^{1/k}$$

37 See, for example, Card and Krueger (1992).
38 The TIMSS (Third International Mathematics and Science Study), conducted in 1995-1996 is a survey of about one-half million students from 41 countries in three grades to determine math and science achievement.
39 The LSAY is a national study of student interests and aptitudes in math and science. The centerpiece is a massive longitudinal survey of schools, students, parents, and teachers from 1986-1994.
40 Simon Board provided this proof.

Chapter 15

1 Identification is particularly important if, as Rivkin, Hanushek, and Kain (2001) find, teacher-specific effects go a long way in explaining the performance of their students.
2 See Koretz et al. (1991) discussed in more detail below. Hoffman, Assaf, and Paris (2001) report on results from Texas Assessment of Academic Skills testing. Using a sample of 200 respondents, they suggest that the Texas exam has negative impacts on the curriculum and on its instructional effectiveness, where eight to ten hours per week on test preparation is typically required of teachers (by their principals) and the curriculum is planned around the test subjects. They also argue that teaching to the test raises test scores without changing underlying knowledge. Jones et al. (1999) study data from North Carolina and conclude from a survey of 236 participants that the high-stakes test induced two-thirds of teachers to spend more time on reading and writing and 56 percent of teachers reported spending more time on math. They also claim that students spend more than 20 percent of instructional time practicing for end-of-grade tests and a significant fraction report a reduction in students' love of learning. In an early study, Meisels (1989) outlines some of the pitfalls of high-stakes testing and suggests adverse effects of the Gesell School Readiness Test and of Georgia's use of the CAT.
3 Beginning with Becker (1968), there is a large amount of literature on optimal incentives for enforcement of the law.
4 Note that $q > P$. When $q = P$, the probability of detection over this range is one. There is no advantage to having a smaller q than P.
5 In the teaching case analyzed below, the loss may be market determined, and then K is given exogenously to the student or teacher. As such, the model with exogenous fines is more appropriate for the main task of the analysis.
6 In a related paper, Eeckhout, Persico, and Todd (2010) take the speeding deterrence approach quite literally and test it using data from Belgium. They find that their model, which uses intuition similar to the one in this chapter, fits the data on speeding quite well.
7 This logic implies that as long as police are costly, there are an optimal number of police. When police locations are secret, it is never optimal to have more police than

$$G = VZ/K,$$

which makes (2) hold with equality so that cheating is completely deterred.

The literature on deterrence that dates back to Becker (1968) notes that it is better to raise the penalty and reduce the number of police in the limit to zero. Since only the expected penalty matters, social costs are saved by reducing the amount of real resources spent on police and increasing the penalty so as to leave the expected fine sufficient to deter all crime.

There have been a number of objections to this rule. One is risk aversion. If false positive errors are made, individuals who are wrongly accused suffer greatly when extreme punishments are doled out. Second, marginal incentives are distorted. An individual who faces the death penalty for a parking violation might take extreme action to avoid arrest, resulting in additional social damage. Third, high penalties create incentive for enforcement officials to engage in extortion. Very high penalties might also encourage extortion by public officials because the penalties to anyone caught are so high that the willingness to pay extortion is increased.

Again, optimal penalties are not the essence of the argument, especially in the context of education where the penalties are likely to be determined exogenously by the market or by some wage structure that is determined in a bargaining context.

8   Some might argue that speeding fines are part of an optimal tax structure. For example, some very small towns set extremely low speed limits to induce speeding so that they can collect revenue from out-of-town motorists.

9   The emphasis here is on the incentive aspect of testing. Another role of testing is to provide information to help in modifying the curriculum. To deal with this component of testing, a dynamic model is required.

10   It is assumed that the same item is never tested twice.

11   Since ability is unobservable, as long as we think of the metric of ability as continuous and monotonic, there is also a transformation of some measure of ability into another that allows the functional form above to hold. This formulation shifts only the mean of the distribution and does not alter higher moments.

12   To see this, it is sufficient to show that the other extreme, of announcing all questions, dominates complete secrecy. It is better to announce the questions when

$$mS(K) + (n - m)S(0) < nS(K\tfrac{m}{n}),$$

which is the same as

$$mS(K) + (n - m)S(0) < nS(0),$$

because $X = Km/n$ is too small to induce learning. The inequality holds because $S(0) > S(K)$.

13   Formally, $S(Km/n) = S(\infty)$; all items are learned. It is better to keep questions secret when

$$mS(K) + (n - m)S(0) > nS(K\tfrac{m}{n}),$$

which is the same as

$$\tfrac{m}{n}S(K) + (1 - \tfrac{m}{n})S(0) > S(\infty),$$

This must hold because $S(\infty) < S(X) \; \forall \; X$ when $\gamma > \max(V)$.

14   For example, McBee and Barnes (1998) claim that a test would have to test a prohibitively high number of tasks to attain acceptable levels of generalizability.

15   There is a large body of literature on learning different skills at different ages. Perhaps best known for these ideas is Piaget and Inhelder (1969).

16   Other issues with teachers and students involve team problems. Because both have an incentive to free ride on the other's effort, the standard result that effort of each party falls short of the optimum holds. But there is little about the student-teacher

team that distinguishes it from other partnership problems, which have been analyzed. See, for example, Holmström (1981) and Chapter 10.

17   See, for example, Lazear (1986, see Chapter 7; 2003).
18   See Chapter 6 as well as Lazear (2000).
19   I thank Thomas Dohmen for pointing out this generalization.
20   Persico (2002) discusses briefly the idea that using differential rates of enforcement may be optimal.

Chapter 16

1   Lazear (1995b) found that those Eastern European economies that grew the fastest during the transition from communism to market economies were those for which new business formation was most rapid.
2   See e.g. the early paper by Evans and Leighton (1989) and the more recent one by Hamilton (2000), who examines the returns to self-employment.
3   The theoretical papers on the subject rarely speak to the issue that is central to this chapter. For example, Otani (1996) examines the theoretical relation of firm size to entrepreneurial ability. Perhaps the closest to this chapter in terms of discussing specialization (although from a very different point of view) is Holmes and Schmitz (1990), where it is argued that certain agents specialize in entrepreneurial skills. This differs from the approach here, where entrepreneurial skills are implicitly defined to be a cross section of all possible skills. De Meza and Southey (1996) build a model where new entrants are excessively optimistic.
4   Landier (2006) argues that the part of the ability distribution from which entrepreneurs are drawn may differ across countries and provides a multiple equilibrium approach in an information framework to discuss the differences.
5   The perfect substitutes/perfect complements income function is extreme, but it is an expository convenience. Any production process that has complementarity of skills for entrepreneurs and substitution of skills for specialists would be consistent with the intuition.
6   Kihlstrom and Laffont (1979) were the first to argue that entrepreneurs tend to be less risk-averse than others in society. Iyigun and Owen (1998) suggest that entrepreneurship is risky and risk-averse agents are less likely to go into entrepreneurship in a developed economy where a larger selection of safer (insured) jobs exists.
7   Becker and Murphy (1992) use a similar notion of specialization. Becker and Mulligan (2002) apply a technology somewhat like the one in this chapter to discuss the difference between market (specialized) and household (generalized) work.
8   Lucas (1978) offers a model in which an individual can choose to work for someone or to be an entrepreneur. The difference between Lucas's model and this one is that, in Lucas, managerial talent is distinct from labor talent. Here, workers and managers have the same two skills, just in different combinations. The complementarity between skills that is the essence of this story is absent from Lucas. Still, Lucas derives implications for the size distribution of firms that are similar to those derived below.
9   One of the skills can be interpreted as the ability to raise capital. This argument is central to Evans and Jovanovic (1989). Holtz-Eakin, Joulfaian, and Rosen (1994) show that capital is important in starting a business by linking the receipt of an inheritance to the likelihood of starting a business. Recent work by Gentry and Hubbard (2004) explores the relation of saving to entrepreneurial investment. Their motivation is growth and macroeconomic factors, but the results are relevant to this study as well. They find that there is an interdependence between entrepreneurial saving and investment.
10   Stopford and Baden-Fuller (1994) list five components (proactiveness, team

orientation, dispute resolution skills, being innovative, and ability to learn) that are important in entrepreneurship. Thus, an entrepreneur might be someone who was highly endowed with each of the five factors.

11   To make statements about groups, it is necessary to show that the propositions are true in a statistical sense at the level of the population. This is derived in the appendix.

12   The response rate was 40%. Some individuals were very old, and others were no longer alive, which accounts for some of the nonresponses.

13   Lentz and Laband (1990) find that there is a higher likelihood of self-employment among the children of the self-employed. They interpret this as human capital that is passed from one generation to the next. There are also papers on the link between education and entrepreneurship. See, e.g., Bates (1985, 1990).

14   One possibility is that those who have been entrepreneurs in the past list many roles when they are entrepreneurs and that entrepreneurship is serially correlated. To check this, NPRIOR was redefined such that each entrepreneurial employment was given one and only one role. The results were substantially unaltered.

15   In fact, because experience brackets contain more than 1 year of experience, it is possible that an individual might enter even the same calculation more than once, say, once with 5 and once with 7 years of experience. Thus, there is not complete independence even within a row of the table.

16   The sorting effect of individuals into different occupations picks up comparative advantage. If entrepreneurs have a comparative disadvantage as specialists, and not merely an absolute advantage, then those who become entrepreneurs should, when they are in training in nonentrepreneurial jobs, earn less than those who choose to be specialists. A regression of earnings in nonentrepreneurial jobs on EXP and a dummy equal to one if the individual ever founds a business in the career yields a negative, albeit insignificant, coefficient on the dummy.

17   The evidence is not dispositive, however. Even if large effects of NAFTER were found, it could be that being an entrepreneur prepares a worker to take on many roles in subsequent employment, precisely because entrepreneurs perform many tasks. Conversely, if entrepreneurship is an absorbing state or close to it, an entrepreneurial spell could be associated with fewer roles after because there are fewer jobs. This is unlikely, however, because entrepreneurs have more roles per year after a given employment spell on average than nonentrepreneurs.

18   For example, suppose that some people like variety. They take many different types of courses and also become entrepreneurs. But those who like variety would only become entrepreneurs if entrepreneurship offered a more varied experience, which says that entrepreneurship is a general rather than specialized occupation.

19   Lucas (1978) uses this production function to discuss income distribution and the size distribution of firms.

Part VII

Personnel Economics – The Past and Future

1   The interpretation of innate ability in these models is somewhat confusing. Individuals may differ in their innate ability, which leads them to follow different skill acquisition paths. It may well be that the varied skill acquisition associated with differences in ability are the key mechanisms through which becoming a well-rounded individual occurs. Still, controlling for fixed effects would wipe out any ability to pick up the actual observation of time-varying skills. Specifically, if individuals are heterogeneous but this heterogeneity also leads them to undertake different training programs while in school, placing fixed effects into the regression will eliminate the effect of the actual skill acquisition on the probability

of becoming an entrepreneur. This does not imply that the skill acquisition per se is unimportant in providing the necessary diversification of attitudes that are necessary to become an entrepreneur.

2   The mechanism that they discuss in terms of variety is somewhat puzzling because there is no obvious reason why a taste for variety should be correlated with a taste to become an entrepreneur. An individual could exercise his or her taste for variety simply by choosing a large number of different wage and salary jobs. It is not necessary or by any means obvious that variety should take the form of choosing to work for oneself. It may well be true that individuals like to work for themselves because of the flexibility this provides, but there is no need nor obvious reasons why that should be correlated with having a large number of skills unless, of course, it is the case that a large number of skills are a necessary ingredient to becoming an entrepreneur. But if that is true, we are right back to the jack-of-all-trades model.

References

Introduction by the Editors

Abeler, J., Altmann, S., Kube, S., Wibral, M. (2010). Gift Exchange and Workers' Fairness Concerns – When Equality Is Unfair, in: Journal of the European Economic Association, 8(6): 1299-1324.

Adams, J. S. (1963). Wage Inequities, Productivity and Work Quality, in: Industrial Relations, 3(1): 9-16.

Altmann, S., Falk, A., Wibral, M. (2011). Promotions and Incentives: The Case of Multi-Stage Elimination Tournaments, in: Journal of Labor Economics, forthcoming.

Amaldoss, W., Rapoport, A. (2009). Excessive Expenditures in Two-Stage Contests: Theory and Experimental Evidence, in: Hangen, I. N., Nilsen, A. S. (Eds.), Game Theory: Strategies, Equilibria and Theorems, New York, NY: Nova Science Publishers, 241-66.

Bandiera, O., Barankay, I., Rasul, I. (2009). Social Connections and Incentives in the Workplace: Evidence from Personnel Data, in: Econometrica, 77(4): 1047-94.

Bognanno, M. L. (2001). Corporate Tournaments, in: Journal of Labor Economics, 19(2): 290-315.

Dohmen, T., Falk, A. (2010). Performance Pay and Multi-Dimensional Sorting – Productivity, Preferences and Gender, in: American Economic Review, forthcoming.

Ehrenberg, R. G., Bognanno, M. L. (1990). Do Tournaments have Incentive Effects?, in: Journal of Political Economy, 98(6): 1307-24.

Eriksson, T. (1999). Executive Pay and Tournament Theory: Empirical Tests on Danish Data, in: Journal of Labor Economics, 17(2): 262-80.

Fehr, E., Falk, A. (2002): Psychological Foundation of Incentives, in: European Economic Review, 46(4-5): 687-724.

Fehr, E., Gächter, S., Kirchsteiger, G. (1997). Reciprocity as a Contract Enforcement Device: Experimental Evidence, in: Econometrica, 65(4): 833-60.

Fehr, E., Klein, A., Schmidt, K. M. (2007). Fairness and Contract Design, in: Econometrica, 75(1): 121-54.

Fließbach, K., Weber, B., Trautner, P., Dohmen, T., Sunde, U., Elger, C. E., Falk, A. (2007). Social Comparison Affects Reward-Related Brain Activity in the Human Ventral Striatum, in: Science, 318(5854): 1305-8.

Grund, C., Sliwka, D. (2005). Envy and Compassion in Tournaments, in: Journal of Economics & Management Strategy, 14(1): 187-207.

Kräkel, M. (2008). Emotions in Tournaments, in: Journal of Economic Behavior & Organization, 67(1): 204-14.

Lazear, E. P. (1986). Salaries and Piece Rates, in: Journal of Business, 59(3): 405-31. [Chapter 7 in this volume]

Lazear, E. P. (1999). Personnel Economics: Past Lessons and Future Directions, in: Journal of Labor Economics, 17(2): 199-236.

References

Lazear, E. P. (2000). Performance Pay and Productivity, in: American Economic Review, 90(5): 1346–61. [Chapter 8 in this volume]

Lazear, E. P. (2005). Entrepreneurship, in: Journal of Labor Economics, 23(4): 649–80. [Chapter 16 in this volume]

Müller, W., Schotter, A. (2010). Workaholics and Dropouts in Organizations, in: Journal of the European Economic Association, 8(4): forthcoming.

Parco, J. E., Rapoport, A., Amaldoss, W. (2005): Two-Stage Contests with Budget Constraints: an Experimental Study, in: Journal of Mathematical Psychology, 49(4): 320–38.

Prendergast, C. (1999). The Provision of Incentives in Firms, in: Journal of Economic Literature, 37(1): 7–63.

Bibliography

Abowd, J., Ashenfelter, O. C. (1981). Anticipated Unemployment, Temporary Layoffs, and Compensating Wage Differentials, in: Rosen, S. (Ed.), Studies in Labor Markets, Chicago: University of Chicago, 141–70.

Acemoglu, D. (1997). Training and Innovation in an Imperfect Labor Market, in: Review of Economic Studies, 64(3): 445–64.

Acemoglu, D., Angrist, J. D. (2001). Consequences of Employment Protection? The Case of the Americans with Disabilities Act, in: Journal of Political Economy, 109(5): 915–57.

Acemoglu, D., Pischke, J.-S. (1998). Why Do Firms Train? Theory and Evidence, in: Quarterly Journal of Economics, 113(1): 79–119.

Addison, J. T., Schnabel, C., Wagner, J. (2001). Works Councils in Germany: Their Effects on Establishment Performance, in: Oxford Economic Papers, 53(4): 659–94.

Adelstein, R. (1994). Order and Planning, Unpublished Manuscript, Wesleyan University.

Aghion, P., Dewatripont, M., Rey, P. (1994). Renegotiation Design with Unverifiable Information, in: Econometrica, 62(2): 257–82.

Akerhielm, K. (1995). Does Class Size Matter?, in: Economics of Education Review, 14(3): 229–41.

Akerlof, G. A. (1976). The Economics of Caste and of the Rat Race and Other Woeful Tales, in: Quarterly Journal of Economics, 90(4): 599–617.

Akerlof, G. A., Kranton, R. E. (2002). Identity and Schooling: Some Lessons for the Economics of Education, in: Journal of Economic Literature, 40(4): 1167–2001.

Akerlof, G. A., Yellen, J. L., (1988). Fairness and Unemployment, in: American Economic Review, 78(2): 44–9.

Alchian, A. A., Demsetz, H. (1972). Production, Information Costs, and Economic Organization, in: American Economic Review, 62(5): 777–95.

Allen, M. P. (1982). The Identification of Interlock Groups in Large Peer Pressure Corporate Networks: Convergent Validation Using Divergent Techniques, in: Social Networks, 4(4): 349–66.

Altonji, J. G., Shakotko, R. A. (1987). Do Wages Rise with Job Seniority?, in: Review of Economic Studies, 54(3): 437–59.

Altonji, J. G., Williams, N. (1997). Do Wages Rise with Job Seniority? A Reassessment, NBER Working Paper No. 6010.

Anderson, R. E., Dubinsky, A. J., Mehta, R. (1999). Sales Managers: Marketing's Best Example of the Peter Principle?, in: Business Horizons, 42(1): 19–26.

Anderson, R. M. (Ed.) (1982). The Population Dynamics of Infectious Diseases: Theory and Applications, London: Chapman & Hall.

Angrist, J., Lavy, V. (1999). Using Maimonides' Rule to Estimate the Effect of Class Size on Scholastic Achievement, in: Quarterly Journal of Economics, 114(2): 533–75.

Angrist, J., Lavy, V. (2009). The Effects of High Stakes High School Achievement Awards: Evidence from a Group-Randomized Trial, in: American Economic Review, 99(4): 1384–414.

References

Antos, J. R., Rosen, S. (1975). Discrimination in the Market for Public School Teachers, in: Journal of Econometrics, 3(2): 123–50.

Aoki, M. (1986). Horizontal vs. Vertical Information Structure of the Firm, in: American Economic Review, 76(5): 971–83.

Arnott, R. J., Stiglitz, J. E. (1981). Labor Turnover, Wage Structures, and Moral Hazard: The Inefficiency of Competitive Markets, Econometric Research Program Research Memorandum 289, Princeton, NJ: Princeton University.

Arnott, R. J., Stiglitz, J. E. (1991). Moral Hazard and Nonmarket Institutions: Dysfunctional Crowding Out or Peer Monitoring, in: American Economic Review, 81(1): 179–90.

Aronstein, C.-S. (Ed.) (1976). International Handbook on Contracts of Employment, Deventer: Kluwer Law and Taxation Publishers.

Asch, B. J. (1990). Do Incentives Matter? The Case of Navy Recruiters, in: Industrial and Labor Relations Review, 43(3), 89–106.

Ashenfelter, O. C., Pencavel, J. H. (1976). A Note on Measuring the Relationship between Changes in Earnings and Changes in Wage Rates, in: British Journal of Industrial Relations, 14(1): 70–6.

Astebro, T., Thompson, P. (2009). Entrepreneurs: Jacks of All Trades or Hobos?, Working Paper No. 0705, Florida International University.

Autor, D. H. (2003). Outsourcing at Will: Unjust Dismissal Doctrine and the Growth of Temporary Help Employment, in: Journal of Labor Economics, 21(1): 1–42.

Autor, D. H., Donohue III, J. J., Schwab, S. J. (2006). The Costs of Wrongful-Discharge Laws, in: Review of Economics and Statistics, 88(2): 211–31.

Azariadis, C. (1975). Implicit Contracts and Underemployment Equilibria, in: Journal of Political Economy, 83(6): 1183–202.

Azariadis, C. (1983). Employment with Asymmetric Information, in: Quarterly Journal of Economics, 98(Supplement): 157–72.

Baily, M. N. (1974). Wages and Employment under Uncertain Demand, in: Review of Economic Studies, 41(1): 37–50.

Baily, M. N. (1977). On the Theory of Layoffs and Unemployment, in: Econometrica, 45(5): 1043–64.

Baker, G. (1992). Incentive Contracts and Performance Measurement, in: Journal of Political Economy, 100(2): 598–614.

Baker, G., Gibbs, M., Holmström, B. (1994). The Internal Economics of the Firm: Evidence from Personnel Data, in: Quarterly Journal of Economics, 109(4): 881–919.

Baker, G., Voicu, C. (2007). Wage Policies and Incentives to Invest in Firm-Specific Human Capital, Unpublished Manuscript, Harvard University.

Bandiera, O., Barankay, I., Rasul, I. (2005). Social Preferences and the Response to Incentives: Evidence from Personnel Data, in: Quarterly Journal of Economics, 120(3): 917–62.

Bandiera, O., Barankay, I., Rasul, I. (2007). Incentives for Managers and Inequality among Workers: Evidence from a Firm-Level Experiment, in: Quarterly Journal of Economics, 122(2): 729–73.

Bandiera, O., Barankay, I., Rasul, I. (2009). Social Connections and Incentives in the Workplace: Evidence from Personnel Data, in: Econometrica, 77(4): 1047–94.

Bandiera, O., Barankay, I., Rasul, I. (2010a). Social Incentives in the Workplace, in: Review of Economic Studies, 77(2): 417–58.

Bandiera, O., Barankay, I., Rasul, I. (2010b). Team Incentives: Evidence from a Field Experiment, Working Paper, London School of Economics.

Bankers Trust (1975). Study of Corporate Pension Plans, New York, NY: Bankers Trust.

Bankers Trust (1976). Study of Corporate Pension Plans, New York, NY: Bankers Trust.

Bankers Trust (1980). Study of Corporate Pension Plans, New York, NY: Bankers Trust.

Bartel, A. P., Borjas, G. J. (1981). Wage Growth and Job Turnover: An Empirical Analysis, in: Rosen, S. (Ed.), Studies in Labor Markets, Chicago, IL: University of Chicago Press, 65–90.

Bates, T. (1985). Entrepreneur Human Capital Endowments and Minority Business Viability, in: Journal of Human Resources, 20(4): 540–54.

References

Bates, T. (1990). Entrepreneur Human Capital Inputs and Small Business Longevity, in: Review of Economics and Statistics, 72(4): 551–59.

Becker, G. S. (1957). The Economics of Discrimination, Chicago, IL: Chicago University Press.

Becker, G. S. (1962). Investment in Human Capital: A Theoretical Analysis, in: Journal of Political Economy, 70(S5): 9–49.

Becker, G. S. (1968). Crime and Punishment: An Economic Approach, in: Journal of Political Economy, 76(2): 169–217.

Becker, G. S. (1975). Human Capital: A Theoretical and Empirical Analysis, with Special Reference to Education, New York, NY: Columbia University Press.

Becker, G. S. (1991). A Treatise on the Family, Cambridge, MA: Harvard University Press.

Becker, G. S., Mulligan, C. (2002). The Division of Labor and Household and Market Economies, Unpublished Manuscript, University of Chicago.

Becker, G. S., Murphy, K. M. (1992). The Division of Labor, Coordination Costs, and Knowledge, in: Quarterly Journal of Economics, 107(4): 1137–60.

Becker, G. S., Murphy, K. M. (2000). Social Markets and Social Economics, Cambridge, MA: Harvard University Press.

Becker, G. S., Stigler, G. (1974). Law Enforcement, Malfeasance, and Compensation of Enforcers, in: Journal of Legal Studies, 3(1): 1–18.

Bedard, K., Brown, W. O., Jr., Helland, E. (1999). School Size and the Distribution of Test Scores, Claremont Colleges Working Paper No. 1999-11.

Bergman, N. K., Jenter, D. (2007). Employee Sentiment and Stock Option Compensation, in: Journal of Financial Economics, 84(3): 667–712.

Bertrand, M., Mullainathan, S. (2001). Are CEOs Rewarded for Luck? The Ones without Principals Are, in: Quarterly Journal of Economics, 116(3): 901–32.

Betts, J. R. (1996a). Is There a Link between School Inputs and Earnings? Fresh Scrutiny of an Old Literature, in: Burtless, G. (Ed.), Does Money Matter? The Effect of School Resources on Student Achievement and Adult Success, Washington, DC: Brookings Institution, 141–91.

Betts, J. R. (1996b). The Role of Homework in Improving School Quality, University of California at San Diego, Economics Working Paper No. 96-16.

Betts, J. R., Shkolnik, J. L. (1999). The Behavioral Effects of Variations in Class Size: The Case of Math Teachers, in: Educational Evaluation and Policy Analysis, 21(2): 193–213.

Bhattacharya, S., Guasch, J. L. (1988). Heterogeneity, Tournaments, and Hierarchies, in: Journal of Political Economy, 96(4): 867–81.

Black, S. E., Lynch, L. M. (2001). How to Compete: The Impact of Workplace Practices and Information Technology on Productivity, in: Review of Economics and Statistics, 83(3): 434–45.

Blake, H. (1954). Class Size: A Summary of Selected Studies in Elementary and Secondary Public Schools, Ph.D. thesis, Columbia University.

Blanchard, O., Portugal, P. (2001). What Hides behind an Unemployment Rate: Comparing Portuguese and U.S. Labor Markets, in: American Economic Review, 91(1): 187–201.

Blanchard, O., Summers, L. (1986). Hysteresis and the European Unemployment Problem, in: Fischer, S. (Ed.), NBER Macroeconomics Annual, Cambridge, MA: M.I.T. Press, 15–78.

Blanpain, R. (Ed.) (various years). International Encyclopedia of Labor Law and Industrial Relations, Deventer: Kluwer Law and Taxation Publishers (supplements 11-12, 1979; 15, 19, 1980; 25-28, 30, 1982; 39, 40, 46, 1984; 48, 52, 58, 1985; 63, 1986).

Blau, F. D. (1984). Occupational Segregation and Labor Market Discrimination, in: Reskin, B. F. (Ed.), Sex Segregation in the Workplace: Trends, Explanations, Remedies, Washington, DC: National Academy Press, 117–43.

Bloom, N., van Reenen, J. (2007). Measuring and Explaining Management Practices across Firms and Countries, in: Quarterly Journal of Economics, 122(4): 1351–408.

Bonin, J. P. (1976). On the Design of Managerial Incentive Structures in a Decentralized Planning Environment, in: American Economic Review, 66(4): 682–7.

Boning, B., Ichniowski, C., Shaw, K. (2007). Opportunity Counts: Teams and the Effectiveness of Production Incentives, in: Journal of Labor Economics, 25(4): 613–50.

Booth, A. L., Frank, J. (1996). Performance Related Pay, CEPR Discussion Paper No. 1593.

Booth, A. L., Chatterji, M. (1998). Unions and Efficient Training, in: Economic Journal, 108(447): 328–43.

Booth, A. L., Zoega, G. (1999). Do Quits Cause Under-Training?, in: Oxford Economic Papers, 51(2): 374–86.

Borjas, G. J. (1985). Assimilation, Changes in Cohort Quality, and the Earnings of Immigrants, in: Journal of Labor Economics, 3(4): 463–89.

Borjas, G. J. (1995). Assimilation and Changes in Cohort Quality Revisited: What Happened to Immigrant Earnings in the 1980s?, in: Journal of Labor Economics, 13(2): 201–45.

Bowen, W. G., Finegan, T. A. (1969). The Economics of Labor Force Participation, Princeton, NJ: Princeton University Press.

Brown, B. W., Saks, D. H. (1975). The Production and Distribution of Cognitive Skills within Schools, in: Journal of Political Economy, 83(3): 571–93.

Brown, C. (1990). Firms' Choice of Method of Pay, in: Industrial and Labor Relations Review, Special Issue, 43(3): 165–82.

Brown, C. (1992). Wage Levels and Methods of Pay, in: RAND Journal of Economics, 23(3): 366–75.

Brown, C., Medoff, J. (1989). The Employer Size-Wage Effect, in: Journal of Political Economy, 97(5): 1027–59.

Brown, M., Philips, P. (1986). The Decline of Piece Rates in California Canneries: 1890-1960, in: Industrial Relations, 25(1): 81–91.

Bull, C., Schotter, A., Weigelt, K. (1987). Tournaments and Piece Rates: An Experimental Study, in: Journal of Political Economy, 95(1): 1–33.

Bulow, J. (1981). Early Retirement Pension Benefits, NBER Working Paper No. 654.

Burkhauser, R. V. (1976). Early Pension Decision and Its Effect on Exit from the Labor Market, Ph.D. thesis, University of Chicago.

Burkhauser, R. V., Quinn, J. F. (1983). The Effect of Pension Plans on the Pattern of Life-Cycle Compensation, in: Triplett, J. E. (Ed.), The Measure of Labor Cost, Conference on Research in Income and Wealth, Studies in Income and Wealth, Vol. 48, Chicago, IL: University of Chicago Press, 395–415.

Burt, R. S. (1987). A Note on the General Social Survey's Ersatz Network Density Item, in: Social Networks, 9(1): 75–85.

Cappelli, P. (2004). Why Do Employers Pay for College?, in: Journal of Econometrics, 121(1-2): 213–41.

Cappelli, P., Neumark, D. (2001). Do "High-Performance" Work Practices Improve Establishment-Level Outcomes?, in: Industrial and Labor Relations Review, 54(4): 737–75.

Card, D., Krueger, A. B. (1992). Does School Quality Matter? Returns to Education and the Characteristics of Public Schools in the United States, in: Journal of Political Economy, 100(1): 1–40.

Carmichael, H. L. (1983a). Firm-Specific Human Capital and Promotion Ladders, in: Bell Journal of Economics, 14(1): 251–58.

Carmichael, H. L. (1983b). The Agent-Agents Problem: Payment by Relative Output, in: Journal of Labor Economics, 1(1): 50-65.

Carmichael, L., MacLeod, W. B. (2003). Caring About Sunk Costs: A Behavioral Solution to Holdup Problems with Small Stakes, in: Journal of Law Economics and Organization, 19(1): 106-18.

Caucutt, E. M. (1996). Peer Group Effects in Applied General Equilibrium, in: Economic Theory, 17(1): 25–51.

Central Bureau of Statistics (various years). Statistical Abstract of Israel, Jerusalem: Central Bureau of Statistics (1957-1984).

Central Statistical Office (various years). Statistical Yearbook of Finland, Helsinki: Central Statistical Office (1978, 1979, 1984, and 1985).

References

Chamber of Commerce (1927). Employee Representation or Works Councils, Washington, DC: Chamber of Commerce.

Chan, W. (1996). External Recruitment versus Internal Promotion, in: Journal of Labor Economics, 14(4): 555–70.

Chan, W. (2006). External Recruitment and Intra-Firm Mobility, in: Economic Inquiry, 44(1): 169–84.

Chang, C., Wang, Y. (1996). Human Capital Investment under Asymmetric Information: The Pigovian Conjecture Revisited, in: Journal of Labor Economics, 14(3): 505–19.

Cheung, S. N. S. (1969). The Theory of Share Tenancy: With Special Application to Asian Agriculture and the First Phase of Taiwan Land Reform. Chicago, IL: University of Chicago Press.

Chiswick, B. R. (1978). The Effect of Americanization on Earnings of Foreign-born Men, in: Journal of Political Economy, 86(5): 897–921.

Chiswick, B. R. (1991). Speaking, Reading, and Earnings among Low-Skilled Immigrants, in: Journal of Labor Economics, 9(2): 149–70.

Chiswick, B. R. (1998). Hebrew Language Usage: Determinants and Effects on Earnings among Immigrants in Israel, in: Journal of Population Economics, 11(2): 253–71.

Chiswick, B. R., Miller, P. W. (1994). Language Choice among Immigrants in a Multilingual Destination, in: Journal of Population Economics, 7(2): 119–31.

Chiswick, B. R., Miller, P. W. (1995). The Endogeneity between Language and Earnings: International Analyses, in: Journal of Labor Economics, 13(2): 246–88.

Chiswick, B. R., Miller, P. W. (1996). Ethnic Networks and Language. Proficiency among Immigrants, in: Journal of Population Economics, 9(1): 19–35.

Church, J., King, I. (1993). Bilingualism and Network Externalities, in: Canadian Journal of Economics, 26(2): 337–45.

Coleman, J. (1961). The Adolescent Society: The Social Life of the Teenager and Its Impact on Education, New York, NY: Free Press.

Coleman, J. (1988). Free Riders and Zealots: The Role of Social Networks, in: Sociological Theory, 6(1): 52–57.

Coleman, J., Hoffer, T. (1987). Public and Private Schools: The Impact on Communities, New York, NY: Basic Books.

Coleman, J., Kilgore, S., Hoffer, T. (1981). Public and Private High Schools, Washington, DC: National Center for Educational Statistics.

Crossley, T. F., Jones, S. R. G., Kuhn, P. (1994). Gender Differences in Displacement Costs, in: Journal of Human Resources, 29(2): 461–80.

Currie, J., Thomas, D. (1996). Could Subsequent School Quality Affect the Long Term Gains from Head Start?, Unpublished Manuscript, University of California, Los Angeles.

David, H. A. (1963). The Method of Paired Comparisons, London: Charles Griffin.

De Leire, T. (2000). The Wage and Employment Effects of the Americans with Disabilities Act, in: Journal of Human Resources, 35(4): 693–715.

De Meza, D., Southey, C. (1996). The Borrower's Curse: Optimism, Finance and Entrepreneurship, in: Economic Journal, 106(435): 375–86.

De Varo, J. (2006). Internal Promotion Competitions in Firms, in: RAND Journal of Economics, 37(3): 521–42.

Deci, E. L. (1971). Effects of Externally Mediated Rewards on Intrinsic Motivation, in: Journal of Personality and Social Psychology, 18(1): 105–15.

Dertouzos, J. N., Karoly, L. A. (1992). Labor-Market Responses to Employer Liability, Santa Monica, CA: The RAND Corporation.

Diamond, P. A., Maskin, E. S. (1979). An Equilibrium Analysis of Search and Breach of Contract, I: Steady States, in: Bell Journal of Economics, 10(1): 282–316.

DiPasquale, D., Glaeser, E. L. (1998). The Los Angeles Riot and the Economics of Urban Unrest, in: Journal of Urban Economics, 43(1): 52–78.

Dismissal Procedures - IX: Japan (1959), in: International Labour Review, 80(2): 528–35.

Doeringer, P., Piore, M. (1971). Internal Labor Markets and Manpower Analysis, Lexington, MA: D. C. Heath.

References

Douglas, P. (1921). Shop Committees: Substitute for, or Supplement to, Trades Unions?, in: Journal of Political Economy, 29(2): 89–107.

Drago, R., Garvey, G. T. (1998). Incentives for Helping on the Job: Theory and Evidence, in: Journal of Labor Economics, 16(1): 1–25.

Drago, R., Heywood, J. S. (1995). The Choice of Payment Schemes: Australian Establishment Data, in: Industrial Relations, 34(4): 507–31.

Duflo, E., Hanna, R., Ryan, S. (2008). Monitoring Works: Getting Teachers to Come to School, CEPR Discussion Paper No. 6682.

Dye, R. A. (1984). The Trouble with Tournaments, in: Economic Inquiry, 22(1): 147–49.

Economides, N., Siow, A. (1988). The Division of Markets Is Limited by the Extent of Liquidity (Spatial Competition with Externalities), in: American Economic Review, 78(1): 108–21.

Eeckhout, J., Persico, N., Todd, P. (2010). A Theory of Optimal Random Crackdowns, in: American Economic Review, forthcoming.

Ehrenberg, R. (1980). Retirement System Characteristics and Compensating Wage Differentials in the Public Sector, in: Industrial and Labor Relations Review, 33(4): 470–83.

Ehrenberg, R. G., Bognanno, M. L. (1990). Do Tournaments Have Incentive Effects?, in: Journal of Political Economy, 98(6): 1307–24.

Emerson, M. (1988). Regulation or Deregulation of the Labor Market: Policy Regimes for the Recruitment and Dismissal of Employees in the Industrialized Countries, in: European Economic Review, 32(4): 775–817.

Epple, D., Romano, R. E. (1998). Competition between Private and Public Schools, Vouchers, and Peer-Group Effects, in: American Economic Review, 88(1): 33–62.

Eriksson, T. (1999). Executive Compensation and Tournament Theory: Empirical Tests on Danish Data, in: Journal of Labor Economics, 17(2): 262–80.

European Communities (1986). Employment and Unemployment, Luxembourg: Office for Official Publications of the European Communities.

Evans, D. S., Jovanovic. B. (1989). An Estimated Model of Entrepreneurial Choice under Liquidity Constraints, in: Journal of Political Economy, 97(4): 808–27.

Evans, D. S., Leighton, L. S. (1989). Some Empirical Aspects of Entrepreneurship, in: American Economic Review, 79(3): 519–35.

Evans, W. N., Schwab, R. M. (1995). Finishing High School and Starting College: Do Catholic Schools Make a Difference?, in: Quarterly Journal of Economics, 110(3): 941–74.

Fairburn, J. A., Malcomson, J. M. (2001). Performance, Promotion, and the Peter Principle, in: Review of Economic Studies, 68(1): 45–66.

Falk, A., Fehr, E., Huffman, D. (2008). The Power and Limits of Tournament Incentives, Working Paper, University of Bonn.

Falk, A., Huffman, D., MacLeod, W. B. (2008). Institutions and Contract Enforcement. IZA Discussion Paper No. 3435.

Falk, A., Ichino, A. (2006). Clean Evidence on Peer Effects, in: Journal of Labor Economics, 24(1): 39–58.

Fama, E. F. (1980). Agency Problems and the Theory of the Firm, in: Journal of Political Economy, 88(2): 288–307.

Fama, E. F. (1991). Time, Salary, and Incentive Payoffs in Labor Contracts, in: Journal of Labor Economics, 9(1): 25–44.

Fama, E. F., Jensen, M. C. (1983a). Agency Problems and Residual Claims, in: Journal of Law and Economics, 26(2): 327–49.

Fama, E. F., Jensen, M. C. (1983b). Separation of Ownership and Control, in: Journal of Law and Economics, 26(2): 301–25.

Fan, L.-S. (1975). On the Reward System, in: American Economic Review, 65(1): 226–29.

Faria, J. R. (2000). An Economic Analysis of the Peter and Dilbert Principles, Working Paper No. 101, Sydney: University of Technology.

Farrell, J., Scotchmer, S. (1988). Partnerships, in: Quarterly Journal of Economics, 103(2): 279–97.

Federal Statistical Office (various years). Statistisches Jahrbuch für die Bundesrepublik Deutschland, Stuttgart: W. Kohlhammer (1976-1983 and 1985).

References

Feldstein, M. S. (1976). Temporary Layoffs in the Theory of Unemployment, in: Journal of Political Economy, 84(5): 937–57.

Fernandez, R., Rogerson, R. (1998). Public Education and Income Distribution: A Dynamic Quantitative Evaluation of Education-Finance Reform, in: American Economic Review, 88(4): 813–33.

Fernie, S., Metcalf, D. (1999). It's Not What You Pay It's the Way That You Pay It and That's What Gets Results: Jockey's Pay and Performance, in: Labour, 13(2): 385–411.

Fields, G., Mitchell, O. (1981). Pensions and Optimal Retirement Behavior. NYSSILR Working Paper No. 27.

Flyer, F., Rosen, S. (1997). The New Economics of Teachers and Education, in: Journal of Labor Economics, 15(1): 104–39.

Frank, R. H. (1984). Are Workers Paid Their Marginal Products?, in: American Economic Review, 74(4): 549–71.

Frank, R. H. (1985). Choosing the Right Pond: Human Behavior and the Quest for Status, New York, NY: Oxford University Press.

Freeman, R. B. (1990). Employee Councils, Worker Participation, and other Squishy Stuff, Proceedings of the 43rd Annual Meeting of the Industrial Relations Research Association, Madison, WI: Wise: Industrial Relations Research Association.

Freeman, R. B., Kleiner, M. M. (2005). The Last American Shoe Manufacturers: Decreasing Productivity and Increasing Profits in the Shift from Piece Rates to Continuous Flow Production, in: Industrial Relations, 44(2): 307–30.

Freeman, R. B., Rogers, J. (1993). Who Speaks for Us: Employee Representation in a Nonunion Labor Market, in: Kaufman, B. E., Kleiner, M. M. (Eds.), Employee Representation: Alternatives and Future Directions, Madison, WI: Wise: Industrial Relations Research Association, 13–39.

Freeman, R. B., Weitzman, M. L. (1987). Bonuses and Employment in Japan, in: Journal of the Japanese and International Economies 1(2): 168–94.

Freeman, S. (1977). Wage Trends as Performance Displays Productive Potential: A Model of Application to Academic Early Retirement, in: Bell Journal of Economics, 8(2): 419–43.

Freixas, X., Guesnerie, R., Tirole, J. (1985). Planning under Incomplete Information and the Ratchet Effect, in: Review of Economic Studies, 52(2): 173–91.

Friedman, M. (1953). Choice, Chance, and the Personal Distribution of Income, in: Journal of Political Economy, 61(4): 277–90.

Galton, F. (1901-2). The Most Suitable Proportion between the Values of First and Second Prizes, in: Biometrika, 1(4): 385–99.

Garicano, L. (2000). Hierarchies and the Organization of Knowledge in Production, in: Journal of Political Economy, 108(5): 874–904.

Garicano, L., Hubbard, T. N. (2009). Specialization, Firms, and Markets: The Division of Labor within and between Law Firms, in: Journal of Law, Economics, & Organization, 25(2): 339–71.

Garicano, L., Rossi-Hansberg, E. (2006). Organization and Inequality in a Knowledge Economy, in: Quarterly Journal of Economics, 121(4): 1383–435.

Gavin, M. (1986). Labor Market Rigidities and Unemployment: The Case of Severance Costs, Board of Governors of the Federal Reserve, Discussion Papers in International Finance No. 284.

Geel, R., Mure, J., Backes-Gellner, U. (2008). Specificity of Occupational Training and Occupational Mobility: An Empirical Study Based on Lazear's Skill-Weights Approach, Swiss Leading House, Working Paper No. 38.

Gentry, W. M., Hubbard, R. G. (2004). Entrepreneurship and Household Saving, in: Advances in Economic Analysis & Policy, 4(1): Article 8.

Gibbons, J. D., Olkin, I., Sobel, M. (1977). Selecting and Ordering Populations: A New Statistical Methodology, New York, NY: Wiley.

Gibbons, R., Katz, L. F. (1991). Layoffs and Lemons, in: Journal of Labor Economics, 9(4): 351–80.

Gibbons, R., Waldman, M. (1999a). Careers in Organizations: Theory and Evidence, in: Ashenfelter, O. C., Card, D. (Eds.), Handbook of Labor Economics, Vol. 3B, Amsterdam: North-Holland, 2373–437.

Gibbons, R., Waldman, M. (1999b). A Theory of Wage and Promotion Dynamics inside Firms, in: Quarterly Journal of Economics, 114(4): 1321–58.

Gibbons, R., Waldman, M. (2004). Task-Specific Human Capital, in: American Economic Review, 94(2): 203–7.

Gibbons, R., Waldman, M. (2006). Enriching a Theory of Wage and Promotion Dynamics inside Firms, in: Journal of Labor Economics, 24(1): 59–107.

Gibbs, M., Hendricks, W. (2004). Do Formal Salary Systems Really Matter?, in: Industrial and Labor Relations Review, 58(1): 71–93.

Glewwe, P., Ilias, N., Kremer, M. (2008). Teacher Incentives, Harvard University Department of Economics working paper.

Gneezy, U., Niederle, M., Rustichini, A. (2003). Performance in Competetive Environments: Gender Differences, in: Quarterly Journal of Economics, 118(3): 1049–74.

Goldin, C. (1986). Monitoring Costs and Occupational Segregation by Sex: A Historical Analysis, in: Journal of Labor Economics, 4(1): 1–27.

Gordon, M. S. (1960). Older Workers and Retirement Policies, in: Monthly Labor Review, 83(6): 577–85.

Gordon, D. F. (1974). A Neoclassical Theory of Keynesian Unemployment, in: Economic Inquiry, 12(4): 431–59.

Green, J., Kahn, C. (1983). Wage-Employment Contracts, in: Quarterly Journal of Economics, 98(Supplement): 173–87.

Green, J. R., Stokey, N. L. (1983). A Comparison of Tournaments and Contracts, in: Journal of Political Economy, 91(3): 349–64.

Grogger, J. (1997). Local Violence and Educational Attainment, in: Journal of Human Resources, 32(4): 659–82.

Grogger, J., Neal, D. (2000). Further Evidence on the Effects of Catholic Secondary Schooling, in: Brookings/Wharton Papers on Urban Affairs, 1: 151–201.

Gronau, R. (1988). Sex-Related Wage Differentials and Women's Interrupted Labor Careers – The Chicken or the Egg, in: Journal of Labor Economics, 6(3): 277–301.

Groshen, E. (1991). The Structure of the Female/Male Wage Differential: Is It Who You Are, What You Do, or Where You Work?, in: Journal of Human Resources, 26(3): 457–72.

Grossman, H. I. (1978). Risk Shifting, Layoffs, and Seniority, in: Journal of Monetary Economics, 4(4): 661–86.

Grossman, S. J., Hart, O. D. (1981). Implicit Contracts, Moral Hazard and Unemployment, in: American Economic Review, 71(2): 301–7.

Grossman, S. J., Hart, O. D. (1983). Implicit Contracts under Asymmetric Information, in: Quarterly Journal of Economics, 98(3): 123–56.

Hall, R. E. (1982). The Importance of Lifetime Jobs in the U.S. Economy, in: American Economic Review, 72(4): 716–24.

Hall, R. E., Lazear, E. P. (1984). The Excess Sensitivity of Layoffs and Quits to Demand, in: Journal of Labor Economics, 2(2): 233–57.

Hamilton, B. H. (2000). Does Entrepreneurship Pay? An Empirical Analysis of the Returns of Self-Employment, in: Journal of Political Economy, 108(3): 604–31.

Hamilton, B. H., Nickerson, J. A., Owan, H. (2003). Team Incentives and Worker Heterogeneity: An Empirical Analysis of the Impact of Teams on Productivity and Participation, in: Journal of Political Economy, 111(3): 465–97.

Hanushek, E. A. (1998). Conclusions and Controversies about the Effectiveness of School Resources, in: Federal Reserve Bank of New York Economic Policy Review, 4(1): 11–27.

Hanushek, E. A., Kain, J. F., Rivkin, S. G. (2004). Disruption versus Tiebout Improvement: the Costs and Benefits of Switching Schools, in: Journal of Public Economics, 88(9-10), 1721–46.

Harris, M., Holmström, B. (1982). A Theory of Wage Dynamics, in: Review of Economic Studies, 49(3): 315–33.

Harris, M., Raviv, A. (1978). Some Results on Incentive Contracts with Applications to Education and Employment, Health Insurance, and Law Enforcement, in: American Economic Review, 68(1): 20–30.

References

Harris, M., Weiss, Y. (1981). Job Matching, Risk Aversion, and Tenure, Kellogg Graduate School of Management, Discussion Paper No. 514.

Hashimoto, M. (1979). Bonus Payments, On-the-Job Training, and Lifetime Employment in Japan, in: Journal of Political Economy, 87(5): 1086–104.

Hausman, J. A., Taylor, W. E. (1981). Panel Data and Unobservable Individual Effects, in: Econometrica, 49 (6): 1377–98.

Hechter, M. (1987). Principles of Group Solidarity, Berkeley, CA: University of California Press.

Heckathorn, D. D. (1988). Collective Sanctions and the Second-Order Free Rider Problem, in: American Journal of Sociology, 94(3): 535–62.

Heckman, J. J. (1999). Doing It Right: Job Training and Education, in: Public Interest, 135(Spring), 86–107.

Heckman, J. J., Lochner, L. (2000). Rethinking Myths about Education and Training: Understanding the Sources of Skill Formation in a Modern Economy, in: Danzinger, S., Waldfogel, J. (Eds.), Securing the Future: Investing in Children from Birth to College, New York, NY: Russell Sage, 47–83.

Heckman, J. J., Scheinkman, J. A. (1987). The Importance of Bundling in a Gorman-Lancaster Model of Earnings, in: Review of Economic Studies, 54(2): 243–55.

Heckman, J. J., Sedlacek, G. (1985). Heterogeneity Aggregation and Market Wage Functions: An Empirical Model of Self-Selection in the Labor Market, in: Journal of Political Economy, 93(6): 1077–125.

Heckman, J. J., Willis, R. (1977). A Beta-Logistic Model for the Analysis of Sequential Labor Force Participation by Married Women, in: Journal of Political Economy, 85(1): 27–58.

Henderson, V., Mieszkowski, P., Sauvageau, Y. (1978). Peer Group Effects and Educational Production Functions, in: Journal of Public Economics, 10(1): 97–106.

Hoffman, J. V., Assaf, L. C., Paris, S. G. (2001). High-Stakes Testing in Reading: Today in Texas, Tomorrow?, in: The Reading Teacher, 54(5): 482–92.

Holländer, H. (1990). A Social Exchange Approach to Voluntary Cooperation, in: American Economic Review, 80(5): 1157–67.

Holmes, T. J., Schmitz, J. A., Jr. (1990). A Theory of Entrepreneurship and its Application to the Study of Business Transfers, in: Journal of Political Economy, 98(2): 265–94.

Holmström, B. (1979). Moral Hazard and Observability, in: Bell Journal of Economics, 10(1): 74–91.

Holmström, B. (1981). Contractual Models of the Labor Market, in: American Economic Review, Papers and Proceedings, 71(2): 308–13.

Holmström, B. (1982). Moral Hazard in Teams, in: Bell Journal of Economics 13(2): 324–40.

Holmström, B., Milgrom, P. (1990). Regulating Trade among Agents, in: Journal of Institutional and Theoretical Economics, 146(1): 85–105.

Holmström, B., Milgrom, P. (1991). Multi-Task Principal-Agent Analyses: Incentive Contracts, Asset Ownership, and Job Design, in: Journal of Law, Economics, & Organization, 7(Special Issue): 24–52.

Holtz-Eakin, D., Joulfaian, D., Rosen, H. S. (1994). Entrepreneurial Decisions and Liquidity Constraints, in: RAND Journal of Economics, 25(2): 334–47.

Hoxby, C. M. (1996). How Teachers' Unions Affect Education Production, in: Quarterly Journal of Economics, 111(3): 671–718.

Hoxby, C. M. (1998). What Do America's 'Traditional' Forms of School Choice Teach Us about School Choice Reforms?, in: Federal Reserve Bank of New York Economic Policy Review, 4(1): 47–59.

Hoxby, C. M. (2000a). The Effects of Class Size on Student Achievement: New Evidence from Natural Population Variation, in: Quarterly Journal of Economics, 115(4): 1239–85.

Hoxby, C. M. (2000b). Peer Effects in the Classroom: Learning from Gender and Race Variation, NBER Working Paper No. 7867.

Hutchens, R. M. (1987). A Test of Lazear's Theory of Delayed Payment Contracts, in: Journal of Labor Economics, 5(4, pt.2): S153-S170.

Iannaccone, L. R. (1992). Sacrifice and Stigma: Reducing Free-riding in Cults, Communes, and Other Collectives, in: Journal of Political Economy, 100(2): 271–91.

Ichniowski, C., Shaw, K., Prennushi, G. (1997). The Effects of Human Resource Management Practices on Productivity: a Study of Steel Finishing Lines, in American Economic Review, 87(3): 291–313.

ILO (various years). Legislative Series, Geneva: International Labour Office Publications, (issues used: 1929, 1931, 1949, 1950, 1955, 1956, 1960, 1961, 1965, 1967-1970, 1972-1977, 1979, 1983 and 1985).

ILO (various years). Yearbook of Labor Statistics, Geneva: International Labour Office Publications, (1957-1975, 1977-1986).

Information Canada (1974). Canada Yearbook, Ottawa: Information Canada.

Institut National de Statistique (1985). Annuaire Statistique de la Belgique, Brussels: Institut National de Statistique.

Instituto Nacional de Estatistica Servicos Centrais (1978). Portugal Annuario Estatistico, Lisbon: Instituto Nacional de Estatistica Servicos Centrais.

Instituto Centrale di Statistico (1974-1984). Annuario Statistico Italiano, Rome: Istituto Centrale di Statistico.

Itoh, H. (1994). Job Design, Delegation and Cooperation: A Principal-Agent Analysis, in: European Economic Review, 38(3-4): 691–700.

Iyigun, M. F., Owen, A. L. (1998). Risk, Entrepreneurship, and Human-Capital Accumulation, in: American Economic Review, Papers and Proceedings, 88(2): 454–7.

Jacobson, L., LaLonde, R. J., Sullivan, D. G. (1993). The Costs of Worker Dislocation, Kalamazoo, MI: W.E. Upjohn Institute.

Japan Statistical Association (various years). Japan Statistical Yearbook, Tokyo: Japan Statistical Association, (1981, 1983 and 1985).

Jensen, M. C., Murphy, K. J. (1990). Performance Pay and Top-Management Incentives, in: Journal of Political Economy, 98(2): 225–64.

John, A., Yi, K.-M. (1997). Language, Learning and Location, Federal Reserve Bank of New York Staff Report No. 26.

Johnson, D. G. (1950). Resource Allocation under Share Contracts, in: Journal of Political Economy, 58(2): 111–23.

Jones, M. G., Jones, B. D., Hardin, B., Chapman, L., Yarbrough, T., Davis, M. (1999). The Impact of High-Stakes Testing on Teachers and Students in North Carolina, in: The Phi Delta Kappan, 81(3): 199–203.

Jones, S. R. G. (1984). The Economics of Conformism, Oxford: Blackwell.

Jovanovic, B. (1979a). Job Matching and the Theory of Turnover, in: Journal of Political Economy, 87(5): 972–90.

Jovanovic, B. (1979b). Firm-Specific Capital and Turnover, in: Journal of Political Economy, 87(6): 1246–60.

Kahn, C., Huberman, G. (1988). Two-Sided Uncertainty and 'Up-or-Out' Contracts, in: Journal of Labor Economics, 6(4): 423–44.

Kandel, E., Lazear, E. P. (1992). Peer Pressure and Partnerships, in: Journal of Political Economy, 100(4): 80–17.

Karthik, M., Sundararaman, V. (2008). Contract Teachers: Experimental Evidence from India, University of California, San Diego.

Katz, K., Matsui, A. (2004). When Trade Requires Coordination, in: Journal of the Japanese and International Economies, 18(3): 440–61.

Katz, L. F., King, J. R., Liebman, J. B. (2001). Moving to Opportunity in Boston: Early Results of a Randomized Housing Mobility Experiment, in: Quarterly Journal of Economics, 116(2): 607–54.

Kaufman, R. (1979). Why the U.S. Unemployment Rate is So High, in: Piore, M. (Ed.), Unemployment and Inflation: Institutionalist and Structural Views, White Plains, NY: M. E. Sharpe.

Kennan, J. (1979). Bonding and Enforcement of Labor Contracts, in: Economics Letters 3(1): 61–6.

Kermack, W. O., McKendrick, A. G. (1927). A Contribution to the Mathematical Theory of Epidemics, in: Proceedings of the Royal Society, Series A, 115(772): 700–21.

509

References

Kihlstrom, R. E., Laffont, J.-J. (1979). A General Equilibrium Entrepreneurial Theory of Firm Formation Based on Risk Aversion, in: Journal of Political Economy, 87(4): 719–48.

Kleiner, M., Bouillon, M. (1988). Providing Business Information in Production Workers: Correlates of Compensation and Profitability, in: Industrial and Labor Relations Review, 41(4): 605–17.

Koike, K. (1989). Intellectual Skill and the Role of Employees as Constituent Members of Large Firms in Contemporary Japan, in: Masahiko A, Gustafsson, B., Williamson, O. (Eds.), The Firm as a Nexus of Treaties, Newbury Park, CA: Sage, 185–208.

Koretz, D. M., Linn, R. L., Dunbar, S. B., Shepard, L. A. (1991). The Effects of High-Stakes Testing on Achievement: Preliminary Findings about Generalization across Tests. Paper presented at the annual meeting of the American Educational Research Association, Chicago, IL.

Kremer, M. (1993). The O-Ring Theory of Economic Development, in: Quarterly Journal of Economics, 108(3): 551–75.

Kreps, D. (1986). Corporate Culture and Economic Theory, in: Tsuchiya, M. (Ed.), Technology Innovation and Business Strategy, Tokyo: Nippon Keizai Shumbunsha Press.

Kreps, J. (1961). A Case Study of Variables in Retirement Policy, in: Monthly Labor Review, 84(6): 587–91.

Krueger, A. B. (1998). Reassessing the View That American Schools Are Broken, in: Federal Reserve Bank of New York Economic Policy Review, 4(1): 29–43.

Krueger, A. B. (1999). Experimental Estimates of Educational Production Functions, in: Quarterly Journal of Economics, 114(2): 497–532.

Krueger, A. B., Whitmore, D. M. (2001). The Effect of Attending a Small Class in the Early Grades on College-Test Taking and Middle School Test Results: Evidence from Project STAR, in: Economic Journal, 111(468): 1–28.

Kugler, A., Saint-Paul, G. (2004). How Do Firing Costs Affect Worker Flows in a World with Adverse Selection, in: Journal of Labor Economics, 22(3): 553–84.

Laitin, D. D. (1994). The Tower of Babel as a Coordination Game: Political Linguistics in Ghana, in: American Political Science Review, 88(3): 622–34.

Landier, A. (2006). Entrepreneurship and the Stigma of Failure, Working Paper, New York University.

Lang, K. (1986). A Language Theory of Discrimination, in: Quarterly Journal of Economics, 101(2): 363–82.

Larkin, I. (2007). The Cost of High-powered Incentives: Salesperson Gaming in Enterprise Software, Working Paper, Harvard University.

Lavy, V. (1999). Using Dual Natural Quasi-Experimental Designs to Evaluate the Effect of School Hours and Class Size on Student Achievement, Unpublished Manuscript, Hebrew University of Jerusalem.

Lavy, V. (2009). Performance Pay and Teachers' Effort, Productivity and Grading Ethics, in: American Economic Review, 99(5): 1979–2011.

Lazear, E. P. (1979). Why is there Mandatory Retirement?, in: Journal of Political Economy 87(6): 1261–84. (Chapter 1 in this volume)

Lazear, E. P. (1980). Corporate Pension Plan Study, New York, NY: Bankers' Trust.

Lazear, E. P. (1981). Agency, Earnings Profiles, Productivity and Hours Restrictions, in: American Economic Review, 71(4): 606–20.

Lazear, E. P. (1982). Severance Pay, Pensions and Efficient Mobility, NBER Working Paper No. 854.

Lazear, E. P. (1983a). Pensions as Severance Pay, in: Bodie, Z., Shoven, J. B. (Eds.), Financial Aspects of the United States Pension System, Chicago, IL: University of Chicago Press, 57–90. [Chapter 2 in this volume]

Lazear, E. P. (1983b). Intergenerational Externalities, in: Canadian Journal of Economics, 16(2): 212–28.

Lazear, E. P. (1984). Incentives and Wage Rigidity, in: American Economic Review, 74(2): 339–44.

Lazear, E. P. (1986a). Raids and Offer Matching, in: Ehrenberg, R. G. (Ed.), Research in Labor Economics, Vol. 8(A), Greenwich, CT: JAI, 141–65.

Lazear, E. P. (1986b). Salaries and Piece Rates, in: Journal of Business, 59(3): 405–31. [Chapter 7 in this volume]

Lazear, E. P. (1987). Employment at Will, Job Security, and Work Incentives, in: Proceedings of the Conference on Employment, Unemployment, and Hours of Work, Science Center Berlin, September 17-19, 1986, London: Allen & Unwin.

Lazear, E. P. (1989). Pay Equality and Industrial Politics, in: Journal of Political Economy, 97(3): 561–80. [Chapter 11 in this volume]

Lazear, E. P. (1990). Job Security Provisions and Employment, in: Quarterly Journal of Economics, 105(3): 699–725. [Chapter 3 in this volume]

Lazear, E. P. (1992a). The Job as a Concept, in: Bruns, Jr., W. J. (Ed.) Performance Measurement, Evaluation, and Incentives, Boston, MA: Harvard Business School Press, 183–216. [Chapter 9 in this volume]

Lazear, E. P. (1992b). Peer Pressure and Partnerships, in: Journal of Political Economy, 100(4): 801–17. [Chapter 10 in this volume]

Lazear, E. P. (1995a). Corporate Culture and the Diffusion of Values, in: Horst Siebert, H. (Ed.), Trends in Business Organization: Do Participation and Cooperation Increase Competitiveness?, Tübingen: J.C.B. Mohr/Paul Siebeck, 89–133.

Lazear, E. P. (1995b). Introduction, in: Lazear, E. P. (Ed.), Economic Transition in Eastern Europe and Russia: Realities of Reform, Hoover Institution Press Publication No. 425, Stanford, CA: Hoover Institution Press.

Lazear, E. P. (1996a). Assimilation: 1900 and Now, Stanford, CA: mimeo.

Lazear, E. P. (1996b). Performance Pay and Productivity, NBER Working Paper No. 5672.

Lazear, E. P. (1999a). Culture and Language, in: Journal of Political Economy, 107(S6): 95–126. [Chapter 12 in this volume]

Lazear, E. P. (1999b). Globalization and the Market for Team-Mates, in: Economic Journal, 109(454): C15–C40.

Lazear, E. P. (2000a). The Future of Personnel Economics, in: Economic Journal, 110(467): F611–F639.

Lazear, E. P. (2000b). Performance Pay and Productivity, in: American Economic Review, 90(5): 1346–61. [Chapter 8 in this volume]

Lazear, E. P. (2000c). Diversity and Immigration, in: Borjas, G. J. (Ed.), Issues in the Economics of Immigration, Chicago, IL: University of Chicago Press, 117–42.

Lazear, E. P. (2000d). The Power of Incentives, in: American Economic Review, 90(2): 410–14.

Lazear, E. P. (2001). Educational Production, in: Quarterly Journal of Economics, 116(3): 777–803. [Chapter 14 in this volume]

Lazear, E. P. (2003). Teacher Incentives, in: Swedish Economic Policy Review, 10(2): 179–214.

Lazear, E. P. (2004a). The Peter Principle: A Theory of Decline, in: Journal of Political Economy, 112(1, pt.2): S141–S163. [Chapter 5 in this volume]

Lazear, E. P. (2004b). Balanced Skills and Entrepreneurship, in: American Economic Review, 94(2): 208–11.

Lazear, E. P. (2004c). Output-Based Pay: Incentives, Retention or Sorting?, in: Polachek, S. W. (Ed.), Research in Labor Economics, Vol. 24, Amsterdam: Elsevier, 1–26.

Lazear, E. P. (2005). Entrepreneurship, in: Journal of Labor Economics, 23(4): 649–80. [Chapter 16 in this volume]

Lazear, E. P. (2006). Speeding, Terrorism, and Teaching to the Test, in: Quarterly Journal of Economics, 121(3), 1029–61. [Chapter 15 in this volume]

Lazear, E. P. (2009). Firm-Specific Human Capital: A Skill-Weights Approach, in: Journal of Political Economy, 117(5): 914–40. [Chapter 13 in this volume]

Lazear, E. P., Freeman, R. B. (1995). An Economic Analysis of Works Councils, in: Roger, J., Streeck, W. (Eds.), Works Councils: Consultation, Representation, and Cooperation in Industrial Relations, Chicago, IL: University of Chicago Press, 27-50. [Chapter 4 in this volume]

Lazear, E. P., Rosen, S. (1981). Rank-Order Tournaments as Optimum Labor Contracts, in: Journal of Political Economy, 89(5): 841–64. [Chapter 6 in this volume]

References

Lazear, E. P., Rosen, S. (1990). Male-Female Wage Differentials in Job Ladders, in: Journal of Labor Economics, 8(1): S106–S123.

Lazear, E. P., Shaw, K. (Eds.) (2008a). The Structure of Wages: An International Comparison, Chicago, IL: University of Chicago Press.

Lazear, E. P., Shaw, K. (2008b). Tenure and Output, in: Labour Economics, 15(4): 710–24.

Lentz, B. F., Laband, D. N. (1990). Entrepreneurial Success and Occupational Inheritance among Proprietors, in: Canadian Journal of Economics, 23(3): 563–79.

Leonard, J. (1989). Career Paths of Executives and Managers, Unpublished Manuscript, University of California, Berkeley.

Lepper, M. R., Greene, D., Nisbett, R. E. (1973). Undermining Children's Intrinsic Interest with Extrinsic Reward: A Test of the 'Overjustification' Hypothesis, in: Journal of Personality and Social Psychology, 28(1): 129–37.

Lewis, H. G. (1983). Union Relative Wage Effects: A Survey of Macro Estimates, in: Journal of Labor Economics, 1(1): 1–27.

Lindbeck, A., Snower, D. J. (1986). Wage Setting, Unemployment, and Insider-Outsider Relations, in: American Economic Review, 76 (2): 235–39.

Lo, D., Ghosh, M., Lafontaine, F. (2006). The Role of Risk, Incentives and Selection in Salesforce Compensation Contracts, Unpublished Manuscript, Ross School of Business, University of Michigan.

Longitudinal Study of American Youth. Bureau of Labor Statistics, Chicago Academy of Science, 2001 N. Clark Street, Chicago, IL 60614, Web site: http://www.bls.gov/nls/.

Lucas, R. E., Jr. (1978). On the Size Distribution of Business Firms, in: Bell Journal of Economics, 9(2): 508–23.

MacLeod, W. B., Malcomson, J. M. (1993). Investments, Holdup, and the Form of Market Contracts, in: American Economic Review, 83(4): 811–37.

Marshall, A. P. (1890). Principles of Economics, New York, NY: Macmillan and Co.

Mas, A., Moretti, E. (2009). Peers at Work, in: American Economics Review, 99(1): 112–45.

May, R. M., Anderson, R. M. (1987). Transmission Dynamics of HIV Infection, in: Nature, 326(6109), 137–42.

Mayer, T. (1960). The Distribution of Ability and Earnings, in: Review of Economics and Statistics, 62(2): 189–95.

McBee, M. M., Barnes, L. L. B. (1998). The Generalizability of a Performance Assessment Measuring Achievement in Eighth-Grade Mathematics, in: Applied Measurement in Education, 11(2): 179–94.

McCue, K. (1990). Intrafirm Mobility and Wage Growth, Ph.D. thesis, University of Chicago.

McManus, W. S., Gould, W., Welch, F. (1983). Earnings of Hispanic Men: The Role of English Language Proficiency, in: Journal of Labor Economics, 1(2): 101–30.

McMillan, R. (2000). Competition, Parental Involvement and Public School Performance, in: National Tax Association Proceedings, 150–55.

McNeill, W. H. (1989). Plagues and Peoples, New York, NY: Doubleday, 1976. Reprint. Garden City, NY: Anchor.

Medoff, J. (1976). Layoffs and Alternatives under Trade Unions in United States Manufacturing, Harvard Institute of Economic Research, Discussion Paper No. 525.

Medoff, J. L., Abraham, K. G. (1980). Experience, Performance, and Earnings, in: Quarterly Journal of Economics, 95(4): 703–36.

Meisels, S. J. (1989). High-Stakes Testing in Kindergarten, in: Educational Leadership, 46(7): 16–22.

Milgrom, P. R. (1986). Quasi Rents, Yale University, Working Paper No. 21.

Miller, F. H. (1982). Wages and Establishment Sizes, Ph.D. thesis, University of Chicago.

Mincer, J. (1962). On-the-Job Training: Costs, Returns, and Some Implications, in: Journal of Political Economy, 70(5), S50–S79.

Mincer, J., Jovanovic, B. (1981). Labor Mobility and Wages, in: Rosen, S. (Ed.), Studies in Labor Markets, Chicago, IL: University of Chicago Press, 21–64.

Mirrlees, J. A. (1976). The Optimal Structure of Incentives and Authority within an Organization, in: Bell Journal of Economics, 7(1): 105–31.

Morishima, M. (1991). Information Sharing and Collective Bargaining in Japan: Effects on Wage Negotiation, in: Industrial and Labor Relations Review, 44(3): 469–87.

Muralidharan, K., Sundararaman, V. (2009). Teacher Performance Pay: Experimental Evidence from India, NBER Working Paper No. 15323.

Murphy, K. J. (1984). Ability, Performance, and Compensation: A Theoretical and Empirical Investigation of Managerial Labor Contracts, in: RAND Journal of Economics, 17(1), 59–76.

Murphy, K. J. (1985). Corporate Performance and Managerial Remuneration, in: Journal of Accounting and Economics, 7(1–3): 11–42.

Murphy, K. J. (1999). Executive Compensation, in: Ashenfelter, O., Card, D. (Eds.), Handbook of Labor Economics, Vol. 3, Amsterdam: North-Holland, 2485–563.

Nalebuff, B. J., Stiglitz, J. E. (1983). Prizes and Incentives: Toward a General Theory of Compensation and Competition, in: Bell Journal of Economics, 14(1): 21–43.

National Industrial Conference Board (1920). A Works Council Manual, Research Report No. 26, Boston, MA: NICB.

National Industrial Conference Board (1922). Experience with Works Councils in the United States, Research Report No. 50, New York, NY: Century.

National Industrial Conference Board, Inc. (1964). Corporate Retirement Policies and Practices, in: Studies in Personnel Policy, 190, New York, NY: NICB.

Neal, D. (1995). Industry-Specific Human Capital: Evidence from Displaced Workers, in: Journal of Labor Economics, 13(4): 653–77.

Neal, D. (1997). The Effects of Catholic Secondary Schooling on Educational Achievement, in: Journal of Labor Economics, 15(1): 98–123.

Neal, D. (1998). What Have We Learned about the Benefits of Private Schooling?, in: Federal Reserve Bank of New York Economic Policy Review, 4(1): 79–86.

Nickell, S. J. (1979). Unemployment and the Structure of Labor Costs, in: Carnegie Rochester Conference Series on Public Policy, 11 (1): 287–22.

Nickell, S. J. (1982). The Determinants of Equilibrium Unemployment in Britain, in: Economic Journal, 92(367): 555–75.

Niederle, M., Segal, C., Vesterlund, L. (2008). How Costly Is Diversity? Affirmative Action in Light of Gender Differences in Competitiveness, NBER Working Paper No. 13923.

Niederle, M., Vesterlund, L. (2007). Do Women Shy away from Competition? Do Men Compete Too Much?, in: Quarterly Journal of Economics, 122(3): 1067–101.

Norton, W. E., Kennedy, P. J. (1985). Australian Economic Statistics 1949-50 to 1984-85: I. Tables, Reserve Bank of Australia Occasional Paper No. 8A.

O'Reilly, C., Williams, K., Barsade, S. (1998). Group Demography and Innovation: Does Diversity Help?, in: Mannix, E., Neale, M. (Eds.), Research on Groups and Teams, Vol. 1, Greenwich, CT: JAI, 183–207.

OECD (various years). National Accounts, Vol. I: Main Aggregates, Paris: OECD Department of Economics and Statistics (1984 and 1986).

OECD (various years). Labor Force Statistics, Paris: OECD Department of Economics and Statistics (1968, 1972, and 1986).

Olson, C. A., Ackerman, D. (2000). High School Inputs and Labor Market Outcomes for Male Workers in Their Mid-Thirties: New Data and New Estimates from Wisconsin, Institute for Research on Poverty Discussion Paper No. 1205-00.

Olson, T. E., Torsvik, G. (2000). Discretion and Incentives in Organizations, in: Journal of Labor Economics, 18(3): 377–404.

Otani, K. (1996). A Human Capital Approach to Entrepreneurial Capacity, in: Economica, 63(250): 273–89.

Oyer, P. (1998). Fiscal Year Ends and Non-Linear Incentive Contracts: The Effect on Business Seasonality, in: Quarterly Journal of Economics, 113(1): 149–85.

Oyer, P., Schaefer, S. (2000). Layoffs and Litigation, in: RAND Journal of Economics, 31(2): 345–58.

References

Oyer, P., Schaefer, S. (2005). Why Do Some Firms Give Stock Options to All Employees?: An Empirical Examination of Alternative Theories, in: Journal of Financial Economics, 76(1): 99–133.

Paarsch, H. J., Shearer, B. S. (1997). Fixed Wages, Piece Rates, and Intertemporal Productivity: A Study of Tree Planters in British Columbia, CIRANO Working Paper No. 97s-01.

Parent, D. (1999). Methods of Pay and Earnings: A Longitudinal Analysis, in: Industrial and Labor Relations Review, 53(1): 71–86.

Parent, D. (2000). Industry-Specific Capital and the Wage Profile: Evidence from the National Longitudinal Survey of Youth and the Panel Study of Income Dynamics, in: Journal of Labor Economics, 18(2): 306–23.

Parsons, D. O. (1972). Specific Human Capital: Application to Quit Rates and Layoff Rates, in: Journal of Political Economy, 80(6): 1120–43.

Parsons, T. (1954). Essays in Sociological Theory, New York, NY: Free Press.

Pencavel, J. H. (1977). Work Effort, On-the-Job Screening, and Alternative Methods of Remuneration, in: Research in Labor Economics, 1: 225–58.

Persico, N. (2002). Racial Profiling, Fairness and Effective Policing, in: American Economic Review, 92(5): 1472–97.

Peter, L. J., Hull, R. (1969). The Peter Principle: Why Things Always Go Wrong, New York, NY: Morrow.

Petersen, T. (1992). Individual, Collective, and Systems Rationality in Work Groups: Dilemmas and Solutions, in: American Journal of Sociology, 98(3): 169–510.

Pfeffer, J. (1990). Incentives in Organizations: The Importance of Social Relations, in: Williamson, O. E. (Ed.), Theory: From Chester Barnard to the Present and Beyond, New York, NY: Oxford University Press.

Piaget, J., Inhelder, B. (1969). The Psychology of the Child, New York, NY: Basic Books.

Pool, J. (1991). The Official Language Problem, in: American Political Science Review, 85(2): 495–514.

Prendergast, C. J. (1995). A Theory of Responsibility in Organizations, in: Journal of Labor Economics, 13(3): 387–400.

Prendergast, C. (1999). The Provision of Incentives in Firms, in: Journal of Economic Literature, 37(1): 7–63.

Prendergast, C. (2000). What Trade-Off of Risk and Incentives?, in: American Economic Review, 90(2): 421–25.

Prendergast, C. (2002a). The Tenuous Trade-Off between Risk and Incentives, in: Journal of Political Economy, 110(5): 1071–102.

Prendergast, C. (2002b). Uncertainty and Incentives, in: Journal of Labor Economics, 20(2): S115–S137.

Prendergast, C., Stole, L. (1999). Restricting the Means of Exchange within Organizations, in: European Economic Review, 43(4): 1007–19.

Radner, R. (1986). Repeated Partnership Games with Imperfect Monitoring and No Discounting, in: Review of Economic Studies, 53(1): 43–57.

Reder, M. W. (1955). Theory of Occupational Wage Differentials, in: American Economic Review, 45(5): 833–52.

Riley, J. G. (1975). Competitive Signaling, in: Journal of Economic Theory, 10(2): 174–86.

Rivkin, S. G., Hanushek, E. A., Kain, J. F. (2001). Teachers, Schools, and Academic Achievement, in: Econometrica, 73(2): 417–58.

Robinson, C. (1988). Language Choice: The Distribution of Language Skills and Earnings in a Dual-Language Economy, in: Ehrenberg, R. G. (Ed.), Research in Labor Economics, Vol. 9, Greenwich, CT: JAI, 53–90.

Rogers, J., Streeck, W. (1991). Works Council Project: Concept Paper and Research Guideline, Unpublished Paper, University of Wisconsin.

Roger J., Streeck, W. (Eds.) (1995). Works Councils: Consultation, Representation, and Cooperation in Industrial Relations, Chicago: University of Chicago Press.

Rogerson, W. P. (1985). Repeated Moral Hazard, in: Econometrica, 53(1): 69–76.

Rogerson, W. P. (1988). Price Advertising and the Deterioration of Product Quality, in: Review of Economic Studies, 55(2): 215–29.

References

Rosen, S. (1972). Learning and Experience in the Labor Market, in: Journal of Human Resources, 7(3): 329–42.

Rosen, S. (1974). Hedonic Prices and Implicit Markets: Product Differentiation in Pure Competition, in: Journal of Political Economy, 82(1): 34–55.

Rosen, S. (1982). Authority, Control, and the Distribution of Earnings, in: Bell Journal of Economics, 13(2): 311–23.

Rosen, S. (1985). Implicit Contracts: A Survey, in: Journal of Economic Literature, 23(3): 1144–75.

Rosen, S. (1986). Prizes and Incentives in Elimination Tournaments, in: American Economic Review, 76(4): 701–15.

Rosen, S. (1987). Some Economics of Teaching, in: Journal of Labor Economics, 5(4): 561–75.

Ross, S. A. (1973). The Economic Theory of Agency: The Principal's Problem, in: American Economic Review, 63(2): 134–39.

Rothschild, M., Stiglitz, J. (1976). Equilibrium in Competitive Insurance Markets: An Essay on the Economics of Imperfect Information, in: Quarterly Journal of Economics, 90(4): 630–49.

Rothschild, M., White, L. (1995). The Analytics of the Pricing of Higher Education and Other Services in Which the Customers Are Inputs, in: Journal of Political Economy, 103(3): 573–86.

Rouse, C. E. (2004). The Effect of Class Size and School Vouchers on Minority Achievement, in: Conrad, C. A. (Ed.), Building Skills for Black Workers: Preparing for the Future Labor Market, Lanham, MD: University Press of America, 15–50.

Sah, R. K., Stiglitz, J. E. (1986). The Architecture of Economic Systems: Hierarchies and Polyarchies, in: American Economic Review, 76(4): 716–27.

Salop, J., Salop, S. (1976). Self-Selection and Turnover in the Labor Market, in: Quarterly Journal of Economics, 90(4): 619–27.

Sander, W. (1997). Catholic High Schools and Rural Academic Achievement, in: American Journal of Agricultural Economics, 79(1): 1–12.

Schelling, T. (1960). The Strategy of Conflict. Cambridge, MA: Harvard University Press.

Schelling, T. (1978). Micromotives and Macrobehavior, New York, NY: Norton.

Schneider, L., Klein, B., Murphy, K. M. (1981). Governmental Regulation of Cigarette Health Information, in: Journal of Law and Economics, 24(3): 575–612.

Schöttner, A. (2007). Relational Contracts, Multitasking, and Job Design, in: Journal of Law, Economics and Organization, 24(1): 138–62.

Seiler, E. (1984). Piece Rate vs. Time Rate: The Effect of Incentives on Earnings, in: Review of Economics & Statistics, 66(3): 363–75.

Shapiro, C., Stiglitz, J. E. (1984). Equilibrium Unemployment as a Worker Discipline Device, in: American Economic Review, 74(3), 433–44.

Shaw, K. (1984). A Formulation of the Earnings Function Using the Concept of Occupational Investment, in: Journal of Human Resources, 19(3): 319–40.

Shearer, B. (2004). Piece Rates, Fixed Wages and Incentives: Evidence from a Field Experiment, in: Review of Economic Studies, 71(2): 513–34.

Silva, O. (2007). The Jack-of-All-Trades Entrepreneur: Innate Talent or Acquired Skill?, in: Economics Letters, 97(2): 118–23.

Slichter, S. (1928). Modern Economic Society, New York, NY: Henry Holt and Co.

Sowell, T. (1994). Race and Culture: A World View, New York, NY: Basic Books.

Spence, A. M. (1973). Job Market Signaling, in: Quarterly Journal of Economics, 87(3): 355–74.

Spitz, J. (1991). Productivity and Wage Relations in Economic Theory and Labor Markets, Ph.D. Thesis, Stanford University Graduate School of Economics.

Staatsuitverij (1979). Statistical Yearbook of the Netherlands, The Hague: Staatsuitverij.

Stevens, M. (1994). A Theoretical Model of On-the-Job Training with Imperfect Competition, in: Oxford Economic Papers, 46(4): 537–62.

Stevens, M. (2003). Earnings Functions, Specific Human Capital, and Job Matching:

References

Tenure Bias is Negative, in: Journal of Labor Economics, 21(4): 783–805.

Stevens, S. S. (1968). Measurement, Statistics, and the Schemapiric View, in: Science 161(3844): 849–56.

Stiglitz, J. (1975). Incentives, Risk, and Information: Notes toward a Theory of Hierarchy, in: Bell Journal of Economics, 6(2): 552–79.

Stiglitz, J. (1981). Contests and Cooperation: Towards a General Theory of Compensation and Competition, Unpublished Manuscript, Princeton University.

Stole, L. A., Zwiebel, J. (1996). Intra-Firm Bargaining under Nonbinding Contracts, in: Review of Economic Studies, 63(3): 375–410.

Stopford, J. M., Baden-Fuller, C. W. F. (1994). Creating Corporate Entrepreneurship, in: Strategic Management Journal, 15(7): 521–36.

Summers, A. A., Wolfe, B. L. (1977). Do Schools Make a Difference?, in: American Economic Review, 67(4): 639–52.

Supply and Services Canada (1981). Canada Yearbook, Quebec: Supply and Services Canada.

Supply and Services Canada (1985). Canada Yearbook, Quebec: Supply and Services Canada.

Teichner, W. A., Luehrman, T. A. (1992). Arundel Partners: The Sequel Project, Harvard Business School Case no. 9-292-140, Boston, MA: Harvard Business School Press.

Third International Mathematics and Science Study (1995-1996). National Center for Education Statistics, 1990 K Street, NW, Washington, DC 20006, USA, Web site: http://nces.ed.gov/pubsearch/getpubcats.asp?sid=073#.

Thurow, L. (1972). Education and Economic Equality, in: Public Interest, 28(Summer): 66–81.

Tirole, J. (1986). Hierarchies and Bureaucracies: On the Role of Collusion in Organizations, in: Journal of Law, Economics, and Organization, 2(2): 181–214.

Topel, R. (1983). On Layoffs and Unemployment Insurance, in: American Economic Review, 73 (4): 541–59.

Topel, R. (1991). Specific Capital, Mobility, and Wages: Wages Rise with Job Seniority, in: Journal of Political Economy, 99(1): 145–76.

Townsend, M. (1985). The Determinants of Labor Union Membership, Ph.D. thesis, University of Chicago.

United Nations (various years). Demographic Yearbook, New York, NY: United Nations Publishing Division (1906, 1965, 1966, 1976, 1981, 1982, 1985 and 1986).

United Nations (1967). National Accounts Statistics, New York, NY: United Nations Publications.

United Nations (1983). National Accounts Statistics, New York, NY: United Nations Publications.

United Nations (various years). Statistical Yearbook for Asia and the Pacific, New York: United Nations Publications (1968-1975, 1977-1979, 1983, 1984 and 1985).

Urquiola, M. (2005). Does School Choice Lead to Sorting? Evidence from Tiebout Variation, in: American Economic Review, 95(4): 1310–26.

U.S. Census Bureau (1974). Current Population Survey, Washington, DC: Bureau of Labor Statistics.

U.S. Census Bureau (1976). Current Population Survey, Washington, DC: Bureau of Labor Statistics.

U.S. Department of Health, Education, and Welfare (1976). Reaching Retirement Age, Social Security Administration Research Report No. 47, Washington, DC: Government Printing Office.

U.S. Department of Labor, Bureau of Labor Statistics (1985). Handbook of Labor Statistics, Washington, DC: U.S. Government Printing Office.

Varian, H. R. (1990). Monitoring Agents with Other Agents, in: Journal for Institutional and Theoretical Economy, 146(1): 153–74.

Various (various years). World Tables, Vol. 1, Economic Data, Baltimore, MD: Johns Hopkins University Press (1980 and 1982).

Wagner, J. (2003). Testing Lazear's Jack-of-All-Trades View of Entrepreneurship with

German Micro Data, in: Applied Economics Letters, 10(11): 687–89.

Wagner, J. (2006). Are Nascent Entrepreneurs Jacks-of-All-Trades? A Test of Lazear's Theory of Entrepreneurship with German Data, in: Applied Economics, 38(20): 2415–419.

Wald, A. (1947). Sequential Analysis, New York, NY: Dover.

Wald, A. (1950). Statistical Decision Functions, New York, NY: Chelsea.

Waldman, M. (1990). Up-or-Out contracts: A Signaling Perspective, in: Journal of Labor Economics, 8(2): 230–50.

Wasmer, E. (2006). General versus Specific Skills in Labor Markets with Search Frictions and Firing Costs, in: American Economic Review, 95(3): 811–31.

Weiss, Y. (1984). Wage Contracts when Output Grows Stochastically: The Role of Mobility Costs and Capital Market Imperfections, in: Journal of Labor Economics, 2(2): 155–74.

Weitzman, M. (1976). The New Soviet Incentive Model, in: Bell Journal of Economics 7(1): 251–7.

Weitzman, M. (1980).The "Ratchet Principle" and Performance Incentives, in: Bell Journal of Economics, 11(1): 302–8.

Weitzman, M. L. (1992). On Diversity, in: Quarterly Journal of Economics, 107(2): 363–405.

Willis, R., Rosen, S. (1979). Education and Self-Selection, in: Journal of Political Economy, 87(5): S7-36.

Wilson, C. A. (1977). A Model of Insurance Markets with Incomplete Information, in: Journal of Economic Theory, 16(2): 167–207.

Wilson, R. B. (1969). Competitive Bidding with Disparate Information, in: Management Science. 15 (7): 446–48.

Yunker, J. A. (1973). A Dynamic Optimization Model of the Soviet Enterprise, in: Economics of Planning, 13(1-2): 33-51.

Zábojník, J. (2002). Centralized and Decentralized Decision Making in Organizations, in: Journal of Labor Economics, 20(1): 1–22.

Index

Index

Index

Index

plan
- conventional 54, 59, 61, 63-4, 68-70
- defined-benefit 54
- defined-contribution 54, 62, 474
- pattern 54, 64, 68-70, 72

political interaction 268
pool effect 355
Pool, J. 488
population 99
- survey 436

Portes, R. 1
portfolio 160
port of entry 238, 245-6, 258-60, 265
Portugal, P. 458
power
- division of 106

Prendergast, C. J. 5, 465, 468, 477, 489
Prennushi, G. 466
present value of
- earnings 27
- marginal product 22, 30
- payments 27
- pension benefits 54, 56
- severance pay 48
- the lifetime marginal product 21-2
- the lifetime wage payment 20, 22
- the pension 51, 59
- the wage stream 21, 48

pressure
- external 275
- internal 275

price
- system 179
- theory
  - standard 8

principal 18, 27, 176, 412-3, 485
principal-agent framework 270
prisoner's dilemma 107, 485
prize
- expected 163-4, 181
- fixed 161
- market-clearing 182
- salary scheme 183
- structure 167, 170, 461, 486
  - competitive 161
  - equilibrium 163
  - optimal 164
  - tournament 167, 180

production
- cost of 231
- educational *see* education
- factor 202, 209, 267, 423
- function 166, 197, 278, 281, 289, 299, 372, 426, 451, 470, 479, 497
  - educational 337, 374, 492

jobs 256, 258, 260, 265
output 4
process 2, 193, 240, 337, 425, 431-2, 466, 470, 496
technology 5, 179, 194, 289, 299, 383, 442
theory 237-8

productivity
- decline 19
- effect 234
- expected 164, 478
- gain 215, 232-4, 458, 481
- log 225-6

profit
- curve
  - firm's 105
- sharing 270-1, 274-6, 281, 285, 475, 484
  - profit-sharing plans 270

promotion
- contest
  - implicit 287
- cutoff 137
- decision 129-30, 133, 137, 140, 143, 146-9, 151, 472
- effect of 251, 482
- internal 265, 461
- level 137
- path 246, 268
- possibilities 20, 140
- rate 256
- rule 130-1, 138, 140, 148, 476
- sequential 138
- standard 129, 134-6, 148

proportional representation 119
psychology 11, 455
public good 368, 370, 386, 484, 491, 492
public policy analysis 9
punishment 51, 270, 275, 278, 281-2, 393, 395, 399, 495

Q

quality 144-5, 185, 200-2, 215, 232-4, 238, 240, 250, 261-2, 276, 282, 340, 369, 385, 409, 424, 463-4, 478-81, 493
- problem 232-3

quantity 185, 200-2, 327, 463
queue
- theory 33, 37

Quinn, J. F. 474

530

Index

salary
  fixed 155, 184, 194, 411
  growth 249
  job 207, 262, 498
  scheme 189, 191
  straight 13, 188-90, 193, 196, 209, 274
  structure 154, 165, 268
  variation 247
Salop, J. 468, 473
Salop, S. 468, 473
sample
  representative 55, 482
Sander, W. 492
Sauvageau, Y. 491
Schaefer, S. 459, 468
Scheinkman, J. A. 490
Schelling, T. 486, 488
Schmidt, K. M. 6
Schmitz, J. A. Jr. 496
Schnabel, C. 459
Schneider, L. 485
school
  Catholic 379,-81, 383, 387, 491, 493
  private 371-2, 376, 379-80, 383, 387,
    492, 493
  public 379-80, 383, 387, 491-3
schooling
  private value of 376
  social value of 376
Schotter, A. 6, 461
Schöttner, A. 465
Schwab, R. M. 492
Schwab, S. J. 458
Scotchmer, S. 483
search
  model 354-5, 489
  problem 479
Sedlacek, G. 490
segregation 297-9, 331, 335, 378-9, 381
Seiler, E. 193, 208, 479-80 .
selection
  worker 336
self-selection
  analyses 473
  Pareto optimal 176
seniority
  effects 145
  rules 110
separation
  decision 47
  efficient 46-7, 71, 188, 345, 489
  firm-worker 23, 473
  inefficient 46, 51-2, 213, 479
  involuntary 350-1
  rates 226-7
  voluntary 345
  worker-initiated 69

severance pay
  arrangement 49
  effects 73, 76, 81, 83, 86, 92-5, 99
  law 74, 77, 88, 94
  legislation 79, 98, 474
  mandatory 76, 78, 94, 99
  requirements 74, 83, 94, 98
  restrictions 16
  rules 79, 82
  state-mandated 73-4, 83
  structure 15
  theory of 43
  voluntary 74
shame 267, 275-6, 279, 285
Shapiro, C. 465
shareholder 274, 276
Shaw, K. 156, 360, 457, 466
Shearer, B. S. 463, 480
shirking 21, 23, 47, 50, 159, 266-7, 276,
  279-82, 338, 463
Shkolnik, J. L. 381, 383, 492
shop committees 107
  see also work councils
signal-to-noise ratio 414
Silva, O. 470
Siow, A. 489
skill
  acquisition 165, 336, 338, 435, 497-8
  balanced skill set 425, 441
  business 431
  development 471
  firm-specific 101, 127, 336
  formation 13, 338, 469
  general 337, 342, 349, 358, 445, 450-1
  level 179, 240
  marginal cost of 162
  requirements 241
  skill-weights
    approach 348, 356, 359, 360
    model 345
  variety of 339-41, 424, 431, 435, 439
Slichter, S. 480
Sliwka, D. 6
Smith, A. 11
Snower, D. J. 80, 475
Sobel, M. 167
social damage
  function 407
social
  gains 113-4, 128
  optimum 105-6, 362, 459, 489
  outcomes 108
  planner 278, 376
  product 105
  return 161, 164
  science 10-1, 271, 455
  security

About the Author...

 ***Edward P. Lazear*** is the Jack Steele Parker Professor of Human Resources Management and Economics at Stanford University since 1995, and Morris A. Cox Senior Fellow at the Hoover Institution since 1985. Previously, he was the Isidore Brown and Gladys J. Brown Professor of Urban and Labor Economics at the University of Chicago's Graduate School of Business (1985-1992). From 2006 until 2009, he chaired the U.S. President's Council of Economic Advisers. Lazear is Founding Editor of the Journal of Labor Economics, Past President of the Society of Labor Economists, a Fellow of the American Academy of Arts and Sciences and of the Econometric Society, and a Research Associate of the National Bureau of Economic Research. He has authored several books, among them "Personnel Economics" (The MIT Press, 1995) and "Personnel Economics for Managers" (New York: John Wiley & Sons, 1998) which has been translated into German, Chinese, and Korean. Lazear has published widely in leading economic journals such as the American Economic Review, the Quarterly Journal of Economics, the Journal of Political Economy, and the Review of Economics and Statistics. He holds honorary doctorates from Albertson College of Idaho, Aarhus School of Business, and the University of Zurich, and has received numerous research and teaching awards, among them the Jacob Mincer Prize for lifetime achievement in the field of labor economics, the Adam Smith Prize from the European Association of Labor Economists, and the Distinguished Teaching Award from Stanford University's Graduate School of Business. Edward Lazear joined IZA as a Research Fellow in June 2002. In 2004 he was awarded the IZA Prize in Labor Economics.

...and the Editors

Steffen Altmann is a Senior Research Associate at IZA and Deputy Program Director for the research area "Behavioral and Personnel Economics". He received his Ph.D. from the Bonn Graduate School of Economics in 2009. Previously, he studied Economics at the Universities of Barcelona and Mannheim, where he also received his Master's degree. His research interests include personnel and labor economics as well as behavioral and experimental economics. In his work, he has studied the influence of economic incentives and psychological motives on workplace behavior. Most recently, he has been working on the impact of non-binding default rules on individual behavior and economic outcomes.

Klaus F. Zimmermann has been Full Professor of Economics at the University of Bonn and Director of the Institute for the Study of Labor (IZA Bonn) since 1998. From 2000 until 2011 he was President of the German Institute for Economic Research (DIW Berlin). Zimmermann is Honorary Professor of Economics at the Free University of Berlin (since 2001) and Honorary Professor at the Renmin University of China (since 2006). He is also Chairman of the Society of the German Economic Research Institutes (ARGE) (since 2005), and a member of the German Academy of Sciences Leopoldina (since 2001), the World Economic Forum's Global Agenda Council on Migration (since 2009) and the Academia Europaea (since 2010).